THE

WORKS

OF THE

RIGHT REVEREND FATHER IN GOD,

THOMAS WILSON, D.D.,

LORD BISHOP OF SODOR AND MAN.

| Saturday   Death | Preparation for Death   240 |

Need a Person who has Rec'd the Sen=
=tence of Death, be persuaded to prepare
for Death? And is not this our case?

Consider Death as appointed by
God, as a Necessary Sentence, as the compleat-
tion of y^e m^r Sacrifice, as a Passage to
a Better Life — as the deliverance
of a Prisoner, as the Recalling of
an Exile from Banishm^t — as the
End of all Mis'rys — and then you
will strive to put much of y^r Service
wch it reqs as accidents as an Accidt
of Nature only —

And then, miserable wise we be, is't Death
surpriseth either doing Evil, or doing nothing,
or doing that wch God does not require of him.
Can we imagine y^t the Immorality of X^n Believer
this Forsooth? —— Suffer me not, O God, to fall
into a Forgetfulness of it.

We complain (with Moses) of the shortness of
Life. He Answers — Dita, si scias uti, longa
est. But then 'tis X^ts only we reach us. time
to use our Life — viz. in working out our own Sal^n
& we are sure 'tis long enough for that, bec. God
wch it has conferred as an Accident has appointed it for y^t very End.

THE

WORKS

OF THE

RIGHT REVEREND FATHER IN GOD,

THOMAS WILSON, D.D.,

LORD BISHOP OF SODOR AND MAN.

VOL. V.

SACRA PRIVATA.—SUPPLEMENT TO SACRA PRIVATA.
MAXIMS OF PIETY AND MORALITY.—SUPPLEMENT TO MAXIMS.

WIPF & STOCK · Eugene, Oregon

Wipf and Stock Publishers
199 W 8th Ave, Suite 3
Eugene, OR 97401

The Works of the Right Reverend Father in God,
Thomas Wilson, D. D., Lord Bishop of Sodor and Man. vol. 5
Sacra Privata. - Supplement to Sacra Privata. Maxims of Piety and Morality.
– Supplement to Maxims.
By Wilson, Thomas, D. D.
ISBN 13: 978-1-60608-138-9
Publication date 3/6/2009
Previously published by John Henry Parker, 1860

PREFACE.

The present volume, printed, with one slight exception, entirely from Bishop Wilson's own MSS., contains two of his works, the *Sacra Privata* and the "Maxims of Piety and Morality," with a Supplement to each.

I. For the *Sacra Privata*, four MSS., all in his own hand, have been collated. The first three are distinguished in this edition by the numbers i., ii., iii.; the fourth, which contains in comparison but few pieces, is referred to by the letters M. H., the initials of Michael Hewetson, Wilson's intimate friend, who gave him the little memorandum-book in which they are contained, at the time of his ordination. MS. i.[a] is the fullest, and largest, and latest in date, and has been generally adopted in this reprint as the basis of the text, the various readings of the other copies being subjoined at the foot of the page. The pages, numbered, if I mistake not, by the Bishop himself, were 312, (the last by a clerical error stands as 112); each page carefully ruled in two columns. Before p. 20, there appears to have been a good deal of insertion and substitution, and hardly any of his own paging. In this part, there are thirty-four pages before we come to his p. 20. After that number the pagination proceeds regularly, with the following exceptions: a leaf inserted after p. 121; another after 141; one omitted after 159; two after 175; two after

[a] A specimen of this MS. faces the title-page.

245; nine after 257, (which have been cut out with scissors,) and two after 305. The whole number of pages now in the book (a good many are blank) is 275. The references in this edition are made to them as they stand, not to Bp. Wilson's paging. Every now and then directions to the printer occur, in the hand-writing of Dr. Wilson, the Bishop's son; and it is plain that this very copy went to the press to form the text of the first edition; with sundry omissions, however, and fresh pieces from the other MSS. This MS. begins, " *Sacra Privata.* Math. vi. 6," and ends, " 5, 6, 12 after Trin." Throughout it bears marks of infirmities increasing with age. But, as Mr. Denton has pointed out in the Preface to his valuable edition, it was properly taken as the "base" of the published text, as being more complete and systematic than either of the others.

MS. ii., so numbered by Dr. Wilson, is the earliest after M. H., and the first in which the heading *Sacra Privata* occurs; and also the arrangement after the days of the week, and the assignment to each of some question in the Consecration Service. It contains, at present, 162 pages, but has had more; bearing marks of mutilation at the beginning and end, and in a few other places, and some insertions also. It begins on the cover, "Ἔργον ἐστὶ," and finishes, " una dies." The last ordination entered in it is dated 1713.

MS. iii. is the most neatly written, and seems to have been more leisurely put together than the others: a good part of it must have been either composed or transcribed in his imprisonment, and shews the first signs of the difficulty of holding his pen, which was caused by an ailment there contracted. It contains 255 pages, of which pp. 192, 255 are slightly mutilated. This MS. begins with " *Sacra Privata.* Math.

vi. 6," and ends with "more than Thine own life." The latest ordination entered in it is in 1726.

The earliest in date, however, and the most interesting of the four MSS., is that which is here denominated "M. H.," being the contents of a little book clasped in brass, which was given to the Bishop on his ordination as deacon, by the friend of his youth, Archdeacon Michael Hewetson. It contains, 1st, in Hewetson's hand (as I suppose), "Memorandums concerning the Consecration of the Church of Kildare," &c., pp. 1—7; 2nd, Personal memoranda of Wilson's own, pp. 7—27; 3rd, (reckoning from the other end of the book, and using Roman numerals,) "Occasional Devotions," Prayers, and a few Meditations, from p. i. to p. ci. The total number of pages (including blank ones from ci. to cxxxi.) is 163. This MS. begins, "Mich. Hewetson's Memorandums," and ends on the cover at the other end, " Ἄριστον εἶναι." On that fly-leaf is written, "Thomas Wilson of Knowsley in Lancashire, 1697. Ἔργον ἐστὶ σπουδαῖον εἶναι. Aristot."—"Prov. xxviii. 9, He y^t turneth away his ear from hearing ye law, even his prayer shall be an abomination. Ἰδιώτου μὲν εἶναι κακίαν, τὸ φαῦλον πράσσειν· ἄρχοντος δὲ, τὸ μὴ ὡς ἄριστον εἶναι." The two latter quotations are plainly of later date than the former, and written since he became a bishop.

The small portion of the *Sacra Privata* not now appearing in any of these MSS. is printed from the original edition of Bp. Wilson's Works, 4to., London, 1781; as is specified in the notes on the several places, particularly at pp. 91, 95. The Supplement is compiled partly from fragmentary portions of the above-mentioned MSS., partly from certain loose papers in Wilson's hand, most kindly communicated for the purpose by the Rev. William Gill, Vicar of Kirk Malew; and partly from the contents of a MS. Book similar to the above-mentioned, by Dr. Wilson, marked No. 10, and now in the possession of Sion College.

In Mr. Gill's papers, and occasionally in the other MSS., mutilations to a certain extent appear, caused, no doubt, by persons allowed to have a sentence or two by way of relic.

II. The "Maxims of Piety and Morality" are given entirely from the original MS., also in possession of Sion College. It consists of two very small books, numbered 5 and 6 by Dr. Wilson. No. 5, mutilated at the beginning, (see p. 375, note o,) contains 168 pages; from 145 to 167 (inclusive) is a blank; and there is some mutilation also at the end. It begins, "Tho. Sodor and Man," and ends, "Be ye perfect, &c."

The continuation, marked by Dr. Wilson "Book 6. Read and approved," begins "Mediis immotus in undis," with the Bishop's motto, "Tuta et Parvula laudo;" and after some fly-leaves, (as described in p. 447,) carries on Dr. Wilson's paging from No. 5, p. 144, to p. 274. Then come blank leaves, with a few stray entries, filling up the number of pages to 302: the last words are, "The world is a Tickle Horse."

The Bishop himself, p. 145, entitles the Book "Maxims of Piety and Morality." Under that title, Cruttwell, authorized by Dr. Wilson, published a large selection from these two MSS., arranging it under alphabetical headings. The whole is now printed in the order itself of the MS., and in general with the abbreviations therein adopted; and with the spelling also, except in palpable cases of clerical error. The Bishop's unstudied way of writing, it was thought, and the manner in which one thing followed another in his MSS., would shew how his mind and heart were employed, and, on the whole, prove more interesting than any selection or new arrangement that could be made; while by a careful index all the purposes of alphabetical order might be secured.

But Sion College supplied another MS. also, with a good deal of interesting matter, none of which has hitherto seen the light: the principal contents of which are here subjoined by way of "Supplement" to the Maxims. An account of this MS. will be found in p. 503. It is by no means a mere commonplace book, although much of it consists of extracts and analyses of what occurred to him in his reading; but in almost every instance they appeared to the Editor to have something of his peculiar touch, so as to make it, on the whole, worth while to publish them *in extenso*. The other contents of the MS., so far as they may require publication, will appear (D.V.) in the concluding "Fasciculus" of Bishop Wilson's Works, together with the *Parochialia* and other interesting tracts, as a second part of the volume reserved for his Life.

The Editor is deeply grateful to the authorities of Sion College for the free use which he has been allowed to make of the precious remains of Bishop Wilson under their care; and to the Rev. W. Denton, the latest editor of *Sacra Privata*, for all kinds of valuable, or rather invaluable, help.

J. K.

March, 1860.

CONTENTS.

	PAGE
SACRA PRIVATA.	
DEVOTION	1
PREPARATORY	3
MATUTINA	8
NOON	39
VESPERTINA	42
SUNDAY, EPISCOPACY	54
SUNDAY LAUDS	84
MONDAY, HOLY SCRIPTURES	100
RESIGNATION	112
TUESDAY [DOCTRINE]	116
TROUBLE AND AFFLICTION	128
WEDNESDAY, SOBER LIFE	143
THURSDAY, CHURCH DISCIPLINE	168
RELIGIOUS DISCOURSE	192
FRIDAY, ORDINATION	198
PENITENCE	220
SATURDAY, ALMS	234
PREPARATION FOR DEATH	254
GRACES AT MEALS	279
EJACULATIONS	281
PASSAGES BY SEA	289
COLLECTS: THEIR TENDENCY	291
SUPPLEMENT TO SACRA PRIVATA	293
MAXIMS	372
SUPPLEMENT TO MAXIMS	504
INDEX TO MAXIMS	635

SACRA PRIVATA.

DEVOTION.

TRUE DEVOTION consists in having our hearts always *devoted* to God, as the sole Fountain of all happiness; and who is ready to hear and help His otherwise helpless, miserable creatures. [i. 2.]

It is to be attained,

First, By earnest Prayer; "He that hungers after righteousness, will certainly be filled."

Secondly, By possessing our hearts with a deep sense of our own misery, our wants, and danger:—This is the grace of *humility*.

[*Thirdly*], By considering God's goodness, power, and readiness to help us:—This is called *faith in God*.

Lastly, By convincing our hearts of the vanity of every thing else to afford us any real help or comfort:—This is to be effected by *self-denial*.

Dying persons are generally more devout than others, because they then see their own misery, that nothing in this world can help them, and that God is their only refuge.

We must change our lives, if we desire to change our hearts. God will have no regard to the prayers of those who have none to His commands.

The Spirit of God will not dwell in a *divided heart*. We cannot feel the pleasures of devotion, while the world is our delight.

Not that all pleasures are criminal: but the closer union we have with the world, the less is our union with God. A Christian, therefore, who strives after devotion, should taste sensual pleasures very sparingly,—should make necessity, not bodily delight, his rule.

In order to dispose our hearts to devotion, the *active* life to be preferred to the *contemplative*.

To be doing good to mankind, disposes the soul most powerfully to devotion.

DEVOTION. And indeed, we are surrounded with motives to piety and devotion, if we would but mind them.

The poor are designed to excite our liberality; the miserable, our pity; the sick, our assistance; the ignorant, our instruction; those that are fallen, our helping hand. In [i. 3.] those that are vain, we see the vanity of this world. In those that are wicked, our own frailty. When we see good men rewarded, it confirms our hope; and when evil men are punished, it excites us to fear.

He that would be devout, must beware of indulging a habit of *wandering in prayer*. It is a crime that will grow upon us, and will deprive us of the blessings we pray for.

Avoid, as much as may be, *multiplicity of business*. Neither the innocency nor the goodness of the employment will excuse us, if it possess our hearts when we are praying to God.

When our Lord bids us to *take no thought for the morrow*, He intended to hinder those cares and fears which are apt to distract our devotions,—which are the more unreasonable, because they never can change the state of things.

Never be curious to know what passes in the world, any further than duty obliges you. It will only distract the mind when it should be better employed.

Never intermit devotion, if you can help it. You will return to your duty, like Samson when his locks were cut, weak and indifferent as other people of the world.

The oftener we renew our intercourse with God, the greater will be our devotion.

Frequent prayer, as it is an exercise of holy thoughts, is a most natural remedy against the power of sin.

Importunity makes no change in God, but it creates in us such dispositions as God thinks fit to reward.

Make it a law to yourself to meditate before you pray: as also to make certain pauses, to see whether your heart goes along with your lips.

They whose hearts desire nothing, pray for nothing.

Give me, O God, the spirit of true devotion, such as may give life to all my prayers, so that they may find acceptance in Thy sight, for Jesus Christ's sake! Amen.

SACRA PRIVATA.

[i. 1; ii. 2; iii. 1.]

Matthew vi. 6. *Thou, when thou prayest, enter into thy closet, and when thou hast shut thy door, pray to thy Father which is in secret; and thy Father, which seeth in secret, shall reward thee openly.* PREPARATORY.

How good is God! who will not only give us what we pray for, but will reward us for going to Him, and laying our wants before Him. [i. 1.]

John xvi. 23. *Verily, verily, I say unto you, Whatsoever ye shall ask the Father in My name, He will give it you.* [iii. 1.]

The lukewarmness of our prayers the source of all our infidelities.

1 John v. 14. *And this is the confidence that we have in Him, that if we ask any thing according to His will, He heareth us.* [ii. 2.]

May I always present myself before God with a firm faith and hope in His promises and mercy; with great reverence to His infinite Majesty; with the humility of an offender; and with a full purpose of keeping all God's commands. [i.1; iii.5.]

May the thoughts of eternity quicken my devotions; my wants make me earnest; my backslidings make me persevere; and ^amay I never wilfully give way to any distracting thoughts.

^bMay I wait with patience, and leave it to Thee^c my God and Father, *how* and *when* to grant^d my petitions^e.

---

^a iii. "let me not."
^b iii. "let me."
^c iii. om. this clause.
^d iii. adds "me."
^e In iii. 5. this prayer stands as follows:—
"That my prayers may be acceptable in Thy sight, grant, O God, that I may always present myself before Thee—with great reverence to Thine infinite Majesty:—with a firm faith and hope in Thy promises and tender mercy:—with the shame and humility of an offender:—and with a full purpose of forsaking every evil way, because Thou hearest not sinners. When I grow indifferent, let the thought of eternity quicken my prayers. Let my sins make me humble, my wants," &c. [as in the text.]

PREPARA- Discover, O Lord, whatever is amiss in me, whether in life
TORY. or principle.
[iii. 5.]

[i. 1.] He that has learned to pray as he ought, has got the *secret* of an holy life.

It is of greater advantage to us than we imagine, that God does not grant our petitions immediately. We learn by that, that whereunto we have already attained, *it was the gift of God.*

The best way to prevent wandering in prayer is not to let the mind wander too much at other times; but to have God always in our minds, in the whole course of our lives.

The end of prayer is not to inform God, but to give man a sight of his own misery; to raise his soul towards Heaven, and to put him in mind that there is his Father and his inheritance.

Matthew vii. 7. *Ask, and it shall be given you.*

Grant me, Lord, a faith which shall make me know my wants, that I may ask them with earnestness and humility, and depend upon Thy gracious promise.

[i. 4.] That man leads a sincere Christian life,

§ 1. Who endeavours to serve and obey God to the best of his understanding and power:

§ 2. Who strives to please his neighbour to edification. Rom. xv. 2:

§ 3. Who endeavours to do his duty in that state of life unto which it has pleased God to call him.

Whoever would continue in the practice of these things unto his life's end, it is necessary that he should call himself often to an account, whether he does [so] or not;—constantly pray for grace to know, and to do his duty;—preserve himself in such a teachable temper, as to be always ready to receive the truth, when it is fairly proposed to him.

THE DUTIES OF A BISHOP,

(The state of life unto which it has pleased God to call me,) by the laws of God and the Church, are, To instruct the people committed to his charge, out of the Holy Scriptures;

and to teach, or maintain, no doctrine but what may be proved from thence. [*Sunday.*]

To exercise himself in those Holy Scriptures; to call upon God for the true understanding of the same. *Monday.*

To use all faithful diligence in driving away all doctrines contrary to God's Word, and to encourage others to do so. *Tuesday.*

To deny all ungodliness and worldly lusts, and to live a sober, righteous, and godly life, so as to be an example unto others. *Wednesday.*

To maintain and set forward, as much as may be, quietness, love, and peace, among all men; and to correct and punish the unruly, criminous, and disobedient, as far as God's Word, and the laws of the land, do require and will warrant. *Thursday.*

To be faithful in ordaining, sending, or laying hands upon others. *Friday.*

To be gentle and merciful, for Christ's sake, to poor and needy people, and to all strangers destitute of help. *Saturday.*

The Prayer.—Almighty God, give me grace and power [i. 5.] faithfully to perform these duties of my high calling; that I may be found perfect and irreprehensible at the last day, through Jesus Christ. Amen.

Prevent, O Lord, the wants of an heart which knows not even how to lay them open before Thee; which does not so much as think of doing it; and which does too often shut out the light and consolation in [of] which it stands in need.

It is a[f] rudeness amongst men to ask a favour, and not [f] [i. 5; ii. init.] stay for an answer. And do we count it no fault to pray for blessings, and never to think of them afterwards,—never to wait for them,—never to give[f] God thanks for them?

Let us not run over our prayers with an insensible and [i. 5.] distracted mind.

Let your prayers be *as particular as may be*,—against the sins of your particular state, and for the graces which you in particular do most stand in need of. This is the best preser-

---

[f] ii. reads "folly and rudeness;" "to stay;" "Him thanks who bestows them."

PREPARA-TORY. vative against sin; makes us best acquainted with our condition; puts us continually in mind of mending what is amiss; lets you see what particular graces you most want,—what are most needful for the cure of your own particular corruption and disorder;—and is the best trial of our hearts. For if I pray for charity, for instance, and for every instance which is necessary to render me truly charitable, I pray for grace to avoid evil-speaking,—to pray for my enemies,—to do them good, &c., and so of all other sins and graces.

God grant that I may never seek His face in vain!

James v. 16. *The effectual fervent prayer of a righteous man availeth much.*

This ought to make me aspire after every possible degree of holiness, that God may hear my prayers for my flock, and for such as have desired my prayers.

Tobit xii. 12. *When thou didst pray, I did bring the remembrance of your prayers before the Holy One; and when thou didst bury the dead, I was with thee.*

May the good Spirit of God assist me in the performance of my duty. Fix my attention, excite my affections, and inflame my devotions, that I may attend upon the Lord with pleasure and without distraction.

Let us make prayer familiar to us; for without the help[g] of God, we are[g] every hour in danger.

[i. 6; iii. 1.] [h]Exodus xxviii. 29. *And Aaron shall bear the names of the children of Israel in the breast-plate of judgment upon his heart, when he goeth in unto the holy place, for a memorial before the Lord continually.*

Let Thy merciful ears, O God, be open unto the prayers of Thy servant for himself, and for the flock over which the Holy Ghost hath made him overseer[i], for the Lord Jesus' sake. Amen.

[i. 6; iii. 1.] O Lord, say Amen to our prayers[k], and grant that my whole flock may[k] be partakers of the blessings we have now prayed for. And may[k] Thy blessing be upon them for ever[k]. Amen.

---

[g] [i. 6. "grace;" "in danger every hour."]
[h] [iii. 1. prefixes, *Intrante in Ecclesiam.*]
[i] iii. adds, "And so lead us in the knowledge and obedience of Thy word, that in the end we may obtain everlasting life, through Christ our Lord."
[k] iii. om. "and;" "partake of;" "let:" add, "For Jesus Christ's sake."

The devil knows, that when we have a relish for prayer, and apply ourselves in good earnest to it,—that we are in the way of life; he therefore strives by all ways possible to divert us.

Luke xi. 1. *Lord, teach us to pray.*

Pour upon us the spirit of supplication and prayer.

God will deny us nothing that we ask in the name of His Son.

Prayers through Jesus Christ.—When we offer our prayers through His mediation, it is then He that prays, His love that intercedes, His blood that pleads, it is He who obtains all from His Father.

[As] "zealous professions of friendship are but the more abominable hypocrisy, for being often repeated, unless there be an [equal] zeal in the heart, so solemn prayers ... are but repeated hypocrisies, unless the heart and mind be conformable to them[1]."

Before Prayer. O Holy Spirit of Grace, help my infirmities. Pour upon me the spirit of grace and supplication[m].

Preparatory Prayer[n].—O Holy Spirit of grace, give us a true sight of our miseries, and a sincere shame and sorrow when we make confession of our sins; a feeling sense of our need of mercy, and a hope of obtaining pardon when we beg it for Thy Son's sake. May we resign our wills to Thee and to Thy goodness, when we pray for temporal things; and when we pray for spiritual graces, may we hunger and thirst after righteousness. Give us a real love for Thy Holy Word, and grace to hear it with attention. May we thankfully close with all the means of grace and salvation. When we praise Thee for Thy works of nature and of grace, and give Thee thanks for Thy mercies, let us do it with high esteem and gratitude. Cause us to hear Thy Holy Word with faith and attention, and to profit by what we hear,—that we may return from Thy Church with a blessing.

---

[1] [Law's] Christian Perfection, p. 419, [c. xii. Works, t. iii. p. 367, ed. 1762.]

[m] [The two last sentences are from i. 6, only a slip has been pasted over them.]

[n] [Evidently before public worship.]

MATUTINA.

MORNING[o].

[i. 7; ii.1; iii. 6.] Joshua xxiv. 15. *Choose you this day whom you will serve.*

Whom have I in heaven but Thee[p], O Lord? and there is none on earth that I desire besides Thee. Thou art my God, and I will thank Thee: Thou art my God, and I will serve [*praise*] Thee[q]. Be Thou my only Ruler and Governor.

[i. 7; ii. 1; iii. 6.] They that have a convenient place to sleep in, and they that have the comfort of sleep, have both great reason to be thankful[r]. And even they that want these mercies ought to bless God, if in the midst of their afflictions He is pleased to refresh them with the comforts of grace.

Gracious God, continue to me these favours so long, and in such a measure, as shall most contribute to Thy honour, and my salvation. And in great mercy support and relieve all that want these blessings.

Ps. cxvi. 12. *What shall I offer unto the Lord for His mercies renewed unto me every morning*[s]*?*—Ps. li. 17. *The sacrifice of God is a broken spirit; a broken and contrite heart God will not despise.*

But most unfit[t] is mine to be to God[t] presented until I have obtained[t] His pardon, through the merits of the Lord Jesus, for the many sins by which it hath been defiled[u].

[i. 7.] Jeremiah iii. 12. *I am merciful, saith the Lord, and I will not keep anger for ever. Only acknowledge thine iniquity, that thou hast transgressed against the Lord thy God.*

[i. 7.] Ps. xxxii. [5.] *I acknowledge my sin unto Thee, O God, and mine iniquities will I not hide.*

---

[o] ii. adds "Devotions;" iii. has "Preces Matutinæ," which occurs as a general heading to p. 30. In i. "Sacra Privata Matutina," is the general heading from p. 7. to p. 27.

[p] ii. om. "O Lord;" "praise Thee."

[q] [Ps. cxviii. 28.]

[r] ii. adds, "They that want no conveniencies of life, &c., have great reason to be fearful, lest in the midst of comforts they forget the God of all comfort."

[s] [iii. adds "Lament. iii. 22, 23."]

[t] ii. and iii. add, "O Lord;" "Thee;" "Thy:" om. "through ... Jesus."

[u] ii. and iii. add, "Lord, pity, and cleanse, and forgive, and accept, and save me, for Thy mercies' sake in Jesus Christ.

"O blessed Physician, [iii.] heal all the naughty inclinations of my soul, and perfect in me a sincere love unto holiness, that I may never again return to folly; which is the desire and the purpose of my heart."

I do therefore implore Thy pardon, and plead Thy gra- MATUTINA.
cious promises, with *full purpose of heart,* by the assistance
of Thy grace, never again to return to folly.

Jeremiah xvii. 9. *The heart is deceitful above all things,* [i. 7; ii. 2; iii. 7.]
and desperately wicked: who can know it?

I cannot answer for my own heart[v]. But there is no
word, O Lord, impossible with Thee; in Thee I do put
my trust; let me never be put to confusion. [i. 8.]

Jeremiah ii. 19. Keep it ever in the heart of Thy servant,
that it is indeed *an evil thing and bitter to offend*[x] *the Lord.*

Keep me from presumptuous sins[y]; that I may never
grieve Thy Holy Spirit, nor provoke Thee to leave me
to myself.

Matthew xxvi. 41. *Watch and pray, that ye enter not into
temptation.*

Lord, make me ever mindful of my infirmities and backslidings, that I may be more watchful, and more importunate for grace for the time to come.

1 Peter v. 8. *Be sober, be vigilant, because your adversary,* [i. 8; ii. 2; iii. 8.]
*the devil, as a roaring lion, walketh about, seeking whom he
may devour*[z].

[a]O Lord, grant that this adversary of our souls may never [i. 8.]
find me off my guard, or from under Thy protection.

Matthew xvi. 24. *If any man will come after Me, let him
deny himself, and take up his cross, and follow Me.*

O my Saviour! how long have I professed to follow Thee,
without following the blessed steps of Thy most holy life,—
Thy patience and humility,—Thy great disregard for the
world, its pleasures, profits, honours, and all its idols.

O Lord, obtain for me the spirit of mortification and
self-denial, that I may follow Thee, as I hope to live
with Thee for ever. Amen.

Matthew vi. 24. *No man can serve two masters. Ye
cannot serve God and mammon.*

---

[v] "I cannot ... But," om. i.
[x] ii. iii., "forsake."
[y] ii. iii. add, "Preserve me always in a serious temper, that being ever mindful of my infirmities and back-slidings, I may be more watchful, more diligent, and more importunate for grace, for the time to come;" and om. the rest.

[z] iii. adds "may be permitted to."
[a] ii. and iii. read, "O grant [iii. grant, O Lord,] that no temptations of the world, the flesh, or the devil, may ever be able to draw me from Thy ser-vice; but that I may continue Thine for ever, continually mortifying my corrupt affections, and daily proceed-ing in virtue and true holiness."

MATUTINA. May my fear and love never be divided between Thee and the world. May I never set up any thing, O God, in competition with Thee in the possession of my heart. May I never attempt to reconcile Thy service with that world which is at enmity with Thee, my God and Father.

Mark x. 17. *What shall I do that I may inherit eternal life?*

Thou shalt love the Lord thy God with all thy heart, and with all thy soul, and with all thy mind; and thou shalt love thy neighbour as thyself.

O that this love of God may be the commanding principle of my soul. May I always have this comfortable proof of His love abiding in me, that I study to please Him and to keep His commandments. And may my love to my [i. 7*; ii. 3; iii. 9.] neighbour be such as He has commanded, that I may forgive, and give, and love, as becomes a disciple of Jesus Christ. Amen.

[i. 7*; ii. 3; iii. 8.] Ecclesiastes xii. 13. *Fear God, and keep His commandments, for this is the whole duty of man;* that is, the happiness of man.

ᵇMay I, great God, continue in Thy fear all the day long. May I keep Thy statutes, and observe Thy laws.

Hebrews iv. 13. *All things are naked and open unto the eyes of Him with whom we have to do.*

Grant that I may always live and act as having Thee, O God, the constant witness of my conduct; for Jesus Christ's sakeᶜ.

Phil. iv. 6. *Be careful for nothing; but in every thing, by prayer and supplication with thanksgiving, let your requests be made known unto God.*

ᵇ ii. and iii. read, "Who would not fear Thee, O God, who can destroy both body and soul in hell? Who would not keep Thy commandments, when in keeping of them there is such reward?"

"O that I may continue in the fear of the Lord all the day long! Accept [iii. Lord] of my imperfect obedience, [and iii.] make me every day more careful of my ways, [and] more concerned to please Thee; and to do my duty in the state of life unto which Thy Providence has called me. [iii. to please Thee, through Jesus Christ our Lord. Amen."]

ᶜ ii. reads, "Grant, O Lord, that such a just sense of this, and such an awful regard for Thy presence and commands may ever accompany me, that I may walk as in Thy sight; continually be given to all good works; that I may be just in all my dealings; that I may act in all things as one who must give an account to Him who sees all my thoughts and deeds; that I may be temperate, chaste, &c., in thought, word, and deed; hurt nobody by word or deed, but continue in perfect charity with all the world."

iii. reads as above down to "good

Matt. vi. 33. *Seek ye first the kingdom of God and His righteousness, and all these things shall be added unto you*[d]. MATUTINA. [ii. 3; iii. 10.]

In this word, O blessed Jesus, is my trust; I do cheerfully leave my temporal concerns to the good Providence of God, to order what He judges to be most convenient for me.

That which I humbly[e] desire is, that I may serve Him without distraction; be content with my condition; not desire by unjust ways to better or secure it; that I may do good to such as are in misery, and by a temperance in all things be ever prepared patiently to endure what His Providence shall bring forth; that so among the sundry and manifold changes of the world, my heart may surely there be fixed, where true joys are to be found. Amen.

Acts xx. 28. *Take heed unto yourselves, and unto all the flock, over which the Holy Ghost hath made you overseers.* [i. 7*; ii. 4; iii. 10.]

Make me, O Lord, a faithful *Overseer*, and all those that labour with me in the work of the ministry, every day more worthy of our calling. And grant unto the people of our flock, that they may profit by us daily, for Jesus Christ's sake, the supreme Bishop and Pastor[f]. Amen.

Blessed God and lover of souls, preserve by Thy grace those that are in the way of life, enlighten the minds of the ignorant, awaken the consciences of the careless, silence the gainsayers, convert the profane, and bring them all to Thine everlasting kingdom. [ii. 5.]

---

works," and then adds only, " through Jesus Christ. Amen."

[d] iii. gives only the text from Phil. iv., and goes on, "O that I could cheerfully" &c.

[e] iii. " earnestly."

[f] ii. reads, " Make me, O God, [iii. adds, 'a faithful overseer,'] and all those that labour with me in the work of the ministry, every way more worthy of this honour to which Thou hast called us: that we may with good success instruct the ignorant, reduce those that [iii. such as] are out of the way; that we may diligently preach the Word, and duly administer godly discipline; that we may be wholesome examples in word, in conversation, in love, in faith, in charity, in purity. And the Lord Jesus Christ be always with us according to His promise.

Matt. xxviii. 20." [An interlined note adds, " Exod. xxviii. 29, to be here inserted." The margin adds, " That I may be a faithful high priest."] " And grant unto the people of our flock, that they may profit by us daily.

" In the meantime, continue to us the blessings of peace and unity, in Church and State.

" Bless the Lord and government of this isle. Let brotherly love and charity increase amongst us, and root out growing vices.

" Supply the necessities of the poor and needy, help and comfort the afflicted, the fatherless and the widow. And sanctify all the dispensations of Thy Providence to the good of this Church and people; for Jesus Christ His sake. Amen."

MATUTINA.
[i. 7.*]

John x. 11. *The good shepherd giveth his life for the sheep.*

O Sovereign Pastor! who gavest Thy life for Thy sheep, grant that I may never sacrifice Thy flock to my own ease, convenience, profit, or pleasure. But that I may employ my time, my substance, my care, my labours, my prayers, for their welfare continually, and thus, at least, *give my life for my sheep.*

Matthew x. 16. *I send you forth as sheep among wolves; be ye therefore wise as serpents, and harmless as doves.*

Give me, O Jesus, this wisdom and simplicity, that the cause of God may never suffer by my ignorance or perverseness. Take me and my flock under Thy protection; and abandon us not to the rage of wolves. Let me never oppose any thing to the violence of man but meekness of spirit.

[i. 7.*; ii. 5; iii. 11.]

1 Timothy iii. 5. *If a man know not how to rule his own house, how shall he take care of the Church of God*[g]*?*

[h] Grant, O Lord, that my care and conduct in the Church of God may appear in the order and piety of my own family.

[i. 8.*]

O heavenly Lord and Master, bless us, and take us under Thy gracious protection; make us an household fearing God, and examples to others of order, diligence, faithfulness, and piety.

Ecclesiastes ix. 10. *Whatsoever thy hand findeth to do, do it with all thy might;—for the night cometh when no man can work.*

Make me, O Lord, ever sensible of the great evil of delaying the work in its season, which Thou hast appointed, lest the night surprise me unawares.

---

[g] ii. adds, "As for me and my house," &c.

[h] ii. reads, "Let Thy grace and blessing, O Lord and Master, be upon myself, my servants and family. Make them *Thy* servants; that they may be more faithful to me; that I may be just and kind to them, and careful of their precious souls: that we may be an household," &c.

"Grant that my conversation among them may be unblameable; my example instructive; my teaching and prayers for them effectual; my reproofs moderate, and my commands equal; ever remembering that I have a Master in heaven.

"To whose mercy and government I commit myself, my child, my relations and family; beseeching Him to pardon and bless and preserve us from sin and danger [iii. 'dangers'], all our days, for Jesus Christ's sake. Amen."

iii. reads, "Give me grace, O Lord, that my conversation in my family may be unblameable, my example instructive, my instructions effectual, my reproofs," &c.

"Make us all Thy servants, that we may be an household," &c.

"Now to God's mercy," &c.

1 St. John v. 14. *This is the confidence we have in God,* MATUTINA. *that if we ask any thing according to His will, He heareth* [i. 8.*] *us*[1].

That it may be unto Thy servant according to this word, I beseech Thee to hear me in the full importance of that holy prayer which Thy blessed Son hath taught us.

Our Father, which art in Heaven;

In whom we live, and move, and have our being; grant that I, and all Christians, may live worthy of this glorious relation, and that we may *not sin, knowing that we are accounted Thine*[k].

We are Thine by adoption; O make us Thine by the choice of our will.

Hallowed be Thy Name.

O God, whose Name is great, wonderful, and holy, grant that I, and all Thy children, may glorify Thee, not only with our lips, but in our lives; that others, seeing our good works, may glorify our Father which is in Heaven.

Thy Kingdom come.

May *the kingdoms of the world become the kingdoms of* [i. 9.] *the Lord and of His Christ*[l]. And may all that own Thee for their King, become Thy faithful subjects, and obey Thy laws.

Dethrone, O God, and destroy Satan and his kingdom; and enlarge the kingdom of grace.

Thy will be done in earth, as it is in Heaven.

We adore Thy goodness, O God, in making Thy will known to us in Thy Holy Word. May this Thy Word be the rule of our will, of our desires, of our lives and actions. May we ever sacrifice our will to Thine; be pleased with all Thy choices for ourselves and others, and adore Thy providence in the government of the world.

Give us this day our daily bread.

O heavenly Father, who knowest what we have need of, give us the necessaries and comforts of this life with Thy blessing; but above all, give us the bread that nourisheth to eternal life.

Acts xvii. [25.] O God, who *giveth* [*givest*] *to all life, and*

---

[1] [For the readings of ii. and iii. in this place, see below.]

[k] Ecclus. [Wisdom xv. 2.]
[l] [Rev. xi. 15.]

MATUTINA. *breath, and all things,* give us grace to impart to such as are in want, of what Thou hast given more than our daily bread.

And forgive us our trespasses as we forgive them that trespass against us.

Make us truly sensible of Thy goodness and mercy and patience towards us, that we may from our hearts forgive every one his brother their trespasses.

May my enemies ever have a place in my prayers, and in Thy mercy.

And lead us not into temptation.

[i. 10.] Support us, O heavenly Father, under all our saving trials, and grant that they may yield us the peaceable fruits of righteousness.

But deliver us from evil.

From all sin and wickedness, from our ghostly enemy, and from everlasting death, good Lord deliver us.

Deliver us from the evil of *sin*, and from the evil of *punishment*.

Deliver us, O heavenly Father, from our evil and corrupt nature, from the temptations and snares of an evil world, and from falling again into the sins we have repented of.

For Thine is the kingdom, the power, and the glory, for ever and ever. Amen.

[m]The whole creation is Thine, and under Thy government[n]. Thine is the *Power*. [o]Thou canst do whatever we pray for, if we resist not Thy will. Thou canst cause Thy Name to be sanctified in all the world[p], and set up Thy kingdom in all[q] our hearts. Thou canst cause Thy will to be done on earth as it is[r] in Heaven. Thou canst give us all things needful[s] for our souls and for our bodies[t]. Thou and Thou alone canst forgive us our sins, and dispose us to forgive one another. Thou canst secure us in the day of temptation, and deliver us from all evil[u].

To Thee, to Thee alone[x] be the glory to all eternity. Amen[y].

[m] [In i. 88, is another copy of this, with a few variations.]
[n] add, "O King of heaven."
[o] om. "Thou . . . will."
[p] "earth."
[q] add, "the world and in all."
[r] add, "done."
[s] "necessary."
[t] add, "as also the grace of contented minds."
[u] "the power of the devil and the corruption of our hearts."
[x] "therefore."
[y] add, "Amen."

By Thy Almighty power, O King of Heaven, for the glory MATUTINA. of Thy Name, and for the love of a Father, grant us all these [i. 11.] blessings which Thy Son hath taught us to pray for.

To God the Creator, the Preserver, and Disposer of all things, be the glory of all the good wrought in us, by us, and upon us.

Rev. vii. 12. *Blessing, and glory, and wisdom, and thanksgiving, and honour, and power, and might, be unto our God for ever and ever. Amen.*

Thine infinite power, wisdom, goodness, faithfulness, and truth, are the only foundation on which we may surely depend. O give us a firm faith in these Thy glorious perfections.

"With angels and archangels, and all the company of heaven, we laud and magnify Thy glorious Name, evermore praising Thee, and saying, Holy, Holy, Holy, Lord God of Hosts, heaven and earth are full of Thy glory. Glory be to Thee, O God most high. Amen."

Jude 24, 25. *Now unto Him that is able to keep us from falling, and to present us faultless before the presence of His glory with exceeding joy, to the only wise God our Saviour, be glory and majesty, dominion and power, both now and ever. Amen.*

Romans xi. 36. *For of Him, and through Him, and to Him, are all things: to whom be glory for ever. Amen.*

Romans xvi. 27. *To God only wise be glory through Jesus Christ, for ever and ever. Amen.*

Ephesians iii. 20, 21. *Now unto Him that is able to do for us abundantly more than we can ask or think, unto Him be glory in the Church by Christ Jesus, throughout all ages, world without end. Amen*[z].

---

[z] [In the two other MSS. the morning paraphrase on the Lord's Prayer stands as follows:—

ii. 6; iii. 12.] "That it may be unto Thy servant according to this word, I most humbly pray,

"*Our Father which art in heaven.* 'As a father pitieth his children, so the Lord pitieth them that fear Him.' [iii. breaks off here.] Psalm ciii. 13. 'God is in heaven and thou upon earth, therefore let thy words be few.' Eccles. v. 2. 'Even as a man spareth his own son that serveth him.'" [Mal. iii. 17.]

[ii. 7; iii. 12.] "*Hallowed be Thy name.* Rev. iv. 11. 'Thou art worthy, O Lord, to receive glory and honour and power, for Thou hast created all things, and for Thy pleasure they are, and were created.' [iii. omits the rest.] Matt. v. 16. That men, 'seeing your good works, may glorify your Father which is in heaven.'

[ii. 7; iii. 13.] "*Thy kingdom come.* Oh that that happy time would come, when Thy will may be done on earth,

MATUTINA. Prov. xvi. 3ª. [*Commit thy works unto the Lord, and thy thoughts shall be established.*]

[i. 12; ii. 8; iii. 15.] ᵇJerem. x. 23. *It is not in man that walketh to direct his steps.* Prov. iii. 6. [*In all thy ways acknowledge Him, and He shall direct thy paths.*]

Ecclus. xxxvii. 13, 14, 15, &c.ᶜ

In all my ways I do acknowledge Thee; do Thou, O Lord,

&c. 'That Thy way may be known upon earth, Thy saving health among all nations.'

[iii. reads.] "*The kingdom of God is within you.* Luke xvii. [21.] i. e. A power subjecting your will to the law of God. O take possession of this Thy kingdom; and command here as Thou dost in heaven.

"*Thy will be done in earth as it is in heaven.* That will, which would have none to perish, but 'would have all men to be saved, and to come to the knowledge of the truth.' 1 Tim. ii. 4.

"Keep my mind in a perfect indifferency towards every thing, [iii. om. these three words], that I may readily [be ready to] close with Thy will as soon as I know it; for thus [so iii.] it is done in heaven. [iii. om. what follows.] Thine angels know not Thy whole will, but when that is known," &c.

[ii. 7; iii. 13.] "*Give us this day our daily bread.* I beg not for the meat that perisheth only, but for that bread which endureth to eternal life. John vi. 27. [iii. om.]

"Having food and raiment, be therewith content." [ii. om.] Gen. xxviii. 20. "If the Lord will [iii. be with me and] give me bread to eat, and raiment to put on, then shall the Lord be my God."

"Take no thought for the morrow," &c. Prov. xxx. 8, 9. "Give me neither poverty nor riches [ii. om.] Feed me with food convenient for me, [ii. om. what follows]: lest I be full and deny Thee, or lest I be poor and steal," &c.

"Not goods for many years," for then we should [forget?] whom we depend on.

"Thou fool, this night shall thy soul," &c.

"*Ours.* By an honest labour. [ii. om.]

[ii. 7; iii. 14.] "*And forgive us our trespasses, as we forgive them that trespass against us.*

"For to what end do we live, but that God may forgive and save us?

"If we confess our sins, He is faithful and just to forgive us." 1 John i. 8. *A Prayer for Enemies, &c.* "With what measure ye mete, it shall be measured to you again." [iii. om. all but this.] "First be reconciled to thy brother, and then come," &c. Matt. v. 24. "Though I give my body to be burned, and have not charity," &c. 1 Cor. xiii. 3.

[ii. 7; iii. 14.] "*And lead us not into temptation.*

"The flesh is weak." "When thou shalt have eaten and art full, then beware lest thou forget God." Deut. vi. 12. [iii. om. all but this.] Withdraw not Thou Thy grace, without which we shall be made an easy prey. Let me never presume upon my own strength, nor upon Thy grace without using my endeavours to avoid occasions. "*Who shall persuade Ahab?*" (1 Kings xxii. 24,) which his former sins deserved. Make me ever watchful; sensible of my own weakness, and of the sufficiency of Thy grace; that I may glorify Thee by my constancy.

[ii. 8; iii. 14.] "*But deliver us from evil.* The evil one, who 'like a roaring lion walketh about, seeking whom he may devour.' 1 Pet. v. 8.

[ii. 8; iii. 15.] "*For Thine is the kingdom, the power and the glory, for ever. Amen.*"

Ecclus. ii. 10. "Did ever any trust in the Lord and was confounded?" [iii. om. the rest.] "Though He kill me, yet will I trust in Him." Job xiii. [v. 15.] "You desire riches, that you may glorify God the more; but is it not your own glory? Glorify God then in the condition His Providence has placed you in."

ᵃ [ii. iii. om.]

ᵇ [ii. has in margin] "Mem. To put the sentences in order for every day, as Proper sentences," &c.

ᶜ [ii. iii. om. these references.]

direct my paths; and teach me to guide my affairs[d], my MATUTINA. designs, my words and actions[e], with charity, discretion, justice, and piety[f].

Ps. cxliii. 8. *Shew Thou me the way that I should walk in*[g]; and give[h] me grace that I may follow the conduct of Thy good Spirit. For Jesus Christ's sake. Amen.

Micah vi. 8. *He hath shewed thee, O man, what is good:* [ii. and iii.] *and what doth the Lord thy God require of thee, but to do justice, to love mercy, and to walk humbly with thy God?*

The Resignation. From sudden death, good Lord, deliver [i. 12.] me, my children and family, and all that have desired my prayers.

May we never be surprised in sin; and may Thy mercy supply whatever shall be wanting in our preparation for death.

For myself: with the submission of a penitent criminal, under the righteous sentence of death, passed upon all mankind, I do most humbly desire to resign my life a sacrifice of obedience in union with that of my Saviour, to Thee, O God; trusting in Thy mercy and goodness and promises, through His merits and mediation, at the hour of death, and in the day of judgment.

Matthew v. 16. *Let your light so shine before men, that they may see your good works, and glorify your Father which is in heaven.*

O my great Master! may I edify others by my example; dispense the light which Thy grace shall vouchsafe me, and in all humility direct all the glory to God.

Matthew v. 48. *Be ye perfect, even as your Father which is in heaven is perfect.*

All my endeavours without Thy assistance, O Jesus, will be ineffectual.

Mark ix. 23. *All things are possible to him that believeth.*

Yes, Lord, and therefore I beg that *faith,* of Him to whom all things are possible, that I may be able to *discover,* to *avoid,* to *resist,* and to *root out,* whatever is evil in me.

---

[d] [iii. adds, " my thoughts."]
[e] [ii. omits all but "affairs."]
[f] [ii. om. " charity."]
[g] [iii. " give grace to follow."]
[h] [ii. om. the rest.]

MATUTINA. O Jesus, obtain this grace for Thy otherwise helpless creature.

Grant that I may this day escape all the snares laid for me, by the devil, the world, or mine own corrupt heart.

Grant that I may this day omit no part of my duty.

[ii. 8.] *A double-minded man* [*is unstable in all his ways.* S. James i. 8].

All things work together for good to those that fear God. Rom. viii. 28. Him therefore will I fear and serve. *Take no thought for the morrow, &c.*

A man's life [and happiness] *consisteth not in the abundance of the things which he possesseth.* Luke xii. 15.

Without Me ye can do nothing. John xv. 5.

Keep thy heart with all diligence, for out of it are the issues of life. Prov. iv. 24.

Resolve to let no sinful, vain, or even suspicious thoughts settle in your heart, for *out of the heart proceed adulteries, &c.* Mat. [Mark vii. 21, 22.]

[ii. and iii.] Prov. x. 9. *He that walketh uprightly walketh surely.* That you may do so, keep, &c.

[ii. 9.] *To do justice and judgment is more acceptable to the Lord than sacrifice.* [Prov.] xxi. 3. *Let not mercy and truth forsake thee; . . . so shalt thou find favour and good success with God and man.* iii. 3. *In the multitude of words there wanteth not sin.* x. 19. *He that answereth a matter before he heareth it, it is folly and shame unto him.* xviii. [13.]

A soft answer turneth away strife, but cruel words stir up anger. xv. i.

He that is slow to anger is better than the mighty, and he that ruleth his spirit, than he that taketh a city. xvi. 32.

It is the glory of a man to pass over a transgression. xix. 11.

Rejoice not when thine enemy falleth. [xxiv. 17.] *Pride goeth before destruction.* xvi. 18.

By humility and the fear of the Lord are riches, honour, and life. [xxii. 4.]

[ii. 10.] *Slothfulness casteth into a deep sleep.* [xix. 5.]

He that loveth pleasures shall be a poor man. xxi. 17.

As we have opportunity, let us do good unto all men. Gal. vi. 10.

To the Angel of the Church, &c. [i]Let me remember my M<small>ATUTINA</small>. character,—and that it is for my life. That all is vanity besides doing one's duty.

Whatever thy hand findeth to do, do it with all thy might; for the night cometh, when no man can work.

To-day if ye will hear His voice, harden not your hearts.

Ecclus. iii. 18. *The greater thou art, the more humble thyself, and thou shalt find favour before the Lord.*

Commit thy way unto the Lord, and He shall [bring it to pass].

Where your treasure is, there will your heart be.

Gentle. *That every man please his brother to edification.*

More blessed to give than to receive.

We must through much tribulation [enter into the kingdom of God.]

If any man suffer as a Christian.

Eccles. [ii. 2.] *Behold, I said of joy, it is madness, and of laughter, it is folly.*

It is better to go to the house of mourning [than to the house of feasting].

Mortify therefore your members that are [on the earth].

Be ye not conformable to this present [world].

Look unto Jesus, the Author and Finisher [of our faith].

Let your light so shine before men that they may see [your good works].

He looked for a city whose builder and maker was God. [ii. 11.]

Who for the joy that was set before Him [endured the Cross].

2 Chron. xii. 20. *We know not what to do, but our eyes are upon Thee.*

Raillery becomes not a clergyman. St. Ambrose.

1 Thess. iv. 6. *Let no man go beyond or defraud his brother in any matter, because the Lord is the Avenger of all such.*

Socrates his character: "*semper eodem incedebat vultu*[k]."

Prov. xi. 3. *The integrity of the upright shall guide them.*

Give us this day our daily bread. For we depend as much

---

[i] [*Prima manu,* " Remember your character ... your life."]

[k] [Vid. Cic. de Off. i. 26; Tusc. Disp. iii. 15; Seneca de Ira, ii. 6.]

MATUTINA. on Thy Providence for our food, as the Israelites did in the wilderness, when Thou gavest them manna every day to eat.

[i. 13; iii. 26, 27.]

Exodus xxviii. 29. *And Aaron shall bear the names of the children of Israel in the breast-plate of judgment upon his breast, for a memorial before the Lord continually*[1].

O God, the God of the spirits of all flesh, have respect unto the prayer of Thy servant on behalf of himself and of this people. Lord, put Thy fear into our hearts, and give us true repentance for our great and crying sins; root out all growing vices, and avert the judgments which we have justly deserved[m].

Preserve this Church in the midst of this[n] uncertain world. Keep us from all wild and dangerous errors, and prepare us for what Thy providence shall bring forth.

Bless the Lord of this isle with a spirit of wisdom, justice, and the fear of God; provide his offices and council[o] with able men, such as fear God, men of truth, hating covetousness.

Endue the clergy with all those graces and abilities, that are necessary to fit them for their high calling[p].

Extend and suit Thy graces to all conditions of men amongst us[q]: that we may all be upright in our dealings, obedient to our governors, peaceable in our lives, sober, honest, temperate, chaste in our conversation, and charitable to the poor, and one towards another.

Increase the number and the graces of all such as love and fear Thee[r].

Enlighten the minds of the ignorant, awaken the con-

---

[1] [i. refers to] Philem. v. 4; 1 Thess. i. 2; Eph. i. 16; Phil. i. 4; Col. i. 9; Rom. i. 9. "*I make mention of you always in my prayers.*"

[m] iii. reads, "... have respect unto the prayers of Thy servant in behalf of this people, whom I have too, too presumptuously undertaken to conduct unto eternal life, through a corrupt world, infinite errors, and powerful enemies. And O that my concern for them may hold some proportion to the value of souls and the account I am to give.
"Lord, pardon all our crying sins, root out," &c.

[n] iii. "an."

[o] "Council and offices," iii.

[p] iii. adds, "Support and bless them in the way of their duty; and make Thy word in their mouth, and Thine ordinances in their hands, effectual for the salvation of the people committed to their charge."

[q] iii. "of men. To the rich, that they may be rich in good works; to the poor, that they may be contented with their lot; that all may be upright in their dealings, obedient to their governors, peaceable in their lives, chaste in their conversations, and charitable one towards another."

[r] iii. "Fear and serve Thee faithfully."

sciences of the careless, silence the gainsayers, convert the MATUTINA. profane, and all that hold the truth in unrighteousness[s].

Rebuke the spirit of antichrist, idolatry, and libertinism,— the sins of drunkenness, whoredom, litigiousness, defrauding the public, and sacrilege, which are broken in amongst us[t].

1721. O God of Peace and Truth, rebuke the spirit of [iii. 17.] antichrist, libertinism, and discord, which is ready to break in upon this Church and nation; rebuke its abettors; and give me grace, like a faithful servant and soldier of Jesus Christ, to stand in the breach, and to omit no part of my duty in this day of danger; for Jesus Christ's sake, the Prince of Peace, and Son of Thy Love.

In tender mercy, remember, O God, all sick and dying [i. 13; iii. 27.] persons[u], that they may omit nothing that is necessary to make their peace with Thee. Be gracious unto all that are in affliction of mind or body, or under any pressing calamity; all desolate widows and fatherless children; all that call upon Thee in their distress, and have none else to help them.

May this memorial be before the Lord continually[x]: that His unworthy servant (who has no hopes of success but in God's gracious assistance) may see the effects of His grace working with him: and that both he, and the flock over which the Holy Ghost hath made him overseer, may become acceptable to God, through Jesus Christ our Lord. Amen, Amen.

Ps. cxxvii. [3.] *Children are an heritage of the Lord.* [i. 14.]

O God, the Father of our Lord Jesus Christ, for His sake be gracious unto my children. Preserve them from dangers and all sad accidents; give and continue to them healthful bodies, understanding souls, and sanctified spirits, that they may remember their Creator all their days.

May Thy restraining grace preserve them from the temptations of an evil world[y].

---

[s] iii. adds, "And grant that such as fall into sins inconsistent with true Christianity, may patiently submit to be reformed by godly discipline."

[t] iii. om. this paragraph.

[u] iii. om. "that they . . . gracious unto."

[x] [The rest of this sentence is from iii. only.]

[y] [Interlined "from the lust of."]

MATUTINA. Endue them, I beseech Thee, with sound principles of virtue, religion, and holiness.

Leave them not to their own choices. Be Thou their Light and Guide, and give them hearts always open to receive the truth.

Direct and bless my son's studies, that he may become wise unto salvation.

O be Thou pleased to be their Father and their portion in this world, and in the world to come, for Jesus Christ His sake, and grant that I may not be wanting in any part of my duty to them.

[In ii. 74; iii. 25, this Prayer stands as follows.]

Children and the fruit of the womb are an heritage and gift that cometh of the Lord. Ps. cxxvii. 4.

Mary, born Sept. 8, 1699[z]. Died Nov. 27, 1712.
Alice, born Feb. 24, 1701. Died June 3, 1703.
Thomas, born Oct. 12, 1700. Died June 8, 1701.
Thomas, born Aug. 24, 1703.

O God the Father of our Lord Jesus Christ, for His sake be gracious unto the child[a] which Thou hast given me: preserve him from dangers and all sad accidents; give him an healthful body, an understanding soul, and a sanctified spirit, that he may remember his Creator all his days.

Let me not be wanting in any part of my duty towards him. Give me grace to instruct him in the true religion, gently to correct his failings, honestly to provide for his necessary support, and to be an example to him of true piety, sobriety, and diligence.

But if I do not live to be and to do this unto him, be Thou, O God, his father, his guide, his support and his portion, in this life and in the life to come.

Let Thy restraining grace preserve him from the temptations of an evil world; let him seriously consider the vows that are upon him, and continue in the state of salvation unto which Thou hast called him, unto his life's end.

And when he has done good in his generation, Lord, receive him into the inheritance of Thy dear Son, for Whose sake I most humbly beg to be heard. Amen.

---

[z] ii. "since dead," no dates.   [a] ii. "children," and so on in the plural.

My children: If I do not live to tell you why I have MATUTINA. saved no more for you out of my Bishoprick, let this satisfy [ii. 75.] you, that the less you have of goods gathered from the Church, the better the rest that I leave you will prosper. For Church livings were never designed to make families, or raise portions out of them, but to maintain our families, to keep up hospitality, to feed the poor, &c. And one day you will be glad that this was my settled opinion. And God grant that I may act accordingly.

Remember that the daughter of a Priest, if taken in a fault, was to be put to death under Moses' law. Levit. xxi. 9.

I never expect, and I thank God I never desire, that you or your children should ever be great; but if ever the Providence of God raiseth any that proceed from my loins to any degree of worldly wealth or honour, I desire they will look back to the place and person from whence they came; this will keep them humble and sober-minded. And above all I desire they will never think themselves too good to be servants, immediate[b].

[On the opposite leaf, iii. 24.] *Adspirationes.*

Imprint on his soul a deep sense of the love and fear that is due to Thee, O God.

Endue him with sound principles of virtue and religion.

Direct him to such thoughts and resolutions, as may lead him to make good the dedication I have made of him to Thee and to Thy service.

Leave him not, O merciful God, to his own choices. Be Thou his light and his guide. Let eternity be ever in his view. Let no worldly respects or interests divert him from Thy service.

Grant that all carnal affections may die in him, and that all things belonging to the Spirit may live and grow in him.

Deliver him, O Lord, from the occasions of sin; from the snares of evil company, and from the infection of evil example.

---

[b] In marg.: "Vid. last page but one of this book," [which is missing. Perhaps the sentence went on, "servants of the Most High God;" *vel tale aliquid.*]

MATUTINA.   Give him an heart always willing to be taught, always open to receive the truth[c].

[i. 14.]   Parents who labour to leave their children in a condition to be independent, to be idle, to live in luxury, &c., do put them in the way of ruin, without a great grace of God, which they are not always careful to pray for.

Our blessed Lord, because He loved the rich young man, directed him to sell what he had, and give to the poor, knowing that riches are a snare, a temptation, and a hindrance to our happiness.

[i. 14; iii. 16.]   Give Thy holy grace to all those for whom I have undertaken at the sacred font: [i. om. what follows.] That they may in their own persons renounce the devil and all his works, and constantly believe Thy holy Word, and obediently keep Thy commandments: that Thou mayest give unto them the blessing of eternal life, and make them partakers of Thine everlasting kingdom.

[i. 15.]   Proverbs xxi. 1. *The King's heart is in the hand of the Lord, as the rivers of water, He turneth it whithersoever He will.*

Let this Thy power, O Lord, be magnified on his Majesty,

---

[c] [iii. 24. as a foot-note after the prayer.] "April 19, 1721. Tommy entered a commoner in C. C. Oxon, under Dr. Criggan [?], senior student."

[The former of the above prayers, that in MS. i., must have been composed while the Bishop had still more than one child, yet when his son was old enough to begin his "studies;" i.e. (as may be seen by the dates relating to his children) between 1709 and 1712. The latter would seem to have been written when he had only one child, i.e. after Mary's death, in 1712; only that it occurs in MS. iii., which is certainly of an earlier date than MS. i. Perhaps the Bishop made it as a special prayer for his only son immediately after his "dedication" of him; whether that word means his baptism, or an inward vow to bring him up (if it might be) a clergyman. Still this does not account for the use of the plural number in MS. i., especially with the following memoranda annexed, the first nine of them apparently of the same date with the transcript of the prayer. "My son born Aug. 24, 1703. Grandson born March 18, 1734. Grandson dyed May 7, 1736. My son ordained deacon, May 28, 1729. My son ordained priest, Dec. 19, 1731. Son made chaplain to the King, rector of St. Stephen's, Walbrook; made his Majesty's sub-almoner April 8, 1743. Made prebend of Westminster, April, 1743;" (these two dates and what follows in a different will, and in the Bishop's older hand.) "My son came to see me June 10, 1743; he went from hence Aug. 10, 1743. Installed prebend of Westm., Dec. 1, 1743." Then in still more tremulous writing: "Aug. 12, 1750, son went off for England from Douglass: [they?] were in danger on board the vessel. God be praised for his deliverance."]

and on the Lord of this Isle, and on all that are put in authority under them, that we may be governed with truth and justice, by men fearing and honouring God, protecting the Christian religion, and punishing evil-doers. In order to this end vouchsafe them, I beseech Thee, all the graces necessary for their high station, and for their eternal happiness.

Colossians iv. 1. *Masters, give unto your servants that which is just and equal, knowing that ye also have a Master in Heaven.* [i. 15.]

O heavenly Lord and Master, direct me to, and bless me with, good and faithful servants. Let Thy blessing be upon them, and upon my affairs committed to their care; and may I never be wanting in any part of my duty to them, for Jesus Christ's sake. Amen.

Burton School[e]. I pray God bless this school, and all that shall be educated in it.

Relations, Benefactors, &c. Be gracious, O Lord, unto my relations, benefactors, enemies, and all that have desired my prayers; all who, by their own labours, do minister to our necessities; together with all the known and unknown benefactors of this diocese. Render, O God, a good reward, and a plentiful return, to all those who have been our benefactors. Grant that we may all so live here, as that we may meet hereafter in the paradise of God.

For myself and labours. Bless all my labours for Thy glory, O Lord, and for the good of Thy Church, and especially those Instructions, which through Thy blessing I have published, and all the glory be to Thee.

[In iii. 17, this stands as follows.] "1707. Bless all my labours for the good of my flock, and especially *that instruction,* which by Thy gracious favour and assistance, I have provided for them."

1 Tim. iv. 15. *Give thyself wholly to these things, that Thy profiting may appear to all.*

God grant that I may do so; and I pray God preserve me from ease, idleness, and trifling away my precious time.

[e] [This entry must have been made in or after 1724.]

MATUTINA. S. John xvi. 23. *Verily I say unto you, Whatsoever ye*
[i. 16.] *shall ask the Father in My Name, He will give it you.*

These are what I ask, O God and Father, above all things, for myself, and for all that have desired my prayers :—That we may be restored to Thy image, and never deface it by our sins; that the image of Satan may be destroyed in us, that all carnal affections may die in us, and that all things belonging to the Spirit may [live and grow in us] : that Christ may dwell in our hearts by faith; that Thy Name, and the Name of our Lord Jesus Christ, may be glorified in us, and we in Him; that our hearts may be entirely Thine; that we may never grieve Thy Holy Spirit; but that we may continue Thine for ever, for Jesus Christ, His sake. Amen.

Conversation. May I never hear with pleasure, never repeat, such things as may dishonour God, or injure my neighbour or my own character and ministry. [This occurs again in i. 24, with the text 1 Cor. xiii., "Charity rejoiceth not in iniquity."]

Ephesians iv. 29. *Let no corrupt communication proceed out of your mouth, but that which is good to the use of edifying, that it may minister grace unto the hearers.*

Grant, O God, that I may delight in Thy law; that my conversation may be truly Christian. Enable me to speak of Thy divine perfections as becomes a Christian bishop, that I may minister grace unto the hearers.

James iv. 11. *Speak not evil one of another.*

Ephesians v. 4. *Foolish talking or jesting are not convenient, but rather giving of thanks.*

Psalm cxxxiii. 3. *Set a watch, O Lord, before my mouth, and keep the door of my lips.*

Matthew xii. 34. *Out of the abundance of the heart the mouth speaketh. How can ye, being evil, speak good things?*

O Holy Spirit of grace, enable me to speak of the things of God, instead of things vain and trifling.

That Thou wouldst effectually reveal thy Son in me.

[i. 17.] John xv. 7. *Ask what ye will, and it shall be done unto you.*

These, O Jesus, are the things that I ask. Intercede for me, that I may be truly sensible of the diseases I labour

under, and thankfully embrace the means which Thy good- MATUTINA
ness hath ordained for my recovery.

Grant that the end of all my actions and designs may be the glory of God.

Enable me to resist all the sinful appetites of my corrupt nature.

Grant that I may hunger and thirst after righteousness.

Vouchsafe me the spirit of adoption—of supplication and prayer—of praise and thanksgiving.

Obtain for me, O Jesus, the graces of mortification and self-denial; the graces of a true humility, and the fear of God.

Grant, O God, that I may never knowingly live one moment under Thy displeasure, or in any known sin.

Grant, O God, that as I have been regenerate, and made Thy child by adoption and grace, I may daily be renewed by Thy Holy Spirit: for Jesus Christ's sake.

2 Pet. i. 4. *Enable me, gracious God, to escape the corruption that is in the world through lust, that I may be partaker of the divine nature.*

Lord, grant me grace to withstand the temptations of the world, the flesh, and the devil; and with a pure heart and mind to follow Thee, the only God, through Jesus Christ our Lord. Amen.

Let Thy love, O God, be shed abroad in my heart, by the power of the Holy Ghost, and grant that it may appear in my life, my conversation, my words, and actions, for Jesus Christ His sake.

Blessed be God that I was admitted into the fellowship of Christ's religion. Grant, O God, that I may eschew all those things that are contrary to my profession, and follow all such things as are agreeable to the same, for Jesus Christ's sake.

Keep me, I beseech Thee, O heavenly Father, under the [i. 18.] protection of Thy good providence, and make me to have a perpetual fear and love of Thy holy Name; through Jesus Christ our Lord.

Grant that I may so pass through things temporal, that I finally lose not the things eternal: for Jesus Christ His sake.

MATUTINA. Pour into my heart such love towards Thee, that I, loving Thee above all things, may obtain Thy promises, which exceed all that we can desire: through Jesus Christ our Lord.

Graft in my heart the love of Thy Name, increase in me true religion; nourish me with all goodness, and of Thy great mercy keep me in the same.

Put away from me all hurtful things, and give me those things that be profitable for me, through Jesus Christ.

Mercifully grant unto me, O God, such a measure of Thy grace, that running the way of Thy commandments, I may obtain Thy gracious promises, and be made partaker of Thy heavenly treasure, through Jesus Christ our Lord. Amen.

Forgive me those things whereof my conscience is afraid, and give me those good things which we are not worthy to ask, but through the merits and mediation of Thy Son Jesus Christ.

That I may obtain that which Thou dost promise, make me to love that which Thou dost command, through Jesus Christ.

Keep me from all things hurtful, and lead me to all things necessary to my salvation, through Jesus Christ.

May Thy Grace, O God, always prevent and follow me, and make me continually to be given to all good works; through Jesus Christ.

2 *Tim. ult.* 18. *Morning.*

The Lord deliver me from every evil work, and preserve me to His heavenly Kingdom; to whom be glory for ever and ever. Amen.

O that Thy Holy Spirit may direct and rule my heart, O God, through Jesus Christ.

Of Thy bountiful goodness, O Lord, keep me, I beseech Thee, from all things that may hurt me, that I may cheerfully accomplish those things which Thou wouldest have done, through Jesus Christ our Lord.

[i. 19.] Grant, O God, that I may be cleansed from all my sin, and serve Thee with a quiet mind, through Jesus Christ our Lord.

Deliver me, O Lord, from the bands of those sins, which

through my frailty I have committed; for Jesus Christ's MATUTINA. sake.

Faith. Grant, O God, that I may so perfectly, and without all doubt, believe in Thy Son Jesus Christ, that my faith in Thy sight may never be reproved, for the sake of the same Jesus Christ.

Against wavering. Grant, O God, that we may not be carried about with every blast of vain doctrine, but that we may be firmly established in the truth of Thy holy Gospel, through—

Jesus Christ the Way, &c. Grant, O God, that I may perfectly know Thy Son Jesus Christ to be the Way, the Truth, and the Life—the Author of the way, the Teacher of the truth, and the Giver of life; that I may steadfastly walk in the way that leadeth to eternal life, through the same Jesus Christ.

Covetousness. Give me grace to forsake all covetous desires, and inordinate love of riches and pleasures; through Jesus Christ. [i. 19.]

Grant that I may both perceive and know what things I ought to do, and also may have grace and power faithfully to fulfil the same, through Jesus Christ.

Grant me, O God, the true circumcision of the Spirit, that my heart and all my members, being mortified from all carnal lusts, I may in all things obey Thy blessed will.

O that we, who know Thee now by faith, may, after this life, have the fruition of Thy glorious Godhead!

In all our dangers and necessities, stretch forth Thy right hand to save and defend us.

Charity. O send Thy Holy Ghost, and pour into my heart that most excellent gift of charity, that very bond of peace and of all virtue, without which, whoever liveth is counted dead before Thee. Grant— [i. 20.]

I do most humbly beseech Thee, O God, that as by Thy special grace preventing me, Thou dost put into my mind good desires, so by Thy continual help I may bring the same to good effect, through, &c.

O everlasting God, grant that as Thy holy Angels always

do Thee service in Heaven, so by Thy appointment they may succour and defend us on earth, through, &c.

Grant me grace so to follow Thy blessed Saints in virtuous and godly living, that I may come to those unspeakable joys, which Thou hast prepared for them that unfeignedly love Thee.

I pray God that my whole spirit, (my understanding, will, and conscience,) my soul, (my appetites, affections, and passions,) and my body, (the tabernacle of my soul,) be preserved blameless unto the coming of our Lord Jesus Christ[t]. 1 Thess. v. 15.

May I take pleasure in abiding in Thy presence, O God; in depending upon Thee; in leaving myself entirely to Thy disposal, as a continual sacrifice to Thy will.

Give me a victory over all my sins and imperfections, increase in me the graces of faith, hope, and charity; of humility, meekness, patience, and resignation, and all other Christian virtues, for Jesus Christ's sake. Amen.

Preserve me, gracious God, from spiritual pride, from ascribing any thing I have done, or can do, to myself, and robbing Thee of the glory of saving me from eternal ruin.

Take possession, O Jesus, of Thy right in my soul, which Thou hast redeemed with Thy most precious blood, and root out all self-righteousness, self-interest, and self-will;—that Thou mayest be my righteousness, and all in me.

[i. 21.] *Repentance.* Give me, O God, such a true sorrow for my sins, as shall enable me to embrace all the necessary means, how bitter soever, for rooting sin [them?] out of my soul.

Faith. O that I may believe in Thee, O God, and put my whole confidence and trust in Thee alone, and not in any thing that I myself can do.

[i. 21, 24.] *Humility.* I have all the reason in the world to be humble. Without God I am nothing[f]. Without His help[g] and grace, I can do nothing that is good[h]. Without His Word,
[i. 21.] I know nothing. Of myself, I deserve nothing but punishment[i]. Of my own, I have nothing but faults, imperfections,

---

[f] i. 24. reads, "Without God I know nothing."
[g] i. 24. om.
[h] i. 24. om. this clause.
[i] i. 24. om. " but punishment."

and sins; an inclination to evil, an aversion to good, unruly senses, ungovernable[k] passions, unreasonable affections[l].   Matutina.

1 Cor. i. 30. O Lord Jesus Christ, who art made unto us of God, our wisdom, by revealing Him and His glorious perfections; our righteousness, by satisfying the justice of God in our nature; our sanctification, by procuring for us the Holy Spirit, and by restoring us, being sinners, to God's favour; our redemption, being in a state of damnation [He?] redeemed us.—O Jesus, for these mighty favours, all love and glory be to Thee, with the Father and the Holy Ghost, for ever. Amen.

Conversation. O Holy Spirit of Grace, enable me to overcome the shame of a degenerate age, which will hear nothing with delight but what concerns this world. O touch my heart with the true love of God, the excellences of His laws, the pleasantness of His service, the wonders of His providences, &c.: that I may edify those that hear me. This I beg for Jesus Christ.

The way of an happy life. Lay nothing too much to [i. 22.] heart; desire nothing too eagerly; rejoice not excessively, nor grieve too much for disasters; be not violently bent on any design; nor let any worldly cares hinder you from taking care of your soul; and remember, that it is necessary to be a Christian (that is, to govern one's self by motives of Christianity) in the most common actions of civil life.

Col. iii. 17. *Whatsoever ye do in word or deed, do all in the name of the Lord Jesus, giving thanks unto God and the Father by Him.*

He that would not fall into temptation, must have a presence of mind, a watchful eye over himself; he must have great things in view, distinguish betwixt time and eternity, or else he will follow what passion, not what reason and religion, suggest.

Christian perfection. Whoever aspires after it, (that is, in being so united to God as to be one spirit with Him,) must resolve to do all things with this sole view, To please God.

---

[k] 924, "wild," and the last two words omitted.

[l] This paragraph is repeated almost word for word in i. 24, with a text prefixed, 1 Pet. v. 5: "God resisteth the proud, and giveth grace to the humble."

MATUTINA. This I purpose, this I forbear, this I undertake, this I do, this I suffer—in obedience to the will of God; and because I believe it will be for His glory. This should be our express purpose, at all times, when we have time to make it; and should be often renewed, lest our own will come to be the motive of our actions.

If I am careful to do this, I shall always have my end, whether I succeed or be disappointed, being convinced it is God's will.

Romans xvi. 14. *Put ye on the Lord Jesus, and make not provision for the flesh, to fulfil the lusts thereof.*

Grant, O Lord, that *I may keep under my body, and bring it into subjection, lest by any means when I have preached to others I myself should be a castaway.* 1 Cor. ix. 27.

1 Peter iii. 8—11. *Be ye all of one mind, having compassion one of another; be pitiful, be courteous; not rendering evil for evil, nor railing for railing, but contrariwise blessing. For he that will love life, and see good days, let him refrain his tongue from evil, and his lips that they speak no guile. Let him eschew evil, and do good; let him seek peace, and ensue it.*

[i. 23.] Give me, O Lord, a wise, a sober, a serious, a religious heart, that I may do Thee honour in a faithful discharge of the duties of my calling.

Give me true Christian courage, that I may never faint in the way of my duty.

Preserve me from evil counsels and rash enterprises. *O make Thy way plain before my face.*

Support me this day under all the difficulties I shall meet with.

I offer myself to Thee, O God, this day, to do in me, and with me, as to Thee seems most meet.

O Lord, sanctify me wholly, and grant that my whole spirit and soul and body may be preserved blameless unto the coming of our Lord Jesus Christ. Amen.

Vouchsafe me, gracious God, the spirit of adoption, whereby I may cry, Abba, Father, and apply to Thee, through Jesus Christ, not as an angry judge, but as to a merciful and loving father.

Treat the world with a holy severity, if you would have it to reverence you.

Remember, that the life of man is only to be valued for its usefulness. MATUTINA. [i. 24.]

Matthew vii. 13, 14. *Enter ye in at the straight gate; for wide, &c.*

Grant, O Jesus, that I may never flatter myself or others on this subject.

John xv. 12. *This is My commandment, that ye love one another.*

O Thou, who hast given me this command and pattern, give me a sincere desire of following, and grace and power to do it.

Resignation. Perfect resignation the surest way to heaven.

Conversation. 1 Cor. xiii. [6.] *Charity rejoiceth not in iniquity.* May I never hear, never repeat with pleasure, any thing that shall dishonour God, or injure my neighbour.

[MS. iii., under the head "Matutina," contains the following paragraphs in addition to those which have been or will be given.]

O. of A. [Oath of Allegiance?] O God of light and truth and goodness, may Thy Holy Spirit direct me in this (to me) perplexing case. Let me faithfully consider what shall be required of me, that I may see my duty, and avoid the paths of error and danger. Let nothing seduce me from a settled purpose of doing what I believe will be most acceptable to Thee. And grant that I may omit nothing that I ought to do in order to be rightly informed. [iii. 16.]

O Lord, be gracious unto my brothers and sisters, and my relations. Grant that they may serve Thee faithfully in this world, and that we may meet in peace in the world to come. [iii. 17.]

[Then a prayer (which is given, p. 30) for his godchildren; then],

Remember, O God, for good, my friends, my benefactors, and all that have desired my prayers.

O God, forgive my enemies, persecutors, and slanderers. Forgive their sins, and turn their hearts, and give me grace to love, to bless, and to do good to them.

Vouchsafe unto all such as are now under the censures of the Church, a *true sense* of their crimes, *true repentance* for them, and Thy *gracious pardon*, that their souls may be saved in the day of the Lord Jesus.

Grant that by Thy Holy Spirit I may have a right judg-

MATUTINA. ment in all things, and evermore rejoice in His comfort, through the merits of Christ Jesus our Saviour.

[iii. 18.] *Difficult times.* Direct me, gracious God, in this difficult time, that I may neither speak nor act anything unbecoming my character, that I may never prostitute my conscience, for any worldly consideration whatever.

[iii. 19.] *Aspirations.* Make me, O God, truly sensible of the affliction of Christ's Church: the want of discipline, of charity, and of zeal for Thy glory; that with the zeal of Elijah I may lay these things before the Throne of Grace.

For one who leads a careless life. O God of mercy, touch the heart, and open the eyes, of this unhappy sinner, that he may see his danger, and that iniquity may not be his ruin.

Call him powerfully from his wicked life, and forgive his sin for Jesus' sake.

O merciful Shepherd, bring him back into Thy fold, that he may obey Thy voice and follow Thee.

Faith. Grant, O God, that I may with humility receive, and with perseverance hold fast, all those truths which Thou hast revealed.

I thank Thee, O God, for Thy holy Word, and for that Thou hast not left us, in the affair of eternity, to the uncertainty of our own reason and judgment.

Defend me against all delusions of error; the snares of wit and learning; the railleries of profane men; and from deserting the truth under oppression.

Grant, O God, that neither education, interest, prejudice, nor passion, may ever hinder me from discerning the truth.

Open the eyes of all that are in error: heal the wounds of the divided Church: that we may be one fold under one Shepherd. Amen.

[iii. 20.] *Despair.* Let Thy infinite mercy deliver me from despair, both now and at the hour of death.

Judgment-day. Grant, O Lord, that I may be of the number of those that shall find mercy at that day.

Zacchæus. The good Lord grant that I may give a proof of the sincerity of my conversion by a change of life.

Hope. Grant, O God, that amidst all the discouragements, difficulties, dangers, distress and darkness of this mortal life,

I may depend upon Thy mercy, and on this build my hopes, as on a sure foundation.

Let the multitude of Thy tender mercies preserve all from despair.

Resignation. Grant that I may receive the punishment of my sins with patience and resignation.

Injuries, Persecution. Give me, O God, an heart to consider that man could have no power against me, unless it were given from above. John xix. 11.

Trouble. Remember me, O God, in the day of trouble. Secure me, by Thy grace, from all excess of fear, concern, and sadness.

(*Prima manu*), "Ὑπὲρ ἐπιστροφῆς τοῦ Δεσπότου νήσου ταυτῆς."

Enemies. Change their hearts by Thy grace, or restrain their malice by Thy power.

Troubles and Afflictions. In Thee, O Blessed Jesus, we find matter of comfort and consolation under every hardship and affliction, which Thou Thyself underwentest. Lord, grant that I may ever imitate Thy patience and resignation.

Oppression in the Gate.

Afflictions. Let the afflictions I meet with be in some measure serviceable towards the appeasing of Thy wrath. Let them prove the happy occasion of forwarding my conversion and salvation.

May I with equal submission and reverence receive the most different dispensations of Thy Providence. We cannot wish one event rather than another without presumption,—without making ourselves judges of secret things which belong to God only, and of future things which God has concealed from us.

Impropriations. O God of truth and justice, restore this [i. 24.] Church to her just rights. Pardon our sins that have brought this calamity upon us. Bless the endeavours of all such as shall assist us to recover our rights. And of Thy goodness touch and turn the hearts of those who would deprive us of them; for Jesus Christ His sake. Amen.

James v. 15. *And the prayer of faith shall save the sick;* [i. 25; iii. 220.]

MATUTINA. *and the Lord shall raise him up; and if he hath committed sins (ἀφεθήσεται αὐτῷ,) he shall be absolved,"* i.e. upon his confession.

O Lord of life and death! have mercy upon all those of my flock, who are now visited with sickness; sanctify this Thy fatherly correction to us all, that we may search our ways, and see whence this visitation cometh.

Have mercy upon all that are appointed to die, and grant that they omit nothing that is necessary to make their peace with Thee, and that they may be delivered from death eternal.

And God grant that we may apply all our hearts to that holy and heavenly wisdom, while we live here, which may in the end bring us to life everlasting: through Jesus Christ our Lord. Amen.

[i. 25.] A.D. 1700. An epidemic distemper, which carried[s] off a great many[t].

A.D. 1724-5. A very sickly spring stitch[u].

A.D. 1728-9. A raging pleurisy, &c.

A.D. 1734. Many people, and some suddenly, and upon very short sickness, especially those in years.

A.D. 1737. A cold and fever carries off very many in all parts of the island.

Nov. 1739. A violent epidemical flux carried off a great many.

April, 1740. The epidemic flux and diarrhœa still continues to carry off a great number of people, &c.

The above distemper still continues (Feb. 1740-41) on the south side, and carries off a great number.

1741. A very great famine. Corn and all other necessaries of life not only at an excessive price, but hardly to be gotten from other countries. Wheat, 8s. or 9s. a-bushel; barley at 5s.; oats at 2s. and 2s. 6d., &c.

Give us, O heavenly Father, in this day of necessity, our daily bread: and give us all grace to impart to such as are in want, of what Thou hast given us more than our daily bread: for Jesus Christ's sake. Amen.

A.D. 1743. A contagious fever, of which many die, and whole families take it.

---

[s] iii. "carries."
[t] iii. "number."
[u] iii. "which takes off very many by a stitch and pleurisy."

Jan. 1747-8. A pleuritic fever, of which very many die, both young and old. MATUTINA. [i. 25.*]

Dec. 1750. *Small-pox.* O Almighty God, to whom alone belong the issues of life and death, look down from heaven, I most humbly beseech Thee, upon all those now visited with this sickness. Visit them, O Lord, with Thy salvation; deliver them in Thy good appointed time from their bodily pain; save their souls for Thy mercy's sake: that if it be Thy good pleasure to prolong their days, they may live to Thee and to Thy glory, by doing good in their generation; or else receive them into the mansions of the blessed, for the sake of Thy Son our Lord Jesus Christ. Amen.

A pleuritic fever which carryeth off a great many, both young and old. 1752.

The Oath administered to the Bishop of Man at his Instalment; administered to me, Apr. 11, 1698. [i. 27; ii. 95; iii. 28.]

My allegiance to the King's Majesty of England, and my former oaths according to the laws there reserved,

I swear to be true to the Right Honourable the Earl of Derby and his heirs, and will perform all such duties unto them as belongs to my place being Bishop here:

And to my power shall defend and maintain the ancient laws, statutes and customs, proper and belonging unto this Isle, and prerogatives due to the Heirs thereof:

And with my best advice and counsel be aiding and assisting to the Captain of this Isle or Governor for the time being, for furtherance of the government and benefit of the said Isle. So, &c.

THO. SODOR AND MAN[x].

[y]O God, the King of all the earth, grant that no[z] breach of this oath may ever[a] rise up in judgment against me.

Look down in mercy upon this part of Thy dominions; put a stop to all[b] growing evils, and to the judgments that must follow[c].

Endue the Lord of this Isle, and all that are put in authority under him, with wisdom from above, that they may

---

[x] ii. adds, "at Peel Castle, April 11th, 1698."
[y] ii. omits this prayer.
[z] iii. "the."
[a] iii. "never."
[b] iii. "the."
[c] iii. "threaten us."

MATUTINA. govern with truth and justice; and that the people, whose duty it is to obey, may do it for conscience' sake.

Give us all a peaceable temper of spirit, that laying aside all partiality, we may study the things that make for peace; and that[p] we may all join in promoting Thy honour, the true religion, and the welfare of this whole nation. For Jesus Christ's sake. Amen.

[iii. 28.] And grant that I may never, by any act or counsel of mine, or by omitting any part of my duty, increase the misunderstandings that are risen among us; but that I may become a peacemaker in word and deed, and may obtain that blessing which Thy Son hath promised to all that truly deserve that character. For whose sake I most humbly beg to be heard. Amen.

[i. 25; ii. 95; iii. 28.] Prov. xxii. 28. *Remove not the ancient landmark which thy fathers have set.*

Isaiah xxx. 1. *Woe unto them that take counsel, but not of Me[q]:*

Prov. xxi. 30. *There is no wisdom, nor understanding, nor counsel, against the Lord.*

[iii. 28.] Ezek. xiv. 4. *Every man that setteth up his idols in his heart, and putteth the stumbling-block of his iniquity before his face, and cometh to the prophet, I the Lord will answer him according to the multitude of his idols[r].*

[ii. 95; iii. 16.] Difficulties[s]. We are to pray for the[t] particular direction of God's[u] Holy Spirit upon all great occasions; we are humbly to depend upon it and cheerfully to expect it[x], which He will manifest, either by some plain event or[y] determination of His providence, or by suggesting such reasons as ought to determine the will to a wise choice.

But to follow the inclinations of the will, without reason, only because we are strongly inclined to a[z] thing, is a very dangerous way, and will engage men in evil[a] practices and endless scruples.

---

[p] iii. adds, "nothing may be done through malice, strife, pride, or vainglory, but that."
[q] iii. adds, "saith the Lord."
[r] The texts in MS. i. come after the prayer; in iii. before. In ii. they are followed by "Aug. 29, 1712. Not to put my hand to anything which I have not well considered."
[s] om. ii.
[t] om. ii.
[u] om. ii.
[x] om. iii.
[y] "and," ii.
[z] "this or that," ii.
[a] "dangerous," ii.

The Spirit of God brings into our minds new lights, sets Matutina. them home, inclines[b] us to attend them[c], &c. [d]But let men take heed of setting up idols in their hearts; and then go and enquire of the Lord—He will answer them.

NOON. [ii. 12.]

1 Timothy ii. 1. *I exhort, that first of all, supplications, prayers, intercessions, and giving of thanks, be made for all men.* N.B. For all Christian Churches.

For we are all of one blood. Acts xvii. 26.

And charity, that *more excellent way*, (1 Cor. xii. 31.) is tender affection for the whole creation of God.

To promote the kingdom of God, is to increase and hasten one's own happiness.

That [e]"man is born to trouble," I see wherever I turn my eyes. I know what pain is by experience; and though I was never in want, yet, from the complaints of others, I see it is grievous, and fit are these things to be laid before the throne of grace.

And since many have desired my prayers, and others have been my benefactors, and do constantly pray for me, I should not neglect to pray for them.

There are also many who cannot, and many who forget to pray for themselves, for whom charity should oblige one [to] pray.

And I should by no means forget the places of my birth, education, and preferment, that I may be some way useful to them, at least desire that God would accept my prayers for them. [ii. 13.]

O God, almighty and merciful, let Thy fatherly kindness be upon all whom Thou hast made. Hear the prayers of all that call upon Thee; open the eyes of them that never pray for themselves: pity the sighs of such as are in misery: deal mercifully with them that are in darkness, and increase the

---

[b] " forces," ii.
[c] om. ii.
[d] ii. " If they are not agreeable to reason and Scripture, they are not from God. And let a man take heed when he goes to enquire of the Lord, that he does not set up idols in his own heart, lest God answer him according to his idols."
[e] ii. interlined, "we are all subject to troubles and wants."

NOON. number and the graces of such as fear and serve Thee daily. Preserve this land from the miseries of war; this Church from all wild and dangerous errors; this people from forgetting Thee, their Lord and Benefactor. Be gracious to all those countries that are made desolate by the sword, famine, pestilence, or persecution. Bless all persons and places to which Thy providence has made me a debtor; all who have been instrumental to my good by their assistance, advice, example, or writings. And make me in my turn useful to others. Let none of those that desire my prayers want Thy mercy, but defend, and comfort, and conduct them through, &c.

[ii. 14.] 1 Thess. v. 18. *In every thing give thanks; for this is the will of God in Christ Jesus concerning you.*

Special favours. That I was born, Dec. 20, of honest and religious parents, in a Christian and a Protestant country.

That I had an early right, Dec. 25, to the covenant of grace.

That I had reason, perfect members and senses, and a sound constitution.

That I had an education and preferments beyond the hopes and abilities of my father's house.

The advantage of honourable and worthy friends; Ed. and H. Finch, M. Hewetson, Col. Cr.; an excellent wife, and four lovely children.

St. Peter's Day, 1686. I was ordained Deacon.

October 20th, 1689. I was ordained Priest.

Aug. 19th, 1692. I was made tutor to James, Lord Strange.

Jan. 16th, 1697, [97-8]. I was consecrated Bishop of Man at the Savoy by the Archbishop of York, assisted by the Bishops of Chester and Norwich.

I was created Dr. of Laws by A.B. of Cant.

March 3, 1707. I was made Dr. in Divinity, in a full convocation of the University of Oxon.

I finished and printed my Manks Catechism.

[In i. 186, and iii. 59, a paper corresponding to this, but enlarged, occurs in the Sunday devotions, which see hereafter.]

Were there not ten cleansed? but where are the nine[z]?   Noon.

   ... Fac, precor,   [ii. 15; iii.
   Jesu benigne, cogitem   62.]
   Hæc semper, ut semper tibi
   Summoque Patri gratias
   Agam, pieque vos colam,
   Totaque mente diligam.

O Lord and Father, I am not worthy of the least of all [ii. 15; iii. 62; i.190.] the mercies which Thou hast shewed Thy servant, neither can I render due thanks and praise for them; but, O Lord, accept of this my [a]sacrifice of praise and thanksgiving, on behalf of myself and all that belong to me[b].

For all the known, and [c]unobserved favours, deliverances, merciful appointments, (?) [d]visitations, opportunities of doing good, chastisements, and graces of Thy Holy Spirit, vouchsafed [e]to myself, my wife, my children, my diocese, my friends, and family, I bless Thy good providence; beseeching Thee to pardon our[f] ingratitude, and that we have passed[g] so many occasions[h] without observing and without acknowledging Thy [i]wonderful Providence and great goodness to Thy most unworthy servants[j].

For when I seriously[k] consider our[l] dependence upon Thee, for life, welfare, health of body, peace of mind, grace, comfort, and salvation, I cannot but[m] be very thankful.

Glory be to God, our Creator; glory be to Jesus, our Redeemer; glory be to the Holy Ghost, our Sanctifier, our Guide, and Comforter:—all glory[n] be to God most high. Amen[o].

And grant, O Lord, that we may be unfeignedly thankful, and shew forth the same, and Thy praise, not only with our

---

[z] iii. om. the text.
[a] ii. prima manu adds "daily."
[b] ii. iii. om. the last clause.
[c] ii. adds, "for all the."
[d] ii. om. this clause.
[e] ii. "unto me and to [my] diocese and family." iii. "unto myself, my diocese, my child," &c.
[f] ii. "my."
[g] ii. om. "have;" iii. "we pass."
[h] "days and years," ii. iii.
[i] ii. iii. om. "wonderful Providence and."
[j] "servant," ii.
[k] "soberly," ii.
[l] "my," and so to the end, ii.

[m] "ought to," ii.
[n] ii. adds, "all love."
[o] [The original editor inserted in this place some additional sentences on thanksgiving, and another of the Bishop's paraphrases on the Lord's Prayer, which do not occur in either of the MSS. at present. Probably they formed part of the 25 pp. which have been torn out of MS. No. 1. (175—201, according to the Bishop's paging): and if so, considering their subject, they must have been annexed to the "Sunday Lauds," to which in this edition they are transferred.]

<small>VESPER-TINA.</small> lips but our lives, by walking before Thee in holiness and righteousness all the days of our life.

[ii. 16.]
EVENING.

What have I done in the way of my duty?

What have I omitted which I might have done?

What have I done amiss in the common duties of Christianity?

What have I omitted?

[i. 28; ii. 16; iii. 31.] Psalm cxli. 2. *Let my prayer be set forth in Thy sight as the incense; and let the lifting up of my hands be an evening sacrifice* º.

That it hath pleased God to add another day to the years of my life;

That none of His judgments, to which for my sins I am justly liable, have fallen upon me;

That by ᴾ His grace He hath kept me from all scandalous sins, and from the dangers of an evil world;

That He ᑫ has given me occasions of doing good, and grace to make use of them;

That ʳ He hath supplied me and my family with the necessaries of this life, and with means of attaining a better:—

Accept, O God, of my unfeigned thanks for these, and for all Thy mercies from day to day bestowed upon me. Add this to all Thy favours, I beseech Thee, that I may never forget to be thankful.

Possess my heart with such a deep sense of my obligations to, and dependence upon Thee, ˢ for life, and health, and grace, and salvation, that religion may be my delight, as well as my duty.

But that I may serve Thee with a quiet mind, forgive me the ᵗ things whereof my conscience is afraid, and ᵘ avert the judgments which I have justly deserved. Remember not the ˣ offences of my youth; and in mercy blot out those of my riper years ʸ. Pardon my sins of the day past, and of my

---

º ii. iii. om. the text.
ᴾ ii. and iii. add, "the power of."
ᑫ ii. "is [iii. 'has been'] pleased to offer me daily [iii. om. 'daily'] opportunities of doing good."
ʳ ii. adds, "with a very bountiful hand."
ˢ iii. om. "for...salvation."
ᵗ "those."
ᵘ "deliver me from those," ii.
ˣ "sins and," ii.
ʸ ii. and iii. read, "which are so

life past, and grant that they may never rise up in judgment against me. Amen. *Vesper-tina.*

1 John ii. 1. *If any man sin, we have an Advocate with the Father, Jesus Christ the righteous, and He is the propitiation for our sins*[z].

O most powerful Advocate, I put my cause into Thy hands; let Thy blood and merits plead for me: and by Thy mighty intercession procure for me a full discharge of all my sins.

John v. 14. *Sin no more, lest a worse thing come unto thee.*

Lord, the frailty of man without Thee cannot but fall. In all temptations, therefore, I beseech Thee to succour me, that no sin may ever get the dominion over me. [i. 29.]

Lord, the frailty, &c. Grant me therefore Thy grace, that in keeping Thy commandments I may please Thee both in will and deed. [ii. 17; iii. 32.]

Give me a true sense of my infirmities, that I may ever look up to Thee for help; and give me grace that I may never despise Thy help, nor grieve Thy Holy Spirit by which I am sanctified.

Remember me of my duty: in mercy correct my backwardness to it: enable me to do what Thou requirest of me: in all temptations succour me, that no wickedness may get the dominion over me, but that I may be blameless and useful in the midst of a crooked and perverse world.

Give me a wise, a sober, a serious, a patient, a courageous, a religious heart, that I may do Thee honour in a faithful discharge of the several duties of the ministry to which I am called.

And O that I may have the example of my great Master ever before mine eyes, to direct, to encourage, to support and to comfort me. *Learn of Me, for I am meek and lowly in heart, &c.*[a]

1 Peter i. 7. *Pass the time of your sojourning here in fear.* [i. 29.]

many that I cannot recount them, so great, that I blush to name them; *Lord, if Thou wilt, Thou canst make me whole,* which I humbly trust to; for this is according to Thy Word by Thy Son Jesus Christ, Who is the propitiation for our sins."

[z] [ii. iii. om this text and prayer.]
[a] iii. om. the text.

VESPER-
TINA.

May God give me a salutary dread of the unfaithfulness of my own heart; and while [a]my duty obliges me to promote the salvation of others, make me always consider my own frailty, and fear for myself.

John xx. 21. *As My Father hath sent Me, even so send I you.*

O my Saviour! I acknowledge Thy goodness in appointing unworthy me a successor of Thy Apostles. Cause me thoroughly to weigh the sanctity of my calling, and to discharge it faithfully.

I have given you an example. Yes, my Lord and Master; but I am ashamed when I consider how far I have come short of this example; how poor my pains have been; how little of my time, my labour, my care, my thoughts, have been spent in Thy service.

O Lord, pardon what is past, and O that I may study Thy spirit and conduct, and follow them more faithfully for the time to come.

[ii. 18; iii. 33.]

2 Cor. v. 10. *We must all appear before the judgment-seat of Christ, that every one may receive the things done in his body, according to that he hath done, whether it be good or bad.*

Gracious God, fit me for that great appearance, and since my calling will oblige me to give a very strict account, let a greater measure of Thy grace ever accompany me.

Let Thy good Spirit incline and assist me every day to examine and to judge myself, that I may not be condemned of the Lord when He cometh to judge the world in righteousness.

Wisd. vi. 5. *A sharp judgment shall be to them that are in high places.* Sharp, i. e. exact and severe[b].

Deut. xxxii. 29. *O that they were wise, that they would consider their latter end.*

My heart is in Thy hands, O Lord, as well as my time. O make me wise unto salvation.

Teach me so to number my days, that I may apply my heart unto wisdom. That I may consider, *in this my day*, the things that belong unto my peace.

[a] [i. prima manu, "I am labouring."] [b] iii. om. this text.

For I am ere long to die: O let not death overtake me unawares. Assist me in my last moments, and receive my spirit[c] for Thy mercies' sake. VESPER-
TINA.

In the meantime, preserve me, I beseech Thee, from all dangers ghostly and bodily.

Residence. John x. 27. *My sheep hear My voice; and I* [i. 29.] *know them, and they follow Me.*

And may I, O Sovereign Pastor, always so speak, as that my flock may hear and understand me; so converse with them, as that I may know *them;* and lead such a life, as that *they* may safely follow me.

1 Timothy iv. 16. *Take heed unto thyself, and to thy doctrine; in so doing, thou shalt both save thyself, and them that hear thee.*

Amen.—The good Lord grant that I may edify the Church [i. 30.*] both by my life and doctrine; that I may faithfully teach the mysteries, defend the faith, and maintain the truths of the Gospel.

2 Timothy ii. 25. *In meekness instructing those that oppose themselves.*

O Jesu, impart to me a portion of that Spirit which prevailed with Thee to preach to a people who regarded Thee not, who rejected, who crucified Thee. Make me always sensible of my own infirmities, that I may treat others with compassion.

Acts vi. 4. *We will give ourselves continually unto the ministry of the word, and to prayer.*

O God, engrave this truth upon my heart, that every moment of my life belongs to Thee. That I may preach Thy word: and may my prayers be evermore acceptable in Thy sight, O Lord, my Strength and my Redeemer!

Luke xxii. 35. *When I sent you without purse, and scrip, and shoes, lacked ye any thing?*

O bountiful Lord and Master! who hast prevented all my wants and necessities to this day; grant that no anxious thoughts and fears for the future, no spirit of infidelity, may ever tempt me to distrust Thy Providence, or to better or secure my condition by any unworthy means.

[c] iii. "soul."

VESPER-TINA.

John xv. 20. *Remember the word that I said unto you; The servant is not greater than his lord.*

My Lord and Master, may I never forget this truth, and then I shall never fear, never complain of injuries, evil treatment, or afflictions.

Hebrews xiii. 17. *They watch for your souls, as they that must give an account.*

[i. 31.*] We cannot answer for ourselves, and yet we stand charged and are accountable for others. Who can think of this without trembling? In mercy, O God, communicate to me a degree of grace, and a zeal, answerable to the work I have undertaken, and the account I am to give.

Luke xii. 37. *Blessed are those servants, whom the Lord when He cometh shall find watching.*

The good Lord grant that I may be ever watchful in the way of my duty, and faithful in performing it. That I may live in the daily expectation of my Lord's coming; and that when I die, I may be made partaker of that blessedness which God hath promised His faithful servants.

[i. 31*; ii. 19; iii. 35.] Psalm xci. 1. *Whoso dwelleth under the defence of the Most High, shall abide under the shadow of the Almighty*[b].

May the Almighty God take me, my family, my children[c] and diocese, my friends, my relations, my benefactors, and my enemies[d], under His gracious[e] protection; give His holy angels charge concerning us; preserve us from the prince and powers of darkness, and from the dangers of the night; and keep us in perpetual peace and safety; through Jesus Christ our Lord. Amen.

Lord, refresh us, &c.

Hear me[f], O God, not according to my weak understanding[g], but according to the full importance of that [h]holy

---

[b] ii. and iii. add, "i. e. under His protection, [iii. 'the protection of One'] who is able to keep him safe, [iii. ' to save him']." After which ii. proceeds, " Ps. xci. 10. *There shall no evil befall thee, neither shall any plague come nigh thy dwelling.* Let it so happen unto Thine unworthy servant, and unto his family. Take us under Thy protection; give Thy holy Angels charge concerning us; preserve us from the dangers of the night; from the prince and powers of darkness; from all filthiness of flesh and spirit; and keep us in perpetual peace and safety, through Jesus Christ our Lord."

[c] iii. "child."
[d] iii. om. " and my enemies."
[e] iii. om. "gracious" and "holy."
[f] ii. " thy servant."
[g] ii. adds, " and performance."
[h] ii. iii., " form of words."

prayer, which Jesus Christ has taught us[j], and which I presume to offer.

Our Father[k].

Our Father, which art in Heaven; hallowed be Thy Name.
God would be glorified in the salvation of souls.

If the Almighty God were not my Father, I might expect vengeance instead of mercy.

May I glorify Thee in a faithful discharge of the duties of my calling.

May I shew by my life that God is my Father.

This earth is not the inheritance of the children of God.

Blessed be God, who dealeth not with us with the authority of a lord over his servants, but with the tenderness of a father over [his children].

Thy Kingdom come. Establish Thy Kingdom in my heart, O God. I own Thee for my King; do Thou make and own me for Thy faithful subject. Grant that by my ministry Thy Kingdom may be enlarged:—that I may be Thy subject out of choice, and ever yield Thee willing obedience. Inflame my heart with an hearty desire of enlarging Thy kingdom. Increase Thy flock, O great Shepherd, for the honour of Thy great Name. May I preserve Thy Kingdom within me, the government of Thy Spirit. Bring me into subjection to Thyself, by Thy grace.

Thy will be done in earth, as it is in heaven.

That Thou mayest have a Church on earth as obedient to Thy will as that is in Heaven.

O heavenly Father, subdue in me whatever is contrary to Thy holy will. Grant that I may ever study to know Thy will, that I may know how to please Thee.

Thy will, O God, is the perfection of justice; let me never prescribe to Thee what Thou oughtest to give me. What Thou dost will, we may be sure, will be best for us; we cannot be sure of what we will for ourselves. Hearken not to the corrupt desires of my heart, but to the voice of Thy own mercy.

Give us this day our daily bread.

Yes, my God, I will have recourse to Thee daily; for on

---

[j] ii. iii. om. the last clause.
[k] i. ii. give the Lord's Prayer in full, and ii. interlines over "our trespasses, as," "A protestation against hatred, malice," &c.

Thee I depend for life, and breath, and grace, and all things.

A Christian prayer is always answered, because nothing is asked but that God's will be done[1].

Give me a true understanding of, and love for, Thy Word, the bread which nourisheth to eternal life.

Give us the bread that nourisheth to eternal life: for Thou, O Lord, hast taught us not to seek that bread which perisheth, but that which endureth to eternal life. John vi. [27.]

And forgive us our trespasses, as we forgive them that trespass against us.

May I ever shew mercy to men, that I may receive it from Thee my God.

Do I value my soul, and think this too hard a condition?

May I never pray with a spirit of malice or revenge, lest I obtain nothing but mine own condemnation.

Thou art all mercy to me; grant that I may be all mercy to my brethren, for Thy sake, O Father.

And lead us not into temptation, but deliver us from evil.

For Thou knowest our infirmities, and the power and malice of our enemies.

2 Peter ii. 9. Thou knowest *how to deliver the godly out of temptation.*

Grant, O God, that I may never run into those temptations which in my prayers I desire to avoid.

Vouchsafe me the gift of perseverance, on which my eternal happiness depends.

Lord, never permit my trials to be above my strength.

O Holy Spirit of grace, be not wanting to me in the hour of temptation.

In all temptations, give us power to resist and overcome.

Leave us not in the power of evil spirits to ruin us.

Support us under all our saving trials and troubles.

For Thine is the Kingdom, the power, and the glory, for ever and ever. Amen.

Let Thy fatherly compassion grant what the Son of Thy love has encouraged us to pray for.

---

[1] [This clause, written at a different time from the preceding and following ones, seems to have been set down by an oversight here instead of under the former petition.]

By Thy Almighty power make good whatever is defective in me. *VESPERTINA.*

[ii. 20. has no descant on the Lord's Prayer, but stands as follows.]

This to be placed before my devotions.

Ps. lxxxv. 8; Hab. ii. 1. *I will hear what the Lord will say concerning me.*

Tantus quisque quantus apud Deum.

Gen. iv. 7. *If thou doest well, shalt thou not be accepted? and if thou doest not well, sin lieth at the door.*

John iii. 20. *Every one that doeth evil hateth the light, neither cometh to the light, lest his deeds should be reproved.*

[*Prima manu,* "And yet"] *there is no darkness where the workers of iniquity may hide themselves.* Job xxxiv. 22.

Lam. iii. 40. [But I will] *search and try my ways, and turn again unto the Lord.*

Whosoever is born of God doth not commit sin, (so as to be a servant of sin. John viii. 34.) *In this the children of God are manifest, and the children of the devil.* 1 John iii. 9.

These things write I unto you that ye sin not; but if any man sin, we have an Advocate with the Father, Jesus Christ the Righteous, and He is the Propitiation for our sins. 1 John ii. 1.

He that saith he is in the light, and hateth his brother, [ii. 21.] (wishing or doing ill to him,) *is in darkness till now.* 1 John ii. 9.

Let us not love in word only, but in deed and in truth, (doing good, as well as giving good words,) *and hereby we know that we are of the truth, and shall assure our heart before Him.* 1 John iii. 19.

Love not the world, nor the things of the world, (set not your heart upon them, nor be unwilling to part with them,) *for he that loveth the world, the love of the Father is not in him.* 1 John ii. 15.

If our heart condemn us, God is greater than our heart, and knoweth all things.

If our heart condemn us not, then have we confidence towards God. 1 John iii. 20.

We fight not against flesh and blood only, but against principalities, against powers, against powers of darkness.

VESPER-
TINA.

Notwithstanding this, *Be sober, be vigilant, because your adversary the devil, as a roaring lion, walketh about, seeking whom he may* (be permitted to) *devour.* 1 Pet. v. 8.

Blessed are those servants, whom the Lord, when He cometh, shall find watching. Luke xii. 37. That is, in the way of their duty.

Who will bring to light the hidden things of darkness, and make manifest the counsels of the hearts. 1 Cor. iv. 5.

Vid. Andrewes's Devotions, left (?) p. 162 [m].

To mind one's faults, and not to regard one's virtues. *Pet. Damianus* [the cotemporary of Gregory VII.; lib. ii. Ep. 2. *Noli frater (quod plerique faciunt) tantummodo siquid est in te virtutis attendere, ut vitia quasi post tergum posita negligas judicare."* Opp. t. i. p. 34, A. Paris, 1642.]

[iii. 35.] *Our Father which art in heaven.* O that I may find mercy at the hands of a merciful Father.

Through Thee have I been holden up ever since I was born. Ps. lxxi.

If ye being evil know, &c. Luke xi. 13. This therefore gives us assurance of being heard.

If sons, then heirs.

I am Thy son, though I have been a prodigal. O cast not off the compassion of a Father.

[iii. 36.] *Hallowed be Thy Name.*

St. Matt. v. 16. *That men seeing your good works may glorify your Father which is in heaven.* John xv. 8. *In this* [two lines below, "Herein"] *is My Father glorified, that ye bring forth* [bear] *much fruit.*

Thy kingdom come.

Thy will be done in earth as it is in heaven.

To will is present with me, but how to perform that will I know not. Rom. vii. 18.

O give me Thy grace, that I may ever do what is acceptable in Thy sight.

Whatever Thou hast in heaven decreed to be done, as best for me, let me—or for this Church, let me—submit to it cheerfully.

[iii. 37.] *Give us this day our daily bread. This day.* Take no

---

[m] The editor has not been able to verify this reference.

thought for to-morrow. Having food and raiment, let us VESPER-
be therewith content. TINA.

And forgive us our trespasses, as we forgive them that trespass against us.

Forgive. Pass by the punishment that is due to our sins.

And lead us not into temptation.

But deliver us from evil. [iii. 38.]

From the devil, the world, and the flesh: from the evil of sin, and from the evil of punishment, good Lord, deliver us.

Deliver me not into the will of mine enemies.

For Thine is the kingdom, the power and the glory, for ever. Amen.

Let not the sun go down upon your wrath.

Examination. Ecclesiasticus xviii. 20. *Before judgment,* [i. 31.] *examine thyself; and in the day of visitation thou shalt find mercy.*

Discover to me, O Thou searcher of hearts, whatever is amiss in me, whether in life or principle.

1 John iii. 20. *If our heart condemn us not, then have we confidence towards God.*

Whosoever is born of God doth not commit sin (so as to be a servant of sin). John viii. 34. *In this the children of God are manifest, and the children of the devil.* [1 John iii. 9, 10.]

Habakkuk ii. 1. [Rather, Ps. lxxxv. 8.] *I will hear what* [i. 32.] *the Lord God will say concerning me.*

If thou doest well, shalt thou not be accepted? If thou doest not well, sin lieth at the door. [Genesis iv. 7.]

Acts vi. 4. *"We will give ourselves continually unto the ministry of the word, and to prayer.*

Have I done so this day?

Have I been mindful of the duties of my proper calling?

Do I make it the great concern of my life to promote the eternal interest of my flock?

Have I read the Holy Scriptures, in order to instruct my people, and to preserve them from error?

Do I call upon God for the true understanding of the Holy Scriptures?

VESPER-
TINA.

Do I deny all ungodliness and worldly lusts, so as to be an example unto others?

Have I endeavoured to keep up the discipline of this Church, by correcting the criminous?

Have I an eye to such as are in holy orders, and to such as are designed for them?

Have I been charitable and kind to poor and needy people?

Do I make the Gospel the rule of my private life, and Jesus Christ my pattern?

Do I endeavour after holiness? live as in God's presence? Is my conversation unblameable?

Do I give the praise of this to God, through Jesus Christ?

Death. The Resignation. Perfect resignation the surest way to heaven[n].

From sudden death good Lord deliver me, my children, and family, and all that have desired my prayers. May we never be surprised in sin; and may Thy mercy supply whatever shall be wanting in our preparation for death.

For myself, with the submission of a penitent sinner, under the righteous sentence of death passed upon all mankind, as the effect of Thy justice, and due to my offence, I beg that I may so live, as that I may with joy resign my life a sacrifice of obedience, in union with that of my Saviour's, to Thee, O Father, trusting in Thy mercy and goodness and promises in Jesus Christ, at the hour of death, and in the day of judgment. Amen.

Ephesians iv. 6. *Let not the sun go down upon your wrath.*

Lord, grant that I may lie down to sleep with the same charitable dispositions with which I desire and hope to die.

I beseech Thee for all that are my enemies, not for judgment and vengeance, but for mercy, for the remission of their sins, and for eternal happiness.

[i. 33.] Psalm xiii. 3. *Lighten mine eyes, O Lord, that I sleep not in death.*

[n] This in pencil, i. 33, in Dr. Wilson's hand.

Psalm xci. *Deliver me from the terrors of the night, and from the pestilence that walketh in darkness.* <small>VESPERTINA.</small>

Let my sleep be free from sin. Preserve me, O Lord, from evil dreams and evil demons.

Into Thy hands I commend myself, my spirit, soul, and body, O Lord, thou God of truth.

Grant that I may remember Thee upon my bed.

Ps. iv. 9. *I will lay me down in peace, and take my rest; for it is Thou, Lord, only that makest me dwell in safety.*

May the Saviour and Guardian of my soul take me under His protection this night and evermore!

I bless Thy love and care, O heavenly Father, for that Thou givest Thy holy angels charge concerning us; give me a lively sense of Thy goodness in their ministration. May I contribute to their joy, by a true conversion, and an holy life.

SUNDAY.

[i. 36; iii. 40.]

EPISCOPACY.

SUNDAY. Quia juxta Scripturæ testimonium, vota nostra tenemur Deo reddere quæ vovemus; decernimus . . . ut Episcopi formam professionis in sua consecratione prolatam, bis in anno coram se legi faciant; ut tanto melius sponsionis propriæ recordentur, quanto sæpius fuerit eorum auribus inculcata: Bis in Anno, viz. in Adventu Domini, et in majori Quadragesima. Steph. et Otho. [ap. Gibson,] Codex Jur. Eccl. Angl. 138.

[i. 36; ii. 25; iii. 41.] [*Consecration of Bishops.*]—*Q. Are you persuaded that you be truly called to this ministration, according to the will of our Lord Jesus Christ, and the order of this realm?*

Answ.—I am so persuaded.

[iii. 41.] °1 St. Pet. v. 2. *Taking the oversight, not by constraint, but willingly; not for filthy lucre, but of a ready mind; neither as being lords over God's heritage, but being ensamples to the flock: and when the chief Shepherd shall appear, ye shall receive a crown of glory that fadeth not away.*

He that doth not find himself endued[p] with a spirit of his calling, hath reason to fear that God never called him.

Rom. x. 15. *How shall they preach, except they be sent?*

Heb. xiii. 17. *For they* (i. e. which have the rule over you) *watch for your souls, as they that must give account.* A dreadful consideration this.

[iii. 42.] N.B. We are ministers of that kingdom which is not of this world. John xviii. 36[q].

Thou who didst put an earnest care of the Church into the heart of Titus, (1 Thess. iv. 9,) give me a true love of souls, from which that care proceeds.

St. John xx. 21. *As My Father sent Me, so I send you.*

St. Matt. xxviii. 20. *Lo, I am with you alway, even unto the end of the world.*

[ii. 24.] [1] Concil. Aurelian. can. xiii. [31.] "Episcopus [Epis-

---

° ii. and iii. insert here the passage from Calvin, *Arcana vocatio, &c.*, and ii. adds the text, Acts vi. 4.; both add, St. John x. 1, &c.: Heb. v. 4.

[p] ii. 24. "is not endued."

[q] iii. adds, St. Matt. xx. 26.

copo,] si infirmitate non fuerit impeditus, Ecclesiæ cui proximus fuerit, die dominico non debet deesse [deesse non liceat." ii. Harduin. 1012.]

Concil. Tarraconense. can. 7. [8. ap. Harduin. ii. 1042.] "Episcopi annuatim diœcesin visitent, et basilicas destitutas restituant, et non nisi tertiam partem de Parochiis accipiant."

Jer. xxiii. 21, 22. vid. loc. [*I have not sent these prophets, &c.*]

2 St. Pet. ii. 15. *Who loved the wages of unrighteousness.*

St. Luke xii. 14. *Who made me a ruler or judge over you?*

Exod. xxviii. 29. *And Aaron shall bear the names, &c.*

Lighten mine eyes, O Lord, that I sleep not in death. Ps. xiii. 3.

Felicitas miseranda: While they that govern, govern for themselves, and love to feel their own power, and enjoy thereby their own lusts the better: not considering that government was never designed to gratify him that is invested with it, but for the comfort of others.

Almighty God, who by Thy [m]providence hast brought me into Thine immediate service; accept of my desire[n] of serving Thee, and grant that in the sincerity of my soul I may perform the several duties of my calling, and the vows that are upon me. [i. 36; ii. 25; iii. 43.]

Blessed be Thy good Spirit, that ever it came into my heart to become Thy minister[o].

May the same good Spirit make me truly sensible of the honour and danger of so great a trust, and of the account I am to give[p].

And give me grace to make amends, by my future diligence, for the many days and years that I have spent unprofitably. And this I beg for Jesus Christ's sake.

" Quanto præ cæteris gradus Episcopalis altior, tanto, si per negligentiam delabatur, gravior ruina est." Amb. de Dignitate Sacerd. cap. 3. [Ed. Bened. iii. 439. The tract is not [ii. 26; iii. 52.]

---

[m] ii. adds, "good."

[n] ii. "ambition:" so iii. 43.

[o] ii. iii. add, "and blessed be Thy holy Name that I attained this great honour without subjecting myself to any unworthy conditions."

[p] ii. and iii. substitute for this, "O Lord, assist and bless mine endeavours, and give me grace to labour hard, and to make some amends by my future diligence, for the many days and years that I have spent unprofitably. Grant this for the sake of Jesus Christ, my great Master. Amen."

SUNDAY. St. Ambrose's, but is supposed to be by Gerbertus, afterwards Pope Sylvester II., towards the end of the 10th century.]

St. Matt. xx. 26. [given hereafter in full by MS. i.]

The greater thou art, the more humble thyself, and thou shalt find favour before the Lord. Ecclus. iii. 18.

Unto the angel of the Church of, &c. Rev. ii. 1.

Concilii [iv.] *Carthaginensis Can.* 15. "Episcopus vilem supellectilem, et mensam, ac victum pauperem habeat, et dignitatis suæ authoritatem fide et vitæ meritis quærat." [ap. Hard. i. 980.]

De Episcopo non transferendo per ambitionem vid. Concil. Carthag. iv. Can. 27. [ap. Hard. ibid.]

Philemon viii. 9. *Wherefore though I might be much bold in Christ,* (i. e. by the power Christ has given me over thee,) *to enjoin thee that which is convenient, yet for love's sake I rather beseech thee.*

[i. 36; ii. 27; iii. 49; M. H. 68.]

April 11, 1698.

When I was enthroned[r] *in the Cathedral*[s] *of St. Germain's, in Peel Castle.*

Tit. i. 7[t]. *A Bishop must be blameless, as the steward of God; not self-willed, not soon angry, not given to wine, no striker, not given to filthy lucre; but a lover of hospitality, a lover of good men* (or things), *sober* (or prudent), *just, holy, temperate, holding fast the faithful word, as he hath been taught, &c.*

In an humble and thankful sense of Thy great goodness to a very sinful and very unworthy creature, I look up unto Thee, O gracious Lord and Benefactor, who from a low obscurity hast called me to this high office, for grace and strength to fit me for it[u].

What am I, or what is my father's house, that Thou shouldst vouchsafe us such[x] instances of Thy notice and favour[y]?

Gen. xxxii. 10. *I am not worthy of the least of all the mercies which Thou hast shewed Thy servant*[z].

---

[r] M. H. "installed."
[s] M. H. "Church in Peel Castle, in the Isle of Man."
[t] [iii. 49. only prefixes this text.]
[u] ii. iii. M. H. "accomplish."
[x] M. H. iii. add "mighty."
[y] M. H. ii. iii. om. "notice and."
[z] om. M. H. ii. iii.

SUNDAY.

O God[a], grant that by a[b] conscientious discharge of my duty, I may profit those over whom I am appointed Thy minister, that[c] I may make such a return as shall be acceptable to Thee.

Give[d] me such a measure of Thy [e]Spirit as shall be sufficient to support me under, and lead me through, all the difficulties I shall meet with.

Command a blessing upon my studies, that I may make full proof of my ministry, and be instrumental in converting many to the truth.

Give me skill and conduct, that with a pious, prudent, and charitable hand, I may lead and govern the people committed to my care: that I may be *watchful* in ruling them, *earnest* in correcting them, *fervent* in loving them, and *patient* in bearing with them.

Let Thy grace and blessing, O Father of mankind, rest upon all those whom I [f]bless in Thy name; and especially upon those who together with me are appointed to watch over Thy flock. [*M. H. om. this clause, and proceeds*],

Guide and govern my mind, that I may lay hands suddenly [M.H.69.] on no man, but faithfully and wisely make choice of fit persons to serve in the sacred ministry of Thy Church. And let not the blood of those that perish be required at my hands through any neglect or default of mine.

To such as shall be ordained to any holy function give Thy grace and heavenly benediction, that both by their life and doctrine they may set forth Thy glory, and set forward the salvation of mankind.

Bless all those of this island who have already given themselves to Thy service, and labour with me in this great work of the ministry: be with us, and guide us, and help us, for Thy promise' sake; for Thine honour's sake; and for the sake of Jesus Christ. That we may teach well, and that we may live well, and be examples of all the holy graces and virtues which we recommend to others[g].

Except Thou buildest the house, their labour is but lost

---

[a] M. H. "My good God."
[b] M. H. ii. iii. "diligent and."
[c] M. H. adds, "by this means."
[d] M. H. "grant."
[e] M. H. ii. iii. add "Holy."
[f] M. H. adds "shall."
[g] In marg. M. H. adds, "1 Tim. iii. 14. *These things write I, that thou mayest know how to behave*," &c.

SUNDAY. that build it; it is but lost labour to rise early and take late rest, if Thou bless not our endeavours who are appointed to watch over Thy flock in this place.

[i. 37; ii. 28; iii. 50; M. H. 70.] Bless every member of this Church: support the weak, confirm and settle those that stand, and [g] feed our flock together with ourselves[h], through Jesus Christ, the chief Shepherd.

Lord, who is sufficient for[i] so great a work? Thou, O Lord[j], canst enable the meanest of Thy creatures[k], to bring to pass what Thou hast determined: be pleased[l] to make me an instrument of great good to this[m] Church and people: and grant that when I have preached to and governed others, I myself may not be lost, or go astray.

Preserve me[n] from the dangers of a prosperous condition; from pride and forgetfulness of Thee[o]; from a proud conceit of myself, and from disdaining others.

Rather turn me out of all [p] earthly possessions, than [q] they should hinder me in the way to heaven.

If affliction is needful for me, let me not want it: only[r] give me grace thankfully to receive and bear[s] Thy fatherly correction; that after this life is ended in Thy immediate service, I may have a place of rest amongst Thy faithful servants in the Paradise of God, in sure hopes of a blessed resurrection, through Jesus Christ. Amen, Amen[t].

[g] M. H. adds, "preserve and."
[h] M. H. "my, ... myself."
[i] M. H. "this;" om. "a."
[j] M. H. "God."
[k] "servants," M. H.
[l] M. H. adds, "if it be Thy gracious will."
[m] ii. iii. "Thy."
[n] M. H. adds, "dear God."
[o] In marg. M.H., "*Beware that thou forget not the Lord thy God, &c.* Deut. viii."
[p] M. H. adds "my."
[q] M. H. adds "that."
[r] M. H. ii. iii. "and."
[s] M. H. ii. iii. om. "and bear."
[t] This sentence stands in M. H., "I may dwell with Thee in life everlasting; for the sake of the blessed Jesus, my great Lord and Master. Amen." In ii. it was, "dwell with Thee in life everlasting," but was corrected first into "be received into the bosom of Abraham:" afterwards, "have a place of rest among thy faithful servants in Paradise." ii. interlines, "*That I may finish my course with joy.* Acts xx. 24."
M. H. subjoins, "Singulis diebus dominicis post preces public. matutinas, prælect. prius offic. de Ordin. Episcop."
ii. 27, 28, subjoins to the prayer the following sentences and texts: 1 Pet. v. 2—4; 1 Sam. xv. 17. *When thou wast little in thine own sight, wast thou not made, &c.*
Vid. Parænesis ad Eccl. &c. § 67. [i. e. "De Bono Unitatis et Ordinis, Disciplinæque ac Obedientiæ, in Ecclesia recte constituta vel constituenda, Ecclesiæ Bohemicæ ad Anglicanam Parænesis; cum præmissa Ordinis ac Disciplinæ in Ecclesiis Fratrum Bohemorum usitatæ Descriptione. Amst. 1660." Bp. Wilson frequently refers to this book. The passage here meant is, "Si ab episcopatu tollatur quod ab initio non fuit, curatus erit morbus. Ecquidnam istuc? Sæcularis dominatus, opes terrenæ . . . .

"Arcana vocatio est cordis nostri testimonium, quod neque ambitione, neque avaritia, neque ulla alia cupiditate, sed sincero Dei timore, et ædificandæ Ecclesiæ studio, oblatum munus recipiamus." Calvin. Instit. iv. 3. [§ 11.] [SUNDAY. ii. 25; iii. 41; i. 37.]

He that doth not find himself endued with a spirit of his calling, hath reason to fear that God never called him. [i. 37.]

John x. 1, &c. *He that entereth not by the door into the sheepfold, but climbeth up some other way, the same is a thief and a robber. But he that entereth in by the door, is the shepherd of the sheep. The sheep hear his voice; he calleth his own sheep by name. He goeth before them, and the sheep follow him; for they know his voice. A stranger will they not follow. I am the door of the sheep. By Me, if any man enter, he shall be saved. The good shepherd giveth his life for the sheep. The hireling seeth the wolf coming, and leaveth the sheep, for he careth not for them.* [i. 38.]

Quesnel. [in loc.] *Marks of a true Pastor.*

A lawful entrance, upon motives which aim at the glory of God, and the good of souls.

An external call and mission, from the apostolic authority of Bishops.

The sheep hear his voice; that is, when he speaks to their hearts, and to their capacities.

He calleth his sheep by name; that is, he knows them so well as to know all their wants.

Christus enim dixit, *Reges dominantur, vos autem non sic. Nolite possidere aurum vel argentum,*" &c.]

Be sure to be steady and fearless in the discharge of your duty, without failing in the respect which is due to the higher powers.

See the character and duty of a bishop in Du Pin's account of Julianus Pomerius at the latter end of the fifth century.

"For even the Son of God came not to be ministered unto, but to minister."

Exod. xxviii. 9, " Aaron shall bear," &c.

See Dr. More's account and description and defence of a good Bishop in his preface to his Mystery of Godliness, p. 21; [iii. gives this at length.]

See Can. i. of the 4th Council of Carthage for the qualifications of a Bishop.

The servant is not greater than his Lord. 1 Tim. iii. 2, 3, &c. *A Bishop then must be blameless, the husband of one wife, &c.* Vid. loc., and Tit. i. 6, 7.

Lev. xxi. 6. *They shall be holy unto their God, and not profane the Name of their God.*

When a bishop loses his gravity, he loses so much of his authority.

Residency. Is. xxx. 20, *Thine eye shall see thy teachers.* Zech. xi. 17; Rom. xii. 7, 8; "Per Vicarium intrabit regnum cælorum."

iii. 53. adds, *The good Shepherd knoweth His flock, and calleth His sheep by name.*

"It is a shrewd symptom of atheism, to think a man less honourable, because he is an immediate servant of the great God and of His Son Jesus Christ.

"O Jesus, let Thy humility teach me to bear the marks of distinction which the world has given me, as a burden rather than an honour."

SUNDAY. *He goeth before them, and they follow him.* He leads such a life as they may safely follow.

A stranger will they not follow; that is, they ought not to follow such as break catholic unity.

I am the door. It is by Jesus Christ, not by us, that the flock is kept in safety; without Him we can do nothing, neither by our learning, our eloquence, or our labours. This is to rob Christ of the glory of saving His sheep: and to enter into the ministry, only to plunder the Church of her revenues.

The good shepherd giveth his life for the sheep; either by spending it in his ministry, or suffering, if there be occasion; never sacrificing the flock to his own ease, avarice, or humours.

The hireling careth not for the sheep. He lords it over them, makes what advantage he can of them, and counts them his own no longer than they are profitable to him. *He* [i. 38.] *leaves them;* that is, when dangers threaten. Then the good shepherd and the hireling are discovered.

Hebrews v. 4. *No man taketh this honour unto himself, but he that is called of God, as was Aaron.*

Hebrews v. 2. *High priest:—who can have compassion on the ignorant, and on them that are out of the way.*

A pastor who is sensible of his own infirmities, will not fail to treat sinners with meekness and compassion.

Hebrews xiii. 17. *They watch for your souls, as they that must give account.*

A most dreadful consideration this; insomuch as that St. Chrysostom[t] said, upon reflecting upon it, "It is a wonder if any ruler in the Church be saved."

It will be work enough for every man to give an account [i. 39.] for himself; but to stand charged, and to be accountable for many others,—who can think of it without trembling? O God! how presumptuous was I, to be persuaded to take upon me this charge[u]!

Who will value himself upon ecclesiastical dignities, who considers that Judas was chosen to be an Apostle?

---

[t] [In loc. ed. Savil. iv. 602, line 28. Θαυμάζω εἰ τινά ἐστι τῶν ἀρχόντων σωθῆναί ποτε. Cf. Bp. Bull, Serm. v. p. 119. Oxford, 1840.]

[u] [ii. 32.] "The holy Fathers stile episcopacy 'A burden dreadful to the shoulders of angels themselves: a source of infinite care and solicitude.'"

O good Shepherd, I beseech Thee, for myself and for my flock, to seek us, to find us, to lead us, to defend us, and to preserve us to life eternal.

If God be satisfied with a pastor, it is of little importance whether he please or displease men.

Titus ii. 15. *These things speak, and exhort, and rebuke with all authority. Let no man despise thee;* that is, for want of exercising ecclesiastical discipline.

The foregoing[x] are truths which cannot be preached too often; viz. the bondage of man by sin—the necessity of a Deliverer—the manner of our redemption—the danger of not closing with it—the power of grace to deliver us, &c.

A pastor should do all this, and act with the dignity of a man who acts by the authority of God[y].

Bishops, &c. We are willing enough to desire to imitate Jesus Christ and his Apostles in their authority, without thinking of following them in their humility, their labours, self-denial, &c.

A bishop is a pastor set over other pastors. They were to ordain elders. They might receive an accusation against an elder. They were to charge them to preach such and such doctrines; to stop the mouths of deceivers; to set in order the things that were wanting; and lastly, this was the form of Church government in all ages. So that to reject this, is to reject an ordinance of God. [i. 40.]

"Talem si nobis Hierarchiam exhibeant, in qua sic emineant episcopi, ut Christo subesse non recusent, et ab illo tanquam unico capite dependeant,—tum vero nullo non anathemate dignos fatear, si qui erunt, qui non eam revereantur, summaque obedientia observent." Calvin. *de Necessit. Eccl. Reform.*, as quoted by Mr. Lesley in his Answer to Bp. of Meux [Meaux] in Dr. Hickes' Letters, p. 320. [*Several Letters which passed between Dr. Hickes and a Popish Priest*, &c. &c., 1705.]

Bp. Sanderson, *Episc. not prejudicial to the Regal Power*, p. 121. [101, 3rd ed. 1683.] "My opinion is, that Epi- [i. 40; iii. 45.]

---

[x] [i. e. *these things*, the truths contained in the preceding verses of Titus, ii. 11—14.]

[y] [These two sentences are taken from Quesnel on the place in Titus.]

SUNDAY. scopal government is not to be derived merely from Apostolical practice or institution; but that it is originally founded in the Person and Office of the Messiah, ... Who being sent by His heavenly Father to be the Great Apostle, (Heb. iii. 1.) Bishop, and Pastor (1 Pet. ii. 25.) of His Church; and anointed to that office immediately after His baptism[z], ... with Power and the Holy Ghost (Acts x. 37, 38.) descending then upon Him in a bodily shape; (Luke iii. 22.) did afterwards, before His Ascension[a], send and empower His holy Apostles, (giving them the Holy Ghost likewise as His Father had given Him,) in like manner as His Father had before sent Him (John xx. 21.) to exercise [execute] the same Apostolical, Episcopal, and Pastoral Office, for the ordering and governing of His Church, until His coming again, and so the same office to continue in them and their successors unto the world's end. (Matt. xxviii. 18—20.)

"This I take to be so clear from these and other like texts of Scripture compared with [between] themselves, and the [b]practice of all the Churches of Christ[c] in all ages, as well as that of the apostles, that there will be little reason for an unprejudiced mind to doubt thereof." [This latter paragraph is quoted in substance, not in the exact words.]

[i. 41; iii. 44.] *The Character of a good Bishop out of Julianus Pomerius. Dupin. Cent.* v. 184. [The passage is found in Prosper *de Vita Contemplativa,* i. 25. See some account of Julianus Pomerius in Cave, Hist. Lit. i. 378.]

He is [d]such as converts sinners to God by his sermons[e] and example; is very humble; free from pride and imperiousness; treating all his flock[f] with the same love and kindness: —who heals the wounds of his people[g] with mild but effectual remedies, and patiently bears with the incurable:—who in his preaching seeks not his own glory, but that of Jesus

---

[z] iii. adds, "by John."
[a] iii. adds, "into heaven."
[b] iii. adds, "following."
[c] iii. proceeds, "as well in the Apostles' times, as in the purest and primitive time nearest thereunto, there will be left little cause why any man should doubt thereof." [Which is very nearly as in Bishop Sanderson's work.]
[d] iii. "they are" such: and so all along.
[e] iii. "preaching."
[f] iii. "who treat all the members of their flock," &c.
[g] "of their sick people," iii.

SUNDAY.

Christ[h]:—who seek not the favour and applause of men, but return it all to God, because it is He who lives and preaches in the bishops[i]:—who comfort the afflicted, nourish the poor, clothe the naked, lodge strangers, redeem captives:—who bring those that err into the way of truth; promise salvation to those that despair; quicken the zeal of such as are in the right way; hasten those that linger; and discharge all the parts[k] of their ministry well.

"These are the true successors of the Apostles; [l]appease the anger of God against His people[m]; defend the faith [n]by their writings, and [o]seal it with their blood, putting their trust in God alone[p]."

The Character of a Bishop by Dr. More. Myst. of Godl. [i. 41; iii. 53.] [1st Ed. 1660.] *Preface*[q]. "A Bishop who rules his own family well, not suffering scandalous attendants on his person or business:—who visits his diocese in his own person; and makes use of his power to punish wickedness without respect of persons:—who is watchful, prudent, and compassionate, and has the art of conversing with such as are of mean capacities:—who has the skill to find out the reason, why the ends of the Gospel are defeated; i. e. whether the pastor or the flock are in the fault:—who is careful to prevent such opinions from spreading, which serve the ends of sin, and encourage to lewdness:—who gravely and severely rebukes bold offenders; and at the same time can have compassion for the failings of the weak; and rejoices to find any [r]in the ways of order and piety[s]:—he that calls such a bishop Antichristian is himself Antichristian[t]."

---

[h] "who employ not their discourses or actions to obtain favour or thanks of men, but who give God all the honour that men bestow on them, because," &c., iii.

[i] iii. adds, "who avoid praises and commendations."

[k] iii. "functions."

[l] iii. adds, "such pastors as these," &c.

[m] iii. adds, "and instruct the people in the knowledge of God."

[n] iii. adds, "of the Church."

[o] iii. adds, "and are ready to."

[p] iii. "Lastly, they hold themselves fast to God only; in whom alone they put their trust."

[q] iii. adds, "page 21."

[r] iii. adds, "people."

[s] iii. adds, "&c."

[t] [This is not literally quoted, but may rather be described as a sort of abstract of the passage; which is omitted (remarkably enough) in the reprints of the book. It stands as follows:—"Wherefore to speak out plainly and at once, if I had said anything of ecclesiastic policy, I should not have forborne to pronounce, that such a bishop as I have hitherto described, and that rules his own family well, not allowing any scandalous servants to attend him, but being a pattern in himself and in all his house of unblamable godliness

SUNDAY.

[i. 42.]

Matthew v. 19. *Whosoever shall do, and teach, &c., shall be called great in the kingdom of God.*

It is in this, the true greatness of a bishop does consist; not in eminence of his see, multitude of attendants, favour of princes, &c.

Bishops were called to sit in parliament, to give their counsel according to God's law, as the civil judges were to give their advice according to the temporal laws in matters of difficulty.

Mark x. 44. *Whosoever of you will be the chiefest, shall be servant of all.*

The greatest prelate in the Church is he who is most conformable to the example of Christ, by humility, charity, and care of his flock; and who, for Christ's sake, will be a servant to the servants of God[n].

O Sovereign Pastor of souls! renew in Thy Church, and especially in me, this spirit of humility; that I may serve Thee in the meanest of Thy servants. If I lie under the necessity of being served by others, let it be with regret, and let me exact no more service than is necessary.

Luke x. 3. *Behold, I send you forth as lambs among wolves.*

and Christianity; that makes his Visitations in his Diocese in his own person, and vibrates that sacred thunder and lightning, the truly dreadful sentence of excommunication, by no other arm but his own, nor to any other aim than the dissipating of vice and wickedness, and all rebellion and disobedience to the known and acknowledged laws of Christ; that inflicts no mulcts but what are bestowed in relief of the poor of the respective parish and the needful repairs or comely adornings of the Church; that is watchful, prudent and compassionate, and has the art and patience of conversing with the meanest capacities, and the skill and sagacity of finding out the reason where he finds the end of the gospel notoriously defeated in any place; that has counsel in readiness and fit applications whether the pastor or his charge be discovered to be in fault; that exhorts everywhere to sobriety and brotherly kindness, and is diligent to pluck up or prevent the growth of such opinions as serve the end of sin, and encourage men to lewdness; that gravely and severely rebukes the bold offender, and affectionately bewails the failings of the weak, and cheerfully expresses his sincere joy wherever he finds a people live orderly and unblamably, and gives the best countenance and encouragement he can devise for the furthering the same; I say, I could not have forborn to pronounce, that to decry such a bishop as this for Antichristian, were an unpardonable piece of Antichristianism; and to murmur against his Visitations, to repine at the annual return of the sun, by whose warmth all things live and flourish. For there is not any effectualler means imaginable to make the people believe in good earnest that religion is worth the looking after, than to find themselves looked after so carefully and affectionately in reference to religion by persons of so honourable rank and quality."—*An Explanation of the grand Mystery of Godliness;* by H. More, D.D. *To the reader,* pp. xx., xxi., fol. Lond. 1660.]

[n] [Quesnel, in loc.]

It belongs to Thee, O Lamb of God, to guard both me SUNDAY. and my flock from wolves who assault us, either openly or in sheep's clothing. I depend entirely upon Thee, in whatever relates to my own preservation, or that of the people committed to my care.

Luke xix. 20. *Lord, behold, here is Thy pound, which I have kept laid up in a napkin.*

O my Saviour, I tremble to think how I have followed the example of this slothful servant and what reason I have to dread his doom. Rest is a crime in one who has promised to labour all the days of his life. And in me, therefore, it is a great evil, not to be always doing good. Pardon me, my God, for what is past; and let me not imagine, that because I am free from gross and scandalous crimes, that therefore I lead a good life.

O Lord, give me grace proportionable to the talents I have received, and to the account I am to give; that I may faithfully perform all the duties belonging to my state. Amen.

Whoever is associated to the priesthood of Christ, ought, in imitation of Him, to sacrifice himself for the advantage of His Church, and for all the designs of God.

Luke xxii. 26. *But ye shall not be so; but he that is greatest among you, let him be as the younger; and he that is chief, as he that doth serve.*

A Bishop does not know his office in the Church, if he pretends to distinguish himself by power, imperiousness, and grandeur; or by any other way than by humility, and by a great concern for souls. Marks of distinction are rather a [i. 43.] burden which he bears out of necessity, but complains of them secretly to God. He considers himself as the servant, not as the lord of souls. Even Jesus Christ made Himself our pattern in this[u].

Translation of Bishops and Pastors. Self-love is too often at the bottom, and not the glory of God, or the good of souls.

When men's labours are attended with tolerable success, yet, because either they can better their temporal condition,

---

[u] [Quesnel in loc.]

F

SUNDAY. or think that a more public station would be more suitable to their great capacities, they leave their station for one more full of dangers, without any prospect of being more serviceable to God, or to His Church, and the souls of men; not considering that this is the voice of pride, self-love, and covetousness, and an evil example to others, to whom we do or should preach humility, as the very foundation of Christianity.

The greater share we have in the authority of Jesus Christ, the greater must we expect to have in His sufferings: the Cross being the reward of faithful pastors.

[i. 46] To leave a clergy and a people to whom one is perfectly well known, to go to another to whom one is a stranger, and this for the sake of riches, which are supposed to have been renounced,—this was unknown to the first ages of Christianity.

'Tis one of the devil's artifices, to cause us to leave a place where we do some, though little good, for one where 'tis uncertain whether, &c.

Translations. Vid. Concil. IV. Carthaginense [Can. 27. Ut Episcopus de loco ignobili ad nobilem per ambitionem non transeat, nec quisquam inferioris ordinis Clericus. Ap. Hard. i. 980, E]. Et Canon. Apost. 14. [13. ἐπίσκοπον μὴ ἐξεῖναι καταλείψαντα τὴν ἑαυτοῦ παροικίαν ἑτέρᾳ ἐπιπηδᾷν. Hard. i. 12, E.] Conc. Aquisgran. (i.) can. xii. [43, 44. from the canons of Nicea (15.) and Chalcedon (5.)] See the Life of Pope Paul II. [by Platina p. 792. ed. 1645.] He removed the more worthy, as he called them, to wealthier sees, by which more annates became due; by which he raised vast sums of money. ["Cum episcopatus vacaret, quo plures annatæ eodem tempore solverentur, digniores (ut ipse ferebat) ad uberiores episcopatus movens, magnam pecuniarum vim undique colligebat."]

[i. 43.] John ix. 34. *Thou wast altogether born in sins, and dost thou teach us? And they cast him out.*

This the character of a wicked pastor;—to treat their flock with imperiousness, and ill language; to be impatient to be told their duty; and to be overhasty in turning men out of communion, and breaking unity[v].

[v] [Quesnel.]

From the time a pastor is mercenary, he has an indifferency for the interests of Christ and His Church, and is ready to give all up upon the prospect of worldly honour and advantage.

On the other hand, nothing renders a pastor more amiable in the sight of God, or draws down more graces and blessings, than a contempt of earthly things, and of the conveniences of life, that he may approve himself a faithful minister of Christ.

He *lays down his life,* who lays down the love thereof, for his flock.

John x. 37. *If I do not the works of My Father, believe Me not.*

Since Jesus Christ put His doctrine upon this issue, let not me expect to be His minister, if I do not shew forth, in my life, the works becoming such a person.

A minister of state talks of nothing but of the interests of his prince, &c.; so should we, if this were most at our hearts [w].

John xiii. 20. *He that receiveth whomsoever I send receiveth Me, &c.*

Men think they reject a mere man in rejecting His Ministers, and yet they reject Jesus Christ.

Acts vi. 2. *It is not reason that we should leave the word of God, and serve tables.*

That is, spiritual affairs must not be left for the sake of [i. 44.] temporal.

They who are the first in authority ought to be the first in discharging their duty, and in setting a good example to others.

2 Corinthians iv. 5. *Ourselves your servants for Jesus' sake.*

An air of imperiousness does not become a servant.

2 Cor. viii. 23. *They are the messengers of the Churches, and the glory of Christ.*

A faithful pastor is the glory of Christ, because his whole life is a continual sacrifice to the glory of Him who has sent him; and because Christ Himself has made him faithful, &c.

A true pastor has but one thing at heart, which is the

[w] [Quesnel.]

performance of his duty; and this is that which secures his peace, his confidence, his hope, &c.

1 Timothy i. 3. *That thou mayest charge some that they teach no other doctrine.*

This is one of the chief duties of a bishop, to be watchful concerning the purity of the doctrine, that none corrupt it, but that they confine themselves to the truths taught by the Apostles, (verse 4,) that they avoid such as only minister to questions, disputes, rather than to godly edifying.

1 Tim. iii. 2—7. *A bishop must be blameless, the husband of one wife, vigilant, sober (modest), of good behaviour, given to hospitality, apt to teach; not given to wine, no striker, not greedy of filthy lucre; but patient, not a brawler, not covetous; one that ruleth well his own house, having his children in subjection with all gravity; not a novice, lest being lifted up with pride he fall into the condemnation of the devil. Moreover he must have a good report of them which are without; lest he fall into reproach and the snare of the devil.*

My God, what qualifications are these! and how rash was I to undertake such a work, without sitting down and counting the cost, whether I was able to finish it! Thou only canst supply all my defects, which I beseech Thee to do.

Enable me, I beseech Thee, to come as near as possible to this character: that I may teach the mysteries, defend the faith, maintain the truths of the gospel; that I may be a pattern to my flock, edify the Church, both by my discourses and example. An hearty zeal for the salvation of souls,—a care to secure my flock from the corruptions of the age. Amen.

Church Government. Col. iv. 5. *Walk in wisdom toward them that are without, redeeming the time.*

Prudence is very necessary in dangerous times; it being no small fault to give occasion to the raising of storms against the Church and her ministers, for want of having a due regard to the times, and to the passions of carnal men.

1 Timothy iv. 16. *Take heed unto thyself, and unto the doctrine; continue in them: for in doing this thou shalt both save thyself, and them that hear thee.*

That is, endeavour first to establish the kingdom of God

in yourself, and then you will be able to do it in your flock; and so both shall be saved. SUNDAY.

Matthew xx. 26, 27. *Whosoever will be great among you, let him be your minister; and whosoever will be chief among you, let him be your servant: even as the Son of man came not to be ministered unto, but to minister.*

God give me a true and prudent humility, to have nothing of the air of secular governors; to attend the flock of Christ as a servant; to look on Him as my pattern; to study His conduct and spirit; to spend and be spent for my flock; that I may never desire to increase my burden, that I may be better qualified to *be ministered unto;* and that I may never strive to live at ease, in plenty, in luxury, repose, and independence. Amen.

The name of a servant ought to be esteemed honourable to the eye of faith, and a real privilege, since Jesus Christ took upon Him the nature of a servant.

Bishops and priests (saith St. Ambrose) are honourable, on account of the sacrifice they offer[x].

The power of the keys, and the exercise of that power; the due use of confirmation and (previous to that) examination; a strict examination into the learning, lives, and characters of such as are designed for holy orders;—are matters of infinite and eternal concern. As also the visitation of parishes, and exercise of Church discipline upon all offenders.

The duties of a Bishop are imposed upon him by divine appointment, and to obstruct him is to oppose Jesus Christ, Who sends him, and has set him his duties.

A man may be ruined by those very means which were designed to enable him to discharge his duty with more convenience. And bishops have too often been put into such easy circumstances, as to forget that they were bishops.

A bishop who has more regard to his temporalties than to the souls of his flock, is fallen into that sad condition.

Matthew xii. 18, 19, &c. *Behold My Servant; He shall*

---

[x] [In Ps. xxxviii. § 25. Vidimus Principem Sacerdotum ad nos venientem, vidimus et audivimus offerentem pro nobis sanguinem suum: sequimur ut possumus sacerdotes, ut offeramus pro populo sacrificium; etsi infirmi merito, tamen honorabiles sacrificio.]

SUNDAY.

[i. 46.]

not strive, nor cry, neither shall any man hear His voice in the streets. A bruised reed shall He not break, &c.

How lovely is this meekness of Christ! how worthy to be imitated by His ministers! their ministry not being a ministry of pride, imperiousness, and violence, but of mildness, peace, &c.[x]

Rev. i. 16. *And He had in His right hand seven stars.*

Make me, O Jesus, a shining star in Thy Church; support me by Thy right hand, guide and direct me by Thy light; let me never become a wandering star.

A primitive bishop will be careful to avoid, as much as possible, worldly equipage and retinue, excess, pomp, and ostentation. To do otherwise would be to establish the kingdom of Satan, which we would destroy; and to destroy the kingdom of Jesus, which we would establish.

When a bishop loseth his gravity, he loseth so much of his authority.

Residence. Nothing can supply the want of a pastor's presence.

Is. xxx. 20. *Thine eyes shall see thy teachers.* [iii. 52. adds] Rom. xii. 7. *Let us wait on our ministering, or he that teacheth, on teaching, &c.*

Zech. xi. 17. *Woe to the idol shepherd that leaveth the flock, &c.*

He is but the vain image of a pastor, (an *idol shepherd,*) who chooses to abandon his flock, and leave them to the conduct of those who have no concern for them; and entrust the salvation of those souls to others, for whom he himself is responsible to God. He may be learned, be employed, &c., but he cannot be a good shepherd[y].

Absence. Leaving the flock. Vid. Willet on 1 Sam. xvii., pp. 77, 78, 79.

[i. 47.]

[p. 154—172. on v. 28. ed. 1607[z].]

Vid. Concilium Francoford. Can. 42. [41. Harduin. iv. 908.] Episcop. extra propriam sedem ultra 3 Hebd. [Ut

---

[x] [Farther on in the same page the same text is quoted, with the note, "To teach us that our ministry is not a ministry of pride, contention, imperiousness, violence; but of humility, mildness, and moderation."]

[y] [ii. 28; iii. 53, subjoin,] " Per vicarium intrabit Regnum Cœlorum. The good Shepherd knoweth his flock, and calleth his sheep by name."

[z] [Andrew Willet was author of *Synopsis Papismi*, and, as is said, of the "Christian Letter" against Hooker.]

nullus episcopus propriam sedem amittat aliubi frequentando, Sunday.
aut in propriis rebus suis manere audeat amplius quam
tres hebdomadas.]

Mission. May I, gracious Lord, take all opportunities of
shewing my mission, by edifying my neighbour, and shewing him the Saviour, on which his salvation depends.

Bishops are called *angels* in the Revelations, intimating [i. 46.]
that he [they] should have no interest on earth at heart so
much as that of the good of the Church, and the honour of
God.

The Holy Fathers[a] stile Episcopacy, "a burden dreadful to [ii. 32.]
the shoulders of Angels themselves;" a source of infinite
cares and solicitudes.

The Bishops in Bastwick's case (Hampton Court Con- [ii. 68.]
ference)[b] declare, that they had not their jurisdiction as
Bishops from any King or Queen.

No authority can deprive a Bishop but such a synodical
assembly as that from which he received his authority.

Apud nos Apostolorum locum Episcopi tenent. St. Jerom. [iii. 45.]
Epist. 4. ad Montanist. [Ep. 41. ad Marcellam. § 3. Ed.
Vallarsii.]

To desire to succeed Jesus Christ, the Sovereign Pastor,
in His authority, and not in His labours and humility, is
folly and impiety[c].

To have received life and education from parents truly [iii. 46.]
Christian is a good presage for a minister of the Church.
This, I bless God, was my case. May I never abuse so great
a blessing by departing from the rules given me by them out
of God's word, and sanctified by their prayers.

It is a shrewd symptom of Atheism, to think a man less [iii. 53.]
honourable because he is an immediate servant of the Great
God, and of His Son Jesus Christ.

Episcopal Power. "Every Bishop hath in the Govern- [iii. 67.]
ment of his own Church, the free power of his will, being
to give an account of his own actions to God." St. Cypr.
[ed. Fell.] Ep. 72 and 76. [Ep. 72. prope finem. "Cum

---

[a] [Concil. Trident. Sess. v. Decr. de Reform. c. i. "Onus Angelicis humeris formidandum."]

[b] [Rather, "in the Star Chamber:" see Laud's Speech as quoted by Collier, E. H. Part ii. b. ix. fol. t. ii. 774, June 16, 1637.]

[c] [The three last words in Dr. Wilson's handwriting.]

SUNDAY. habeat in Ecclesiæ administratione voluntatis suæ arbitrium liberum unusquisque præpositus, rationem actus sui Domino redditurus." [Ep. (not 76, but) 73.] ad fin. " nemini præscribentes . . . quo minus unusquisque Episcoporum quod putat faciat, habens arbitrii sui liberam potestatem.]

Elections of Bishops, Priests and Deacons in the Primitive Church were by the generality of the faithful, or nominated by the Bishop with their consent, and by him consecrated—viz. the Inferior Clergy; and the Superior by the Comprovincial Bishops, or Metropolitan.

[i. 47.] *Intercession for my flock.* He who bewails not the sins of his people, and does not, by his own tears, make as it were some amends for their impenitency, is not worthy to be their mediator with God.

For a Criminal under Sentence of Death. O merciful God, our only help in time of need; hear me, I beseech Thee, for this miserable sinner.

Touch his heart most powerfully from above, that he may give glory to Thee in a full and free confession of his crimes, and of Thy justice and mercy in bringing them to light.

Give him a true sense and knowledge of all his sins, and true repentance for them, that they may be done away by Thy mercy, and his pardon sealed in Heaven before he go hence, and be no more seen.

Grant that with a firm faith and trust in Thy mercy, he may lay hold of Thy promises for Jesus Christ's sake to all that repent and believe.

Look upon the work of Thine own hands. Let not his sins obstruct Thy mercy. Suffer him not to overlook this day of visitation, nor to die in his sins.

[i. 48.] O blessed Jesus, O powerful Advocate, undertake for this sinner; by Thy Cross and Passion deliver him from the bitter pains of eternal death, as Thou didst the penitent thief, even at the last hour. Amen.

God often grants to the faith and prayers of others, the conversion of a sinner, who himself doth not think of God.

Gracious God, look down in mercy upon the miserable case of these whom I now present before thee. Touch their hearts most powerfully from above, that they may see, before

SACRA PRIVATA. 73

it be too late, the danger of living without God in the world; SUNDAY.
for Jesus Christ his sake. Amen.

Briefs. Consider the uncertainty of human affairs. Who knows whose turn it may be next, to suffer by fire, by loss of friends, sickness, &c. so as to want the charity of others?

Catechising. See Mr. Herbert, p. 66. [§ xxi.]

Seriousness in a clergyman. Nothing more unbecoming us than too much mirth. Sin and miseries, which we meet with at every turn: God dishonoured and man afflicted, is sufficient to make, &c. [See Country Parson, c. 27.]

An holy unblameable life. Where a man is despised, his instructions will be despised also. He that would gain respect must respect others.

Reproving. To be able to reprove others with success, a man must, &c.

Preaching. Watts *on the Passions*, pt. ii. 149. [i. 49.]

We do not sufficiently consider that gravity in discourse [?] is necessary to gain us respect, and cause us to be...especially if we design to instruct others.

N.B. Benzelius hath (1743) been Bishop of Upsal now forty-five years[d].

LORD'S SUPPER.

[iii. prefixes by way of title], Private devotions at the Altar, taken out of the most ancient offices of the Church; to render our present Communion-service more agreeable to Apostolic usage, and more acceptable (I hope) to God, and beneficial to all that partake thereof. Until it shall please Him to put it into the hearts and power of such as ought to do it, to restore to us the First Service of Edw. VI. Or such as shall be more conformable to the appointment of

---

[d] [He was therefore consecrated in the same year with Bp. Wilson himself, 1697 8. But it would seem as if it were a mistake to say he had been Bishop of *Upsal* so long; for he probably is the Ericus Benzelius, Bishop of *Linkoping*, who wrote a Preface to Serenius' English, Latin, and Swedish Dictionary, published at Hamburgh, 1734; in which he speaks of himself as growing old, and as having been a friend of Hickes, Hudson, Dodwell, Tho. Smith, Grabe, and complains of the taste for " Literæ Septentrionales" having so far abated in England, from what it had been thirty years before, that he could not publish there an edition of Ulphilas' Gospels, which he had prepared. He had been *Librarian* at Upsal twenty years and more, which might account for Bp. Wilson's mistake.]

SUNDAY. Christ and His Apostles and their successors. Which may the Divine Majesty vouchsafe to grant, for His sake Who first ordained this holy Sacrament. Amen.

[i. 50; iii. 219.] *Before Service begins*[c]. May it please Thee, O God, who hast called us to this ministry, to make us worthy to offer unto Thee *this Sacrifice,* for our own sins, and for the sins of Thy people.

Accept our service and our persons, through our Lord Jesus Christ, who liveth and reigneth, with Thee and the Holy Ghost, one God, world without end. Amen.

O, reject not this people for me, and for my sins[d].

Upon placing the Alms upon the Altar[e]. All that we possess is the effect of Thy bounty, O God; and of Thy own do we give Thee. Pardon all our vain expenses; and accept of this testimony of our gratitude to Thee, our Benefactor, for the Lord Jesus' sake[f]. Who remembered us when we were without hope and without God in the world, and hath made us His brethren and heirs of His kingdom.

[i. 50; iii. 220.] *Upon placing the Elements*[g] *upon the Altar.* Vouchsafe to receive these Thy creatures from the hands of us sinners, O Thou self-sufficient[h] God!

Immediately after the [i] *Consecration.* We offer unto Thee, our King and our God, this bread and this cup.

We give Thee thanks for these and for[j] all Thy mercies, beseeching Thee to send down Thy Holy Spirit upon this sacrifice, that He may make this bread the Body of Thy Christ, and this cup the Blood of Thy Christ: and that all we, who are partakers thereof, may thereby obtain remission of our sins, and all other benefits of His Passion.

And, together with us, remember, O God, for good, the whole mystical Body of Thy Son[k]: that such as are yet alive may finish their course with joy; and that we, with all[l] such

---

[c] iii. adds, *kneeling at the altar.*
[d] om. i i.
[e] iii. "When the alms are placed."
[f] iii. "Of Thy own, O Lord, do we give Thee. Pardon all our vain expenses, and teach us so to husband the riches with which we are entrusted, that we may always have to offer a testimony of our gratitude to Thee our Benefactor, through Jesus Christ. Amen."
[g] iii. "the bread and wine and water."
[h] [ἀνενδεής: from the Apostolical Constitutions, viii. 12. t. i. p. 407. ed. Cotelerii. Perhaps "self-sufficing" would be a more satisfactory rendering.]
[i] iii. adds, "Prayer of."
[j] iii. om. "these and for."
[k] iii. *prima manu,* adds, "Whether on earth or in Paradise."
[l] iii. om. "that we, with all."

as are dead in the Lord, may rest in hope and rise in glory, SUNDAY.
for Thy Son's[m] sake, whose death we now commemorate.
Amen.

May I atone Thee, O God, by offering to Thee the pure [i. 50.]
and unbloody sacrifice, which Thou hast ordained by Jesus
Christ. Amen.

But how should I dare to offer Thee this sacrifice, if I had
not first offered myself a sacrifice to Thee, my God.

May I never offer the prayers of the faithful with polluted [i. 51.]
lips, nor distribute the bread of life with unclean hands!

I acknowledge and receive Thee, O Jesus, as sent of God,
a Prophet, to make His will known to us, and His merciful
purpose to save us; as our Priest, who offered Himself an
acceptable sacrifice for us, to satisfy the divine justice, and
to make intercession for us; and as our King, to rule and
defend us against all our enemies.

O good Saviour, who remembered us when we were lost
and undone for ever.

We live unmindful of a mercy by which we have been redeemed from eternal death and misery.

Thy death, burial (?), resurrection, and ascension, and
meriting for [us?] the inestimable gift of the Holy Ghost
......A Prophet to instruct;—a Priest to intercede for;—
a King to govern...

May I always receive the holy Sacrament in the same
meaning, intention, and blessed effect, with which Jesus
Christ administered it to His Apostles in His last Supper.

CONFIRMATION. [i. 72.]

By faith we receive the Spirit, which is of God. *I will put
My Spirit within you*, saith God. [Ezekiel xxxvi. 27.]

We are truly Christians, by receiving the Spirit of Christ.
He that hath not received this Spirit, and doth not keep
it, is no Christian.

This is the great blessing of the gospel, the fellowship of
the Holy Ghost, with the desire of which we conclude our
daily prayers, with the grace of our Lord Jesus Christ.

[m] iii. "the Lord's."

SUNDAY.

By the imposition of hands is signified to us, that God by His own minister takes possession of us anew; that He unites us to Himself by His Holy Spirit; that He will keep us in His hand, and under His protection. How can Christians neglect so great a blessing, upon which their salvation so much depends?

By laying on of hands was given them the fruits of the Holy Ghost, that is, all the graces and virtues necessary [for] them to lead a godly and Christian life; without which graces and helps we can do nothing that is good. Such fruits as these: love, joy, peace, &c. Gal. v. [22.] To enable us to cast off the works of darkness: to crucify the flesh with its affections and lusts.

The love of God will be shed abroad in your hearts, by the Holy Ghost that is given you, if you do not resist nor grieve Him, but follow the good thoughts He puts in your hearts.

This love of God for you will lead you to love of your neighbour. By the same Spirit you will be led to every good work, to be just to all, charitable, &c. &c.

[i. 73.]

By the same Holy Ghost, or Spirit, you will be kept from pride, lust, malice, and every evil temper which makes God our enemy. It is by this good Spirit that you will be taught to pray, and to do every thing which you believe will please God, and avoid what you know will offend Him.

The effect and blessing of Confirmation. It is to convey the inestimable blessing of the Holy Spirit of God, by prayer, and the imposition of the hands of God's minister, that He may dwell in you, and keep you from the temptations of the world, the flesh, and the devil.

Confirmation is the perfection of baptism. The Holy Ghost descends invisibly upon such as are rightly prepared to receive such a blessing, as at the first He came visibly upon those that had been baptized.

By imposition of the hands of God's minister, God takes as it were possession of [you] as His own peculiar treasure; He sanctifies and consecrates you again to Himself—engages to keep you continually in His hand—and makes us partakers of the divine graces and virtues.

[i. 52; ii. 96; iii. 68.]

Acts viii. 7. *Then laid they* (that is, Peter and John) *their hands on them,* (namely, whom Philip had baptized,) *and they received the Holy Ghost.*

O God, who hast called me to this high office, to confirm and bless the people in Thy name, let Thy blessing[1] be dispensed, not according to my unworthiness, but according to Thine own goodness, and the appointments of Thy Church.

O Lord, graciously behold Thy servants, on whom I am now[m] going to lay my hands.

Possess their hearts with [n]a lively sense of Thy great mercy, in bringing them from the power of Satan[o], in giving them an early right to [p]the covenant of grace; that with the full consent of their will[q] they may devote themselves to Thee and [r]Thy service; that they may receive the fulness of Thy grace, and be able to withstand the temptations of the world, the flesh, and the devil.

Keep[s] them, O Lord, in the unity of the Church, and grant that they may improve all the means of grace vouchsafed them in this Church, of which they are now to be made complete members[t].

Increase their knowledge, confirm their faith, and strengthen them in all goodness. Preserve in their minds a constant remembrance of that vow which they are going to renew before Thee and Thy Church[u]; that knowing that they are the servants of the living God, they may walk as in Thy[x] sight, avoid all such things as are contrary to their profession, and follow all such things as are agreeable unto the same.

O Lord, who hast made them Thy children by adoption, bring them in Thy good time to Thine everlasting kingdom, through Jesus Christ our Lord. Amen. [ii. only], That by their good lives they may bring honour to Thee, and benefit to their own souls. [i. 52; ii. 96; iii. 64.]

Confirmation. O Lord, who hast called Thy unworthy servant to this high office in Thy holy Church, *to confirm and bless the people in Thy Name;* let not any unworthiness in [M.H. lxvii.]

---

[1] "blessings," ii. iii.
[m] om. ii.
[n] ii. adds "such."
[o] "unto God," ii. iii.
[p] iii. "Thy holy covenant, and an early knowledge of their duty."
[q] ii. "wills."
[r] iii. adds "to."
[s] ii. "continue."
[t] ii. "are members."
[u] The rest of this sentence in iii. only.
[x] ii. "His."

me, I most humbly beseech Thee, hinder the current of Thy blessings from descending upon them.

It is great presumption in me, who am myself subject to so many and great infirmities, to exercise this office: but Thy favours and blessings, O great Creator, are not dispensed according to our merit, but according to Thy own infinite goodness and mercy to the work of Thy hands. It is this consideration, O God, and in hopes of the pardon of my own sins by the blood of Jesus Christ, which makes me bold to do that office to which I am now separated and appointed by Thy Church.

For the sake of the same Jesus Christ, my great Master, and whose example I desire to imitate in all other acts of goodness and charity—for the sake of Jesus Christ hear me, I most humbly beseech Thee, and grant the petitions which I now offer to the throne of grace on behalf of those on whom I am going to lay my hands.

Possess them, O God, with such a lively sense of Thy great mercy, in sending Thy Son to be the Saviour of the world; in bringing them into the world in such a place where the Christian religion is purely taught, and Thy sacraments duly administered; in giving them such an early knowledge of God, and in laying upon them so many and such strong obligations to be happy by obeying Him; and in affording them such powerful assistances of the Holy Spirit to attain the happiness which we all so passionately desire: that they may believe in Thee, that they may love, fear and obey Thee, all the days of their lives.

To this end give them grace, O blessed God, that with the deliberate and full consent of their own wills they may this day devote themselves to Thee, and to Thy service: preserve in their minds a constant remembrance of that vow which they shall this day renew before Thee and Thy Church, that so they may not wilfully offend against so many forceable reasons obliging them to their duty.

And by the power of Thy Holy Spirit (which I earnestly beg for Christ's sake may attend me in the offices of this day) confirm and settle them in all goodness, and of Thy great mercy keep them in the same, until they come to Thy everlasting kingdom. Amen.

And O that the performances of these offices of my calling Sunday. may constantly leave a greater sense of Thee and of my duty upon my soul, that I may have a better sense and taste of piety and holiness, and may by Thy grace become such as Thou canst approve and delight in for ever. Amen, Amen.

The Jews' custom was, when children were thirteen years old, and had learnt the law, &c., and their prayers, to bring them before the congregation, upon which they were declared sons of the precept, and were now to answer for their own sins, &c. Buxtorf, Synag. Jud. cap. 7.

This usage was so reasonable and necessary, that it is probable it had its origin from God Himself; as we are sure confirmation had from Christ.

See Can. 60. Of the Antiquity of Confirmation in the Church of God. ["It hath been a solemn, ancient, and laudable custom in the Church of God, continued from the Apostles' times."]

Can. 61. Bishops shall confirm in their visitation. Ministers shall prepare children for confirmation.

xiv. of Car. II. [i. e. the Prayer Book according to the Act of Uniformity of 1661, in which for the first time was inserted the following.] Minister shall give the names of such as are to be confirmed to the bishop, and if the bishop approve of them, [&c.] As also the Rubric after the Catechism[y].

Jo. Calvin in Heb. vi. 2. "Hic unus locus abunde testatur [i. 53; ii. hujus cæremoniæ originem fluxisse ab Apostolis." Idem in 97; iii.64.] Institut. lib. iv. cap. 19, § 4. ["Talem ergo manuum impositionem, quæ simpliciter loco benedictionis fiat, laudo, et restitutam hodie in purum usum velim."] et 13. ["Utinam vero morem retineremus, quam apud veteres fuisse admonui ...non enim esset Confirmatio talis qualem isti fingunt, quæ sine Baptismi injuria ne nominari quidem potest, sed Catechesis qua pueri aut adolescentiæ proximi fidei suæ rationem coram Ecclesia exponerent."] Beza in locum. [..."doctrinæ explicationem compendiariam, quæ in baptismis et impositione manuum tradi rudibus præsertim solebat."] Tertull. lib. de Baptismo, cap. viii. ["Dehinc manus imponitur, per

---

[y] [This reference is an oversight, being in fact the same with the preceding.]

SUNDAY. benedictionem advocans et invitans Spiritum Sanctum."]
Cypr. Ep. lxxiii. ad Jubaianum. [" Quod deerat, id a Petro et a Joanne factum est, ut oratione pro eis habita, et manu imposita, invocaretur et infunderetur super eos Spiritus Sanctus. Quod nunc quoque apud nos geritur, ut qui in Ecclesia baptizantur Præpositis Ecclesiæ offerantur, et per nostram orationem ac manus impositionem Spiritum Sanctum consequantur, et signaculo Domini consummentur.] St. Je-
[i. 53.] rom. Dial. advers. Lucif. [§ 8.] If you ask where this is ordered, I refer you to the Acts of the Apostles. But if the Scriptures were silent, the consent of all the world in this particular is instead of a command[z].

[i. 53; iii. 64.] Bp. Beveridge's Sermons. "How any bishops in our age dare neglect so considerable a part of their office, I know not, but I fear they will have no good account to give of it, when they come to give account before God[a]." [vol. i. p. 23, ed. 1709[b].]

Acts viii. 14. It appears from hence, that even in the Apostles' times, confirmation was necessary, as well as baptism, that persons might become complete members of the [c]Church, and partakers of the grace of Christ: and that these graces were conferred by peculiar hands; for though Philip had the power of miracles[d], yet he could not do that which belonged to an higher order:—so great a regard had the Spirit of God to order and discipline.

"The same," saith St. Cyprian, [ubi sup.] " is [e]practised among us. They who have been baptized are brought unto the presidents of the Church, that by our prayer and imposition of hands, they may receive the Holy Ghost, and be consummated with the Lord's seal."

[i. 53.] The imposition of hands signifies to us, that God takes possession of His creature anew, in order to sanctify it by His invisible residence; that He unites it to Himself by His Spirit, &c.[f] ["Submits it to Himself by the power of His grace, and holds it in His hand to fulfil in it what He purposes."]

[z] [om. iii.]
[a] [iii. "stand before God's (our Lord's) tribunal."]
[b] [i. adds, "How any clergyman can give it under his hand."]
[c] [iii. "body, or."]
[d] iii. "and was himself inspired, yet being of an inferior degree, he could not do that which belonged to an higher order." So the sentence ends.
[e] iii. om. "now."
[f] Quesnel in Acts viii. 17.

As the Holy Spirit is present in our baptism, to seal the   SUNDAY.
remission of sins, and to infuse the seeds of Christian life; so
is He present in confirmation, to shed further influences on
those that receive it, for stirring up the gift of God bestowed
in baptism, &c.

Acts viii. 17. Confirmation, in the primitive times, was
often attended with external signs. The Holy Spirit de-
scended visibly upon the faithful, that we may know that He
descends invisibly now into those who are duly confirmed
and prepared for Confirmation. [Quesnel in loc.]

See Reeves's Use of the Fathers, [prefixed to his Transla- [i. 53; ii.
tion of the Apologies of Justin Martyr, &c., 1709,] p. 93.   97.]

It is necessary to make young Christians sensible of the
danger of doing any thing to deserve Church censures. Shew
them the advantage of being permitted to partake of the holy
Sacrament, &c.; that if they sin publicly, they will be deprived of it; if privately, they will be deprived of heaven.
[This is in MS. ii.; i. reads, "Shew young Christians the
advantage of receiving the Lord's Supper, &c. And that if
they sin presumptuously, they will be deprived both of that,
and of heaven."]

[*Prayer after Confirmation.*] Matthew xix. 15. *And He* [i. 53.]
laid His hands on them.

Could the laying on of Christ's hands be without a powerful effect, and can it be without effect for those who have His
authority to do the same[c]?

O Holy Spirit of Grace, I make my humble supplication [i. 54.]
to Thee, in behalf of those Thy servants on whom I have this
day laid my hands. Be Thou their *wisdom,* to give them the
knowledge of religion;—their *understanding,* to know their
duty;—their *counsel,* in all their doubts;—their *strength,*
against all temptations;—their *knowledge,* in what belongs to
the state of life in which Thy providence shall place them;
—their *piety* and *godliness* in all their actions; and be Thou
their *fear,* all their life long, for Jesus Christ's sake. Amen.

The Prayer at Confirmation. The spirit of wisdom, to
choose aright;—of understanding, to know our duty;—of

---

[c] See Wensley's Sermon on the Catechism of the Church of England, a small bound octavo.

counsel, to give or take advice;—of knowledge, to understand divine truths;—of godliness, to practise them;—of holiness, to be conformed to the image of God, in which we were at first created, and to which to restore us Christ came Himself and sent His Holy Spirit.

See Mr. Wheatley his comment upon the Common Prayers, in loc.

See Quesnel, Acts viii. 15, 16, 17.

Imposition of hands. Deut. xxvi. 17. You have this day publicly acknowledged and declared the Lord to be your God, and that you will walk in His ways, and keep His commands, and hearken unto His voice. And the Lord hath owned and received you to be His servants, and to reward you with eternal life and happiness, if you continue to serve Him faithfully unto your life's end.

To enable you to do so, He hath given you His Holy Spirit, who will assist and govern you all your days, that you may be holy unto the Lord, and be for ever happy when you die.

Take heed, therefore, that you do not grieve that Holy Spirit, nor force Him to forsake you, and leave you to yourselves, which will be the greatest judgment that can befall you; for then the evil spirits will get power over you, and without a speedy repentance, and return to God, they will at last bring you to destruction both of soul and body.

The only way to prevent this sad judgment is, to beg of God every day to keep you from all wilful and known sin. For he that liveth in any known sin, the good Spirit of God will at last forsake him most certainly.

When the Holy Ghost puts into your heart any good thought, or good purposes, or your conscience tells you that you have done, or are going to do, any [thing that] will displease a holy God, be assured it is the voice of God, and have a care of neglecting to hear, as you value your salvation.

Lastly; Remember to beg of God to direct and bless you in all your ways. And forget not this safe direction and rule:—That if you cannot have the confidence to pray for God's blessing upon any work you are about, or going to undertake, that work is unlawful, and will be unprosperous, and a curse and not a blessing to you.

Another Exhortation. The Church, dear children, takes SUNDAY. this way to convince you, that the service which we owe to [iii. 65.] God should be free and voluntary.

You have promised, with your own mouths, to serve God faithfully all your days.

It behoves you, therefore, to have these promises always before your eyes, that you may remember and perform them; otherwise it would have been better for you that you had never been baptized—never been born.

Your everlasting salvation or damnation depends upon your keeping or forgetting the promise you have made this day.

Your duty therefore it is to pray daily to God for grace and strength to fulfil the same unto your lives' end, that you may be happy for ever; which God grant, for Jesus Christ's sake. Amen.

You are come into a very corrupt world; you will meet with very many temptations; you are naturally weak, and prone to evil continually; so that without God's assistance you are sure to be undone.

St. Luke xiv. 28. *Which of you intending to build a tower, &c.*

You are much likelier to become apostates than good Christians, if you have not well considered, and understand, the faith and duties of Christianity.

God stands in need of nobody's service in this world. It is for our sake alone that He calls us to His service; but then He would have none but such as engage themselves in His service freely and of their own choice.

Confirmed, A.D. 1737—566.   [i. 55.]
1738—117.
1739—126.
1740—390.
1741—119.
1742—483.
1743—126.
1744—219.
1745—272.
1746—348.

2766.

SUNDAY LAUDS.

It becometh well the just to be thankful.
1 Thess. v. 18. *In every thing give thanks.*
Special Favours.

That I was born of parents fearing God, and in a Christian and in a Protestant country, Dec. 20, 1663.

An early right to the covenant of grace, baptized by Mr. Litherland, Dec. 25, 1663.

Reason, perfect members and senses, and an healthful constitution.

An education above the abilities of my family.

Entered in Trinity College, Dublin, 1681.

Ordained deacon by Dr. Moreton, Bp. of Kildear (sic), at the consecration of the Quire, June 29, 1686.

Curate of New Church, Winwick, Feb. 10.

Ordained Priest by Bishop Stratford, Oct. 20, 1689.

Tutor to James, Lord Strange, Aug. 19, 1692.

The advantage of worthy friends.

Forced to accept the Bishoprick of Man, Nov. 27, 1697.

Dr. of Laws, Jan. 10, 1697.

Consecrated in the Savoy Chapel, by Abp. of York, (Dr. Sharp), Chester and Norwich, Jan. 16, 1697.

Married to M. Patten, an excellent woman, Oct. 27, 1698.

Dr. in Divinity, full Convocation, Oxon, March 3, 1707.

Finished and printed Manks Catechism, May 30, 1707.

Dr. Divinity, Cambridge, Dr. Balderson, Vice-Can., June 2, 1707.

Lord Viscount Weymouth, £20, for Bibles, &c., May 27, 1707.

Lady Westmorland £10, Mr. Hoar books.

Member of the Society for Promoting Christian Knowledge, May 15, 1707.

Imprisoned for a faithful discharge (I hope) of my duty, June 29, 1722.

His Majesty reversed all proceedings of the officers, July 4, 1724.

Sept. 10, 1723. Being engaged, by the advice of the Archbishop, &c., in an expensive controversy for defence of the discipline of the Church, Mr. Dean Harris, chaplain to the Prince of Wales, proposed (without my knowledge) that

SUNDAY LAUDS.

a contribution should be made to enable me to go through with it, it being the common cause of the Church. Upon which Dr. Marshal, jun., undertook to manage it, and has paid me as follows: Mr. Dean Harris, £5 5s., Dean of York and Mr. Finch, £42; Lord Thanet, £21; Lord Anglesea, £21; Mr. Auditor Harley, £21; Dean of Poles' [St. Paul's], £5 5s. [15s.]; from Dean of York, £50; Dr. Sherlock, Dean of Chichester, £10 10s.; Mr. Jennings, £5 5s.; Dr. Pelling, Canon of Windsor, £5 5s.; Sir John Phillips, £5 5s.; Mr. Hoar, £5 5s.; Mr. Witham, £5 5s.; Dr. Marshall, £5 5s.; Mr. Annesley, £5 5s.; Lady B. Hastings, £31 10s.; Sir Thos. Veasy, Lord Bishop of Ossory, £20. In all, £264 15s.

May the God of Heaven return it sevenfold into their bosoms.

[In iii. 59, 58, this stands as follows (still as part of the Sunday Devotions)].

1 Thess. v. 18. *In every thing give thanks.*

Special Favours.

That I was born of honest parents fearing God, and in a Christian and Protestant country, Dec. 20, Sunday, 1663.

That I had an early right to the covenant of grace, Dec. 25, 1663.

That I had reason, perfect members and senses, and a sound constitution.

That I had an education beyond the abilities of my father's house.

The advantage of worthy friends.

Entered in the University of Trinity Coll. Dublin, 1681.

I was ordained deacon by Bp. of Kildare, June 29, 1686.

I was licenced curate of New Church, Feb. 10, 1686.

I was ordained priest, Oct. 20, 1689.

I was made tutor to James, Lord Strange, Aug. 19, 1692.

My Lord Derby even forced me to accept the bishoprick, Nov. 27, 1697.

I was created Doctor of Laws, Jan. 10, 1697.

I was consecrated Bishop of Man in the Savoy Church by Dr. Jo. Sharp, Abp. of York, Bps. of Chester and Norwich, Jan. 16, 1697.

I was marry'd to M. Patten, an excellent woman, Oct. 27, 1698; by whom I have had four lovely children.

SUNDAY LAUDS.

I was made Dr. in Divinity in a full Convocation of the University of Oxford, March 3, 1707.

I finished and printed my Manx Catechism, May 30, 1707.

The Univ. of Cambridge honoured me with my degree of Dr. in Divinity. Dr. James presented me to Dr. Balderson, Vice-Chancellor, June 11, 1707.

Lord Vic^t. Weymouth sent me £20 for Bibles, May 27, 1707.

Mr. H. Hoar made me a present of books for my diocese, May 16, 1707.

Lady Westmoreland, £10.

I had the honour of being imprisoned for a faithful discharge of my duty, June 29, 1722.

Admitted a member of the Society for Propagating Christian Knowledge, May 15, 1707.

The King in council reversed all the proceedings of the officers of the Isle, July 4, 1724.

[iii. 58.] Sept. 10, 1723. Having engaged myself by the advice of A Bp., &c., in an expensive controversy for the defence of the discipline of the Church, in which I have already spent above £300, Mr. Dean Harris, chaplain to the Prince of Wales, as Dr. Marshall tells me in his of the 5th instant, proposed that, without my knowledge of it, a contribution should be made to enable us to carry on this suit, which being the common cause of the Church, he said 'twas not fit I should bear the whole burden myself. He therefore laid down five guineas, and Dr. Marshall very kindly undertook to manage it, and as far as I can yet be let into the secret, there is £200 given or subscribed—such as are come to my knowledge are—[then follows the list as before: only to Lord Anglesea's name is added "&c.," and (*prima manu*) "by Mr. Annesley;" to Mr. Harley's name, "June 23, 1724." "Pole's" is spelt "Paule's;" with the sum £5 15s., and there are no words of prayer at the foot.

See before, p. 51, for the list of "Special Favours" as it occurs in MS. ii. In i. 186-7, it proceeds as follows.]

June 22, 1730. Mrs. Levinz, my predecessor's widow, at the request of my son, sent me £50 towards purchasing land for the use of clergymen's widows and their children.

[i. 187.] Directions to an Academick Youth, June, 1727.

My son ordained Deacon by Bp. of Oxford, May 28, 1727.

June, 1735. At my son's request, Sir John Cheshire gave me £20 for pious uses, which I intend to lay out, part on a vicar's house in Kirk Lonan, part towards a vicar's house in Kirk Germain.

June, 1735. Dr. Hales sent me £20 from an unknown lady (the Lady Grace Butler), to buy Bibles, &c.

June, 1735. One Mr. Williams gave my son £16, to be laid out in my books on the Sacrament.

June, 1735. The Lady Harrold, sister and executrix of the late Lord Weymouth, [Thanet?[d]] at my son's request, and upon his representation, gave me £100 towards augmenting the fund I have made for the widows and orphans of my clergy.

March, 1740. The Lady Eliz. Hastings, who died Dec. 22, 1739, by her last will, (God blessing my labours and representation of the want of encouragement for petty schools in the Isle of Man,) has left £20 a-year for ever for this pious use. Blessed be God for His mercies.

April 28, 1736. By a letter from my daughter-in-law, I have an account of my son's recovery from the small-pox, for which I can never be sufficiently thankful.

Dec. 1, 1737. By a letter from my son, he has with exceeding pains found the deeds for securing to my clergy the impropriations, which are enrolled in the Chancery Records in the Chapel of the Rolls.

Dec. 9, 1737. This day my Lord High Chancellor of Great Britain, upon the request of Sir Joseph Jekyl, Master of the Rolls, to present my son to the living of St. Stephen's, Walbrook, worth about £200 per annum. [From the three foregoing entries, special reference is made by asterisks to the two following.]

Thanksgiving. Blessing, and glory, and wisdom, and thanksgiving, and honour, and power, and might, be to our God for ever and ever. Amen.

Remember, O God, for good, our known and unknown

---

[d] [See Jacobs' Peerage, ii. 549. Lady Mary Tufton, 4th daughter of Thomas, sixth Earl of Thanet, (who died 1729,) married Anthony, Earl of Harrold, son of Henry Grey, the last Duke of Kent of that family; she afterwards married the first Earl Gower, and is no doubt the lady here referred to. The Bishop must have written "Weymouth" by a slip of the pen.]

benefactors; for Jesus Christ's sake, our greatest and best Benefactor. Amen. [Between the two last entries is inserted],

1743. Aug. and Sept. *Eye-sight.* God's most especial favour in restoring me to my sight when I was in the greatest fear of losing it.

A dangerous rupture perfectly cured.

2 Cor. i. 10: *Who delivered us from so great a death, and doth deliver: in whom we trust that He will still deliver us.*

Mercies and[e] extraordinary deliverances[f].

From the dangerous wounds I received in my head and thigh, when a child.

From gunpowder.

From drowning at Acton Bridge.

From a pin[g] swallowed in my meat. Feb. 10, 1703.

From fire. Dec. 9, 1700.

From great troubles going to befal me on account of A.D. Marsden, Acad. Place[h]. Aug. 1701.

From the dangers of the sea, Whitehaven[i], Sept. 5, 1704.

From a temptation which had ruined me, had I not been surprisingly delivered by a sensible power of God, upon my humble request to Him for grace and strength[j].

From a [k]dangerous fall off my horse, March 6, 1711.

From the dangers of the sea, (Jan. 25, 1719,) a leaky vessel, and violent storm, which followed my landing, in which two vessels were lost at Hylake.

[iii. gives it thus.] From the great danger I escaped in returning to the Island in a very leaky vessel, (of which I knew nothing till after I landed,) and from the violent storm which immediately followed my coming ashore, in which two vessels were lost.

From the dangers I escaped (Feb. 2, 1720,) returning from Douglass, in the snow.

---

[e] "mercies and" om. iii.
[f] i. *prima manu*, added, "and merciful disappointments."
[g] iii. adds, "which I."
[h] iii. reads, "From the great troubles going to befal me on account of the Academick Place by Archdeacon Marsden."
[i] iii. om. "Whitehaven."
[j] This blotted in iii. His last words seem to have been, "upon my making my humble request to Him for grace."
[k] iii. adds "very."

[iii.] Returning to Douglass, I was in great danger of being lost in the snow, or hurt by my mare, while I lay in the snow, &c. Feb. 2, 1720.

^{SUNDAY LAUDS.}

Jan. 1, 1725. My dear child was in a tempest driven to [i. 188.] the coast of Ireland, and there shipwrecked; the master and he left on board by the boat, the master drowned, and by the mercy of God he was saved; and this day (Jan. 16) I have a letter from him. Blessed be God for this miraculous [deliverance?]

[iii. has], Jan. 1, 1725. My dear child coming to see me from Liverpool, was in tempest driven to the coast of Ireland, and there shipwrecked, but by the great mercy of God his life was saved, and this day (Jan. 16) I have a letter under his own hand: the Lord make me truly thankful.

May, 1734. From the troubles threatened, and in some[1] measure begun, by our unreasonable Governor Horton, denying me right of appointing my own Vicars-general; which Lord Derby (as he says) has restored me to my rights without my applying to him. May God make the Governor sensible of the great evil he has done, in putting a stop to justice, &c.; and me ever thankful for His mercies to those that call upon [Him] in their distress.

April 21 and 28, 1735. In a violent storm both these days (in the last of which a bark and the men in her were lost), God was pleased to deliver me from the dangers of the seas.

Nov. 2, 1735. My chair overturned coming from Lezaire. But blessed be God, I got no hurt.

The very many times I have been hindered from such steps as might in all probability have been to my great disadvantage, both with respect to my temporal as well as spiritual condition.

Sept. 1738. My son delivered from very great danger of his life by a fall from his horse. And from many [?] fits of sickness.

May 5, 1739. Lighting from my horse, my foot stuck in the stirrup, but through the favour of God the horse, though young, stood still, though I lay upon the ground a good while.

---

[1] iii. places here the text, 2 Cor. i. 10.

SUNDAY LAUDS.

Aug, 17, 1746. My chaise-horse, by a fright, had like to run [away with?] me: but God be praised, &c.

[i. 189;
iii. 61.]

Job xxxiii. 14. *God speaketh once, yea twice, yet man perceiveth it not.*
Merciful Visitations, Chastisements, and Disappointments.
An afflicting melancholy in my youth.

Sept. 8, 1692. A shock of an earthquake, with an affecting circumstance never[m] to be forgotten.

Sept. 29, 1693. A [n]dangerous fever.

A long indisposition, from which I recovered in 1698.

March 7, 1704. The loss of my dear wife, with a circumstance *very peculiar,* which shewed the love and the justice of God.

[iii. reads], The loss of my dear wife, and three of my children, with circumstances very peculiar, and which shewed the love and the justice as well as providence of God. March 7, 1704; June 8, 1701; June 3, 1703; Nov. 27, 1712.

Nov. 9, 1705. A most merciful visitation, when I was surprisingly awaked out of sleep, and most powerfully stirred up to a more diligent discharge of my duty. [This, and the next entry, all but the date, are cut out of MS. iii.]

April 13, 1716. The like visitation.

St. Peter's Day, 1722. I and my two Vicars-general were fined £90, and imprisoned nine weeks, for censuring, and refusing to take off the censures of certain offenders. [iii. adds], June 29, 1722. Which punishment and contempt I desire to receive from God as a means of humbling me, &c.

Nov. 22, 1722. Mr. St. acquainted me with a most scandalous lie, propagated by —— and ——. The good Lord rebuke them—make them sensible of their error, and forgive their sin. [This not in iii. The entry in the corresponding place is cut out, all but " Jan." in the margin, (which might be part of the next following date,) and the following line :—
" for bodily ease, and He gave me spiritual pleasure."]

Jan. 9, '25. A most merciful visitation, &c. [iii. om. as also what follows, to the prayer.]

March 29, 1727. By a letter of T. Hd. (so God makes all things serve to His own purpose), I was in the visitations of

---

[m] iii. om. these four words.   [n] iii. adds "very."

the night awakened to the performance of a branch of my duty, which I had sadly neglected, viz. publishing the great sin of defrauding the King of his customs. God grant that I may now do it effectually.

Nothing more provoking to God, than mercies forgot, or abused.

Friday, July 6, 1744. A merciful visitation in the night, by which I was put in remembrance of the sins of youth, and by the good Spirit of God moved to repent of them in a peculiar manner.

Sept. 1743. *Eye-sight.* God's great mercy in restoring me to my sight, when I was in great danger of losing it.

The stack of chimneys falling down over my son's house.

Cause us, O God, to profit by all the visitations of Thy grace and mercy.

It becometh well the just to be thankful. [Here follows the thanksgiving as in p. 41, at Noon.] [i.190.]

Let us never ascribe any thing to ourselves, but all to the grace of God, and render to Him all the glory of His works.

Let Thy present favours to us be a pledge and earnest of Thine eternal mercy.

Preserve me, O God, from the insensibility of those who receive Thy favours without being affected with them, and from the ingratitude of those who look upon them as a debt.

Psalm xcii. 1, 2. *It is a good thing to give thanks unto the Lord; and to sing praises unto Thy Name, O Most High! To shew forth Thy loving-kindness in the morning, and Thy faithfulness every night.*

For delivering me from the dominion and power of Satan, and my own corrupt nature, and vouchsafing the grace of a true conversion.

º Many and great have been the favours and blessings which Thou hast bestowed upon this place, and upon parti- [1st ed. i. p. 200.]

º [At this point, the foot of p. 190, MS. i. breaks off, having lost 25 pages, as appears by the paging in the Bishop's own hand: and what follows to the end of the next paraphrase on the Lord's Prayer, having been contained, no doubt, in some of those missing pages, the Editor has not been able to find anywhere in either of the MSS. It is corrected here from Cruttwell's original edition, 4to. Bath, 1781, p. 200, 201.]

Sunday Lauds.

cular families. If they have forgot to praise Thee for them, I bless and praise Thee for them in their stead.

Bless the Lord, O my soul, and forget not all thy benefits.
Our Father, which art in Heaven. Acts xvii. 28. *In Thee we live, and move, and have our being.*

Grant, O Father, that all Christians may live worthy of this glorious relation.

O that we may not sin, knowing that we are accounted Thy children[p].

Grant that we may love Thee with all our heart, and mind, and soul, and strength.

Blessed be God, who dealeth with us with the tenderness of a father.

O that we may remember that our Father and our inheritance is in Heaven.

I commit myself, and all that belongs to me, to Thy fatherly care and love.

"*Verily*, whatever ye ask the Father in My Name, He will give it you[q]." This is the great support and comfort of sinners. Hear us, for Thy Son's sake; for, as sinners, we have no right to ask any favour.

What manner of love is it, that we should be called the sons of God[r]!

Hallowed be Thy Name.
Thou art worthy, O Lord, to receive honour, and power, and glory; for Thou hast created all things.
In this is My Father glorified, that ye bring forth much fruit.

May Thy children have a great regard for every thing that belongs to Thee.

May I never dishonour Thee, O heavenly Father, by word or deed.

May I glorify Thee daily by a good life. Fill my heart with a great concern and zeal for Thy glory.

Let every thing that hath breath praise the Lord.
They that honour Me, I will also honour.

How little have I done to promote Thy glory! God be merciful unto me.

[p] Wisdom xv. [2.]   [q] 1 John [iii. 1.]   [r] John xvi. [23.]

Thy Kingdom come.   SUNDAY LAUDS.

May all the kingdoms of the world obey Thy laws, and submit to Thy providence, and become the kingdoms of the Lord, and of His Christ!

May all that own Thee for their King, become Thy faithful subjects!

Bless the pious endeavours of all those that strive to propagate the gospel of Thy Kingdom.

Vouchsafe to reign in my heart; and let not Satan ever have dominion over me. [1st ed. i. p. 201.]

Grant that by my ministry Thy kingdom may be enlarged.

Fit us, O God, for the coming of Thy Kingdom. May I submit and rejoice to be governed by Thee.

O that Thy Holy Spirit may direct and rule my heart. Subdue in me all pride and covetousness, hatred, malice, envy, lust, and all uncleanness, and whatever shall offend Thee.

Thy will be done in earth as it is in heaven.

1 Thess. iv. 3. *This is the will of God, even your sanctification.*

Thou hast sent us into the world, not to do our own will, but Thine.

O subject my will to Thine.

May Thy Name be honoured by the good lives of Christians.

O that I may have respect unto all Thy commands.

May Thy will, revealed unto us in Thy holy Word, be the rule of my will, of my desires, of my words, life, and actions.

Give us this day our daily bread.

John vi. 27. *Labour not for the meat which perisheth, but for that meat which endureth unto everlasting life.*

Give us the bread which came down from Heaven, and giveth life unto the world.

Lord, give us evermore this bread. May we never deprive ourselves of this food, which will preserve our souls from death, and restore life unto our bodies.

Give us the necessaries of life; but, above all, the bread that nourisheth to eternal life.

Sunday Lauds.

And forgive us our trespasses as we forgive them that trespass against us.

Luke vi. 37. *Forgive, and ye shall be forgiven.*

Grant, O heavenly Father, that I may close with this merciful condition of pardon.

Thou hast been all mercy to me, O God, grant that I may be so to all others.

Blessed be the Lord, who has put our salvation into our own hands. May Thy grace, O Father, give me an heart ever ready to forgive!

And lead us not into temptation.

1 Corinthians x. 13. *Let him that thinketh he standeth* (firm), *take heed lest he fall.*

Let not any confidence in ourselves provoke Thee, O God, to leave us to ourselves.

2 Peter ii. 9. *The Lord knoweth how to deliver the godly out of temptation.*

Thou, O Father, knowest my infirmities, and the power of my enemies; be not wanting to me in the hour of temptation.

Matthew xxvi. 41. *Watch and pray, that ye enter not into temptation.*

Make me mindful of my weakness, that I may be more watchful and importunate for grace.

Fortify my soul against the temptations of the world, the flesh, and the devil, for Jesus Christ His sake.

But deliver us from evil.

1 Peter v. 8. *Be sober, be vigilant, because your adversary the devil, as a roaring lion, walketh about seeking whom he may devour.*

Grant, O heavenly Father, that this adversary may never find me off my guard, or from under Thy protection.

In all my saving trials, give me grace and power to overcome, to Thy glory.

For Thine is the Kingdom, the power, and the glory, for ever and ever. Amen.

To Thee, to Thee alone, and to Thy Son, and Holy Spirit, be glory for ever and ever. Amen[s].

A Daily Form of Thanksgiving.

[1st ed. 263.]

O ALMIGHTY God and most merciful Father, who, day after day, dost minister to sinful man infinite occasions of praising Thee, accept of my unfeigned thanks for all the blessings I have, and every day receive, from Thy good providence.

That of Thine own mere goodness, and without any merit of mine, or of my forefathers, [t]Thou hast given me a being from honest and religious parents, and in such a part of the world where the Christian religion is purely taught, and Thy sacraments duly administered. M.H.lxxv.

That Thou didst endue me with reason[u] and perfect senses; and, to make these more comfortable to me, didst [x]give me a sound and healthful body.

That Thou didst preside over my education, and gavest me an early knowledge of Thee, my Creator and Redeemer.

That Thou hast preserved me ever since my birth, and vouchsafed me health and liberty, and a competency of means to support[y] me.

That Thou hast redeemed me by Thy Son, and given me a share in His merits; sanctified me by Thy Holy Spirit; called me to Thy *immediate* service; raised me above the level of my father's house, and continually hast heaped unexpected favours upon me.

That Thou hast given me honourable and honest friends, to admonish, to counsel, to encourage, to support me, by their interest and advice.

That Thou hast been my refuge in tribulation, and my defence in all adversities, delivering me from dangers, infamy, and troubles. For all the known or unobserved deliverances,

---

[s] [From hence to the end of the Sunday Devotions occurs in neither MS. of the Sacra Privata. Probably it, with some devotions (which will be given) for Mondays and Tuesdays, made part of the missing 25 pp. in MS. i.]

[t] [Here the portion of this Thanksgiving now to be found in M.H. commences.]

[u] M. H. "and didst also give me perfect members and senses."

[x] M. H. adds, "likewise."

[y] M. H. "maintain."

SUNDAY LAUDS.

[1st ed. p. 263; M.H. lxxvi.]

I praise Thy good providence, and for the guard Thy holy Angels keep over me.

When I went astray, Thou didst reduce me; when I was sad, Thou didst comfort me; when I offended Thee, Thou didst forbear and gently correct me, and didst long expect my repentance; and when, for the grievousness of my sins, I was ready to despair, Thou didst keep me from utter ruin; Thou hast delivered me from the snares and assaults of the devil; Thou hast not only preserved my soul, but my body, from destruction, when sicknesses and infirmities took hold of me.

O Lord and Father, I cannot render due thanks and praise for all these mercies bestowed upon me: such as I have, I give Thee; and humbly beseech Thee to accept of *this my daily sacrifice of thanksgiving.*

Pardon, dear God, all my former ingratitude; and that [z]I have passed so many days without observing, without admiring, without acknowledging and confessing, Thy wonderful goodness to the most unworthy of all Thy servants.

For (now I soberly consider my dependence upon Thee) as there is no hour of my life that I do not enjoy Thy favours, and taste of Thy goodness, so (if my frailty would permit) I would spend no part of my life without remembering them.

Praise the Lord, then, O my soul, and all that is within me praise His holy Name.

Glory be to Thee, O Lord, my Creator. Glory be to Thee, O Jesus, my Redeemer. Glory be to the Holy Ghost, my Sanctifier, my Guide and Comforter.

All love, all glory, be to the high and undivided Trinity, whose works are inseparable, and whose dominion endureth world without end. Amen [a].

A confession of God's glory [b]. When I seriously consider, great God, my dependence upon Thy providence, and that the favours and mercies I have received are infinitely more in number than the acknowledgments I have made, I am justly ashamed of my ingratitude, and afraid lest my un-

---

[z] M. H. *prima manu*, "I lived so long in the world."

[a] [The first ed. and M. H. insert here the verses beginning "Fac, precor," as in p. 40. M.H. prefixes "for Sunday."]

[b] May 11, 1705, after a voyage of fifty hours. (M. H. omits this.)

thankfulness should provoke Thee to hinder the current of Thy blessings from descending upon me. SUNDAY LAUDS.

Forgive me, O merciful Father, my past negligences, and give me grace for the time to come to observe and to value Thy kindnesses, as becomes one who has received so much more than he deserves.

Accept of my hearty thanks, O God, for Thy late mercies vouchsafed me, in delivering me from the dangers of the seas, in giving me a safe and a speedy passage, and in bringing me to my friends in peace.

It is the desire of my soul, and shall be my great endeavour, that this life, which Thou hast preserved, should be dedicated to Thy immediate service, to which, by my repeated vows, I have bound myself: ^cthat we, whom Thou hast preserved, may serve Thee all our days.

Preserve in my soul, dear God, such a constant and clear sense of my obligations to Thee, that upon the receipt of every favour, I may immediately turn my eyes to Him from whom cometh my salvation. That Thy manifold blessings may fix such lasting impressions upon my soul, that I may always praise Thee faithfully here on earth, until it shall please Thee, of Thy unbounded mercy, to call me nearer the place of Thy heavenly habitation, to praise my Lord and Deliverer to all eternity. Amen^d. [1st ed. p. 264; M.H. lxxviii.]

A THANKSGIVING FOR ST. PETER'S DAY, WHEN MY FATHER AND TWO OF MY BROTHERS MOST WONDERFULLY ESCAPED BEING DROWNED. [1st ed. p. 264; M.H. xxi, xxii.]

O eternal and most merciful God; who hast made us happy in the knowledge of Thy providence, which governs

---

^c 1st ed. om. this clause.

^d [M. H. subjoins], "I humbly ascribe my whole preservation to Thy favour and blessing. April 9, 1698, I landed in Derby haven, being the first time I came to the Island. September [30, to Liverpool, vid. i. 273]. April 7, 1699, being Good Fryday, I landed with my family in Derby haven. April 18, 1701, Good Fryday, I landed at Hylake after twelve hours' sail. September 16, 1701, I with my family landed safe in Derby haven after a favourable passage of 24 houres. Aug. 7, 1703, after a favourable passage of 26 houres, I landed at Hylake with D^d. [? David] Christian. Sept. 11, 1703, after a favourable passage of 36 houres I landed 1704, after a passage of about 5 hours, at Douglass with D. Christian. Sept. 5, I and my [sick wife landed at Whitehaven, see i. 273]. May 11, 1705, after a voyage of 50 houres, I landed at St. Maughold."

H

<small>SUNDAY LAUDS.</small>

and preserves all things both in heaven and earth; by whose goodness my father and two of my brothers were, as on this day, delivered from sudden and untimely deaths: accept of my hearty thanks and praise for this great mercy vouchsafed to the whole family; and grant that none of us may, while we live, forget these wonderful expressions of Thy loving-kindness to us, the most undeserving of all Thy people.

We had sinned many ways against Thee, O Lord, and this was a loud, a distinct, and merciful call of Thine, to every one of us, to repentance, which I most humbly beseech Thee give us grace to hear, to remember, and obey.

[1st ed. p. 264; M.H. xxi.] The greatest happiness, O merciful Father, which I can desire, either for myself or those who were sharers in this great deliverance, is what I now humbly beg for; that we may all of us gratefully acknowledge[e] Thy great love to us; meditate on Thy tender mercies; magnify Thy great and good providence; and by these mighty favours be reduced to an obedience becoming our redemption.

Pass by and pardon the ingratitude we have any of us been guilty of; and give us grace to consider, that by the merciful goodness of God we are delivered from a world of dangers, which would otherwise overwhelm us.

And according to Thy wonted mercies preserve us for the time to come, to serve Thee. May the same watchful providence, which has aforetime[f] defended us from such imminent dangers, guard us the remainder of our days, through all the changes and chances of this mortal life. This I most humbly beseech Thee to grant, for Thy own goodness' sake, and for the merits of our Saviour Christ Jesus. Amen.

Praise the Lord, O my soul, and all that is within me praise His holy Name.

[1st ed. p. 265; M.H. xxii.] Praise the Lord, O my soul, and forget not all His benefits, who saved thy life from destruction.

Lord, what is man, that Thou art mindful of him; or the sons of men, that Thou so regardest them?

But what is my father's house, that Thou shouldst have such respect to so poor, so sinful a cottage?

I am oppressed with the load of mercies we have received from Thee.

---

[e] "resent," M. H.   [f] "beforetime," M.H.

PROVIDENCE.

God has more ways of providing for us, of helping us, than we can possibly imagine; it is infidelity to desire to confine Him to our ways and methods. [1st ed. p. 265.]

Matthew viii. 25. *Lord, save us, we perish.*

Nothing can better express our own inability, and our whole dependence upon God: two sure conditions of obtaining help.

Since Thy mercy, O God, is ever ready to help all that call upon Thee in time of distress, let Thy goodness answer my wants.

Keep me under the protection of Thy good providence, and make me to have a perpetual fear and love of Thy holy Name, through Jesus Christ[g].

The more destitute we are of human aid, the more ought we to trust to that providence which God is pleased to exert in extreme necessity.

O God, give me grace never to condemn Thy providence; let me adore the wisdom of Thy conduct, the holiness of Thy ways, and the power of Thy grace.

How many sins should we commit, if God did not vouchsafe to oppose our corrupt will! Blessed be His holy Name, for not leaving me to my own choices.

Lord's Day. Amos viii. 5. *When will the Sabbath be gone, that we may sell wheat?* [1st ed. p. 266.]

Deliver us, gracious God, from this sin of covetousness,— from being weary of Thy Sabbaths, which are ordained to preserve in our hearts the knowledge of Thee, and of Thy Son Jesus Christ.

O that we may desire, and rejoice in the return of this day, and serve Thee faithfully on it; and that we may enjoy an everlasting Sabbath with Thy saints, for Jesus Christ His sake. Amen.

O that I may be glad when they say unto me, Come, let us go to the house of God!

[g] Second Sunday after Trinity.

[i. 56; ii. 29; iii. 69.]

MONDAY.

HOLY SCRIPTURES.

Q.—Are you persuaded that the Holy Scriptures contain sufficiently all doctrine required of necessity to eternal salvation through faith in Jesus Christ? And are you determined out of the same Holy Scriptures, to instruct the people committed to your charge, and to teach or maintain nothing as required of necessity to eternal salvation, but that which you shall be persuaded may be concluded and proved by the same?

A.—I am so persuaded and determined by God's grace.

Q.—Will you then faithfully exercise yourself in the same Holy Scriptures, and call upon God by prayer for the true understanding of the same; so as you may be able by them to teach and exhort with wholesome doctrine, and to withstand and convince gainsayers?

A.—I will so do by the help of God.

MONDAY. [i. 56; ii. 29; iii. 72.]
[a] O GOD, the fountain of all wisdom, [b] enlighten my mind, that I [c] myself may see, and be able to teach others the wonders of Thy Law; that I may learn from Thee, what I ought to think and speak concerning Thee; and that whatever in Thy holy word I shall profitably learn, I may indeed fulfil the same [d].

Direct and bless all my labours [e]; give me a discerning spirit, a sound judgment, and an honest and a religious heart, that in all my studies, my first aim may be, to set forth Thy glory, [f] by setting forward the salvation of men.

And if, by my ministry, Thy kingdom shall be enlarged [g],

---

[a] [ii. has here, "Acts vi. 4; xx. 31; 1 Cor. ix. 16, 17; 2 Tim. iv. 3." iii. has certain texts and sentences, which will be given hereafter.

[b] ii. adds, "I most humbly beseech Thee to."

[c] ii. "may see myself and teach others."

[d] ii. adds, "through Jesus Christ our Lord. Amen."

[e] ii. and iii. add, "without which I shall disquiet myself in vain."

[f] ii. iii., "and to set forward the salvation of mankind."

[g] ii. iii. add, "which God grant."

let me, in all humility, ascribe the success, not unto myself, MONDAY. but unto Thy good Spirit, which enables us both to will and to do what is acceptable to Thee, through Jesus Christ our Lord. Amen.

[The original draft of this prayer is in M. H. iii. as follows.]

Before Study. James i. 5. " Will you diligently exercise yourself in the same Holy Scripture," &c. Vid. Consecration.

O God the Fountain of all Wisdom, in a deep sense of my own ignorance, and of the great charge which lies upon me, I am constrained to come often before Thee, from whom I have learned whatever I know, to ask that help without which I shall disquiet myself in vain: most humbly beseeching Thee to guide me with Thine eye, to enlighten my mind, that I may see myself, and teach others, the wonders of Thy Law; that I may learn from Thee what I ought to think and speak concerning Thee. Direct and bless all the labours of my mind; give me a discerning spirit, a sound judgment, and an honest and a religious heart; and grant that in all my studies, my *first* aim may be to set forth Thy glory and to set forward the salvation of mankind; that I may give a comfortable account of my time at the great day when all our labours shall be tried. And if Thou art pleased that by *my ministry* sinners should be converted, and Thy kingdom enlarged, give me the grace of *humility*, that I may never ascribe the success to myself, but to Thy Holy Spirit, which enables me to will and to do according to Thy good pleasure. Grant this, O Father of all light and truth, for the sake of Jesus Christ. Amen.

Acts vi. 4. *But we will give ourselves continually unto prayer, and to the ministry of the word.* [i. 56; iii. 69; ii. 30.]

2 Tim. iv. 2. *Preach the word, be instant in season, out of season; reprove, rebuke, exhort with all long-suffering and doctrine.*

[h]N.B. We deceive ourselves, if we fancy that we have done our duty when we have given our people a sermon one day in seven: we must try all ways to gain a soul.

Luke vi. 39. *Can the blind lead the blind? Shall they not both fall into the ditch?*

[h] om. iii.

MONDAY.
[i. 57; iii. 69.]

1 Timothy iv. 13. *Give attendance to reading, to exhortation, to doctrine.*

[i]Quesnel.—Not to read, is to tempt God; to do nothing but study, is to forget the ministry. To read in order to appear more learned, is a sinful vanity. But to read in order to exhort and to instruct with wholesome doctrine, this is according to God's will and word.

James i. 5. *If any of you lack wisdom, let him ask of God, who giveth to every man liberally, and upbraideth not, and it shall be given him.*

[j]Wisdom being the gift of God, and this gift the fruit of prayer; a prayer that is humble, earnest, and persevering, will assuredly be blessed with this excellent gift.

[i. 57; ii. 30; iii. 69.]

St. Luke xxiv. 45. *Then opened He their understanding, that they might understand the Scriptures.*

[k]O Jesus, cause *me* to read, to understand, to love, to practise, and to preach Thy word.

John vii. 17. [l]*If any man will do* (that is, is disposed[m], desires to do,) *His will, he shall know of the doctrine, whether it be of God, or whether I speak of Myself.*

[n]Light and truth discover themselves to such as desire to follow them.

Psalm xxv. 14. *The secret of the Lord is among them that fear Him, and He will shew them His covenant*[o].

It was the saying of a learned man, saith Dr. Lightfoot, that he[p] got more knowledge by his prayers[q] than by all his studies[r].

---

[i] om. iii.
[j] om. ii. iii.
[k] om. ii. iii.
[l] ii. inserts, " 1 [2] Tim. ii. 7. *The Lord give thee understanding in all things.*"
[m] "is disposed," om. ii. iii.
[n] om. ii. iii.
[o] ii. inserts, " Job [xxxiv. 32.] The things I am ignorant of, do Thou teach me." [*That which I see not, teach Thou me.*] " Whatever I shall know to be Thy will, do Thou, O Lord, enable me to receive and practise accordingly."
[p] ii. reads, " I," " my."
[q] ii. " by prayer."
[r] [ii. iii. insert], " Cujus vitæ despicitur, restat ut ejus prædicatio contemnatur." St. Greg. [Mag. in Evang. Homil. xii. sub init.]
[ii. 33 inserts], Matt. x 16. *Behold, I send you forth as lambs in the midst of wolves, be ye therefore wise as serpents, and harmless as doves.*
St. Luke xii. 42. *Who then is that faithful and wise steward, whom his Lord shall make ruler over his household, to give them their portion of meat in due season?*
Blessed is that servant whom his Lord when He cometh shall find so doing. [Also 1 Tim. iv. 13; and a reference to 1 Thess. iv. 9; both given elsewhere.]

St. Matt. xi. 25. *I thank Thee, O Father, Lord of heaven* MONDAY.
and earth, because Thou hast hid these things from the wise
and prudent, and hast revealed them unto babes.

^sMy God and Saviour, imprint on my heart the amiable [i. 57; iii. 70.]
characters of simplicity and humility, which are the marks
of Thy elect, of such to whom Thou wilt reveal Thyself.

It is a ^tdangerous mistake to think that any man can have
a right understanding of divine things, without being illu-
minated by divine grace, and without leading an^u holy life.

[iii. inserts], *Ordination.* 2 Tim. i. 7. *For God hath given*
us (viz. at our Ordination, v. 6.) *the spirit of Power,* (whereby
we are enabled to overcome the world, the flesh, and the devil):
of Love, (whereby we are excited to discharge our duty both
to God and man), *and of a sound Mind,* (whereby we judge
aright of the will of God).

[iii. inserts], Heb. v. 2. High Priest. *Who can have com-*
passion on the ignorant, and on them that are out of the way.

Psalm cxix. 19, [99, 100.] *I have more understanding*
than my teachers,...because I keep Thy Commandments.

There is a light arising from a sincere good life, which dis-
pelleth all darkness, and is the best defence against ^xerror
and sophistry.

[iii. inserts], Matt. v. 6. *Blessed are they that do hunger*
and thirst after righteousness, (not after that knowledge which
puffeth up but never satisfieth,) *for they shall be filled.*

Psalm xxv. 10. *All the paths of the Lord are mercy and*
truth unto such as keep His covenant and His testimonies.

That is^y; to such as do so, all the ways of God, and what- [i. 58; iii. 71.]
ever He hath revealed, will appear to be the effect of infinite
wisdom, goodness, justice, and truth.

He giveth light and understanding unto the simple.

Matthew v. 8. *Blessed are the pure in heart, for they^z shall*
see God.

" Qui vult plene et sapide Christi verba intelligere, oportet
ut totam vitam suam illi studeat conformare." [Thos. à
Kempis, de Imit. Christi, lib. i. c. 1.]

---

^s iii. om.
^t iii. "a most dangerous error."
^u iii. "a pious."
^x iii. "all the efforts of sophistry."
^y iii. "all that God hath command-
ed, revealed, &c., will to such appear
to be the effects of infinite mercy, wisdom, and truth."
^z iii. adds, "and they only."

MONDAY. Erasmus, [ep. 207, tom. iii. 189. B. Lugd. Bat. 1703]. Gaudium suum ob renascentes literas non sine metu exprimet. "Unus scrupulus habet animum meum, ne sub obtentu priscæ literaturæ caput erigere tentet Paganismus... Optarim frigidas istas argutias" (humanæ eloquentiæ, logicarumque subtilitatum) "amputari prorsus, Christumque illum simplicem et parum restitue, penitusque humanis mentibus inseri."

"Self-love, amongst its other cheats, hinders us from studying Christian morality, because that would let us see how vile and frail we are; and therefore to divert us, it carries us impetuously to study other sciences, wherein we may admire our own wit and sagacity." Mackenzie, p. 411. ["Essays upon several Moral Subjects. By Sir George Mackenzie, Knt.," (the distinguished Scottish lawyer,) "London, 1713."]

"O that famous arts
Should raise men's wits, and yet debase their hearts[a]."

Psyche.

[iii. inserts here], Ἂν διὰ παντὸς, &c. Si semper in Scripturis versemur, et doctrinam veram et vitam piam sciemus. St. Chr.

Μή μοι λογισμοὺς [καὶ συλλογίσμους ἀνθρωπίνους προσενέγκῃς· ἐγὼ γὰρ μόνῃ πειθόμαι τῇ θείᾳ γραφῇ.] "Ne mihi rationes et argumentationes humanas offeras, ego enim soli Scripturæ divinæ credo." Theodoret. [Dial. Ἄτρεπτος, t. iv. 18. ed. Schulze.]

[i. 58; iii. 71.] Τοῖς ἐρευνῶσι τὰς γραφὰς, κ.τ.λ. [om. i.] "Illis qui Scripturas scrutantur opus est cœlesti lumine, ut et quod quærunt inveniant, et inventa custodiant."

[iii. 71.] Τοῖς γεγραμμένοις πίστευε· τὰ μὴ γεγραμμένα μὴ ἐννόει, μηδὲ ζήτει. Euseb.

[a] [The whole stanza is (speaking of St. Andrew):
"Thence into Greece the restless preacher came,
Arrogant Greece; who though she ranks her own
Quite counter to the scorn'd Barbarian name,
Yet now more cruel was and salvage grown
Than Thrace or Scythia: O that, &c.
From "Psyche, or Love's Mystery: displaying the intercourse betwixt Christ and the soul." By Joseph Beaumont, D.D., late King's Professor of Divinity, and Master of St. Peter's Coll. Cambridge. 2d ed. 1702. Canto x. st. 126.]

Luke xxii. 32. *When thou art converted, strengthen thy brethren.* MONDAY. [i. 58; iii. 72.]

God grant that [b] we may all of us consider the *absurdity* of going about to *convert others*, without being *converted ourselves* [b].

To understand the Holy[c] Scriptures aright, is to understand them as the Primitive Church did.

Speak, Lord, for Thy servant heareth. Speak to my *heart, that I may obey Thy word. Teach me to do Thy will, for Thou art my God.*

[iii. inserts], Let Thy love, O Lord, inflame my heart, that I may not meet with darkness in the midst of the light which Thou hast afforded us.

It belongs to God to give the true understanding of His own word[d].

There is a sacred obscurity in the Holy Scriptures, which we ought to value them for: because that convinceth us that we [e] are not to hope to understand them without a light from God: that God never designed that the carnal mind should see the truth: and that we must ask light of God, and fit ourselves to receive it.

Matthew vii. 5. *Thou hypocrite, first cast out the beam out of thine own eye; and then shalt thou see clearly to cast out the mote out of thy brother's eye.* [i. 59.]

That is; purify your own heart from all worldly aims; mortify your own passions, which are the cause of our blindness; study that word which alone can enlighten you; and lay aside all prejudices which are contrary to piety.

A pastor should never undertake to teach a virtue which he has never practised himself.

Luke v. 5. *We have toiled all the night, and have taken nothing.*

So does every preacher who does not beg God's blessing upon his labours.

[b] "I may ever...myself."
[c] iii. om. "holy."
[d] iii. "Scriptures."
[e] iii. "must have a light from God to understand them: that the carnal mind is incapable of seeing the truth; that God never designed it should: that we must ask light from God."
[iii. 173, adds], "Let us read the Gospel, not so much to know what truths it contains, but as we say our prayers—that we may possess our hearts with the same spirit which Jesus Christ discovers in them: observing His actions, and manner of life, and striving continually to imitate them; to follow His instructions; to believe His promises and threatenings."

MONDAY.   It is impossible for any man to *teach* well, who does not *live* well.

[Hos. iv. 6.] *My people perish for want of knowledge.*

The design of religion being to lead men to God,—how He is to be *served, appeased, attained,*—the business of a preacher should be, to shew how all the parts of religion contribute to these ends.

He that reads the Scriptures, and understands the things concerning the kingdom of God, and the way of conducting men thither, need not complain for want of learning.

In preaching, we must speak to the *heart,* as well as to the *understanding* and to the *ear.*

The end of preaching is to turn men from sin unto God, that they may be saved. He that has not this in his view, will do little good.

A preacher should accustom himself to give a practical turn to every thing.

He that leaves it to his hearers to apply what he has said, leaves to them the greatest part of his own duty.

To be heartily in love with the truth one recommends, is the great secret of becoming a good preacher.

A good preacher's sermons must be *instructions,* not *declamations.*

John vii. 16. *My doctrine is not Mine, but His that sent Me.* To preach our own thoughts, forsaking God's word, is like an ambassador who neglects his prince's instructions, and follows his own fancy.

With what truth can it be said, that *the sheep hear his voice,* when the shepherd speaks of things, or in such a manner, as is above their capacity?

Grant, O Lord, that I may read Thy word with the same Spirit with which it was written.

[i. 60.]   *Learning* does not always lead men to God; it often carries them from Him. Indeed when they study to find out, and correct their own weaknesses, their folly, and the corruption of their nature; to be convinced of the evil of sin, of the vanity of the world; to fill their souls with heavenly wisdom and devout affections towards God; and all this, that they may be better able to convince and edify their neighbour:—such learning leads men indeed to God. The rest MONDAY. is folly.

Have mercy upon all that sit in darkness; and may these saving truths be received in all the world!

He that sets his heart upon the world is not in a capacity of understanding the Gospel.

Give me that true wisdom, which consists in knowing how to save myself and them that hear me.

Remember that a man may have the knowledge of the word, without the Spirit.

Obscurity of Scriptures serves to subdue the pride of man; to convince us, that to understand them we have need of a light superior to reason; and that we may apply to God for help.

May I ever understand the true language of Thy word, O Lord, and profit by it!

Vouchsafe, O God, to give me a love for Thy Scriptures, and a true understanding of them, that I may see therein the wonders of Thy conduct, and Thy love for us Thy miserable creatures.

Sermons should be instructions, not declamations, or displaying curious thoughts, which may amuse, but not edify Christians.

If God suffers even an holy pastor not presently to see the fruits of his labours, it is to convince him that the success of his labours belongs to God: that he ought to humble himself, and pray much, and fear lest the fault should be in himself.

Pride and irreligion meet with darkness in the midst of light, raise vain disputes, unprofitable reflections and enquiries; while humility attains to light in the midst of darkness and difficulties.

Whenever God vouchsafes to open the heart, be the understanding and parts never so small, we see the reasonableness and beauty of His word, we taste the sweetness and feel the power thereof.

John xii. 16. *These things understood not His disciples at* [i. 61.] *the first: but when, &c.*

We often read the Scripture, without comprehending its full meaning; however let us not be discouraged; the light

MONDAY. in God's good time will break out, and disperse the darkness, and we shall see the mysteries of the gospel.

Grant me, O Lord, a persevering love of Thy word, and so much light as is necessary for myself, and those that hear me.

John xii. 30. *Jesus said, This voice came not for Me, but for your sakes.*

The way to profit by reading the Scriptures is, to apply to ourselves that which is spoken in general to all. This truth, this command, this threat, this promise, this intimation,—is to me.

John xii. 49. *I have not spoken of Myself, but the Father which sent Me gave Me a command, what I should say, and how I should speak.*

He preaches with a well-grounded confidence, who advances nothing merely of his own head, but what he has received from God. He may then expect a blessing. But then let him take care not to disguise it, by a language foreign from God's word.

O Holy Spirit of Grace, cause me both to understand and love Thy word.

Acts i. 1. *The former treatise have I made of all that Jesus began both to do and teach.*

This is the whole of a pastor's life. For a man to preach the gospel before he has practised it, is to be a very bad imitator of the Prince of Pastors.

Lord, grant that I may imitate Thee by a life conformable to Thine, by all ways becoming my station in the Church; and lay hold of all the opportunities which Thou shalt put into my hands.

It is God who does all good by the labours of His ministers. To Him therefore must be all the praise.

More sinners are converted by holy, than by learned men.

Inflame my heart, O God, with an ardent love for Thy word, an ardent zeal for Thy glory, with a pure and disinterested love for Thy Church, and with an hearty desire of establishing Thy kingdom.

Who can say, it is not owing to himself that his flock are ignorant of their duty?

Romans ii. 21. *Thou therefore which teachest another, teachest thou not thyself?*

MONDAY. [i. 62.]

Unhappy that person who has in his hands the rule of knowledge and of the truth, and makes no other use thereof, but to set up for a teacher of others, without applying to himself those truths with which his mind is filled. A mind full of light, and a heart full of darkness,—how dreadful is that man's condition!

1 Tim. iv. 13. *Give attendance to reading, to exhortation, to doctrine.*

Without holiness no man shall see,—shall know,—the Lord.

In all our studies, we should take care to beg of God to preserve us from error, and to lead us to, and keep us in, all truths necessary to salvation, by His Holy Spirit.

^kI AM: i. e. self-existent. *God.* Exod. iii. 14. Rom. [ix. 5. See Bp. Wilson's note on Exod. iii. 14.]

Colossians iv. 4. *That I may make it manifest,* (that is, the mystery of the gospel,) *as I ought to speak.* All preachers do not speak as they ought. A man may have the skill to give Christian truths a turn agreeable to the hearers, without affecting their hearts. Human learning will enable him to do this. It is prayer only that can enable him so to speak as to convert the heart.

May I ever speak to the hearts and to the capacities of my flock.

2 Timothy iv. 1, 2, 3, &c. *I charge thee, before God, &c., preach the word. Be instant in season, out of season;—reprove, rebuke, exhort, with all long-suffering and gravity. For the time will come when they will not endure sound doctrine; and they shall turn away their ears from the truth. But watch thou in all things, endure afflictions, make full proof of* (or fulfil) *thy ministry.*

N.B. Preaching is a duty, but not the only duty of a pastor. He is to take all occasions to *instruct* those that seek the truth; refute such as oppose it; reprove those that do not practise it; and confirm such as have embraced it. [i. 63.] And the more we perceive the times of apostacy approaching, the more zealous ought we to be to defend sound doctrine.

It will be no comfort to a pastor, that the world praises

---

^k [This entry is in the Bishop's latest handwriting.]

MONDAY. him for some one part of his duty, while God condemns him for the neglect of another.

1 Peter iv. 11. *If any man speak, let him speak as the oracles of God.* That is, worthy of God, not weakening it by softening interpretations, not altering it by human inventions, nor degrading it by a profane eloquence.

If we find that people do not attend to the Scriptures, as the word of God, with eagerness and attention, we ought to fear that the fault is in those that preach it, after such a manner as is not proper or likely to make them believe it to be the word of God.

Let us always remember, that to understand the language of God, we stand in need of a light superior to reason.

It is good to know what God has revealed, and to be ignorant of what He has not thought fit to make known to us.

[i. 64.] *Ejaculations before reading the Holy Scriptures.* Give me, O God, a love for Thy Scriptures, and a true understanding of them.

O Jesus, open my understanding; cause me to love Thy word, and to order my faith and life according to it.

May I, O Jesus, love Thy word, make Thy gospel my delight, and continue in the practice of Thy law unto my life's end.

John xvi. 13. *The Holy Spirit shall guide you into all truth.*

O Holy Spirit, make me to understand, embrace, and love the truths of the gospel.

Give, O God, Thy blessing unto Thy word, that it may become effectual to my conversion and salvation, and to the salvation of all that read or hear it.

Give me grace to read Thy holy word with reverence and respect becoming the gracious manifestation of Thy will to men; submitting my understanding and will to Thine.

Let Thy gracious promises, O God, contained in Thy word, quicken my obedience. Let Thy dreadful threatenings, and judgments upon sinners, fright me from sin, and oblige me to a speedy repentance: for Jesus Christ His sake.

Cause me, O God, to believe Thy word, to obey Thy commands, to fear Thy judgments, and to hope in and depend upon Thy gracious promises contained in Thy holy word: MONDAY. for Jesus Christ's sake.

Grant, O Lord, that in reading Thy holy word I may never prefer my private sentiments before those of the Church in the purely ancient times of Christianity.

Give me a full persuasion of those great truths, which Thou hast revealed in Thy holy word.

The gospel will not be a means of salvation to him who reads or hears it only, but to him who reads, loves, remembers, and practises it by a lively faith.

Cause me, O God, rightly to understand, and constantly to walk in, the way of Thy commandments.

Grant us in this world knowledge of Thy truth, and in the world to come life everlasting, for Jesus Christ's sake. Amen. [i. 65.]

From hardness of heart, and contempt of Thy word, good Lord, deliver us.

Give us all grace to hear meekly Thy word, to receive it with pure affection, and to bring forth the fruits of the Spirit: —to amend our lives according to Thy holy word.

Luke xxiv. 45. *Then opened He their understanding, that they might understand the Scriptures.* Unless Thou, O Jesus, openest our understanding, all our pains, all our learning, will signify little.

Matthew xiii. 36. *Declare unto us this parable.* This should instruct us, that the knowledge of God's word, and the mysteries of the gospel, are favours which we must always beg of God.

Against Sloth. Proverbs xix. 5. *Slothfulness casteth into a deep sleep.* [M.H. xc.; ii. 31; iii. 75.]

O God, who hast given me an active spirit, and many opportunities of doing Thee service; give me grace to make use of all occasions of serving Thee[1], and of doing good in my generation.

Make me to abhor that sloth which would lead me into an insensibility, and forgetfulness of Thee and of my duty[m].

Keep me from idleness, which would expose me to temptations, enfeeble my mind, and cover me with rags.

---

[1] "faithfully," M. H.   [m] "errand into this world," M. H.

MONDAY. Make me ever sensible of the great evil of delaying to do the work in its season which Thou hast appointed me; that whatever my hand, by Thy providence, findeth to do, I may do it with all my might; and that whenever I am called to give an account of my labours to my great Master, I may not be found[n] an unprofitable servant. [o]Accept of my ambition of serving Thee, great God; and O grant that when my Lord comes He may find me so doing. Amen.

[iii. 77.] *Duties of a Clergyman. Visiting the Sick.*
Lev. xiii. 46. [*He is unclean: he shall dwell alone.*] Let it be here observed that the leprosy here spoken of was infectious to all but the priests, who being by God appointed to judge concerning it, were always preserved by a miracle from contagion.

Jer. xv. 20, 21. *And I will make thee unto this people a fenced brazen wall, and they shall fight against thee, but they shall not prevail against thee; for I am with thee, to save thee, and to deliver thee, saith the Lord. And I will deliver thee out of the hand of the wicked, and I will deliver thee out of the hand of the terrible.*

N.B. A standing rule for God's ministers;—viz. To do their duty faithfully, and to depend on God's protection.

To the glory of God be it remembered, that on the day this portion of Scripture was read in the Church, I was attacked by one I had excommunicated for enormous crimes, and threatened, &c. This has often happened, and I believe by the special providence of God, for the comfort and direction of His faithful servants.

[1st ed. 268; iii. 130.]

RESIGNATION[p].

Castle Ryssin (*sic*), Aug. 5, 1722[q].

[r]Luke xxii. 42. *Nevertheless, not My will, but Thine be done.*

O God, who takest delight in helping the afflicted, help a soul too often distressed with an inward rebellion against Thy just appointments.

---

[n] "judged," M. H.
[o] This sentence om. iii. ii.
[p] 1st ed. adds, "*to the will of God.*"
[q] 1st ed., "When prisoner in Castle-Rushin, Aug. 5, 1722."
[r] iii. inserts here the paragraph beginning "to the glory of God."

MONDAY.

ˢWho am I, that I should make exceptions against the will of God, infinitely great, and wise, and good?

I know not the things that are for my own ᵗ good.

My most earnest desires, ᵘif granted, may prove my ruin.

The things I complain of, ˣand fear, may be the effects of the greatest mercy.

The disappointments I meet with may be absolutely necessary for my eternal welfare.

I do therefore protest against the ʸsin and madness of desiring to have my ᶻ will done, and not the will of God.

ᵃGrant, gracious Father, that I may never dispute the reasonableness of Thy will, but ever ᵇclose with it, as the best that can happen.

Prepare me always for what Thy providence shall ᶜbring forth.

ᵈLet me never murmur, be dejected, or impatient, under any of the troubles of this life; but ᵉever find rest and comfort in this; *this is the will of my Father, and of my God:* ᶠgrant this for Jesus Christ's sake. Amen.

To the glory of God and justification of His infinite goodness, I ᵍdo here acknowledge, that in all the dispensations of Providence which have befallen me, to this day, however uneasyʰ to flesh and blood, I have notwithstandingⁱ experienced the kindness of a father forᵏ his child; and am convinced that it would have been much worse for me ˡhad I had my own choices.

ᵐO God, grant that for the time to come I may yield a cheerful obedience to all Thy appointments. Amen.

[1st ed. 268; iii. 130.]

ˢ iii. om. this sentence.
ᵗ iii. om. " own."
ᵘ om. "if granted."
ˣ iii. om. " and fear."
ʸ iii. " folly."
ᶻ iii. " my own will done, and not Thine, O God."
ᵃ iii. "O may I never."
ᵇ iii. " embrace it."
ᶜ iii. adds, " permit or."
ᵈ iii. " Grant that I may set no greater value upon this world than it deserves.
" Let me never be eager or positive in my desires, so that I may readily embrace the appointments of Thy will.
" Let my dependence be upon Thee, and never upon myself, or upon the power, the wisdom, or counsels of men.
" Who am I, that I should make exceptions against the will of God, infinitely great, and wise, and good?
" Lord, Thy will be done: and grant that I may be ever pleased it should be so "
ᵉ iii. adds, " let me."
ᶠ iii. om. " grant...Amen."
ᵍ iii. " must own."
ʰ iii. " unwelcome."
ⁱ iii. " yet."
ᵏ iii. " correcting."
ˡ iii. " if I had."
ᵐ iii. " How just therefore is it, to yield a cheerful submission to all God's appointments for the time to come."

MONDAY.   [n]Philip. iv. 6. *Be careful for nothing, but in every thing, by prayer and supplication with thanksgiving let your requests be made known unto God.*

Corrupt nature cannot comprehend that afflictions are the effects of the Divine love. It must be Thy grace, [o]O lover of souls, which must work in me this conviction, which I beseech Thee to vouchsafe me.

Never set a greater value upon this world than it deserves.

If a man is not eager or positive in his desires, he will more readily embrace the appointments of providence.

If we place our hopes, or our dependence, upon the power, the wisdom, the counsel, or the interest we have in man, and not in God only, we shall surely be disappointed.

Job xiii. 15. *Though He slay me, yet will I trust in Him.*

[1st ed. 268.]
O my crucified King and Saviour, let my submission to whatever afflictions shall befall me, for Thy sake, or by Thy appointment, be to me a pledge and an assurance of my fidelity to Thee, and conformity to Thy sufferings.

It is a favour to be punished and to suffer in this life, when a man makes a good use of his sufferings. But to suffer by constraint, is to suffer without comfort and without benefit.

Our union and conformity with the will of God ought to be instead of all consolation.

[1st ed. 269.]
Grant, O God, that I may always accept of the punishment of my sins with resignation to Thy good pleasure.

Remember me, O Lord, in the day of trouble; keep me from all excess of fear, concern, and sadness.

Grant me an humble and a resigned heart, that with perfect content I may ever acquiesce in all the methods of Thy grace, that I may never frustrate the designs of Thy mercy, by unreasonable fears, by sloth, or self-love. Amen.

Think often of God, and of His attributes, His mercy, compassion, fidelity, fatherly care, goodness, protection. Dwell on these thoughts till they produce such a well-grounded confidence as will support us under all difficulties, and assure us that He cannot possibly forsake those that depend on Him.

When God deprives us of any thing that is most dear to

---

[n] 1st ed. om.   [o] iii. "O God, that must do it: which I beseech Thee to vouchsafe."

us,—health, ease, conveniences of life, friends, wife, children, &c., we should immediately say, *This is God's will;* I am by Him commanded to part with so much; let me not therefore murmur or be dejected, for then it would appear that I did love that thing more than God's will.

When God thus visits us, let us immediately look inwards, and, lest our sins should be the occasion, let us take care that we seriously repent, and endeavour to make our peace with God, and then He will either deliver or support us, and will convince us that we suffer in justice for our faults; or for our trial, and to humble us; or for God's glory, and to sanctify us.

1 Peter v. 5. *Be clothed with humility; for God resisteth the proud, but giveth grace to the humble.*

Give me grace, O God, to study, to love, to adore, and to imitate that humility which Thy blessed Son hath taught us both by His word and by His most holy example.

Ephes. v. 17. *Understanding what the will of the Lord is.*

To engage in any business of importance without knowing this, and taking counsel of God, may cost us dear.

Isaiah xxx. 1. *Woe to them that take counsel, but not of Me, saith the Lord.*

But then, let a man take heed that when he goes to enquire of the Lord, he does not set up idols in his own heart, lest God answer him according to his idols.

We are to pray for the direction of God's Spirit upon all great occasions; especially, we are humbly to depend on His direction, and cheerfully to expect it, which He will manifest, either by some plain event of His providence, or by suggesting such reasons as ought to determine the will to a wise choice.

But to follow the inclinations of the will without reason, only because we find ourselves strongly inclined to this or that, is a very dangerous way, and may engage us in very dangerous practices.

Master, Servant. Death, in a very little time, may make the master and the servant equal. Let us anticipate this equality, by treating our servants with compassion; having respect to Christ in the person of our servant,—to Christ, who took upon Him the form of a servant for our sakes.

TUESDAY.

Q.—Are you ready, with all faithful diligence, to banish and drive away all erroneous and strange doctrine, contrary to God's word; and both privately and openly to call upon and encourage others to do the same?
A.—I am ready, the Lord being my helper.

TUESDAY. Blessed be the good providence of God, who, in great compassion to ᵃthis Church and nation, has hitherto preserved us from heresies and schisms.

O Lord, continue to us this great mercy, and grant ᵇ that we, who are appointed to watch over Thy flock, may employ our learning and our time in promoting of true piety; that we may never grow secure and careless, but that we may ᶜendeavour to secure the power, as well as the form of godliness.

Have pity upon all Christian Churches that are distracted by contending parties, and reduce all that wander out of the way.

[ii. iii.] Have mercy upon all Jews, Turks, and Infidels; fetch them home, and make them one fold under one Shepherd.

Enable usᵈ to preserve this Churchᵉ in peace and unity, by all means becoming the spirit of the gospel.

ᶠKeep usᵍ steadfast in the faith, that ᵍwe may never be tossed about with any wind of doctrine, or the craft of men.

[ii. iii. insert], And make me a lively example of all the graces and virtues which we [ii. I] recommend to others.

Let the zeal and industry of those that are in error provoke usʰ to be zealously affected in a righteous cause; in

---

ᵃ ii. iii. "to the circumstances of."
ᵇ ii. "give us grace."
ᶜ ii. iii. "preserve the power."
ᵈ ii. iii. "me."
ᵉ ii. iii. add, "committed to my care."
ᶠ ii. iii. add, "to this end."
ᵍ ii. iii. "me...I."
ʰ ii. iii. "me."

labouring to make men good, and in converting sinners from TUESDAY. the error of their ways; which God grant for Jesus Christ's sake. Amen.

Can. lxvi. Eccles. Angl. "Sed et ipsum Episcopum (quan- [i. 76; ii. 37; iii. 96.] tum per arduas occupationes licuerit) summo studio contendere, ut docendo, persuadendo, modisque blandis et benignis omnibus, tum dictos recusantes, tum omnes infra suam diæcesin sic affectos, a suis erroribus deducat."

Tertull. ad Scap. "Sed nec religionis est cogere." [§ 2.]

2 Timothy iv. 3. *The time will come when they will not endure sound doctrine, but after their own lusts shall they heap to themselves teachers, having itching ears.*

N.B. We are now in these sad times, and it behoves all faithful pastors to know it.—It is not the doctrine of the gospel, if it favours men's lusts.—They that will not receive, or [who] reject, the truth, are often judicially punished with a greediness to receive errors, falsehoods, and fables—(see v. 4.)

v. 5. *Watch thou in all things, endure afflictions, make full proof of* (or fulfil) *thy ministry.*

He that is wanting in any essential part is wanting to his own salvation.

Ammianus Marcellinus, lib. xxii. [c. 5] tells us, that [i. 77.] Julian's contrivance for destroying Christianity was, "Ut quisque, nullo vetante, religioni suæ serviret intrepidus:" "To give every one leave to follow his own fancy, and serve the interests of his own party in religion."

"Every bishop in his own diocese may condemn an heresy, and forbid communion with such as he judges to be heretics, and this his flock ought to submit to: this being matter of discipline. But the faith he cannot alter." Mr. Lesley's letter amongst Dr. Hickes' Letters, p. 324. [Leslie's exact words are: "Every bishop as supreme in his own church, and a council of bishops assembled, may condemn such an heresie, and forbid communion with such and such, or not, as they shall find it expedient for the saving of their own flocks, and the general good of the Catholic Church. For this is matter of discipline. And in this they have authority, to which their flocks ought to submit: and this they may alter, retain, or relax, according to the variation of times

TUESDAY. and circumstances. But the faith they cannot alter, only bear witness to it."].

Lord, Thou art just in all the troubles which Thou hast brought upon this Church and nation: yet, O Lord, have mercy upon us, and restore to us that peace and unity which we once enjoyed.

Matthew vii. 20. *By their fruits ye shall know them.*

This rule, though given by Christ Himself, is seldom observed. The best fruits are counted as nothing, are overlooked, and often condemned, by those who have none good to shew. Hence all the evils the Church suffers.

Matthew xiii. 25. *But while men slept, his enemy came and sowed tares among the wheat.*

O Jesu, awaken the pastors of Thy flock, and open their eyes, that they may perceive the tares which choke the seed, the wolves which destroy Thy sheep.

A mixture of good and bad in the Church is necessary to instruct, exercise, purify, sanctify, and keep the righteous in humility.

Matthew xiii. 29. *Nay, lest while ye gather up the tares, ye root up also the wheat with them.*

A zeal not regulated by this prohibition allows no time to the good to grow strong in goodness, or to the wicked to forsake their evil ways; but chooses rather to destroy the good, provided they can but destroy the bad.

Revelations ii. 14, 20. *I have a few things against thee, because thou hast there them that hold the doctrine of Balaam,* [i. 78.] *who taught Balak to cast a stumbling-block before the children of Israel, to eat things sacrificed unto idols, and to commit fornication... Thou sufferest that woman Jezebel to teach and to seduce My servants to commit fornication.*

How dreadful is the government of the Church, wherein a man must answer for those sins which he does not hinder!

To tolerate by silence those who favour and promote sin, Jesus Christ rebukes in the persons of these bishops.

A.D. 1727. Let me consider these words as spoken to myself at this time, when popery and profaneness meet with so much countenance from the civil government.

O my Saviour! Thou who givest me this warning, enable me to profit by it. Assist me, in this day of trial, effectually to oppose and suppress that spirit of impurity, idolatry, profaneness, and irreligion, which is broken in upon us. *Tuesday.*

If for fear of offending men, or from a false love of peace, we forbear to defend the truth, we betray it, and abandon it, &c.

Acts xxviii. 29. *And when He had said these things, the Jews had great reasonings among themselves.*

A preacher of the truth is not to be blamed for the contests which it gives occasion to carnal men to raise. Even Christ Himself could not preach without disturbing sinners; and if He came not to bring peace on earth, but a sword of division, His ministers ought to expect to do the same.

It is not by the heat of disputation, but by the gentleness of charity, that souls are gained over to God.

And when controversy is necessary, as sometimes it is, let it never be managed with harshness, bitterness, or severity, lest it exasperate and harden, more than convert and edify.

A prudent condescension has often prevailed upon the weak, and rendered them capable of hearkening to reason, when the contrary conduct would have removed them farther from the light.

We ought to avoid evil men and seducers, in order to shame them; to deprive them of that credit whereby they may do hurt; to make them to return to a right mind; and that we may avoid the snare ourselves.

Disputes. The primitive fathers were ever modest upon [i. 79.] religious questions. They contented themselves with resolving such questions as were proposed to them, without starting new ones; and carefully suppressed the curious, restless temper.

May I receive from Thee, O God, at all times, the rules of my behaviour on these occasions.

God judges otherwise than we do of these things. He knows the good He intends to bring out of evil, either for the sanctification of the righteous, conversion of the wicked by His goodness in bearing with them, or leaving them without excuse.

One single soul is worth the utmost pains of the greatest minister of Christ. But then let us take care, that when it

TUESDAY. is brought into the fold, that he be a better Christian than before,—that he be not twofold more the child of hell than before.

Protect me, O Lord, among the manifold sects, errors, heresies, schisms of this loose world, that attempt the foundation of Thy Holy Religion.

[i. 80.] THE LORD'S PRAYER PARAPHRASED.

Our Father, which art in Heaven.
In whom we live, and move, and have our being.
What manner of love is this, that we should be called the children of God? 1 St. John iii. 1.
We will not sin, knowing that we are accounted Thine. Wisd. xv. [2.]
May we ever love, and serve, and fear Thee, not as slaves, but as children.
May we always live worthy of this glorious relation!
We depend upon Thy fatherly *goodness,* to do ever what is best for us, upon Thy *wisdom* to choose for us, and upon Thy *power* to help us.
My Father, I have sinned against Heaven, and in Thy sight, and am not worthy to be called Thy son.
Look upon us, O Father, as poor, weak, ignorant, froward, and helpless children, and pity us according to Thy goodness, for Jesus Christ's sake, the Son of Thy love.
As a father pitieth his own [children,] so the Lord pitieth them that fear Him.
Malach. i. 6. *If I be a Father, where is Mine honour?*
Be ye followers of God, as dear children. Ephesians v. 1.
In this the children of God are manifest, and the children of the devil. Whoever doth not righteousness, is not of God. 1 John iii. [10.]
As He that hath called you is holy, so be ye holy in all manner of conversation. 1 Peter i. [15.]
Blameless as the sons of God, in the midst of a crooked and perverse nation, &c. Phil. ii. 15.
I am Thine by adoption: O make me Thine by the choice of my will.

What love, O God, is due from us to Thee, for so much [love] to us?   TUESDAY.

O that we may love Thee with all our heart and mind, and soul and strength!

Hallowed be Thy Name. [i. 81.]

For Thou hast created all things, and by Thy will they all subsist.

O that I, and all His children, may give the Lord the honour due unto His Name, which is great, wonderful, and holy.

May we all glorify Thee in a faithful discharge of the duties of our several callings.

Increase the number and the graces of all such as love, and fear, and honour Thy holy Name.

May Thou, O heavenly Father, have the glory of saving a miserable sinner, such as I have been.

O that we may glorify Thy Name, by walking before Thee in righteousness and holiness all our days.

O that we may glorify Thee not only with our lips but in our lives, by bringing forth much fruit: and that men seeing our good works may glorify our Father which is in heaven.

May I never dishonour Thy holy Name in word or deed.

1 Chron. xvi. 29. *Give unto the Lord the glory due unto His Name.*

That men may see your good works, and glorify your Father which is, &c.

Do all to the praise and glory of God.

A son honoureth his father, and a servant his master. If I be a Father, where is My honour? If I be a Master, where is My fear? Malach. i. 6.

John xv. 8. *In this is My Father glorified, that ye bring forth much fruit.*

May we thus glorify Thee, O heavenly Father, not only with our lips, but in our lives.

O that Thy Name, and the Name of our Lord Jesus Christ, may be glorified in us, and we in Him.

Let every thing that hath breath praise the Lord.

Holy, holy, holy, Lord God Almighty, which was, and is, and is to come.

TUESDAY.   May the end of all our designs and actions be to the glory of God.

[i. 82.]   *Thy kingdom come.*

May the kingdoms of this world become the kingdoms of the Lord and of His Christ, that He may reign for ever and ever. Rev. xi. 15.

O that the saving laws of Thy kingdom may be received in all the world.

Take possession of my heart, O King of Heaven, and subdue whatever is amiss in me.

Make me instrumental in promoting the interests of Thy kingdom, that truth and righteousness may be established in this place.

Make all the ministers of Thy kingdom zealous in advancing Thy honour, and the welfare of all Thy subjects.

Do Thou, O King of saints, establish Thy kingdom of grace in all our hearts, that we may be Thy subjects out of choice, and ever yield Thee willing obedience.

Rebuke all the enemies of Thy kingdom, and all such as would not have Thee to reign over them.

May the heathen fear Thy Name, O God, and all the kings of the earth Thy Majesty.

May all that own Thee for their King, become Thy faithful subjects.

Bless the pious endeavours of all such as strive to propagate the gospel of Christ; and may its saving truths be received in all the world.

Deliver the world, O Jesus, in Thy good time, from the tyranny of Satan, that all nations may obey and glorify Thy holy Name.

O that Satan may never set up his kingdom in this place.

O God, recover Thy whole right and dominion over my soul, and rule in me by Thy holy, all-powerful Spirit.

Set up, O God, Thy throne in our hearts, and reign for ever and ever.

[i. 83.]   *Thy will be done in earth as it is in heaven.*

O heavenly Father, give us light to see, an heart to close with, and a power to do Thy will at all times.

Grant that we may cheerfully accomplish those things which Thou wouldest have done, through Jesus Christ.

Let it ever be the desire of my soul to do Thy will, and to be pleased with all Thy choices for myself and others. Tuesday.

May I ever sacrifice my will to Thine, to do in me and with me as to Thee seemeth most meet.

May I ever submit my understanding and my will to Thine, for Jesus Christ His sake.

Subdue in us that natural aversion which we have to do Thy holy will, O God.

May Thy will, made known in Thy threatenings and promises, have its saving effects upon our hearts.

Keep our minds in such a temper, that we may close with Thy will whenever it is made known to us.

May this be the constant practice of our lives, to be pleased with all Thy choices, for ourselves and others.

Luke xxii. 42. *Not my will, but Thine be done.*

It is the Lord, let Him do what seemeth Him good. 1 Samuel iii. [18.]

Ps. xxxix. 10. *I was dumb, and opened not my mouth, because it was Thy doing.*

Thou art righteous in all Thy ways, and holy in all Thy works.

Keep us, O Lord, from having our own wills, whenever they are not agreeable to Thine.

Colossians i. 9. *Grant that we may be filled with the knowledge of Thy will in all wisdom and spiritual understanding.*

We adore Thy goodness in making Thy will known to us, and the way to attain everlasting life.

May we never question the goodness of Thy will and choices, but ever close with Thy will, as the best that can be ordered for ourselves or others.

What are we, that we should make exceptions against the will of a God infinitely wise, and just, and good?

Enable me to live according to Thy will.

Make it the joy and pleasure of my heart to do Thy will.

Give us this day our daily bread. [i. 84.]

O heavenly Father, give us the necessaries and comforts of this life, with Thy blessing, but above all things give us the bread that nourisheth to eternal life.

TUESDAY. Give us grace, that we may never use any unlawful ways to get our daily bread.

That we may be content and thankful for our present condition, to which, as sinners, we have no right.

Give us grace to impart to such as are in want of what Thou givest us more than our daily bread.

O that we may seek Thy kingdom, and the righteousness thereof, and then we are sure we shall want nothing that is necessary for this life.

We will cast all our care upon Thee, for Thou carest for us.

[1 Timothy vi. 8.] *Having food and raiment, let us be therewith content.*

We beseech Thee, O Father, not for ourselves only, but for all our brethren.

Cast all your care upon Him, for He careth for you. 1 St. Peter v. 7.

Thou, O heavenly Father, knowest what we have need of.

Give us the bread that came down from heaven—the bread that giveth life unto the world—the bread that nourisheth unto eternal life.

O that Thy grace may render me worthy of this bread.

Let us ever remember that we depend upon Thee for life, and breath, and all things.

[i. 85.] *And forgive us our trespasses, as we forgive them that trespass against us.*

O that we may *be kindly affectioned one towards another, tender-hearted, forgiving one another, even as God, for Christ's sake, hath forgiven us.* Ephesians iv. 3.

May we ever remember Thy goodness, Thy mercy, Thy patience towards us, and the multitude of our offences against Thee, that we may, from our hearts, forgive all that have offended us.

Grant, O God, that I [may] make all my prayers in the spirit of love and charity.

O that that mercy and pardon, which we hope for from Thee, may lead us to forgive all that have injured or offended us.

Give us grace to imitate Thy goodness, that we may *for-*

give, and *give,* and *love,* as becomes the disciples of Jesus Christ. TUESDAY.

Give us all, O God, such forgiving tempers, that we may close with this merciful condition of pardon.

Even the power to perform this must be from Thy grace.

Colossians iii. 13. *As Christ forgave you, so also do ye.*

Luke vi. 38. *Judge not, and ye shall not be judged. Condemn not, and ye shall not be condemned.—Forgive, and ye shall be forgiven.—Give, and it shall be given unto you. For with the same measure that ye mete withal, it shall be measured to you again.*

Thou, O God, art all mercy towards us, O make us all so to one another, for Thy sake, and for our own.

We beseech Thee for all that are our enemies, not for judgment and vengeance, but for mercy, for the remission of their sins, and for their eternal happiness.

And lead us not into temptation: but deliver us from evil. [i. 86.]

Support us, O all-powerful God, under all our saving trials, and grant that they may yield the peaceable fruit of righteousness.

May we never provoke Thee to withdraw Thy grace, and permit us to be tempted above what we are able.

Give us, O heavenly Father, grace to flee from all occasions of sin, and be not wanting to us in the hour of temptation. Leave us not to ourselves, and to our own choices.

Enable us to make the right use of all Thy trials, and to profit by them.

Restrain the power of Satan, and the many temptations we are liable to, and grant that we may never be found from under Thy protection.

In all temptations, we beseech Thee, O heavenly Father, to succour us, that no sin may ever get the dominion over us.

Let not our faith fail us in the day of temptation and trial.

Thou, O Lord, only knowest how to deliver the godly out of temptation.

Deliver us, O God, from the evil of sin, and from the evil of punishment. Deliver us, O heavenly Father, from the author of evil—from the evils of our corrupt nature—from

TUESDAY. an evil and corrupt world—and from falling into the sins and evils we have repented of.

[i. 87.] *For Thine is the kingdom, and the power, and the glory, for ever and ever. Amen.*

May all that own Thee for their *King* become Thy faithful subjects.

By Thine Almighty *power* subdue whatever is amiss in us.

Eph. iii. 21. *Unto Him that is able to do for us exceeding abundantly more than we can ask or think...unto Him be glory in the Church by Christ Jesus, throughout all ages, world without end. Amen.*

1 Timothy i. 17. *To the King eternal, immortal, invisible, the only wise God, be honour and glory for ever and ever. Amen.*

Isaiah vi. 3. *Holy, holy, holy, Lord God of Hosts. The whole earth is full of His glory.*

To Thee, O God, the Creator, the Preserver, and the Disposer of all things—to Thee belongeth all the glory of all the good wrought in us, by us, and for us.

Let my whole dependence be upon Thee, and Thy grace, O heavenly Father.

By Thy Almighty *power*, O King of Heaven; for the *glory* of Thy Name, and for the love of a Father; grant all these things which the Son of Thy love hath taught us to pray for.

To Thee, O King of Heaven, we pray; on Thee we depend; for Thou only hast power to help and defend us. To Thee, therefore, we give the glory of all the blessings we enjoy or hope for in this world, or in the world to come, through Jesus Christ our Saviour. Amen.

Thou, O heavenly Father, art able to do more for us than we can ask or think. To Thee be glory for ever. Amen.

Thy *power*, Thy *wisdom*, Thy *goodness*, O God, are the only sure foundation on which we may depend. Give us, we beseech Thee, a firm and lively faith in these Thy glorious perfections: through Jesus Christ. Amen[1].

---

[1] [MS. i. 88, repeats here the descant on the Doxology, from the Preces Matutinæ, p. 30, with a few variations, there noticed in the margin.]

Against Anger. Ecclesiastes vii. 9. *Be not hasty in thy spirit to be angry, for anger resteth in the bosom of fools.* [TUESDAY. [ii. 38; iii, 100.]

The Lord, who is a God ready to pardon, slow to anger, and of great kindness, remove far from me all occasions and effects of causeless and immoderate anger; all pride and prejudice, and too much concern for the things of this world; all intemperate speeches, and indecent[j] passions.

Give me, O Lord, a mild, a peaceable, a meek, and an humble spirit, that, remembering my own infirmities, I may bear with those of others; that considering my character, I may rebuke with all long-suffering and gravity; that I may think lowly of myself, and not be angry when others do so also; that I may be patient towards all men, gentle and easy to be entreated; that God, for Christ's sake, may be so towards me. Amen[k].

Ephesians iv. 26. *Be angry, and sin not:—Let not the sun go down upon your wrath.*

Proverbs xix. 11. *The discretion of a man deferreth his anger.* [ii. 39; iii. 101.]

Prov. xv. 1. *A soft answer turneth away strife.*

Prov. xvi. 32. *He that is slow to anger is better than the mighty; and he that ruleth his spirit than he that taketh a city.*

Romans xii. 10. *Be kindly affectioned one towards another.*

Suppress the very beginnings of anger.

Do not use to[l] indulge it even where there are real faults; but try the gentle way, which may[m] probably succeed better, and, to be sure, with more ease by far.

Seldom do people vex us on purpose, and yet prejudice very often makes us think that[n] they do.

[o]A sense of one's own integrity will make one pass by injuries more easily. [ii. 39; iii. 102.]

Be not too[p] much concerned to tell the injuries you have received.

Accustom yourself to silence, if you would learn to govern your tongue.

---

[j] ii. "undecent."
[k] ii. om. "Amen."
[l] ii. om. "use to."
[m] ii. "will very."
[n] ii. om. "that."
[o] ii. adds, "If one is sincere in all his ways."
[p] ii. om. "too."

TUESDAY. *Nemo consilium cum clamore dat.*—Seneca.

[iii. 102.] *Passions.* Deliver me, O God, from all violent and sinful passions, and give me grace to stand against them.

Matthew v. 4. *Blessed are the meek.*

Instruct me, Lord, in this Christian virtue; Thou who art the Master and Teacher of it.

[iii. 104.] Matt. vi. 14, 15. *If ye forgive men their trespasses, your heavenly Father will also forgive you; but if ye forgive not men their, &c.*

O God, who alone canst order the unruly wills and affections of sinful men, shew mercy to Thy servant, in forcing my corrupt nature to be obedient to Thy commands.

O God, who hast made it my everlasting interest as well as duty, to forgive my neighbour whatever wrong he has done me; help me to overcome all the difficulties I have to struggle with, all pride, prejudice, and desire of rendering evil for evil, that I may not deprive my soul of that mercy which Thine infinite goodness has offered to sinners.

He shall have judgment without mercy, that hath shewed no mercy. [James ii. 13.]

O blessed God, help me in this great concern, that I may never fall under Thy wrath for want of shewing mercy to others. O blessed Jesus, grant that in this I may be Thy disciple.

[1st ed. 270; iii. 128.]

TUESDAY MEDITATIONS.

TROUBLE AND AFFLICTIONS.

Psalm l. 15. *Call upon Me in the time of trouble, so will I hear thee, and thou shalt praise Me.*

O God, who seest all our[q] weaknesses, and the troubles we[r] labour under, have regard unto the prayers of Thy servant, who stands in need of Thy comfort, Thy direction[s], and Thy help.

[t]Grant that I may suffer like a Christian, and not grieve like an unbeliever: that I may receive troubles as a punish-

---

[q] " my," iii.
[r] " I," iii.
[s] " Thy direction," om. iii.

[t] iii. " Give me grace to receive this trouble as a punishment," &c.

TUESDAY.

ment due to my past offences, as an exercise of my faith, and patience, and humility, and as a trial of my obedience; and^u that I may improve all my afflictions to the good of my soul, and Thy glory.

Thou alone knowest what is best for us^v: let me never^w dispute Thy wisdom or Thy goodness^x. [1st. ed. 270; iii. 128.]

Direct my reason, subdue my passions, put a stop to my roving thoughts and fears, and let me have the comfort of Thy promise, and of Thy protection, both now and ever, ^yfor Jesus Christ's sake. Amen.

O Jesu, who hast known what troubles and sorrows are, have compassion upon me in my trouble. Thou who wast despised and rejected of men—whose life was sought for by Herod—who was tempted by the devil—who wast hated by the world which Thou camest to save, and set at nought by Thy own people—who wast called a deceiver and a dealer with the devil—who wast driven from place to place, and hadst not where to lay Thy Head—who wast betrayed by one Disciple and forsaken by all the rest—wast falsely accused, spitted on, and scourged—set at nought by Herod and his men of war—given up by Pilate to the will of the Jews—hadst a murderer preferred before Thee—wast condemned to a most shameful death—crucified betwixt two thieves—reviled by those that passed by—had gall and vinegar given Thee to drink, and suffered a most bitter and most shameful death, submitting with patience to the Will of Thy Father:—O Jesu, who now sittest at the right Hand of God to succour all those that suffer for righteousness' sake: be my advocate with God for grace, that in all my sufferings I may follow Thy example, and be supported under all the difficulties and discouragements with which He shall think fit to exercise the patience and fidelity of His poor servant. Amen. [iii. 128. (for Wednesday.)]

Hebrews xii. 7. *If ye endure chastening, God dealeth with you as with sons; for what son is he whom the father chasten-* [1st ed. 270; iii. 129.]

^u This clause om. iii.
^v om. iii.
^w "not," iii.
^x iii. adds, "for this is not the effect of chance, but according to Thy just appointment. Grant, O God, that I may suffer like a Christian, and not grieve like an unbeliever."
^y iii. om. "for...sake." and adds, " Grant that I may improve this and all other afflictions to the good of my soul."

K

TUESDAY. *eth not? But if ye be without chastisement, whereof all are partakers, then are ye bastards, and not sons.*

[Micah vii. 9.] *I will bear the indignation of the Lord, because I have sinned against Him.*

[iii. adds], Matt. x. 24. *The disciple is not above his master, nor the servant above his lord. If they call the Master Beelzebub, &c.*

[z]If I am despised or slighted, I ought to consider it as a favour, since this is a mark of God's children; and therefore I ought to thank Him for it, and not be angry with those whom He makes His instruments to subdue and mortify my pride.

1 Peter iv. 13. *Rejoice, inasmuch as ye are made partakers of the sufferings of Christ; that when His glory shall be revealed, ye may be glad also with exceeding joy.*—viz. because[a] your reward will be proportionable to your sufferings.

[iii. adds], v. 16. *If any man suffer as a Christian, let him not be ashamed, &c.*

Matthew v. 11, 12. *Blessed are ye when men shall revile you, and persecute you, and shall say all manner of evil against you falsely for My sake. Rejoice, and be exceeding glad; for great is your reward in heaven; for so persecuted they the prophets which were before you.*

The mystery of the Cross is to be learned under the Cross.

Matthew x. 28, 29. *Fear not them which kill the body, but are not able to kill the soul: but rather fear Him which is able to destroy both body and soul in hell. Are not two sparrows sold for a farthing? and one of them shall not fall to the ground without your Father. The very hairs of your head are all numbered.*

[iii. 130. adds], *Rejoicing in tribulation.* This is indeed an heroic virtue. O God, enable me to attain to it.

1 Pet. v. 6, 7. *Humble yourselves under the mighty hand of God* (i.e. great[b] afflictions which He suffers to befall you,) *that He may exalt you in due time; casting all your care upon Him; for He careth for you.*

[1st ed. 270; M.H. ɪl.; ii. 88.] Matthew vi. 10. *Thy will[c] be done.*

[z] iii. om. this sentence.
[a] iii. " since."
[b] iii. " the."
[c] " God's will," M. H.

It is just, great God, it should be so; for who should[c] TUESDAY. govern the world but He that made it? And yet we poor creatures[d] repine[e] when any thing crosses our hopes or[f] designs. What strange unthoughtfulness! what presumption is this! And it is[g] Thy great mercy that any of us are sensible of this folly, and become willing to be governed by[h] Thee.

With all my heart and soul, O[i] God, I thank Thee, that[k] in all the changes and chances of this mortal life, I[l] can look up to Thee, and [m] cheerfully resign my will to Thine.

ii. adds, "O Lord, grant that it may be ever so with me.

"Why should such creatures as we expect or desire that our will should be done? is it not sufficient that His will be done, Whose will is most wise and just?"

It is the desire of my soul, and my humble petition, that I [1st ed. may [n] always be ready and willing to submit to Thy provi- 271; M.H. dence, that Thou mayest order what Thou judgest to be most xliii.] convenient for me.

I have trusted Thee, dear Father, with myself; my soul is in Thy hand[o], which I verily believe Thou wilt preserve to eternal happiness: my body, and all that belongs to it, are of much less value. I do therefore, with as great security and satisfaction, trust all I have to Thee, hoping Thou wilt preserve me from all things hurtful, and lead me to all things profitable to my salvation.

I will love Thee, O God; and then I am satisfied that all things, however strange and irksome they appear, shall work together for good to those that do so.

I know in whom I have believed; I have a Saviour at Thy right hand, full of kindness, full of care, full of power; He has prayed for me, that this faith fail me not; and by this faith I am persuaded, that neither tribulation, nor anguish, nor persecution, nor famine, nor nakedness, nor peril, nor sword, nor death which I may fear, nor life which

---

[c] M. H. "can order and."
[d] "mortals," M. H.
[e] M. H. adds, "and blame Thy wisdom and goodness."
[f] M. H. "and."
[g] M. H. adds "of."
[h] "so wise and just a Power," M.H.
[i] M. H. "dear God."
[k] M. H. adds, "that Thou hast given me grace."
[l] M. H. "to look."
[m] M. H. "and to resign my will entirely and cheerfully to Thine."
[n] M. H. "be always willing and ready."
[o] M. H. "hands."

TUESDAY. I may hope for, nor things present which I feel, nor things to come which I may apprehend, shall ever prevail so far over me, as to make me not to resign my will entirely to Thee°.

[M. H. inserts here ᵖ],

"Thou art too great to delight in grieving us poor mortals; and hast other ways of procuring to Thyself pleasure, than by our misery and disappointments; I do therefore freely resign all my thoughts and hopes and desires to Thee, and resolve, by Thy gracious assistance, to rest contented with whatever Thou shalt appoint.

"Blessed be Thy Name, who hast continued to me so long the enjoyment of so many good things. Blessed be God that I had any thing to part withal, any hopes to lose, whereby I may testify my faith in Thee and affection to Thee. Blessed be the goodness of God, that I have so many of the comforts of this life still remaining; I have nothing too dear or too great to be resigned to Thee; from whose bounty I have received all I have; and who art my best and my eternal Friend.

"Help me to think wherein I have offended Thee, and carefully to amend it: to lay up my treasure and hopes in Heaven, and to place my desires and affections on things more certain.

"Increase my faith, O God, that I may acknowledge at all times, and upon all such occasions as these, Thy wise and merciful Providence; which, by ways most contrary to our desires, doth bring us to endless and undisturbed bliss."

[1st ed. 271; M.H. xlv.] In an humble, quiet, and dutiful submission ᵠ, ʳlet me faithfully run the race that is set before me, looking unto Jesus, the Author and Finisher of our faith, who, for the joy that was set before Him, despised the shame, endured the Cross, and is now seated ˢ at the right hand of God; to whom I most humbly beseech Thee to bring me in Thy good time; and for whatever shall fall out in the mean while, THY WILL BE DONE. Amen.

[M. H. inserts, apparently in another hand], 'Tis a dan-

° [See Hooker, end of Sermon on Certainty of Faith in the Elect, t. iii. p. 598. ed. 1836.]

ᵖ [The inverted commas are in the MS.]

ᵠ M. H. adds, "to Thee."

ʳ M. H. "I go on in the race," &c.

ˢ M. H. "set down."

gerous mistake we are liable to, when we conclude that TUESDAY. being troubled at the crosses and disappointments of life is only an injury to ourselves, we fancy there is no hurt in it, only a little disturbance to our minds. But consider: 'tis a sin against God, and for which we are as much liable to punishment as for a breach of any other of His laws. For the very nature of sin consists in our having wills contrary to the will of God. Now if God, by ordering any thing to befall us, declares that 'tis His will it should be so, I certainly oppose His will if I am not pleased with it, and consequently I sin.

Look unto Jesus. He was despised and rejected of men; [1st ed. 271.] His life was sought for by Herod; He was tempted by Satan: hated by that world which He came to save; set at nought by His own people; called a deceiver and a dealer with the devil; was driven from place to place, and had not where to lay His head; betrayed by one disciple, and forsaken by all the rest; falsely accused, spit upon and scourged; set at nought by Herod and his men of war; given up by Pilate to the will of His enemies; had a murderer preferred before Him; condemned to a most cruel and shameful death; crucified between two thieves; reviled in the midst of His torments; had gall and vinegar given Him to drink; suffered a most bitter death, submitting with patience to the will of His Father.

O Jesu, who now sittest at the right hand of God, to succour all who suffer in a righteous way; be Thou my advocate for grace, that, in all my sufferings, I may follow Thy example, and run with patience the race that is set before me. Amen.

ᵗTake all things that befall you as coming from God's [1st ed. 271; iii. 127.] providence, for your particular profit. ᵘAnd though they are evil in themselves, yet as He permits, or does not think fit to hinder them, they may be referred to Him.

[iii. inserts],

" Remember, that it is God's will that you should willingly bear the afflictions that befall you, whether by others' faults or your own: and especially injuries from such as you have obliged.

"See Spiritual Combat, p. 143." [ch. 32. p. 90, 91, Engl.

ᵗ iii. prefixes " *Afflictions*."   ᵘ iii. " i. e."

TUESDAY. Tr. 1846. "He will receive thee and embrace thee the more lovingly, the more thou .... delightest to be esteemed vile by others .... Fail not to return Him continual thanks for it, and hold thyself obliged to those who have given thee occasion to humble thyself, and still more to those who have trampled upon thee," &c.]

[1st ed. 271.] God no sooner discovers in your heart an ardent desire of well-doing, and of submitting to His will, but He prepares for you occasions of trying your virtue; and therefore, confident of His love, receive cheerfully a medicine prepared by a physician that cannot be mistaken, and cannot give you any thing but what will be for your good.

See Ecclus. chap. ii. The whole chapter.

[1st ed. 272.] N. B. This chapter was the lesson for the day, March 25th, 1727, at a time when I was much perplexed about the attempts made upon the episcopal jurisdiction; and this I cannot but remark, since to my exceeding great comfort and direction, it has often so happened, I am persuaded, by a special providence of God.

Lord, prepare my heart, that no afflictions may ever so surprise, as to overbear me.

Dispose me at all times to a readiness to suffer what Thy providence shall order or permit.

It is the same cup which Jesus Christ drank of; it is He sends it. He sees it absolutely necessary that I must be first partaker of His sufferings, and then of His glories.

Matthew x. 22. *And ye shall be hated of all men for My Name's sake; but he that shall endure to the end shall be saved.*

It is indeed grievous to nature to be thus treated; but when it is for Thy Name's sake, O Jesus, and for the sake of Thy truth, and for being true to Thee; how lovely is this hatred; and how advantageous when salvation is the reward!

Matthew x. 24. *The disciple is not above his master, nor the servant above his lord.*

He who keeps this saying in his heart, will never complain of what he suffers, nor seek for any other way to save himself, but by humiliation and the Cross.

Suffering. The Lord grant that whenever I suffer, it may be for being faithful to God, and without drawing it unseasonably upon myself.

St. Luke ii. 35. *Yea, a sword shall pierce through thine own soul also.* Thus God treated the Mother of His Son, and thus He treats those whom He loves;—He mingles bitters with their sweets.

He who is called to the ministry of the Word, is called to suffer the contradiction of the world, and if occasion be, to seal the truth with his blood.

This should always be our support and comfort, that the tongues, the ill-will, the evil designs of men, are always subject to the power of God: let us therefore be intent upon our duty, and leave the rest to God, who continually watches over His faithful servants. *Even the hairs of your head are all numbered.*

We are in God's hands; we often take ourselves out of His hands, by trusting to the help and protection of men, more than that of God.

My God, settle in my heart a firm belief in Thy Providence, and dependence upon Thy will and designs, that I may consider nothing but my duty, and fear no evil, but only lest I should not faithfully discharge my duty in all respects.

God can render none miserable but those whom He finds sinners. Let us apply this to ourselves when in affliction, but not unto others, or to their personal faults.

Acts ix. 29. *He preached boldly in the Name of the Lord Jesus, but they went about to kill him.* When a man is treated as Jesus Christ was for preaching, it is a good sign that he preaches by His Spirit, and that this is the beginning of his reward; and indeed opposition and evil treatment are less to be feared by a minister of Christ than applause and commendation. *Woe unto you when all men shall speak well of you.*

Rev. iii. 19. *As many as I love, I rebuke and chasten; be zealous therefore, and repent.*

Blessed be God, who vouchsafes, by salutary chastisements, to awaken us when we fall asleep through sloth and lukewarmness. Grant that I may with a true zeal, and timely repentance, make good use of all Thy rebukes.

2 Cor. iv. 8, 9. *We are troubled on every side, yet not distressed; we are perplexed, but not in despair; persecuted,*

TUESDAY.

[1st ed. 273.]

but not forsaken; cast down, but not destroyed. Observe here an apostolical disposition in the midst of persecution;—liberty of spirit and joy of heart;—an invincible courage;—a lively belief of the care of God;—a full trust in His assistance in the lowest abyss of trouble;—casting the eyes of faith upon the sufferings of the Lord Jesus;—counting himself happy in fulfilling them in His mystical body.

Philip. i. 12. *The things which happened unto me have fallen out rather unto the furtherance of the Gospel.* He who loses courage under oppositions is even yet a stranger to the ways of the Gospel. God can and does make His greatest enemies contribute to His work and glory. Let us leave God to act, and follow His guidance.

2 Tim. iv. 17. *Notwithstanding, the Lord stood with me and strengthened me.* The more a minister of Christ is forsaken by men the more conformable he is to Christ, and the greater consolation he may expect from God.

Heb. xii. 3. *Consider Him that endured such contradiction of sinners against Himself, lest ye be wearied and faint in your minds.* If the world, which rose up against Christ, suffer us to be quiet, we should have reason to fear that we do not follow His steps, and that the world is pleased with us.

Whom the Lord loveth He chasteneth. If nature were innocent, a Father so just and so good would not impose a condition so hard upon His children, were it not necessary to our salvation. We are treated as bastards, if we are not chastened, but left to our own libertinism;—too sure a sign of reprobation. Grant, O Lord, that I may submit to, and even be pleased with, these temporal evils, which lead to eternal happiness.

1 Pet. ii. 19. *This is thankworthy, if a man for conscience towards God endure grief, suffering wrongfully.*

He who can be content to have God for a witness of his patience and sufferings, has found the secret to make God his friend.

We complain of unjust sufferings, and they are the things which we ought most to value.

A Christian, whose whole care is to avoid sufferings, has forgot his pattern; and that we are Christians in order to be crucified with Christ.

We see in Jesus Christ innocence and holiness itself suffering; and yet we complain of hardships. _{TUESDAY.}

The meekness of Christ, when in the hands of His enemies, and when He had power to have delivered Himself, is what we are alway to remember.

1 Pet. iii. 14. *If ye suffer for righteousness' sake, happy are ye; and be not afraid of their terror.*

It is plain we do not know the happiness of suffering, when we speak of it with abhorrence, and shun it with all our might.

Nothing but Thy love, O Lord, can suppress in our hearts the fear of men.

1 Pet. iv. 14. *If ye be reproached for the name of Christ, happy are ye: for the spirit of glory and of God resteth upon you.*

No worldly glory equals this;—nothing causes His Spirit to rest upon us more perseveringly;—God will not account of sufferings brought upon a man's self by his own fault; and yet Christian grace can sanctify even such crimes, when a criminal suffers in the spirit of repentance, and submission to the will of God.

To be purified by afflictions is a great mercy,—to be abandoned to prosperity till death, is an instance of God's anger.

1 Pet. iv. 19. *Wherefore let them that suffer according to the will of God, commit the keeping of their souls to Him in well-doing, as unto a faithful Creator.*

1 John iii. 13. *Marvel not, my brethren, if the world hate you.* Let us rather fear that we do not belong to God, if the world spare us.

Grant, O God, that I may never murmur at Thy appointments, or be exasperated against the ministers of Thy providence. [1st ed. 274.]

2 Cor. i. 7. *As ye are partakers of the sufferings, so shall ye be also of the consolations.* O Lord, remove from me all inward disquiet, and grant that with an entire submission to Thy will, I may ever preserve a peace of mind, and leave my deliverance to Thy choice.

The more the world deprives us of its protection for our adherence to God, the more He espouseth our interest, and declares on our side.

TUESDAY.   It is the part of the minister of Christ to labour without ceasing, to suffer without resentment, and to leave his cause in the hands of God, with full trust in Him.

In Thee, O Jesus, we find matter of consolation in every affliction that can possibly befall us.

All visitations are from God. He is not delighted with the miseries of His poor creatures; afflictions are therefore designed for our good. He will either shew you the reason of this visitation, or make you reap the fruits of it.

People that may be well disposed, may yet live under the power of some evil custom, which is displeasing to God; a man may have been guilty of some great sin which he has yet never truly repented of, or been truly humbled for. This was the case of the sons of Jacob; they had attempted the life of, and afterwards sold, their brother, and endangered the life of their aged father; under which guilt they passed their life well enough for many years, till God visited them; and then they thought of their sin, confessed, and repented.

God, by afflictions, often fits us for greater degrees of grace which He is going to bestow.

"Though I suffer, yet I am well, because I am what God would have me to be."

[ii. 89. continues this quotation[u].] "For when we will not be what He wills, 'tis we that are in fault, and not He, who neither wills nor permits any thing but what is just." St. Aug. ep. xxxviii. to Profuturus, § 1. ["Etiam sic, quoniam id Domino placet, recte sumus. Potius enim, si id nolumus quod ille vult, nos culpandi sumus, quam ille non recte aliquid vel facere vel sinere existimandus est." The same occurs, MS. iii. 237, with the addition, "And what He will turn to His glory and our good, if we do not rebel against His will."]

Lord, do not permit my trials to be above my strength, and do Thou vouchsafe to be my strength and comfort in the time of trial.

Grant, O Lord, that I may never be wanting to the cause

---

[u] [prefixing to it], "Quisquis detrahit famæ meæ, addit mercedi meæ." Augustine. [De Bono Viduitatis, § 27, ad fin. in substance.] "The servant is not greater than his Lord."

of truth, nor expose it by any indiscretion, or unseasonable transports of zeal. <small>TUESDAY.</small>

Jesus Christ avoids persecution[x]. To suffer for righteousness' sake is well-pleasing to God; but then it must be done according to the appointment of God, not out of a proud zeal.

Give me grace to take in good part whatever shall befall me, and let my heart acknowledge it to be the Lord's doing, and to come from His providence, and not by chance.

Afflictions. These God makes use of, sometimes by way of prevention; *lest I should be exalted,* said St. Paul[y]:—to reform them; *before I was afflicted, I went astray*[z]:—to perfect them; patience, courage, submission to the will of God, are graces not so much as understood by people who meet with no adversities; *we must through much tribulation enter into the kingdom of God*[a]:—to prove men, and shew them for examples; if a man had no enemies, how could he shew his charity in forgiving them?

Never consider so much the instrument of your afflictions as the meaning of the good providence of God in these things.

John xi. 5. Afflictions no marks of God's displeasure. *Jesus loved Mary and Lazarus,* yet they were both afflicted.

Punishment is due to sin. We must be punished here or hereafter; it is the cause of all afflictions, and designed by our gracious God to bring us to repentance.

Prosperity a most dangerous state; we fancy it is owing to our merit, and it is followed with pride, neglect of duty, fearlessness.

It is happy for us when God counts us worthy to suffer for His Name's sake; to contend with Satan, as Job did, and be able, through God's grace, to overcome so powerful a spirit. [1st ed. 275.]

Afflictions, undergone with resignation, the great test of our love of God; when we love Him then He chastens us. May God sanctify all our afflictions to us all!

Afflictions are always useful when they oblige us to go to God.

[x] John vii. 1.
[y] 2 Cor. xii. 7.
[z] Psalm cxix. 67.
[a] Acts xiv. 22.

TUESDAY.   May I receive every thing from Thy hand with patience and with joy!

[iii. 20, 21.]   *Despair.* Let Thine infinite mercy in Christ Jesus deliver me from despair, both now and at the hour of death.

Hope. Grant, O God, that, amidst all the discouragements, difficulties, dangers, distress, and darkness of this mortal life, I may depend upon Thy mercy, and on this build my hopes, as on a sure foundation.

Let the multitude of Thy tender mercies preserve all from despair.

Resignation. Grant that I may receive the punishment of my sins with patience and resignation.

Injuries, Persecution. Give me, O God, a heart to consider, that man could have no power against me, unless it were given from above[b].

Trouble. Remember me, O God, in the day of trouble. Secure me, by Thy grace, from all excess of fear, concern, and sadness[c].

Enemies. Change their hearts by Thy grace, or restrain their malice by Thy power.

Troubles and Afflictions. In Thee, O blessed Jesus, we find matter of comfort and consolation under every hardship and affliction which Thou Thyself underwentest: Lord, grant that we may ever imitate Thy patience and resignation.

Oppression in the Gate[d]: [i.e. probably, in the place where justice should be.]

Afflictions. Let the afflictions I meet with be in some measure serviceable towards the appeasing of Thy wrath. Let them prove the happy occasion of forwarding my conversion and salvation.

May I with equal submission and reverence receive the most different dispensations of Thy Providence. We cannot wish one event rather than another without presumption— without making ourselves judges of secret things which belong to God only, and of future things which God has concealed from us.

---

[b] St. John xix. 11.

[c] iii. has here, with a line drawn across it, Ὑπὲρ ἐπιστροφῆς τοῦ Δεσπότου Νήσου ταύτης.

[d] [Prov. xxii. 22. "Rob not the poor, because he is poor: neither *oppress* the afflicted *in the gate.*"]

Enemies. A Christian should not discover that he has enemies any other way than by doing more good to them than to others. *If thine enemy hunger, feed him, &c.* He will therefore be careful not to lose such occasions. [TUESDAY. 1st ed. 275.]

O Jesu! whose charity all the malice of Thy bitterest enemies could not overcome, shed abroad in my heart that most excellent gift of charity.

Ecclus. viii. 7. *Rejoice not over thy greatest enemy being dead; but remember that we die all.*

Our enemies are our benefactors, procuring for us a new right to Heaven.

I pray God convert all those who hate us without cause.

I beseech Thee for my enemies, not for vengeance, but for mercy; that Thou wouldst change their hearts by Thy grace, or restrain their malice by Thy power.

Wars. O Sovereign Lord! who for our sins art justly displeased, I prostrate myself before Thee, confessing my own sin and the sin of this people; acknowledging the justice of any scourge which Thou shalt think fit to bring upon us; and trembling to think how much I may have contributed toward it.

Thou hast already spoken to us both by Thy judgments and mercies, both by the scarcity and plenty of bread; and we have not regarded it. Thou hast taken away the lives of many, very many, in their very sins, by which numerous widows and fatherless children have been left miserable.

The sins of whoredom and drunkenness; of swearing, lying, and perjury; of litigiousness, injustice, defrauding the public, and sacrilege, are made light of.

The sins of impiety, of profaneness, of despising the means of grace and salvation, are too common amongst us.

What shall I say, to prevail with God to avert the judgments which these sins deserve?

God be merciful unto us, and put a stop to this torrent of wickedness; put Thy fear into all our hearts, that we may return to Thee; that we may repent, and bring forth fruit meet for repentance; and that iniquity may not be our ruin.

TUESDAY.   May the dread of Thy now threatened judgments deter us from evil; may Thy goodness and patience lead us to repentance; weaken the power of Satan; take from among us the spirit of slumber, of ignorance, and inconsideration.

Let every one of us see and feel the plague of his own heart, and say, *What have I done* to bring these evils upon us? So that bringing forth fruits answerable to amendment of life, we may escape Thy judgment now hanging over our heads, and above all, Thy judgments against sinners in the world to come. And this I beg for Jesus Christ His sake. Amen.

[iii. 20; 2nd ed. p. 425.]   *Judgment Day.* Grant, O Lord, that I may be of the number of those that shall find mercy at that day.

Zacchæus. The good Lord grant that I may give a proof of the sincerity of my conversion by a change of life.

WEDNESDAY MEDITATIONS.

SOBER LIFE.

Q.—Will you deny all ungodliness and worldly lusts, and live soberly, righteously, and godly, in this present world, that you may shew yourself in all things an example of good works unto others, that the adversary may be ashamed, having nothing to say against you?

A.—I will so do, the Lord being my helper.

[a]ALMIGHTY God, who hast made me a guide to others, suffer me not to go astray myself; give me grace that I may never follow the inclinations of corrupted nature, nor govern myself according to the maxims of an evil world; but give me the spirit, as well as the character, of a minister of Jesus Christ.

O Holy Spirit of Grace[b], sanctify my *heart,* that no base or impure thoughts, no mean and covetous affections, may lodge there.

Govern my *tongue,* that no corrupt communication may proceed out of my mouth.

Guard my *eyes,* purify my *hands,* guide my *feet.*

Conduct my whole life, that by all instances of a good example, I may lead the people committed to my care, in the ways of truth and of eternal life; and that no irregularity in my conversation may ever make my instructions ineffectual, or the ways of religion to be evil spoken of.

O Lord Jesus Christ, without whom we can do nothing, be Thou my[c] Advocate with God as well as my example, that I may *live* and *be* as Thou wouldst have me. Amen[d].

1 Corinthians ix. 27. *I keep under my body, and bring it*

---

[a] [iii. prefixes the sentences to the prayer.]
[b] ii. iii. om. " O...Grace."
[c] ii. iii. " Helper as well."

[d] ii. adds, " Josh. xxiv. 15. *But as for me and my house, we will serve the Lord.*"

WEDNES-DAY.

into subjection, lest by any means, when I have preached to others, I myself should be a castaway.

Εἰ δὲ Παῦλος, τί ἂν εἴποιμεν ἡμεῖς[e];

When a man has given himself[f] to the immediate service of[g] God, he is no longer at liberty to follow his own inclinations, whether in study, profit, recreation, &c.

[i. 97; ii. 43; iii. 120.]

Gal. v. 24. *They that are Christ's have crucified the flesh with the affections and lusts.*

"Voluptatis causa aliquid agere, his relinquit qui vulgarem vitam sequuntur." Boeth. de Cons. Philosoph. Mor. v.

Funcii Epitaphium.

"Disce meo exemplo mandato munere fungi,
Et fuge ceu pestem τὴν πολυπραγμοσύνην[h]."

Nature is content with a[i] little, grace with less.

James iii. 13. *Who is a wise man, let him shew out of a good conversation his works with meekness of wisdom;* that is, let him shew his wisdom in his life[k].

Temperance consists in neither eating nor drinking more than is necessary, and in not seeking for exquisite dainties and liquors[l].

Ecclus. xix. 30. *A man's attire, excessive laughter, and gait, shew what he is.*

Tit. i. 7. *A bishop must be blameless, as the steward of God; not self-willed, not soon angry, not given to wine, no striker, not given to filthy lucre, but a lover of hospitality, a lover of good men;* sober (prudent,) *just, holy, temperate; holding fast the faithful word, as he hath been taught.*

Whoever loves pomp, superiority and riches in episcopacy, cannot avoid the haughtiness of pride; but he who looks

---

[e] [S. Chrys. on 1 Cor. ix. 27. Hom. 23.]

[f] ii. adds, " or is called."

[g] ii. iii. add " his." ii. " reading, studies, profit," &c. iii. " reading, study, profit, recreation," &c.

[h] [John Funck, born 1518 at Werden near Nuremberg, a Lutheran divine, son-in-law and partizan of Osiander: author also of a large work on Chronology, sometime in much repute. Duke Albert of Prussia made him his almoner; and interfering in political matters, he was tried and beheaded at Knigsburg through the influence of the nobles, and a few minutes before his death composed the distich here quoted; Oct. 28, 1566. Biogr. Dict. and Encycl. Metropolit. 12, 450.]

[i] ii. om. " a," and adds " and."

[k] iii. " Let him shew it in his life, which is true Christian wisdom." ii. om. the whole.

[l] Julian Pomerius, [al. Prosper, de Vita Contemplativa, lib. iii. c. 19. " Temperantia intemperantiam nostram ad honestum modum redigit in cibo ipso vel potu, ut contenti simus appositis."]

upon it as a *burden* and a *charge*, for which he must strictly account, cannot but be ever fearful and humble. Quesnel [in loc.]

Malachi ii. 8, 9. *But ye are departed out of the way; ye have caused many to stumble at the law; ye have corrupted the covenant of Levi, saith the Lord of Hosts; therefore have I made you contemptible and base before all the people; according as ye have not kept My ways, but have been partial in the law, &c.*

The good Lord keep His servant from bringing *contempt upon the clergy,* by any irregularity or fault of mine.

Titus ii. 15. *Let no man despise thee.*

That is; demean thyself agreeable to the authority which thou hast received from Jesus Christ, not making thy office contemptible by any mean action, but act with the dignity of one who stands in the place of God.

They that recommend eternal possessions and happiness [i. 98.] to others, ought to shew that they are verily persuaded themselves of the vanity of all earthly enjoyments, avoiding superfluities, and not being over-concerned for necessaries. Jesus Christ thus preached the contempt of the world, by contemning it Himself.

John viii. 46. *Which of you convinceth Me of sin?*

O Jesus, the only Priest free from all sin, make me Thy servant as blameless and holy as the frailty of my nature will suffer me to be.

The reputation of a minister is not his own, but the Church's, as the reputation of an ambassador is his prince's.

Leviticus iv. 3. *If the priest that is anointed do sin, &c.*

N.B. That the same sin in a single priest, is to have as great a sacrifice as a sin of the whole people of Israel[m], v. 13 [and 14.]

The flesh never thrives but at the cost of the soul.

Let us ever remember, that *mortification* must go further than the body. Self-love, pride, envy, jealousy, hatred, malice, avarice, ambition, must all be *mortified,* by avoiding and ceasing from the occasions of them.

---

[m] [See St. Chrys. de Sacerdotio. Serm. vi. ed. Savil., t. vi. p. 50. l. 32. δεῖξαι βουλόμενος ὅτι τὰ ἁμαρτήματα μείζονα ἐκδέχεται πολλῷ τὴν τιμωρίαν, ὅταν ὑπὸ τῶν ἱερέων γένηται, ἢ ὅταν ὑπὸ τῶν ἰδιωτῶν, προστάττει τοσαύτην ὑπὲρ τῶν ἱερέων προσάγεσθαι τὴν θυσίαν, ὅσην ὑπὲρ παντὸς τοῦ λαοῦ.]

WEDNES-DAY. The sobriety of the soul consists in humility, and in being content with necessaries.

O Thou who hast made me a servant in Thy house, give me grace that I may never dishonour Thy service.

Failings of good men. God permits these, that we may plainly see that there is no person in whom nature is not corrupted.

A man may hide from the world some of his good works; but a *Christian life* ought to be seen; it is a public testimony which we owe to our faith, and an example which Christianity requires of us. *Let your light, &c.*

It is not only in the Church that a minister of Christ should be mindful of his character, but in his converse with the world.

Ecclesiasticus xviii. 31. *If thou givest thy soul the desires that please her, she will make thee a laughing-stock to thine enemies that malign thee.*

Ecclesiasticus xix. 5. *He that resisteth pleasures crowneth his life.*

[i. 99.] *Self-denial* is a duty contrary to *self-pleasing*. Vouchsafe me, gracious God, the graces of mortification and self-denial, that my affections and flesh being subdued unto the Spirit, and my heart and all my members being mortified from all carnal and worldly lusts, I may ever obey Thy blessed will, through Jesus Christ our Lord. Amen.

Grant that no day of my life may pass without my endeavouring to mortify some evil affections, some evil habit, some bad inclination, &c., that the whole body of sin may be destroyed.

Instances of self-denial. To deny our *sinful appetites:* such as when denied will not hurt us, but help to bring our bodies in subjection to our souls.

Not to please ourselves in any things which will not profit us;—*Jesus Christ pleased not Himself.*

To deny the love of riches and the pleasures they furnish us with. Proof of this. Charity to the poor. Blessed are the merciful[n].

[i. 100.] Matthew xvi. 24. *If any man will come after Me, let him deny himself, and take up his cross, and follow Me.*

[n] [These seem to be heads of a sermon.]

O my Saviour! let me not profess to follow Thee, without complying with the terms which Thou requirest of them that desire to do so sincerely.

Matthew vii. 14. *Strait is the gate and narrow is the way that leadeth unto life, and few there be that find it.*

But if the difficulties of an holy life affright us, let us consider, *who can dwell with everlasting burnings?*

All mankind being under the sentence of death, certain to be executed, and at an hour we know not of; a state of penance and self-denial, of being dead and crucified to the world, is certainly the most suitable, the most becoming temper that we can be found in, when that sentence comes to be executed; that is, when we come to die.

Especially when we consider, that this short and uncertain time, allowed us betwixt the sentence and execution, will determine our condition for eternity.

If this is the case of fallen man, as most certainly it is; then mirth and pleasure is the greatest indecency; a fondness for the world, the greatest folly; and self-indulgence, downright madness.

And consequently the contrary to these, namely, a constant seriousness of temper; an universal care and exactness of life, an indifference for the world; self-denial, sobriety, and watchfulness, must be our greatest wisdom.

And this discovers to us the reason and the necessity of all the duties of Christianity, and of God's dealings with fallen man in this state of trial.

For instance:—Jesus Christ commands us to *deny ourselves,* and to *take up our cross daily,* not because He can command what He pleases, (for He is infinite goodness, and can command nothing but what is good for His creatures,) but because the corruption of our nature requires that we should be forbid every thing which would increase our disorder.

And because this disorder has spread itself through all the powers of our souls and bodies, and inclines us to evil continually, He requires that our self-denial should reach as far as our corruption.

He commands us therefore to deny our own wisdom, because we are really blind as to what concerns our own

WEDNESDAY — true good, and should infallibly ruin ourselves, if left to our own choices.

He commands us to deny our *appetites*, because intemperance would ruin us.

He forbids us to give way to our *passions*, because a thousand evils will follow if we should do so.

He obliges us to keep a very strict watch over our hearts, because from thence proceed hypocrisy, covetousness, malice, and a thousand other evils.

We are forbid to set our hearts upon the world, and every thing in it, because our eternal happiness depends upon loving God with all our heart and soul.

We are obliged to love our neighbour, and our very enemies; and are forbid to hate, to contend, to hurt, to go to law with him; because this would exasperate our minds, and grieve the Holy Spirit of God by which we are sanctified, being against that charity which God delights in.

We are forbid all repining when God afflicts us, because, as sinners, suffering is due to us.

And, because our bodies have a very great influence over our souls, we are commanded to *fast*, and to be strictly temperate at all times, and to deny ourselves the love of sensual pleasures, and self-indulgence.

We are commanded to deny all the ways of folly, vanity, and false satisfactions, that we may be able to take satisfaction and pleasure in the ways of God.

In short: in whatever instances we are commanded to deny ourselves, it is because it is absolutely necessary; either to cure our corruption, or to qualify us for the grace of God, or to hinder us from grieving God's Holy Spirit, and forcing Him to forsake us.

The more we deny ourselves, the freer we shall be from sin, and the more dear to God.

God appoints us to sufferings, that we may keep close to Him; and that we may value the sufferings of His Son, which we should have but a low notion of, did not our own experience teach us what it is to suffer.

[i. 102.]

They that deny themselves will be sure to find their strength increased, their affections raised, and their inward peace continually advanced.

Had there been any better, any easier way to heaven, Jesus Christ would have chosen it for Himself and for His followers.   *WEDNESDAY.*

The more you love God, expect you must give the greater proofs of it; and you may expect greater assistance and consolation.

Luke vi. 25. *Woe unto you that are full, for ye have received your consolation.*

If this be the life of the reprobate, who would not dread the pleasures of a prosperous condition?

1 Timothy vi. 8. *Having food and raiment, let us be therewith content.*

Let us not imagine that excess, luxury, and superfluity, and the love of pleasures, are less criminal because they are so common.

Afflictions bring us the nearest way to God.

Take up the Cross. This is designed as a peculiar favour to Christians, as indeed are all Christ's commands. Miseries are the unavoidable portion of fallen man. All the difference is, Christians suffering in obedience to the will of God, it makes them easy: unbelievers suffer the same things, but with an uneasy will and mind.

To follow our own will, our passions, and our senses, is that which makes us miserable. It is for this reason, and that we may have a remedy for all our evils, that Jesus Christ obliges us to submit our will, our passions, &c., to God.

The good Christian is not one who has no inclination to sin, (for we have all the seed of sin in us,) but who, being sensible of such inclinations, denieth them continually, and suffers them not to grow into evil actions.

No pleasure can be innocent which hinders us from minding our salvation.

We need but taste any pleasure a very little while, to become a slave to it.

The only way to overcome our corrupt affections, is absolutely to deny their cravings.

We seldom laugh without crime.

We have reason to suspect every doctrine which would teach us to avoid sin without suffering, since the Holy

WEDNES- Scriptures speak so much of self-denial, of the difficulty of
DAY. working out our salvation.

Self-denial [is] absolutely necessary to prepare us to receive the grace of God; it was therefore necessary that John Baptist should prepare the way, by preaching repentance and self-denial.

[i. 103.] Men need not be at pains to go to hell; if they will not deny themselves,—make no resistance,—they will go there of course.

It will be great presumption to go to the utmost bounds of what is allowed, because the bounds which separate what is allowed and forbidden, are often not perceived.

One does not begin to fall when the fall becomes sensible.

Diversions are too apt to make us lose the remembrance of the dangers that encompass us, which is the ready way to ruin: fear being as necessary as any other grace.

Where there is a real abhorrence of evil, there will be a proportionable care to avoid it.

They that are Christ's have crucified the flesh, with the affections and lusts. This is the only true test of being truly Christians.

Afflictions may make men esteem us less; but God loves us the more for them, if we bear them with resignation; which if we do, it is a certain sign of His grace and care of us.

All we aim at is to be easy: the Gospel saith, *Blessed are they that mourn; enter ye in at the strait gate, &c.*

The yoke of Christ is not only safer but even easier than that liberty we are naturally fond of. It makes the practice of virtue pleasant; frees us from the violence of corruption, from being ruined by false pleasures.

Crosses make[n] death less frightful. And indeed, he that will not obey Jesus Christ, must obey his own passions, the world, its customs, humours,—which are the worst of tyrants, and downright slavery.

Every day deny yourself some satisfaction; your *eyes*, objects of mere curiosity; your *tongue*, every thing that may feed vanity, or vent enmity; the *palate*, dainties; the *ears*,

---

[n] MS. "makes."

flattery, and whatever corrupts the heart; the *body*, ease and luxury: bearing all the inconveniences of life, (for the love of God,) cold, hunger, restless nights, ill health, unwelcome news, the faults of servants, contempt, ingratitude of friends, malice of enemies, calumnies, our own failings, lowness of spirits, the struggle in overcoming our corruptions;—bearing all these with patience and resignation to the will of God. Do all this as unto God, with the greatest privacy, &c. {WEDNESDAY.}

All ways are indifferent to one who has heaven in his eye: as a traveller does not choose the pleasantest, but the shortest and safest way to his journey's end; and that is, if we were to choose for ourselves, the way of the Cross, which Jesus Christ made choice of, and sanctified it to all His followers. [i. 104.]

It being much more easy to prevent than to mortify a lust, a prudent Christian will set a guard upon his senses. One unguarded look betrayed David. Job made a covenant with his eyes. *Evil communications corrupt good manners*[o].

Sensuality unfits us for the joys of heaven.

If that concupiscence which opposes virtue be lessened, a less degree of grace will secure our innocence.

Take up the Cross. Can God, who loves us, take pleasure in our sufferings? Could He not shew us a way to good without afflicting us?

We are to judge of what is best, and what is necessary, by what He does, and what He requires.

We are in a fallen state, and in order to be restored it is necessary we be humble and depend entirely on God,—deny our own wisdom, and our own will, because they lead us from God. We must believe Him, put our whole trust in Him, wean our hearts from the world, &c. We will not do this ourselves, God in love to us, does this for us; He disappoints us, He suffers men to injure us, lets us fall into sin, to shew us our own weakness.

Self-love would wish to be made perfect at once; but self-love is what God would destroy by a course of wholesome trials.

Our disorder is an excessive love for ourselves, and for

---

[o] 1 Cor. xv. 33.

WEDNES-DAY.

this world; God orders or permits a train of events to cure us of this self-love. The cure is painful, but it is necessary. We suffer from His love; He is a Father, and cannot take pleasure in our misery. If He deprives us of any thing we love, 'tis that we may love Him, who is our happiness. He corrects, that He may amend us. We would ruin ourselves, and He hinders us. We are deprived of a child, or a friend, and we are sorry, i. e. we are sorry that he is got out of a world of sin and vanity. In short, God would cure our disorders, and we are in distress for it. And yet Jesus Christ was made a Man of Sorrows, that He might convince us how necessary they are for fallen man.

[i. 105.] The most consummate wisdom made choice of the *Cross*, of *poverty* and *meanness*.

All ways are indifferent to one who has heaven in his eye.

He that does not practise the duty of self-denial, does not put himself into the way to receive the grace of God.

Self-denial has respect to the good estate of the soul, as it hinders her from being carried away to the lower pleasures of sense, that she may relish heavenly pleasures.

Matthew viii. 20. *The Son of Man has not where to lay His head.*

This should fill us with confusion, whenever we are overmuch concerned for the conveniences of life.

Our affections being very strongly inclined to sensible good, for the sake of which we are often tempted to evil, and fall into great disorders, we should resolve to sacrifice our will to reason, and reason to the Word of God.

God does not require it of us, that we should not feel any uneasiness under the Cross, but that we should strive to overcome it by His grace.

Virtues of an holy life. Fervency in devotion; frequency in prayer; aspiring after the love of God continually; striving to get above the world and the body; loving silence and solitude, as far as one's condition will permit; humble and affable to all; patient in suffering affronts and contradictions; glad of occasions of doing good even to enemies; doing the will of God, and promoting His honour to the utmost of one's power; resolving never to offend Him willingly, for any temporal *pleasure, profit,* or *loss.* These are virtues highly pleasing to God.

Dr. Hen. More. "A choice receipt for those that will use it; the greatest that one friend can communicate to another, viz. every day to deny one's self in things indifferent, (consistent with health and civility to others,) and not to please one's self in any thing."

There is no pleasure comparable to the not being captivated to any external thing whatever.

Self-denial does not consist in fasting and other mortifications only, but in an *indifference for the world,* its *profits,* [i. 106.] *pleasures, honours,* and its other idols.

It is a part of special prudence, never to do any thing because one has an inclination to it; but because it is one's duty, or it is reasonable; for he who follows his inclination, *because he wills,* in one thing, will do it in another.

He that will not command his thoughts and his will, will soon lose the command of his actions.

Always suspect yourself, when your inclinations are strong and importunate.

It is necessary that we deny ourselves in little and indifferent things, when reason and conscience, which is the voice of God, suggests it to us, as ever we hope to get the rule over our own will.

Say not, "it is a trifle, and not fit to make a sacrifice of to God." He that will not sacrifice a little affection will hardly offer a greater. It is not the thing, but the reason and manner of doing it, namely, for God's sake, and that I may accustom myself to obey His voice, that God regards, and rewards with greater degrees of grace[p].

Romans xv. 3. *Even Jesus Christ pleased not Himself.* As appears in the meanness of His birth, relations, form of a servant, the company He kept, His life, death, &c.

The greater your self-denial, the firmer your faith, and more acceptable to God. The sincere devotion of the rich; the alms of the poor; the humility of the great; the faith of such whose condition is desperate; the contemning the world when one can command it at pleasure; continuing instant in prayer even when we want the consolation we expected:

[p] Life of Mr. Bonnel, p. 122. [123...128. ed. 1842.]

WEDNES- these, and such like instances of self-denial, God will greatly
DAY. reward.

They who imagine that self-denial intrenches upon our liberty, do not know that it is this only that can make us free indeed; giving us the victory over ourselves; setting us free from the bondage of our corruption; enabling us to bear afflictions, (which will come one time or other;) to foresee them without amazement; enlightening the mind, sanctifying the will, and making us to slight those baubles which others so eagerly contend for.

Mortification consists in "such a sparing use of the creatures, as may deaden our love for them, and make us more indifferent in the enjoyment of them." This lessens the weight of concupiscence, which carries us to evil, and so makes the grace of God " more effectual to turn the balance of the will q."

[i. 107.] It is the greatest mercy, that God does not consult our inclinations, in laying upon us the Cross, which is the only way to happiness. Jesus Christ crucified would have few imitators, if God did not lay it upon us, by the hands of men, and by His providence.

Matthew xxvii. 43. *Let Him deliver Him now, if He love Him.*

Carnal man cannot comprehend that God loves those whom He permits to suffer; but faith teaches us, that the Cross is the gift of His love, the foundation of our hope, the mark of His children, and the title of an inheritance in heaven. But unless God sanctify it by His Spirit, it becomes an insupportable burden, a subject of murmuring, and an occasion of sin r.

Luke xvi. 19. *There was a certain rich man, which was clothed in purple and fine linen, and fared sumptuously every day, &c.*

For a man then to be rich, to be clothed magnificently, to fare sumptuously, and to take no care of the poor, is sufficient to send him to hell: because he cannot lead a Christian life. Repentance, mortification, and the Cross, are utterly inconsistent with a soft, sensual, voluptuous

---

q Norris's Christian Prudence, p. 300.   r [From Quesnel, *in loc.*]

life; the desire of happiness, with the love of this present life[s].

It is therefore a most miserable state, for a man to have every thing according to his desire, and quietly to enjoy the pleasures of life. There needs no more to expose him to eternal misery[t].

John xii. 25. *He that loveth his life shall lose it; and he that hateth his life in this world shall keep it unto life eternal.*

He that loveth life (that is, is fond of it) for the sake of the pleasures, advantages, it affords, will soon lose the love of heavenly things; the love of God, of his soul, and of the duty he owes to them. He hates it, who does not value it in comparison of eternal life, which he hopes for. A Christian gives proof of this, by mortifying himself; a pastor, in spending his life in the works of the ministry, &c.

Those whom God loves in order to an happy eternity, He weans from the pleasures of this present life.

Temperance consists in a sober use of all earthly, visible things, and in confining ourselves within the compass of what is necessary.

With God all things are possible.

The Almighty God enable me to conquer the temptations of riches, and to get above the allurements of this present life.

There is much more reason for a man to humble himself, on account of his self-denial, than to boast of it, since the corruption of his nature is so great, that he cannot follow even the lawful dictates of nature, without hazarding his soul. [i. 108.]

Christian self-denial is, to resist and crucify in ourselves the spirit and inclinations of Adam,—the flesh, its affections and lusts;—to die to our passions, in order to follow the motions of the Spirit.

Humility. Far be from me that pride which would not have me impute to myself the faults and unfruitfulness of my ministry. [i. 109.]

Fasting. Necessary to bring our hearts to a penitent, holy, and devout temper. [i. 110.]

---

[s] [Quesnel, *in loc.*]   [t] [Id. on St. Luke xvi. 25.]

WEDNES-
DAY.

Our Church requires this, and appoints days, and times, &c.; and it has been the honour of this Church, that she hath kept up to her rules, when others have shamefully neglected them.

Fasting necessary to perform the vows that are upon us all.

By *fasting*, by *alms*, and by *prayers*, we dedicate our *bodies*, *goods*, and *souls*, to God in a particular manner.

[i. 192; ii. 40; iii. 124.]

Covetousness. Ash-Wednesday. Matthew iv. 9, 10. *All these things will I give Thee. Get thee hence, Satan, for it is written, Thou shalt worship the Lord thy God, and Him only shalt thou serve.*

Great and[u] glorious God, who alone art worthy of our love and service, cure me of, and preserve me from, the sin and vanity of admiring this world.

Give me grace to renounce all covetous desires, all [v]love of riches and pleasures; to desire only what is necessary, and to be content with what Thou, O Lord, thinkest so;—

Not to be [w]troubled at the loss [x]or want of any thing besides Thy favour;—

That no business, no pleasures, may divert me from the thoughts of the world to come;—

That I may cheerfully part with all these things when Thou requirest it of me;—

And that I may ever[y] be prepared to do so, dispose me to a temperance in all things, and to lay up my treasure in heaven[z], for Jesus Christ's sake. Amen.

[ii. 40; iii. 125.]

1 Tim. vi. 9. *They that will be rich, fall into temptation and a snare, and into many foolish and hurtful lusts, which drown men in destruction and perdition: but thou, O man of God, flee these things.*

St. Mark [Luke] viii. 14. *That which fell among thorns are they, which when they have heard go forth, and are choked with cares, and riches, and pleasures of this world, and bring no fruit to perfection.*

[u] ii. om. "great and."
[v] ii. iii. add, "inordinate."
[w] ii. iii. add, "too much."
[x] ii. iii. om. "or want."

[y] ii. iii. "always."
[z] ii. iii. add, "to which place the God of mercy bring me."

SACRA PRIVATA. 157

St. Luke x. 23. *How hardly shall they that have riches enter into the kingdom of heaven.* WEDNES-DAY.
[ii. 43; iii. 125.]

St. Luke xii. 20. *Thou fool, this night shall thy soul be required of thee, then whose shall those things be which thou hast provided?*

St. Luke xvi. 25. *Remember that thou in thy lifetime receivedst thy good things.*

Remember Lot's wife: i. e. look not on the poor transitory things of this world, when your soul is at stake.

2 Tim. vi. 7. *We brought nothing into this world, and it is certain we shall carry nothing out.*

Foxes have holes and the birds of the air have nests, but the Son of Man has not where to lay His head. Which[a] poor estate being matter of choice in [b] our Lord, it ought to convince us of what little account the goods of this world are [c] in comparison of the blessings of heaven, and another world.

[ii. 44; iii. 126.]

St. Luke xxii. 35. *When I sent you without purse, and scrip, and shoes, lacked ye any thing? They said, Nothing.*

[ii. 43; iii. 126.]

Nemo militans Deo implicat se negotiis sæcularibus[d].

It will be convenient[e],

1. To discharge one's retirements of all worldly business. 2. To talk of it abroad as little as may be. 3. Not to be solicitous for many [f] worldly conveniences, nor [g] delighted with them. 4. To give reasonable orders, and to leave them to their success. 5. Not to be afflicted[h] too much with disappointments, for even these are from God.

Terram calcare didici, non adorare[i].

It is better, and safer too, to be a favourite of heaven, than to be the darling creature of the greatest man on earth.

[ii. 44.]

Vid. S. Cypr. *de Simplicitate Prælatorum,* [i. e. *de Unitate Ecclesiæ*[k]].

"Certum itaque est, eminentiam episcopalem non in eo sitam, prædia possidere multa, splendere auro," &c. Vid. *Parænesis ad Eccl. Anglican.* § 73, 74.

---

[a] ii. " This."
[b] ii. " Christ."
[c] ii. adds, " to be esteemed."
[d] ii. iii. add, " Funcius, his epitaph," [vid. p. 144.]
[e] ii. adds, " therefore."
[f] ii. om. " worldly."
[g] ii. adds, " to be."
[h] ii. " afflicted at disappointments."
[i] [ii. 67 repeats this, adding,] "Clem. Alex." [Protrept. ad Gentes, c. iv. § 56. γῆν δὲ ἐγὼ πατεῖν, οὐ προσκυνεῖν μεμελέτηκα.]
[k] [The reference may be to the first section: " Neque enim persecutio sola metuenda est," &c.]

**WEDNES-
DAY.**
[iii. 127.]

World. Deliver me from the love of creatures, lest they steal my heart from Thee, my God: whom I desire to love with all my heart.

O Jesu, take full possession of my soul.

[i. 192.]

Luke vi. 24. *Woe unto you that are rich, for ye have received your consolation.*

A man must have but little faith, who can read these words, and yet love riches, and the pleasures they afford.

Lord, grant that I may resist every temptation to the love of creatures; lest they steal my heart from Thee, my God, whom I desire to love with all my soul.

I know that I must renounce all other objects of my affection, in order to love Thee with all my heart. Lord, give me grace and strength to put this in practice.

1 John ii. 15. *Love not the world, nor the things that are in the world; if any man love the world, the love of the Father is not in him.*

Grant, O Lord, that I may never hope to reconcile two things so inconsistent as the love of Thee and the world.

Matthew v. 3. To be *poor in spirit*, is to be disengaged from wealth; to use it as a poor man; to look upon it as a burden, or as a trust.

1 Timothy vi. 8. *Having food and raiment, let us be therewith content.*

And yet even the Christian world is not content without superfluities and excess. These disorders are not less criminal because so common.

2 Peter ii. 15. *Following the way of Balaam.*

Nothing is more to be dreaded by a minister of God than covetousness; when a man has his heart upon his own interests, he easily forgets those of his Great Master.

Give me, O Lord, the eyes of faith, that I may see the world just as it is; the vanity of its promises, the folly of its pleasures, the unprofitableness of its rewards, the multitude of its snares, and the dangers of its temptations.

[i. 194;
iii. 133.]

Lent. Ash-Wednesday. Retirement. The primitive bishops had places of retirement near their cities, that they might separate themselves from the world; lest teaching others [1]their

---

[1] iii. om. "their duty."

duty, they should forget ᵐtheir own; lest they should lose the spirit of piety themselves while they were endeavouring to fix it in others.

Prosper, O God, the good thoughts, the good purposes, ⁿthe good resolutions, which Thou Thyself shalt inspire, ᵒthis day.

§ 1. I acknowledge Thy goodness, which has raised me above my brethren, and ᵖhas appointed me to be *a Successor of Thy Apostles.*

ᑫMay I ever act agreeably to this character: may I never profane a character so holy and so divine: lest God should pour down His vengeance upon my ungrateful head.

Pardon me, ʳgracious Lord, whereinsoever I have been wanting ˢto my duty to Thee and to Thy Church, and give me grace to be more careful for the time to come. Amen.

§ 2. How am I bound to adore Thy ᵗgreat goodness, my Lord and Master! Thou hast set me in office amongst the chief of Thy servants: ᵘO that for Thy sake I may make myself ˣa servant to the meanest of Thy servants.

By ʸus Thou ᶻteachest Thy people the truth; by our hands Thou adoptest Thy children in baptism; feedest them with Thy body; ᵃcommunicatest Thy graces; comfortest them in affliction; armest them against the fear of death; and fittest them for a blessed eternity.

O that ᵇwe may ᵇthoroughly weigh the sanctity of ᵇour calling, and faithfully discharge it! ᶜThat others may weigh and value it, and bless Thee for so great a blessing. Amen.

§ 3. I am appointed to sanctify others: ᵈLord, grant that I may first sanctify myself; that I may separate myself from this world, its profits, pleasures, honours, and all its idols.

Let my zealᵉ be answerable to the account ᵉI must give; let me not see Thy laws broken, hear Thy Name blasphemed,

---

ᵐ iii. "themselves."
ⁿ om. this clause.
ᵒ om. "this day."
ᵖ om. "has"—"to be."
ᑫ add, "O."
ʳ om. this clause.
ˢ "in the sacred duties of my calling."
ᵗ "goodness, my great Master."
ᵘ "but I will for Thy sake make."
ˣ "the servant of."
ʸ "me...my."
ᶻ "communicatest Thy grace in the Sacraments—by me Thou teachest," &c.
ᵃ om. this clause.
ᵇ "I...truly...my."
ᶜ add "O," om. "and value."
ᵈ "O."
ᵉ add, "O my Lord and Master"..."which I must one day give."

<small>WEDNES-DAY.</small>

Thy word despised, Thine ordinances set at nought, with patience, ᶠor a sinful silence.

Let me remember what was once said by Christ Himself to a Christian bishop: *Because thou art neither cold nor hot, I will spue thee out of My mouth.* (Rev. iii. 16.) ᵍHe that is indifferent for God, no wonder if God is sick of him.

<small>[i. 193; iii. 132.]</small>

ʰO Lord, inspire me with such a firmness of mind, that I may fear no man when Thy honour and my duty call me: that no worldly considerations may ⁱdiscourage me when my office obliges me to stand in the gapᵏ.

§ 4. Give me such holy dispositions of soul, whenever I approach Thine altar, ˡin some measure proportionable to the holiness of the work I am about:—Of presenting the prayers of the faithful; of offering a spiritual sacrifice to God; in order to ᵐcommunicate the true bread of God to all His members.

Give me the same intentions that Jesus Christ had when He instituted this Sacrament. To acknowledge the mercies of God, to satisfy His justice, and to pay the debt that is due from a creature to his Creator. None can do this effectually but Jesus Christ. Him therefore, and His merits, I present to God in this Sacrament.

iii. gives this paragraph as follows:—

"Give me, when I commemorate the same sacrifice which Jesus Christ once offered, give me the same intentions that He had,—To satisfy the justice of God,—to acknowledge His mercies,—and to pay all the debt which a creature owes to his Creator. None can do this effectually but Jesus Christ. Him therefore we present to God, in this holy Sacrament. O Thou, who hast made me a servant in Thy house, give me such dispositions, as that I may never dishonour Thy service. Amen."

§ 5. I am a sinner, and yet I am appointed to offer up prayers for othersⁿ. To me the Church ᵒof Christ, His

---

ᶠ om. this clause.
ᵍ om. this sentence.
ʰ "Inspire my heart with such holy resolution and courage...not fear any man."
ⁱ "hinder."
ᵏ add "Amen."

ˡ "as may...be."
ᵐ "convey the body and blood of Christ, the true bread of life."
ⁿ add, "'Tis to (sic) the great God to whom I offer these prayers."
ᵒ "the spouse of Christ."

spouse, entrusts her *desires*, her *interests*, her ᵖ*wants*, and her *thanks*. ᑫMay I never betray so great a trust, nor obstruct the mercies of God by a formal service. ʳBut let me speak from God, of God, and to God: with *attention*, with *fear*, with *love*, with *respect*, with *purity of heart*, and with *unpolluted lips*. Amen.

WEDNESDAY.

§ 6. The office of a shepherd of souls is full of difficulty. Consider what ˢJesus Christ underwent; what reproaches, what contempt, ᵗwhat pains, what despite, and from those ᵘvery persons to whom He preached the most concerning truths! and last of all laying down His life for His sheep. I am astonished and ˣashamed when I consider how ʸfar I come short of this pattern,—how poor my pains have been, how little of my time, ᶻmy devotion, my care, my thoughts, ᵃhas been spent in this service.

O ᵇgreat Shepherd and Bishop of souls, communicate to me the meanest of Thy ᶜservants such a degree of ᵈgrace and concern as may ᵉqualify me for this great work. ᶠPardon my negligence, and lay not to my charge the evils that may have happened thereby. Amen.

§ 7. Transcribe the example of your great Master; the patience and compassion with which He treated sinners: and then, if any of your flock are perverse, you will bear with them, and strive to reduce them even against their will.

But alas! this has not been my way. How impatient have I been when any of my flock have not been bettered by my endeavours! and this, I fear, from self-love, (not from the love of God and of souls,) as if my labours should not be in vain. And yet how often has God spoken to myself, and I regarded it not!

O Jesu, impart to me a portion of that spirit of meekness,

ᵖ " necessities."
ᑫ " What a trust is this! O may I never betray it—may I never obstruct Thy mercies to Thy Church by," &c.
ʳ " Let me ever speak to God, and from God: with attention, with love, with respect, with fear, with," &c.
ˢ add " toil."
ᵗ om. " what pains."
ᵘ om. " very."
ˣ add " greatly."
ʸ add " very."
ᶻ om. this clause.
ᵃ " have."
ᵇ " chief shepherd, and bishop."
ᶜ " herdsmen."
ᵈ om. " grace and."
ᵉ add " thoroughly."
ᶠ " And pardon my past," &c.

WEDNES-DAY.

which prevailed with Thee to preach to a people who regarded Thee not, who rejected, who crucified Thee.

[iii. 134 reads], § 7. Consider the patience of your Great Master; with what compassion He treated sinners. Transcribe His example; and if any of your flock are perverse, froward, obstinate—bear with them—condescend to their weakness, and strive to reduce them even against their wills.

But has this been my way?—very far from it. I have been impatient when any of my flock have not been bettered by my care and pains. And this, not from a true zeal for the glory of God, and good of souls, but too often, alas! from a principle of *self-love;* angry because I have been so conceited as to think *my* labours should not be in vain.

And yet how often has God spoke to me myself, and I regarded it not? How long was His grace ineffectual even [to] myself!

O Jesu, impart to me a portion of that spirit of meekness which prevailed with Thee to preach to a people who regarded Thee not,—who despised, who crucified Thee. Then why should I, who am a sinner, complain of my unfruitful labours?

Forgive, gracious God, the faults I have committed in this great work of the ministry; and let no unworthiness in me hinder Thy blessings from descending upon the souls committed to my care. Amen.

§ 8. A watchman who saith, Peace, peace, when there is none; who gives the children's bread to dogs, and administers the sacrament of reconciliation to the impenitent: what account has he to give? Lord, keep Thy servant from this sin. Amen.

[iii. 135 reads], § 8. Reflect seriously what a dreadful account you have to give, if you say *Peace, peace, when there is no peace;* or if you give the children's bread to dogs, i.e. admit to the holy table those that are unworthy of such a favour. This would be to lay men asleep in their sin. Lord, preserve Thy servant from this sin. Amen.

§ 9. *I have given you an example, that ye should do as I have done.*

O Saviour! that I could say this to my flock! that I could say, " Be ye serious and devout, as ye see me so: do ye forgive, as ye see me ready to forgive: despise the world; set your affections on things above, as ye," &c.

I am not only answerable for my own personal offences, but for any ill example I give others.

Lord, suffer me not to follow mine own will, but give me light to see, and grace to amend where I have done amiss. Amen.

[iii. 135 reads (after the text)],

O Lord, that I could say this to the flock over which the Holy Ghost hath made me *overseer*. That I could say, "Be ye devout, as ye see me devout. Do ye forgive one another, as ye see me ready to forgive. Despise the world, &c., as ye see me do it."

Let me seriously consider that I am not only answerable for my own personal offences;—I sin every time I cause others to sin by my example.

What reparation can be made, what answer can be given, when Christ requires our flock at our hand?

Lord, suffer me not to follow my own will. Reform me, that I may reform others. Give me light to discover, and grace to amend, where I have done amiss.

§ 10. Let your conversation be such as [g]becometh, not only the Gospel, but ministers of the Gospel; to whom all that is *curious, useless, light* and *vain*, is forbidden: [h]foolish talking, &c.

Have it always in your thoughts[i] to leave some impression of piety, something that is holy, useful, or edifying, upon the minds of such with whom you converse. Jesus Christ did do so always[k]. O Lord, that I had followed Thy example! God be merciful unto me!

§ 11. I am only a *steward*, not a *proprietor*, of the *revenues of the Church*. If motives of pride, or vanity, or covetousness, govern me in disposing of them, I should be as criminal as those laymen who sacrilegiously invade them. And it is

---

[g] iii. "becomes."
[h] "all scurrilous language, idle stories," &c.
[i] "endeavour to leave some impression of piety upon the minds of those," &c.
[k] iii. inserts, "Make no distinction betwixt the rich and the poor, as to converse with one and not with the other;"—and goes on, "Lord, that Thy example may ever be before me; and my conversation holy, useful, and edifying."

WEDNES-
DAY.

probable that the wrong use the clergy made of them encouraged the laity to do the same.

O my blessed Master, who hast given me much more of this world's goods than Thou tookest Thyself; grant that I may apply the goods of the Church to Thy glory, and to the support of Thy poor members: and in mercy pardon all my vain expenses. Amen.

[iii. 136], § 11. As to the disposal of the *Church's revenues:* the suggestions of avarice, of vanity, of pleasure, and of the world, ought not to govern me. I am only a steward, not a proprietor; and should be as criminal as those laymen that invade them, if I convert them to lay and secular uses: which sin of sacrilege, very probably, took its rise from others observing the Church's revenues put to secular uses. Grant, O my Lord, who hast given me much more of this world's goods than Thou tookest Thyself,—grant that I may apply the goods of Thy Church to Thy glory, and the support of Thy poor members. And pardon all my vain expenses. Amen.

[i. 196;
iii. 136.]

§ 12. *He,* and especially the minister, *that hath not the spirit of Christ, is none of His.* He ought to perform all ¹duties in the name of Christ; by His authority and power; and offer all to God through Him. ᵐHe ought to adore Jesus Christ as *preaching, praying,* ⁿ*blessing, absolving, comforting*° His people, by you His minister.

ᵖGrant, Lord, that I may direct all my labours to Thy glory; ᑫand that I may so live and speak, that my words and actions may be worthy of Thee, and that Thou mayest call them Thine. Amen.

§ 13. *The Priest's lips should keep knowledge.* Whence this knowledge but from Scriptures? but then these are not to be understood without the light of God's Spirit, and a knowledge of the maladies men are subject to, in order to apply them safely. If men read the Scriptures as *judges,* not as *disciples,* the consequence will be error, heresy, &c.

Grant, O God, that when I read Thy Word I may do it

---

¹ "his duties in Christ's Name."
ᵐ om. "he ought to."
ⁿ om. "blessing."
° "comforting, &c. by you."

ᵖ " Lord, that I may set Thee ever before me—that I may direct," &c.
ᑫ " Let me so speak and so live."

with a spirit crucified to the world, to [r]*curiosity*, to vanity, to interest, and to prejudices.

Cure me, [s]O great Physician of souls, that I may be able to relieve the maladies of my flock, and that [t]they may be presented to Thee both sound and lovely. Amen.

[iii. reads],..." Scriptures? which alone make us sound in doctrine, and able to convince gainsayers.

But even these are not to be understood without the light of God's Spirit, a diligent reading of them, and a knowledge of the maladies men are subject to, in order to apply them wisely and safely.

Men read the Gospel as judges rather than as disciples, which is the rise of all errors both in life and doctrine.

Grant, O Lord, &c."

§ 14. *Covetousness* is idolatry in every man, but it is abominable in a minister of Jesus Christ,—who [u]affected *poverty* rather than *wealth*,—who lived upon charity, and [x]expressly forbid His disciples superfluities, when He sent them to preach the Gospel.

He that takes care of the fowls of the air, will [y]not fail to provide for His own Ministers. [z]May I, O Lord, depend upon Thy word, and that no spirit of infidelity may ever possess my soul. Amen.

§ 15. *Purity of soul and body* is so necessary in a minister of Jesus Christ, that it must be the most provoking sin to offer the prayers of the faithful with polluted lips,—to break the bread of life with unclean hands, &c. *Blessed are the pure in heart, &c.* Lord God, keep Thy servant from such presumptuous sins. Amen.

[iii. 137.] *Purity* of soul and body is a most necessary qualification in a Minister of Jesus Christ. To offer the prayers of the faithful to God with polluted lips—to break the bread of life with unclean hands—to receive the bread into a soul defiled with unchaste thoughts—how dreadfully provoking must it needs be.

---

[r] add " my" before these nouns.
[s] " O blessed Physician, first, and then teach me to know and relieve."
[t] " I may present them sound and lovely in Thy sight."
[u] add " ever."
[x] om. " expressly."
[y] " never."
[z] " 'Tis therefore infidelity to be over careful for this world. God grant that I may ever depend upon the providence of God."

WEDNES-DAY.

A blindness of spirit—an alienation from divine things—an incapacity to receive them—are the necessary effects of impurity.

The natural man receiveth not the things of the Spirit.—"Into a malicious soul wisdom, &c.—The pure in heart, for they shall see God."

§ 16. A Priest, who in the exercise of his [a]ministry has an eye to [b]grandeur, repute, esteem of the great, &c., worldly advantages, &c., [c]greatly perverts the design of the ministry.

O Lord, grant that I may regard nothing [d]so much as Thy glory, that I may act and live for Thee alone. That my [e]love to Thee, and for the good of souls, may be the [f]commanding principle of my life. Amen.

[iii. 138.] Who will value himself upon ecclesiastical dignities, who considers that Judas was chosen to be an apostle? Dignities and benefices, without a life answerable, are only a curse.

[i. 198.] *Fasting.* St. Mark ix. 29. *This kind can come forth by nothing but by prayer and fasting.* These a minister of God must make use of, in converting sinners, as ever he hopes to succeed.

Those who are by God, or His Church, put into the hands of the executioner, for their crimes or contumacy, have need of very powerful solicitations to obtain their pardon. These are, prayer and fasting.

Jesus Christ spared not His innocent flesh, but fasted: the sinner cherisheth his continually, refusing it nothing.

Fasting is in some sense a punishment and expiation for past sins, a remedy for present temptations, and a preservative against future.

Psalm cii. 4. *My heart is smitten, and withered like grass, so that I forget to eat my bread.*

The humble and afflicted soul is not much concerned to please the appetite.

Luke vi. 25. *Woe unto you that are full, for ye shall hunger.* That is, ye whose daily meals are feasts, who make

---

[a] "function."
[b] "the grandeur, repute, esteem of great men, presumptuous authority over the conscience of others, worldly," &c.
[c] om. "greatly."
[d] "nothing but."
[e] "zeal for Thy glory."
[f] "chief motive of all my actions."

profession of a life of sensuality, who know not what it is to fast, even when the Church requires it :—Woe to such Christians!

Blessed are they that mourn. O that I may be as deeply concerned for the glory of God and for the dishonour done to Him and His laws, as Thou, O Jesus, wast, when on earth, for Thy own people! I should then mourn day and night for the evils we commit daily, and for the judgments we have reason to fear; and for the dishonour [done] to God by the people committed to my [charge]. *Blessed are the poor in spirit.*

Judge yourselves, that ye be not judged. If we judge ourselves with severity, *we* shall be judged with mercy. [i. 199.]

Temptation. We are exposed to temptation all our days. Men are never more dangerously tempted, than when they think themselves secure from temptation. This is a proof of the power the devil has over them.

We tempt God when we expose ourselves unnecessarily to dangers, through a false confidence of His assistance.

THURSDAY.

CHURCH DISCIPLINE.

Q.—Will you maintain and set forward, as much as in you lieth, quietness, love, and peace, among all men; and such as be unquiet, disobedient, and criminous, within your diocese, correct and punish, according to such authority as you have by God's word, and as to you shall be committed by the [a]ordinance of this realm[b]?

A.—I will so do by the help of God.

O GOD of peace and love, make me, Thy minister[c], a messenger and instrument of peace to this people to whom I am sent; that by Thy gracious assistance, I may root out all strife and variance, hatred and malice, and that this Church and nation may enjoy a blessed tranquillity.

[d]Bless the discipline of this Church in my hands, and make it effectual for the conviction of wicked men and gainsayers.

Assist me, by Thy good Spirit, that I may apply a proper cure to every disorder; that I may reprove with mildness, censure with equity, and punish with compassion.

O merciful God, who wouldest not the death of a sinner, but that he should be converted and live, bring into the right way all such as are gone astray from Thy commandments.

Vouchsafe unto all penitents (*and especially unto all such as are now under the censures of the Church*) a true sense of their crimes, true repentance for them, and Thy gracious

---

[a] ii. "laws of your country."

[b] MS. i. adds, "see p. 117," i.e. according to the numbering here used, 132. "This can never be looked upon as any limitation of the power received from Christ, but only as directing the exercise thereof, as to the manner, form, and circumstance."

[c] "servant," ii.

[d] ii. adds, "O Lord and Master."

pardon, that their souls may be saved in the day of the Lord Jesus. [e]Amen.

Church Discipline. "However the Church be, in some respects, incorporated with the commonwealth in a Christian state, yet its fundamental rights remain distinct from it. Of which this is one of the chief: to receive into, and to exclude out of the Church, such persons which, according to the laws of the[f] Christian society, are fit to be taken in or shut out[g]."

And when[h] temporal laws interpose, it is temporal punishment only which they design to [i]inflict, or set aside.

Ezek. ii. 6. *And thou, son of man, be not afraid of them, neither be afraid of their words; thou shalt speak My words unto them, whether they will hear, or whether they will forbear.*

2 Cor. xiii. 10. *Lest I should use sharpness, according to the power* (namely, of binding and loosing) *which God hath given me, to edification, and not to destruction*[j].

THURSDAY.
[i. 116; iii. 149.]

---

[e] iii. adds, "for Jesus' sake."
[f] iii. "a."
[g] Bishop Stillingfleet, Answ. to N. O., p. 267. ["The New Way of answering examined in a reply to two late Pamphlets," &c., 1672. N. O., the author of the second of the two pamphlets, was Abr. Woodhead, sometime Fellow of Univ. Coll. Oxford; and the pamphlet is "Dr. Stillingfleet's principles, giving an account of the faith of Protestants, considered," 1671.]
[h] "where," iii.
[i] "set aside or suspend," iii.
[j] ii. 49, has "*the power...destruction*," om. the parenthesis: and goes on as follows:—
"The Bishops excommunicating sinners are interpreters of the will of God, and do only separate them from the Communion whom God hath already condemned; for if they do it unjustly their sentence will not be confirmed." The Author of the Book attributed to Dionysius the Areopagite. [De Ecclesiast. Hierarch. c. vii. § 7. τὰς ἀφοριστικὰς ἔχουσιν οἱ ἱεράρχαι δυνάμεις, οὐκ ὡς ταῖς αὐτῶν ἀλόγοις ὁρμαῖς τῆς πανσόφου θεαρχίας (εὐφήμως εἰπεῖν) ὑπηρετικῶς ἑπομένης, ἀλλ' ὡς αὐτῶν ὑποφητικῶς ὑποκινοῦντι τῷ τελεταρχικῷ Πνεύματι τοὺς κεκριμένους Θεῷ κατ' ἀξίαν ἀφοριζόντων.]
See an Epistle of Pet. Damienus [Damianus], Ep. 12. to Pope Alex. II. about the danger of inconsiderate excommunication.

"Præterea duo quædam apud Apostolicam sedem frequens usus obtinuit, quæ si sancta prudentia vestra judicat, ut nobis videtur, omnino digna sunt corrigi. Unum, quia cunctis fere Decretalibus paginis anathema subjungitur; alterum, quia cujuslibet Ecclesiæ filius, sive clericus sit, sive laicus, exponere proprii excessus Antistitis prohibetur; quorum primum quam sit humanæ salutis immane periculum, et infinite patens vorago labentium, ac pernicies animorum, clementiæ vestræ pietas non ignorat. Dicitur enim, quisquis hæc vel illa non fecerit; sive certe quisquis hoc, quod superius statutum est, irritum duxerit, vel in aliquo violaverit; anathema sit. Ubi notandum quam lubrica, quam præceps subito ruendi illic procuretur occasio, ut ante quis in æternæ mortis barathrum corruat, quam se vel leviter impegisse cognoscat: et substratæ quodammodo tendiculæ jam pes ejus innectitur, dum se liberis adhuc incedere gressibus arbitratur. Delinquit itaque quisquis ille est, in illud Apostolicæ constitutionis edictum, et aliquando levi quadam, ac perexigua offensione transgreditur: et continuo velut hæreticus, et tamquam cunctis criminibus teneatur obnoxius, anathematis sententia condemnatur. Et cum, dictante justitia, alia sit ultione plectendus, qui plus delinquit, alia qui minus excedit: hic graviter, leviterque peccantibus æqua cunctis, et indifferens pœna solius sci-

THURSDAY.
[i. 117; iii. 146.]

1 Tim. i. 20. *Whom I have delivered unto Satan, that,* &c.

"O admirable use and command of Satan! He is God's enemy, and yet does Him service; and an adversary to man, and yet helps to save him. He is the author of blasphemy, and yet teacheth not to blaspheme; that is, one that is stronger than he directs his malice to ends which he did not intend. Satan is set on work to take him down by terror and despair, whom before he had tempted to sin. But while Satan thinks to drive him to destruction by despair, God stops his course when the sinner is sufficiently humbled: and then, as it was with Christ, Satan is dismissed, and angels come and minister unto him[k].''

licet anathematis, irrogatur. Non tribunalium more, vel forensis examinis, aut libertas ceditur aut possessio confiscatur, nec pecuniariæ mulctæ reus adducitur, sed Deo potius, omnium scilicet bonorum auctore, privatur. Hanc itaque homo de homine pœnam sumit, quam de sui transgressione mandati ipse quoque Deus omnipotens non præsumit. *Qui amat,* inquit, *patrem, aut matrem plusquam me,* non continuo addidit, sit anathematizatus vel maledictus, sed tantum ait, *non est me dignus.* Et in lege, *Oculus pro oculo, Dens pro dente, percussura pro percussura, adustio pro adustione,* duntaxat exigitur, nec continuo qui reus est de synagoga projicitur, vel maledictione damnatur. Non enim secundum Stoicos, omnia peccata sunt paria, atque idcirco indifferenti sunt ultione plectenda, sed juxta modum culpæ temperanda semper est mensura vindictæ. Porro nec beatus papa Gregorius, vel ceteri patres, qui diversis temporibus in Apostolicæ sedis regimine floruerunt, hunc morem in suis reperiuntur observasse Decretis, et vix eorum aliquando statutis anathema subnectitur, nisi cum Catholicæ fidei clausula terminatur. Quamobrem si sanctæ prudentiæ vestræ placet, hunc morem de cetero a Decretalibus paganis amoveri præcipiat, et vel damni pecuniæ vel alterius cujuslibet ultionis calculum in earum transgressione præfigit; ne, quod aliis est ad tuitionis munimenta provisum, aliis ad perniciem proveniat animarum.

Petri Damiani Opp. ed. Bassan. 1783, tom. i. coll. 12, 13.

The opposition and discouragements I meet with in discharge of this part of my office ought by no means to discourage me. I should be apt to be too proud of my own performances and authority, if all these things succeeded according to *my* will: therefore it is in mercy that I am sometimes opposed.

"Quomodo potest Præses Ecclesiæ auferre malum de medio ejus, qui in delicto simili corruerat [corruerit]? aut qua libertate corripere peccantem potest, cum tacitus sibi ipsi respondeat, eadem admisisse quæ corripit?" St. Jerom. on Tit. [i. 6.]

[k] Rouse, p. 188. [The passage stands thus: "O admirable use and command of Satan! He is an enemy to God, yet doth Him service; he is an adversary to man, and yet helps him. A strange thing it is, that Satan should help the incestuous Corinthian, to the destruction of his flesh and the edification of his soul. A strange thing that Satan should teach Hymenæus and Alexander not to blaspheme. His kingdom is seated in the flesh, and yet the flesh he destroys. He is the author of blasphemy, and yet he teacheth not to blaspheme. But is Satan contrary to himself, and is his kingdom divided in itself? No, surely. But One that is stronger than he, both in wisdom and power, manageth both his craft and malice to ends which himself intendeth not. The devil is one and the same still, even purely malicious. And in this malice he tempts men being in high blood into a presumption of sinning. And by the same malice, he tempts the same men, being cast down, into a despair of mercy. Now as remedies are by contraries, so a measure of despair is medicinable to a measure of presumption. And just so

"Disciplina Ecclesiæ debet esse proportionata regno Christi, quod totum est spirituale. Ergo probra, proscriptiones, mulctæ pecuniariæ, carceres, cippi, (supplicia quæ sunt civilis speciei pœnæ) non sunt arma militiæ nostræ;— sed commonefactio, confusio, terror, tandemque judicio Divino, executorique hujus Satanæ, traditio." Vid. *Parœn. ad Eccl. Ang.* § 44, 46, 47.

"*Quos diligo*, inquit Dominus (Apoc. iii. 19) *redarguo et castigo*: sic oportet et Dei sacerdotem non obsequis decipientibus fallere, sed remediis salutaribus providere." St. Cypr. *de Lapsis.* [edit. Fell, Oxon. p. 128.]

"Contra evangelii vigorem, contra Domini et Dei legem, temeritate quorundam laxatur incautis communicatio; irrita et falsa pax, periculosa dantibus, et nihil accipientibus profutura." *ibid.* . . . .

"Et quod non statim Domini Corpus inquinatis manibus accipiat, aut ore polluto sanguinem Domini bibat, sacerdotibus sacrilegus irascitur. Irasceris ei qui abs te avertere iram Dei nititur,...qui pro te misericordiam Domini deprecatur, qui vulnus tuum sentit, quod ipse non sentio, qui pro te lacrymas fundit." *ibid.* [p. 131.]

"Quam multi quotidie pœnitentiam non agentes, nec delicti sui conscientiam confitentes, immundis spiritibus adimplentur! quam multi usque ad insaniam mentis excordes dementiæ furore quatiuntur." *ibid.* [p. 133.]

"Confiteantur singuli...delictum suum, dum adhuc qui deliquit in sæculo est; dum admitti confessio ejus potest; dum satisfactio et remissio facta per sacerdotes apud Dominum grata est." *ibid.* [p. 134.]

"Pacem in antecessum datam intuitu pœnitentiæ secuturæ rem esse ab institutis veteris Ecclesiæ prorsus abhorrentem,

---

far doth God suffer Satan to go on in his temptation, as temptation is profitable, and no farther. Therefore, while Satan is driving the offender to despair, God stops his course when the sinner is come to due humiliation. And then as it was with Christ in the wilderness, so it is with the humbled sinner; Satan is dismissed, and angels come and minister to him."

Treatises and Meditations by Francis Rous, Esq., London, 1657, pp. 188, 9.

Lord Clarendon, Hist. of Reb. iii. 648, (Oxf. 1819), says, "They" (Barebones' Parliament) "made choice of one *Rouse* to be their Speaker, an old gentleman of Devonshire, who had been a member of the former parliament, and in that time preferred and made Provost of the College of Eton, which office he then enjoyed, with an opinion of having some knowledge in the Latin and Greek tongues, but of a very mean understanding, but thoroughly engaged in the guilt of the times." Cf. Antony Wood, Ath. Oxon., t. ii. n. 159.]

THURSDAY. et non nisi post Caroli Magni tempora in usu receptam." *ibid.* [Bp. Fell's note] in verb. " Dom. satisfacere[k]."

"Pacem sibi ultro, nemine dante, sumpserunt." *ibid.* p.127.

"Justis operibus incumbe, [incumbere] quibus peccata purgantur; eleemosynis frequenter insistito, [insistere] quibus a morte animæ liberentur." *ibid.* p. 138.

"What great man shall we now find, who will not take it ill to be reproved? And yet David, a prince and favourite of God, when he was reproved even by a subject, did not turn away in a rage, but confessed his fault, and repented truly of his sin[1]."

[i. 118; iii. 149.]
[i. 119; iii. 147.]

The same God who has given princes the government of the world, has given bishops the government of the Church.

"The very office of consecration, so often confirmed by act of parliament, does warrant every bishop, in the clearest and most express terms, to claim authority, by the Word of God, [m]to exercise all manner of spiritual discipline within his own diocese[n]."

[iii. 147.]

And yet it must be acknowledged that the external administration of discipline in established courts and forms, &c., is in subordination to the royal supremacy. *ibid.*

[i. 119; iii. 147.]

Gen. xviii. 21. *I will go down and see.* " [Ipse quippe ut nos a præcipitata sententiæ prolatione compesceret, cum omnia nuda et aperta sint oculis ejus, mala tamen Sodomæ noluit audita judicare:...ut gravitatis nobis exemplum proponat, ne mala hominum ante præsumamus credere, quam probare." This is the correct reading. MS. i. reads], "Cum omnia nuda et aperta sunt, [sint, iii.] mala tamen Sodomæ noluit ante judicare quam probare; nos instruere, ne mala hominum ante præsumeremus credere, quam probare." Greg. in loc. [iii. reads, " Hom. xvii. in Evang." The true place is, Moral. xix. in Job. § 46. Cf. Epist. vii. 14.]

"Judicare magno cum pondere, ut apud certos de Dei conspectu[o]. Tert. [Apol. § 39.]"

---

[k] [MS. i. reads, "res est ab institutis veteris Ecclesiæ prorsus abhorrens."]

[1] St. Ambrose, Apolog. David, [§ 5. "Quem mihi nunc facile reperias honoratum ac divitem, qui si arguatur alicujus culpæ reus, non moleste ferat? At ille regio clarus imperio, tot divinis probatus oraculis, cum a privato homine corriperetur,... non indignatus infremuit, sed confessus ingemuit culpæ dolore."]

[m] iii. " for the exercise of."

[n] [Gibson,] Codex Jur. Eccl. Angl., p. 18.

[o] i. om. this sentence.

[THURSDAY]

[p]Men should be [q]persuaded, not forced, to forsake their sins; because God rewards not those who[r] through necessity [s]forsake their sins, but [t]such as do so voluntarily[u].

[v]Be steady and fearless in the discharge of [x]duty, without failing in that respect which is due to higher powers. [i. 119; iii. 148.]

Grant, O [y]Lord, that I may have an eye to duty only, that I may fear no temporal[z] evil, and be concerned only lest I should not, in all respects, [a]please Thee, my God.

St. Matt. xviii. 17. *If he neglect to hear the Church, let him be unto thee* (and consequently unto the whole Church) *as an heathen man and a publican.* [i. 119.]

That is, let him be reduced into the state of infidels, as he was before baptism. Which may be done by a judicial authority, which God declares He will ratify. So that there is the same authority for excommunication as for baptism: and if one is a real privilege, the other is a real punishment. 'Tis indeed a sentence passed by men, but by men commissioned by God Himself, i.e. by the Holy Ghost.

See St. Matt. xviii. 17, and my notes upon it. [iii. 149]

Deut. i. 17. *The judgment is God's.* [i. 119; iii. 149.]

As this should oblige all people to be afraid of a [b]judgment or censure passed by men commissioned by God, so it should make us very[c] careful [d]that our judgment be such as is worthy of God, and agreeable to His will and word.

If we expect assistance from the civil power to back our censures, then that power has a right to judge of the reasonableness of what is desired, and how far it is consistent with public good. As to the spiritual power, *that* the magistrate has nothing to do with: it is part of the ministry of the Church, and it would be persecution to obstruct it. [iii. 149.]

Our duty is to watch, as well as to preach and administer the sacraments. The same God who has given princes the

---

[p] iii. adds, " St. Chrysostom says that."
[q] iii. adds, " only."
[r] iii. " that upon."
[s] iii. " abstain from evil."
[t] iii. " only those that do it."
[u] Chrysostom. [iii. adds, "περὶ ἱερωσ. lib. ii." t. vi. p. 9, 10. ed. Savile; οὐ βιαζόμενον, ἀλλὰ πείθοντα δεῖ ποιεῖν ἀμείνω... οὐ τοὺς ἀνάγκῃ τῆς κακίας, ἀλλὰ τοὺς προαιρέσει ταύτης ἀπεχομένους στεφανοῦντος τοῦ Θεοῦ.]
[v] iii. adds, " Be sure to."
[x] iii. adds, "your."
[y] iii. adds, " my."
[z] iii. om. " temporal."
[a] iii. " discharge that duty."
[b] iii. " our censures, so."
[c] iii. " very very."
[d] iii. " what judgment we pass, that it be agreeable to God's word and will."

THURSDAY. government of the world, has given bishops the government of the Church.

[i. 119.] 1 Cor. xvi. 22. *If any man love not the Lord Jesus Christ, let him be Anathema Maranatha.*

Here is a positive direction to the Church to excommunicate all such as plainly discover that they have no love for Jesus Christ, who are scandalous or profane.

^eSince we are to give^f an account of the souls committed to our charge, we cannot be debarred of^g making use ^hof all the means enjoined us by the Gospel to reduce sinners.

The civil magistrate has a right to do what he judges necessary to secure theⁱ society over which he is set. If he mistakes in doing this, and prosecutes his own ^jwill, he is answerable to God^k. All that we have to do is to submit with patience, this not being the world we were made for.

[i. 120; iii. 149.] We ought^l to be thankful for the favours we have received from religious princes; but if our benefactors require of us what is inconsistent with our trust, we then know whom we are to obey.

[i. 120.] 2 John 10, 11. *If there come any unto you, and bring not this doctrine, receive him not into your house, neither bid him God speed; for he that biddeth him God speed, is partaker of his evil deeds.*

Not to shew our abhorrence of sin, is to consent to it. Men do not sufficiently consider the guilt of this, when they converse with notorious offenders without scruple. They partake with them in their sins; they harden the sinner; they forget the fidelity they owe to God and to His laws; and greatly hazard their own salvation.

[iii. 149.] N.B. The primitive Christians were not allowed to salute any one that was excommunicated. Capitul. Carol. Magni, lib. v. ch. 42. ["Nec ejus munera quisquam accipere debet, vel osculum porrigere, nec in oratione se jungere, nec salutare." fol. Francof. 1613.]

[i. 120; iii. 150.] *Excommunication* never pronounced except where the case

---

^e iii. "If."
^f iii. "render."
^g iii. om. "of."
^h iii. "of all enjoined us to reduce sinners," &c.

ⁱ iii. adds "civil;" om. "over ... set."
^j iii. "wilful humour."
^k iii. "but we are to submit," &c.
^l iii. "are very."

was desperate, by the obstinacy of the party in refusing ad- THURSDAY.
monition, ᵐ and to submit to disciplineⁿ.

Clinics. Of dealing with them, see Penit. Discipl. 104, 211, [77, 78; 152, 3]; App. p. 14, 40, [194, 219, &c.]: and Concil. Carthag. iv. can. 78. ["Pœnitentes, qui in infirmitate viaticum Eucharistiæ acceperint, non se credant absolutos sine manus impositione, si supervixerint." Harduin. i. 983.]

St. Luke xv. 2. *The Scribes and the Pharisees murmured,* [i. 120.] *saying, This man receiveth sinners, and eateth with them.*

On some occasions, we ought to avoid sinners; for fear of being corrupted; or to put them to shame, in order to their conversionº. But to converse with them as our Lord did, in order to teach them their duty, to encourage them in the way of piety, &c., this is godlike.

Mark viii. 33. *Get thee behind Me, Satan; thou savourest not the things that be of God, but the things that be of men.*

How dangerous is tenderness in matters of salvation! To spare a penitent, is to ruin him by a fatal kindnessᵖ.

How perilous is the government of the Church, wherein a man becomes guilty of those things which he does not hinder. Rev. ii. 20. *I have a few things against thee, because thou sufferedst that woman Jezebel to teach and to seduce my servants, &c.*

2 Cor. x. 4. *For the weapons of our warfare are not carnal, but mighty through God, to the pulling down of strong holds.*

We surely mistake the spirit of the Gospel, when we would establish and defend the Church by human policy and carnal means, by friendship of great men, credit, reputation, splendour, riches, &c.

God will have us to use other sort of arms; namely, [i. 121.] patience, humility, meekness, prayer, suffering, and spiritual censures, to which God will join His own almighty power.

No human laws can deprive the Church of the power of admitting persons into her communion, and of shutting them out of it. Mr. Nelson, *Christian Sacrifice,* 89 ۹.

ᵐ iii. om. "and...discipline."
ⁿ [Marshall's] Penit. Disc., p. 41, 42, 75, 120. [in Anglo-Cath. Lib., pp. 32, 33, 48, 87.]
º [Quesnel, *in loc.*]
ᵖ [Ibid.]
۹ [The Editor has been unable to verify this.]

THURSDAY. All mankind are agreed, that human legislators can only dispense and make laws in cases purely human.

There is a public absolution which is no more than a relaxation of a censure. There is no relation betwixt that and the absolution of sins.

We derive no spiritual jurisdiction from the crown. We hold our benefices from the crown, but our offices from Christ. Bp. Bramhall, [*Just Vindication*, &c., c. ix. §. v. n. 4. t. i. 272. Anglo-Cath. ed.]

God ratifies in heaven the judgments of His ministers upon earth, when they judge by the rules prescribed by His word and His Church.

Whenever Church discipline meets with discountenance, impieties of all kinds are sure to get head and abound. And impieties unpunished, do always draw down judgments.

The experience of this made princes, &c.

The same Jesus Christ who appointed baptism for the receiving of men into His Church and family, has appointed excommunication to shut such out as are judged unworthy to continue in it. St. Matt. xviii. 15, &c.

When once an offender's crimes come before the Church, and he refuses to be reformed by that, let him no longer be looked upon as a member of that society, but as an heathen. And Christ will ratify whatever sentence the Church passes.

So that if baptism be a blessing, excommunication is a real punishment. And if men ridicule it, they do it at the peril of their souls.

In short; this authority is necessary, if it is necessary to preserve the honour of religion. It is appointed by Jesus Christ. The ends proposed by it are, to reform wicked men, and to remove scandals. If the sentence is duly executed, the offender is really deprived of the ordinary means of salvation.

If it is erroneously passed, yet it is not to be despised without great sin, because it is passed by men commissioned by Christ.

The authority of Christ is to be respected in the meanest of His ministers.

[i. 122.] *Excommunication*, the most dreadful punishment which a Christian can suffer, becomes less feared than it ought to be, through the countenance which excommunicated persons meet with, contrary to the express command of God, *With such a one no not to eat.* [2 Thess. iii. 6.]

A true penitent will be willing to bear the shame of his sins (where he has given offence) before men, that he may escape the confusion of them hereafter. But then he ought to know, that to submit to the outward part of penance, is not to submit to God, unless it proceed from the fear and love of God.

A man may see his sin, confess it, abhor it, and yet be a false penitent. Judas did all this. What he wanted was the grace of God, to see the mercy of God, as well as His justice.

Those who are the first to lead men into sinful courses, seldom trouble themselves to recover them out of them. The ministers of Christ must do it, or they must die in their sin.

Mark v. 40. *And they laughed Him to scorn.*

O my Lord and Master! let me not be driven from my duty, by the infidelity and scoffs of the world.

How desperate soever the condition of a sinner may appear, we must neither insult over it, nor despair of his conversion.

A person who has offended and scandalised others by his sins, ought, before he be admitted to the peace of the Church and to receive sacraments, to give some good assurance, by a sober life, that he is a true penitent.

Mark vi. 11. *Shake off the dust, &c.*

Jesus Christ permits not His apostles to avenge themselves by their apostolical power, nor even to desire that He should do it; but to leave their cause to God, with full confidence in Him[r].

Luke xix. 8. *And if I have taken any thing from any man by false accusation, I restore him fourfold.*

The judgment which of his own accord this penitent passes upon himself, will condemn those who reject all the remedies offered, and all methods made use of for their conversion, and who will not make the least atonement for their crimes[s].

Men shew very plainly that they love sin, when they will [i. 123.] not suffer any one to put a stop to it, to remove the occasions

[r] Quesnel. [s] Quesnel.

THURSDAY. thereof, and to shame, to reprove, and to punish the sinner. This is a sin which draws after it great judgments.

If a pastor hopes to do his duty without reproving the world, (without testifying that *the works thereof are evil*[t],) or to reprove it without being hated by it, he will deceive himself; he may carry it fair with men, but will be condemned by Jesus Christ.

John viii. 7. *He that is without sin among you, let him first cast a stone at her.*

They whose duty it is to punish offenders, should take great care not to be influenced by pride, hypocrisy, passion, false zeal, or malice; but to punish with reluctancy, with compassion, as having a sense of their own misery and weakness, which perhaps render them more guilty in the sight of God[u].

Let ecclesiastical judges always remember, that the Holy Ghost, to whom it belongs to bind and loose, never makes Himself the minister of the passions of men.

John xii. 43. *They loved the praise of men more than the glory of God.*

And this is the cause that men count it more shameful to acknowledge their crimes than it was to be guilty of them.

We must never insult a sinner; but without extenuating his sin, we must comfort him, by shewing him the good which God may bring out of it.

Acts viii. 3. *As for Saul, he made havoc of the Church, &c.*

The designs of God towards Saul should teach us not to despair of any man's conversion, but to pray for it, and to use our best endeavours, &c., instead of being angry, and using them ill[v].

Acts ix. 9. *And Saul was three days without sight, and neither did eat nor drink.*

Jesus Christ Himself, in this instance, teaches His ministers not to be hasty in receiving penitents, but to let them fast and pray, and bear the sense of their sin, and of their bad condition, before they be reconciled. It teaches penitents to fast and pray, and to bear with patience the fruit of their own doings[w].

[t] John vii. 7.
[u] [Quesnel.]
[v] [Quesnel.]
[w] [Quesnel.]

Acts xix. 18. *Many that believed came, and confessed their deeds, &c.*

The Spirit of Grace always inclines men to *confess* their evil deeds, and humble themselves for their sins. There could not be a more shameful one than dealing with the devil, &c., yet this did not hinder them,—or from sacrificing the most valuable things that had been instruments in their wickedness. This is a proof of a true conversion, &c.[x]

The fall of others is for us a great instruction, and a lesson which we ought to study, not in order to insult our neighbour, but to fear for and amend ourselves.

Let us not despise any sinner; God has sometimes very great designs in relation to those who are at present most opposite to Him.

To reprove, when persons are not in a proper disposition for amendment, would be to give both them and ourselves trouble without any prospect of advantage.

To make reproof beneficial, they to whom it is given should see that it does not proceed from humour, or from a design to vex them, but from a true zeal and love for their souls.

A true charity will never insult those that are gone astray, but will use the greatest sinners mildly, lest they should be driven to despair by too great severity.

The Church forgives sins in the person of Christ[y]. She remits the temporal punishments of them also, because Christ is the sovereign High-priest, and because it belongs to God alone to recede from the strictness of His justice, in what manner He thinks fit.

An ecclesiastical governor should endeavour to preserve discipline, and the esteem of his people at the same time, by acts of tenderness, &c.

2 Cor. x. 8. *For though I should boast of my authority, (which the Lord hath given us for edification and not for destruction,) I should not be ashamed.*

It is necessary, sometimes, to extol the dignity of our office.

N.B. Pastors are appointed by Christ for to edify the Church; they must therefore be honoured and obeyed.

[x] [Ibid.]   [y] 2 Cor. ii. 10.

Thursday. The disorders which a good pastor observes in his flock will always be matter of humiliation to him, because he will always impute them to himself.

A pastor, a priest, who does not with tears and supplications bewail the sins of his people, cannot call himself their mediator with God.

It is the greatest comfort of a good pastor to find himself obliged to use nothing but good advice, and the mild part only of his authority; but when that will not do, &c. He must use sharpness; but still with this view, that it be for their edification, not for their destruction.

[i. 125.] It seldom happens that great men, whether clergy or laity, reform their lives, because they seldom meet with persons of courage to oppose them or to tell them of their faults. A bishop who is not restrained by any earthly engagements, will not spare any man whose conduct is prejudicial to the faith.

Gal. v. 12. *I would they were even cut off which trouble you.*

To wish shame, or some temporal evil, for the salvation of my neighbour's soul, is not contrary to charity. It seems, matters were come to a great height of evil, when St. Paul was forced to wish that to be done, which he did not in prudence think fit to do.

Ecclus. viii. 5. *Reproach not a man that turneth from sin, but remember that we are all worthy of punishment.*

2 Thess. iii. 6. *Now we command you,* (and the same authority subsists still in the governors of the Church,) *in the name of our Lord Jesus Christ, that ye withdraw yourselves from every brother that walketh disorderly.*

Nothing is there which the faithful ought more carefully to avoid, than disorderly livers [living?]; nothing which pastors ought more earnestly to warn their flocks of.

May I ever observe the rules of a holy and charitable severity.

2 Thess. iii. 14. *And if any man obey not our word, note that man, and have no company with him, that he may be ashamed; yet count him not as an enemy, but admonish as a brother.*

Excommunication is only for the contumacious, not to *insult,* but to *cure.*

1 Tim. v. 19. *Against an elder receive not an accusation,* THURSDAY *but before two or three witnesses.*

A pastor ought not lightly to be exposed to the revenge of those whom it is probable he has or shall have occasion to reprove.

1 Tim. v. 20. *Them that sin rebuke before all, that others also may fear.*

That is, who sin grievously, and are convinced before two or three witnesses; let such be censured before, or by the consent of all the congregation.

2 Tim. ii. 25. *In meekness instructing* (reproving) *those that oppose themselves, if God peradventure will give them repentance, &c.*

When we consider that repentance is the gift of God, that the wiles of the devil are many, and corruption of nature very strong, we shall compassionate instead of insulting a sinner.

We shall adore the mercy of God towards ourselves, and hope for it for others. We shall fear for ourselves, and pray [i. 126.] for them. They may recover, and be saved: we may fall, and be lost for ever.

When men will not take care of their own salvation, the Church owes this care to her children, to hinder them as much as possible from ruining others.

If excommunication is perpetual, it is caused by the obstinacy of the offender, not by the laws of Christ or His Church; which only deprive wicked men of the benefit of communion for a time, to bring them to a sense of their duty.

"*If any man come unworthily,*—though he be a general, or lieutenant,—nay, though he wears the imperial diadem, stop him: you have more power than he in this respect. If you dare not do it yourself," (speaking to the priest,) "leave him to me: I will not permit such things to be done...I would rather spend my own blood than profuse [profane?] such tremendous Blood against right and reason." St. Chrys. Homil. in Matt. [lxxxii. p. 789, C. ed. Bened. κἂν στρατηγός τις ᾖ, κἂν ὕπαρχος, κἂν αὐτὸς ὁ τὸ διάδημα περικείμενος, ἀναξίως δε, προσίῃ, κώλυσον· μείζονα ἐκείνου τὴν ἐξουσίαν ἔχεις . . . . εἰ δὲ αὐτὸς οὐ τολμᾷς, ἐμοὶ πρόσαγε· οὐ συγχω-

THURSDAY. ῥήσω ταῦτα τολμᾶσθαι . . . . τὸ αἷμα τὸ ἐμαυτοῦ προήσομαι πρότερον, ἢ μεταδώσω αἵματος οὕτω φρικώδους παρὰ τὸ προσῆκον.]

Church discipline is for the *honour of God*, for the *safety of religion*, the *good of sinners*, and for *the public weal;* that Christians may not run headlong to ruin without being made sensible of their danger; that others may see, and fear, and not go on presumptuously in their evil ways; that the house of God may not become a den of thieves: and that judgments may not be poured down upon the whole community. *Did not Achan commit a trespass, and wrath fell on all the congregation*[v]*?*

The most effectual way of answering these ends is, to exercise a strict, impartial discipline. First, to withhold from Christians the benefit of the holy Sacrament, till they behave themselves so as to be worthy of so great a blessing. And, secondly, if they continue obstinate, (all proper methods being used to reclaim them,) to excommunicate them; and to oblige all sober Christians not to hold familiar conversation with them.

But first of all, Christians should be made sensible of what blessings they are deprived, when they are debarred the Communion: even the greatest on earth; without which they can have no hopes of salvation, but must perish eternally. St. John vi. 53.

[i. 127.] He that understands and believes this, will submit to any hardships, rather than incur, rather than continue under a sentence so full of terror: and a sentence passed by one commissioned by God, and bound, at the peril of his soul, to pass it; it being the greatest indignity to Christ and the divine ordinance, to prostitute the Body and Blood of Christ to notorious evil livers.

God has therefore lodged a power in the pastors of His Church to repel all such; and it is a mercy even to them to be hindered from increasing their guilt and their damnation.

Nor can any prince, governor, nor human law, hinder a Christian bishop from exercising this power, because he is under an obligation to the King of kings, and Lord of lords, to do his duty in this respect.

[v] Joshua xxii. 20.

THURSDAY.

Nor must it be pretended, that the punishment which Christian magistrates inflict may supersede this discipline.

Those punishments only affect the body, and keep the outward man in order. These are designed to purify the soul, and to save that from destruction.

Excommunication being, as St. Paul tells us, *for the destruction of the flesh, that the soul may be saved;* that is, to mortify the corruptions of nature,—*lust, pride, intemperance,* &c.; this being the only way to save the soul of the sinner, and to bring him to reason; that is, to repentance.

For upon a sinner's repentance, (unless where he has incurred this sentence more than once,) the Church is ready to receive him into her bosom with open arms.

But then by repentance must be understood, *not a bare change of mind*, not an acknowledgment of the sin and scandal, not a serious behaviour for a few days; all which may soon wear off; but a course of public penance, a long trial of sincerity, such as may satisfy a man's self, and all sober Christians, that the sinner is a true penitent; that he has forsaken all his evil ways, evil companies, evil habits; that he is grown habitually serious, devout, and religious; and that by fasting and prayer he has in some good measure got the mastery of his corrupt nature, and has begun a repentance not to be repented of.

For want of this care and method, many Christians are [i. 128.] ruined eternally. They sin, and repent, and sin again, and think all is safe, because they have repented, as they think, and are pardoned.

There are people who are in the same sad case with those that stand excommunicate, though no sentence has passed upon them; namely, such as live in a contempt of the public worship of God. They cannot properly be turned out of the Church, who never come into it; but they keep themselves out of the ark, and consequently *must* perish.

Excommunication, in the primitive times, was pronounced in the congregation to which the offender belonged. After which, they gave notice to all other Churches; namely, "Let no temple of God be open to him; let none converse with him;" &c.[x]

[x] [Synesius ap. Bingham, Eccl. Antiq. xvi. ii. 8.]

THURSDAY. 2 Samuel xii. 13, 14. *And David said unto Nathan, I have sinned against the Lord. And Nathan said, The Lord also hath put away thy sin; thou shalt not die. Howbeit, because by this deed thou hast given occasion to the enemies of the Lord to blaspheme, &c.*

The Divine Justice punisheth every sin, either in this world or the next.

A sinner's willingness to undergo any punishment which shall be appointed by the minister of God, in order to make proof of and to establish his repentance, is a sure sign that God has not withdrawn His grace, notwithstanding his sin.

[Hebrews xiii. 4.] *Whoremongers and adulterers God will judge.*

You dare not say that this is not true. What can you say to your own mind to make it easy? Nothing but this *can* make you easy; to take shame to yourself, to confess your sin, to fast, and to pray earnestly to God for pardon, &c., and to let others know *what an evil thing and bitter it is to forsake the Lord.*

This visitation will either do you much good or much hurt; you will from this time grow much better or much worse.

Since you did not blush to sin, do not blush to own your faults.

Let it be matter of joy and thankfulness to you, that we are concerned for you so much.

Grace, indeed, we cannot give; that is the gift of God. We can only pray for you, and do our duty in admonishing you, &c.

[i. 129.] If you submit for fear only, and not for conscience' sake, you will suffer both here and hereafter.

Where excommunication or Church censures are ridiculed, the most damnable sins become the subject of mirth, rather than of sorrow and shame: a sure symptom of approaching judgments.

When men, and especially men in any authority, are not content to neglect their own salvation, but are industrious to ruin others, they may depend upon it, they are very near filling up the measure of their iniquities, and consequently THURSDAY. their destruction is not far off.

Our charity to offenders ought to be like that of God, not in flattering them by a cruel indulgence, but in putting them, by a merciful severity, in the way of obtaining pardon.

In the primitive Church, great offenders were not restored to communion till they had, by their behaviour, given all possible demonstrations of the sincerity of their repentance not to be repented of; and this by a long trial of mortification, &c.

For a short repentance too seldom ends in amendment of life; and he who fancies that his mind may effectually be changed in a short time, will deceive himself and the Church, unless he shews this change by fasting, alms-deed, retirement, &c., and that for a considerable time.

Will any man say that he loves Christ, and His Church, when he opposes the authority of her pastors; when he opposes her discipline; or when he weakens her unity?

When we consider, that God is absolute Master of men's hearts, we should not think any man incapable of salvation.

My God! let me always fear for myself, when I am labouring to promote the salvation of others.

Common fame. St. Paul (1 Cor. v. 1.) proceeded to censure persons upon common fame. *It is reported,* saith he, *that there is fornication, &c.,* which is sure a good and a safe example to follow.

The lesser excommunication is in order to prevent the greater.

Remissness in Church discipline is owing, sometimes, to indulgence and an easy temper, not caring to trouble others, or be troubled; sometimes by being satisfied to go on in the track trodden by their predecessors, not considering what [i. 130.] duty obliges them to, but what was done before; others, out of downright neglect, not caring how things go, give opportunity to the enemy to sow tares while they are thus asleep. Thus corruption gets head, and is like to do so, until God

THURSDAY. awakens the governors both in Church and State, and makes them see, that they are answerable for all the sins occasioned by their negligence; and that they have more souls besides their own to account for; which is one day to fall heavy upon them.

Lord, awaken all that are in power; and me, Thy unworthy servant; that we may all discharge our duty more faithfully.

There may be people bold enough to make a mock of sin, to submit to public penance with contempt of the authority that enjoins it, and not to be bettered by such Christian methods for the restoring sinners to the peace of God; but it is to be hoped all are not so hardened; and that Christian discipline is, notwithstanding, a mighty check upon sin, and keeps many under a fear of committing such crimes as must oblige them to take shame to themselves before the face of men.

"Qui habere possunt (viz. excommunicationem) moderate ea utantur; et caveant a rigore: quia ob infirmitatem humanam, eventusque dubios, medicina est, ut valde dolorifica, sic admodum periculosa." Paræus on 1 Cor. vi. 5. [rather on cap. v. ad fin. p. 281. Francofurti, 1609.]

Convocation, 1536. [in Bp. Lloyd's "Formularies of Faith in the reign of Henry VIII.," p. 8.] That " perfect penance which Christ requireth, consists of contrition, confession, and amendment of former life, and an obedient reconciliation to the laws and will of God." See also the Homilies [of Repentance, p. 590, 92, 95, 97, ed. 1833].

Absolution. "Our Church ascribeth not the power of remission of sin to any but to God only. She holds, that faith and repentance are the necessary conditions of receiving this blessing. And she asserts, what is most true, that Christ's ministers have a special commission, which other believers have not, authoritatively to declare this absolution, for the comfort of true penitents; and which absolution, if duly dispensed, will have a real effect from the promise of Christ. John xx. 23[y]."

[y] Puller, Moderation [of the Church of England, c. xi. n. 5. § 4. p. 318, ed. 1679.]

Authority of the Church is only *spiritual* and *ministerial*, THURSDAY. (the Head and Author being in heaven). She does not, therefore, call her orders *laws*, but *rules, canons;* and her inflictions, not *punishments*, but *censures*. She acknowledges, that whatever power she has besides spiritual, is either from the favour or injunctions of princes. But (Article 37) we give not our princes (and they have always disclaimed it) the power of administering God's word or the sacraments. And although our spiritual power be from God, yet is this power subject to be inhibited, limited, regulated, in the *outward* [i. 131.] *exercises*, by the laws and customs of the land. By this moderation both powers are preserved *entire* and *distinct*. We neither claim a power of jurisdiction over the prince, nor pretend to be exempt from his.

Ante-nuptial Fornication. Those who enter into marriage only to conceal their shame ought to give public satisfaction, as well as expiate their sin by open penance.

The greatest care ought to be taken concerning the sincerity of penitents; till that be done, penance will only be a form without a power, or any real benefit.

In the primitive Church, every thing was done with advice, because their great aim was to have reason and the will of God prevail. A despotic power was forbid by Christ Himself: *It shall not be so among you.* He that is humble and charitable will take the mildest and surest way, and will not be troubled, provided the end be obtained.

Penance. Sin is the disease of the soul. Diseases are not to be cured in a moment; it will take time to root out their causes, and to prevent their effects; so will it require time to prove the sincerity of our resolutions. We solemnly profess that we repent, and we are not sure but that we lie to God.

Discipline. As discipline slackened, men's manners grew more and more corrupt, even in the primitive times. There were never more infidels converted (saith Fleury[z]) than when catechumens were most strictly examined, and baptized Christians put to open penance for their sins.

They that are for making still more concessions to human

---

[z] [Hist. Eccl. t. viii. Disc. sur l'Histoire des 6 Premières Siècles, §§ 8. p. 22 ed. 1740.]

THURSDAY. frailty, will at last set aside the Christian religion, which is established upon maxims of eternal truth, and not on human policy; and instead of gaining or securing the bad, they will lose the better sort.

A flattering physician is for giving palliating medicines, to ease the pain, without taking away the cause; which will occasion relapses, until at last they destroy the patient. But a good man will prescribe what he believes necessary to remove the cause, though uneasy to his patient, and will have nothing to do with such as will not submit to the necessary methods of cure.

Penances, in the primitive Church, were never granted but unto such as desired them, and such as desired to be converted. None were forced; but such as would not submit were excommunicated.

Discipline impracticable. This cannot be, when it was practised for so many years in the primitive Church. And what if it be one of those things which Christ hath commanded His followers to observe so strictly, (Matt. xxviii. 19, 20,) and which He had learned of the Father? (John xv. 15; xvi. 13.) The commands of Christ cannot be impracticable. That would be to tax Him with ignorance or weakness. When He promised to be with His Church to the end of the world, He engaged to give such graces as were necessary to raise us above our natural weaknesses.

[i. 132.]

Penances forced are seldom lasting.

The priest, under the law, could not accept the offering of a leper, nor allow him to partake of the sacrifice, till he had received convincing tokens of his cleanness; no more ought the Christian priest to treat sinners as cured, till he sees the proof[a].

Con. Afric. [Code of African Church], can. 29. [Harduin, i. 879.] "If any excommunicate presumes to go to the Lord's table, let him be judged to have pronounced the sentence of damnation upon himself."

Matt. xvi. 19. *Whatsoever thou shalt bind on earth, &c.* Those ministers that know not what it is to bind and loose sinners, reject one half of their commission.

Excommunication is the last remedy, reserved for the in-

---

[a] Quesnel, [on St. Matt. viii. 4.]

corrigible, in case of enormous sins. They who despise it, <u>Thursday.</u> know not what it is to be a heathen in God's sight,—to be without God for a Father, Christ for a Saviour, the Church for a mother, and Christians for brethren.

A true penitent is always willing to bear the shame and confusion of his sin and folly before men, that he may escape, &c.

Heb. xii. 15. *Looking diligently, lest any man fall from the grace of God; lest any root of bitterness springing up trouble you, and thereby many be defiled. Lest there be any fornicator, or profane person, as was Esau, &c.;* that is, such as for a short pleasure, forfeit their eternal inheritance.

Happy that sinner, whom God does not abandon to the hardness of his heart, but awakens him by His judgments, or the visitations of His grace.

Luke viii. 28. *I beseech thee, torment me not.* These were the words of the devil to our Lord, and these are his suggestions in the hearts of all sinners, wherever he has got possession. When a minister of Christ, by his sermons, rebukes, &c., or the Church by her discipline, attempts to disturb the sinner, they are looked upon as his mortal enemy; and they treat both the Church and her ministers worse than this legion did Jesus Christ. They despise their power, set at nought their persons, and threaten and persecute them for their good-will[b].

There is not any greater or more dreadful sign of the wrath of God, than when He abandons a sinner to his lusts, and permits him to find means of satisfying them.

The public good is the sole end of Church discipline. The interest of the governors of the Church is no way concerned in it, but only the advantage of their flock: that sinners may be converted; that contagion may be hindered from spreading; that every one may be kept to his duty, and in obedience to the laws of God; that judgments may be averted from the public; and that God in all things may be glorified; that differences among neighbours may be made up, and charity improved, &c.

Discipline (saith our Homily of the right use of the Church, part 2,) in the primitive Church was practised, not only upon

[b] Vid. Quesnel, [on St. Mark vii. 7.]

THURSDAY. mean persons, but upon the rich, the noble, and the mighty; and *such*, as St. Paul saith, *were even given to Satan for a time, &c.*

[i. 133.] Those that make a *mock*, a *sport*, a *jest* of sin, too plainly betray a love of wickedness in themselves.

Exemption. A legal exemption cannot free a man from guilt, beyond the extent of that power which grants the exemption. If it be a human power, it can extend no further than to exempt a man from human penalties, not from those that are purely spiritual.

Ecclus. viii. 5. *Reproach not a man that turneth from sin.*

They whom fear renders cowardly in the exercise of their ministry, forget that they act in the name and place of Christ, and are to account to Him for the mischief the Church receives thereby.

[i. 134; iii. 156.] Deut. i. 17. *Ye shall not be afraid of the face of man, for the judgment is God's.*

O righteous Judge of the world, give me and my substitutes grace, patiently to hear, and impartially to weigh, every cause that shall come before us in judgment.

Give us a spirit to discern, and courage to execute true judgment, that all our sentences may be ^capproved by Thee our Lord and Judge. Amen.

Deut. xxiv. 17. *Thou shalt not pervert the judgment of the stranger, nor of the fatherless*^d.

Isaiah i. 23. *Every one loveth gifts: they judge not the fatherless.* That is, ^ethey are poor, and cannot bribe them.

[iii. inserts], Jer. xxii. 3. *Thus saith the Lord, Execute ye judgment and righteousness, and deliver the spoiled out of the hand of the oppressor, and do no wrong, no violence, &c.*

Exod. xxiii. 2, 3. *Thou shalt not follow a multitude to do evil;...neither shalt thou speak in a cause, to decline after many, to wrest judgment. Neither shalt thou countenance a poor man in his cause*^f.

[iii. inserts], v. 8. *Thou shalt take no gift, for the gift blindeth the wise, and perverteth the word of the righteous.*

---

^c iii. "such as Thou shalt approve and confirm at the great day, to the glory of Thy Name, and the justification of Thy unworthy ministers; for Jesus Christ's sake. Amen."

^d iii. adds, " &c."

^e iii. adds, " because."

^f iii. adds, " Ps. lxxii. 2," &c.

Deut. xix. 15. *Thou shalt not respect the person of the poor, nor honour the person of the mighty; but in righteousness shalt thou judge thy neighbour.* THURSDAY.

[iii. inserts], Deut. xxvii. 19. *Cursed be he that perverteth the judgment of the fatherless, the stranger and widow, &c.... Amen.*

Prov. xxiv. 23. *It is not good to have respect of persons in judgment.*

The judgment of the multitude is[g] no rule of justice. *Then cried they all, Not this man, but Barabbas*[h]. [i. 134; iii. 157.]

John xix. 12. *If thou let this man go, thou art not Cæsar's friend:* when Pilate [i]heard that saying, [j]then he resolved to sacrifice his conscience, rather than [k]lose his prince's favour.

[iii. inserts], Exod. xviii. 21. *Thou shalt provide...able men, such as fear God, hating covetousness.*

2 Chron. xix. 6. *And he said unto the judges, Take heed what ye do: for ye judge not for man, but for the Lord, who is with you in the judgment.*

Prov. xvii. 13. *He that justifieth the wicked, and he that condemneth the just, even they both are an abomination to the Lord.*

John xix. 11. *Unless given thee from above.* But although the magistrate's authority is from God, yet [l]he is answerable to God for the due[m] execution of it.

Prov. xxi. 3. *To do justice and judgment is more acceptable to the Lord than sacrifice.* Ps. l. 8; Is. i. 11; Hos. vi. 6; Mich. vi. 7, 8.

The Jews had a rule, that if a rich man and a poor man had a controversy, they must both of them stand or sit, to avoid partiality. [i. 135.]

Virtue would hardly be distinguished from a kind of sensuality, if there were no labour, no opposition, no difficulty, in doing our duty. *Dulce est periculum sequi Deum.*

The duty of a judge may oblige him to punish according to the law; but it is the part of a Christian injured to forgive according to the charity of the Gospel.

---

[g] iii. om. "is."
[h] iii. adds, John xviii. [40.]
[i] iii. adds, "therefore."
[j] iii. reads, "&c., i. e. he resolved."
[k] iii. "displease his prince."
[l] iii. "the magistrate."
[m] iii. "undue."

THURSDAY. A judge is not the master but the minister of the law; for the public good, not for his own interest, passion, or will.

A good judge will never desire to make himself feared by his power; but will rather be afraid of abusing it.

The civil magistrate is liable to be excluded from Church communion for such reasons as the spiritual governors shall judge necessary; they are to determine for him, and not he for them, in matters merely spiritual.

Concerning the denying relapsers and great offenders, the Sacrament and absolution at the hour of death, &c., see Bingham, vol. viii. p. 276, and book xviii. c. 4. [n. 4.]

Give me, O Lord, the spirit of judgment[m], that I may govern this Church with wisdom.

Ecclus. iv. 9. *Be not faint-hearted when thou sittest in judgment.*

A lover of the law will always have an eye to the intent of the law[n].

Excommunication is a most dreadful punishment; but sin, of which this is the punishment and remedy, is sure more dreadful.

[iii. 151.] *Aspirations.* O God, who desirest not the death of a sinner, have mercy upon these Thy creatures which have forsaken Thee. Let not their iniquities obstruct Thy mercy. Convince them of the extreme danger of their sins. O Lord Jesus, who came [camest] into the world to save sinners, fill my heart with a great concern for every one of my flock; and especially for these that are gone astray.

[i. 202 ; ii. 50; iii. 152.]
Religious Discourse in Ordinary Conversation.
Foolish jesting, which is not convenient.

Ephes. iv. 29. *Let no corrupt communication proceed out of your mouth, but that which is good to the use of edifying, that it may minister grace unto the hearers.*

[o]Preserve me, O God, from a vain conversation. Give me grace never to be ashamed or afraid to speak of Thee, and of Thy law.

Give me a lively sense of the value of religion, and make it [p]the delight of my heart; that I may speak of it with great

---

[m] Isaiah xxviii. 6.
[n] Matt. xii. 3.
[o] ii. iii. "deliver."
[p] ii. iii. add, " I beseech Thee."

judgment, seriousness, and affection, and at all seasonable times. [THURSDAY.]

May that good Spirit, which appeared in the likeness of tongues of fire, warm my heart, direct my thoughts, and guide my tongue, and give a power to persuade; that by my conversation and example, as well as by my sermons qand writings, I may promote the kingdom and interests of my great Master r. Amen.

Malachi iii. 10. *Then they that feared the Lord spake often one to another.* [i. 202; iii. 152.]

Matt. xii. 34. *Out of the abundance of the heart the mouth speaketh.—How can ye, being evil, speak good things?—By thy words thou shalt be justified, and by thy words thou shalt be condemned.* [i. 202.]

We count words for nothing, and yet eternity depends upon them.

[Psalm cxli. 3.] *Set a guard, O Lord, upon my mouth, and keep the door of my lips.*

[Psalm xxxvii. 30.] *The mouth of the righteous seeketh wisdom, and his tongue talketh of judgment.*

It is strange that that which is every body's greatest concern should be nobody's discourse.

The want of religious discourse in common conversation, one of the chief causes of the decay of Christian piety.

Hearts truly touched with the love of God, will communicate their light and heat to others in their ordinary conversation,—will speak honourably of God, of His perfections, His justice, goodness, wisdom, and power; the excellency of His laws, the pleasantness of His service, the instances of His love; the rewards He has promised to His friends, and the punishments He has prepared for His enemies, &c.

And by doing so, we shall recommend God and religion to those that we converse with—win over subjects to Him, &c., and add to our own happiness. [i. 203.]

Matt. v. 16. *Let your light so shine before men;—that they may see your good works, and glorify your Father which is in heaven.*

Col. iv. 6. *Let your speech be always with grace, seasoned with salt, that ye may know how ye ought to answer every*

---

q ii. iii. om. "and writings." r ii. iii. add, "the Lord Jesus."

THURSDAY. *man.* One mild, prudent, and edifying conversation has often gained more souls than many sermons.

1 Thess. v. 11. *Wherefore comfort yourselves together, and edify one another.* These are two express duties of Christian conversation.

Heb. x. 24. *Let us consider one another, to provoke unto love, and to good works.*

The more spiritual our minds are, the more heavenly will our conversation be with those we discourse with.

We, of all men, should desire to talk, and to be talked to, in our own way, and of things relating to our own profession; and so we should, if our profession is [were] most at our heart.

Love is a talkative passion, and yet the divine lover is backward to talk of the very delight of his soul.

Ps. cxix. [46.] *I will speak of Thy testimonies even before kings, and will not be ashamed.*

Rules. Never talk of religion but when you think seriously of it. Not to betray the want of it by one's discourse of it, which should be *decent, grave, sober, prudent.*

That our discourse of religion be practical rather than notional, or disputing; that it be devout, edifying after a hearty and affectionate manner.

That it be seasonable; that is, when men are like to be the better for it. Not in promiscuous company; not mixed with sports, hurry, business, nor with drink. Nor to cast pearls before swine.

That we join a good life to our religious discourses; and never to contradict our tongue by our deeds.

Luke xxiv. 30. *As He sat at meat, He took bread, and blessed it, and brake, and gave to them, and their eyes were opened, &c.*

We may know religious persons, not only in the exercise of religious actions, but even in the most common actions of life, which they convert into holy actions, by the manner of doing them, the holiness of their dispositions, by prayer, &c.

We always do good or harm to others by the manner of our conversation; we either confirm them in sin, or awaken them to piety.

A minister of state talks of nothing but the interests of his prince—the way to make him be obeyed, beloved, &c., and how to make his subjects happy: and so should we, if the interests of our Lord and King were most at heart. THURSDAY. [i. 204.]

It is too true, that some evil passion or other, and to gratify our corruption, is the aim of most conversations. We love to speak of past troubles; hatred and ill-will make us take pleasure in relating the evil actions of our enemies. We compare, with some degrees of pride, the advantages we have over others. We recount, with too sensible a pleasure, the worldly happiness we enjoy. This strengthens our passions, and increases our corruption. God grant that I may watch against a weakness, which has so evil consequences.

Ecclus. iv. 23. *Refrain not to speak when there is an occasion to do good.*

It is an extraordinary talent to be able to improve conversation to the advantage of religion, by taking some fit occasion to say something that is edifying and beneficial.

The great subject of a Christian's discourse should be, about the true way of attaining the grace of God, through the blood of Christ, and by the assistance of the Holy Spirit. But then they must say no more than what they are sure of, lest they should lead men into error. For the Lord will not hold him guiltless that taketh His name in vain, and speaketh not the truth as it is in Jesus.

Let us take all opportunities of communicating our belief of Christ to others, both to bear witness and confess Him before men, and to increase our own faith and reward.

May I never hear, never repeat with pleasure, such things as may dishonour God, hurt my own character, or injure my neighbour.

Joel ii. 28, 29. *I will pour out My Spirit upon all flesh; and your sons and your daughters shall prophesy, &c.*

That is; their discourse shall be chiefly upon subjects of practical Christianity, of Jesus Christ, and what He has done and suffered for us, and of the way to attain eternal happiness.

See a little tract, "Meditations on Poverty," from p. 5 to p. 20.

THURSDAY.   Vid. Isaiah l. 4. [*The Lord God hath given me the tongue of the learned, that I should know how to speak* **a** *word in season to him that is weary.*]

[i. 205.]   James iv. 11. *Speak not evil one of another.*

True humility makes us see our own faults, without concerning ourselves with the faults of others.

Prov. xv. 23. *A word spoken in due season, how good is it!*

Charity. (1 Cor. xiii. 6.) *Rejoiceth not in iniquity.* May I never hear, &c. [as above.]

[i. 210.]   *Uncharitableness.* Envy makes us see what will serve to accuse others, and not perceive what may justify them.

St. Matt. xii. 3. [*Have ye not read what David did, &c.*]

A truly good man is always disposed to excuse what is evil in his brethren, as far as truth will suffer him.

Slander. Matt. xi. 19. *The Son of Man came eating and drinking, and they say, Behold a man gluttonous, &c.*

And shall I sinner fret and repine when, &c.

Whatever measures a good man takes, he will hardly escape the censures of the world; the best way is, not to be concerned at them.

It is an instance of humility silently to bear the calumnies which are raised against us, when they relate to ourselves only; but it is a duty of prudence and charity modestly to vindicate ourselves, when the honour of God and the Church are concerned.

St. Luke vii. 33, 34. Both Jesus Christ and John Baptist were slandered; who then will complain that they cannot satisfy the world, and stop men's mouths?

[iii. 158.]   Psalm cxx. 2. *Deliver my soul, O Lord, from lying lips, and from a deceitful tongue.*

Nov. 2, 1722. Mr. Stevenson informed me this day of a most malicious, false, and groundless story set about by ——, and propagated by ——. As, that when I was tutor to Lord Strange, about twenty-six years ago, * * * *:—pretending that Lord Strange told him so, twenty-five years ago. We immediately went to evening prayer, when, to my great comfort, the history of Susanna was the lesson appointed to be read; in which, viz. v. 42, 43, Susanna, *as I can truly do,* appealed to God in these words: *O everlasting God, who knowest secrets, Thou knowest that they have borne false wit-*

ness against me, whereas I never did such things as these men THURSDAY. *have maliciously invented against me.*

But although in this thing I am very much wronged, as Thou, O Lord, knowest, yet my very very many great and crying sins have deserved this and a much greater punishment.

I will therefore hold my peace, and not open my mouth, because it is Thy doing and my deserving.

Lord, give me true repentance for all the sins of my life past, and especially for those which may have been the occasion of this sad reproach.

The good Lord grant that the ministry may not be blamed, nor His Church suffer, while I receive the due reward of my sins.

And give me grace to look upon the authors of this wrong, as Thy servant David did on Shimei when he cursed him bitterly—as instruments in Thy hand for manifesting Thy glorious attributes of mercy and justice.

Lord, forgive them, for they know not what they do.

But, grant, O Lord, that I may know and acknowledge Thy voice in this dispensation, and that I may make the best use of this severe trial and treatment;—that my sins may be forgiven, and my pardon sealed in heaven, before I go from hence and be no more seen. For Jesus Christ's sake. Amen.

The use I purpose to make of this affliction, by God's grace:

Most seriously to *consider*, to *avoid*, and to *repent of*, the sin of detraction.

This great sin (for such St. Paul accounts it, and such all men account it when they themselves are sufferers) being against all the laws of the Gospel—justice, charity, peace,

[i. 136; ii. 52; iii. 164.]

FRIDAY.

ORDINATION.

Q.—Will you be faithful in ordaining, sending, or laying hands upon others?
A.—I will so be, by the help of God.

FRIDAY. [a] ALMIGHTY God, who knowest the hearts of men, govern my mind[b], that I may faithfully discharge this *great trust;* that neither through *fear, favour, interest,* or *negligence,* I may ever promote any person to the sacred charge of Christ's flock[c].

Bless all those[d] who have already given themselves to Thy immediate service, and labour with me in this [e]ministration; be *with* us, and *guide* us, and *help* us, for Thy *promise sake,* for *Thine honour's* sake, and for the *sake of Jesus Christ,* that we may teach well[f], and that we may be *examples* of all the *graces* and *virtues* which we recommend to others[g].

Direct [h] all such as are designed to serve at Thine altar; sanctify their *persons,* their *studies,* their *intentions,* and *affections*[i].

And grant[j] that no unworthiness in *me* may ever hinder *Thy gifts and graces* from descending upon those whom I shall ordain to Thy service. For Jesus Christ's sake. Amen[k].

Jer. iii. 15. *O Lord, give us pastors according to Thine own heart, which shall feed us with knowledge, &c.*

---

[a] [iii. inserts before the prayer some sentences from holy Scripture, and others, given hereafter.]

[b] ii. iii. add, "I most humbly beseech Thee."

[c] ii. iii. add, "That I may not be partaker of other men's sins, and that the blood of those that perish may not be required at my hands through any neglect of mine."

[d] ii. iii. add, "of my diocese."

[e] ii. iii., "great work of the ministry."

[f] ii. iii. add, "and that we may *live* well."

[g] ii. "Amen:" ending the Collect here.

[h] iii. adds, "and bless."

[i] iii. adds, "that they may be honoured for their piety, for their charity, for their zeal, and for their endowments."

[j] iii. adds, "O Lord."

[k] iii. subjoins here the references to the Canons, given below.

St. Luke vi. 12. *And it came to pass that in those days* FRIDAY. *He went into a mountain to pray, and continued all night in* [i. 136.] *prayer to God; and when it was day, He called unto Him His disciples, and out of them He chose twelve, whom also He named* Apostles: viz. that their very title might put them in mind of their *mission*[k].

Ministers being the officers of God's household, we must depend upon Him in the choice of them, and not upon human motives.

Acts xiii. 3. *And when they had fasted and prayed, and laid their hands on them, they sent them away.*

All Christians being concerned in this affair, all ought to fast and pray, in order to have faithful pastors[l].

Apostolical usages ought to be kept up to, as proceeding from Jesus Christ Himself.

2 Tim. ii. 2. *The things which thou hast heard of me among* [iii. 164.] *many witnesses, the same commit thou to faithful men, who shall be able to teach others also.*

Men should consider upon what principles and motives they enter into holy orders, and to what uses they design to employ their revenues.

Matt. ix. 38. *Pray ye the Lord of the harvest, that He* [i. 137.] *will send forth labourers into His harvest.*

[m]O gracious Lord, look down in mercy upon this Church, at this time. Provide it with faithful labourers, such as shall have a true compassion for the souls committed to their care, and a knowledge and zeal answerable to the account they are to give.

Grant that we may all preach *the truth as it is in Jesus*[n].

Give a blessing to our labours, that we may see the fruits of them in the repentance and conversion of ourselves and of all sinners that hear us.

Make us truly sensible, that when we labour for our flock, we labour for ourselves, and for Thy glory.

And pardon us, gracious God, whereinsoever we have been wanting in any part of our duty.

---

[k] iii. has the text alone.
[l] Quesnel.
[m] i. has here, in a later hand, and the pen drawn across it, "Give us, O Lord, pastors according to Thine own heart;"

iii. has the text only.
[n] i. adds, in a later hand, "and that knowledge and that learning which is after godliness."

FRIDAY.

Awaken, and touch all our hearts most powerfully from above, that we may not forget our ordination vows.

And for Jesus Christ's sake, grant that I may not be answerable for the sins, and the dreadful mischiefs that may follow, if not hindered by Thy grace. Amen.

The conversion of souls is Thine, O Lord, and not ours; prosper Thou Thine own work. It is not in us to save souls. Let us not sacrifice to our own net, but use the means, and ascribe all the glory to God; we of ourselves have nothing whereof to glory.

[i. 138; M.H. lxii.]

ⁿO blessed Lord and Master, let Thy tender regard for Thy Church make me everᵒ solicitous at the throne of grace, in behalf of thoseᵖ I send into Thy vineyard; andᵠ grant that no unworthiness in me may hinder Thy gifts and graces from descending uponʳ those whom I shall ordain to Thy service.

ˢFor the sake of this Church, which Thou hast purchased with Thy most precious blood, enable them for the work unto which they are called, that they may *teach* well, and that they may *live* well, and be *examples* of all the holy graces and virtues which they shall recommend to others.

Sanctify ᵗtheir personsᵘ and their labours, that they may be respected by their people: andᵛ, for Thy authority in them, be heard and obeyed, that they may be able to give a comfortable account at the great day. Amen.

John xxi. 15. *Jesus said unto Peter, Lovest thou Me?... Yea, Lord, Thou knowest that I love Thee... Feed My sheep.*

O Sovereign Pastor, who lovedst and gavest Thy life for us, make our love for Thee, and our care of Thy sheep, so great and sincere, that we may feed them constantly, and dili-

---

ⁿ i. repeats here the text, St. Luke vi. 12, and M. H. adds, " Matt. ix. 38."

ᵒ M. H., " O blessed Jesus, my great Lord and Master, whose example I desire to imitate as far as my frailty will suffer me; let Thy great care and tender regard for Thy Church move me to be solicitous."

ᵖ M. H., " labourers which I am going to send."

ᵠ M. H., " O good God, grant."

ʳ M. H., " them."

ˢ M. H., " but for Thy promise' sake, for Thine honour's sake, for the sake of Thy Church which Thou hast purchased with Thy blood, pour down upon them such gifts of Thy Holy Spirit as shall enable them."

ᵗ M. H. adds, " O God."

ᵘ M. H., " their studies, their labours."

ᵛ M. H., " honoured for their endowments, and for their works' sake be heard and obeyed, that they may give a comfortable account of their time when all our labours shall be tried."

gently watch over them; that not one of them may be lost through my neglect, or the fault of those whom I send into Thy service. **FRIDAY.**

Make us every day more mindful of our charge, and every day more able to perform it, remembering the account we must give. Grant this for the glory of Thy grace, and the good of Thy Church, which Thou hast purchased with Thy most precious blood.

Ἀγαπᾷς με; Ποίμαινε τὰ πρόβατά μου. O Thou good Shepherd, may these persons, whom I am going to send into Thy service, love Thee so passionately, that for Thy sake they may have a tender regard for Thy flock; that they may feed them constantly, and diligently watch over them; that no danger, no enemy, may rob Thee of this handful of sheep which Thou hast so dearly purchased. *They are Thine:* O save them for Thy mercy's sake, and let not one of them, dear God, perish or go astray, through any neglect or fault of mine, or of those whom I send into Thy service. [M.H. lxiii.]

Assist me, O heavenly Father, in all the duties of my calling: make me every day more sensible than other (sic) of the great charge which lies upon me; and make me, O God, every day more and more able to perform it; for the honour of Thy Name, and for the good of Thy Holy Church. O good God, say Amen to my prayers, and though I am unworthy to be heard for my own sake, for the sake of my dear Master, hear me, I beseech Thee.

Jesus said unto him the third time, Lovest thou Me?— John xxi. 17.^x [i. 139; iii. 164]

Though Jesus Christ knew St. Peter's heart, yet He asked him three times *whether he loved Him?* To teach those to whom the power of ordaining belongs, to be very solicitous and^y careful, and not to content themselves with a slight enquiry into the dispositions and qualifications of those who are to have the care of souls committed to them^z.

It being entirely at the Bishop's discretion whether he will

---

x [i. two pages after, repeats this text, and the sentence as follows: "J. C. repeats this question several times, to teach those whose duty it is to ordain Pastors, not to content themselves with a slight enquiry into the qualifications of those who are to undertake the cure of souls."]

y iii. "solicitous and," om.

z [See Quesnel on St. John xxi. 16.]

FRIDAY. admit any one to the order of priest or deacon, and [he] being not obliged to give any reason for his refusal[y]; he will be more accountable to God, both for ordaining unfit persons, and for any prejudice against such as are worthy.

Canon 31. Ordinations shall be on Sundays immediately succeeding the Jejunia quatuor Temporum; where the Bishop resideth, and in presence of the Archdeacon, and four other grave persons allowed to be public Preachers, [also in iii. 166; ii. 53.]

Can. 33. None to be ordained but in order to be a curate, or incumbent, or to have some minister's place in some Church; or except he be a fellow, conduct, or some chaplain in some college in the University; or be Master of Arts of five years standing, and live there at his own cost. [iii. 166. In ii. 53 it stands, "Neminem sine certo Titulo ordinandum. Siquis Episcopus aliter fecerit, per integrum annum suspendetur."]

Can. 34. A bishop not to ordain any who is not of his own diocese, without letters dimissory, &c. See [Gibson,] Codex, 164. "Rules for letters dimissory." [iii. 166; ii. 53, has, "Siquis ausus fuerit aliquem qui ad alterum pertinet ordinare in sua Ecclesia, cum non habeat consensum Episcopi ipsius a quo recessit clericus, irrita erit hujusmodi ordinatio. Concilii Nicæn. can. 17," [or 16. Hard. i. 330, 332.]

Every person to be ordained deacon shall be twenty-three years, and priest twenty-four, complete; and be examined according to the Thirty-nine Articles, which they shall also subscribe; and shall exhibit letters testimonial from college or neighbouring ministers.

Can. 35. Bishop shall examine in presence of such as shall assist him at ordination. [iii. 166.]

Can. 36. Persons to be ordained shall subscribe the Royal Supremacy, the Book of Common Prayer, the Thirty-nine Articles.

There shall be a sermon or exhortation, explaining the office of a deacon, and concerning the order of priests.

[i. 138*.] Can. 32. [iii. prefixes, "No person whatever to be made deacon and priest in one day."] A deacon may be made priest within the year, if the bishop see cause.

[y] Vide [iii. 167, and] Clergyman's Vade-Mecum, p. i. p. 42.

Can. 135. No fees[z] for orders[a], more than 10s. for seal, &c.   FRIDAY.
"That neither a bishop, nor his officers for registering [ii. 53.] their names, shall take nothing from persons ordained. Counc. of Bourges, Anno. 1031. Can. 3." [Hard. vi. part 1. 849.]

Nich. Clemangis (1440) has a most excellent discourse, entitled 'Simoniacal Prelates,' against taking, or suffering others to take, fees for ordination, i.e. for letters, seals, &c.; and indeed there are so many councils expressly against this usage, that one who would not be led by custom into an error, would be afraid of this practice, which, &c.[b]]

[c]N.B. Parish clerks were anciently, both here and in Eng- [i. 138*.] land, real clerks.

Resignation. None valid but what admitted by the bishop. [Gibson], Cod. 833.

Institution. Ordinary shall have twenty-eight days to inquire into the sufficiency of the clerk, p. 847.

None to be instituted till in priests' orders, 849. To exhibit orders, testimonials, &c., 850. To subscribe the Thirty-nine Articles, 852. No minister to serve till licensed by the bishop. Can. 42, Cod. 934, 5.

Lev. xxi. 16, 17, &c. [*Whosoever he be of Thy seed in their* [ii. 53.] *generations, that hath any blemish, let him not approach to offer the bread of his God*]. Though this law was made for the people of Israel, and perhaps does not in strictness [ii. 54.] bind us, surely some regard ought to be had to the reason of the thing, and why a Christian priest that is deformed is not an offence as well as a Jewish, I cannot see the difference.

Lev. xxi. 6. *They shall not profane the Name of their God.*

Ps. cxxxii. 9. *Let Thy priests be clothed with righteousness.* Is. lvi. 10. *His watchmen are blind, they are all ignorant, dumb dogs, sleeping, lying down, loving to slumber, looking to their own way, every one for his gain from his quarter.* Ezek. xxxiv. 4. *Woe be to the shepherds.... The diseased have ye not strengthened, neither have healed that which was sick, neither have ye bound up that which was broken, neither have ye brought again that which was driven*

---

[z] iii. "shall be taken."
[a] "by bishops or others."
[b] [This occurs again, i. 143, referring to Du Pin, 15 cent. p. 78.]
[c] i. gives here the title of Can. 32, as above.

FRIDAY. *away, neither have ye sought that which was lost; but with force and with cruelty have ye ruled them.*

Mal. ii. 6. [see after.]

[i. 138.*]. As we consult God, as Jesus Christ Himself did, when we ordain men to His service, so should we consult Jesus Christ, when we assign them a place in His family. Would Jesus Christ have given this man the charge of the souls of this parish?

That we may have the comfort of knowing that we enter into the ministry by a choice which proceeded from God, we must have some assurance from our own hearts, that the glory of God, the good of souls, was in our intention, and that we were called regularly, and according to the intention of the Church.

Ember week. All persons being concerned in the choice of pastors, every body ought to pray for good pastors.

1 Cor. i. 1. *Paul, called to be an apostle of Jesus Christ through the will of God, &c.* Not through his own will—not through motives of worldly lucre, &c.

Deacons. 1 Tim. iii. 10. *Let these first be proved; then let them use the office of a deacon, being found blameless.*

It is not sufficient to secure the dignity of the ministry even in its lower ministries, that men have taken up virtuous resolutions, unless they be also proved, to see whether those resolutions will continue, &c.

N.B. To give every person I ordain some short hints, *in writing,* of the nature, dignity, several branches, hazard of not discharging them faithfully, &c. of the ministry.

Matt. xxviii. [20.] *Lo! I am with you.*

The chief care of a minister of Christ should be, not to render himself unworthy to have Christ present with him in the exercise of his ministry.

John xvii. 16. *They are not of the world, even as I am not of the world.*

The repetition of this truth ought to make us sensible how different our life ought to be from that of worldly people. (Quesnel in loc.)

[i. 139.*] *The true Pastor.* 1 Pet. v. 1—4. *The elders I exhort:*...

---

d [In ii. 54, marg. opposite this text, is written "Sunday:" perhaps because the text may seem to belong to the Bishop's duty as a Governor, rather than as an Ordainer: i.e. to the Sunday rather than the Friday meditation.]

Feed the flock of God, which is among you, taking the oversight not by constraint, but willingly; not for filthy lucre, but of a ready mind; neither as being lords over God's heritage, but being ensamples to the flock. And when the Chief Shepherd shall appear, ye shall receive a crown of glory that passeth not away.   FRIDAY.

N.B. We must feed the flock, not live in idleness;—not with imperiousness, as over subjects, but with love, as over brethren; not with an eye to self-interest, but with regard to an heavenly reward.

Apostles, (Envoys). So Jesus Christ called the Twelve; that the world might know from whom they had their mission, and that such as are not sent by Him, and by those that have their powers from Him, are not His Apostles.

Luke vi. 16. *And Judas Iscariot, which also was the traitor.*

A man may have a lawful call to the priesthood, to dignities and benefices; and yet, for want of answering the ends of his calling, may be a traitor to the Church, to Christ, and to his own soul. The good Lord grant that I may often think of this with great seriousness!

Luke vi. 39. *Can the blind lead the blind?*

It belongs to Thee, O Holy Spirit of Grace, to send such guides into Thy Church, as may lead Thy people in the right way, and to be the guide of those guides. O do so, for Thy mercies' sake, to this Church and people.

Ignorance in pastors, forasmuch as it is likely to destroy the foundation, is sometimes worse than vice itself; being the occasion of superstition, disorders, and infinite evil consequences, teaching error for truth, and truth for error.

ᵉN.B. Remember, that a minister of Christ can save himself, but only by labouring to save others.

Happy that pastor, whose life and zeal and labours do all testify that he loves his flock, and that he loves them for Christ's sake.

They whom God, by a terrible judgment, leaves to enter [i. 140.] into the ministry solely of themselves, are generally puffed up with a carnal notion of its dignity; while they that through His mercy are called to it, at the same time that

---

ᵉ i. repeats here the reference to St. John xxi. 17, and the remark on it.

FRIDAY. they know its dignity, are humbled under a sense of its weight, and the account, &c.

Such as the heart of the pastor is, such is his behaviour.

He who suffers the priesthood to become vile in his own person, does not remember that he is an ambassador of Christ. The dignity is great, and so ought the sanctity to be, of one who is in Christ's stead. (2 Cor. v. 20.)

2 Cor. vi. 3. *Giving no offence in any thing, that the ministry be not blamed.*

A pastor's life must not contradict his doctrine. He must preach by his actions.

2 Cor. vi. 4, 5, &c. *In all things approving ourselves as the ministers of God, in much patience, in afflictions, in necessities, in distresses, in stripes, in imprisonments, in tumults, in labours, in watchings, in fastings; by pureness, by knowledge, by long-suffering, by kindness, by the Holy Ghost, by love unfeigned, by the word of truth,* [preaching it sincerely,] *by the power of God,* [depending entirely upon His assistance,] *by the armour of righteousness on the right hand and on the left,* [defending us both in prosperity and adversity,] *by honour and dishonour, by evil report and good report; as deceivers, and yet true; as unknown, but yet well known; as dying, and behold we live; as chastened, and not killed;* [believing that God chastens His servants not to destroy them;] *as sorrowful, yet always rejoicing;* [rejoicing in afflictions;] *as poor, yet making many rich;* [with true, not perishing riches;] *as having nothing, and yet possessing all things;* [possessing all things in depending upon God.]

1 Tim. v. 22. *Lay hands suddenly on no man, &c.* A bishop engages to answer before God for such persons as he by advice, ordination, &c., causes to enter into a state of life so very hazardous, and which requires so great a stock of virtues.

[i. 141.] It is happy for a minister of God, that the life he is to lead, and the very outward acts he has vowed to perform, will help to change his heart, and create in him those dispositions which will make him like his great Master. For instance: he has solemnly promised to read the Scriptures daily; he will therefore have daily before his eyes the precepts, the instructions, the example of Christ; the rewards and punishments of the life to come. He is obliged to *catechize;* and the more careful he is to instruct others, the more effectually he will learn himself, how far we are fallen from God, and what pains we must take to be restored to the image and favour of God. *He has promised to lead an holy and exemplary life.* If he does not do this sincerely, he will be the scorn of men now, and of devils hereafter. It will be impossible to converse with *poor and needy people,* and to seek out for help for them, without partaking of the spirit and compassion of the blessed Jesus, who laid down His life for them. If he is careful to *read divine service* distinctly, with deliberation and gravity, it will beget devotion in himself, as well as those that hear him. If his *sermons* be plain and practical, they will affect his own heart, as well as those he preaches to. Every child he *baptizes* puts him in mind of the vows that are upon himself. And he cannot administer the other Sacrament as he ought to do, but it must needs fill his soul with a thousand holy ideas and devout thoughts;—with an holy *fear,* lest he should offer the prayers of the faithful with polluted lips, or distribute the bread of life with unclean hands;—with an ardent love for Jesus Christ, whose love and death he commemorates;—with a perfect charity for all the world, for whom He died. And the oftener he administers this Sacrament, the more he will find his graces increased.

In visiting sick and dying persons, he will be put in mind of his own mortality; and in fitting them as he ought to do for the account they are going to give, he will be put in mind of the much greater he is himself to give.

When he *exhorts, reproves, admonishes* others, it will bring to his mind the words of the apostle, *Thou that teachest another, teachest thou not thyself? &c.*

When he calls to mind, that he has promised *all faithful diligence, &c.,* he will give himself *wholly* to these things, and will be ashamed to be found wholly taken up with business which no way relates to the salvation of souls.

If he is *diligent in prayer,* which he promised to be, God will certainly enlighten his mind with saving truth and grace.

In short, if he has an ardent desire to save souls, and really strives to do it as effectually as he can, he will be be-

FRIDAY. loved of God, assisted by His Spirit; he will see of the fruit of his labours; he will secure his own peace and hope, and will give an account with joy when his Lord calls for him.

One of the most certain marks of a divine call is, when it is the full purpose of a man's heart to live for Jesus Christ and His Church.

[i. 142.] John xvii. 16. *They are not of the world, even as I am not of the world.*

O Lord, make us truly sensible how very different our lives ought to be from the lives of worldly people, that we may avoid their maxims,—all that is curious, useless, light, and vain,—and live up to our character.

Mercy and tenderness for sinners, and faithfulness to the justice of God, are characters inseparable in a true pastor.

John x. 11. *The good shepherd giveth his life, &c.*

He gives his life by giving his labour, in taking all occasions of instructing them; in employing his thoughts for their good; in praying for them continually, and rendering God propitious to them; in sacrificing his ease and peace for them, by delivering truths which the world will not receive without unkind returns. He gives up the dearest friendships, when they stand in competition with truth and righteousness. He gives up all worldly satisfactions, when he does not look upon what is *lawful*, but what is *expedient*[e]. He sacrifices his inclinations, though never so innocent, rather than offend any. He submits to the humility and poverty of the gospel, that he may give no example of pride and luxury to his flock. He dares not be even a witness of disorders, lest he should encourage them by his presence. It is thus he must be the light of the world, and without this he cannot satisfy the duties of his charge; and it is thus he is to give his life for his sheep.

Mark vi. 8. *Nothing for their journey, &c.*

The ecclesiastical ministry requires a great disengagement from the world, to take away all suspicion that the clergy act only out of self-interest. Whoever is not ready to part with all, rather than be wanting to his duty, is not worthy to be a successor to the Apostles.

Deut. xxxiii. 11. *Smite through the loins of all that hate*

[e] [1 Cor. x. 23.]

them, of all that rise up against them, &c. i. e. Make them FRIDAY. childless, who would destroy the succession of the priesthood.

The Blessing of Levi. Deut. xxxiii. 11. *Bless, Lord, his* [i. 153.] *substance, and accept the work of his hands. Smite through the loins of them that rise up against him, and of them that hate him, that they rise not again.* N.B. This is a prophetical declaration of the dreadful [punishment] of such as shall oppose the priesthood.

1 Cor. iv. 1. *Ministers of Christ.* Then none can appoint [i. 142.] them but Christ; or those whom He appoints.

We shall never be able to establish the kingdom of God in the hearts of men, so long as we do not appear fully persuaded of those truths which we preach.

Fees. Can. 135. No fee or money shall be received, either [i. 143.] by the archbishop or any bishop, either directly or indirectly, for admitting of any into sacred orders, nor any to his servants or officers above ten shillings for parchment, wax, sealing, &c.

For ^f"letters testimonial of ordination are no part of the ordination, but only taken afterwards for the security of the person ordained," which if he neglect to take, it is at his own peril.

Preachers, Lecturers, Licenses. No minister shall serve in any place without licence from the bishop, nor without testimony of the bishop of the diocese whence they came, of their honesty, ability, and conformity to the ecclesiastical laws. Can. 48.

None shall be suffered to preach, or be a lecturer in any church, till he is licensed by the Bishop or Archbishop, Can. 36; and subscribe the three Articles and take the oaths.

Ordination. The example of Jesus Christ, before He ordained the Apostles, shews us, that in this choice we ought to depend upon God, and pray for His direction and blessing.

Catechising. Can. 59. Minister shall, every Sunday evening and holy-day, for half an hour at least, examine and instruct in the Church Catechism; and he that neglects to do so, after reproof, to be first suspended, afterwards excommunicated.

^f [Gibson,] Codex Can. Eccl. Ang., p. 177.

FRIDAY.
[i. 144.]

Institution. Persons to be instituted shall exhibit orders and testimonials, and be examined[g].

Reasons for refusing Institution. i. *Lack of learning;* of which the Bishop is the sole judge, and not accountable to any temporal court, but only to a superior spiritual judge. And a person's being ordained, licensed, and approved by another Bishop, does not take away the right which every Bishop has to examine and judge[h].

Lack of language; which renders a person uncapable of the cure. Nor does it avail, that the language may be learnt, or that the duty might be discharged by a curate. And the canon law requires, that where there are [is] a mixture of languages, the priest shall understand both[i].

Other causes. Whatever is sufficient to deprive, is sufficient cause to refuse institution.

Mala in se: Incontinence, drunkenness, murder, manslaughter, heresy, schism, simony, perjury.

The bishop must signify the cause of his refusal, specially, that the proper court, if application is made elsewhere, may be able to judge whether the refusal be just: except in the case of insufficiency; for it has been judged in parliament, that it is sufficient to set forth, *Quod persona in literaturâ minus sufficiens* [*sit*], *seu capax ad habendam dictam ecclesiam.*

The Bishop, having the care of all the souls in his diocese, is bound in conscience to see them well taken care of, by committing them to fit persons.

Persons instituted or licensed to preach shall subscribe the Thirty-nine Articles, and take the oaths of allegiance, supremacy, &c.

Resignation. None valid till accepted by the proper ordinary. Codex, p. 869.

Acts i. 24. *And they prayed and said, Thou, Lord, who knowest the hearts of all men, shew whether of these two Thou hast chosen, &c.*

Should not this make patrons and Bishops to tremble, to see with what caution, devotion, &c., even the Apostles themselves proceeded in the choice of fit persons to serve in the sacred ministry of the Church?

A Christian Priest. Heb. v. Let him remember, that he

[g] Can. 39.   [h] Codex, p. 850.   [i] Codex, p. 851.

himself is a man and a sinner; that he is ordained for men FRIDAY. *only* in things pertaining to God; that he is not to live an idle life, but to offer, &c., that is, to perform the duties of his calling; to appease the justice of God, by offering the prayers, the oblations, &c., of the people; to have bowels of compassion towards sinners; to instruct the ignorant, and them that are out of the way; never to forget his own infir- [i. 145.] mities, that he may treat sinners with compassion; to pray much for himself and for his people; to stay till he is called into the ministry.—It is an honour, and to be conferred, as it was on Aaron.—To keep his flock, by his vigilance, from falling into ignorance in relation to the truths of Christianity; to suit his instructions to the capacities of his hearers, and to their peculiar wants; and not to fill their heads with vain amusement, which signify little to their salvation.

O Lord, abandon not Thy flock to wolves, but send them pastors after Thine own heart.

Numbers xviii. 1. *The Lord said unto Aaron, Thou and thy sons shall bear the iniquity of the sanctuary.* That is, they shall carry them away by the sacrifices which they shall offer for them, especially on the day of expiation.

Ecclus. vii. 29. *Fear the Lord with all thy soul, and reverence His priests. Love Him that made thee, with all thy strength, and forsake not His ministers; but give Him his portion as it is commanded.*

Manners of the Clergy. "Si clericus verba scurrilia, jocularia, risumque moventia loquitur, acerrime corripiatur." Conc. African. [fors. iv. Carthag. can. 60. "Clericum scurrilem, et verbis turpibus jocularem, ab officio retrahendum.]"

Our business is to preach, to make men love, and to confirm them in, the truths of the Gospel.

Nothing can supply the want of a pastor's presence[k].

Call. A lawful call affords us a good ground to hope for [i. 146.] all necessary assistance, and grace to do our duty, and for mercy for all our involuntary defects.

Clergy. I beseech Thee, O God, for them, and for myself; that, in the exercise of our ministry, we may depend much

---

[k] [i. has here by way of memorandum, "*Convocation. Lifeless Sermons.* See Watts on the Passions, part ii. p. 140, and 149, &c." i. e. perhaps the topic was to be mentioned in a Convocation Charge.]

FRIDAY. on Thee; that we may learn from Thee what we ought to speak concerning Thee; that we may constantly speak the truth, boldly rebuke vice, and patiently suffer for righteousness' sake; that we may live and act as in the place of Christ, doing nothing unbecoming that character; and that we may preserve an apostolical firmness of mind under the vexations and persecutions of this world. Amen.

[i. 147.] *Faults of the Clergy.* Let it be considered what is the great design of the generality of the clergy of these days:— To appear learned rather than pious; to get preferment, riches, and to live at ease. This makes them satisfied with a mere speculative knowledge in divinity.

Luke v. 5. *We have toiled all the night, and have taken nothing.* And it is much to be feared that the little good we see done by our sermons, is owing to the neglect of praying for God's blessing upon our labours.

Sermons should be plain, practical, and tending to the salvation of those that hear them.

Remember, that all useful truth must come from the Spirit of truth, and therefore to be prayed for.

No man can teach well who does not live well.

My people perish for want of knowledge.

Do holy things after an holy manner. He that reads the service negligently, betrays a great want of piety in himself, and begets contempt and indevotion in others.

Catechising. The neglect of this duty makes the discourses of the pulpit of very little use. People do not understand the very words made use of in the Gospel.

The Lord's Supper. Christians are too often admitted without knowing, &c. The consequence—they fancy they are good Christians, and are in danger of perishing without knowing it.

Lives of the Clergy. They should consider that they are taken from amongst men to minister in things pertaining to God, and therefore are not to live like those from whom they are taken. They are restrained from many things which others practise without reproach or scruple.

The maxims of the world are not to be our rule. To desire to be esteemed; to get as much of this world as we well can; to stick at nothing to gain an end; to despise those below us; to live without taking the cross, self-denial, &c.;

to admire what the world admires:—by these things the ministry is blamed and brought into contempt.

Lives of the Clergy. Look at home, a sad reproach, where occasion is given.

Remember that a contempt of the clergy will be attended with a contempt of the gospel, and of God Himself at last.

More sinners have been converted by holy than by learned men.

The greatest presumption to pretend to heal others of a distemper I labour under myself.

John viii. 46. *Which of you convinceth me of sin?* Here is [the] pattern of a pastor.

He who would edify by his sermons, must be that same virtuous, sober, serious, pious man in his life and conversation; he will then be heard with respect and reverence.

If a clergyman be eager after pleasures, the world and its idols, trifling and vain in life, all he says out of the pulpit will signify nothing.

He that religiously practises himself what he teaches others,—he then preaches effectually.

No man can teach well, who does not live well.

It is true, the faith is not built upon the lives of those that preach it, but upon the word of God; but a bad life exposes Christians to great temptations, &c.

Simon, lovest thou Me? &c. This should teach us, that nothing but a sincere love for God, and for the souls of men, which He loved so well as to redeem them by His own Son, can carry us through the work of the ministry.

How shall we attain to such a love? By prayer; by reading the Scriptures; by instructing the poor, the youth, after such a manner as to affect our own hearts; by visiting, relieving, comforting sick and needy people, &c. These will pray for you, and God will hear their prayers, and increase His love, &c.

Difficulties. If the motives which determined you to take Holy Orders were the glory of God, and the good of souls, He will enable you to bear and get the better of all difficulties.

Preacher. Sermons. The design of religion being to lead men to the knowledge of God, how He is to be worshipped, appeased, honoured; and to make men holy, that they may

FRIDAY. be capable of being happy when they die; the great business of a preacher should be, to shew how the Christian religion and all its parts contribute to this end.

They that recommended eternal possessions to others, ought to shew by their lives that they are themselves verily persuaded of the vanity of all earthly pleasures, avoiding superfluities, &c. Jesus Christ preached up the contempt of the world, by contemning it Himself.

A pastor's knowledge need not extend so far as is imagined. If he knows the Scriptures, and what concerns the kingdom of God, and the way of leading souls thither, he, &c.

[i. 148.] We must speak to the heart as well as to the understanding. While we attack the men's reason only, they will hear with patience; but when we attack the heart and its corruption, then they are uneasy.

I would rather send away a hearer smiting his breast, than please the most learned audience with a fine sermon against any vice.

The end of preaching is to turn men from sin unto God. He that has not this in his aim, &c. to convince men of the reality of a future state of happiness or misery, and how to avoid the one and gain the other, &c.

Let people feel that you are in earnest, that you believe and are deeply affected with the great truths you would recommend.

Avoid such discourses and subjects as would divert the mind without instructing it.

Never consult your own fancy in the choice of subjects, but the necessities of your flock.

Necessary Subjects. A concern for what may come hereafter; a firm hope of immortality; a fear of a judgment to come,—of hell torments.

Remember, that your own salvation depends very much upon the salvation of your flock.

A man may flatter himself with keeping fair with the world, by not telling them the danger they are in. This was not the way of Jesus Christ[1].

A preacher ought to advance nothing but what he has

[1] John vii. 7.

received from Jesus Christ. *My doctrine is not Mine, but His that sent Me*[m]. FRIDAY.

To pursue our own thoughts, forsaking those of the Gospel, is like an ambassador who neglects his prince's instructions, and follows his own fancy.

With what truth can it be said, that your sheep hear your voice, when you speak of matters above their capacity, or in a language or terms which they do not understand?

Can any man imitate a greater master of eloquence than Jesus Christ was, whose great excellence appears in making great truths understood by the meanest capacity?

The great end of our ministry, and should be our great design, to destroy the kingdom of Satan.

To have an eye to the learned part of our audience, who will not very likely profit by you, rather than to the poor in spirit, whom God designs to save, is very wrong, and yet is what, &c.

1 Cor. iii. 7. Q. [i. e. Quesnel in loc.] We must depend on God for success, nor take that to ourselves which belongs to God alone.

2 Cor. ii. 17. He that considers that he is God's ambassador to His people; that he speaks from God to them; that Jesus Christ speaks by him; will, &c.

God would have all men see that the success of the gospel depends upon His grace, and therefore preachers [should be] humble, meek, &c.

It is too often that preachers perplex those whom they should instruct, either by proving things which want no proof,—the being of a God, &c.,—or by proposing useless questions and doubts, or speaking of things above the capacities of the common people.

There is a great deal of difference betwixt people admiring a preacher, and being edified by his sermons.

Test of a good Preacher. We count him a good physician whose patients we see cured. If the people are cured of their intemperance, lying, &c., his works will speak for him.

A saying of Bishop Hall: "The sins of teachers are teachers of sin."

1 Cor. iii. 7. *Neither is he that planteth any thing, neither he that watereth, but God which giveth the increase.* [i. 149.]

[m] John vii. 16.

FRIDAY.

It is God who gives His ministers, *such as are humble*, power over the hearts and souls of men; when distrusting themselves, they ascribe all the glory to God.

We take the work out of the hands of God, when we are pleased with what we have done, and rob Him of the honour due to Him alone.

There have been many, who, without any great learning or eloquence, yet by their communication in a humble and low way, have instructed and converted more than famous preachers; for that they preached not themselves, but Christ Jesus, placing all their confidence in God.

[i. 150.] *Irregularities in Ordination.* Bishop Burnet, Hist. Ref., vol. i. p. 267, [484. Oxf. 1816,] tells us that Henry VIII. [A.D. 1539,] gave Bonner "a strange commission," (as he truly calls it,) "to ordain in the King's stead such as he found worthy,—to present and give institution, with all other parts of the episcopal authority," &c. ["Præter et ultra ea quæ tibi ex sacris literis divinitus commissa esse dignoscantur." Records in Burnet, i. part ii. b. iii. no. xiv. p. 285.]

Priests not to engage in secular business. "Singuli divino sacerdotio honorati non nisi altari et sacrificiis deservire, et precibus et orationibus vacare debeant." Cypr. ep. lxvi. ed. Rigalt. [ep. i. ed. Fell.]

[i. 151.] *Ordination.* St. Luke vi. 12, 13, [as given above]. Blessed Jesus, my Lord and Master, may I ever follow Thy example as far as my frailty will permit.

O let Thy great and tender care and regard for Thy Church, make me solicitous at the throne of grace on behalf of those labourers whom I shall at any time send into Thy vineyard, and especially to [for?] ——. They are to be the immediate servants of Thy family: in the choice of them, therefore, we depend upon Thee.

For Thy promise' sake, for Thine honour's sake, and for the sake of the Church which Thou hast purchased with Thy blood, pour upon them such gifts of Thy Holy Spirit, as may enable them for the work unto which they are called;—that they may teach well, and that they may live well, and be examples of all those graces and virtues which they recommend to others.

Sanctify their persons, their studies, their labours: that

they may be respected by their people, honoured for their endowments, and for their work's sake be heard and obeyed, and that they may give a comfortable account of their time when all our works shall be tried. [FRIDAY.]

And grant, O God, that no unworthiness in me may ever hinder Thy gifts and graces from descending upon those whom I shall ordain to Thy service: for Jesus Christ His sake. Amen.

Institution. St. John xxi. 17, [as before]. O great and good Shepherd, may this person whom I am going to send into Thy service love Thee so sincerely, that for Thy sake He may have a tender concern for Thy flock: that he may diligently feed and watch over them, that the enemy may not rob Thee of any of those sheep which Thou hast purchased with Thy blood. They are Thine, O save them for Thy mercy's sake, and let none of them be lost or go astray through any fault of mine, or of those whom I send into Thy service. [i. 152.]

Make me every day more sensible of the great charge which lieth upon me, and every day more able and desirous to perform it, for the glory of Thy Name and for the good of Thy Church, through Jesus Christ Thy Son and my Lord and Master. Amen[m].

Persons ordained by me. [M. H. 26; i. 154, 5; ii. 55; iii. 188, 189.]

1. Matth. Curghy, Presb., Sept. 25, 1698.
2. Ch. Wattleworth, Deacon, eod. die.
3. Wm. Gell, Deacon, same time.
4. Jo. Christian, Deacon, Sept. 24, 1699.
5. Wm. Walker, Deacon, March 11, 1700.
   Wm. Gell, Presbyt., May 31, 1702.
   Wm. Walker, Presbyt., same day.
   Charles Wattleworth, Presbyter.
   Jo. Christian, Presbyt., Dec. 19, 1703.
6. Henry Allen, Deacon, Sept. 22, 1706.
7. Wm. Ross, Deacon, May 30, 1708[n].
   Wm. Ross, Presbyt., March 30, 1712.
   Hen. Allen, Presbyter, same day.
8. Wm. Brideson, Deacon, same day.

[m] [MS. i. inserts here the texts, Matt. ix. 38; Deut xxxiii. 11.]
[n] [Here ends the list in MS. M. H.]

218   SACRA PRIVATA.

FRIDAY.
    9. Jo. Quayle, Deacon, Sept. 21, 1712.
  10. Robt. Parr, Deacon, Apr. 19, 1713.
      Wm. Brideson, Presbyt., Feb. 21, 1713º.
      Jo. Quayle, Presbyt., Feb. 26, 1715.
      Robt. Parr, Presbyt., eod. die.
  11. Anth. Halshal, Deacon, Mar. 24, 1716.
  12. Jo. Woods, Deacon, June 8, 1718.
  13. Jo. Coshnahan, Deacon, same day.
p 14. Fran. Yeates, of Whitehaven, D., Sept. 25, 1720.
      Jo. Coshnahan, Presbyt., Sept. 24, 1721.
      Jo. Woods, Presbyt., Sept. 24, 1721.
      Edw. Moor, D., same day.
      Edw. Moor, Presbyt., Feb. 21, 1724.
      Jo. Annyan q, Curate of Pilling, Presbyt., eod. die.
      Matth. Curghy, D., eod. die.
      Wm. Rosse, jun., D., June 5, 1726 r.
      Matth. Curghy, Presb., Mar. 17, 1727.
      Rob. Radclif, Deacon, same day, 17 of Mar.
      Wm. Heyton, curate of Plumland, Deacon, Dec. 22, 1728.
      Robt. Radcliff, Presbyt. ⎫
      Paul Crebin, Deacon. ⎬ Apr. 20, 1729 s.
      Phil. Moor, Deacon. ⎭
      Paul Crebin, Presbyt., May 24, 1730.
      John Allen, Deacon, May 24, 1730.
      Tho. Burket, Deacon, ⎫
      Tho. Christian, Deacon, ⎬ June 13, 1731.
      Tho. Mathew, A.B., Carliolensis, Sept. 26, 1731.
      John Allen, (above,) Priest, Mar. 5, 1731.
      Brian Lancaster, Deacon, Mar. 18, 1732.
      Nich. Christian, Deac n., Dec. 23, 1733.
      Josias Relph, Mar. 10, 1733, Deacon, upon letters dimissory from the Bishop of Carlisle, and letters, testimonials, &c.
      Mr. Thos. Christian, Priest, Mar. 25, 1735. ⎫
      Mr. Nath. Curghy, Deacon, Mar. 25, 1735. ⎬

º [Here the list in MS. ii. ceases.]
p [The numerals, which terminate here, occur only in MS. iii.]
q [iii. Anyon.]
r [Here the list in MS. iii. ceases.]

s Two livings being destitute of curates by the deaths of Ch. Wattleworth and Robert Parr, I was obliged to this ordination, the necessities of the Church requiring it.

Tho. Allen, Deacon, Trin. Sund. 1736.   FRIDAY.
John Crane, Deacon at Peel, Oct. 15, 1738.
John Mackenzie, at Kk. Mich., Feb. 25, 1738, [i. 155.]
  Deacon,—bound for North Carolina, Cape Fare,
  [? Fear],—Batchelor of Arts, Dublin Coll.
Sept. 23, 1739, Mr. Philip Moor, Priest, in Douglass
  Chapel.
May 4, 1740, Jo. Moor, Deacon.
June 21, 1741, Jo. Crane, Priest.
Eod. die, Edward Kippax, Deacon, upon letters
  dimissory from the Abp. of Dublin.
Sept. 19, 1742, K. Michael, Tho. Allen, Priest,
  James Wilks, Deacon.
James Wilks, Priest, ⎫
Wm. Crebbin, Deacon, ⎬ Trin. Sunday, May 29, 1743.
Saml. Gill, Deacon,   ⎭
Mr. Tho. Bacon, Deacon, Septemb. 23, 1744, at K.
  Mich., by permission of the Bishop of London,
  for a missionary.
March 10, 1744-5, Mr. Thos. Bacon, Priest, in order
  to go into the Plantations, (Bp. of London,) &c.
Eod. die, Mr. Wm. Mylrea, Deacon.
Sept. 22, 1745, Mr. Sam. Gell, Priest, in order to
  assist his infirm father.
Sept. 21, 1746, ordained Mr. Wm. Mylrea, Priest.
Mr. Tho. Woodes, Deacon.
Mr. Michael Smith, Deacon.
Sept. 20, 1747.
  Mr. Nich. Christian, of Ryshen, Presbyt.
  Mr. Jo. More, of Arbory, Presbyt.
  Mr. Tho. Woodes, of Ramsea, Presb.
  Mr. Jos. Coshnahan, Deacon.
  Mr. James Ansdell, Jan. 27, 1750-51, Deacon.
October, 1751. Deacons ordained in my chapel, I being indisposed:—Mr. Cleve Quayle, Deacon; Mr. Gill, Deacon; Mr. — Christian.
July 5, 1752. Robert Drew, of K. Maliew, in my own chapel, I being very infirm with the gout.
  Acolythi, individ. comites Episcoporum.   [ii. 55.]

FRIDAY. 1 Tim. v. 22; 2 Tim. ii. 2; Acts viii. 20; 2 St. Peter ii. 3[s].

"Ars artium est cura animarum," St. Greg. [Reg. Past. i. 1.] This is the true *Priestcraft*.

Sanctify them by Thy truth. Grant that before I separate others, I may separate myself from this world and its delights, &c.

Quo quis inter vos majorem in Ecclesia dignitatem obtinebit, eo sciat tibi non plus imperii concessum, sed plus oneris, injunctum. Grot. on St. Matt. xxiii.

Nequis sacerdotes ad sæcularem molestiam devocet, &c. Vid. Cyprian, ep. i. ed. Oxon.

The husbandman is never better pleased than when his harvest is great, and consequently his pains must be so.

[iii. 163.] To see a man entirely devoted to the world, to sin and vanity, under an habit that consecrates him to God!

[iii. 168.] *Let no man despise thee.* Tit. ii. 15.

Mal. ii. 8, 9. *But ye are departed out of the way; ye have caused many to stumble at the law; ye have corrupted the covenant of Levi, saith the Lord of Hosts: Therefore have I also made you contemptible and base before all the people according as you have not kept My ways, but have been partial in the law, &c.* And 'tis to be much feared that this is the origin of the *contempt of the clergy*.

PENITENCE.

[M.H. xlvii; ii. 62; iii. 172; 1st ed. 283.]

Luke xviii. 13. [t]*The publican standing afar off, would not so much as lift up his eyes to heaven; but smote upon his breast, saying, God be merciful to me a sinner.*

What would become of *me*, if Thou, O God, shouldst not have mercy upon me?

When I seriously consider these dreadful truths,—"That all they are *accursed* who do *err* and go astray *from Thy commandments*[u]:—"That *the unprofitable servant* was *cast into outer darkness*[x]:"—"That we *watch for the souls* of our

---

[s] [ii. gives the texts in full.]
[t] [ii. "God be mérciful to me a sinner." iii. Luke xviii. 18. Ὁ Θεὸς ἱλάσθητι μοί τῷ ἁμαρτωλῷ. i. wants two pages here. M.H. Ὁ Θεὸς, κ.τ.λ.; Matt. vi. 14, 15.]
[u] Ps. cxix. 21.
[x] Matt. xxv. 30.

FRIDAY.

flock, *as they that must give an account;*"—When I think of these things, I cannot but fear for myself, and tremble to think of the account I have to give.

[M. H. ii. iii. give the following prayer, after the text, Luke xviii. 13.]

What would become of me, if Thou, O Father of mankind, shouldst not have mercy upon[y] me; it had been better for me that I had never been born, than that I should live[z] to have offended Thee[a] *as I have done*, and should not live to repent of it, and to appease my angry [b]Judge.

[c]When I consider, O King of Heaven, what Thou hast [d]so plainly declared,—[e]That all they are accursed who do err and go astray from Thy commandments[f], (Ps. cxix. 21;) That it is a fearful thing to fall into the hands of the living God, who can destroy both body and soul in hell, where the worm dieth not, and the fire is not quenched:—When I think of this, my soul is sore troubled, and I am justly afraid of Thy judgments hanging over my head.

For the sake of Jesus Christ avert them: or [g]if it be Thy pleasure, [h]O Lord, to stay Thy hand, that Thy great mercy and forbearance may oblige me to [i]repent, and to bring forth fruits meet for repentance[k]. I do earnestly repent, and am heartily sorry for my sad misdoings. I am sorry that I have offended Thee, and provoked Thy wrath and indignation against me; that I have abused Thy long-suffering, despised the means of grace, and so long did put off my conversion.

---

[y] iii. "on."
[z] M. H. "have lived."
[a] M. H. "Thy Majesty."
[b] "Lord and," iii.; M. H. "God."
[c] M. H. inserts, "O give me true repentance for all the errors of my life past, and stedfast faith in Thy Son Jesus Christ, that my sins may be forgiven, and my pardon sealed in heaven before I go hence and be no more seen. Ὁ Θεὸς, κ.τ.λ.
"I know, O Lord, that there is no word impossible with Thee, and though my sins," &c. [as below.]
[d] M.H. "positively;" iii. om. "so plainly."
[e] M. H. adds, "That no whoremonger nor adulterer, nor covetous person —that none who wrongs his neighbour in body, goods, or name,—that neither the drunkard nor the profane, can enter into Thy kingdom:—When I do seriously consider."
[f] M. H. goes on, "My very soul is distracted with fear, and I am justly," &c.
[g] M. H. "or, good Lord, let it be Thy pleasure to stay," &c.
[h] iii. om. "O Lord."
[i] M.H. om. "repent, and."
[k] M. H. goes on with the text, 1 John ii. 1, and adds, "Great God, what comfort hast Thou given me in this revelation! though my transgressions have been many and great, yet I may still hope for mercy by the merits and intercession of Jesus Christ the righteous."

FRIDAY. O Lamb of God, that takest away the sins of the world[m], &c.

Speak the word only, and Thy servant shall be whole.

If any man sin, we have an advocate with the Father, Jesus Christ the Righteous, [n] *and He is the propitiation for our sins*[o].

So God loved the world, that He gave His only-begotten Son, to the end that all that believe in Him should not perish, but have everlasting life.

Blessed be God for this instance of His love, for this gracious revelation of His will, so very comfortable to miserable mankind wearied with the burden of their sins.

Though my sins are so many that I cannot recount them; though they are of such a foul nature that I blush to name them; though they have left such [p]a stain upon my soul as may make [me] to be [q]abhorred of Thee; yet [r]if Thou wilt Thou canst make me whole: which I most humbly beg for Jesus Christ His sake.

[s]O blessed[t] Advocate, look upon [u]a penitent who earnestly desires pardon and forgiveness; receive a sinful prodigal, who [x]by Thy grace is sensible of and returning from his folly.

[y]Perfect, O Lord, what Thou hast begun in me: create in me a new heart, that I may feel the effects of Thy grace, in the constancy of my devotions, in the care of my soul, in the discharge of the several parts of my duty; in the sincere performance of the vows that are upon me, and in all such acts of mercy and charity by which I shall be judged at the latter day.

And let not [z]the Lord be angry with His servant, who presumes to beg[a] the same [b]pardon and grace for others that I ask for myself; and especially for those[c] unfortunate people

---

[m] iii. " have mercy upon me."
[n] iii. om. " and He...sins."
[o] iii. inserts, " O Blessed Advocate, look upon a penitent, who puts his cause into Thy hands,—who earnestly prays for pardon and forgiveness.
" Receive a sinful prodigal," &c., [as below.]
[p] M. H. " base impressions."
[q] M. H. adds, " justly."
[r] iii. " the price of Thy Son's blood is sufficient to procure me a full discharge of all my sins."

[s] "iii. om. this sentence.]
[t] M. H. " dear."
[u] M. H. " an afflicted."
[x] M. H. om. " by Thy grace," and adds, " O Lamb of God, that takest away, &c., and let not," &c.
[y] iii. " And may the good Lord perfect what He has;" M. H. om. this sentence.
[z] M. H. " my God."
[a] iii. " ask."
[b] iii. " grace and pardon."
[c] " such," iii.

—who by my example, ^dat my instance, by my neglect of my duty, may have been led^e to commit such wickedness^f as I now repent^g and confess.

O Lord, lay not these sins to their charge; give them grace, before it is too late, to forsake the evil^h of their ways, to turn to Thee in weeping, fasting, and prayer; that Thou mayest have mercy upon *them*, and that ⁱI may be delivered from the guilt of their sins, for Jesus Christ His sake. Amen.

[ii. subjoins], "Faciam, Aselle, ut non amplius calcitres; nec te hordeo alam, sed paleis; fame et siti te conficiam." St. Hilarion [in his life by S. Jerome, § 5].

Matt. ix. 15. *But the days will come, when the Bridegroom shall be taken from them, and then shall they fast.*

Acts xiii. 3. *And when they had fasted and prayed, and laid their hands on them, they sent them away.*

[M. H. xlix. subjoins], Κύριε, ἐὰν θέλῃς, δύνασαί με καθαρίσαι· Κύριε, σῶσον με, ἀπόλλυμαι. "For Thy Name's sake be merciful unto my sin, for it is great."

Though my sins are very many, and of a deep dye, yet I should have done worse, and fallen into much greater, if the merciful God had not prevented me by His gracious Providence.

If through the frailty of my nature and temptation of the devil I at any time forget these good purposes, Lord, reduce me to my duty by what wholesome methods shall seem best to Thee.

Lord, I make my prayer unto Thee, I hope, in acceptable time. [M. H. l.], Κύριε, τὶ με θέλεις ποίησαι.

Isaiah lxvi. 2. *To this man will I look, even to him that is poor and of a contrite spirit, and trembleth at My word.*

Psalm xxxiv. 18. *The Lord is nigh unto them that are of a contrite heart; and will save such as be of an humble spirit.*

Look upon me, gracious Lord, with an eye of mercy.

Psalm xxv. 2. *For Thy Name's sake, O Lord, pardon mine iniquities, for they are great.*

My only comfort is, they are not too great for Thy mercy.

---

^d M. H. "by my advice."
^e M. H. "tempted."
^f "sins," iii.
^g "lament," iii. M. H.
^h M. H. "wickedness."
ⁱ M. H. "that Thou mayest deliver *me*," &c.

FRIDAY.

And the Lord Jesus our Advocate has assured us, even with an oath, That *all sins shall be forgiven unto the sons of men*[k]. That is, that with hearty repentance and true faith turn unto God.

O most powerful Advocate! I put my cause into Thy hands; let it be unto Thy servant according to this word; let Thy blood and merits plead for my pardon; say unto me, as Thou didst unto the penitent in Thy gospel, *Thy sins are forgiven*. And grant that I may live to bring forth fruits meet for repentance.

[i. 211.] Matt. vi. 14. *If ye forgive men their trespasses, your heavenly Father will also forgive your trespasses.*

Even the power to perform this most kind condition, must be from Thy grace, O Jesus!

And I trust Thou wilt grant me this grace, because the very will to ask it is from Thee, and from Thy will, which wills nothing in vain.

Perfect, therefore, O my Saviour, the work which Thou hast begun in me; and let me feel the effects of Thy grace in the constancy of my devotions,—in the care of my soul,—in the faithful discharge of my duty and the vows that are upon me; and in all such acts of righteousness, piety, and charity, by which I shall be judged at the last day.

And let not the Lord be angry with His servant, who presumes to ask the same pardon and grace for others, as I ask for myself: and especially for all such as by my example, or neglect of my duty, may have been offended or led to such sins as I now lament and confess.

Lord, lay not their sin to their charge, but give them grace to repent; that Thou mayest have mercy upon them, and that I may not be answerable for the sin and ruin of others.

John v. 14. *Sin no more, lest a worse thing come unto thee.*

Make me, O Lord, ever mindful of my infirmities and backslidings, that I may be more watchful, and more importunate for grace for the time to come.

Matt. v. 7. *Blessed are the merciful, for they shall obtain mercy.*

---

[k] Mark iii. 22.

Give me, O Lord, a true compassion for the wants and miseries, both temporal and spiritual, of others, that Thou mayest have compassion upon me. *Friday.*

Luke xv. 10. *There is joy in the presence of God over one sinner that repenteth.* [i. 212.]

Lord God, increase the number of penitents, and the joys of heaven, in delivering myself and all sinners from the power of the devil, and in vouchsafing us the grace of a true conversion.

Matt. v. 4. *Blessed are they that mourn, for they shall be comforted.*

O Lord, grant that I may seek for comfort, not in the things of this world, but in a sincere repentance for my own sins, and for the sins of the flock committed to my charge, by which God is dishonoured, and His judgments hanging over our heads.

Luke xix. 10. *The Son of Man is come to seek and to save that which was lost.*

O comfortable words for lost sinners! God Himself seeks to save them. O Thou, who sought me when I was astray, save me for Thy mercy's sake; preserve that which Thou hast sought and found.

Matt. xi. 28. *Come unto Me, all ye that labour and are heavy laden, and I will, &c.*

O Jesu, conduct and keep me to Thyself, or I shall surely miss the way.

Phil. ii. 12. *Work out your own salvation with fear and trembling; for it is God that worketh in you both to will and to do of His good pleasure.*

It was not in myself, O God, to begin the work of my conversion;—finish, I beseech Thee, what Thou hast begun in me;—may I close with Thy grace, and persevere unto my life's end.

Micah vii. 18. *God retaineth not His anger for ever, because He delighteth in mercy.*

Ezra ix. 15. *O Lord God, behold, we are before Thee in our trespasses; we cannot stand before Thee for this.*

Ps. xxiv. [25.] 11. *For Thy Name's sake, O Lord, pardon mine iniquity, for it is great.*

FRIDAY. Numbers xiv. 19. *Pardon, I beseech Thee, the iniquity of Thy servant, according to the greatness of Thy mercy.*

O say unto me as Thou didst unto Moses, *I have pardoned thee*[1].

Ezekiel xviii. 22. *All his iniquities that he hath committed, they shall not be mentioned unto him.*

[i. 213.] Lord, be merciful unto me, for I have sinned in the midst of light, and even against light; in contempt of the grace we received at our baptism.

1 John i. 9. *If we confess our sins, He is faithful, &c.*

These are comfortable words to one whom the sight of his sins hath cast into a dread of the judgments of God. Both that dread, and the hatred of sin, and the dependence upon the promise of God, and the love that that produces in the soul, are owing entirely to the blood of Jesus Christ.

2 Sam. ix. 8. *What is Thy servant, that Thou shouldst look upon such a dead dog as I am?*

St. Luke xv. 19. *I am* now *no more worthy to be called Thy son,* much less Thy minister.

1 Cor. xv. 9. *I am not meet to be called an apostle.*

My only support is, that my sins have not put me out of the reach of that mercy which is infinite.

[iii. 214.] *Repentance.* Who can understand his errors? O cleanse Thou me from my secret faults.

O Lord, be favourable unto me; pardon and deliver me from all my sins.

Grant that my great sins may never rise up in judgment against me, nor bring shame and confusion of face upon me.

My soul truly waiteth still upon God, for of Him cometh my salvation.

[2nd ed. 433.] John vi. 20. *It is I, be not afraid.*

Lord Jesus, in all the troubles that shall befall me, speak these comfortable words to my soul, *It is I, be not afraid;* and then I shall be secure both from presumption and despair.

John viii. 24. *If ye believe not that I am He,* (that is, the Messiah, the Son of God,) *ye shall die in your sins.*

O Jesus, the only refuge of sinners, does the world know what it is to die in sin? I believe; Lord, increase my

---

[1] [i. inserts here again the text, Is. lxvi. 2.]

faith, and deliver us all from the dreadful state of final impenitency. FRIDAY.

John viii. 31. *If ye continue in My word, then are ye My disciples indeed.*

May I, O Jesus, love the truths of Thy word; make the gospel my delight; and continue in the practice of them to my life's end.

John viii. 51. *If a man keep My saying, he shall never see death.*

O Jesus, Thou hast made known to us another death, besides that which separates the soul from the body. O may Thy grace and mercy secure us from the bitter pains of eternal death.

Luke vii. 7. *Say the word, and my servant shall be healed.*

I acknowledge, O Jesu, the almighty power of Thy grace, to heal all the disorders of my soul; O deal with me according to the multitude of Thy mercies, and heal my soul of its sad disorders.

John iii. 24. *God is a Spirit: and they that worship Him must worship Him in spirit and in truth.*

Give me, O Jesus, an inward disposition to holiness, an humble and contrite heart, a dependence on the will of God, an acknowledgment of His goodness, and a zeal for His glory; to which all the ordinances of the law and gospel should lead us.

Good use of Time. Grant, O Lord, that as I have but a short time to live, and an eternal interest depending, I may not squander away one moment in vanity, or in that which will not profit me in the day of adversity.

[m] *Intercession.* 1 Tim. ii. 1. *I exhort, that first of all, supplications, prayers, intercessions, and giving of thanks, be made for all men.* [iii. 176; i. 214.]

[n] O God, almighty and merciful, let Thy fatherly kindness be upon all that Thou hast made.

Have mercy upon all Jews, Turks, Infidels, and Heretics;

---

[m] [This prayer is appointed in both MSS. for *Friday*. The first edition assigns it to *Sunday*, but gives it apparently from MS. iii. It *may* have been in the portion of MS. i. now missing, but if so, there was less variation in the two copies than the Bishop usually made.]

[n] i. om. this, and begins with, "O God, the Creator," &c. (as below).

Friday.

and ᵒgrant that none may deprive themselves of that happiness which Jesus Christ has purchased by His death.

Bless the pious endeavours of all those who strive to propagate the gospel of Christ; and may its saving truths be received in all the world.

Preserve Thy Church in the midst of the dangers that surround it; purge it from all corruptions, heal its divisions, that all Christian people may unite and love as becomes the disciples of ᵖ Jesus Christ.

Grant that ᑫall bishops and pastors may be careful to observe the sacred rights committed to theirʳ trust:—

[1st ed. p. 266; iii. 177; i. 214.]

That godly discipline may be restored and countenanced:—

That Christians may not content themselves with ˢbare shadows of religion and piety; but endeavour after that holiness without which no man can see the Lord:—

ᵗThat such as are in authorityᵘ may govern with truth and justice; and that thoseˣ whose duty it is to obey, may do it for conscience' sakeʸ.

Let all that sincerely seek the truth, be led into it by Thy Holy Spirit; and to all such as are destitute of necessary instruction, vouchsafe a greater measure of Thy grace.

ᶻSupport and comfort all that labour under trials and afflictionsᵃ, all that suffer wrongfully; and by Thy mighty grace succour all those that are tempted.

Give unto all sinners a true sense of their unhappy stateᵇ, and grace and strength to break their bonds.

Visit, with Thy ᶜfatherly comforts, all ᵈsuch as are now in their last sickness, that they may omit nothing that is necessary to make their peace with Thee.

ᵒ i. om. this down to "grant."
ᵖ 1st ed. om. "Jesus."
ᑫ i. adds, "I and."
ʳ 1st ed., "that."
ˢ i. om. "bare," and "and piety."
ᵗ i. adds, "Bless our gracious King, and the lord of this Isle, and make them both faithful patrons of Thy Church, and of the truth."
ᵘ "grant that all," i.
ˣ i. "such."
ʸ i. adds, "Pity all them that are in error, and deliver them out of it."
ᶻ The two next sentences transposed, i.
ᵃ i. "All that are in pain of body, or anguish of mind—all that are in danger of falling into despair—all that are in slavery, under persecution, oppression, in poverty, or in prison. And give them all grace according to the difficulties they labour under. By Thy mighty grace succour all such as are under temptation."
ᵇ i. adds, "a fear of Thy judgments."
ᶜ i. adds, "good and."
ᵈ i. "that are."

Be gracious to all those countries that are ᵉmade desolate by the sword, famine, pestilence, or persecution.

And sanctify the miseries of this life, to the everlasting benefit of all that suffer.

Preserve this land from the ᶠmiseries of war; this Church from persecution, and from ᵍ all wild and dangerous errors; and ʰthis people from forgetting Thee, their Lord and Benefactor.

[i. 215; 1st. ed. 267; iii. 177.]

Avert the judgments which we have justly deserved; and mercifully prevent the ruin that threatens us; and grant that we may be ever prepared for what Thy providence shall bring forth.

Bless all persons and places to which Thy providence has made me a debtor; all who have been instrumental to my good, by their assistance, advice, example, or writings; and make me in my turn useful to others.

Let none of those that have desired my prayers, want Thy mercy; but defend, and comfort, and conduct them through this dangerous world, that we may meet in paradise, to praise our God for ever and ever. Amen.

ⁱEnlighten the minds, and pardon the sin, of all that err through simplicity.

Let the wickedness of the wicked come to an end, but guide Thou the just.

[1st ed. 267; iii. 179.]

Relieve and comfort all that are troubled in mind or conscience; all that are in danger of falling into despair; all that are in any dangerous error; all that are in prison, in slavery, or under persecution for a righteous cause; all that are in any distress whatever, that all may improve under their sufferings.

Have mercy upon and reclaim all that are engaged in sinful courses, in youthful lusts, in unchristian quarrels, and in unrighteous lawsuits.

Direct all that are in doubt, all that seek the truth.

ᵉ i. "in distress."
ᶠ i. "judgments that our sins have deserved."
ᵍ i. "error."
ʰ i. "This people from forgetting Thee: and grant that we may ever be prepared," &c.
ⁱ i. om. the rest of the prayer; and adds "*Enemies.* May my enemies ever have a place in my prayers, and in Thy mercy."

FRIDAY.

[i. 215; iii. 179.]

O God, the Creator and Redeemer of all, have mercy upon all whom Thou hast made and redeemed. Amen.

Rom. xi. 16. *Blindness in part is happened to Israel, until the fulness of the Gentiles be come in, and so all Israel shall be saved*[j].

O God, the God of Abraham, look upon Thine everlasting covenant[k]: cause the captivity of Judah and of Israel to return. They were[l] Thy people; O be Thou their Saviour! that all who love Jerusalem, and mourn for her, may rejoice with her[m]; for Jesus Christ's sake, their Saviour and ours. Amen.

June 10, 1727. *This whole country labouring under great distractions.* O sovereign Lord! I prostrate myself before Thee confessing my own sin, and the sin of the people committed to my charge; acknowledging the justice of any scourge which Thou shalt bring upon us; and trembling to think how much I may have contributed towards it; beseeching Thee to have compassion on us, in these days of confusion. For we are, for our sins, delivered up to distraction and oppression.

[i. 216.]

O Lord, prevent the judgments that threaten us; purge this nation from all such crimes as may be the cause of Thy heavy displeasure against us;—from whoredom and drunkenness; from swearing, lying, and perjury; from sacrilege, injustice, fraud, disobedience, malice, and uncharitableness. Take from among us the spirit of atheism, irreligion, and profaneness; and in mercy rebuke and convert all such as give encouragement to any of these vices, which may provoke Thee to give us up to infidelity or destruction. O let Thine anger be turned away from us; give us not over unto the will of our adversaries, and unto such as strive to bring all things into confusion. Preserve this Church in the midst of the dangers that surround us; and restore unto us that peace and unity which we formerly enjoyed; and grant us grace to make a better use of these blessings, for the time to come: for Jesus Christ's sake. Amen.

---

[j] iii. adds, "or 'called to a state of salvation.'"
[k] Genesis xvii. 7.
[l] iii. "are."
[m] Isaiah lxvi. 11.

We complain of oppression, of our laws being perverted, <u>Friday.</u> trampled upon; of arbitrary government, &c. Let us not be wiser than God, who judges these things to be necessary; to exercise the good; to punish the wicked; to reclaim the sinner; to recover those that are going astray; to make all serious. Let us not impeach the ways of Providence, who brings good out of evil; but reverence and submit to His will, His wisdom, and justice.

Proverbs xxviii. 2. *For the transgression of a land, many are the princes thereof:* that is, it is punished with a confused government.

Isai. lxii. 6. *Ye that are the Lord's remembrancers, keep* [i. 217.] *not silence; give Him no rest, till He establish, and till He make Jerusalem (His Church) a praise in the earth.*

Thy kingdom come. Rev. xi. 15. *May the kingdoms of this world become the kingdoms of the Lord and of His Christ. O take unto Thee Thy great power, and reign for ever and ever.* Rev. xi. 17. Though we are altogether unworthy of the good times Thou hast promised Thy Church, yet we beseech Thee deprive us not of them.

O Lord, hear; O Lord, forgive; O Lord, hearken and do; defer not these good days, for Thine own sake, O our God[n].

We hope a day is coming when all the world will come and worship Thee, O God.

See Jeremiah xxxi.—The whole chapter.

Wars. Ezek. xxi. 9, 10. *A sword, a sword is sharpened:* [i. 218.] *should we then make mirth?*

Isai. xxii. 12, 13, 14. *In that day did the Lord call to mourning, &c., and behold joy and gladness, eating flesh and drinking wine. Let us eat and drink, for to-morrow we shall die. This iniquity shall not be purged from you till ye die, saith the Lord God of hosts.*

A sword hath been sharpened for many years past in all the four quarters of the world. Christians against Christians, Turks against Turks, Mahometans against Mahometans, &c. Papists against Protestants.

A war with Spain.

A war with France: declared by France, Mar. 1743-4.

[n] [Dan. ix. 19.]

FRIDAY.

A rebellion in Scotland, begun Aug. 1745, the 10th, the Pretender's son landed.

An invasion threatened from France and Spain, 1745.

April 16, 1746. The rebels in Scotland defeated.

[ii. 99, 101.]

In time of war, or any public calamity. Ezek. xxi. 9, 10. *A sword, a sword is sharpened, and also furbished: it is sharpened to make a sore slaughter; it is furbished that it may glitter: should we then make mirth?*

O God, terrible in judgment, make me and my flock truly serious and affected and penitent in these days of danger: that now fear is on every side, our hope may be in Thee; and when Thy judgments are in the world, we, and all that feel, and all that fear them, may learn righteousness.

We know, O Lord, that Thy judgments are just; and that they are designed in mercy for our amendment. O God, that they may have this blessed effect upon us; and we will depend upon Thy goodness for our deliverance.

In the mean time, we commend unto Thy tender mercy, O God, all that suffer wrongfully, all that flee to Thee for succour, all that have none else to help them. Give them patience under their afflictions, and profit by them.

Compass the righteous with Thy favour as with a shield. Let not those that fall die in their sins unrepented of. Enlighten the minds of such as through simplicity have engaged in an unrighteous cause. Let the wickedness of the wicked come to an end, but establish Thou the just.

Preserve Thy Church in the midst of this uncertain world...

[iii. 180.]

The Plague in France, A.D. 1720.

Numb. xvi. 48. *And Aaron stood between the dead and the living; and the plague was stayed.*

O God, terrible in judgment, let the atonement of Thy Son's blood, infinitely more prevailing than the incense of Aaron, put a stop to the plague which is begun.

In the midst of judgment remember mercy, and for Jesus' sake have regard unto the miseries and cries of all that feel and fear Thy heavy displeasure.

Have mercy upon all those that are appointed to die, and grant that they may omit nothing that is necessary to make their peace with Thee, before they go hence and be no more seen. FRIDAY.

And may this dreadful visitation have this blessed effect upon us all,—to awaken us into a deep sense of our manifold sins, which have deserved the severest punishment; that every one of us may feel the plague of his own heart, and see the reason, and confess the justice of this scourge; that we may turn unto the Lord our God, and that He may have mercy upon us, and command the destroying angel to stay his hand and save our life from destruction.

And grant, O God, that I may omit no part of my duty in this day of danger, but that performing all the offices of a faithful shepherd and watchman, both I and my flock may be ever prepared for the day of death and judgment: for Jesus Christ's sake, who is our life, and health, and Saviour. Amen.

God grant that we may all take notice of the wholesome warnings of Heaven, and profit by them. [iii. 181.]

No kind of death is to be feared by him that has lived well. S. Greg.

SATURDAY.

ALMS.

[M.H. vii.; i. 156; ii. 62; iii. 193.]

Q.—Will you shew yourself gentle, and be merciful for Christ's sake, to poor and needy people, and to all strangers destitute of help?

A.—I will so shew myself, by God's help.

Upon one of the days of the week[p], *(κατὰ μίαν Σαββάτων,) let every one of you lay by him in store as God hath prospered him*[q].

[r]It is by Thy bounty and providence, O God, that I want nothing that is needful either for my soul or body.

Be pleased [s]to receive *this* [t]*acknowledgment* of my gratitude[u] for the many favours [x]I have received. And give me grace, that while I am able, I never turn away my face from any poor man [y]or any good work, that Thy face, and the light of Thy countenance, may never be turned away from me.

---

[p] *Every first day of the week*, ii.
[q] 1 Corinthians xvi. 2.
[r] ii. prefixes "The Prayer;" iii. "The Dedication;" M. H. "Vid. Questions before Consecration of Bishops, &c.
"Give unto God the things that are God's.
"Before laying aside of alms for the poor. Deut. xv. 7; Luke xiv. 14; 2 Tim. i. 17; Prov. iii. 17 [27]: *Withhold not good from them to whom it is due, when it is in the power of thine hand to do it;* Prov. xix. 17. *He that hath pity on the poor lendeth unto the Lord: and look, what he layeth out, it shall be paid him again.*
"1 St. John iii. 17. *Whoso hath this world's good, and seeth his brother have need, and shutteth up his compassion from him,—how dwelleth the love of God in him?* Psalm xli. 1. *Blessed be the man that provideth for the sick and needy, the Lord shall deliver him in the time of trouble.* St. Matt. v. 7."
[s] M. H. and ii. add, "in mercy."
[t] "small," M.H.
[u] "thankfulness," M.H.
[x] M.H. "which by Thy goodness I every day meet with." ii. iii. "I every day meet with."
[y] ii. iii. om. "or any good work."

O Lord my God, whatever I have prepared [z]cometh of SATURDAY. Thee, and of Thine own do I give Thee. Pardon all my vain expenses, and teach me so to husband the riches [a]wherewith I am entrusted[b], that I may always have [c]to offer a testimony of my duty [d]to my great Benefactor, to be bestowed on [e]such poor people [f]and pious works as [g]His providence shall direct to me for relief.

[h]And the good Lord direct my hand, that I may give where there is most need, and after such a way as shall most please Thee, [i]and be for Thine honour.

Give a blessing to what I distribute, that it may do Thy poor good, and that they may own Thy hand in it.

And grant [k]that if it should ever be Thy good[l] pleasure to change my circumstances into a lower condition, [m]that I may bear it patiently, believing[n] assuredly that [o]I have a treasure in heaven: to which place I most humbly beseech Thee to bring me, [p]and the people committed to my care, for the sake of Jesus Christ. Amen[q].

Gen. xxviii. 20. [r]*And Jacob vowed a vow, saying, If God will be with me, and will keep me in the way that I go, and will give me bread to eat, and raiment to put on, then shall the Lord be my God; and of all that Thou shalt give me, I will surely give the tenth unto Thee*[s].

Knowsley[t], *Easter-Day*, 1693. [u]It having pleased God to [v]give me a temporal income [x]above my hopes, and the hopes [M.H. ix.; i. 157; ii. 62; iii. 191.]

---

[z] "for Thy poor," M.H.
[a] M H. "with which I am blessed."
[b] Prima manu, "blessed;" ii. "trusted."
[c] M.H. "wherewith."
[d] M.H. "and gratitude."
[e] M.H. "those poor people whom Thou shalt direct me to relieve."
[f] ii. iii. om. "and pious works."
[g] ii. "Thy good" (prima manu) "Spirit."
[h] These two sentences om. M.H.
[i] ii. iii. om. last clause.
[k] "O Lord," M.H.
[l] M.H. om. "good."
[m] M.H. adds, "give me grace."
[n] "knowing," M.H.
[o] "my treasure is."
[p] "and my family," ii.
[q] M.H. adds, "The Lord give a blessing to what I offer, that it may do the poor good, and that they may own Thy hand to it." Also in the margin, "And I thank God that before I knew it I pitched upon the proportion which comes near to what the Jews were bound to give."
[r] Also in M.H. ix.
[s] M.H. adds, "It shall fight for thee" (saith Sirach's son) "more than [a mighty shield and strong spear." Ecclus. xxix. 33.]
[t] M.H. and ii. om. "Knowsley."
[u] ii. adds "Now," [in reference to the text from Genesis, quoted above].
[v] M.H. "of His mere bounty and goodness to bless me with;" ii. "trust me with;" [prima manu, "bless me, (and that of His mere goodness, without my help,) with;"] iii. "bless me with."
[x] M.H. iii. "far above my hopes or deserts;" ii. "far above my deserts or my very desires."

SATURDAY. of my father's house, and ʸhaving hitherto ᶻgiven a tenth only, ᵃI now devote one fifth of my income to pious uses.

[M.H. x.] *August*, 1693. The God that gave me a will to make this solemn purpose, has given me grace not to repent of it, and He will give me grace to my life's end. Amen. *Though I give my goods to feed the poor, and have not charity, &c.*

Prov. iii. 9. *Honour Him with thy substance, and with the first-fruits of all thine increase.*

It having pleased God to bring me to the bishoprick of Man, I find my house in ruins, which obliges me to interrupt my charity to the poor in some measure, &c.

[i. 157; iii. 191.] *Bishop's Court, Jan.* 6, 1716. ᵇHaving enough and to spare ᶜabove a decent hospitality ᵈof a Christian bishop, I do therefore ᵉdedicate ᶠto the glory of my great Benefactor three-tenths ᵍ to pious uses. As also one-tenth of the profits of the demesnes ʰto be turned into corn for poor families. And two-tenths of ⁱ my English estate, till I can purchase the ʲimpropriate tithes for the use of the vicar, and after that one-tenth ᵏ.

[iii. 191; i. 157.] *Bishop's Court, Feb.* 18, 1718. ˡ*To the glory of God.* I find by constant experience that God will be no man's debtor. I find that I have enough and to spare: so that for the future I dedicate four-tenths ᵐ to pious uses, one-tenth of the ⁿ demesnes and customs which I receive in money, and of

---

ʸ M.H. ii. add, " I."

ᶻ M.H. "but given one-tenth part of my income to the poor;" ii. "given but a tenth;" iii. "but given a tenth."

ᵃ M.H. "I do therefore purpose, and I thank God for putting it into my heart, that of all the profits which it shall [please] God to give me, and which shall become due to me [from the] 5th of August next, (after which time I hope to have paid my small debts,) I do purpose to separate the fifth part of all my incomes, as I shall receive them, to pious uses, and particularly for the poor;" ii. "I do for the time to come purpose to give a fifth to pious uses: and out of the demesnes and tenants of the bishoprick which are properly for his housekeeping, I hope to give the same proportion in daily alms and kindness to the poor, the widow and the fatherless;" iii. "I do for the future purpose to give one-fifth part."

ᵇ iii. " Finding that I have."

ᶜ iii. adds, "over and."

ᵈ iii. om. "of…bishop," and adds, "besides what I formerly gave to pious uses, and being convinced that I am no proprietor, but only a steward of the Church's patrimony."

ᵉ iii. adds, "to the glory of God."

ᶠ iii. om. "to…Benefactor."

ᵍ iii. adds, "of my rents."

ʰ iii. om. "to…families."

ⁱ iii. adds, "the profits of."

ʲ iii. "impropriation of the estate, which I intend to do, and give it to the Church."

ᵏ iii. adds, "besides."

ˡ i. "From this time forwards I dedicate," &c.

ᵐ i. adds, "of my ecclesiastical incomes and rents."

ⁿ i. "profit of the demesnes in corn, and of customs, and English estate as before."

my English estate as above. And the Lord accept His poor servant in this service, for Christ's sake. Amen°.

Bishop's Court, St. Thomas's Eve, 1721. To the glory of God. I dedicate the interest of all my monies to pious uses, so long as I have wherewithal to live on besides. Blessed be God for giving me an heart and will to do so. [iii. 191.]

[Same date.] I do this day in gratitude to my bountiful Creator dedicate the whole interest of what monies I have at use, to pious uses, while I have to live on besides. Blessed be God for giving me an heart, &c. [i. 157.]

Bishop's Court, Dec. 23, 1722. I made the above dedications when I had enough and to spare, ᵖand this I did in a grateful return to God for the undeserved bounties He had heaped upon me. It has now pleased ᑫHim to suffer me to fall into ʳtroubles, and an expensive law-suit, ˢto defend the discipline of this Church, and the episcopal jurisdiction. He is the same great and good God, who can either shorten my troubles or lessen my expenses, or make good my losses in another life. In sureᵗ confidence of which, and as a testimony of my firm faith in ᵘHis power, truth and goodness, I do ˣfor the future dedicate five-tenths of ʸall my ecclesiastical rents to pious uses; and the rest as above ᶻ. And blessed be the good Spirit of God, who at this time has put this thing into my heart, as an earnest of His purpose ᵃof weaning my affections from the world. Amen. [iii. 191; i. 157.]

ᵇAnd God has not disappointedᶜ His servant, but has raised up such friends to countenance my righteous cause, as has brought it to a good end, and has always raised me up such friends (many of them unknown to me) as hath made the burden of my expenses tolerable, which would otherwise have almost sunk me. Blessed be God for this mighty favour. [iii. 192; i. 158.]

° i. om. the last sentence.
ᵖ i. om. "and...upon me."
ᑫ i. "God."
ʳ i. om. "troubles and."
ˢ i. "in defence of the discipline and jurisdiction of this Church."
ᵗ i. om. "sure."
ᵘ i. "in Him."
ˣ ii. "dedicate this day."
ʸ i. "my rents ecclesiastical."
ᶻ i. "before."
ᵃ i. "to wean my affections from the world and its idols."
ᵇ i. adds, "N.B. Sept. 10, 1723." om. "And."
ᶜ i. "my trust in Him; for He has raised up friends unknown to me, who have made my expenses more tolerable than otherwise they would have been."

SATURDAY.
[i. 158.]

Warrington, Sept. 21, 1729. If God shall bring me to my flock and to my home in peace, I purpose through His grace to be much more liberal to all such as stand in need of my help. And in kindness to my clergy, I will take no deductions for my expense and trouble in getting for them the royal bounty.

Bishop's Court, 1730. Blessed be God, I have by my own and the charity of Bishop Crowe's widow and Bishop Levinz's widow, &c., established a small fund for the widows and orphans of my clergy.

Easter-Day, 1735. St. Luke xix. 8. *Behold, Lord, the half of Thy goods (for indeed they are Thine and of Thine own) I do give to Thee and to Thy poor.*

The Lord having convinced me, by an experience of more than forty years, that He will be no man's debtor, and having in every station of life in which His Providence has placed me, given me much more than was necessary for a decent support: in an humble gratitude to my gracious Benefactor, I do from henceforward dedicate one-half of my rents to pious uses; as also the whole interest of all my monies; one-tenth, in corn, of the profits of the demesnes, and of all customs paid in monies.

O Lord Christ, say unto me, as Thou didst unto this happy convert, *Salvation is come unto this house.* Amen.

[i. 159; ii. 67; iii. 192.]

St. Luke xi. 41. *But rather give alms of such things as you have,* (or, as you are able[d],) *and all things are clean unto you.* That is, proportion your alms to your estate, lest God proportion your estate to your alms[e].

[i. 159.]

St. Luke xii. 33. *Sell that ye have, and give alms*[f]*: provide yourselves bags which wax not old; a treasure in the heavens that faileth not, where no thief approacheth, neither moth corrupteth. For where your treasure is, there will your heart be also.*

---

[d] iii. adds, "τὰ ἔνοντα."

[e] Bishop Beveridge [Sermons, vol. xii. § 2. ed. 1714. "Be sure to observe this rule, even always to proportion your charity to your estates, otherwise God may justly proportion your estates to your charity."]

[f] [On this text, MS. ii. 67, has the following:—" And shall I think of purchasing? God grant that my Master's words may have more weight with me." iii. 192 has,—"O my Lord and Master, I am ashamed when I consider how much I forgot this command (for such they are to me) [sic], but by Thy grace I will make amends for this wrong step."]

N.B. This is still a necessary Christian duty, whatever men think of it,—to part with our worldly enjoyments for the sake of Christ.

To sell all; that is, to renounce all the pleasures, and pomp, and enjoyment, which wealth affords, as if we had actually parted with it; to take to a man's self no more of his estate than necessity requires; and to make the remainder the support of the poor and distressed;—it being utterly impossible to take delight in the enjoyments of riches, and to love God with all the soul.

If God is our only happiness, we shall of course be *dead, crucified,* to the world.

Give to the poor, said our Lord to the rich young man whom He loved. Had there been a better way of disposing of his estate, He would certainly have told him.

St. Matthew vi. 1, 2. *Take heed that ye do not your alms before men, to be seen of them.—Let not thy left hand know what thy right hand doeth.—Thy Father, which seeth in secret, Himself shall reward thee openly.*

By *vanity* we lose both our riches and our reward. It is vanity to boast of our alms, and it is vanity to take pleasure in reflecting upon them. It is sufficient that God will remember them.

Tobit xii. 8. *It is better to give alms than to lay up gold.*

Deuteronomy xv. 7. *If there shall be a poor man within any of thy gates, thou shalt not harden thy heart from thy poor brother; but thou shalt open thine hand* wide *unto him, and lend him sufficient for his need. Thy heart shall not be grieved when thou givest unto him, because that* for this thing *the Lord thy God shall bless thee in thy works.*

Psalm xli. 1. *Blessed be the man that provideth for the sick and needy: the Lord shall deliver him in the time of trouble.* [i. 160.]

St. Matthew v. 7. *Blessed are the merciful, for they shall obtain mercy.*

Ecclesiasticus iv. 8. *Bow down thine ear to the poor, and give him a friendly answer with meekness; be as a father unto the fatherless, and as a husband to the widow; so shalt thou be as the Son of the Most High, and he shall love thee more than thy mother doth.*

SATURDAY. **Ecclesiasticus xxix. 11.** *Lay up Thy treasure according to the commandment. It shall bring thee profit, it shall deliver thee, it shall fight for thee, &c.*

Isaiah lviii. 10, 11. *If thou draw out thy soul to the hungry, and satisfy the afflicted soul, then shall thy light rise in obscurity, and thy darkness be as the noon-day. And the Lord shall guide thee continually, and satisfy thy soul in drought, and make fat thy bones; and thou shalt be like a watered garden, and like a spring of water, whose waters fail not.*

[i. 160; ii. 66; iii. 195.] St. Bernard, Ep. 2. [ad Fulconem. § ii. "Quæ sunt illa tua? Beneficia Ecclesiæ...Dignum est ut qui altario deservit, de altario vivat...non autem ut de altario luxurieris."]

Do not imagine that all that belongs to your Church belongs to you. You have indeed a right to live by the altar, but not in luxury.

All above an honest maintenance is sacrilege[g].

"Gravius est qui propria dare debuit aliena surripere."

"Nihil Ecclesia sibi nisi fidem possidet: Possessio Ecclesiæ sumptus est egenorum." S. Ambros. 2.

"Christum debitorem habere, plus est quam omnia possidere[h]."

N.B. The Church has not had worse enemies, than such as have been raised to estates out of her patrimony. This should open the eyes of those who make no other use of Church livings than to provide portions, raise estates and families, enrich relations, &c. From which practices the good Lord keep me[i].

"[j]Non tua sunt quæ possides, sed dispensatio tibi credita est."

---

[g] ["Quicquid præter necessarium victum ac simplicem vestitum de altario retines, tuum non est: rapina est, sacrilegium est."]

[h] ii. iii. add, "Greg. Naz.," and ii. subjoins, "Is. xliv. and ch. lviii."]

[i] [ii. and iii. give this as follows:—
"It has been long observed that[a] the Church has not had worse enemies than such as have been raised out of her patrimony, [b]for these, viper-like, tear out the bowels of that parent which made them what they are. [c]And perhaps it is a just judgment of God, and should open the eyes of such as make no other use of Church livings, than to provide portions, make[d] families, enrich relations, &c., from which[e] God preserve His servant."

ii. adds, "Those who follow the crime of Judas, and take that to themselves which belongs to the poor, must not hope not to fall into a condemnation something like this.

"2 Cor. xi. 8. *Taking wages of them, to serve you.*"

[j] iii. adds to this, "Clem. Alex." [in Tract. "Quis Dives salvatur," ii. 953.]

[a] iii. om. "It...that."
[b] iii. adds, "For."
[c] iii. "And it is often."
[d] iii. "raise."
[e] iii. adds, "crimes."

SATURDAY.

The goods of this world, much more the goods of the Church, are mere *depositums*, put into the hands of men for the common good—of the Church and of mankind[k].

Colossians iii. 2. *Set your affections on things above.* [i. 161.]

It is more for our advantage to have the prayers of a poor, good man, than the smiles of the greatest man on earth.

Deuteronomy x. 18, 19. *The Lord loveth the stranger; love ye therefore the stranger, &c.*

St. Mark x. 21. *Sell what thou hast, and give to the poor; and thou shalt have treasure in heaven; and come, take up thy cross, and follow Me.*

My God! we think we love Thee above all things, when, without being sensible of it, we love a thousand things better; but as we hope for heaven, we must sacrifice even what we love most. This is a necessary duty now: and though it be a very, very difficult one, yet to Thee all things are possible.

Sell all: i.e. part with the enjoyment of riches from yourself, and make them the support of those that want, with the same freedom of mind as if you had really sold your estate, and it were no longer yours. This is what all rich men are obliged to do, however strange the doctrine be to flesh and blood; viz. to part with the splendid enjoyment of riches— to make them the support of the poor and distressed.

To sell, is only an expression for a disregard for riches; such as are, "being *dead* to the world," "crucified," "born again," "overcome the world;" all which denote that temper which Christianity requires.

Matt. xxv. 40. *Inasmuch* (Fr.[1] "as often") *as ye have done it unto one of the least of these My brethren, ye have done it unto Me.*

As often!—Who then would miss any occasion? *The least:*—Who then would despise any object? *To Me:*—So

---

[k] Dr. More's Divine Dialogues; [ii. adds "p. 16," and om. "much... Church."]

["It is a great and general error in mankind, that they think all their acquisitions are of right for themselves, whether it be power, or riches, or wisdom, and conceit they are no farther obliged than to fortify or adorn themselves with them: whereas they are in truth mere *depositums*, put into their hands by Providence for the common good." Part i. p. 16, Lond. 1668.]

[1] [i. e. Quesnel's French version, "autant de fois:" Vulgate, "quamdiu."]

SATURDAY. that in serving the poor, we serve Jesus Christ. O comfortable declaration!

It is not out of cruelty or indigence, that Christ suffers any of His members to want or be in misery, but to give others an opportunity of exercising their faith and their love, and of making some amends for their mis-expenses by their alms.

Mark ix. 41. *Whosoever shall give you a cup of water to drink in My Name, because ye belong to Christ; verily* (with an oath He assures us) *he shall not lose his reward.*

[i. 162.] This should always, if possible, be our intention:—This poor, oppressed, this miserable man, belongs to Christ. This would wonderfully enhance the value of our good deeds before God[i].

Mercy is a natural debt, not left to our discretion. He that stands in need of our help is to have it. Inclination, friendship, vain generosity, are selfish motives.

The last refuge of a sinner is Alms: it is an art of turning our Master's goods innocently to our own advantage, and "making to ourselves friends of His;" heaven being the patrimony and inheritance of the poor; and by our alms we engage them to solicit the mercy of God for us. This is the only way to sanctify riches, which are almost always either the fruit, or the seed of unrighteousness and injustice. And indeed we are more obliged to the poor than they to us[k].

Earthly riches are almost always abused without an extraordinary grace.

Luke xviii. 12. Be very careful not to be puffed up with the thoughts of your alms. *I give tithes of all that I possess,* was the effect of a pride more prejudicial than the sins of a publican. It is a stratagem of the devil to set before us a sight of our own good works, and to deprive us of that humility which alone can render us acceptable to God.

Luke xxi. 3. *And Jesus said, Of a truth I say unto you, that this poor widow hath cast in more than they all.*

God judges not by the greatness of the gift, but by the heart that offers it[l].

The applause which the great gifts of the rich receive, the

---

[i] [Quesnel in loc.] [k] [cf. Quesnel in St. Luke xvi. 6, 9.]

complacency they take in them, and the little religion where- SATURDAY. with they are too often companied, lessen them in the sight of God[1].

The rich indeed may give much, and reserve much for themselves. The poor, who gives all, reserves nothing to himself, but faith in God's providence[m].

Shut my heart, O Jesus, against the love of worldly riches.

Romans xv. 25. *But now I go unto Jerusalem to minister* (that is, to carry alms) *unto the saints.*

So great an apostle is not at all afraid that he should debase his character in carrying of alms.

A Christian, who considers all other Christians as one body in Jesus Christ, will cheerfully contribute even to the necessities of the greatest, remotest strangers.

God often spares the rich for the sake of the poor. To the poor, therefore, the rich stand indebted.

A rich man, if a good man, is more afraid of not finding fit persons to receive his alms, than a poor man is of not finding persons to bestow alms upon him.

The very best of men are only instruments in God's hands, [i. 163.] to receive and to give what God bestows upon them. And this they should do without any desire of glory or self-interest.

Let us make light of money and riches, and send [them] before us into the heavenly treasures, where neither moth nor rust doth corrupt; where neither tyrants nor thieves can take it from us; but where it will be kept to our eternal advantage, under the custody of God Himself[n].

Tobit xii. 8. *It is better to give alms, than to lay up gold.*

Thou, O Lord, hast been all mercy to me; grant that I may be all mercy to others for Thy sake.

We honour Jesus Christ in His poor, when we treat them kindly and help them.

Upon giving of Alms. Not unto me, but unto Thee, O God, be the thanks and praise and glory.

---

[1] [Quesnel in loc.]
[m] [Quesnel.]
[n] Lactantius, Epit. ch. vii. [Epitome Divin. Instit. c. 65, ap. Galland. Biblioth. iv. 390. "Contemnenda est pecunia, et ad cœlestes transferenda thesauros, ubi nec fur effodiat, nec rubigo consumat, nec tyrannus eripiat; sed nobis ad æternam opulentiam, Deo custode, servetur."]

SATURDAY. Matt. xv. [37]. *And they took of the fragments seven baskets full.* Here is a true emblem of alms: we receive more than we give.

See Allen of Justification, fol. p. 168-9, &c., 170, 171°.

[i. 164; ii. 64; iii. 195.] p *Tithes. So hath the Lord* (viz. Jesus Christ q) *ordained that they which preach the gospel should live of the gospel.* 1 Cor. ix. 14.

° [Works of William Allen, vicar of Bridgewater, Lond. 1707. "A View of Justification," §§ 13, 14, 15. Bishop Wilson is giving the substance of three folio pages.]

p [ii. iii. or both, add the following texts under the head of Alms.] Luke xiv. 13. "Call the poor...And thou shalt be blessed, for they cannot recompense thee." 2 Tim. i. 17. "Onesiphorus...sought me out very diligently, and oft refreshed me." Ecclus. xii. 3. "There can no good thing come to him that giveth no alms." "Terram calcare didici, non adorare." Clem. Alex. [Cohortatio ad Gentes, t. i. p. 50, ed. Potter. γῆν δὲ ἐγὼ πατεῖν, οὐ προσκυνεῖν μεμελέτηκα.] "It is required in stewards that a man be found faithful." 1 Cor. iv. 2. "If thine enemy hunger, feed him," &c. Rom. xii. 20. "He that sheweth mercy, let him do it with cheerfulness." Rom. xii. 8. "Nudam crucem nudus sequar." Hieron. [ep. lii. § 5.] Vid. Paraenesin ad Ecclesiam Anglican. § 68; item § 70, de Pompa Ecclesiastica.

Three-tenths of £5:

The first tenth, .. 10s. ⎫
The second tenth, 9s. ⎬ Total, 1l. 7s.
The third tenth, . 8s.   ⎭

[The above occur, ii. 64, 67; iii. 196 adds], " Eminentia Episcopalis non in eo sita est, prædia possidere multa, splendere auro, cingi satellitio, vehi pilentis, vestiri serico, &c....Sed esse intima pietate, plenum divinæ lucis, cum zelo pro gloria Dei et Ecclesiæ salute, debitaque rerum experientia, et privati commodi ejuratione:—hæc sunt, quæ veri Episcopi ideam absolvunt. Externi vero characteres sunt,—esse multum in labore, in ærumna, in vigiliis, in fame et siti, in jejuniis, et sollicitum esse pro omnibus ecclesiis: cum infirmis infirmari, alienis offendiculis uri," &c. Jo. Am. Comen. Paraenesis ad Eccl. Angl. § 73.

[iii. 197.] Numb. xxxi. 48, &c. "And the officers... said, Thy servants have taken the number of the soldiers under our charge, and there lacketh not one man of us; we have therefore brought an oblation for the Lord,—To make an atonement for our souls,—For a memorial before the Lord."

Luke xiv. 13. "When thou makest a feast, call the poor, the maimed," &c. In these a Christian finds his brethren, his kinsmen, his neighbours, and his friends—because in them he finds Jesus Christ.

Jesus Christ is answerable for whatever one gives to the poor, and our security, if we give as we should do: whatever is given to them is given to Him.

The goods of the Church. Father Paul [of Ecclesiastical Benefices and Revenues, Eng. Tr. 1736, abridged from § 2, 6, 7, 11.]

"Till the year 470, the clergy and poor lived upon the oblations of the faithful, which were divided by the deacons by the direction of the Bishop, as every one had need. About that time it was ordained, that they should be divided into four parts. One, the Bishop's, for hospitality, &c.: 2. For other ministers: 3. For the fabric of the Church, and church houses, and hospitals: 4. For the poor of the place.

"750. The Bishops becoming powerful, and finding soldiers for the wars, or going in person themselves, in many places seized all the revenues themselves. In the meantime the inferior clergy were distressed, and the laity, out of devotion, gave them part of their own, till at length it began to be canvassed what part that should be, which introduced the paying of a tenth or tithes." Quære.

q Matt. x. 10.

SATURDAY.

O Lord[r], who hast graciously allowed us a recompense for our labours, make me [s]a faithful steward of that part of Thy revenues committed to my charge, that I may give Thy servants their portion of meat in due season; and that I may not feed myself or[t] family with that which belongs to Thy poor.

But, above all, I pray[u] God [v]give me grace to *preach* the gospel as well as live of it; and that when my Lord cometh, He may find me so doing. Amen[x].   [i. 164.]

By what right can those who do nothing at all claim a share of those tithes which are by Jesus Christ appointed for the propagation of the Gospel? To satisfy avarice, ambition, luxury, or pleasures, with these, is no better than sacrilege.

"Omnium negotiorum ecclesiasticorum episcopus habeat ["curam, φροντιδα,"] et ea, velut Deo contemplante, dispenset." Can. Apost. 37. [Hard. i. 20.]

Numb. xviii. 26. *When ye take of the children of Israel the tithes, which I have given you from them for your inheritance, then you shall offer up an heave-offering of it for the Lord, even a tenth part of the tithe.*

Deut. xviii. 2. *The Lord* (that is, that which God hath reserved unto Himself) *is their inheritance.*

This is said to shew, that the priests had as good a right to the tithes and offerings as any of the other tribes had to their land, they being both the gift of God.

Deut. xxvii. 12, 13, 15. *When thou hast made an end of tithing all the tithes of thine increase, and hast given it unto the Levite, &c., then thou shalt say before the Lord, I have brought away the hallowed things out of mine house, &c. Look down from Thy holy habitation, and bless Thy people.*   [i. 165.]

What care is here taken, that men shall not confound the things that belong to God with those that they may lawfully convert to their own use[y]! and indeed a great deal more depends on this than men are aware of, or are willing to believe.

---

[r] "God," ii. iii.
[s] ii. adds, "I humbly beseech Thee;" iii. "I beseech Thee."
[t] ii. iii. "nor."
[u] ii. "beseech."
[v] ii. iii. add, "to."
[x] iii. adds, 1 Pet. v. 2. "Taking the oversight not for filthy lucre."
[y] [This sentence and the text before it are repeated, i. 170.]

SATURDAY. Matt. x. 10. *The workman is worthy of his meat.*

This is a matter of justice as well as of Divine right. But then observe, it is only he that *labours,* not he that is idle, who has a right to the revenues of the Church.

Men that are liberal, even to profuseness, to the ministers of their pleasures,—that think nothing too much which is laid out upon the body, upon trifles and vanity,—will yet grudge him that has the care of their souls, and who stands accountable for them, a very small part of their incomes.

After all, it is God who maintains His own ministers, and not the people; He who gives all, having reserved to His own disposal a part of every man's estate, labour, &c.

Prov. iii. 9, 10. *Honour the Lord with thy substance, and with the first-fruits* (the best) *of all thine increase; so shall thy barns be filled, &c.*

Gal. vi. 6. *Let him* (that is, he is bound by his Christianity) *that is taught in the word communicate to him that teacheth in all good things.*

When God left out the tribe of Levi in the division of the land, He did it for his advantage: for He gave him a tenth instead of a twelfth part; and even this under such conditions as freed him from bodily labour.

May my gracious God, who has blessed me with wealth, may He bless me with humility and gratitude, and with a perseverance in the most lovely grace of charity.

1 Cor. ix. 14. *So hath the Lord ordained, &c. Live of the Gospel:* i. e. out of the labours and revenues of those to whom they preach the Gospel. And this (upon principles of justice as well as of religion: if thou hast much, give plenteously) as God has prospered you, that is, proportionably to your incomes. *This no human law can set aside.*

There being a great deal of difference betwixt being exempt by law and exempt in conscience.

Every one is bound to help the poor, not just as he is assessed by human laws, but according to his ability, as God has prospered him; and if he will do no more than he can be compelled by law, he will have but a bad account to make.

Prescriptions are therefore unlawful.

Ezekiel xliv. 30. *And the first of the first-fruits of all things, &c., ye shall give unto the priest, that he may cause* SATURDAY. *the blessing to rest in thine house.*

Ecclus. vii. 9. *Say not, God will look upon the multitude of my oblations,* (that is, if we wilfully break His laws,) *and when I offer to the Most High God, He will accept it.*

Tithes. Deut. xii. 19: and all the texts referred to, and my notes upon many of them.

God has no need of our help to relieve the poor. He [i. 166.] commands us, for our own profit, that we may help one another; we them with our riches, they us with their prayers. We give nothing to the poor but what we have received from God. How well is a man paid for his alms, when they obtain for him the grace of God! not to mention a reward in temporal blessings.

2 Cor. ix. 12. Many good fruits of this charity: God is adored and praised by them that receive benefit by it: the benefits they receive are many, &c.

1 Tim. v. 8. *But if any provide not for his own, and especially for those of his own house* (kindred), *he hath denied the faith, and is worse than an infidel.*

A very terrible sentence! And will not this awaken *pastors, masters, parents,* now fast asleep in a deplorable neglect of those who stand related to them, both as to temporals and spirituals?

We rob the poor, when we leave to others the care of maintaining our poor relations, when we ourselves are able to do it, and thereby give those charitable persons the means of supporting other poor persons.

John xii. 6. *This Judas said, not that he cared for the poor, but because he was a thief, and had the bag, and bare* (the money) *which was put therein.*

Our Lord trusts a thief with the little money that He had for His own, or His disciples' necessities, and for the poor, because He values it not much[z]. My Saviour, Thou who hast entrusted me with the revenues of Thy poor, make me a faithful steward; let me not be proud of the trust, since Judas himself had once the same office; but let me dread being unfaithful, lest I draw upon me his cursed fate and end!

[z] [Quesnel.]

SATURDAY. They who are united in an expectation of an eternal reward, ought to have very little regard to those external advantages which distinguish men.

We ought to look upon it as a certain truth, that it is God who sends to us His friends in the persons of the poor and strangers.

Ecclus. xxxv. 9. *In all thy gifts shew a cheerful countenance, and dedicate thy tithes with gladness.*

[i. 167.] *Give unto the Most High according as He hath enriched thee. For the Lord thy God recompenseth, and will give thee seven times as much. But do not think to corrupt* (viz. God) *with gifts, nor trust to unrighteous sacrifices, for the Lord is judge.*

Remember to give to those that are ashamed to ask; and do not forget your poor relations, lest you be worse than an infidel.

"Gloria Episcopi est, pauperum opibus providere: ignominia omnium sacerdotum, propriis studere divitiis." St. Hieron. ad Nepotianum. [ep. lii. 6, ed. Vallarsii.]

Rom. xii. 18. *He that sheweth mercy, let him do it with cheerfulness.*

The good Lord preserve me from vanity, and from seeking applause for my charity.

N.B. To lend is sometimes better than to give, because it flatters not our vanity; it puts not the receiver to the blush; and gives not encouragement to idleness and sloth.

Jesus Christ has left the poor in His place, and has in them continual wants and necessities to be supplied.

There is danger in letting our thoughts run too much upon the good we do, lest we should at last come to fancy that God is in our debt; and that He should reward us in this life.

The merits of the poor is not to be the rule of our charity. *If thine enemy hunger, feed him, &c. I was a stranger, and ye took me not in.* God Himself maketh His sun to shine upon the evil, &c.

We should always have enough for the poor, if we would but moderate our vanity, and live according to the spirit of the gospel.

It will one day be found true, that the measure of the

SATURDAY.

riches which any man possesseth should have been the measure of his charity. *If thou hast much, &c.*

Ecclus. xl. 24. *Brethren and help are against the time of trouble: but alms delivereth more than them both.*

Tobit xiv. 10. *Manasses gave alms, and escaped the snares of death which they had set for him.*

Ecclus. iii. 30. *Alms maketh an atonement for sin.*

2 Cor. ix. 7. *God loveth a cheerful giver.*

St. Luke vi. 38. *Give, and it shall be given unto you:* GOOD MEASURE, PRESSED DOWN, SHAKEN TOGETHER, and RUNNING OVER, &c.

What an heap of arguments and expressions are here to encourage men to charity!

He who gives to receive glory of men, is as great but [a] worse beggar than any he gives to.

Send Thy blessing upon my labours and my substance, and continue to me a willing mind to help such as have need according to my ability.

Ecclus. xviii. 15, 16. *My son, blemish not thy good deeds, neither use uncomfortable words when thou givest any thing. Shall not the dew assuage the heat? so is a word better than a gift. A word is better than a gift; but both are with a gracious man.*

Prov. xi. 24. *There is that scattereth, and yet increaseth; and there is that withholdeth more than is meet, but it tendeth to poverty.*

Whenever we relieve the wants of the body, we ought not [i. 168.] to forget the necessities of the soul. Good advice, and devout petitions for their eternal welfare, will then be most proper and acceptable to God.

O God, who knowest the necessities of all Thy creatures, give Thy poor the spiritual graces they stand in need of.

Lord Jesus, conduct this poor blind person in the way of light and peace everlasting.

Support Thy poor members, O Jesu, under all their difficulties, and sanctify their bodily wants to the salvation of their souls.

May Thy poor, O Lord, engage Thee, by a life of resignation and piety, to make them amends in the next world for what they want in this,

SATURDAY. Let Thy poor have a particular share of Thy grace and mercy, that they may appear for me at the day of judgment.

Let these poor people have Thy grace, whatever else Thou deniest them.

May the wants of Thy poor here help to increase their happiness hereafter.

Lord, grant that these may bear their poor estate with patience and resignation, and that we may one day meet in the paradise of God.

Give me, O my Lord and Benefactor, an abhorrence of making a trade of Thy gifts, of which I am only a dispenser.

Matt. x. 8. *Freely ye have received, freely give.*

Prov. xvii. 5, xiv. 31. *He that mocketh and he that oppresseth the poor reproacheth his Maker.* As if He did not order what is best for all His creatures.

May this Thy poor member, O Lord, make a Christian use of this condition in which Thy providence hath placed him.

Jesus Christ is continually humbled in His members; some are poor, in prison, sick, naked, hungry, &c. Let me, O Lord, see and help Thee in all these objects.

[i. 169.] *Hospitality* does not consist in keeping a plentiful table, and making great entertainments; but in providing a sober and suitable refreshment for such as are in want, and for such as come to visit us.

[i. 170.] A man that has faith will be glad to discharge himself of the burden (some part at least) of temporal goods, in order to secure those that are eternal; and to be in some sense the preserver of his brethren.

Charity treats the most unknown and remote like brethren, as being children of the same heavenly Father, and members of the same body.

1 Cor. xiii. 3. *Though I bestow all my goods to feed the poor, and have not charity, it profiteth me nothing.*

If external acts of charity do not proceed from charity, that is, from a love of God, and of our neighbour for His sake, they are as nothing in the sight of God. My God, pour into my heart this most excellent gift, the very bond of peace and of all virtue.

The apostles and their successors are the proper trustees for the charity of Christ.

Galatians vi. 10. *Let us do good unto all men.*

He who seeks for Jesus Christ in the poor, in order to relieve and assist Him, will not be too solicitous to find any other merit in them than that of Jesus Christ.

For our earthly things, O Lord, give us heavenly: for temporal, eternal.

1 Pet. iv. 10. *As every man has received the gift, even to minister the same one to another, as stewards of the manifold grace of God.*

N.B. We have received them freely not for ourselves but for others. No man is excused. As stewards we are accountable. Every man should be content with his own talents.

Luke iii. 11. *He that hath two coats, let him impart to him that hath none.*

That is, let him that hath plenty—to spare—of any thing necessary for life, let him give to him that wants.

Matt. x. 42. *Whosoever shall give a cup of cold water in the name of a disciple, &c.*

We should, in all our charities, direct our eye towards Christ in His members; it is this which heightens the smallest gifts. Men reward what is done on human motives; God such as are done for His sake.

The more a man gives to the poor, the more he receives from God. The increase is like that of the five loaves and two fishes, which produced twelve baskets of fragments, after five thousand were filled.

He that for his good actions expects the applause of men, runs the hazard of losing the reward of God.

Matt. xviii. 5. *Whoso shall receive one such little child in My Name, receiveth Me.*

Jesus Christ is received in the persons of the poor. These must be received not out of human respects, nor ostentation, nor for our own satisfaction, but in the name and for the sake of Christ. This renders our hospitality truly Christian. [i. 171.]

The poor are, as it were, the receivers of the rights and dues belonging to God; we must have a care of defrauding them.

St. Luke xxi. 3. *And Jesus said, Of a truth I say unto you that this poor widow hath cast in more than they all: for all these of their abundance have cast in unto the offerings of*

SATURDAY. *God, but she of her penury hath cast in all the living that she had.*

From hence it appears that God judges of the gift by the heart that offers it.

Lessen not the value of your alms by the applause you receive, nor by taking too much pleasure in them.

When a rich man gives a great deal, he has still a great deal left: but when a poor man gives much, he has nothing left but confidence in God.

God magnifies the power of His grace in disengaging a soul from the love of riches; O my God, manifest this power upon me; raise my soul above the fear of poverty, and let me have the greatest part of my treasure in heaven.

Deut. xxvii. 12, 13[a]. By this it appears that the proportion of charity appointed by God Himself to His own people for the relief of the poor, was every year a thirtieth part of all their incomes, or a tenth every third year; to be laid up every third year as a fund for charitable uses.

This was the Jews' proportion. He that came short of this was a breaker of the law, and without repentance and restitution had no hopes of pardon.

The Christian's proportion ought to be greater, as his hopes and reward will be greater.

Prov. xi. 24. *There is that scattereth and yet increaseth.*

Almsgiving never lessened but rather increaseth a man's estate. Mal. iii. 10. *Bring me all the tithes, &c., and prove me, &c.*

May my gracious God, who has blessed me with wealth, may He bless me with humility and gratitude, and with a perseverance in the most lovely grace of charity.

Psalm cxii. [5.] *A good* (i.e. a charitable) *man will guide his affairs with discretion.* That is, he will cut off, and retrench all needless expenses in apparel, diet, diversions, &c., that he may give to him that needeth.

[i. 172.] In alms and charity to the poor, and good works, a good Christian will always endeavour to be better than he appears to the world to be.

"That thine alms may be in secret" as much as may be.

Charity; or, the love of God and our neighbour. 1 Cor.

---

[a] [See before, p. 249.]

xiii. [3]. *Though I give my goods to feed the poor, and have* SATURDAY. *not charity, it profiteth me nothing.* [i. 174.]

It is but the first essay of charity to give alms.

Whoever shews mercy to men will certainly receive from God.

1 John iii. 15. *Whosoever hateth his brother is a murderer.*

A man has already killed him in his heart, whose life is grievous to him, and at whose death he would rejoice.

1 John iii. 14. *He that loveth not his brother, abideth in death.*

Can we believe that it is God that saith this, and delay one moment to be reconciled?

1 John iii. 19. *And hereby* (that is, by a true charity) *we shall assure our hearts before Him.* Namely, at His coming, when His sentence will be founded upon the exercise or omission of this duty.

It is not enough to love our brethren; we must love them upon a principle of faith, in the name, for the sake, and as members of Jesus Christ.

Forgive, and it shall be forgiven you, &c.

Give me, O my God, an heart full of Christian meekness and charity, that I may willingly forgive the evil I have received, and be always disposed to do good to others.

Neighbour. We love our neighbour after a Christian [i. 175.] manner, when we love him for God's sake, and for God's sake do him good.

Oct. 26, 1750. Now and before to Mr. Gell, towards [i. 177.] Vicarage-house, 4 guineas.

Nov., 1750. To my clergy, towards recovering their impropriations, 50 pounds.

Aug. 21, 1748. The parish church of K. Michael, the roof broken, I gave £7 towards.

Ramsea Chapel. May 21, 1746. I laid the foundation of this chapel, 20 yards long and 20 feet broad in the clear. God grant it may be for His glory and the good of His Church. To the building and adorning, plate, &c., of which my son and I gave, &c. The good Lord accept it to His glory. [This comes after a leaf torn out, in which might be many like entries.]

SATURDAY.

[i. 220;
iii. 201.]

PREPARATION FOR DEATH[b].

[c]Deut. xxxii. 29. *O that they were wise, that they would consider their latter end.*

St. John ix. 4. *The night cometh, when no man can work.*

A very gracious [d]intimation. Lord, grant that I may never forget it; and that *now, now*[e], is the time in which to provide for eternity.

What a wise man then when he comes to die, would wish he had done, that he ought to do forthwith; for death is [f]at hand, and the consequences of a surprise most dreadful. He will then [g]wish, if he has not done it, with all his soul,—

1st. That he had made a just and Christian settlement of his worldly[h] concerns; so as not to be distracted with the cares of this world, when all his thoughts should be upon another:

2ndly. That he had made his peace with God by a timely repentance:

3rdly. That he had [i]faithfully discharged the duties of his calling:

4thly. That he had weaned his affections from things temporal, and [j]loosened the ties which fasten us to the world[k]:

---

[b] iii. 199, 200, prefixes to these devotions, 1. a list of departed friends, down to the year 1728, [see hereafter].
2. The following texts and sentences:—
Ecclus. ix. 9. *Whatsoever thy hand findeth to do, do it with all thy might; for there is no work, nor device, nor knowledge, nor wisdom, in the grave whither thou goest.* Heb. ix. 27. *It is appointed unto men once to die, but after this the judgment.* 2 Cor. vi. 2. *Now is the accepted time, now is the day of salvation.* Ecclus. vii. 36. *Whatsoever thou takest in hand, remember the end, and thou shalt never do amiss.* St. Luke xii. 20. *Thou fool, this night shall thy soul be, &c.* Deplorable is our unthoughtfulness. We own that death is inevitable, and yet we turn our eyes from seeing the consequence. St. Matt. xxiv. 44. *Therefore be ye also ready, &c.* We own that we are miserable, and yet we are afraid of that hour which will deliver us. The true way of preparing for the night is to spend the day well. *They that sow in tears shall reap in joy.* Ps. cxxv. 5. Foolish man would reap without sowing. To hope much and do little is what self-love aims at. And yet the kingdom of heaven suffers violence, and the violent only enter into it. St. Luke xii. 36. *And ye yourselves like unto men who wait for their Lord.* Grant, O Lord, that I may ever be in that state in which I desire to be found when Thou comest to take me hence. The only happiness of this life is to be secure of a blessed eternity. It is our duty to resign ourselves up to death, as one condemned to it in Adam;—to expect it every moment.

[c] iii. om. this text.
[d] iii. adds, "and seasonable."
[e] iii. om. the second "now."
[f] iii. adds, "ever."
[g] iii. adds, "for instance;" and om. "if he has not done it."
[h] iii. "temporal."
[i] iii. "lived to God's glory, in discharging faithfully."
[j] iii. adds, "had."
[k] iii. adds, "to this end."

SATURDAY.

5thly. That he had crucified the flesh with its[1] affections and lusts; so[m] that being weary of this life, he might be more desirous of a better:

6thly. That by acts of justice, mercy, charity, and alms, he may be entitled to the mercy of God at the hour of death[n]:

7thly. That he had got such habits of patience and resignation [o]to the will of God, during his health, as may render death, with all the train of miseries[p] leading to it, less frightful and amazing:

8thly and lastly. That by a constant practice of devotion preparatory for death, he had learned what to pray for, what to hope for, what to depend on, in his last sickness.

And this, gracious Lord, is what I wish for, what I pray for, and what I purpose shall be the constant practice of my life. Amen[q].

§ 1. 2 Kings xx. 1. *Set thine house in order, for thou shalt die, and not live.* [i. 221; ii. 202.]

O that they were wise. Deut. xxxii.[r]

[s]May God, who has every way provided for me, and put it into my power to be just to all men, charitable to the poor, grateful to my friends, kind to my servants, and a benefactor to the public: [t]may He add this to all His favours, and grant that in making my last will, I may [u]faithfully discharge all these engagements; and that for want of that, no curse may cleave to myself, or to any thing I shall leave behind me[v]. Amen.

[x]But, above all things, I beg of Thee, O God, to enable me to set my inward house, my soul, in order, before I die.

---

[1] iii. "the."
[m] iii. om. "so."
[n] iii. reads, "That by acts of mercy and charity he had entitled himself to the mercy of God, at the hour of death, and at the day of judgment, when he will most stand in need of it."
[o] iii. om. "to the will of God."
[p] iii. "evils."
[q] iii. om. "Amen."
[r] iii. om. the text.
[s] iii. "O Lord, what am I, that Thou hast heaped upon me so many favours? Thou hast every way," &c.
[t] iii. "add this to all Thy favours, I beseech Thee, that in making," &c.
[u] iii. "so faithfully...that no curse may cleave to any thing," &c.
[v] iii. adds, "And when my will shall become of force, may I, gracious God, hear those joyful words, Well done, good and faithful servant. Amen. Amen. Thou hast been faithful over a few things, I will," &c.
[x] iii. om. these two sentences.

SATURDAY. Give me true repentance for all the errors of my life past, and steadfast faith in Thy Son Jesus Christ; that my sins may be done away by Thy mercy, and my pardon sealed in heaven, &c.

§ 2. Proverbs xxviii. 13. *Whoso confesseth, and forsaketh his sin, shall have mercy.*

Behold, O God, a creature liable every moment to death, prostrate before Thee, begging, for Jesus' sake, that [y]faith and repentance to which Thou hast promised mercy and pardon.

Discover to me, O Thou searcher of hearts, the charge that is against me, that I may know, and confess, and bewail, and abhor, and forsake, [z]and repent of all the evils I have been guilty of[a].

Have mercy upon me, have mercy upon me, most merciful Father, who desirest not the death of a sinner[b]; for Thy Son Jesus Christ's sake, forgive me all that is past.

And, O blessed Advocate, [c]who art able to save them for ever who come unto God by Thee, seeing Thou ever livest to make intercession for us;—I put my cause into Thy hands; let Thy power defend me; Thy blood and merits[d] plead for me; supply all the defects of my repentance; procure for me a full discharge of all my sins [e]before I die; and by Thy mighty grace confirm and strengthen me in all goodness, during the remainder of my life, that my death may be a blessing to me, and that I may find mercy at the great day. Amen.

[i. 222; iii. 204.]

§ 3. Eph. iv. 24. *Put on the new man, which after God is created in righteousness and true holiness.*

This, O God, is what I [f]desire and purpose, by Thy grace,

---

[y] iii. om. "faith and."
[z] iii. om. "and repent of."
[a] iii. adds, "That my sins may be done away by Thy mercy, and my pardon sealed in heaven, before I go hence, and be no more seen.

"For Thy Name's sake, O Lord, pardon my sin, for it is very great.

"I have been ever backward to please Thee, ever ready to offend Thee; fond of the pleasures of this life; unthoughtful of that which is to come.

"I have neglected the duties of my calling, and the vows that are upon me; I have indulged all my passions and appetites, and grieved Thy Holy Spirit by sins so *many* that I cannot recount them, so *great* that I blush to name them. The remembrance of which makes my flesh to tremble, my heart to ache."

[b] iii. om. "who...sinner."
[c] iii. "who by Thy death hast destroyed death, Thou art able," &c.
[d] iii. "mercy."
[e] iii. om. "before I die," and "during ...life."
[f] iii. "I fully purpose."

to do; and do again renew the vows which I have so often made[g], and too often broke.

SATURDAY.
[i. 222;
iii. 205.]

I renounce the devil and all his works; the vain pomp and glory of the world, with all covetous desires of the same, and the carnal desires of the flesh; resolving, by Thy [h]grace, neither to follow nor be led by them.

I desire, and purpose, to redeem my misspent time, to exercise myself in all the duties of my sacred calling.

And, O God, assist me, that neither sloth nor corruption may ever make me lay aside or forget these resolutions; but that I may live to Thee; be an instrument of Thy glory, by serving Thee faithfully, and by doing good in my generation; [i]and that I may be found so doing when Thou art pleased to call me hence: for Jesus Christ's sake. Amen.

§ 4. Colossians iii. 2. *Set your affections on things above, not on things on the earth.*

And may Almighty God, who alone can do it, effectually convince me of the vanity of all that is desirable in this present life; that I may not, like an unbeliever, look for happiness here.

Give me, O [k]Lord, a perfect indifference for the world, its *profits, pleasures, honours, fame,* and all its *idols.*

Represent Thyself unto me as my true happiness, that I may love Thee with all my *heart*, and *soul*, and *strength*; so that when I am called out of this world, I may rejoice in hope[l] of going to the paradise of God, where the souls of the faithful enjoy [m]rest and felicity, [n]in hopes of a blessed resurrection, through Jesus Christ our Saviour. Amen.

§ 5. Luke ix. 23. *If any man will come after Me, let him deny himself, and take up his cross daily, and follow Me.*

[i. 223;
ii. 206.]

Blessed Jesus, who pleasedst not Thyself, but tookest upon Thee the form of a servant, to teach mankind the great duty[o] and blessing of self-denial; assist me[p] to follow [q]Thy commands and Thy holy example, though I should be obliged to lose any thing as dear as a right hand or a right eye.

---

[g] iii. om. "made...often."
[h] iii. "assistance."
[i] iii. om. "and...hence."
[k] iii. "God."
[l] iii. "hopes."
[m] iii. adds, "perpetual."

[n] iii. om. "in hopes," &c., and adds, "Grant this for Jesus Christ's sake."
[o] iii. "mighty secret."
[p] iii. adds, "by Thy grace."
[q] iii. om. "Thy commands and."

SATURDAY.   *Give me resolution* to deny my inclinations for the good things of this world, even while I may command them; to subdue my corrupt affections, and* to take revenge upon myself—for my intemperance, by *mortification; for misspending my *time, by retirement; for the *errors of my tongue, by silence; for the *great neglect of duty, by a laborious diligence for the time to come; and for all the sins *of my life, by a deep humiliation, patiently submitting to all the troubles with which Thou shalt think fit to exercise or punish me; so that being effectually weaned from this world, and weary of its corruptions, I may be satisfied *to repose in the grave, in hopes of a better life, through Thy mercy and merits, O Lord Jesus Christ. Amen.

[i. 223; iii. 207.]

§ 6. 1 Peter iv. 8. *Charity covereth the multitude of sins.*

Possess my soul*, O God, with a sincere love for Thee, and for all mankind*.

*Let no malice or ill-will abide in me. Give me grace to forgive all that have offended me; and forgive *my many offences against Thee, and against my neighbour.

Make me ever ready to give, and glad to distribute, that Thy gifts, passing through my hands, may procure for me the prayers of the poor; and that I may lay up in store for myself a good foundation against the time to come, that I may attain eternal life, through Jesus Christ our Lord. Amen.

§ 7. *Thy will be done*. Fortify my soul, blessed Jesus, with the same spirit of submission with which Thou underwentest the death of the Cross, that I may receive all events with resignation *to the will of God; that I may receive troubles, afflictions, disappointments, sickness, and death itself, without amazement; these being the appointment of

---

r iii. adds, " To this end."
s iii. adds, " and strength."
t iii. om. " and."
u iii. adds, " fasting and."
v iii. adds, " precious."
x iii. adds, " many."
y iii. "many duties I have neglected."
z iii. " I have committed, by a most deep sorrow and humiliation; submitting with patience and resignation."
a iii. " long to repose myself in the grave, in sure and certain hopes of a joyful resurrection, through Jesus Christ our Lord."
b iii. " heart."
c iii. " the world."
d iii. " Permit ... to abide in my heart."
e iii. " gracious God, my many offences against my neighbour."
f iii. adds, " *in earth as it is in heaven.*"
g iii. om. " to...God."

Thy justice for the punishment of sin, and of Thy mercy for the salvation of sinners. SATURDAY. [i. 224; iii. 208.]

Let this be the constant practice of my life, to be pleased with all Thy choices[h], that when sickness and death approach[i], I may be prepared to submit my will to the will of my Maker.

And O that, in the meantime, my heart may always go along with my lips in this petition,—*Thy will be done.* Amen[k].

[1][§ 8.] Heb. ix. 27. *It is appointed unto men once to die; but after this the judgment.* [i. 224.]

May the thoughts of death, and of what must follow, by the grace of God, mortify in me all carnal security, and fondness for this world, and all that is in it, the lust of the flesh, the lust of the eye, and the pride of life. And O that I may make my calling and election sure, that I may die in peace, and rest in the mansions of glory, in hopes of a blessed resurrection, and a favourable judgment at the great day.

And may the consideration of a judgment to come oblige me to examine, to try, and to judge myself, that I may prevent a severe judgment of God by a true repentance, and lead a life answerable to true repentance[m], and that I may find mercy at the great day.

John v. 28. *All that are in the graves shall hear His voice, and come forth; they that have done good, unto the resurrection of life; and they that have done evil, unto the resurrection of damnation.*

May that dreadful word oblige me to work out my salvation with fear and trembling, that through the merits of Jesus Christ, I may escape that dreadful doom.

And may the hopes of heaven and happiness sweeten all the troubles of this mortal life.

O Lord Jesus, [who] hast redeemed us with Thy precious blood, make me to be numbered with [Thy] saints in glory everlasting. Amen.

---

[h] iii. adds, "never to charge God foolishly."
[i] iii. "it may be no new thing to me."
[k] iii. om.

[1] [This § as it stands in MS. iii. is given entire below, on account of the number of various readings.]
[m] prima manu, "amendment of life."

SATURDAY.   O let my name be found written in the Lamb's book of life at the great day.

[i. 225.]   I thank the Lord, for all the favours of my life, and especially for that He has vouchsafed me time and a will to *think of and prepare for death*, while I am in my full strength, while I may redeem my misspent time, and bring forth fruits meet for repentance.

Let us consider death as a punishment, to which, as sinners, we are justly condemned.

But then let us look on it in another view, namely, as a *sacrifice* for sin, which God will mercifully accept of, in union with that of His Son, if we submit to it *as due to our offences*.

It being a *sacrifice*, it ought to be voluntary; being a *debt*, it ought to be made out of love to justice; and being a *satisfaction*, [we?] must be humbly resigned.

My God, I humbly submit to it, and to Thy *justice;* and trust in Thy *mercy* and *goodness* and *promises*, both now and at the hour of death.

Death is inevitable; the time uncertain; the judgment which follows without appeal; and followed by an eternity of happiness or misery.

Lord, grant that I may consider this as I ought to do.

Let me remember that I shall come forth out of the grave just as I go in; either the object of God's *mercy*, or of His *wrath*, to all *eternity*.

He lives to no purpose, who is not glorifying God.

Our greatest hopes should lie beyond the grave.

No man must go to heaven when he dies, who has not sent his heart thither while he lives.

Our greatest security is to be derived from duty, and our only confidence from the mercy of God, through Jesus Christ.

Sickness,—if you consider it as painful to nature, and not as a favour from God, it will be a torment to you. To make it really comfortable, believe it to be ordered by a loving Father, a wise Physician; that it is the effect of His mercy for your salvation; that, being fastened to the Cross, you be-

[i. 226.]   come dearer to God, as being most like His own Son. God will loose you when it is best for you.

SATURDAY.

We often hinder our recovery by trusting to physic more than to God. Means succeed just as far as God pleases. If He sends diseases as a remedy to cure the disorders of the soul, He only can cure them. While you are chastened, you are sure God loves you; you are not sure of that, when you are without chastisement.

A timely preparation for death frees us from the fear of death, and from all other fears.

A true Christian is neither *fond* of life nor *weary* of it.

The sting of death is sin; therefore an holy life is the *only* cure for the fear of death. We ought to fear sin more than death, because death cannot hurt us but by sin.

To me to die is gain. Philippians i. 21.

O that I may be able to say this, when I come to die; and so I shall, if I live as becomes a Christian; if I employ and spend my life in the service of Christ.

Holiness being a necessary qualification for happiness, it follows that the holiest man will be the happiest, (for there are certainly degrees of glory:) therefore a Christian should lose no time to gain all the degrees of virtue and holiness he possibly can; and he that does not do so is in a fair way of not being happy at all.

It concerns us more than our life is worth, to know what will become of us when we die.

Who will pretend to say that he is not in a very few days to die?

The only happiness of this life is to be secure of a blessed eternity.

Now is the time in which we are to choose *where* and *what* we are to be to all eternity. There is therefore no time to be lost to make this choice.

No kind of death is to be feared by him who lives well.

If we consider death as the night of that day which is given us to work in, in which to work out our salvation; and that when the night is come, no man can work; how frightful must death be to such as are not prepared for it! And if we consider it as the beginning of eternity, it is still more dreadful. It is for this reason called the "King of Terrors[n];" and the Psalmist, when he would express the

[n] Job xviii. 14.

SATURDAY. worst of evils, saith, *The terrors of death are fallen upon*
[i. 227.] *me*[o].

Judges xiii. 23. *If the Lord were pleased to kill us, He would not have received a burnt-offering at our hands, neither would He have shewed us all these things.*

And this is the comfort of all God's servants: if He gives them opportunities of renewing their vows, and a will to do it; if He accepts their alms and their good deeds, that is, gives them a heart to do such; if He touches their hearts with a sense of their unworthiness; if He opens their ear to discipline; if He chastises them with afflictions; if He visits them with His Holy Spirit, &c. All these are reasons for a Christian to hope that these graces are not in vain, but that God will crown them with pardon, favour, and happiness eternal. Amen.

Matt. xxv. 6. *And at midnight there was a cry made, Behold, the bridegroom cometh, go ye out to meet him.*

A terrible voice to all such as shall meet Him not as a Bridegroom, but as an inexorable Judge.

Grant, O Lord, that I may not be of the number of those who dread Thy coming, who cannot but with regret submit to the necessity of dying, and who have neglected to prepare for death till the last hour.

Matt. xxv. 10. *And the door was shut.*

Death shuts the door. No more to be done. It is then too late to repent, to resolve, to promise, and to do any thing.

Matt. xxv. 13. *Watch, therefore, for ye know neither the day nor the hour wherein the Son of Man cometh.*

A person whose life is full of good works, whose heart is devoted to God, whose faith and hope are pure and sincere, will never be surprised by death.

Matt. xxvii. 50. *Jesus Christ yielded up the ghost.*—And so His death became a voluntary sacrifice. Let mine be so, O blessed Jesus! Let Thy death sanctify me; and let my spirit be received with Thine!

Rom. v. 1. *Being justified by faith, we have peace with God, through our Lord Jesus Christ.*

Give me, O Lord, that desire and earnest longing, which

[o] Psalm lv. 4.

I ought to have, for that happy moment which is to release SATURDAY. me from this state of banishment, and translate me to a better place; and grant that I may never lose the sight of that important moment.

Let me, O God, have my lot and portion with Thy saints.

When we come to die, the great enemy of our souls will [i. 228.] then attack us with all his stratagems. It is good therefore to be prepared.

If he attacks your faith, say with St. Paul[p], *I know whom I have believed, and am persuaded that He is able to keep that which I have committed unto Him against that day.*

I believe in God the Father, who hath made me and all the world.

I believe in God the Son, who hath redeemed me and all mankind.

I believe in God the Holy Ghost, who hath sanctified me and all the elect people of God.

I give Thee hearty thanks, O heavenly Father, that Thou hast vouchsafed to call me to the knowledge of Thy grace, and faith in Thee. Confirm this faith in me evermore; grant that I may die in this faith, and in the peace and communion of Thy holy Church; and that I may be united to Jesus, the Head of this Church, and to all His members, by a love that shall never end. Amen.

John iii. 15. *Whosoever believeth in Jesus Christ shall not perish, but have eternal life.*

I believe:—Lord, increase my faith; and let it be unto Thy servant according to this word.

Luke xxiii. 43. *This day shalt thou be with Me in paradise.*

O blessed Jesu! support my spirit when I come to die, with this comfortable promise, *This day shalt thou be in paradise.*

We indeed suffer justly the sentence of death. O Thou, who didst nothing amiss, and yet didst suffer for me; *remember me, O Lord, now Thou art in Thy kingdom.*

What terror, what affliction, can equal that of a Christian, who has never thought of weaning his heart from the world till he comes to die:—who can find nothing in his life, but

---

[p] 2 Tim. i. 12.

SATURDAY.

[i. 229.]

what must render him unworthy of mercy? But the greatest of all miseries would be to despair of mercy, and not to have recourse to it.

Need a person, who has received the sentence of death, be persuaded to prepare for death? And is not this our case?

Consider death as appointed by God, as a necessary penance, as the completion of the Christian sacrifice, as a passage to a better life, as the deliverance of a prisoner, as the recalling of an exile from banishment, as the end of all miseries:—and then you will strip it of much of that terror which it has when considered as an accident of nature only.

Luke xii. 36. *And ye yourselves like unto men that wait for their lord.*

He who waits for his master will always endeavour to be in that state in which he desires to be found.

A Christian should not look upon death with anxiety, but with the satisfaction of a good servant, who waits with impatience for his master's return, in hopes of being approved of, &c.

Luke xii. 40. *Be ye ready also, for the Son of Man cometh at an hour when ye think not.*

And are not so many sudden deaths sufficient to convince us of the folly of assuring ourselves of one day? Let every one of us, therefore, count himself of the number of those that are to be surprised by death; this will make us watchful.

Luke xii. 43. *Blessed is that servant, whom his lord, when he cometh, shall find so doing,*—that is, doing his duty.

And then, miserable will he be, whom death surpriseth either doing *evil*, or doing *nothing*, or doing that which God does not require of him. Can one imagine that the generality of Christians believe this truth? Suffer me not, O God, to fall into a forgetfulness of it.

We complain (saith Seneca) of the shortness of life; he answers, *Vita, si scias uti, longa est.* "Life is long, if you know how to use it." But then it is Christianity only can teach us how to use our life; namely, "in working out our own salvation;" and we are sure it is long enough for *that*, because God has appointed it for that very end.

As Christianity alone can take from us the love of life, so SATURDAY. it is this alone that can free us from the fear of death.

Life. It is not one pin a matter how a man spends his life and his time, if he does not employ them in securing a blessed eternity.

Eternity adds an infinite weight to all our actions, whether good or bad.

If we desire that our death should, like that of Jesus Christ, be a sacrifice of love and obedience, we must take care to make our life so too.

Acts ix. 39. *This woman was full of good works and almsdeeds;—and she died, &c.*

Happy that soul which death finds rich, not in gold, furniture, learning, reputation, or barren purposes and desires, but in good works.

Acts vii. 59. *And they stoned Stephen, calling upon God,* [i. 230.] *and saying, Lord Jesus, receive my spirit.*

O my God, enable me to live to Thee, that when the hour of death shall come, I may thus with confidence offer up my spirit to Jesus Christ.

Rev. iii. 3. *Thou shalt not know what hour I will come upon thee.*

Is it not then the highest presumption to persuade ourselves that we have always time sufficient, when Jesus Christ Himself declares that we have not one moment certain?

Death being the effect and punishment of sin, we ought to expect it with great submission, since it honours God by expiating of sin, and saves the man by punishing the sinner.

It is purely for want of faith that we tremble at the approach of our Deliverer; and which is to destroy in us the reign of sin, and instate us in that of glory.

Let us resign up ourselves to God, as to the manner in which it shall please Him to determine our lives, praying only that it may be to His glory and our salvation.

What does it signify how this house of clay perisheth, which hinders the perfect renovation of the soul, and the sight of God?

2 Cor. v. 1. *For we know that if our earthly house of this tabernacle were dissolved, we have a building of God, an house not made with hands, eternal in the heavens.*

SATURDAY. We know, we believe, we promise ourselves this, but we think too seldom of it, and we make still less use of what we know, in order to wean our hearts from this world.

Would we look upon our bodies as houses of clay just ready to fall, we should think of that eternal house; we should sigh after our native country, and be willing to leave a place of misery and banishment.

Remember that death is the punishment of sin; we ought therefore to resign ourselves up to it in a Christian manner, looking upon ourselves as condemned to it in Adam.

Consider well, that life is given and continued for no other end but to glorify God in working out our own salvation.

[i. 231.] He who has lived and looked on earth as in a place of banishment, will look upon death as a gracious deliverance from it.

A man goes with confidence to meet the bridegroom, when he has been faithful to him, and believes him to be his friend.

Heb. ii. 15. *And deliver them who through fear of death were all their life long subject to bondage.*

Bondage is the sentence of rebellious slaves; we were condemned to it in Adam; we being under this sentence of death and the Divine justice, we ought to expect it with submission, and be always preparing for it. This is the only way to be secure, and from fearing death when it comes.

Gather us, O God, to the number of Thine elect, at what time and in what manner Thou pleasest; only let us be without reproach, and blameless; let faith, and love, and peace, accompany our last periods.

We look upon a body without a soul with horror. We can see a body with a soul which is like to die eternally, without concern.

Wretched man that I am, who shall deliver me from the body of this death? I thank God (I am delivered) *through Jesus Christ our Lord.*

Grant, O Lord, that though my outward man decays daily, yet that my inward man may grow and increase unto the day of my death.

He that hath lived best will stand in need of mercy at the hour of death, and in the day of judgment; and he that hath lived the worst has not sinned beyond the efficacy of the SATURDAY. blood of Christ, provided his repentance be sincere.

My God! let Thy glory be magnified by saving a sinner, by redeeming a captive slave, by enlightening an heart overwhelmed in darkness, by changing a wicked heart, by pardoning innumerable transgressions, iniquities, and sins.

If my hopes were placed upon any thing but the infinite mercies of God, in Jesus Christ, which can never fail, I should utterly despair.

Acts ii. 21. *Whosoever shall call on the Name of the Lord, shall be saved.*

These, my God, are Thine own words; give me leave to trust in them, to depend on them, both now and at the hour of death.

John xvii. 4. *I have finished the work which Thou gavest* [i. 232.] *Me to do.*

O Lord, the very best of men come infinitely short of this pattern; how then shall I, an unprofitable servant, appear before my Lord and Judge?

Genesis iii. 15. *The seed of the woman shall bruise the serpent's head.*

This, my God, is Thy sure, Thy eternal promise; I believe it; I trust in it; I will hold me fast by it.

Phil. ii. 16. *That I may rejoice in the day of Christ, that I have not laboured in vain.*

Luke xxii. 16. *Nevertheless not My will, but Thine be done.*

May I, O blessed Jesus, when my death approaches, breathe out my last with these words, and with the same spirit of submission.

Death of Friends. Let us cast our eyes upon sin, which is the cause of death, and then we shall weep with reason.

Preserve in us a lively sense of the world to come.

And when I shall not be able to pray for myself, the good Lord favourably hear the prayers of His Church for me.

Grant that the sins which I have committed in this world may not be imputed unto me; but that escaping the gates of hell, I may dwell in the regions of light, with Abraham, Isaac, and Jacob, until the day of the general resurrection, and that

SATURDAY. then I may hear those joyful words of Thy Son,—*Come ye blessed children, &c.*

Grant that I may have perfect conquest against the devil, sin, and death, through Christ, who by His death hath overcome him who hath the power of death.

Luke xxiii. 43. *This day shalt thou, &c.*

O Jesus, who hadst compassion on this thief, even at the hour of death, have mercy upon me, who now repent of all my misdoings. Suffer not the gates of paradise to be shut against me when I die, Thou that hast opened the kingdom of Heaven to all believers.

Restore my soul at the great day to life eternal.

Give me the patience of Job, the faith of Abraham, the courage of Peter, and the comfort of Paul, and a true submission to Thy will.

Apply to my soul all the wholesome medicines of Thy Son's passion, death, and resurrection, against the powers of Satan, against all unreasonable fears and despair, and ease my careful conscience.

Hear the prayers of Thy Church for me, and for all in my condition, for Jesus Christ's sake.

[iii. 208.] § 8. *Prayers, Profession of Faith, Intercessions, &c., Preparatory for Death.*

I believe in God the Father, who made me and all the world.

I believe in God the Son, who hath redeemed me and all mankind.

I believe in God the Holy Ghost, who sanctifieth me and all the elect people of God.

I give Thee hearty thanks, O heavenly Father, that Thou hast vouchsafed to call me to the knowledge of Thy grace and faith in Thee. Increase this knowledge and confirm this faith in me evermore. Grant that I may die in this faith, and in the peace and communion of Thy holy Church; that I may be united to Jesus the Head of this Church, and to all His members, by a love that shall never end.

[209.] Grant, O Lord, that for the remainder of my life I may exercise a firm faith, a sincere repentance, an assured hope, a lively charity, a true courage, a profound humility, an unwearied patience, a perfect resignation; so that I may be ever prepared for my last summons.

In the midst of life we are in death, &c., [from the Burial Service].

From the guilt and burden of my sins; from impatience, presumption, and despair; from the prince and powers of darkness; from a false peace; from sudden and from eternal death, and from the dreadful judgment of the last day: good Lord, deliver me. [210.]

The souls of the righteous are in the hand of God, and no torment shall touch them. Wisd. iii. 1.

Though I walk through the valley of the shadow of death, yet will I fear no evil, for Thou art with me.

Be merciful unto me, O God, be merciful unto me; for my soul trusteth in Thee, and under the shadow of Thy wings shall be my refuge until this calamity be overpast.

Why art thou so full of heaviness, O my soul? and why art thou so disquieted within me? Put thy trust in God, for I will yet give Him thanks for the help of His countenance.

Like as a father pitieth his own children, even so is the Lord merciful unto them that fear Him: for He knoweth whereof we are made, He remembereth that we are but dust.

The Lord shall preserve me from all evil, it is even He that shall keep thy soul.

O say unto my soul, I am thy salvation. [211.]

Blessed are the dead which die in the Lord, for they rest from their labours, and their works do follow them.

And God shall wipe away all tears from their eyes. And there shall be no more death, neither sorrow, nor crying; neither shall there be any more pain.

Vouchsafe me, O Lord, in my last sickness, the prayers of the faithful, the comforts of the Holy Sacrament, the ministry of absolution, and the assistance of my friends.

O blessed Jesus, when my soul shall depart from my body, do Thou give Thy holy angels charge concerning it, to guard it from the prince and powers of darkness, to conduct it through the unknown paths of death, and to carry it safe to the paradise of God, there to wait for Thy coming. And O that I may there meet my departed friends and children, to praise Thee to all eternity.

SATURDAY.   I thank Thee, O God, for all the favours of my life, and especially for that Thou hast vouchsafed me *time* and a *will* to think of, and to prepare for death, while I am in my full strength, while I may redeem my misspent time, and bring forth fruits meet for repentance.

[iii. 212.]   *Death.* May the continual thoughts of death mortify in me all pride and vanity, all covetousness and worldly-mindedness, all carnal security, and fondness for this life, and oblige me to a strict watchfulness, while I continue in this state of banishment.

Judgment. May the consideration of a judgment to come oblige me to a sincere holiness; make me careful of my thoughts, designs, words, and actions; oblige me to try, to examine, and to judge myself; and to endeavour to appease my Judge by prayers, by tears, by alms, by mortification, and all other expressions of a true repentance; that in the day of visitation I may find mercy.

Hell. And if the difficulties of a holy life affright me, if
[iii. 213.]   the commands of Jesus Christ seem hard to flesh and blood, then consider, *Who can dwell with everlasting burnings?* The good Lord give me grace that I may suffer and take pains *now*, and that I may escape the bitter pains of eternal death.

Heaven. This day shalt thou be with Me in Paradise. O may the constant expectation of that happy day, and a faith and hope full of immortality, sweeten all the troubles of this mortal life.

Raise, O Lord, my sense and value for the joys of Paradise so high, that I may no longer dote upon the short appearances of happiness I meet with here.

O Thou, who hast redeemed me with Thy precious blood, make me to be numbered with Thy saints in glory everlasting. Amen, Amen.

[i. 233.]   *Death. Ejaculations.* Psalm lxxi. 9. *Cast me not away in the time of age; forsake me not when my strength faileth me.*

Grant, O Lord, that the end of my life may be truly Christian; without sin, without shame, and, if it so please Thee, without pain.

Psalm lxiii. 26. *My flesh and my heart faileth; but God is the strength of my heart, and my portion for ever.*

1 Samuel iii. 18. *It is the Lord; let Him do what seemeth* SATURDAY. *Him good.*

Lord, be merciful unto me; heal my soul, for I have sinned against Thee.

I confess my wickedness, and am sorry for my sin.

For Thy Name's sake, O Lord, be merciful unto my sin, for it is great.

The Lord is nigh unto them that are of a contrite heart, and will save such as are of an humble spirit.

Psalm xxxix. 8. *And now, Lord, what is my hope? truly my hope is in Thee.*

Psalm ciii. 14. *Lord, Thou knowest whereof we are made: that we are but dust.*

Let my misery, my fear, my sorrow, move Thee to compassion.

Despise not, O Lord, the work of Thine own hands.

I freely forgive all that have offended me.

O Thou that never failest them that seek Thee, have pity on me.

Nevertheless, though I am sometime afraid, yet put I my trust in Thee.

O Lord, I beseech Thee, deliver my soul. Gracious is the Lord and righteous, yea, our God is merciful.

O go not far from me, for trouble is at hand, and there is none to help me.

The sorrows of my heart are enlarged; O bring Thou me out of my troubles.

O keep my soul, and deliver me; let me not be confounded, for I have put my trust in Thee.

Withdraw not Thy mercy from me, O Lord; let Thy loving-kindness and Thy truth alway preserve me.

O Lord, let it be Thy pleasure to deliver me; make haste, O Lord, to help me.

Shew Thy servant the light of Thy countenance, and save me for Thy mercy's sake.

O deliver me, for I am helpless and poor, and my heart is wounded within me.

Wherefore hidest Thou Thy face, and forgettest our misery and trouble?

My God, save Thy servant, who putteth his trust in Thee.

SATURDAY. Thou, O Lord, art full of compassion and mercy, long-
[i. 234.] suffering, plenteous in goodness and truth.

When I am in heaviness, I will think upon God; when my heart is vexed, I will complain.

Will the Lord absent Himself for ever? Will He be no more entreated?

Hath God forgotten to be gracious? And I said, it is mine own infirmity; but I will remember the years of the right hand of the Most High.

[iii. 213.] *Aspirations.* Grant, O Lord, that I may finish my course with joy, and that having served Thee in my generation, I may be gathered unto my fathers, who died in the true faith, and in the fear of God.

[iii. 214.] Wean my affections from the world. Take from me the fear of death, and fit me for the day of my dissolution.

Death. Grant, gracious God, that for the time I have yet to live, I may live to Thee; without which life and length of days will be no blessing.

Repentance. Who can understand his errors? O cleanse Thou me from my secret faults.

O Lord, be favourable unto me: pardon and deliver me from all my sins.

Grant that my great sins may never rise up in judgment against me, nor bring shame and confusion of face upon me.

My soul truly waiteth still upon God, for of Him cometh my salvation.

Grant, O God, that I may die in peace, and rest in hope, and rise in glory.

Grant, O Lord, that I may daily improve in good works, so that in the last moments of my life I may find mercy and comfort.

Forsake me not at the hour of death, but then increase my faith, and give me a firm trust in Thy mercy and promises when I shall most stand in need of it.

[iii. 215.] Ps. xxxi. 6. *Into Thy hands I commend my spirit; for Thou hast redeemed me, O Lord, Thou God of Truth.*

St. John iii. 15. *Whosoever believeth in Him* (Jesus Christ) *shall not perish, but have eternal life.*

SATURDAY.

I believe: Lord, increase my faith; and let it be unto Thy servant according to this word.

St. John iii. 36. *He that believeth on the Son hath everlasting life.*

Rom. x. 9. *If thou shalt confess with thy mouth the Lord Jesus, and shalt believe in thine heart that God hath raised Him from the dead, thou shalt be saved.*

Rom. x. 13. *Whosoever shall call upon the name of the Lord* (Christ) *shall be saved.*

Gen. iii. 15. *The seed of the woman shall break the serpent's head.*

Acts x. 43. Whosoever believeth in Him shall receive remission of sins.

S. John xvii. 4. *I have finished the work which Thou gavest Me to do.* Lord, grant that I may so discharge the duties of my calling, as to be able to say this at the hour of death.

Our life should not be torn from us as by violence. It is a *sacrifice*, and therefore ought to be voluntary. It is an *homage*, and therefore full of submission. It is a *debt*, and to be made out of love to justice. It is a satisfaction, and therefore it must be humbly resigned.

Let us remember that we shall come forth out of our graves just as we enter in, either to life or death eternal.

Ps. xxii. 19. *Be not Thou far from me, O Lord. Thou art my succour, haste Thee to help me.* [iii. 216.]

Suffer me never to fall into a forgetfulness of these things: Heaven, Hell, Death, and Judgment.

Grant that I may so live as that I may look upon death as a desirable sacrifice.

Let me look upon death as a punishment to which I am justly condemned, but yet which God will accept as a sacrifice for sin, if I accept of it, and submit to it as due to my offences.

I accept of it, O God, in union with the sacrifice of my Saviour, and [in] whatever manner I am to suffer this sentence of death, justly passed upon me and upon all mankind.

O Thou who hast overcome the sharpness of death, and hast opened the kingdom of heaven to all believers, increase my faith *now*, and at the hour of death let it be perfect and unshaken.

SATURDAY. Ps. lxxi. The greatest part proper for a dying person, to express our trust in God, and want of His help.

How shall I appear when I am called to give an account of my stewardship?

Let us consider death as a punishment to which, as sinners, we are justly condemned.

But then let us consider it in another view, viz., as a sacrifice for sin, which God will mercifully accept of in union with the death and sacrifice of His Son—if we submit to it as due to us for our offences.

My God, I submit to it, and to Thy justice; and I hope in Thy mercy, now, at the hour of death, and in the day of judgment.

Death is inevitable—the time uncertain—the judgment without appeal—and followed by an eternity of happiness or misery.

Who considers this as he ought to do?

[iii. 217, in pencil.] I have the greatest assurance of mercy and pardon. *For He that spared not His own Son—Take and eat this*—May this be the bread of life to me—*Drink this in remembrance*—May I never thirst after the things of this world. May this satisfy my thirst after Thee, and effectually quench my thirst—effectually hinder me from thirsting after this world.

A short and plain Account of the Lord's Supper, and such as the meanest Christian may understand, with proper assistances for such as desire to receive it worthily: containing the Communion service of the Church, with instructions how to use it to the most devout purposes q.

[i. 234.] THE LITANY.—BISHOP ANDREWES.

O God the Father of Heaven; have mercy upon me, keep and defend me.

O God the Son, Redeemer of the world; have mercy upon me, save and deliver me.

O God the Holy Ghost; have mercy upon me, strengthen and comfort me.

---

q This is clearly a memorandum for the title of the Bishop's book on the Lord's Supper, which came out in 1734.]

Remember not, Lord, mine offences, nor the offences, &c. SATURDAY.

From Thy wrath and heavy indignation; from the guilt and burden of my sins; from the dreadful sentence of the last judgment;

Good Lord, deliver me.

From the sting and terrors of conscience; from impatience, distrust, or despair; from extremity of sickness and pain, which may withdraw my mind from God;

Good Lord, deliver me.

From the bitter pangs of eternal death; from the gates of hell; from the powers of darkness; and from the illusions of Satan;

Good Lord, deliver me.

By Thy manifold and great mercies; by Thy manifold and great merits; by Thine agony and bloody sweat; by Thy bitter cross and passion; by Thy mighty resurrection; by Thy glorious ascension, and most acceptable intercession; and by the graces of the Holy Ghost;

Good Lord, deliver me.

For the glory of Thy Name; for Thy loving mercy and truth's sake;

Good Lord, deliver me.

In my last and greatest need; in the hour of death, and in the day of judgment;

Good Lord, deliver me.

As Thou hast delivered all Thy saints and servants which called upon Thee in their extremity;

Good Lord, deliver me;—and receive my soul for Thy mercy's sake[r].

Deliver my soul from the power of the enemy, lest he tear it in pieces, if there be none to help. [1st ed. p. 294.]

Be merciful unto me, and forgive me all my sins, which, by the malice of the devil, or by my own frailty, I have at any time of my life committed against Thee.

Lay not to my charge, what in the lust of the eye, the pride of life or vanity, I have committed against Thee; what by an angry spirit, by vain and idle words, by foolish jesting, I have committed against Thee.

[r] [Here MS. i. fails—two leaves torn out.   The rest of this Litany is given from the 1st edition.]

SATURDAY.

Make me partaker of all Thy mercies and promises in Christ Jesus.

Vouchsafe my soul a place of rest in the Paradise of God, with all Thy blessed Saints; and my body a part in the blessed resurrection.

[1st ed. p. 295.]

O Lord God, Lamb of God, that takest away the sins of the world;

Have mercy upon me.

Thou that takest away the sins of the world,

Grant me Thy peace.

Thou that sittest at the right hand of God,

Have mercy upon me.

Have mercy upon me, and receive my prayer; even the prayer which Thou hast taught me:—

Our Father, which art in Heaven, &c.

O Lord, deal not with me after my sins; neither reward me after mine iniquities.

O God, merciful Father, that despisest not the sighing of a contrite heart, nor the desire of such as be sorrowful; mercifully assist my prayers which I make before Thee—at such times especially as I am preparing for death and for eternity. And, O Lord, graciously hear me, that those evils, those illusions, and assaults, which my great enemy worketh against me, may be brought to nought, and by the providence of Thy goodness they may be dispersed; that Thy servant, being delivered from all temptations, may give thanks to Thee, with Thy holy Church, to all eternity. Amen.

Let us endeavour, by a timely repentance, to prevent the reproaches which otherwise our conscience will cast upon us at the hour of death.

The support of a Penitent at the hour of Death. John iii. 16. *God so loved the world, that He gave His only-begotten Son, that whosoever believeth in Him should not perish, but have everlasting life*[s].

1 John ii. 1. *We have an Advocate with the Father, Jesus Christ the righteous,* who came into the world to save sinners, who died for us when we were His enemies, that He might offer us unto God.

[s] [These two sentences are not in the 4to. edition.]

It is our Judge Himself who hath assured us that "all sins shall be forgiven unto the sons of men[c]." SATURDAY.

The memory of the Just is blessed. [i. 235; iii. 199.]

My kind and pious uncle, Dr. Rich[d]. Sherlock[t], June 20, 1689.
My first Thomas[u] died June 8, 1701.
My dear father died May 29, 1702, aged 75.
My daughter [x]Alice died June 3, 1703.
My wife, my dear wife, died Mar. 7, 1704.
My dear mother died Aug. 16, 1708, aged 84.
My worthy[y] friend, Mr. Christian, of Lewagne (?), May 28, 1712.
My daughter Mary[z] died Nov. 27, 1712[a].
My eldest brother, Samuel, Sept. 6, 1719, aged 70.
My uncle, John Leigh, Sept. 10, 1719.
My dear mother-in-law, Apr. 19, 1720, aged 78.
My sister Sarah,   1721, aged 66.
My god-daughter, R.[b] Murray, Sept. 6, 1722, 17.
My kind brother-in-law, Mr. Thos. Patten, Ap. 2, 1726, aged 64.
My hon[ble] [c] friend the Dean of York[c], Aug. 1728, 65[d].
Honest Mr. Phil. Hooper, Dec. 29, 1728, 78.
Dr. Walker, Jan. 18, 1729, 49 years and 6 months.
Dr. Tho. Bray, our great benefactor, 1729.
Dr. Nath. Marshal, Feb. 5, 1729.
My dear brother Joseph, June 8, 1730, aged 74.
Mrs. El. Murray, Jan. 6, 1730, aged 89.
My dear cousin, Susannah Murray, Mar. 17, 1730.
Mr. Wm. Heyward, Dec. 11, 1731.
Mr. Edw. Allanson, of Neston, Dec. 23, 1731.
Jenny Patten, Feb. 13, 1731, a good Christian.
My sister-in-law, Margt. Patten, July 16, 1734, 65.
My brother Wm. Patten's wife died Dec. 20, 1734.
Sister Mary Faulconer, Jan. 1734, aged 69.
Cousin Hugh Patten, Apr. 16, 1736.

---

[t] iii. inserts "Rector of Winwick."
[u] iii. "Tommy."
[x] iii. "little."
[y] iii. "good."
[z] iii. "pretty daughter Molly."
[a] iii. adds, "13:" i. e. "aged 13."
[b] iii. "Rachael."
[c] iii. adds, "and worthy"..."Mr. Finch."
[d] iii. breaks off here.

SATURDAY. My pretty grandson, T. W., died May 7, 1736, aged one year.

Blessed are the dead which die in the Lord.

Mr. Hen. Finch, Dean of York, my most kind and worthy friend for 30 years, died Aug.   , 1728, aged 68.

Sir John Philips, a good and worthy friend, died in a good old age, 1737.

Mr. Edw. Finch, my old and worthy friend, died Feb. 14, 1737, aged 77.

The Queen died 20 of Nov. 1737, 55.

The excellent, pious, and charitable, the Lady Eliz. Hastings, died Dec. 22, 1739.

Mr. Vicar-general John Woodes, Ap. 17, 1740.

My most dear brother, Mr. Wm. Patten, to whom the clergy of this Isle have been so much indebted, died Oct. 5, A.D. 1740, aged 71.

My dear brother Benjamin, died Sept. 1, 1741, aged 80.

Mrs. Eliz. Butler, a most pious lady and great benefactress to my diocese, died June 9, 1741, aged 58.

My worthy friend Edw. Harley, Esq., died Aug. 30, 1755, ætat. 71.

Mr. John Murray, merchant, Oct. 5, 1741, ætat. 70.

Dr. George Cheyne, a most excellent religious physician and philosopher; for whose excellent works I and many more stand obliged.

Rev. xxi. 27. May the names of all these, O God, who died with the sign of faith, be found written in [the Lamb's] Book of Life at the [great day]. Amen. Together...[e]

[i. 244 (A.)
248 (B.)]
[f]*Midnight Meditations.* St. Matt. xxv. 6. *At midnight there was a cry made, Behold, the Bridegroom cometh, go ye out to meet Him.*

Grant, O Jesus[g], that I may not be of the number of those that dread Thy coming; who with regret submit to the ne-

---

[e] [In MS. i. this is followed in p. 236 by a paragraph headed "Obligations;" and in p. 240 by one headed "Act of Settlement:" both which in this edition are transposed to the Bishop's Life; as is also one in MS. i. p. 252, headed "Remarkables."]
[f] B. prefixes, "Hours of Prayer."
[g] B. "Lord."

cessity of dying[h], and who neglect to prepare for death till SATURDAY. the last hour.

St. Mark xiii. 35. *Watch ye, for ye know not when the Master of the house cometh: at even, or at midnight, or at cock-crowing, or in the morning.*

Let the remembrance of my death, gracious Lord, and the account I am then to give, [i]be ever present with me. O suffer me not to fall into a forgetfulness of death; or ever to presume that I have time sufficient to prepare for death, when Jesus Christ assures us, Rev. iii. 3, that we have not one hour certain[k].

Psalm cxxxix. *Thou art about my path and about my bed, and spiest out all my ways. The darkness is no darkness with Thee, the darkness and light to Thee are both alike.*

Lighten mine eyes, O Lord, that I sleep not in death.

Shew the light of Thy countenance upon Thy servant, and save me for, &c.

Rev. iv. [8.] *They rest not day and night, saying, Holy, Holy, Holy, Lord God Almighty, which was, and is, and is to come. Thou art worthy to receive glory and honour and power: for Thou hast created all things, and it is by Thy will that they subsist.*

O holy and blessed Trinity, three Persons and one God, vouchsafe to make me worthy in Thy good time, to join with these blessed [ones?] in praising Thee for ever and ever. Amen.

Grant, gracious Lord, that my name may be found written in the Lamb's Book of Life, (Rev. xxi. 27,) and that I may find mercy at the great day.

Lord make me ever ready for the coming of the Bridegroom.

GRACES BEFORE AND AFTER MEAL. [i. 257.]

O God, who givest food unto all flesh, grant that we may receive these Thy gifts with Thy blessing, and use them with sobriety and thankfulness[l]: through Jesus Christ our Lord. Amen.

After meat. May God, who hath given us bodily food, give

---

[h] A. om. this clause.
[i] A. continues, "Since Thou, O Jesus, hast assured us, Rev. iii. 3, that we have not one moment certain."
[k] Here MS. B. breaks off.
[l] As repeated below, "thankful hearts."

GRACES AT MEALS.

us also spiritual food and life, through Jesus Christ our Lord. Amen.

O eternal God, who feedest with Thy blessing every living thing: give us this day our daily bread, and grant that we may receive these Thy gifts with Thy blessing, and use them with sobriety and thankful hearts: through Jesus Christ.

Let not our table become a snare to us. Let us not abuse the good creatures which Thou hast given us.

That we may never dishonour Thee by abusing these Thy good creatures which Thou hast bestowed upon us; through Jesus Christ our Lord. Amen.

O God, who givest food, &c. (as above).

Blessed be God for providing so well for us: and may He who hath given us bodily food give us also spiritual food, and eternal life through Jesus Christ: and make us mindful of the wants of others, for Jesus Christ's sake. Amen.

Ungrateful creatures! to partake of His creatures by which we live, and yet not thank Him for them, and that openly!

The devil is never likelier to ensnare us than at our meals. Intemperance, idle and sinful mirth, forgetting God who feeds us, forgetting those that hunger, &c. Starving the soul, while feeding the body.

O God, who hast taught us that man does not live by bread alone, but by, &c. Grant that we may receive these Thy gifts with Thy blessing: through Jesus Christ.

O God, who givest, &c. [as above].

Blessed be God for providing so well for us: and may God who hath given us bodily food give us also spiritual food, and make us ever mindful of the wants of others, for Jesus Christ's sake. Amen. But above all give us the bread that nourisheth to eternal life.

May God, who has given us bodily food, vouchsafe us also the food of our souls, the bread that nourisheth to eternal life.

[ii. 1.*] *That He might make thee know that man doth not live by bread alone.* Deut. viii. 3.

May the blessing of God, by which we live, sanctify unto us our daily bread. The Lord dispose us to a temperate use of the good things of this world, that we may not forget the world to come: through Jesus Christ our Lord. Amen.

When thou hast eaten and art full, then thou shalt bless the Graces at Meals.
Lord thy God. Deut. viii. 10.

Blessed be God, by whose goodness we live. The Lord make us mindful of those that are in want, and dispose us by His favours to relieve their necessities. Continue to us the means of grace, the blessings of a peaceable government in Church and State, and fit us for the happiness of a better life, through Jesus Christ our Lord. Amen.

Bless us, O God, and grant that we may receive these Thy gifts with Thy blessing: through Jesus Christ our Lord. Amen. [i. 258; iii. 251.]

EJACULATIONS.

Take from me all evil imaginations, all impurity of thought, all inclinations to lust, all envy, pride, and hypocrisy, all falsehood, deceit, and an irregular life, all covetousness, vainglory, and sloth, all malice, anger, and wrath, all remembrance of injuries, every thing that is contrary to Thy will, O Most Holy God. [i. 258.]

O King of peace, give us Thy peace, keep us in love and charity.

Make Thyself, O God, the absolute master of my heart.

Love of God, &c. Bless me, O God, with the love of Thee, and of my neighbour. Give me peace of conscience, the command of my affections; and for the rest, *Thy will be done,* and not mine.

They that be whole, need not a physician, &c. It belongs to Thee, O sovereign Physician, both to make us sensible of our maladies, and to go to Thee for help. O say unto my soul this word of salvation, *Behold, thou art made whole!*

Without Me ye can do nothing. Miserable indeed is he who pretends to walk without Thee. O give me light to see, an heart to close with, and a power to do Thy will. From Thy Spirit I hope to receive these graces.

St. John x. *He goeth before them, and the sheep follow him.* O my Saviour, grant that I may lead such a life as that my sheep may safely follow me.

1 Cor. iv. 16, [and xi. 1.] *Wherefore I beseech you, be ye followers of me, as I myself am of Jesus Christ.* O Jesu, grant that I may in some measure follow the pattern which

Thou hast set me; that I may with some confidence desire my flock to be followers of me.

Love not the world, &c. O Lord, give me the eyes of faith, that I may see the world such as it really is: the vanity of its promises, the folly of its pleasures, the unprofitableness of its rewards, the multitude of its snares, and the dangers of its temptations.

Let me have no fear in this world, but only the fear of displeasing Thee my God.

[i. 259.] John xii. 26. *If any man serve Me, let him follow Me; and him will My Father honour.*

Let me never flatter myself that I serve Thee, my Saviour, unless I follow Thy example at the expense of every thing I love or fear besides. O keep my heart fixed upon that *honour* which God has prepared for those that follow Thee.

St. Matt. x. 8. *Freely ye have received, freely give.* Give me, O my Lord and Benefactor, an abhorrence of making a trade of Thy gifts, of which I am only a dispenser.

O Divine Spirit, render me worthy of Thy presence and consolation.

Fill my heart with an holy dread of Thy judgments.

Give me a true sense and knowledge of the danger and the evil of sin.

Make Thyself, O God, the absolute Master of my heart.

Grant, O my Saviour, that I may seek Thy interests, and the interests of Thy Church in the first place, and labour with all my might to establish the truths and the piety of the Gospel: and then with a prudent moderation be concerned for the temporal rights of my diocese.

Jesus Christ is always in His temple, and near you; (if your soul is fit for Him to dwell in.) To Him apply on all occasions:—

As your *Master*; for grace to study, to love, to teach, and to follow, His instructions. He requires nothing but what He first practised Himself.

As your *Lord*; that you may love and serve Him faithfully, and fulfil all His commands.

As your *Pattern*; that you may follow His example, and imitate His virtues.

As your *Saviour.* . . . .

As your *King;* that He may give laws to my soul, and that I may surrender myself to His commands; never rebel, or resist His authority.

EJACULA-
TIONS.

As your *Shepherd.* Keep me in Thy flock by Thy almighty grace. I am one of the lost sheep which Thou camest to seek. O take me on Thy shoulders, and restore me to Thy fold. Increase Thy flock for the honour of Thy Name.

Thy will be done. It is most just, O God, it should be so: for who should govern the world but He that made it? And yet we poor creatures repine when our hopes or desires are crossed. My God, cure this folly and presumption in me. [i. 260.]

Wilful sin. Let me rather choose to die, than to sin against my conscience.

My flock. Lord, make it the great concern of my life to promote the eternal interest of my flock.

Penitent. I am ashamed to come before Thee, but I must come or perish. I know that Thou art angry with me for my sins, but I know too that Thou pitiest me, or why do I yet live? Make me full of sorrow for my sin, and full of hopes of Thy mercy and pardon. Look upon the infirmities of Thy servant, and consider his weakness. Sensible of my own sad condition, weak and miserable, sinful and ignorant, liable to eternal death, I prostrate myself before Thee, imploring Thy help and pardon.

Holy Scriptures. Grant, O God, that I may always read them with the same Spirit with which they were written.

Give me, O God, a sincere love for the truths of the Gospel, a teachable heart, and an obedient will.

Gracious God, never abandon me to the opposition I shall at any time make to Thy grace.

Blessed be God, that He has so often prevented me, and not left me to the desires of my own heart.

Put a stop to the torrent of wickedness and profaneness which carries all before it.

Let it be reckoned amongst Thy miracles, that Thou hast saved me, a miserable sinner.

I confess my sins unto Thee, my God; do Thou hide them from all the world.

Eternity. Lord, imprint upon my heart a lively idea of

eternity, that the sorrowful passages of this life, which are so uneasy and frightful to nature, may vanish, or be borne with patience.

Example. Pardon my sin, and forgive all such as have been misled by any evil example of mine.

Matt. v. 48. *Be ye perfect, even as your Father which is in heaven is perfect.*

O Divine repairer of our corrupt nature, may Thy all-powerful grace make me as perfect as Thou hast commanded me to be.

Matt. x. 20. *It is not ye that speak, but the Holy Spirit that speaketh in you.* O Holy Spirit, speak in me on all occasions, that I may always speak as a Christian.

Matt. x. 19. *It shall be given you in that same hour what ye shall speak.* Let no incredulity, O Jesus, hinder the effects of so positive a promise: that neither want of talents, nor any other defect or surprise may hurt Thy cause.

Matt. x. 16. *Behold, I send you forth as sheep among wolves.*

My Saviour, give me grace to oppose nothing to the violence of men, but the meekness and simplicity of that creature.

Matt. x. 24. *The disciple is not above his Master, nor the servant, &c.*

St. John xv. 20. *Remember this word, &c.*

O Thou great Master of humility and of suffering, how unwilling are we to follow this maxim, and imitate Thy conduct! O let me *remember*—learn from Thee never to murmur, never to complain. I can never suffer anything but what Thou hast suffered.

Mark iv. 38. *Carest Thou not that we perish?*

Lord, give me always a great concern for the Church, a true compassion for its evils, and a sure confidence in Thee. O Lord Jesus, Thou seest our afflictions, our troubles, and our wants. Haste Thee to help us, O Lord God of our salvation.

Holiness. O God, who hast called me to a high degree of holiness, give me a firm faith in Thy power, through our Lord Jesus Christ, that by this assistance I may get the mastery over all my sins and corruptions; that I may be redeemed from *all* iniquity; that I may be holy, as He who has called me is holy.

EJACULA-
TIONS.

JESUS—Saviour.—This Name shall ever be my refuge and confidence, my strength and support, my peace and consolation. O JESU, be my Saviour, now and at the hour of death.

We glorify Thee, O Lord, for Thy mercy towards sinners, and we beg the same for ourselves.

Possess my soul with an earnest desire of pleasing Thee, and with a fear of offending Thee.

Let me be ever ready to forgive injuries, and backward to offer any.

Give me, O Lord, faith and patience, that I may neither murmur at Thy appointments, nor be angry against the instruments of Thy justice.

Deliver me from the errors and vices of the age we live in; [i. 161.] from infidelity, wicked principles; from profaneness, heresies, and schism.

I most heartily thank God for His perpetual care over me; for all His mercies bestowed upon me; for the blessings of nature and of grace.

Give a blessing to those means which Thou Thyself hast appointed.

Grant, O God, that I may never receive Thy grace in vain, but that I may live like one who believes and hopes for the joys of heaven.

Aspirations. Church. Let not our sins force Thee to re- [i. 262.] move our candlestick from us.

St. Matt. xx. 22, [32.] *What will ye that I should do unto you?* O JESUS, Thou knowest my will, for it is Thou who hast wrought in me this desire:—that the eyes of my mind may be opened; that Thou wouldst have the same compassion on me as Thou hadst on these blind men; that I may recover the sight that sin has deprived me of; that I may see Thee, and love Thee, and follow Thee, all the days of my life.

Let me ever be sorry for my sins, thankful for Thy blessings,—fear Thy judgments, love Thy mercies, remember Thy presence.

Vouchsafe me Thy Holy Spirit to bear witness with my spirit, that I am Thy child.

EJACULA-TIONS.

Give me an humble mind, a godly fear, and a quiet conscience.

Weaken, O Lord, the power of Satan in this place, and the tyranny of his ministers.

In time of Pestilence or Danger. Set Thy saving mark upon our houses, and give order to the destroyer not to hurt us.

[2nd ed. p. 443.]

St. John xvi. 23. *Verily, verily, I say unto you, Whatsoever ye shall ask the Father in My Name, He will give it you*[m].

Upon this promise, blessed Lord, I depend; beseeching Thee, O Heavenly Father, for Thy dear Son's sake, to give me the graces I most stand in need of.

Before rising in the morning. Raise me up, O Lord, at the last day to life everlasting.

For Magistrates. Make them instruments of Thy glory and the public good.

After prayers. Vouchsafe us those graces and blessings which Thou knowest to be needful for us, notwithstanding our great unworthiness.

Riches. Shut my heart, O Lord, against the love of worldly riches, lest I betray Thee as Judas did.

May I never render myself unworthy of Thy graces.

May Thy Holy Spirit, O God, fill my heart, that it may appear in all my words and actions, that I am governed by it.

[i. 263.]

Luke x. O Jesus, the true Samaritan, look upon the wounds which sin hath caused in my soul, and have compassion on me.

May I always resign my will and my desires to Him who knows what is good for us better than we ourselves do.

Give me, gracious God, a passionate desire for the salvation of souls which Thou hast redeemed with Thy most precious blood.

Perseverance. Finish, O my God, the work of mercy and conversion, which Thou hast begun in me.

Save, O Lord Jesus, a soul which Thou hast redeemed by Thy blood.

What good canst Thou, O Lord, find in me, unless Thou first cause it in me?

---

[m] [Ed. ii. fol. p. 443, inserts here, Matt. viii. 2, 3. *Lord, if Thou wilt, Thou canst make me clean.—I will, be thou clean.*

There is no merit in me, O God, to attract Thy mercy and goodness, but only my great misery and blindness. May I make a suitable return by an holy life.

According to the greatness of Thy goodness, and the multitude of Thy mercies, look upon me.

Sanctify my soul and body with Thy heavenly blessings, that they may be made Thy holy habitation, and that nothing may be found in me, that may offend the eyes of Thy Majesty.

Protect and keep me in the midst of the dangers of this corrupt world; and by Thy light and grace direct me in the way to everlasting life, through Jesus Christ, &c.

St. John xi. 3. A proper and prevailing way of addressing Christ for ourselves or others. "Behold, Lord, *him whom Thou lovest*, him for whom Thou sheddest Thy precious blood," &c.

Sight of Sin. This is my case, my sin: Lord, help me to break my bonds.

New Birth. Forgive me, gracious God, the many sins by which I have broken the covenant I made with Thee at my baptism: deliver me from the chains of those sins with which I am bound, that I may love and obey Thee, and glorify Thy goodness to all eternity.

Aspirations. Jesus Christ our example and pattern. O that [i. 264.] I may have my eyes continually fixed upon that example and pattern which Thou, O Lord Jesu Christ, hast left and set us, and grant that I may daily endeavour to follow Thee[n].

Scripture Examples. Persecution for righteousness' sake. [i. 268.] Such the Lord never forsakes.

Gen. xxxix. 21. *But the Lord was with Joseph, and shewed him mercy, and gave him favour in the sight of the keeper of the prison.*

Christ's patience. What sorrows did He undergo, and with what patience did suffer them! Patient when Judas unworthily betrayed Him with a kiss; patient when Caiaphas despitefully used Him; patient when hurried from one place to another; patient when Herod with his men of war set Him at nought; patient when Pilate so unrighteously

---

[n] [Another copy of this, i. 266, reads, "O that my eyes may ever be fixed upon that example that our blessed Lord hath left us, and that I may daily endeavour to follow Him. Amen."]

condemned Him; patient when scourged and crowned with thorns; patient when His cross was laid upon Him, when He was reviled, reproached, scoffed at, and every way abused. Lord Jesus, grant me patience, after this example, to bear Thy holy will in all things.

Christ's love and charity. Where shall we take our pattern but from Thee? Thou callest Thy followers Thy friends. Thou didst stoop down to wash their feet who were not worthy to untie Thy shoe. Thou forgavest and restored [didst restore] Peter, when he had abjured Thee. Thou didst vouchsafe to satisfy Thomas, who would not believe but upon his own terms. Thou didst forgive and pray for Thy bloody persecutors. O Thou fountain and pattern of love, grant that I may love Thee above all things, and my neighbour as myself.

[i. 270.] *Verily, verily, I say unto you, Whatsoever ye shall ask the Father in My Name, He will give it you.* These, O heavenly Father, are the things which I ask in Thy Son's Name, for myself, my children and family, and for all that desire my prayers.

[i. 266.]

EJACULATIONS DAILY.

Morning. I laid me down and slept, and rose again, for the Lord sustained me. Blessed be the Name of the Lord.

Raise me up, O Lord, at the last day, to life and happiness everlasting.

Blessed be the Lord for His mercies renewed unto me every morning.

[2nd ed. 443.] 1 Cor. vii. 35. *Attend upon the Lord without distraction.*

O Holy Spirit of Grace, help my infirmities, that I may fix my thoughts upon my duty; and that I may serve Thee with all my heart and mind.

That I may never give way to wandering thoughts, but watch against them continually.

Look upon me, O Lord, and pity me; make me, and let me be, Thine by the choice of my will!

Make me serious and thoughtful at all times, that I may not fail being so when I attend upon God.

Let not my heart, O God, be inclined to any evil thing. Keep me, O God, from every thing that may displease Thee. O make me wise unto salvation.

Phil. ii. 21. *For all seek their own, not the things which are Christ's.*

The good Lord deliver me from this dreadful judgment.

Phil. iv. 14. *I can do all things through Christ, which strengtheneth me.*

O that I may never forfeit this power by presumption or want of faith.

John xx. 28. *Thomas said, My Lord and my God!*

Thou art indeed, O Jesus, my Lord, for Thou hast redeemed me by Thy precious blood; Thou art my God, for I am dedicated to Thee, and sanctified by Thy Spirit.

Acts ii. 44. *And all that believed were together, and had all things common.*

May God grant, that as we are all members of the same body, have one and the same Father, the same Saviour, the same Spirit, and hope to meet in the same paradise; that we may live in unity and godly love, and be charitable to the poor according to our ability, and as every one hath need.

The good Lord grant that in the day of Christ I may rejoice that I have not run in vain, nor laboured in vain.

Occasional Meditations and Ejaculations. The necessity and the power of the Holy Ghost to sanctify and change our nature.

Who will say, he doth not want the assistance of God's Holy Spirit?

Passages by Sea.

Apr. 6, 1698, landed at Derby Haven.
Sept. 30, 1698, at Lirpool, (sic) 24 Houres.
Apr. 7, 1699, wth my wife Derby Haven.
Apr. 18, 1701, at Hylake wth my wife. 24.
Sept. 16, 1701, Derby Haven wth my wife. 24.
Augt. 7, 1703, Hylake—Act of Settlem^t.
Sept. 11, 1703, Douglass 26 Hours°.

° [In iii. these seven entries stand as follows: (the dates being the same.)]
"I landed at Derby Haven, the first time I came hither."
"At Lirpool after 24 Houres sayl."
"Good Fryday—with my Family in Derby Haven 24 Hours."
"Good Friday—at Hylake with my wife 12 H."
"In Derby Haven with my wife and child. 24 H."
"Hylake. 26 Hours. Act of Settlement then passed."
"Returned to Douglass, having assisted in the A. of Settlem^t. 26 H."

PASSAGES BY SEA.

Sept. 5, 1704, Whitehaven, with my sick wife, 6 H. a great deliverance[p].

May 11, 1705, Maughold's Head, wife buried[q].

Feb. 25, 1706, Beaumorris, with my daughter, &c.[r]

[s]Sept. 19, 1707, Derby Haven, 20 hours.

Augt. 1, 1710, Kilcudbright, 9 H.[t]

July 17, 1711, Laxy, London, about the Customs[u].

May 17, 1713, Hylake, Captn. Leigh, 13 H.[x]

Sept. 13, 1713, Derby Haven, Col. Stanley[y].

Ap. 18, 1719, Lirpool, 12 H., M. Hendrick. [iii. "Mary Hendrick's affair."]

Jan. 25, 1720, Douglass, 48 H.—leaky vessel. A storm followed—vessels lost at Hylake[z].

Ap. 8, 1723, at Hylake, 24, Mr. Stevenson. ["I landed at Hylake wth Mr. Stevenson, after 24 H."]

Oct. 4, 1724, (after having been 18 m. absent from my diocese, to my grief[a] and charge, to defend [b]the Episc. Jurisdiction, and having gained my cause[c], blessed be God), at Douglass, 24 H.

July 14, 1729, at Douglass, on board Captn. Richmond in 48 houres at Lirpool. Blessed be God.

Sept. 29, 1729, at Lirpool, on board Capt. Richmond,—landed next day at Douglas. Deo gratias.

Sept. 7, 1731, I parted with my dear child, he going for England. May our gracious God send us a happy meeting in this or a better world.

June 18, 1733, I went off with Oliver Gardiner, and after

---

[p] iii. "after a short passage of six hours, I and my wife came to Whitehaven."

[q] "Having buryed my dear wife, I returned to my dear children, and landed at St. Maughold's-head."

[r] "I landed at Beaumories, and went to Warrington."

[s] iii. adds "Fryday...I landed at."

[t] "After nine hours in a fishing boat in the night, I landed with Mr. Murray in the hills of Ard, within three miles of Kilcudbright."

[u] "After 30 hours I landed near Laxy, having spent half-a-year in London, serving Lord Derby and the country."

[x] "After having preached at Ballaugh, I went on board Capt. Fr. Leigh, and landed at Hylake after 13 houres."

[y] "I preached Wallysee [Wallasey, in Cheshire], landed (with Col. Stanley) at Derby Haven, 17."

[z] "Jan. 25. 1719. After a voyage of 48 Houres, I landed at Douglass, in a leaky vessel, a storm immediately followed, in wch 2 ships lost at Hylake."

[a] "Very much to my sorrow."

[b] "the jurisdiction and episcopal authority."

[c] "I took shipping at Hylake, and the next day, after a very fine passage, I landed safe at Douglas. Blessed be God for these great mercies."

[Here the list in MS. iii. ends.]

a rough passage of 24 H., landed at Lirpool. Blessed be God. <small>PASSAGES BY SEA.</small>

Sept. 14, 1733. Having the day before parted with my dear son and friends at Lirpool, I landed this day, after 22 houres, with Capt. Richmond, at Douglass. D. Gr.

Apr. 28, 1735. The 21, I took ship with Captn. Richmond, (Cor. Murray, &c.) We met with a very great storm that night, and were driven to Peel Foudray (sic) where we stayd till yesterday, when setting sail, we met with another storm, (in which a small bark and two men were lost), but blessed be God we came safe to Lirpool. May I never forget God's repeated favours to me.

Sept. 7, 1735, I went on board Oliver Gardiner's new vessel, and with great difficulty and not without some danger we landed at Derby Haven the day following in 30 houres.

COLLECTS:

THEIR TENDENCY.

Comfort of the Holy Ghost	First Sunday after Ascension.
Humiliation [? Illumination]	Whitsunday.
Direction of the Holy Ghost	Nineteenth Sunday after Trinity.
Manifold gifts of the Holy Ghost ...	St. Barnabas.
Means of Grace; Hearing	St. Bartholomew. / St. Luke.
——————— Reading	Second Sunday in Advent.
——————— Fasting	First Sunday in Lent. / Tenth and twenty-third after Trinity[d].
To convert us from sin	First in Advent. / First after Easter. / St. Andrew. / St. James. / St. Matthew.
Pardon of sin, and acceptance with God	Twelfth, twenty-first, and twenty-fourth after Trinity. / Purification. / Second after Epiphany.
To rescue us from temptation	Fourth in Advent. / Fourth after Epiphany. / Eighteenth Trinity.

[d] [The mention of these two would seem more appropriate if *Prayer* had been joined with *Fasting*.]

292 SACRA PRIVATA.

COLLECTS: THEIR TENDENCY.

To enable us to do good	Fifth Easter. First, ninth, eleventh, thirteenth, seventeenth, and twenty-fifth Trinity.
To bring us to glory	Epiphany. Sixth after Epiphany.]
Regeneration	Christmas Day.
Charity	Quinquagesima.
Mortification	Circumcision. Easter Eve.
Contrition	Ash Wednesday.
Sincerity	Third after Easter.
Love of God and His laws	Fourth after Easter. Sixth and fourteenth after Trinity.
Heavenly desires	Ascension.
Faith, right	Trinity Sunday.
Faith, firm	Seventh Sunday after Trinity. St. Thomas. St. Mark.
Imitation of Christ	Sixth in Lent. Second after Easter.
Imitation of Saints	St. Stephen. St. Paul. St. Philip and Jacob. St. John Baptist. Innocents. All-Saints.
Guarding of Angels and God's providence	Second, third, fourth, and twentieth after Trinity. St. Michael.
Deliverance from enemies	Third in Lent.
Deliverance from judgments	Sexagesima. Septuagesima. Fourth in Lent.
Support under afflictions	Third and fourth after Epiphany.
Defence from evil, and supply of good	Eighth and fifteenth after Trinity.
For Jews, Turks, &c.	Collect for Good Friday.
Ministers may be fit, diligent, successful	St. Matthias. St. Peter. Third in Advent.
That the people may be kept in truth, unity, and peace	First Collect, Good Friday. St. John. St. Simon and Jude. Fifth, sixth, twelfth after Trinity.

SUPPLEMENT.

I.

Before prayers publick. Let ye words of my mouth, and y^e [M. H. i.] meditations of my heart, be always acceptable in Thy sight, O Lord, my Strength and my Redeem^r.

Hear us, O King of Heaven, w^n we call upon Thee in ye name of o^r Ld J. X^t.

Let Thy H. Sp^t. teach us how to pray: give us just apprehensions of o^r wants, and just resentments of Thy mercies; y^t o^r pray^{rs} may be heard, and o^r requests be granted, to Thy hon^r and ye salvation of o^r soules.

After prayers publick. The Good God say Amen to o^r prayers; and pardon every one y^t has now set his heart to seek ye Lord, tho' he was not prepar'd according to ye purity wch is required of those y^t tread His courts.

II.

Before prayers private. My Good God grant, y^t as oft as I p^{e}sent myself bef. Thee, Thy good Sp^t may be wth me, to dispose me unto, and to assist me in Thy service. Keep my mind stedfast in ye duty I am ab^t, y^t no sinfull distractions may carry me away fr. Thee; y^t I may serve Thee wth my heart as well as wth my body; and y^t my pray^{rs} in ye name of J. X^t. may be heard, and my petit^{ns} granted.

After prayers private. Good God say Amen to my pray^{rs} [M.H. ii.] if it be Thy gracious will; but if in any thing I have ask'd or done amiss, pardon mine infirmities, and answer my necessities, for Jesus and His mercies' sake.

Ecclus. xviii. 23. *Before thou prayest prepare thyself, and* [ii. 3*.]

SUPPLE- *be not as one that tempteth the Lord:* i.e. expecting His
MENT
No. II. blessings without using the means of obtaining them.

May the good Spirit of God dispose me unto, and assist me in His service, that now[a] I present myself before the Majesty of Heaven and earth, no sinful distractions may carry me from the duty I am about, but that I may serve Him with my heart as well as with my body.

St. Matt. v. 6. *Blessed are they that do hunger and thirst after righteousness, for they shall be filled.*

Blessed God, who never gavest a regular appetite but Thou didst provide for it, satisfy my soul, I beseech Thee, with what Thou hast made me long for—such a love for Thee and for Thy service as shall make me *think* of Thee with pleasure, *pray* to Thee with attention, and *serve* Thee with joyfulness and gladness of heart.

Give me a just sense of mine iniquities, of *my* wants, and of *Thy* mercies, that I may with all humility present my supplications before Thee, depend upon Thy goodness and truth, and be satisfied with the pleasures of Thy house, even of Thine holy temple. Amen.

Matt. vi. 21. *Where your treasure is, there will your heart be also. What things soever ye desire when ye pray, believe that ye receive them, and ye shall have them.* Mark xi. 24.

The Lord increase my faith, that it may be unto His servant according to this word. Lord, pardon mine infirmities, and answer my necessities for Jesus Christ His sake.

III.

[M.H. ii.; *Before sermon in the pulpit, private.*
ii. 2*.]
John xxi. 17. *Jesus said unto him, Feed My sheep*[b].

O Thou[c] Good Shepheard, and my Great Master, behold *this flock* for w[ch] Thou wast contented to suffer; feed them by me Thy unworthy servant, and preserve y[m] by Thy grace, to[d] y[e] day of Thy coming to judge y[e] world.

After sermon in y[e] pulpit, private.

The Good God, fr. whom alone cometh y[e] increase of all our labours, and who alone can[st] order y[e] unruly wills and

---

[a] [prima manu, "when."] [c] iii. om. "Thou."
[b] M.H. adds, "Before Catechising, [d] ii. "to life eternal."
Feed my Lambs."

affections of sinful men; give a blessing (if it be Thy gracious will) to all my endeav{rs} wch are directed to Thy hon{r}, and ye good of mankind; for ye sake of J. Xt., my Master and Saviour. Amen.

[ii. 2* reads], *Except the Lord build the house, they labour in vain that build it.* The good God, from whom cometh the increase of all our labours, give His blessing to what I have now spoken; direct and rule my heart and actions, that I may instruct as well [by] my life as by my sermons; through Jesus Christ our Lord. Amen.

Put words into my mouth, and make this people to understand their meaning.

I came not to seek my own glory, but the glory of Him that sent me.

IV.

Prayer before Study. James i. 5.   [M.H. iii.]

"Will you diligently exercise yourself in the same H. Ss. &c." vid. Consecration.

O God, the Fountain of all wisdom, in a deep sense of my own ignorance, and of that great charge which lies upon me, I am constrained to come often before Thee, from whom I have learned whatever I know, to ask that help without which I shall disquiet myself in vain: most humbly beseeching Thee to guide me with Thine eye; to enlighten my mind, that I may see myself, and teach others the wonders of Thy law; that I may learn from Thee what I ought to think and speak concerning Thee. Direct and bless all the labours of my mind, give me a discerning spirit, a sound judgment, and an honest and a religious heart. And grant that, in all my studies, my *first* aim may be to set forth Thy glory, and to set forward the salvation of mankind; that I may give a comfortable account of my time at the great day, when all our labours shall be tried.

And if Thou art pleased that by *my ministry* sinners shall be converted, and Thy kingdom enlarged, give me the grace of *humility*, that I may never ascribe the success to myself, but to Thy Holy Spirit, which enables me to will and to do according to Thy good pleasure. Grant this, O Father of all light and truth, for the sake of Jesus Christ. Amen.

V.

Prayer before Sermon.

Prevent us, O Lord, in all our doings, &c., [as in the Communion service.]...Through Jesus Christ:

For whose merits we beg the acceptance of those prayers which we have already made, and all other devotions both public and private, which we offer according to Thy will to Thy Divine Majesty. And deny us not, for Thy gracious goodness' sake, those things which Thou mightest justly deny to our unworthiness.

And that our prayers may be more acceptable in Thy sight, we most humbly present them together with all the good prayers which are this day offered to the Throne of Grace; the intercession of our Lord, and the supplications of all Thy servants. Beseeching Thee, O Father of mankind, to hear and accept them for all Jews, Turks, and Heathens, that they may be converted to the truth, and with us be made partakers of the blessing of the Gospel of Christ.—For all Christian Churches throughout the world, that they may be united in religion.—For our Church in particular, that whatever is amiss in it may be mended.—For all Christian Kingdoms and Commonwealths [that all violent spirits by which the Christian world is unjustly disturbed, may be suppressed, and] that truth and justice, true religion and piety, may be established in them and countenanced: and that all atheism and profaneness, and whatever else opposes Thy Divine will revealed to us, may be discouraged, punished, and rooted out of the world.

More especially we beg that this blessed Reformation may be promoted in *these kingdoms;* that they may flourish in peace and in Thy favour. To which end we offer up our prayers—For the King's Majesty and his prosperity, that he may do those things which shall be acceptable to Thee and profitable for his people.—That the Royal Family may be happy and prosper, and that Thou wouldst give them the blessings of this life, and of that which is to come.—That [the Parliament now assembled, and] his Majesty's Council, may be blessed, in all their undertakings for Thy honour and glory, with good success.—That the Nobility, the Gentry, and the Magistrates, may in their several places, both by their example and authority, promote Thy honour, the ease, and welfare and happiness of all below them [E. D.ᵉ]

Give Thy blessing to the Clergy, that they may teach well, and that they may live well—that their labours may be blessed, and that the people may follow their good instructions. [Bish.] We humbly pray unto Thee for the prosperous education of youth in all universities and schools, that those places may answer the end of their foundations, the glory of God, and the good of mankind.—For the prosperous and good success of all merchants, husbandmen, and tradesmen; and that they may diligently and with an upright conscience follow their several vocations. [Cit. and Corp.]

We humbly beseech Thee to hear us for all those that desire our prayers, and especially for such as are in affliction of mind or body, in danger or want; in prison or persecution for a righteous cause; that Thou wouldst in mercy look upon all such; support them under, and graciously deliver them out of all their distresses.

We offer up our prayers for all those who never pray for themselves: open their eyes that they may see their own wants, and how much they stand in need of Thy gracious and powerful assistance and defence—that they may consider, before it be too late, whither their unwary steps will lead them: that we and they may all with one heart and voice beg of Thee such things as we stand in need of, and all with one heart and voice praise that infinite goodness which bestows them on us.

And, good God, give us grace that *we* may never forget to praise Thy Holy Name, for all the mercies and blessings we have, and every day receive from Thy good Providence: but let the sense of Thy kindness create in us a true and lively faith and gratitude: that we may have such thoughts of God as becomes us; for His power in creating us; for His wonderful providence in preserving us; for His great goodness in redeeming us by Jesus Christ. For whose Gospel and example we bless Thy Holy Name, and for the examples of all those who by Thy grace followed His doctrine, and through

ᵉ [i.e. Mention was to be made, in the Isle of Man, of the Earl of Derby as Lord thereof. So afterwards the Bishop of the Diocese and Heads of the City or Corporation are indicated.]

faith in His promises have attained eternal happiness. Most humbly beseeching Thee to give us grace so to follow the blessed Saints in all virtuous and godly living, that we may come to those unspeakable joys which Thou hast prepared for them that unfeignedly love Thee.

These things, and whatever else our necessities or our charity obliges us to pray for, we most humbly beg, in the Name and Words of our blessed Saviour. Our Father, &c.

VI.

Birthday.

[MSS. ii. and iii. prefix.] I was born Dec. 20, 1663[a], being Sunday, in the evening about 4 o'clock, and[b] baptized on Friday following, being Christmas Day.

Psalm xc. 12. *So teach us to number our days, that we may apply our hearts unto wisdom.*

Blessed be[c] God for my creation [d]and birth; for giving me a being from honest parents, [e]fearing God, and in a Christian and Protestant country; for giving me perfect members and senses, a sound reason, and an healthful constitution; for the means of grace, the[f] assistance of the Holy Spirit, and for the hopes[g] of glory; for my good education[h] and preferments, above the hopes and abilities of my father's house, and that I attained to it without any [i]sordid methods; for all the known or unobserved favours, [j]providences and deliverances, by which my life has hitherto been preserved; [k]most humbly beseeching [l]Thee, my God and Father, to pardon my neglect or abuse of any of [m]Thy favours, and that I have so [n]very much forgotten Thee[o], in whom I live, and move, and have my being.

[p]Good Lord, forgive me the great waste of my precious

---

[a] iii. "Sunday evening, 'twixt 4 and 5."
[b] iii. "baptized Christmas-day."
[c] ii. "the God of heaven."
[d] ii. iii. om. "and birth."
[e] ii. "parents, and in such a part of the world where the Christian religion is purely taught, and without persecution professed." iii. "such...professed without persecution."
[f] iii. "assistances of His."
[g] iii. "hope."
[h] ii. iii. "education and preferment, and that I," &c.
[i] iii. "unworthy."
[j] ii. iii. om. "providences."
[k] ii. adds, "I bless the good providence of God."
[l] ii. "Him to pardon."
[m] ii. "His mercies;" iii. "Thy mercies."
[n] iii. om. "very."
[o] ii. adds, "my Creator."
[p] "The good Lord forgive," &c., ii. iii.

time; the many days ^qand years of health, and ^rthe many opportunities of doing good, which I have lost; and give me grace, that for the time to come I may be truly wise, that I may consider my latter end, ^sand work out my salvation with fear and trembling, ever remembering "that the night cometh when no man can work;" that the day of my death may be better to me than the day of my birth.

O gracious God^t, grant that before Thou takest from me that breath which Thou^u gavest me, I may truly^v repent of the errors of my life past; that my sins may be forgiven^w, and my pardon sealed in heaven; so that I may have a place of rest^x in paradise with Thy faithful servants, till the general resurrection; when the good Lord vouchsafe me a better and an everlasting life, through Jesus Christ. Amen.

[ii. adds], 20th of December, 1663. I was born on Sunday evening, Christmas being the Friday afterwards, when I was baptized by Mr. Bethel.

[M. H. page c., reads this as follows.]

Birthday. St. Thomas's Eve, 1663.

God, the Creator of all things, who as on this day ordered me to be born, to glorify Him among the rest of His creatures, receive the humble thanks of His servant, for my creation and preservation and for all the blessings of my life.

Blessed be God for giving me a being from honest and religious parents, and in such a part of the world where the Christian religion is purely taught and without persecution professed:

For my regeneration by water and the Holy Ghost: (O that I may become a new creature indeed!)

For my perfect members and senses, and sound constitution:

For all the known and all the unobserved blessings and deliverances hitherto vouchsafed to me.

Blessed be God for preventing me betimes with His grace; for my education, and for my preferment, and [that] it pleased Him to bring me to it without my making use [of]

---

^q iii. om. "and years."
^r ii. om. "the many."
^s iii. om. "and...work."
^t iii. adds, "and Father."
^u iii. "didst give."
^v iii. "repent me of all the."
^w ii. adds, "by Thy mercy."
^x ii. iii. "rest among Thy faithful servants in the paradise of God."

sordid or unlawful means: the Lord pardon [me herein, that?] I have abused those mercies:

Pardon my ingratitude, that I have at any time forgotten my Creator, in Whom and by Whom I live and move and have my being.

[M. H. ci.] If by Thy favour I shall live another year, grant that I may do nothing of which I may be ashamed at the great day of account.

Before Thou shalt call for the breath which Thou hast given me, Lord, give me true repentance for all the errors of my life past, that my sins may be forgiven and my pardon sealed in heaven, before I go hence and be no more seen: that I may be numbered amongst Thy saints in glory everlasting.

For those that desire my prayers. Thou who art everywhere present, and seest the necessities of all Thy creatures, &c.

VII.

New-Year's Day.[y] Blessed be God, who has[z] brought me safe to the beginning of another year.

Blessed be God, that I am of the number of those who have time and space for repentance yet given them.

My [a]God, make me truly sensible of this mercy, and give me grace to consider [b]often how short and how uncertain my time is: that there is one year more of a short life passed over my head; and that I am so much nearer eternity; that I may in good earnest think of another life, and be so prepared for it, as that death may not overtake me unawares.

[c]Lord, pardon all my misspent time, and make me more diligent and careful [d]to redeem it for the time to come, that when I come to the end of my days[e], I may look back with comfort on the days that are past[f].

Grant that I may begin this new year with new resolutions of serving[g] Thee more faithfully; and if, through infirmity or

[y] ii. inserts Ps. xc. 12.
[z] ii. "safely brought me."
[a] ii. "gracious."
[b] ii. om. "often."
[c] ii. "The good Lord pardon."
[d] ii. om. "to redeem it."
[e] ii. "years."
[f] ii. *prima manu* adds, "and have some comfortable hope of everlasting life."
[g] ii. "God." Then, *prima manu*, "in the state of life unto which He hath called me."

negligence, I forget these good purposes, the [h]good Lord awaken in me a sense of my danger.

My heart is in Thy hands, O God, as well as my time; O make me wise unto salvation; that I may consider in this my day the things that belong unto my peace: and that [i]I may pass this, and all the years[j] I have yet to live, in a comfortable hope of[j] a blessed eternity, for the Lord Jesus' sake. Amen.

VIII.

[*In a time of sickness.*] [M.H. lxxix.]

Ps. cvi. 30. *Then stood up Phineas, and executed judgment, (or prayed) and so the plague was stayed.*

O gracious Lord and Master! who from an obscure family and low condition hast call'd me forth to feed Thy sheep, and hast honoured me with the charge and oversight of this part of Thy flock, give me grace that I may with all imaginable faithfulness and diligence discharge the trust which Thou hast reposed in me.

Let Thy love, O blessed Jesus, and Thy example, be my pattern; that I may do all the good I possibly can while Thou art pleased to continue me in this charge; that I may lead Thy flock in the way they should go; that I may stand in the gap when Thou art angry, and by Thy merits and intercession have power with God to turn away His wrath from them.

For the sake of Thy Son Jesus Christ, O merciful God, have mercy upon all those who are now visited with Thy hand; sanctify Thy fatherly correction to them, and to us, who have yet escaped this sickness.

Look down in mercy upon all those to whom this sickness shall be unto death; give them true repentance for the errors of their life past, and stedfast faith in Thy Son Jesus Christ, that their sins may be forgiven, and their pardon sealed in heaven, before they go hence and are no more seen; that they may be delivered from death eternal in that day when Thou shalt judge the world in righteousness.

Give us all grace that we may search our ways, and see

---

[h] ii. "the Lord in mercy awaken me to a just."
[i] ii. adds, " serving Thee with joyfulness of heart."
[j] ii. " of my life...eternal happiness."

whence this evil comes, for though we are born to trouble, yet affliction comes not out of the dust.

But more especially I beg this grace for myself, and for all those who with me are appointed to watch over Thy flock in this place, that we may neglect no duty incumbent upon us in these times of danger, when Thou seemest to be displeased with Thy people. Blessed be Thy holy Name that Thy displeasure is not greater,— that Thou hast not yet punished us according to the multitude of our transgressions.

Teach us, O God, who by Thy goodness yet survive, in the daily spectacles of mortality to see how frail our own condition is, and so to number our days, that we may seriously apply our hearts to that holy and heavenly wisdom, while we live here, which may in the end bring us to life everlasting. Make us all (like the wise servant) ever ready and prepared for the coming of our Lord; that we may receive the blessings of faithful servants.

If it be Thy good pleasure, preserve my family from sickness; but give us grace that we may not abuse Thy mercy, either by neglecting those that are in misery, and want that assistance which we can give them, or by forgetting that Thy goodness and forbearance ought to lead us to repentance.

O Thou who hast made it my duty to pray for others, (for otherways it would be great presumption in me to take upon me to intercede with Thee for those that are more worthy than myself,) hear me, I most humbly beseech Thee, for Jesus Christ His sake, my Great Master, and the Saviour of men. Amen.

[In ii. 93, this prayer stands thus.]

Job xxxiii. 19, &c. *He is chastened with pain upon his bed, and the multitude of his bones with strong pain.*

Yea, his soul draweth near to the grave, and his life to the destroyers.

If there be a messenger *with him, one among a thousand, to shew unto man his uprightness, &c.*

He shall pray unto God, and He will be favourable unto him, &c.

Almighty God, who dost not afflict willingly, nor grieve the children of men, have mercy upon all those who are now visited with Thy hand; sanctify Thy fatherly correction to them; and to us, and to all such as have yet escaped this sickness. Give us all grace that we may search our ways and see whence this evil cometh: for though we are *born to trouble,* yet affliction cometh not out of the dust.

Look down in mercy upon all those unto whom this sickness shall be unto death: give them true repentance for all the errors of their lives past, and stedfast faith in Thy Son Jesus Christ, that their sins may be done away by Thy mercy, and their pardon sealed in heaven before they go hence and be no more seen; that they may be delivered from death eternal in that day when Thou shalt judge the world in righteousness.

And teach us, who by Thy goodness yet survive, in the daily spectacles of mortality, to see how frail and how uncertain our own condition is, and so to number our days, that we may apply our hearts to that holy and heavenly wisdom whilst we live here which may in the end bring us to life everlasting.

Grant, O Lord, that we, who are appointed to watch over Thy flock in this place, may not neglect any duty incumbent upon us in times of danger.

Gracious Lord and Master, save us and our flocks which Thou hast purchased with Thy most precious blood. Amen, Amen.

IX.

[Advice to an afflicted person.]

Heb. xii. 5, 6. *My son, despise not thou the chastening of the Lord, nor faint when thou art rebuked of Him. For whom the Lord loveth He chasteneth, &c.*

Consider

That this visitation is certainly from God. That He cannot be delighted with the miseries of His poor creatures, and therefore it is not without reason that you are afflicted.

It may be you cannot for the present see the reason of this visitation; but if you submit to God's dealings with you, you'll either see the reasons, or reap the fruits of it, which will be as good for you.

I'll put you in mind of some of the reasons of God's thus dealing with men.

SUPPLE-
MENT
No. IX.

1. Some people (who are otherwise well disposed) do yet live under the power [of], and give way to, some passion, or custom, or prejudice, which is very displeasing to God, though they are not aware of it; now afflictions are proper to put people upon considering what is amiss in them, of calling their own ways to remembrance, and putting on resolutions of better obedience for the time to come.

2. A person may lie under the guilt of some sin which he had never (it may be) truly repented of—has never been truly humbled for it. This was the case of Jacob's children: they had sold their brother, endangered the life of their aged father, had like to have brought down his grey hairs with sorrow to the grave; under which guilt they passed their time well enough for fourteen years, till God visited them in Egypt, where being treated for spies, they called to remembrance and heartily lamented their sin. *We are verily guilty concerning our brother, &c.*

3. It may be God is designing by this affliction to fit your soul for greater degrees of grace or knowledge. This was God's way from the beginning...... [h]

X.

[ii. 128.]

[*For a penitent woman.*]

Remember not, Lord, our offences, nor, &c.

O most merciful God, who according to the multitude of Thy mercies and promises in Jesus Christ, dost so put away the sins of those who truly repent, that Thou rememberest them no more; open Thine eye of mercy upon this Thy servant, who being sensible of her error, most earnestly desires pardon and forgiveness. Renew in her (most loving Father) whatsoever hath been depraved by the fraud and malice of the devil, or by her own carnal will and frailty. Preserve and continue her in the unity of the Church: suffer her not to fall into any temptation whereby she may be prevailed upon to forsake or offend Thee by any wilful sin, but enable her by Thy grace to resist and overcome all the snares of

---

[h] [This passage is followed in the MS. by a Form of Prayer to be used before Sermon; which is not given here, having been already printed in this edition of the Bishop's works, vol. iv. p. 326—28.]

the devil, the world, and the evil inclinations of corrupt nature.

And blessed be Thy holy Name, for those favours which Thou hast already vouchsafed her in delivering her from the snare of the devil. Continue Thy mercies to her, O God, and give her such measure of preventing, restraining, and assisting grace, whereby she may be enabled to conquer all delusions for the time to come.

Strengthen her, O Lord, with the Holy Ghost the Comforter, and daily increase in her and in us all Thy manifold gifts of grace, the spirit of wisdom and understanding, the spirit of counsel and ghostly strength, the spirit of knowledge and true godliness; and fill us, O Lord, &c. Let Thy Fatherly hand, O merciful God, ever be over us, &c.[i]

XI.

Public Works. A.D. 1698, &c. I rebuilt the house, barnes, out-houses, &c., erected a new miln, planted orchards, gardens, and fenced the whole demesnes, all which has cost me upwards of £1200.

Sept. 6, 1703. I was I hope on this day an happy instrument in bringing the Lord of this Isle and his people to an agreement: vide the Act of Settlement. What the consequence may be, I know not, but this I know, that I acted in this affair uprightly, and God be praised for it.

July 16, 1698. I laid the corner-stone of a new Chapel at Castletowne. Built with the episcopal revenues.

Aug. 4, 1704. I finished the body of St. John's Chapel which I began to build in 1699, at my own expense: it cost me near £40, and the 24 Keys are besides indebted to me, £6 18s., for the north isle.

St. Patrick's new Church. St. Peter's-day, 1714. This day I dedicated this Church, having built it new from the ground, and added £50 towards mending the endowment.

---

[i] [The leaf opposite this has the following:—
"Meditations and Prayers for Saturday evening—Preparation for Death—vid. Nelson's *Easter Eve, Moulin,* Soliloquie y⁰ last.
"When the last day of my life shall come, O let Thy servant depart in peace.
"O blessed Jesus, say unto me, as Thou once didst to the sick of the palsy, *Son, thy sins be forgiven thee.*
"*But we had the sentence of death in ourselves,*" &c.

SUPPLE-
MENT
No. XI.

The year following I built the school, and recovered the glebe, which had been leased out by Governor Ireland.

Douglass Chapel. Sept. 21, 1708. I consecrated this Chapel, having contributed £10 towards the building, and begged from Lord D. and others £60 more.

Kirk Braddon chancel rendred, flagg'd, new East window, &c., 1704.

Kirk Braddon church-house new built, to which I gave £6. A.D. 1705.

New Library of Castletowne, April 2, 1710, then finished; it cost £83 5s. 6d. Towards which I got subscriptions, £14 6s. 3d.

[iii. 55.] *Chappel at Ramsea* rebuilt, to which I contributed £5, A.D....

Kirk Christ Lezair, Church and Chapel rebuilt and enlarged, to which I contributed about £5, A.D....

Kirk Christ Lezair glebe. I made interest with Dr. Crow, Bishop of Cloyn, to add a small estate of his to the glebe, of which the Vicar is this year, A.D. 1722, in actual possession.

Kirk Christ Lezair, a new school-house, to which I have and will [give] £3 : 1722-3.

Sulby School, to which I have promised £5 : 1715.

A.D. 1697. The Royal Bounty having been unpaid for some years, I made interest to get the arrears, with part of which I paid the fine of £130, payable every thirty years.

Parochial Librarys, 1699. By the encouragement of my worthy friend, Dr. Thos. Bray, I began this year a foundation of parochial libraries in this diocese, which by the good blessing of God upon His servant, I have been improving ever since with books both practical and devotional.

Impropriations, 1715. These having been sadly mismanaged, and the Lord's rents unpaid, I took the management into my own hands, and now, A.D. 1722, I have not only paid the arrears, but have raised already £70 towards paying the fine of £130, payable in 1726.

Ballaugh Church. June 19, 1717. I then laid the foundation of an addition of seven yards to this Church, which being much too little for the parishioners, the worthy Rector and I engaged to finish it, the parish furnishing £12, which we have done, and built a new steeple, at our own expense.

Kirk Arbory Vicarage-house, A.D. 1712. I supply'd the cure of souls by the neighbouring clergy, and applied the incomes toward building a new house: with this and what I begged, and gave myself, viz. £2 10s., and with the assistance of the parish, we have erected one of the best houses in the diocese.

Ryshin Vicarage-house. A.D. 1715. Rebuilt, to which I gave £2, &c.

Kirk Saint Anne Vicarage-house. A.D. 1722. Began to be rebuilt, to which I have given and am to give £5.

Kirk Michael Vicarage-house. Having supplied the parish by a curate, I have raised £12 or £14 towards this work, and have and purpose to give £5 myself, if not much more. May 1722, the foundation laid.

A.D. 1724. This year I built a school-house at Burton in Werrall, which cost me about £120. I have and am to marle twenty stat. acres for a perpetual endowment, which when inclosed, will make the school worth £20 a-year. I have already laid out £138 upon marling.

March 1725. Towards the steeple of Kirk St. Anne, £1.

A very small page will serve for the number of our good works, when vast volumes will not contain our evil deeds.

XII.

Lord's Prayer paraphrased.

Mark ix. 24. *I believe: help Thou mine unbelief.* Let Thy goodness supply what I want of such a faith as Thou requirest.

Charity will oblige us to intercede for the greatest sinners. Thus did Moses for the idolatrous Israelites. Exod. xxxii. 12, 13.

Our Father.

I thank Thee, O God, that Thou hast permitted me to call Thee *Father*. For I now know assuredly, as a father pitieth his child, He will hear my prayer: give me what is best for me; defend me [from] evil; correct me when I do amiss; direct me in the way I should go; lastly, He will give me an inheritance amongst His children. I will therefore strive to please Him.

_{SUPPLE-
MENT
No. XII.} Hear me for all Thy children, for we are all brethren: and hear their prayers for me.

Whom have I in Heaven but Thee? &c.

Call upon Me in the time of trouble.

See the Homily of Prayer.

I will trust to Thy love, O heavenly Father.

[iii. 234.] *Our Father, which art in Heaven.*

As a father pitieth his own children, so the Lord pitieth them that fear Him.

O cast not off the compassion of a Father, though I have been an undutiful child.

I will arise and go to my Father, and will say to him, Father, &c.

O Father, who hast brought me to a sense of my folly, receive a returning prodigal.

If ye being evil know how to give good gifts unto your children, how much more will your heavenly Father, &c.

Happy am I, for now I am sure to be heard. I will therefore ask with faith, not wavering. (Jam. i. 6.) I will go boldly to the throne of grace.

What son is he whom the father chasteneth not?

I will therefore with joy receive Thy Fatherly correction, which I know will consist with the tenderness of a father.

Behold what manner of love the Father has bestowed upon us, that we should be called the sons of God.—And if sons, then heirs.

O happy redemption, which has made me better than I was by nature. O may I never forfeit this blessed title and privilege.

And all ye are brethren. Even the poorest—even the worst—even my enemies. O that Thy love may extend to all these my brethren, and that we may meet in Heaven to praise Thee for ever.

I know not what to ask for myself. Do Thou teach me; I am Thy child; give me what is best for me, either crosses or comforts.

[iii. 235.] *Hallowed be Thy Name.*

That God in all things may be glorified. May I, great

God, ever glorify Thee, by promoting the knowledge of Thy glorious attributes—by shewing respect to whatever is called by Thy Name—by an holy life.

That the Name of God be not blasphemed. Lord, grant that this may never happen through any neglect or fault of mine.

Grant that I may never profane Thy holy Name, and pardon wherever I have done so.

To pray that God's Name may be hallowed, and not to do it in our words, by promoting His glory in conversation....

Thy kingdom come. [iii. 236.]

It is your Father's good pleasure to give you the kingdom. Luke xii. 32.

O fit me by Thy grace for Thy Kingdom. Destroy all the powers of darkness within me. Let my heart and eye be there where my treasure is.

The Kingdom of God is within (or *among*) *you:* i.e. a power subjecting our will to the will of God.

O take possession of this Thy kingdom, and govern here as Thou dost in heaven.

May the Gospel be received and have its saving effects in all the world: that being brought from the power of Satan unto God, we may all become one fold under one Shepherd and King, the Lord Jesus.

Let me not only pray for this blessing, but strive to advance it.

May all Thy subjects, O King of Heaven, shew to whom they belong, by their good works.

N.B. The *Kingdom of God within us,* is the rule of the, Spirit of God in the soul, directing all her powers and affections according to His will—i.e. to that which is ever best, —subduing all corruption, &c.

Cure that wickedness which hinders the increase of Thy Kingdom, and bring in everlasting righteousness in Thy good time.

All wicked men do in effect say, We will not have God to rule over us.

Establish Thy Kingdom in our hearts, root out all that oppose Thee.

SUPPLE-
MENT
No. XII.

Let us every one in our several places endeavour to establish the Kingdom of God, by opposing the corruption of the world.

I own Thee for my King, do Thou make and own me for Thy faithful subject.

[iii. 237.] *Thy will be done in earth as it is in heaven.*

Keep my mind [k] in such a temper, that I may readily close with Thy will whenever I know it, for so it is done in Heaven.

Direct me by Thy laws, and restrain me by Thy grace. For it is Thou, O God, that must give us both to will and to do of Thy good pleasure.

As it is in Heaven. May this ever be my pattern. Let no sinful customs, no earthly example, be my rule.

O manifest Thy will to me, and let me ever obey Thy will, whether made known to me by reason or revelation.

Let me never desire to do what is good in my own eyes. Let me renounce my own will, that I may cheerfully submit to Thine.

Nothing is done on earth, any more than in Heaven, but according to God's will. But men do not love that will and close with it, because it thwarts their desires.

It is Thine, O God, to *will,* and mine to obey. Let all my actions be done in obedience to Thee, then shall my whole life be one continual sacrifice.

Teach me to do Thy will, for Thou art my God. Ps. ciii. [cxliii.] Thy will, Thou who art most wise and most just.

Who should govern the world but He that made it?

Though I suffer, yet I am well, because I am what God would have me to be, God,—who neither wills nor permits but what is just, and what He will turn to His glory and our good, if we do not rebel against His will.

Thy will be done. Thus we pray, but when God manifests His will by events which do not please us, we repine, and in effect pray that His will may not be done, but ours. A great sin. For [Thou] knowest what is always best for us.

[iii. 238.] *Give us this day our daily bread.*

My eyes wait on Thee, O Father; (Ps. cxlv. 15) my de-

---

[k] *prima manu,* "in a perfect indifferency."

pendance is on Thee alone; for *in Thee we live, and move, and have our being.*

I desire only what is necessary, but above all a contented mind.

I will take no thought (no anxious care) *for to-morrow : for to-morrow I may have for asking.*

I desire only what is necessary for *this day* only, lest I should forget my dependance upon Thee, my God, and neglect to pray to Thee daily.

I depend upon Thee for a blessing upon all my labours, I will therefore never take any unjust ways to obtain my desires.

May Thy fear be ever in my heart, *and then I am sure to want no manner of thing that is good.*

That bread, which nourisheth to eternal life—that food which cometh from God. *Give us,*—for Thou art the Giver of all goodness—*this day*—for we cannot subsist—be happy one day without—*our daily bread.* For *man doth not live by bread alone.* Deut. viii. 5.

Thou feedest the fowls of the air, and clothest the lilies of the field.

I will depend upon Thy love, O heavenly Father, and upon Thy word: but I will not give myself up to sloth and negligence, which will displease Thee.

And forgive us our debts, as we forgive our debtors. [iii. 239.]

Thy mercy in Jesus Christ is infinite, O may that be my pattern.

Here corrupt nature rebels; but Thy grace is sufficient to subdue her. O give me Thy grace.

I will bless them that curse me, and pray for them that despitefully use me, and persecute me, and then I am sure my God will change the inward disposition of my soul.

I will not hate the instruments which Thou makest use of to punish or to prevent sin. This would be rebellion against my God, and the greatest injury to myself.

God is provoked every day. He spares us when we deserve punishment; and shall not I forgive a man like myself?

Our sins have hid His face from us, that He will not hear. Is. lix. 2.

SUPPLE-
MENT
No. XII.
As we forgive them. So far as they have wronged us; neither avenging ourselves, nor bearing them ill will.

That trespass—which is nothing in comparison of what we hope to be forgiven.

Against us—their fellow-creatures.

N.B. The measure of forgiveness here required must be consistent with other duties. I am obliged to [shew?] my enemy all good offices, pray for him, not speak evil of him, &c., and yet not to treat him as a favourite or confident as formerly.

Eccl. xxviii. 1, 2, &c.; Matth. vii. 2.

[iii. 240.] *Lead us not into temptation.*

These being trials of my faithfulness to Thee, my God, I do not beg to be wholly free from them. But that I may not be tempted above what I am able to bear; that I may never rashly run into temptation; that I may watch and pray against the dangers that attend a careless life; that by Thy grace I may be able to go through the trials appointed as the necessary consequence of our fallen state.

May I faithfully persevere under all my trials, preferring God's will to my own; depend upon His power, and goodness, and promises, that the temptations I am exercised with may yield the peaceable fruits of righteousness. Heb. xii. 11.

And grant that I may ever have a tender regard for all others that are tempted.

Deliver me from such temptations as are most likely to overcome if I should fall into them.

Let not Satan try his full power upon me.

Into temptation—from our own corrupt hearts—from others enticing us—from the devil.

"In all dangers and necessities let Thy right hand" . . . .

God very often answers this petition when He denies us what we wish for most impatiently.

[iii. 241.] *Deliver us from evil.* "The evil one"—the author of all evil.

I thank Thee, O God, that the power of the prince of this world is abridged, though not destroyed.

May I ever watch and pray against the sins which he

tempts us to: especially against pride, infidelity, and despair.

1. *Pride.* Let me never presume upon my own merit or self-dependance; lest I fall into the condemnation of the devil, the same guilt and punishment (Isaiah xiv. 13) with him. 1 Tim. iii. 6.

2. *Infidelity.* Let that wicked one never be able to take away the seed sown in my heart, or mix tares with it. Let me never hold the truth in unrighteousness, or any dangerous and damnable errors.

3. *Dejection of spirit.* Preserve me, Holy Lord, from this delusion of the devil.

Deliver us: for in Thee is our help. Hos. xiii. 9. Make a way for us to escape.

XIII.

[Ejaculations, and Hints for Prayer.]

Create in me a constant desire of pleasing Thee, and a fear of offending Thee.

Let me remember that Thou art every where present: make me careful of my ways.

Make me ready to forgive injuries, and backward to offer any.

Keep Thy servant from presumptuous sins.

Deliver me from the errors and vices of the age: from wicked principles, heresy, and schism: from evil company.

I most heartily thank Thee for Thy care over me—for all Thy mercies bestowed upon me—for the blessings of nature and of grace.

Luke vii. 5. Ἀγαπᾷ γὰρ τὸ ἔθνος ἡμῶν.

For my diocese. Rom. x. 1. *My heart's desire and prayer to God for Israel is, that they might be saved.*

Thunder. O Lord, before whom the pillars of heaven tremble, and are astonished at Thy reproof. Job xxvi. 11.

With whom is terrible majesty. Job xxxvii. 22.

That all the earth might fear Thee, and all the inhabitants of the world stand in awe of Thee. Ps. xxxiii. 7.

Sea. Thou rulest the raging of the sea; when the waves thereof arise, Thou stillest them. Ps. lxxxix. 9.

Thunder. Who is able *to abide Thine indignation?* Jer. x. 10.

Sea. O God, the confidence of them that are afar off upon the seas. Ps. lxv. 5.

Before Prayers. That I may never seek Thy face in vain.

Clergy. That they may save themselves and them that hear them. Tit. ii. 7. [1 Tim. iv. 16.]

Intercession. For all those countries that are made desolate, by the sword, by the persecutions, &c. For all such as have been instrumental to our good, by their assistance, advice, writings, &c.

Church. Keep us from all wild and dangerous errors.

Before preaching, &c. I came not to seek My own glory, but the glory of Him that sent Me.

To be inserted into Evening Prayer, private. *Let not the sun go down upon your wrath.*

Ordination. "Si quis ausus fuerit aliquem qui ad alterum pertinet ordinare in sua Ecclesia, cum non habeat consensum Episcopi ipsius a quo recessit Clericus, irrita erit hujusmodi Ordinatio." Concilii Nicæn., can. 17. [16. Routh, Script. Eccles. Opusc. i. 380.]

Grace before meat. Blessed be God who bringeth food out of the earth.

After meat. Blessed be God by whose goodness we live.

Sickness, light-headed. And since he is not able to pray for himself, the good Lord favourably hear our prayers for him.

Give us grace to see how frail our condition, that we may prepare ourselves for that time, when not only our reason but our life will forsake us.

Increase the number of those that serve Thee daily.

After Sermon. That as they have heard how they ought to walk and to please God, they may continue to do so unto their lives' end.

A Prayer for religious conversation. That I may speak of holy things with boldness, discretion, and success, at all seasonable times. "Grant unto Thy servant that with all boldness he may speak Thy Word." Acts iv. 29.

Voyage. Bless us with seasonable weather, a prosperous voyage, and be Thou our haven at the last.

Fleres si scires unum tua tempora mensem,
Rides cum non sit forsitan una dies.

Certain things to be done, if God shall enable me, and think me worthy to accomplish them.

SUPPLEMENT No. XIII.
[iii. 252.]

To have public prayers in all parishes upon all Ember-days, with a discourse the Sunday before, or Mr. Nelson's discourse. And by that means to introduce prayers, at least the Litany, on all Wednesdays and Fridays throughout the year.

Grace before meat. O God, who givest food unto all flesh, [iii. 253.] grant that we may receive these Thy creatures with Thy blessing. Through Jesus Christ.

Meanes of Grace. Pour down a blessing upon those means which Thou Thyself hast appointed.

Omniscience. May I always live and act as having Thee the constant witness of my conduct.

Love of Christ. Thou hast loved us, O blessed Lord, more than Thine own life.

[In pencil]. I confess before God that I for my sins deserve the death which Jesus Christ suffered, and even eternal death. But since He was so good and compassionate to lay down His life to redeem mine...

I remember His love at this time when all...

Since God has laid on Him the iniquity of us all, I humbly intreat Him, that my sins may be placed to His account.

XIV.

[*Fragments communicated by the Rev. William Gill, Vicar of Kirk Malew.*] [No. xiv.]

[1. [1]*Love of God.*]

Do I know this offendes ye God I Love—far be...from Me to be pleased with ye Man, His actions &c. y^t offends G.

Dos Wickedness abound in ye Land? Rivers of Tears run down my eyes bec. men break Thy Laws. Ps. cxix. 158.

A Lover of G. avoids as much as may be ye Company of Wicked Men, vain Diversions, Plays, &c.

Holy Love silences every Murmur ag^t. Providences &c. y^t are uneasy to Flesh and blood. He always concludes y^t ye Righteous and good God has reason and Love in every thing.

[1] [Consisting apparently of notes for sermons.]

SUPPLEMENT No. XIV.

Test. W^n ye Love of God is the Governing Passion of all ye rest of ye Passions of ye Soul—w^n we Fear, Desire, Hate w^t we sh^d do, &c. If our Hopes, Fears, Desires, &c. are exercised upon the things of this world, be sure there is little Love for God &c.

If Ambition &c. is ye subject of our Hopes and Feares &c. or if Sensual Pleasures, Amusements &c. there can be no Love [?] of God.

[2.] [*Renouncing the World.*] Com. 2d. Who love Me and keep my Com.—So y^t to....and to keep His Com. is ye same thing, so saith Xt...

If I give way to my Passions, I cannot expect y^t the Love of God will abide long in my Heart.

The Love of ye World, and the Love of God are not to be found in the same Heart. A worldly minded m. has no sense of ye Love of God, no Delight &c.

Love of Company, Diversions, Pleasure, doe soon draw the Heart from loving God.

I can have no satisfaction, no security in .... until I can bring myself to love God. I Pray y^t His Love may ever possess my Heart.

There is no other sure proof of my loving God but this y^t I strive to please Him and to keep His C.

We often say tis our Duty to love God wthout considering...

To love God, is to desire to know what will please Him, To live as in His sight, To love His Word and w^{t}ever belongs to Him. *Motives*, God loves me, He pitys my Sad Condition, is always ready to Help me, To pardon me w^n I am penitent, He forbids me Nothing but w^d really Hurt me, and commands me no.. ......

[3.] *Fear.* There is a Godly Fear necessary for our safety—And there is an unreasonable Fear wch we sh^d strive to cast off—being a Trick [?] of Satan to distress and distract fearful X^{ns}. and to weaken their Faith in God's Goodn. and Promises &c.

If yor Feares w^d suffer you to make use of yor [Reason?] you w^d argue with yo^{r}self after some such way [as this:]

Shall I imagine that I offend God, w^n He knows that I [am afraid?] of offending Him? W^n I Pray y^t I may not offend Him, [w^n?] I am sorry w^n I have done it, and desire to do w^t will please [Him?] Even a Good Man, knowing me to be thus disposed, w^d not be angry with me, much less a gracious God, who permits me to call Him Fath^r, y^t He may convince me how much He loves [me] ....
..... As a good X^n will do to [?] any oth. affliction—And say, God's will be done—He knows what is best for me, &c.

But ag^n I advise you, do not give way to y^m, do not [indulge] y^m. Sitt not much alone. Read not too......

I will depend upon Thy mercy, O God, for I know Thou w^{dst} not continue me alive, but y^t I may glorify Thee in one state or oth^r.

[The] very Sparrowes—the very Hair of my Head—are Thy care. [I] will therefore put my Trust in Thee. I know Thou wilt not reject a Child y^t cryes to Thee for Help.

*But y^t wch above all I recommend to you, and beg you will give me credit......

[4.] [*Love of y^r Neighbour.*] When we consider that God has placed this duty next to ye love we owe to Him ...... [fulfilling] of it.

Observe ye great stress y^t is laid upon this Duty, 1 Jo. iv. 21. This Com. have we fr. God, y^t who (sic) loveth God love his neighbour also. .

Our Neighb^r is every Man wth w^m we have to do, or who may be benefited by our Love. Every man for whom Xt dyed, i. e.

Effects. As we have opportunity, let us do good unto all men, especially—Follow Peace with all Men. Be Patient towards all Men. Make Supplications for all Men.

We may most easily know the particular .....

Whoever dos not forgive is shut out of all Hopes of Pardon fr. G. His own sins will not be forgiven—His Pray^r will not be heard.

If we once can wean our Hearts from ye world, we should [shall] have little to fall out ab^t.

If we consider the Love of God and of Xt for us, we shall

SUPPLE-
MENT
No. XIV.

have the strongest motive to do w^t they had [have] com.—to love one ano. .... W^n *Men shall be lovers of their own selves*, with^t any Regard to their neighb^{rs}. This is ye caract^r of ye last and worst ti. . . . .

Let us not fall [? fail] to command our outward Actions, and then our Inward dispositions, thro' ye grace of God, will follow of course. Let us be just—courteous—speak well of others; or be silent when we cannot wth Truth. Let us Pray for our N. These outward actions are some p[roof] of our desire to have our Hearts changed.

[5. *Formal Xn.*]^m

Preserve me, O God, fr. ye Judgm^t of enjoying ye means of Grace and Salv^n, with^t growing better by y^m.

Outward Ordinances, meanes to lead us to a Godly, Righteous and Sober Life. See y^e

People do often live under ye Observ. of outward Ordin^s, and yet continue to be very bad men, and in ye way of Damnat^n. To be com̃on Swearers, Drunkards, Adult.—to live in [Malice?] &c. &c.

Whether we will believe it or not, such are in ye way of Ruin. We have ye sure Word of God for it, "not every one" . . . .

Therefore [as] on one Hand, we must not despise or neglect ye outward Ordinances, w^h are appointed by God as powerful means of Salv. [?] of obt. the Graces and Blessings we stand continually in need of—so ye strictest obs. of y^m will neither please God nor [? profit] ourselves, without an Holy Life.

We go to Ch. to learn how to live so as to please G^d and save our Souls, and obtain such Help and Grace as are necessary to [? amend] our lives. If we content ourselves wth going to Ch. &c. with^t an Inward change—

W^n we beg pardon for our sins, let us beg and resolve at ye same time y^t we may bring forth fruits meet for R.—W^n we professe to Be . . . .

*Our Relig^n like a Tree by its fruit, must be known wheth^r it be good or bad.

^{m} [This on different paper, and in a hand bearing marks of age.]

We have confessd our sins—We have heard on w^t conditions G^d will pardon us, we have recd. Absolute (sic) f^m one appointed by God to do so (a Blessing not to be despised). We have Heard ye Word of God—We praised Him in Psalmes and Hym[ns?]—We have Pray'd for many blessings —We pleaded ye Promise of J Xt to be our Adv.—We have rec^d ye L^{ds} Supp^r as a Pledge of My [? Mercy] and lastly, we have recd. ye solemn blessing of God's Minister appointed by God to bless in His Name.—What is all this for? why, y^t we may keep in our mindes—That we are Sinners, and y^t with^t God's Mercy we shall be lost for ever.—That [therefore?] we shd. thankfully remember and acknowledge God's wonderful goodness and mercy in sending His only Son to redeem us, hoping for Pardon and Salv. thro' His Mercy—Taking care not to grieve His Holy Sp^t by wch we have been sealed.

We have [beg'd?] God's Blessing upon ourselves, our children, our Labours — Our Govern^{rs}, our Church, our Teachers, &c.

Appointed by G^d To bless ye People in His Name—This will be a g^t and sure Blessing to every Soul y^t receives it wth an Heart disposed and Resolved to live as becomes ye Gospel of Xt.

God being ye constant witness of all our Designes, Works, and   —We shall live as in His Sight, fearing to do w^t we know [will] offend Him, rejoycing to do w^t [we] believe will please Him.

Faith. These are ye effects of a Saving Faith—To live as if you did indeed believe His Alm. Power, to bless those y^t Love, Fear to offend Him—To punish such as dare to despise His commands—To give entire credit, &c., to Trust in His Word and Promises, &c. &c.

Satan Himself will be well pleased y^t we sh^d go constantly to Ch. to ye Sacram^t &c. Provided He can prevail wth you to be content wth ye name of a Xⁿ. y^t He can govern you ye week after.

Jer. vii. 9. Will ye steal, and commit Adult. &c. Vid—

A Xⁿ by Profession and an Heathen in Life—How dreadful is y^t man's case?

W^d you profit by going to Ch.—Put on a serious temper.

SUPPLE-
MENT
No. XIV. Tis for y^or Soul—Tis [Here should come another leaf, which is lost.]

[6.] *Holy Communion.* The devout and constant use of this H. Ordinance is one of the most effectual meanes of obtaining the Grace of a true and lasting Conversion—and an Habit of true Devotion—For Instance—Every one who considers the blessing of being a X^n will be oblig'd, before He goes to this Sacr^t, to consid^r ye conditions upon wch He was made a X^n and How He hath performd [observ'd?] y^m—to beg pardon for our Failings and Backsliding and Negligence, To Resolve to look better to our ways for ye time to come —To Renew the vowes wch we often made and too often neglected.

Tis one of ye greatest meanes of Grace and Salv^n—of obtaining ye Gr. of a true Conversion, and of Preserving a Devout Temper.

One of ye most solemn Dutys of ye Xn. Relig^n and Services wch we owe to God.

It concerns therefore every Xn. to be careful not to profane so Holy an Ordinance either before or after Receiving.

The D—l is in nothing more earnest than to tempt Men to profane this Sacr. either before or after receiving.

Bless this Thine own Ordinance as an effectual meanes of Gr. God gives us all the Benefits and Blessings of His Son's Death.

The 2 gr^t ends of this Sacram^t, Atonem^t of Sin and Acceptance wth God.

Our security lies in the careful use of ye meanes of Grace wch God has ap[pointed].

God will have no regard to the Request [Pray^r] of those who have no regard to His commands.

Scripture. Who profess to know (and to wors^p) *God, but in works deny Him.* Tit. i. 16.

Hath a Name to live but is dead.

Jo. viii. 31. *If ye continue in My Word, then are ye My disciples indeed.*

Isaiah i. 11, 12, &c., and my Notes. *Who hath required this,* &c. with^t Hearts devoutly disposed, and with^t full purposes of obeying My laws.

St. Luk. xviii. 9. *Who trusted in y^{ms}* (were well persuaded) *y^t they were Righteous*, and consequently, will make a false Judgment of their own State.

Jo. xviii. 17. *Art not thou one [of] Xt's disciples?* Peter said, *I am not,* so saith every one . . . .

Heb. x. 25. The Forsaking the Assembly is an over [overt] Act of Apostacy, and a natural meanes [?] of leading to it.

Give me the Spt. as well as the Name of a Xn.

Rom. i. 18. *Who hold the Truth in unrighteousness—*

Rom. ii. 13. *Not y^e hearers of y^e Law, but y_e doers, &c.*

Vid. Dr. Chere's Catechis. Sacram^{nts}, p. 11, 12.ⁿ

This Sacrament being a distinguishing mark, or sign ordained by Xt. Himself, by wch His Servants are to be known from Heathens, and Unbeliever[s], it is no Wonder y^t most Xtns (or y^e Generality of Xtns.) cannot be easy w^{tht} observing it, &c. This is ye very case of ye Jews, who depended upon an outward Righteousness for Justification, or being accepted of God, wch our L^d and His Apostles endeavour'd to cure y^m of. Rom. ix. &c.

God's Righteousness, wh. is Faith in Xt. and obedience. Rom. x. 3. *The Right. of y Jewes* an Outward Observatⁿ of Circumcision and Passover—no work of ours can be ye cause of our Justificatⁿ.

[7.] *Dutys of Parents and Children.*

Both Nature and Grace obliges Parents to take care of their own Children—To Instruct, To Restrain and to correct y^m. And the neglect of this, by a just judgmt. of God, brings Grief to the Parents, and a Curse upon the Land, by breeding up so many Agents of Hell to Corrupt their Neighbors.

If any body should tell any of you that is a Fath^r or a Mother, your Child will to-morrow be carry'd a Slave to the West Indies—How w^d it startle you, How w^d it afflict you— But wⁿ we tell you that Son of yours is going Directly to Hell, if you don't take better Care of Him,—you take the

---

ⁿ ["The Church Catechism with a brief and easie explanation, &c., by T. C., D.D., 8vo., London, 1683. But the pages relating to the Sacraments are 26—32.]

SUPPLEMENT No. XIV.
ready way to have y[t] Daught[r] of yo[rs] ruin'd body and soul for ever—You make her proud—You let her have Her own will and ways—You let Her keep loose Company, &c.—w[n] you are assur'd of this, you never mind it.

Math. iv. 8. Parents do to their Children w[t] the D—l did to X[t] w[n] He shew'd Him the Glory and Pomp of y[e] World, They Praise, They cause them to Admire Riches, Finery, Esteem &c. Doing by this the Devil [Devil's] offices &c.

Math. x. 30. *A Man's Foes shall be they of His own Household.*

And indeed Relations are too often y[e] greatest enemies Men have. Some Heap up Riches not well got, w[ch] become a Curse—Others leave Estates w[ch] only serve to Corrupt, &c. Others put their Friends into a way of Life full of Snares and Tempt. Others by a Cruel Indulgence suffer y[m] to go on &c. Others breed y[r] Ch. in Excess and Vanity.

Math. xix. 13, 2. [? 13 &c.]

If ye are more Careful to leave y[m] fortunes than to have y[m] taught to Fear God—you may live to see y[m] squander away y[t] by a wicked life w[ch] &c.

Take notice y[t] yo[r] Children are a Charge for w[ch] you must give acc[t] to God.

With[t] a good educat[n], a good example—Correction &c., They will be ruined.

Be watchful over their ways—Pray for y[m] daily—One w[d] think y[t] Parents sh[d] not need to be advised to take care of their Children's Manners, since they see with their own eyes so many young People taking the ready road to Hell,—Drunkards, Whoremasters, Swearers, Profaners of y[e] Lord's day—How w[d] they lament if they sh[d] see their Children Banish'd into a Strange Land, and yet can be content to see y[m] going to Hell.

Too much Severity in Parents is unnatural, it makes Ch. obstinate and hate advice.

Too much Fondness is as mischievous, makes Children Headstrong, Humorsome &c.

Parents who cannot see their Children's Faults, may live to see y[m] disobedient, and a grief to y[ms] [themselves] w[n] they grow up, neither minding their Commands, nor their Teares.

He y^t dos not keep His Children under Command, as Nature and God has ordained, may have the Sorrow to see Their children Govern y^m.

Train y^m up in ye Fear of God—See y^t they say their Prayers Morning and Evening devoutly upon their knees, not Hurrying y^m over as if it were a Task upon y^m.

Oblige them to go to Church,—Suffer y^m not to take God's name in vain upon any acc^t,—Keep y^m out of Bad Company as you value their Soules.

W^n you put y^m to trades, or marry y^m, Have an eye to their Salvat^n rather than to Worldly Advantages, lest w^n . . .

Warn y^m often and often agst ye vices of ye age. — Deprive not yor Children of a Comfortable Support by your own Prodigality........Tis no better than Robbing yor Children of........tho' Lawes will not Hang a Man for such Injustice, for God will Call Him to an acc^t He may depend upon it.

'Tis a Crime so Barbarous, so cruel, so unnatural for a Parent, who brought y^m into ye world, to deprive y^m of a comfortable way of Living, That a Thief in Comparison of such Parents is a better Man—A better Man than He who games away—Drinks away—Bargains away His Children's bread—Leaving y^m to Hardships and Misery—To take unlawful ways to get a Livelyhood—To temptation of cursing their Parents.

It is a common and mournful thing to see, Parents in disposing of their children, to leave God out of a concern w^h is to last for Life.—How Few put their Children upon Begging God's Direction and Blessing in Disposing of y^{ms} in marriage. How few Pray God to Direct y^{ms} on such occasions.

And this, I will take upon me to say, is ye true occasion of so many unhappy Match's—God's Direction and Blessing were neither thought of, nor prayd for, either by the Parents or their children, and this provokes God to leave y^m to y^{ms}, and to their own rash unhappy Choices.— And very often [He] Punishes them wth disobedient Children—Taking ill ways—Hence the Disorders and Ruin of many Familys.

To keep Children in Awe, That they do not grow Headstrong, Stubborn, Self will'd &c.

SUPPLE-
MENT
No. XIV.

Consider w^t a terrible thing it is to be ye ruin of yor own Ch.

If after all yor care children will take ill ways, you will have the Comfort of Knowing it has not been yor fault.

Math. xx. 22. *Ye know not w^t ye ask.* Indeed we do not when we ask for our selves and for our Children, Riches, Hon^{rs}, High Places &c.; i. e. we desire to put y^m into ye way of Temptation, of being answerable for a great deal &c.

[A sentence cut out.]

There cannot be a surer way of entailing a curse instead of an inheritance upon a Man's children and family than by leaving y^m Lands or Goods got by. . . .

Children. How many [hurtful Le]gacys do Par. leave their Childⁿ [wⁿ they] leave y^m ill gotten goods, or wⁿ they leave y^m to be visited for *their* crying sins, and Injurys, and wrongs done to others, for wch God has declared He will visit, &c.

The Follye of leaving goods unjustly gotten to their Children. Jeremiah xxxii. 18. See Ecclus. ch. 3. [9..11.]

Rebellious and Disobedient Son. See the Punishment under the Law of Moses. Deut^r. xxi. 18, 19, 20.

We see in Potiphar's Wife, y^t wⁿ a Woman hath lost Her Modesty she is capable of any Wickedness—How careful therefore sh^d parents be, &c.

Josh. iv. 21, 22. This shews it to be Parents' duty to put their children in mind &c.

See 2 Sam. xxi. 9. My Notes.

See Matth. x. 35, 36, 37. And Quesnel upon it.

Parents often take more paines to make their Children Rich, &c., than to bring y^m up in ye Fear of God,—we see the Sad Consequences of this in ye disobedience, loose and wicked lives of &c.

Parents (that are Pious) do receive the [reward] of their Care of their Children.

Children's Duty and Piety a most invaluable Comfort.

Children. See Ecclus. iii. 1, 2, 3, 4, &c. &c.

Parents are a sort of Trustees for their Children and Posterity,—both for their good and evil.—The Posterity of Abraham were blessed for His Piety,—and the Posterity of

Ham were made Slaves for His Impiety and Sin, and so in many Instances we find it by Experience.

A Succession of Blessings and Curses, of threats, ...

[Something cut out.]

[8.] *Baptism, Regeneration.*

We derive from our Parents a Naāl Life only, by y^t we can never arrive at Heaven,—we are therfore Baptized, and thereby receive ye Sp^t of God, a Principle of a New Life,— we are therby made Members of X^t, &c.

Regeneration. Jo. iii. 3. *Verily* (a most solemn oath) *Except a Man be born ag^n* (or fr. above) *He* &c.

This is the very first Thing we ought to know, to be convinced of, viz. The Corruption of our Nat. and the absolute necessity of our being renewed by J. X^t. Vid. Quesn. The 21 verse of this ch.

He y^t is born of the Flesh, (i. e. who is in a state of Nature only, who has nothing but his Naāl Reason to Direct Him, and has nothing but His own Strength to Support Him) *is Flesh,* &c.

This shews ye Absolute Necessity of being born ag^n.

See Coloss. ii. 11, 12, 13, 14, 15. Quesnel.

When God appointes Meanes, He evermore gives Power and Virtue to those Means,—viz. an Inward and Spiritual Grace for ye Cleansing of the Soul.

Mark i. 9. Where J. X^t condemnes by His Example the State^m of those who will not go out of their Houses to ye Ch. to be Baptized, w^n He went even to anoth^r Province.

The *Sacraments* assure us of God's favour to us. And they engage us to do w^t God requires of us. And they are attended with Sure Blessings w^n we receive them with Sincere purposes of doing w^t God requires of us.

Baptism. By this we are Rec^d into ye Society of X^{ns} wch is the Church of God, and also into Covenant with God.

All such as do believe the truths of X^{ty}, are sincerely disposed to become X^{ns}, and to be the servants of the True and only God, are Wash'd or Sprinkled with Water, in the Name of &c. [n]

---

[m] [i. e. the affected dignity.]
[n] [Vid. Just. Mart. Apol. ii. p. 93, 94. Ed. Paris. 1636.]

SUPPLE-
MENT
No. XIV.

Math. [Mark] xvi. 16. *He y^t Believth and is Baptized shall &c.*

That as Water Cleanses the body, as [so] surely dos the Holy Spirit then given Cleanse the Soul.

Such as are Baptised do engage to live like as X^{ns} ought to do, and as all good X^{ns} do,—Righteous, Soberly and Godly, in this World.

Every X^n ought to be very thankful to God for His Mercy, in Receiving us into His Ch. and Covenant, and giving us a Title to Eternal Life and Happss.

You cannot be a true X^n with^t knowing the Reasons, and with^t making it yor choice.

Baptismal Vow and Promise. That you live as becomes a X^n. To make a solemn and sincere Resolution agst all sin and wickedness.

Agst having any God but &c.

World. Agst the sins wch reign in ye world.

Flesh. All sinful Lust and Passion.

He ought faithfully [to] resolve to observe the Commands of God, as far as they are made known to Him, To do nothing y^t He is persuaded will displease Him.

Confirmation, Regeneration, Conversion.

If the Confirmation of ye Heart dos not precede that of ye laying on of ye Hands, or Confirmation of the Bishop, The person confirm'd has no reason to expect the Graces of God's Sp^t therby conferred.

Ecclus. iv. 19. If He go wrong, she (ye Sp^t) will forsake Him, and give Him over to His utter Ruin.

Baptism. You must come to receive B. wth a firm Faith or Belief in God your Creator—In His Son J. X^t your Redeem^r; and in the H. Sp. ye Sanctifier of all such as shall be saved—with a full purpose thro' ye assistance of ye H. Sp^t to lead an Holy Life—To avoid all such wayes and things as you know and believe will displease God—or dishon^r yor H. profession—And Rember y^t into a wicked soul ye Sp^t will not enter, nor Remain in a body, &c. Wisd. i.

The Flesh will oppose the Sp^t and ye Sp^t ye Flesh, and thus it will be till one gets ye better.—Now the H. Sp^t is given us at Bap^t for this end y^t we may be able to get y^e

better of ye Flesh and its attempts to ruin us, with^t this no man living *can* be saved.

Regeneration, Conversion. Shall I be plain with you, one of the great Hindrances of a true Conversion is the satisfying ones self with an outward Form, and Observance of Religious Worship.

A true *Conversion* begets a sensible change in the Heart and Life—Acts ii. 37. *They were pricked in their hearts, &c.* They were sensible of their Danger, and the necessity of a New Life &c.

[9.] *Pastors and their Flock.*

A dreadful judgm^t. Pastors, who have the knowleg of ye S. S. and do not profit by them—To shew the way of salvatⁿ to others and not walk in it thems.

To take the name of a Pastor, with^t minding ye Flock— How impertinent, How wicked, How provoking must it be in the sight of God.

Math. xiv. 4. *John said, It is not lawful for Thee to have thy Brother's Wife.* The best service one can do to sinners, is, clearly and plainly to lay before y^m w^t God forbids, and w^t He commands, with^t ye Flourishes of Discourse, as if we were afraid to awaken y^m out of their sin &c.

Consider How many Graces and Fav^{rs} and Blessings must of necessity pass thro' their Hands, and you will never despise y^m, you will most highly value y^m.

If we w^d take away fr. ye People all suspicion that we act only out of Self-Interest, we must renounce Ambition and Avarice, wch ruin a Preacher and all His Labours.

They y^t complain and crye out agst negligent Pastors, sh^d consider whether they y^m selves have done their Duty, and prayd as our Lord has commanded (Luke x. 2,) y^t God w^d *send Labourers into His Harvest,* For want of w^{ch}, we have reason to fear, Judgment &c.

God stands not in need of ye Ministry of men, being able to change ye Hearts of ye Wicked, and enlighten ye minds of ye Ignorant, but He w^d have ye whole Body of ye Church to depend one Part and Member upon another.

To be deprived of the assistance of God's Ministry is a greater punishm^t than men imagine. *Shake off ye dust of y^r Feet, as a Testimony ag^t such.—He y^t Heareth you Heareth*

SUPPLE-
MENT
No. XIV.

Me, saith X^t, *and He y^t despiseth &c.* How very dangerous is it, not to Hear those who are appointed by God to teach us our duty. W^n we Hear God's Ministers, we Hear God Himself and His Son J. Xt.

A Pastor ought to Preach in such a Manner y^t any of His Flock might safely and cheerfully put His Cause into His Hands to prevent going to Law.

How can a Pastor recover those soules wh. have been lost thro' His negligence? An astonishing consideration.

St. Luk. xvii. 14. *Go shew yourselves unto the Priests— And as they went they were cleansed.* Dos not our Lord Himself shew us in this Instance, the great regard that is to be had to God's Priests?—And y^t it is thro' their Hands Sinners must expect Health and Reconciliation wth God? Those are ye ordinary Meanes of Salvation put into their hands. He causes their Authority to be acknowleg'd tho' they wer a corrupt generat^n.

We seldom admonish wicked men with^t suffering for it. But then we must not forbear doing our duty at our per[il. 'Tis our] part of ye Cross &c.

Caracter of a Bad Pastor—To treat ye poor of his Flock with haughtiness—To be impatient to be put in mind of his duty—To be over hasty in driving from ye Fold.

[A sentence cut out.]

It is a terrible Judgm^t w^n Pastors by their evil Lives...... confirm their Flock in Impiety or error, and even autorise y^m in their Wickedness.

The Advice of Holy Men, and especially of a Pastor, is seldom or never despis'd or neglected wth impunity, it being in effect to despise Providence.

Wo to ye person who being entrusted with ye care of serving and ...... the Flock committed to Him dos not discharge His Duty. Rom. xii. 7. *Or ministry, let us wait on our ministry, or He y^t Teacheth on Teaching*—J. Xt.

[Some cut out.]

The Carracter, Dutys, &c. of a Pastor. Ephes. c. ii. (? iv.)
The Duty of a Preacher. See Eph. vi. 19, 20. Quesnel.
A Pastor purchases a livlyhood at a very dear rate, who

for it parts with the Liberty to Preach ye Truths of ye Gospel, to Reprove, Rebuke, to refuse favours y^t are Unjust, &c.

2 Thess. iii. 6. *Now we command you &c.* 'Tis the same Authority wch is lodged in the Successors of ye Apostles, and ye same respect is due to their Authority—w .... [when they] Act in ye name of Xt.

[Some torn.]

Pastors and Their Flock.

Why are you afraid of your Teachers? I'll tell you the true Reason—They are bound at the Peril of their Soules to represent unto your mindes Truths. ...

[Some cut out.]

[Minist]ers of God, are in a more especiall manner to be Holy in their Lives, that they may render Religion venerable in ye eyes of ye People, who will learn to be Holy by ye H. Example and Lives of their Teach^rs, and that nothing must be seen in ye Lives of &c. wch may expose Rel. to contempt &c.

Prov. xxix. 18. Where there is no vision (no teachers of God's will) the People perish &c.

[Ezech.] ix. 6. *Begin at My Sanctuary.* This was God's command to ye destroyer. And indeed w^n the Ministers of God fall into ye sins of ye common people, or neglect their Duty, they have reason to fear y^t God will [begin] in Judgm^t with them. Vid. 1 Pet. [iv. 17.]

[Some cut out.]

[Hos. iv.] 6, 7, 8, 9. Their *(sic) like people like priest.*— My People perish for want of knowledge.

Zechar. xi. 5. *Their own shepherds pity y^m not.*

Non Resident. Zech. xi. ult. Wo to the Idol shepherd that leaveth the Flock, &c. His punishm^t.

.... alt [*Salt*] *of the Earth.* Designed to keep ye world from corruption.—He y^t is not such will be the very .. fuse [refuse] of the [Earth]—and Dealt with as such—be trodden. ...

[Some torn out.]

Dutys of The Flock. Ecclus. vii. 30, 31, 32.—See Numb. xvi. and Margin, Luk. iv. 33, 34. Those y^t Live in any known Sin, cannot bear to have that Sin touched upon, bec. it disturbes their miserable peace.

We cannot, indeed, as Xt. did, cure sicknesses, but we can visit those that are sick, we can Pray for y^m. Assist, relieve and Pray for y^m, so far we do our duty.

Tythes. See Reading, Third Sund. after Epiph. Morning. pag. 87, 89.

Tinwald. ^{n}Malachi, ye chapt. for the day &c. Deut. xii. 19, vid.

This being perhaps ye last time I shall ever speak in this place, I think it my duty to leave a Testimony of my true concern for ye good of ye People by whose Labours I have eat my bread these 40 yeares.

For their *Good* I say, for I am convinced that very many of the Temporal calamities are owing &c.

We know what many will think, and some perhaps will say—That we are preaching for ourselves—But God is the witness of my Heart and Designe in what I am going to say, [that it] is not for our own but your sakes only—That He may bless you, and make His Promises good — And therefore I will not use one Argument but what God Himself hath made use of in His Holy Word.

[A long interval.]

[10.] *Repentance* ...... for the Sake of His Repentance or on y^e [acc^t] of His   —But only thro' Faith in the-blood of Xt. and on acc^t of His Sacrifice and Intercession.

Repentance. A serious Resolution to amend when we know we have done amiss, with a full purpose to lead a Xn. —a Holy life.

W^n People think of Repentance, they [? comonly] consider only the great sins, and such as are criminal [?] in the eye of ye world, that they have been guilty of—Seldom considering the Dutys they owe to God, and have neglected—Such as Faith in God—Fear and Love—Submission, Resignation, Prayer, Thanksgiving—Worship Publick and Private &c.—Why, the omissions of those Dutys are sins w^h will shut men out of Heaven as well as Adultery, Theivery, &c.

^{n} [This is plainly a note for a sermon before the Court of Tynwald in 1738.]

XN. PERFECTION. Primitive Christianity...in this world, but to do their Duty, and to get out of it as [blameless?] as they could, yᵗ they might enjoy a much better Life (?).... {SUPPLEMENT No. XIV.}

Sober in Apparel. A vain garb, a certain indi.... of a vain mind. A Xⁿ ought to be such in everything, in His dress &c. They wi[thout] condemning yᵗ Distinction in Apparel, as well of .... and quality, and employmᵗ, ... Excess and Singularity [they?] avoided, conforming yᵐˢ to yᵉ Decent manner [of the place?] they lived in. Vanity, Costlyness, and Finery they gua[rded against?] as was consistent wᵗʰ yᵉ Former rules. Emulation mi[schievous.] "Must we not live like ourselves?" Yes, but be sure [your souls?] have renounced yᵉ Pride of Life; lest they shᵈ. be[come?] inflam[ed] ...... either with unlawful Passions or Envy, and be a cause of [sin.] "The attire of an Harlot," has some meaning in it, sure; [what can it be] but such as may entice, ensnare &c. A Painted Face [can in no] sense be call'd yᵉ Image of God—Softness and Lux......

[11.] *Regeneration. Hopkins.*

Regeneration or *New Birth* is that whereby [we are] begotten agⁿ to a lively Hope of being yᵉ Children of God. [Bapt]ism is the Sacramᵗ of Regeneration, by which [outw]ard Ceremony we are brought within yᵉ Bond of yᵉ Covenᵗ. [The outw]ard Ceremony entitles none to Etern. Life, unless the [Spirit working] upon the inward man cleanseth it from sin, as [water] the outward Man from filth. Or as Fire pu[rifieth] from dross; Math. iii. 11.—Whereby the *Understanding,* [*will,* and *affec*]*tions,* are Rectify'd wᵗʰ new habits of virtue, &c.

[*Regeneratio*]*n* doth not consist in the Profession of a True [Faith. This] may be done, and men may still be Infidels in [Heart.] And wⁿ Sᵗ. Jo. saith, ch. 5, *He that Believeth that Jesus* [*is the Xt is bo*]*rn of God;* He had regard to those times, when [those who own]'d this Faith, could not but be sincere, since they [were s]ure to suffer for it. [Neither doth] it consist in a man's amending his life— This may be yᵉ fruit of Prudence, [or of] Interest°.

° [Abridged from Bp. Hopkins, Serm. xi. on the Nat. and Necess. of Regeneration. Works, 1701, p. 518...21.]

SUPPLE-
MENT
No. XIV.

[12.] *Dutys we owe to ourselves.*
Self Denyal. The Cross. Mortification.

The World. We are strictly required not to Set our Hearts upon the world—bec. we can neither understand, nor mind the concerns of our soules while we do so.

If God sh^d consult our inclinations, and never lay the Cross upon us, but w^n we sh^d choose it, we sh^d never be in a capacity of going to Heaven.

Had there been any other more easy way to Heaven, J. Xt. w^d have chosen it for Himself and for His Followers.

The concern for a Man's Family perhaps may seem to require that he sh^d continue in a business full of snares and dangers, but if His Eternal Salvation require y^t He sh^d leave it, is there any room for deliberation?

If Thy Right Hand offend Thee Cut it off.

This at first sight seems a severe command. 'Tis bec. we do not consider it as we sh^d do, and y^t we have no other choice but Obey God or Perish.

'Tis uneasy to Flesh and Blood, but Flesh and Blood must be oppos'd or we must be undone.

Swearing, drinking, evil company are become a second nature.—Well, but you must leave them or lay aside all Hopes of Heaven.

If I cannot get so good an estate as I propose with^t following a business full of snares and danger, if not Sin—Why then I must be content to go to Heaven with^t an estate—or go to Hell with one.

God com[mands] self denyal—not bec. He can and will, but bec. He knows 'tis absolutely necessary to restore [us] to His Image—with^t wch. we shall infallibly be ruin'd.

Men need not be at pains to be ruin'd &c.

A X^n is not oblig'd to seek for Crosses, Calamity, &c. If He will be true to His profession, follow after Righteousness, &c. Not conform Himself to ye world—He will meet wth enough to exercise His Patience—Besides the Corruption of His own Nature, wch will furnish Him wth continual Occasions &c. Add to these the Tryals with wch God proves ye Sincerity of His best Servants; Reproaches of Friends and Enem. Afflictions—Sickness—Disappointments—Losses—Death of Freindes &c.

Our duty is, as Xns, as Xt's followers—Humbly to receive all occasion of sufferings, wch eith^r the Provid. of G. or ye Wickedness of Men, or ye indiscretion or evil of our own Conduct has brought upon us.

2 Tim. iii. 12. *All y^t will live godly in Xt. J. shall suffer Persec.* The very nature and designe of ye X^n R. supposes this. If X^ns will do their Duty in a wicked world—They must of necessity meet wth hardships—Reproches — Injustice—&c. If He is serious (as His relig^n requires Him to be) He's call'd an Hypocrite—if He reproves Vice &c. &c. &c.

The mystery of the Cross is to be learned under the Cross. Where y^e ✠ is, there is Light, i.e. where 'tis [there is] Resignation and Love to God.

The X^n Relig^n is far fr. denying us [any satisfaction] of our Appetites (which God [hath permitted] and set bounds to) but the Vicious and Heathenish abuse them.—Which forbidden Liberty [is slavery:] for He is properly a slave. . . . He dos ill, and yet is [unable] to forbear w^t His. . . .

Fasting. Self Denyal.

Numb. vi. concerning the Law of Nazarites. See the margin in my Bible.

Wisd. [Ecclus.] xxxiv. 25, 26. *So is a man y^t Fasteth for his sins, and then goeth and doth ye same, who will hear His prayer, or w^t doth His Humbling profit Him?*

St. Luke xvii. 27. *They did eat, they drank &c.*

This seems to intimate that the disuse of Fasting &c. was the first beginning and occasion of those sins wch brought destruction upon ye wicked world.

Self Denyal. See Pr[act.] Catech. Hamond p. 32; [p. 71. Oxf. 1847.]

Dutys we owe to our selves. See Watts on the Passions. No man can be said to be Just to Himself who is not concern'd, and dos not take pains to know His Duty.

Jesus Xt. having prescribed Rules for Fasting as well as Prayer and Almes, Tis plain He has made Fasting a Duty as well as the other—not only Publick but private Fasts, wch are here meant, to dispose us for Humiliation and Pray^r.

Instances of Self Denyal.

The being fond of Bad company, whether for their wit. . . .

SUPPLE-
MENT
No. XIV.

In [finite] are the Number of such as have been ruin'd by This. . . . Therefore to [be] denyed as we Hope. . .

Merchants and Traders . . . . Such gain as covetousness in our corrupt state. .

Defrauding His Ministers, Tythes, &c.

Both Rich and Poor ly under great Tempta[tion to this] evil, wch must be deny'd, or . . . .

Mortification—Self Denyal.

Let us never set up our own Reason, subject as it is to errors, agst God's word.

Let us deny the Friendship of a Profane World, rather than lose the Fav^r and Friendship of God.

[A long interval.]

[13.] *The Lord's Supper*

Is to us w^t the Tree of Life was to Adam while in Paradise. W^n He was deprived of y^t He was reduced to a State of Nature.

And w^n a X^n deprives Himself of ye Lord's Supper, He is left to His pure naãl cond. wthout ye Grace of God—And wanting a Principle of Life and Immortality, wch is absolutely necessary to fit us for Heaven, we are sure never to go there.

Is not this plainly to undervalue J. Xt. and all y^t He has done and suffer'd for us ?

Jo. vi. 48. I AM THE BREAD OF LIFE, (i.e. The Principle, the Support of the Spiritual Life), as Adam was of death—w^{tht} which it cannot be preserved.

Lay hold of this surest of all Remedys.

May I live to Thy Honour who didst dye for me. May I dayly increase in Thy Holy Sp^t, ever more and more, until . . . . . .

If any man sin we have an Advocate—Let Thy Blood and Merits plead for me.

Come unto Me &c. Make me truly sensible of my sins, that I may come to Thee more cheerfully.

Preparation. Go to God as ye Publican did, *God be merciful unto me &c.*—Or as the Leper, *Lord if Thou wilt &c.*

God has made the Salvation of the whole world to depend on This Sacrif.

Jo. xiii. 1. *Having loved His own He loved y^m unto ye end.* The Institution of this Sacram^t.—This was ye greatest Instance of His Love, wⁿ He was going to part wth y^m.

<small>SUPPLEMENT No. XIV.</small>

How unworthy soever we are of God's Fav^{rs}, yet wⁿ He offers y^m we ought......

Jo. xiii. 10. *And ye are clean but not all.*—If J. X^t, who knew the Heart, pronounces this sentence upon all His Apostles (except Judas) *Ye are clean,* i.e. well qualify'd for Receiving this Sacram^t, altho' their Faith was weak, and they were all subject to many Infirmities (as appeared afterwards) what comfort is this to us, y^t J. Xt. will receive us, tho' we are not so perfect as we would and hope somtime to be!

J. Xt. offer'd himself to become a Sacrifice for our Sins, God has accepted of y^t Sacr. If we lose the Benefit of this Sacram^t in wch we represent this Sacrifice, we despise ye Fav^r of God, and our own Happss.—For 'tis by This we plead the Coven^t wch God has made in Xt. with us, viz. To pardon us upon our Rep.—To Hear our Prayers—To receive us into Fav^r—To Remember [y^t Covēnt] in Heaven as we do on Earth &c. by wch we preserve a continual correspondence wth. Heaven.

The Memorial of our Redemption—By wch we engage our selves to love and obey God, without wch we never can be happy.

This is our prevailing argum^t wth God—That J. Xt. has made our Peace with Him by the Blood of His Cross.

It was necessary that ye sin be expiated by ye Death of ye true Sacrifice, before He [we] could be reconciled to God— The Memorial of this is what we are to commemorate.

God hides the Treasures of His Grace and Power under very plain and common things — Imposition of Hands— Bread and Wine &c.

Bread and wine with ye Blessing of God, can effect such things as pass our Understanding.

End of—One great end of this Ordinance is to testifye to all ye world y^t we are Xt's disciples. Remember how many Teares it cost St. Pet. for saying " I am not this man's disciple:" every one who turns his back on ye Table says ye same in effect.

SUPPLE-
MENT
No. XIV.

To preserve the memory of X^t crucified in ye Ch.

We derive from Adam a naāl life only, by that we can never [reach] Heaven, we are therefore Baptised, y^t by y^t Sacram^t we may obtain a Principle of a new and Heavenly Life.

In this Sacrament we represent to God ye Death and Sacr[ifice] of His Son, we plead His covenant and His gracious Promises.

Bread and Wine by Consecration Receive such divine virtues as do impart to devout Receivers all ye Benefits of Xt's Death.

...Great end of this Sacram^t was to preserve ye memory of Xt Crucified, ye greatest Act of Goodness and Mercy y^t ever was known.

As there was no hope of Life for an Israelite who had not ye Blood of ye Paschal Lamb upon His door, so no X^n can......

Preparation.

A serious meditation upon our Lord's Suffering. He is crown'd with Thorns.—His meekness before Herod is call'd Stupidity—Cloth'd in contempt with a White Garment—Let us adore Him in these circumstances, and learn from Him to bear contempt with Patience.

Crucifye Him, crucify Him—Lord grant y^t I may never out of weakness comply with others to do a wicked thing.

The Soldiers knew not w^t they did, w^n they crucify'd Thee, but I have no excuse if I crucifye Thee &c.....

I see all this with the eye of Faith, and I adore Thee O Jesus, while they mock and abuse Thee—and thro' Thy Grace I will learn to bear wth submission to ye will of God Contempt, Afflictions and Reproaches.

Shall I read these things with^t being sensible y^t my sins was the occasion of all this? If I do, I am no better than a Jew.

His [He] bare His Cross. Prepare me Gracious Lord to bear all the evils, wch Thou shalt think fit to lay upon me.

Simon the Cyrenian. Thou must help me, O Jesus, to bear my Cross, or I shall sink under it.

Weep not for Me. But I will, O Jesus, by Thy Grace, weep for those sins of mine wch caused Thee these sorrows.

Crucify'd, betwixt 2 Theeves, to make the unthoughtfull world beleive that He was equally guilty wth y^m.

As ye Devil took possession of ye unworthy Judas, so dos ye Sp^t of Jesus take possession of every worthy. . . .

Do this.—This shewes the Minister of God's Commission to Consecrate with effect these [*sic*] Bread and Wine.

Spiritual Advantages. See Campbel, p. 296 & 307.[p]

A X^n can have no solid Hopes of Salvat^n who dos not hold communion wth X^t after this manner, no more than the Branch of a Tree can grow and bear fruit, w^n separated from the Tree, so saith our Lord himself.

By representing to God ye sacrifice of His Son we prevail with Him to Hear us.

This Holy ordinance ye most acceptable way of worshipping God—The surest way of obtaining the pardon of our sins—of obtaining ye Gr. of God, and of securing our Salvation.

Believe it X^ns y^t ye Forgiveness of yor Sins is the greatest blessing you can ask of God. He y^t is not pardoned will infallibly be damned.

We may indeed do as Naaman did—Question whether—we may for want of Faith question whether—an Action so plain and easy can be attended with so great blessings. And we may thro' Infidelity lose these blessings, as he w^d have done, had He not been better advised.

Lord's Supper. Spiritual Communion[q].

Our Church (see Rubrick after Com. of Sick) for the comfort of such as thro' any just impediment, are hinderd from Receiving the Sacram^t Has given Us this Instruction, That if we do truly repent us of our sins,—If we have a lively Faith in God's Mercy thro' X^t with a thankful remembrance of His Death, we do eat and drink the Body and Blood of our Sav^r profitably and to our Soul's Health. Altho' we do not Receive the Sacram^t with our Mouth.

Now for as much as many Pious soules w^d very willingly preserve ye memory of X^ts death in their Soules, and reap

---

[p] ["An Essay upon the Holy Eucharist," being the last of "Six small Treatises," in "A Preservative against several of the Errors of the Romish Church," subjoined to "The Doctrine of a Middle State," &c., by the Hon. Archibald Campbell, 1721.]

[q] [Evidently the rough draught of the passage on this subject in the Introduction to the Lord's Supper.]

> SUPPLE-
> MENT
> No XIV.

the Benefit therof, by Receiving ye Sacram^t according to X^ts Institution, but have this *Just Impediment*, for want of an opportunity: I have here added a short Form of Prayer wch any well disposed X^n may make use of to His soule's Health and Comfort on Sundays, Holydays, or as often as He thinks fit. And whoever dos so will surely find, y^t this is the best way of preparing Himself for y^t Holy ordinance, w^n 'tis administered in ye Publick Congregation.

Sin. W^d you have a true knowlege of Sin, see How severly God punished it in His beloved Son, when He undertook to Satisfye His Justice for our Sins.

J. X^t sufferd all this contempt to shew us w^t we ought to suffer for our Rebellion ag^nst God.

SPIRITUAL COMMUNION. We can expect no blessing to our Selves, no Answer to our Prayers, no security of dying in ye Peace of God, but for ye sake of ye Sacrifice of His Body and Blood, and therfore the oftener we repeat ye Memorial of His Death the stronger will be our Faith and Hope, and surer our Pardon.

All Faithful Communicants do as truly partake of the Benefit of X^ts Sufferings, as if they had indeed sufferd in their own persons w^t He sufferd.

Sacr. Ordaind. To preserve ye Memory &c. To apply ye merits of X^ts death to every communicant—y^t X^ns may call y^ms to an Account concerning their Repentance—Faith and Love towards God and X^t.

A Token y^t we still resolve to continue X^ts Faithful Servants and Members of His Ch. and Family.

Our Alms an outward Testimony of our sincere Charity.

Oblations. A publick Acknowlegm^t y^t all we eat and drink and our very lives are owing to God's Goodness and Bounty.

THE BLOOD OF XT. CLEANSETH US FROM ALL SIN. 1 Jo. i. 7.

This shewes the Fulness of Pardoning Grace.

How many Blessings and Favours have X^ns procured for them by ye Death of X^t. But then w^t Judgments are they to expect who slight these mercys, and live like Heathens in ye midst of X^ty.

Such is y^e *exceeding Benefit* of X^ts death wch we commemorate, That the Divine Justice cannot punish us for the sins we have repented of, no more than if we had never sin'd or done any thing amiss.

To Live in any Known Sin, after we have been at y̅ᵉ Sacramᵗ is to be guilty of y̅ᵉ Death of Xᵗ.

Ends. The Remembrance of Xᵗˢ Death, mentioned by Xᵗ Hims. 2ˡʸ. To Testifye our Union with Xᵗ and Communion with one anothʳ, mentioned by St. Paul.

Do this; i.e. This yᵗ I do—Offer Bread and Wine as a Sacrif. to God (wⁿ consecrated). They could not offer His real Body—but only His Sacr. Body—as a Memorial of His Real Body.

A meanes of conveying to us all y̅ᵉ Blessings of Xts. Death and Sacrifice—to all worthy Communicants, viz. Grace and Pardon.

We have no way of obtaining Pardon after we have broke our Baptismal Covenᵗ. but by this Sacramᵗ.

Wⁿ the Bread and Wine are, by Consecration, made the Sacramental Body and Bl. of Xt., we have then a Sacrifice to offer wʰ is worthy to be recᵈ. and to prevail wᵗʰ God &c.

The Power of y̅ᵉ H. Sp. accompanys these elements, and makes y̅ᵐ effectual Meanes of Grace and Salvation, this is what we are to believe &c.—This y̅ᵉ very life of. . . .

They have a Supernatural power communicated by y̅ᵉ Spt.

Christ's Spiritual Body, i.e. made such by y̅ᵉ Spᵗ of God.

Not by y̅ᵉ Faith of y̅ᵉ Receiver, for they were such before.

Whatever Promises are made to Prayʳ—It is always to be supposed—To Prayer offer'd to God thro' J. Xt. commemorated in y̅ᵉ Sacr. As all y̅ᵉ Prayers made by every Jew, was [were] accepted in Union with y̅ᵉ daily Sacrifice.

Those who turn their backs upon y̅ᵉ Sacramᵗ wᵈ tremble if they knew y̅ᵉ danger they are in, viz. That all their Prayers for pardon, for grace, for comfort, for Salvⁿ will be rejected.

Every worthy Receiver obtaines these 3 blessings. 1. The pardon of all his past sins. Math. xxvi. 28. *His blood shed for y̅ᵉ Remission of Sins.* He is absolved by this Sacr. 2. Grace and Power to amend his Life. 3. An Assurance of an Happy Resurr. Jo. vi. 48. *He yᵗ Feedeth on this Bread*

SUPPLE-
MENT
No. XIV.

shall live for ever.—It was ye Tree of Life, in Paradise, wch was to make Him [Adam] Immortal—Tis This Food must make us so, or &c.

Dutys on our part — *Obedience* and *Charity.* He who comes not to ye Sacr. dos in effect say—eith^r "I will not obey God"—or "I am not in charity."

J. Xt. has made this Ordinance necessary to Salvatⁿ. He has at ye same time commanded—*If Thou bring thy gift to ye Altar &c.*—making it necessary to be in charity before a Man must Hope for Salvation.

As Bp. Burnet observes—As Wax tho' by putting a Seal to it continues wax still, yet if ye seal put to it brings you a Pardon for your Life, you do not consider it as a common thing^r.

In this Sacram^t we make a publick profession y^t we firmly believe what is said in the Gospel that J. Xt. has done and suffer'd for us, and w^t He taught and commanded, and that we resolve to order our life according.

Consider what is the Ordinary Practice and settled course of y^r Life.

Do This in Remembrance of Me—i.e. Of the Holy example I have set you—OF the Holy Doctrine I taught you—OF the Bitter death I suffer'd for you, And of my coming again to punish my Enemys and Reward my Freinds.

Charity. And bec. there is nothing but Love and Peace and good agreem^t in Heavⁿ, We are therefore to resolve and strive to bring our selves to this temper before we dye.

We are all equally God's Creatures and all Redeemd by Son's Blood.

The Xⁿ Sacrifice designed to render God favourable to us, by representing unto His divine Majesty w^t His Son has suffer'd and done for us.

Tis also design'd and was ordained to preserve the Remembrance of Xts. love for us.

---

^r [Exposition of the Ch. Catechism, 1710. p. 321.

"The elements in the Sacrament, the bread and wine, after they are blessed and consecrated, are still in their nature what they formerly were, and what our senses do discover to us evidently that they still are. But yet they are exalted to a high and spiritual use by the institution: for as wax, by putting a seal to it, does not change its nature, but is still wax as it was before; yet it gives every thing that is contained in the paper or parchment to which it is affixed, by a real and certain title, &c."

The Lord's Supper is a publick and solemn Acknowlegem^t of our being in Communion with Xt. and His Church—and used as a means of living as becomes the Gospel of Xt.

Txts. 1 Cor. xi. 26. *For as often as ye eat this bread &c.*

Benefits. Pardon of all our sins—Admitted to all ye Blessings of ye new Covenant—An assurance of grace and assistance to do our duty—An assurance of a Blessed resurrection—Jo. 6. 54—*Whoso eateth my Flesh, &c. and I will raise Him up at ye last day.*

Those y^t turn their backs on ye H. S. deprive ym^s of ye greatest blessings in ye world—The Pardon of their Sins—The Fav^r of God—The Peace of Conscience, and ye Assurance of Happss w^n they dye.

Preparation.

The best preparation is an H. Life. A Resolution to Live in the Fear of God with a desire to please Him—The way to put this Resolution in Practice, is this, or something like it, viz. To say to y^r self upon every Occasion—This I do, this I undertake, this I suffer, bec. I believe it will please God. This I forbear to do, this I avoid, bec. I believe it will displease God, if I sh^d do it—And w^never you perceive y^t you have done any thing wch you ought not to have [done], (wch y^or conscience will tell you, if you do not stifle it) then immediatly beg of God to forgive you; and remember...... until you have done so, you lye under ye guilt of ye sin, and under ye displeasure of God.

The End of Preparation is to bring a man to such a sense of His Sins, as y^t He may not be guilty of y^m again.

If you have done any man wrong &c. We must not expect Fav^r and Forgivness fr. God, if we do [not] forgive others.

At the Celebration. Say nothing aloud, but w^t all ye People are directed [to] say—lest you disturb those y^t are near you—do not repeat ye Absolution after ye Minister, but attend, and say [Amen] to it.

After Receiving. Give God thanks for this meanes of grace and.... beg ye assistance of His Grace to enable you to [live] as becomes a X^n. And especially for such graces as you know [you] most stand in need of—Now is a proper [time] to pray for yor Freinds—Children—Benefactors, En-

SUPPLE-
MENT
No. XIV.

[emies] .... ᵃobtain those graces wch are necessary to fit us for Heaven, nor are they affected with this Love of J. Xt. thus dying for us—so as to resolve to follow His H. example, and to do what He has commanded us.

This Sacram^{t} is a Seal of God's Covent^{t}—And it is intended to increase our Faith in God's Promises and Faithfulness to His Covenant—As also to put us in mind of our part of ye Cov. made at Bap. and to put us upon renewing it.

Examination. The Jewes were used to search and clean their Houses of Leaven before ye Passover. This sh^{d} teach X^{ns} to search diligently whether there be not some Sin or Lust, harbouring secretly in their Hearts.

In Remembrance of Me—Suppose y^{r}self at ye foot of ye Cross—J. Xt. speaking to you—"These Torments I suffer for y^{r} sake, To Reconcile you to God, to make atonem^{t} for your sins. To Deliver you fr. eternal death &c." W^{t} w^{d} your thoughts and answ^{rs} be—"I abhorr those sins for wch you bleed and dye—I am amazed at yor Love—for so poor a creature as I am—I am thankful with all my soul—Your Love passeth all acknowlegments on our part," &c.

[In a larger and feebler hand, still Bishop Wilson's.]

By a Participation of these Divine Mysterys we are united to, and made one Body wth Him—or as the Body is to ye Head.

[A good deal cut out.]

Lord's Supper.

[Still in the Bishop's larger character.]

If you have been brought up in a Xn. manner, and have done this, you have done well, and are in ye way of Salvat^{n}.—If you have not, or have led an unthoughtful and ungodly life, you must not attempt to go to the Lord's Table, till you [have] Repented and Forsaken all y^{r} sins, and sincerely purposed to lead a Xn. and good life for ye time to come. When you are come to this Resolution, you must get Instructed in ye meaning, use and blessings of This H. Sacrament.—Besides this, it will be requir'd y^{t} by an Outward sober life you give a proof of the sincerity of your purposes of leading a good and Xn. life, according to God's Commdm^{ts}.

ᵃ [Some lines cut out here.]

N.B. An Holy X^n Life a continual Preparat^n for the Lord's Supper; and for Death.   SUPPLEMENT No. XIV.

Xn. with^t Xty. Ps. l. 17, 21. *Why dost thou take my covenant in thy [mouth?] whereas ....*

[A good deal cut out.]

[14.] *Perseverance—Conversion.*

Say often to y^{r}self—" My Hearts desire is—That I may be saved—My great concern, by the Grace of G. shall be, y^t I may not perish eternally."

Of Regeneration—And this is effected by ye Sp^t of God, convincing us of our own vileness and of ye vanity of the things we are so fond of nãally, and seting before us the vast advantage it will be to obey God's will and commands. Here the will is free, freely choosing w^t the H. Sp^t hath represented to ye mind to be the best thing in the world it can choose.

But then this Conviction is not Regeneration, if it shall rest in a bare wishing to be Regenerate—with^t using the meanes to be such.

Marks or Signes or Tests of [saving?] Grace.

1. A willingness to be tryed—*He that doth evil hateth the light, lest His deeds sh^d be reprov'd.* Jo. iii. 20.

2. A real regard for good men, in w^m the Spirit of God appears—*We have passed fr. death unto life bec. we love the Brethren.* 1 Jo. iii. 13.

He y^t loves the Image of God in others, has a good share of it in Himself.

3. An universal obedience to all God's cõmands. 1 Jo. ii. 3. *Hereby we know that we know Him &c.* A sincere desire and endeav^r to keep the Law of God.

And tho' our obedience be imperfect—yet if we aspire after Perfect^n both by fervent Pray^r and earnest endeav^{rs} it is a sign of the work of Grace in our Hearts.—Such sincerity in God's acc^t passeth for perfection.

Now this obedience must be both Inward and Outward—*Out of the Heart proceedeth, &c.* We must not say our Hearts are right, w^n our actions are bad.

Our obedience also must be universal, with regard both to God and Man—*Herein,* saith St. Paul, [Acts xxiv. 16.] *do I*

SUPPLE-
MENT
No. XIV.

exercise myself, to keep a conscience void of offence towards God and Man.

4. Not to *commit sin*, another Test of Grace. 1 Jo. iii. 9, 10. W^n a man, with David, [Ps. cxix. 104.] *Hateth every evil way.*—Doth not knowingly allow of any sin, any evil Thoughts, Desires, Lusts—Sins of the Heart.

To oppose these the surest way to secure the life.—Especially such as Pride, Envy, Malice, Hatred of God and Goodness, these being sins wch come nearest to ye sins of Hell.

A Regenerate Person will not only abstain from sin, but fr. all temptations to sin, and Occasions of sin.

5. Test. They that have Grace must be fruitful in good works—They that are born of God must live as do the children of God, must have ye affections of God's children. A Sonlike Fear and Love of God.

Imitating Him in His Goodness to all—Take His Chastismts patiently and thankfully.

Such as are yet *unconverted* sh^d consid^r their dang^r and not delude themselves with false Hopes of Heaven and Happss—Who w^d not disdain to be asked—Do you really Hope to go to Heav^n?—The Drunkard, the Profane, the Proud, the Covetous &c. to a Man w^d &c.

W^t do you rely upon? X^{ts} merits? He will save none but such as are Regenerate.

Is it ye mercy of God? God is merciful, and yet both Men and Angels have been sent to Hell.

It is therefore absolutely necessary as ever we hope for H. to lab^r with all our might to be Regenerated.—To prepare our Souls to Receive this Grace.—And remember—That now is the Accepted time, now is the Day of Salv.

Two necessary Directions—*First*, Most Earnest *Prayer*. *Secondly*. A sincere Improvement of the Means of Grace.

[1 S. John iii. 9.] *Regeneration.*

Such only are regenerate as are under such a constant sense of their Duty, have such an Inclination to Holyness, as they cannot knowingly commit sin—Such as have gain'd a victory over the world and its Lusts.

Regeneration. A Spiritual Birth—By wch our nature is renew'd and the Image of God restor'd in us, from wch we were sadly faln.—By Regen. we become the children of God.

Regeneration. A change of Man's Heart, is one of the greatt Miracles wch God works—But this He doth in a na̅al way—by our endeav{rs} as well as by His all powerful Grace—Ezek. xviii. 31. *Make you a new Heart, &c.*

SUPPLE-
MENT
No. XIV.

Mr. Mead. p. 138.

None can be Heires of the K. of Heaven, but ye sons of GOD—None are sons of God, but by Regen. or a new Birth —So saith our Lord. Jo. iii. 3. *Except, &c.*

Now Regen. consists in this—Repentance towards GOD, and *Faith* toward our Ld J. X{t}.—By the first we return to God, from whom we are gone astray—By the second we are reconcild to God, and are enabled to serve Him acceptably.

Repentance. A turning of the whole Heart from Satan (whose servant every one who lives in sin is) To serve God in newness of Life. Acts xxvi. 8.[18.]

Dying to Sin (Contrition) is a Sorrow of Heart, joyned with a full purpose of Heart to forsake the sin wch has given us so much sorrow.

This attended with *Fear, Grief,* and *Hate.*

Fear. Occasion by these words of X{t}. Math. xxv. 42. *Go ye cursed into Everlasting Fire*—&c.

Greif. For having lost ye Fav{r} of so gracious a God and the Happiness He has prepard for ym that love and obey Him.

Hate. By wch we hate sin, and loathe our selves for &c.

The natural effect of this *Fear, Greif, Hatred* is Confession. Vid. loc. p. 141. And *Turning unto God.*

Now when Repentance is come thus far—w{n} a man *trembles* and *Feares* for Himself, is greived for His Sins, *Hates* the thoughts of them, Confesses them befor God—Purposes to forsake them—The same Grace (wch from the begining moved the Heart all those steps) Directs us to Flye to J. X{t} by Faith, who Invites such, and none but such (for the *whole need not* &c.) to come to Him and He will give them ease —And follow by degrees :—

A Love for God who has been so good to Him—A Delight in the ways of Relig{n}—A Firm Hope of the Reward promised, and Lastly Good Works—Works of Relig{n} and Piety towards God, and of Righteousness towards men :—all these will be the fruits of a true Conversion.

SUPPLE-
MENT
No. XIV.

Thus much concerning Repentance, *the first* part of Regeneration—we come now to consid-r the *Second*, wch is *Faith*—REPENT AND BELIEVE Y^e GOSPEL.

Now the Gospel is the glad tidings of Salvat^n, to be obtain'd by J. Xt.—Who hath taken away our sins by sacrificing Himself—Reconcil'd us to God, and that by His grace we might turn unto, and perform such Obedience as may make us meet to be Partakers of Et. Life.

Regeneration or Spiritual Generation.

Now there is a *False Faith*, w^n men hope for salv. by Xt. otherways than God has ordained, viz. without Obedience and Good Works.

2. There is a *true Faith*, w^n men believe the Gospel as it is deliver'd to us, but do not act accordingly.

3. There is a *Saving Faith*, or *Justifying Faith*, w^n we do not only believe and embrace the Gospel, but apply ourselves to Xt, Relye upon Him, and perform such Works of Obedience as God hath promised to reward with Eternal Life.

A true X^{tn} must be crucify'd unto ye world and the world to Him, be dead to ye world, and ye world to Him—i.e. to the Lust of ye Flesh, gluttony, Drunkeness, Letchery—To the Lusts of ye Eyes—i.e. Covetousness or a Desire of every thing we see—The Pride of Life—Ambition, State, the Praise of Men, Power, &c.

How must these be mortify'd? By a constant denyal of their cravings.—Deny vain-glory in words and actions and Pride will dye—Give not vent to thy Anger—Hearken not to ye cravings of Lust &c. And these sins will at last forsake thee.

The New Creature, is the Image of God in ye Soul of Man, —to be Holy, Just, and Wise.

Regeneration. We were first born according to nature, our [bodies] and soules united by the Father of Life—W^n the Divine Nature, the Spirit of God, is added to these, we are then perfect, and Born ag^n. And a Man being thus born ag^n by the Spirit, is as different from the Naāl Man, as the Natural Man is from a Beast.

W^n a Man is govern'd wth new Principles, new desires &c. He may be justly call'd a New Man.—To be one Will wth God, will entitle us to be the sons of God.

The Word of God is the Cause of our Regeneration, that is *the Living Word*—(The Seed of the Soul—) or J. Xt. the Son of God, Described Heb. iv. 12, 13.—*The Word of God is quick and Powerful, and sharper than any two-edged sword, and a Discerner of ye Thoughts—Neither is there any Creature that is not manifest in His Sight, but all things are naked &c.*—The Attributes belong only to the Incarnat Word.

Therefore in a Real conversion to God, in true Repentance—In this New Birth,—God Himself by His *Living Word* is the immediate cause of Regeneration.

We see then that the Seed wch produces this New Creature is *The Son of God*, by Union wth w^m we become the Children of God. Dr. Hen. More[t].

They that hope for salv. must, besides their X^n Baptism, seriously take X^{ty} upon themselves, and continue therein unto the end of their days—leaving off all known Sin, and following y^e rules of their $Relig^n$.—*The Spt.* must *bear witness with our Spt. that we are the children of God.*

Fruits of the Spirit. Love, Joy, Peace &c. N.B. These are call'd the Fruits of y^e H. Sp^t not oures. Ours are described before (Gal. v. 19, 20, 21). *Adultery, Fornication* &c. These are the Natural Fruit and product of Original Sin.

[In another, a female, hand. Qu. Bp. W.'s composition?]

Pleasure.

Kinds. 1. Sensual pleasures—of ye eye, ear, taste, smell, ease, indulgence &c. 2. pleasures of ye heart—attachments, entanglements, creature love, unmortified friendships. 3. pleasures of ye mind—curious books, deep researches, speculations, hankerings after news—wit—fine language. 4. the pleasures of ye imagination—schemes, fancies, suppositions.

To be denied, because, 1. God will have ye heart. 2. there is no solid union with God, until, in a X^n Sense, we are dead to creature comforts. 3. God is purity. 4. God calls us to shew our faith and love by a sp^t of sacrifice. Pleas. is Isaac.

5. Denying ourselves, hating &c. are gospel precepts—as is cuttg. off &c. plucking &c. 6. God makes no exceptions. All ye offending Members must be cut off &c. 7. Pleasures

[t] [Mystery of Iniquity, ch. iv. § 2. Works, Lond. 1708, p. 394, (in substance)].

SUPPLE-
MENT
No. XIV.
render yᵉ soul incapable of yᵉ operations of yᵉ Spt. and obstruct divine consolations. If nature is pampered, grace must be starved. Earthly Pleasures are of a corrupting nature —betrays with a kiss &c. Indulgence enervates, and renders us incapable of suffering fᵐ God, men, devils or self, and stands in yᵉ way of our doing as well as suffering yᵉ will of God. He must walk steadily who wᵈ walk safely on yᵉ brink of a precipice. The earthly senses must be spiritualized; yᵉ sensual heart purified; yᵉ wandering mind fixed; yᵉ foolish imagination made sober.

[Put not off from] day to day, for suddenly &c.—and in thy [security thou shalt] perish, &c. Ecclus. v. 7.

Ecclus. vii. 8. *Bind not one sin upon another; for in one thou shalt not be unpunished.*

Ecclus. viii. 5. *Reproach not a man yᵗ turneth from sin, but remember that we are all worthy of punishmᵗ.* Ecclus. xxxiv. 15, 16.

The Holy Sc. use yᵉ severest expressions to explain *Repentance.* To mortifye the Flesh—To crucifye the Flesh with its affections and lusts—To be crucifyed to yᵉ world—To be crucifyed wᵗʰ Xt. Rom. vi. 6.—To dye to sin—To be dead with Xt—A broken heart—A bruised spirit—To Rend yᵉ Heart &c.—To Hate our selves—To deny our selves—All wᶜʰ is necessary to fit us for receiving by Faith the Gospel of Xt.

Repent—implies a sense of, and an acknowlegmt of, yᵉ sad estate wᶜʰ our sins have brought us into—A sincere sorrow for yᵐ—An Hatred of yᵐ—A Resolution not to commit any more—And to shew yᵗ our purposes are real and sincere, by a new obedience.

[15.] *As our selves—*

...... love one another—As such Love yᵐs.—to such only this is a direction how they shᵈ love their neighbʳ.,

God is our common Fathʳ, and all we are brethren—Nothing dos more effectually recommend us to yᵉ Favʳ of God than a tender regard for our neighbʳ.

As our self. i.e. Sincerely, as in the sight of God. They know w^t satisfac^n they take in their own welfare, how much they are concerned for their own misfortunes, how careful to supply their own wants—how tender of their own Reputation —how careful to hide their own faults—how ready to find excuses for their own Mistakes and Failings—how well disposed to pardon y^{m}s. w^n they have done amiss—Dos my Heart stand thus affected to my neighb^r? If not I am condemned by this Law.

How shall we express our Love? Thou shalt not suffer sin upon him—Lev. xix. [17.] For y^t w^d be to hate him—God punishes sinners, bec. He Loves y^m.—He dos it wth Regret and Pities y^m at ye same time—And receives y^m wth Joy w^n they return to their Duty.

Our Lord calls this His Law—To make ye greater Impression upon our Mindes—and y^t we may strive to understand and obey it—And y^t we may obey it for His sake— And bec. He has commanded us—And bec. He can and will Reward or Punish us as we obey or neglect this command.

If I consider this seriously, I shall not say, "This man has not deserved it [at] my Hands—That man has injured me, and I'll not forgive Him, I'll do as He has done to me —Such a man has spoken evil of me and I'll not forget it— I do not like such a man and I'll not speak to Him." Why now this is ye language not of X^{ns} but of Heathens and Infidels.—A X^n being bound at the peril of His soul, and in obedience to ye command of X^t to lay aside all .... at God's command—And to lye down to sleep every night, wth ye same charitable dispositions with wch He desires and Hopes to dye: wch is ye meaning of, *Let not the sun &c.*

I will for God's sake, and bec. He has commanded Me, and bec. I beleive it will please God, do my neighb^r no wrong, tho' I could propose ye greatest gain to myself—I will not render evil for evil, tho' Revenge is sweet to Flesh and Blood —I will not bear Malice in my Heart, tho' I could never so well conceal it from the eyes of men—I will forgive such an enemy, however [great the] expense of doing so—I will bear with ye Infirmities of ye weak, tho' pride w^d not have me do so.—These things, done in obedience to ye will and command

SUPPLEMENT No. XIV.

of God, are a most acceptable sacrifice to the Divine Majesty.

The man y^t wants this grace of Charity, cannot enter into ye K. of H.

If men live in envy and malice, if they Bite and devour one anoth^r—If they imagine mischief agst their neighb^r—If they will oppress, vex and domineer over oth^{rs}—If they will wrong him in Body, Goods or Good Name—If they will defraud—Bear false witness &c. No man with these dispositions can possibly be Happy w^n he dyes.

Instances of Charity. I will not despise any man living—He y^t despiseth His neighb^r sinneth—Prov. xiv. 21.—For he is God's creature—and we are all a Race of poor, vile, sinful creatures—and subject to ye same misfortunes, ye same Failings, even to every thing y^t can make any man contemptible.

I will not wrong my Neighb^r.—*Love worketh no ill to His Neighb^r.*—I will not trouble nor vex my Neighb^r wthout cause—I will not overreach nor defraud my N.—I will not slander my N.—I will not rashly Judge my N.—I will not Tempt my Neighb^r to sins wch will ruin Him, Whoredom, Drunkeness &c.

I will have a concern for ye Interest of my N. I will condole and comfort Him w^n any thing sad or calamitous befalls Him.

I will not greive ye Heart of ye afflicted, nor add Sorrow to his Burden.

I will endeav^r to do Good—as well as give good Words to my Neighb^r.

I will be ready to forgive my worst Enemies, and bring my Heart to love y^m. Upon this depends our Pardon hereafter.—*If ye forgive men*, Math. vi. 14.

Math. xviii. The Lord was more offended wth His ungrateful Servants Uncharitableness than wth ye Loss of 10,000 Talents.

Meanes of obtaining this Grace. Our Lord knew very well, y^t while men placed their Happss in the Things of this world, they could never Love as they ought to do.

What a comfort is it for an unlearned X^n y^t the Duty he owes to his Neighb^r and upon wch depends his own salvation is comprehended in so few Words—*Thou shalt love &c.*—and yet yᵉ Apostle affirms it to be so—*Love is yᵉ Fulfilling &c.*

Common Civility is not this Love—yᵗ may proceed from Interest, Fondness &c. Fear, Hope &c. Vanity, or a Love (?) to be admired—All this is self-love.

If I really love my Neighbʳ I shall never desire to injure him, nor do him any injustice.

Consider J. Xt. in every Neighbʳ—Whatever is done to yᵐ is done to Xt. whose Members they are.

I will Pray yᵗ *he may find mercy at yᵗ day.* Tho' he shᵈ be wicked, yet he is miserable, and as such I will recommend him to yᵉ Mercy of G.

We never despise others but wⁿ we do not reflect upon ourselves. Pardon is not to be had but at the Price of Pardon.

He who goes to his knees without a forgiving Temper obtains nothing but his own condemnation.

If you profess to be a Follower of Him who dyed for His enemies, you will most chearfully forgive yoʳˢ.

He yᵗ is not concern'd to keep his Neighbʳ from perishing is in danger of perishing Himself.

We love our N. as our selves when we are concern'd for his salvation. To Love our N. is more our own Interest than His. We know yᵗ we have passed fr. death unto Life, bec. we love the Brethren.

Signs of Want of Ch. An aversion to their Company, Joy in their Misfortunes—Satisfaction in hearing yᵐ evil spoken of.

God grant yᵗ I may never be satisfyd, but by the effects my Love produceth, yᵗ I love My Neighbʳ as my Self.

.... Success—That our Good Name be not hurt—we never envy ourselves any good—we are troubled and sorry wⁿ any evil or mischief befalls our selves.

We are reconcil'd to our selves upon very reasonable termes.

We do not sift our own faults wᵗʰ Rigour.

We shᵈ not aggravate our Neighbʳˢ failings—Slander his good Name—Delight to spread abroad his faults.

SUPPLE-
MENT
No. XIV.

We sh^d love our Neighb^r as we desire and expect he sh^d love us, i.e. as Himself.

In this consists ye comforts and Blessings of Society—If I love my self better than my Neighb^r I shall be always thinking and striving to better myself and lessen Him.

My neighbour has as great a share in God's Love as I have.

I will impart my substance to such as want.

I will do no evil to my N.

I will beg of God ye Sp^t of Love—i.e. His H. Sp^t.

It behoves us to understand a Law on wch so much depends. An express and an indispensible Law of God, a Law by wch we shall be judged at ye last day.

Church Discipline.

[16.] WHOSE SOEVER SINS YE REMIT &c.

These words give a Pow^r of excluding out of the Church scandalous offenders, and of Receiving them agⁿ upon their Repentance.

This Power lodged in ye Govern^{rs} of ye Ch. Jo. xx. 22. Gal. v. 12. *I w^d they were cut off*, (i.e. excom.) *y^t trouble you.*

§. Wⁿ people fell into scandalous sins, some time was always thought necessary to prove the sincerity of their Rep.

§. Tho' we sh^d always stand oblig'd to the Civil Magistrates for their Protectⁿ, And enforcing the D. of ye Ch. upon those upon w^m Conscience has no power—Yet we must still look upon Ch. D. and depend upon it as ye surest method of Reclaiming Sinners, and wch X^t and His Apostles intended for ye Governm^t of His Subjects—A power *mighty thro' God for ye pulling down &c.* [2 Cor. x. 4.], much more efficacious than any Temporal Penalty.

§. 'Tis a vile Prostitution of Ch. D. wⁿ 'tis used in causes merely secular, and not wth regard purely to Religⁿ and ye Soules of Men.

§. The Ch. is founded upon ye Power of ye Keyes. *Do not ye Judge them y^t are within*, [1 Cor. v. 12.]—i.e. wthin ye Church.

§. Wⁿ X^{ns} are made sensible y^t Excom. is a sentence passed by men commissioned by God, who at the peril of their souls are to act agreable to ye Word of God &c.

§. *I have a few things agst Thee, bec. thou sufferest Jezebel to seduce my servants.* Rev. ii. 20.

SUPPLEMENT No. XIV.

§. We may carry it fair wth Men, but J. X^t will most surely condemn us, if we neglect this sacred Deposite.

§. Ch. D. is for ye Hon^r of God, for ye Security of X^{tns} and for ye benefit of Sinners, and Edificat^n of ye whole Ch.

§. Whatever Power the Ch. has (besides purely Spirit.) tis a Burden laid upon us by ye Civil Magistrate.

§. If the Enemy, thro' our negligence, sowes Tares by Pestilent bookes, and we give not warning, we shall be answerable for ye sad effects they occasion.

§. We have our Authority as much from God as ye Civil Magistrate has His—He is ye Minister of God, and so are Pastors.

§. That w^h brought Ch. D. into Contempt was ye Unrighteous use made of Her Power, by ye Ch. in Her corrupt estate, w^n She took advantage of the Just dread wch from the beginning X^{ns} had of Ch. censures, and this she did both to secure and to enlarge Her Temporal Interests.

§. And now this is come upon us wch was foretold by Malachi (ii. 8.) *Ye have corrupted ye Covenant of Levi, ye are departed out of ye way &c.* Ye have depended upon a Secular Arm, *Therefore have I made you contemptible &c.*

§. We find by sad Experience How ineffectual Temp. Penalties are to Reclaim Sinners—Some are too Gr^t to be come at, some too Cunning, some too Rich and others too poor to be cared for—while none are exempt from Ch. D. High and Low, Rich and Poor are subject to be censured, and are [*sic*] sufficient to bring into Captivity every Imagination, every High thing y^t exalteth it self against the knowledge of God.

§. The Ch. of Scotland (whatever other Defects she labours under) has kept out Play Houses, Masquerades, Gladiators &c. By asserting Her Right of Discipline as Inherent in Her Pastors.

§. And tho' ye Ch. of Eng. has more, and more Powerful adversaries than ever she had since the Reformation, and tho' Iniquity aboundes, and J. X^t and His Gospel are Blasphemed in bookes &c. yet we have no reason to fear, but [by] a vigourous execution of Discipline, this Infidelity w^d

SUPPLE-
MENT
No. XIV.

be Humbled—and the Spirits and Powers of Darkness wch possess so many w^d be cast out, and brought into subjection.

§. St. Cyprian, nor St. Chrysost. w^d not have given the Sacram^t to such as frequented Playes.

§. W^n we hope to secure the Ch. by Human Policy, by Worldly Meanes, by the Power, Interest, Freindship of Men, God often leaves us to feel the Folly of our *own* choices, and Departing from *His*.

§. The Church owes this to Her Children. To keep them, if possible, from ruining y^{m}selves, and from running headlong to destruct^n wthout b̄ made sensible of their Danger.

§. Not to exercise Ch. D. is to lay aside one half of our Commission.

§. Heb. xii. 15. *Looking diligently lest any fall from the Gr. of G^d, lest any root of Bitterness springing up trouble you.*

§. The Ch. as a Spiritual Society is to be Govern^d and preservd by pure Spiritual Methods, such as affect ye Conscience—such as X^t will bless—being—....

§. 1 Tim. i. 20. *That they may learn not to Blaspheme.*

§. These are Truthes not to be questioned—That J. X^t appointed Lawes for ye Governm^t of His Ch. wth respect to the Spiritual Concernes of its Members—That ye Bps and Pastors stand chargd wth these Lawes—That they are oblig'd to do all in their power to preserve these Lawes.

§. There was never more need, and never less concern to restore it.

✠ This we may be sure of, that ye world will always oppose an Authority and a Doctrine wch condemns its maxims and its Practices.

W^n wicked men cannot excuse their crimes, and cannot bear to be reproved, they do w^t they can to ruin the Authority of their Pastors—*By w^t Authority*, say ye Cheif Preists to X^t. Luk. xx. 2.

God by visiting men with Temporal evils, constraines men to have recourse to Him—The Church imitates this conduct of God by Her Discipline.

2 Cor. vii. 10. *Godly sorrow worketh Rep. not to be re-*

pented of. Those who make repent. an easy work, seek to please men for a moment, not to save y^m for ever.

Too much indulgence ye cause of Relapses.

It is ye great thing we sh^d aim at in Ch. Discipline to convince sinners y^t we aim at nothing but their salvation.

1 Tim. v. 20. *Them that sin rebuke before all, that others may Fear.*

Every good Pastor wishes y^t His Sermons might be heard and followd, but wⁿ that will not do He is directed to use Sharpness, but still with an eye and. . . .

Letters of Discipline.

Prov. xxix. 1. *He that being often reproved hardeneth His neck, shall suddenly fall and that wthout Remedy.*

Endeav^r to make Him sensible of ye Damnable condition into wch His wickedness has brought Him. That by a true and sincere Repentance He may be restor'd to the Peace of the Church and continue a more faithful member of it than He has been.

It will be y^r Duty to have a watchful eye over His Conduct and Life for the time to come, considering w^t a reproch it w^d be to the Discipline of ye Church to see Sinners so little bettered by the severest censures.

People under Church Censures are apt to think y^t all is over, and they have no more to do, but to submit to w^t ye Church requires in order to remove the scandal and offence they have given, with^t considering y^t it is their Repentance and Conversion, and Eternal Salvⁿ y^t is aimed at, and to prevent their Damnation.

For God's sake endeav^r to make Him sensible, y^t if He is not sensible of the great Sin He has been guilty of, and Repeated—If He doth [not] from His Heart Abhorr it, and the offence He has given by it to God and M.. . . .

[17.] *Prayer. Lord's Prayer.*

GRACE BEFORE AND AFTER MEAT. 1 Tim. iv. 4, 5.

Every creature of G. is good, if rec^d wth Thanksgiving, for it is Sanctified by ye word of God and Prayer. What a pass

SUPPLEMENT No. XIV. are ye X^n world come to, y^t people are ashamed to own that they depend upon God for their daily Bread, and scorn, as it were, to give Him thanks for it—And w^t is more, dare eat ye meal w^h if not sanctifyd by Prayer, can do y^m no good —nor contribute to the nourishm^t of our bodys. Vid. S...

Math. ix. 32. *A Dumb man possessd wth a Devil.* And are not all such who never open their mouths to Praise God for His mercys, nor to beg His Blessing?

Solemn Blessing of ye People by ye Bp. or Preist of God. See Numb. vi. 24, &c., &c., and my notes in margine.

Scriptures relating to Prayer. Ps. l. 15. *Call upon me in ye day of Trouble, and I will deliver thee, and Thou shalt glorifye Me.*

Math. vii. 7. *Every one y^t asketh receiveth &c.*

Jo. ix. 31. *God heareth not sinners.*

Is. i. 15. *W^n ye spread forth yor hands, I will not Hear &c.*

He will give ye H. Sp^t to y^m y^t ask Him, wch will enable us to—.... p.

Math. viii. 2. *Lord if Thou wilt Thou canst make me clean.* Here is a Pattern of a Pray^r.—Humble, Plain and full of assurance in God's Goodness and Power.

The efficacy of Pray^r consists in being sensible of w^t we want, and in [representing our wants to God].

Lord's Prayer. In this Pray^r we Pray for all men as well as for our selves.—*Hallowed*—That G. may be Honourd by ye good lives of Men—*Thy Kingdom.* May all ye world become ye subjects of X^t.—*Thy Will.* May we all be pleased with Thy Choices for our Selves and oth^{rs}.—*Give.* The necessarys of Life, and the bread y^t nourish[eth] to Et. Life. —And *Forgive*—And grace to forgive oth^{rs} as—*And lead us not*, Suffer us not to be tempted above &c. *Deliver us*— From ye D—l and ye Corruption of our own corrupt......

We are to learn from God, how we are to Pray, and what to ask for—so as not to displease Him, or ask in vain.

We learn in this Prayer of our Lords to ask for such things as are for the Glory of God and our own Happss. These sh^d be ye subjects of all our Pray^r.

Our Father wch art in Heavn.

Supplement No. XIV.

O y^t we may live worthy of this Relation w^{ch} &c. O God who dealest wth us wth ye tenderness of a Father, grant y^t we may &c.

Ps. ciii. 17. *As a Father pityeth his own children*—Look upon us, Gracious Father, as indeed we are, poor, weak, ignorant, froward children, and pity us &c.

I beseech Thee, not for myself only, but for all Thy Children, y^t we may live worthy of ye relation wch we bear to Thee, that we may never wilfully offend so good, so tender, so gracious a Father—That we may love Thee, put our whole trust in Thee, depend upon Thy Power, Wisdom, Goodness and Prom. to Help us.

That we may serve Thee with pleasure—and in prospect of an Inheritance in Heaven.

That we may Fear thee not as slaves, but as children.

That we may abhorr and avoid every thing y^t may displease Thee.

Our Father—Thou who art ye Father of X^{ns} in a more especial manner—

Joyn^{ng} wth all other X^{ns} we are sure to be Heard—begging ye same Blessings for y^m as for our selves and as they do for us—

The Fath^r of X^{ns}.

Hallowed be Thy Name.

May all that call Thee Father walk worthy of y^t Relation—Glorify Thee by bearing *much fruit.* John xv. 8. *How excellent is Thy Name in all ye world. As for me I will be talking of Thy Praise &c.*

May the Name of God never be blasphemed thro' any word or deed or Fault of Me.

May we speak of Thee wth ye Reverence of Children. *Let every thing that hath breath praise ye Lord—Thou art worthy, O Lord, to receive Glory and Hon^r and Power, for Thou hast created all things*—Fill all our Hearts wth a zeal for Thy Glory. May we Glorify Thy Name, by leading Holy and X^n Lives, and by having a great regard for every thing that belongs to Thee, Thy Name, Thy Day, Thy Word, Thy House, Thine Ordinances, Thy Ministers—That others seeing our good works may Glorify Thee.

SUPPLEMENT No. XIV.

As we are Thy children it is our Duty to be concerned for Thy Glory and Hon^r.—

That we may shew ye greatest Hon^r and Respect to Thee and to whatever belongs to Thee—

God is pleased to place His Glory in ye good lives of X^{ns}.

Thy Kingdom Come.

Rule in my Heart as in Thy K.—govern me by Thy Laws and by Thy Sp^t—subdue our wills entirely to Thine.

May all ye Kings of ye Earth become Thy faithful subjects.

May all ye earth stand in [awe] of Thee and Fear Thy Name.

Subdue the Power of Satan and His Agents—Convert or Confound all ye enemies of Thy K.

May all ye unbelieving nations be converted—Make us Thy Subjects out of choice and love—

Prepare us O God for the coming of thy K. y^t we may pray for it more Heartily.

Bring us in Thy good time to the K. of Glory.

Subdue ye wickedness y^t hinders the increase and coming of. . . .

How dreadful is ye case of those y^t will not have Thee to Rule over y^m.

Hasten the time wch thou hast foretold, y^t *all nations w^m Thou hast made shall come and worship Thee and glorify Thy Name.*

Let all y^t own Thee for their K. become Thy faithful subjects.

Bless the pious endeav^{rs} of all those y^t strive to propagate—and prepare the Hearts of all men to receive—ye Gospel of [Thy] K.

The more His name is known ye more it will be Hallowd.

That His K. may be established in ye whole world—Let us endeav^r to expect it with comfort.

Subject us to Thyself daily more and more.

Reduce us into the way of obedience, and re-establish ye K. of G.

[18.] *Death, Sickness.*

Every Wise Man will be often thinking, w^t may become of Him w^n He dyes.

Certainty in this is a very desirable thing.

Death Bed. It is then a Man w^d give all ye world for Salvat^n, and yet while He has it in His Power to secure it, He will not be prevailed [on] to think of it. I hope I shall be no longer deaf to this call to a Timely Repentance, lest I sh^d never have ye Grace to Hearken to anoth^r.

I will (as I have been this day exhorted) consider ye condition of a Man, who w^n he comes to dye, has no will made, but leaves Contention and Law Suites for a Legacy to those y^t come after—who cannot comfort himself with any good He has done—who has done abundance of mischief, evil, Injustice, &c. &c. and has no more time to &c. &c.

Is it not an happss to be often put in mind of those things wch will come whether we think of y^m or not, and wch will render us Happy or Miserable for ever?

W^t an astonishing thing is it, to be surprised by Death eith^r in a course of Sin [or] in ye midst of Pleasures—in an utter forgetfulness of God and the Duty we owe to Him.

We sh^d never lose ye Thoughts, ye Sight of Death, bec. 'tis y^t wch must determine our Fate for ever.

Funeral. You are returning fr. a Fun. consider y^t for aught you know you may be ye next.

Death is coming fast upon us, and shall I not—

If I hope to dye well I must resolve to Live [well].

Here is a man y^t is gone to a much better or much worse place than this—His condition is not now to be mended or changed.

I will no longer flatter my self, y^t my time, my Repent. my Salv. will be always in my own power—This is ye time of Tryal, of Grace, of Rep. of Mercy.

If you have attended to w^t you have heard upon this Subj. it will teach you more than you are aware of, not to be over fond of a world, and Pleasures &c. wch you are so soon to leave—not to be proud, or gallant. . . .

[Some lines cut out.]

Death, Funeral, Sickness.

. . . . that of our Sav^r will satisfye the Justice of God. That it may be, if tis not our own fault, a passage to a much [better] world—As the deliverance of a Prisoner—As an End [of] all worldly troubles.

SUPPLE-
MENT
No. XIV.

W^t a sad condition must y^t man be in, who upon his death bed looks back and can see nothing in his life but w^t must render him unworthy of ye mercy of God.

As ever you hope to dye well, take care to Live well. The moment you dye, your condition is fix'd for ever.

Who amongst us will pretend to say y^t He is not in a few days to dye, and to go—

Our Happss or Misery beginning wⁿ we dye.

We are continued here only to be purify'd, our nature mended, [y^t] we may be made worthy and capable of ye Happss for wch God has designed us.

Sickness. That Sickness may not be a Torment to you, consider it as order'd by a Loving Father for your good. He could have taken you wthout notice. If He gives you time to...'tis ye effect of God's mercy—You are just w^t you sh^d be while you are chasten'd and bear wth Patience. You are sure God loves you, you are not so sure of y^t wⁿ you are wthout Chastism^t.

DEATH. A Timely Prepar. for Death frees us from all feares. If I spend my Life as I sh^d do, I shall be [able] to say wth St. Paul, *To me to dye is gain.* Phil. [i. 21.]

If we consider Death as ye night of ye day wch God has given us as a State of Tryal, to work out our [Salvation] and y^t after ye night no man [can] work—How serious sh^d this make us, least &c. And if we consider [also?] y^t [it is?] the begining of Eternity—Tis still more dreadful to one who is not prepar'd for it—Tis for this reason death is call'd ye K. of Terrors—*The Terrors of Death,* ye greatest of all Terrors, *are faln upon Me.*

And at Midnight there was a crye, The Bridegroom cometh. See my Priv. Devot^{ns} p. 238.^s

And ye Door was shut, see p. 238, ibid. We stay too [late?] wⁿ we stay till ye door is shut.

I hope I shall never lose ye sight of y^t Important [?] hour, wⁿ &c.

What Terror, w^t afflicting thoughts will arise in his Breast, wⁿ he comes to dye, who has done no good.

I see y^t ye Sentence of Death is already pass'd upon Me. See Private Devotions, p. 250.^s

^s [These references are made to MS. i. Sacra Privata.]

W⁴ you strip death of its Terror? Consider it then as a Righteous Sentence pass'd by God upon all men for their offences—and wᶜʰ He will accept of, in Union with yᵗ [of His Son?] for all our offences yᵗ we have truly repented of. That [then it?] will be no more than yᵉ Release of a Prisoner, and end of all Miserys of Life—As a Passage to a better World—as going to receive our Wages &c.

SUPPLEMENT No. XIV.

Luk. xii. 36. *And ye yoʳselves as Men waiting for their Lord.* Who will always endeavʳ to be found in yᵉ way of their duty, yᵗ yᵉ Lord may say, *Well done, faithful Servant.*

Luke xii. 40. *Be ye ready—For yᵉ Son of Man cometh at an Hour wⁿ ye think not*—Is not this and yᵉ unexpected Deaths of so many enough to convince us, yᵗ it is yᵉ greatest folly to assure our selves of one Year, of one Month, of one Day? Let us rather count our selves of yᵉ Number of those who &c.

Miserable, very miserable will yᵗ man be wᵐ death overtakes eithʳ doing evil, or doing nothing yᵗ he ought to do—can we say yᵗ yᵉ generality of Xⁿˢ believe this?

Happy yᵗ soul wᶜʰ Death finds Rich in Good works, not a pin matter then, whethʳ they were Rich in Gold, in Lands, &c.

Rev. iii. 3. *Thou shalt not know wᵗ Hour I will come—* Xt. says this—yᵗ we have not one Hour certain.

Preserve in us a lively sense of yᵉ world to come.

Let us endeavʳ by a sincere repentance to prevent those Reproches wᶜʰ otherwise our consciences will upbraid us wᵗʰ at yᵉ Hour of Death.

I was sent into yᵉ world upon Tryal, let me seriously consider, How I have lived—

The consequence of a Surprise will be most dreadful. Have I made my Peace wᵗʰ God? do I hope for Mercy? Have I wean'd my affections from this world?

Have I got rid of all those evil Habits wᶜʰ I contracted?

Shall I live as if I came into yᵉ world only to lead a useless life?

We are all hastening towards Death—as the day dos towards evening.

The sentence of death is already passed upon every one of

us, and God only knows w^n y^t sentence will be put in execution.

Then follows Eternity—Eternity of Happss if &c. Shall I not consider why God sent me into the world?

He y^t dos not think of these things till a few days before He dyes, has but a few days to make His Acc^{ts} and His Peace wth God.

W^t argum^{ts} can be made use of to comfort a man who has lived an unthoughtful, useless, sinful life? and is just going to give an Acc^t?

God may be provoked to shorten my days w^n He sees y^t I make so ill use of y^m.

I will not say, w^n I dye there is an end of me, so far from y^t that then begins our Happss or Misery. *They y^t have done good, &c.*

I will not, I dare not depend upon ye goodness of God, if I go on to abuse His Goodness. God is just as well as merciful—And He has declar'd how far His Mercy, and to w^m it shall be shewed.

We are Inform'd of Esau y^t He *found no Place for Repentance tho' he sought it wth Tears.*

The termes of Salv. are fix't and certain. *With^t Holiness no man shall see ye Lord.*

Death, Funeral, Sickness.

If I deferr my Rep. my Case will grow every day more desperate.

I will remember ye Judgm^t of ye unfruitful Tree—*Cut it down, why* &c. This may be passed upon me w^n I least think of it.

My Case may be so bad, y^t tho' Noah, Danl. . . . I cannot with^t astonishm^t think of being for ever miserable.

I will just tell you w^t a wise man will wish He had done w^n He comes to dye—See ye Serm. *The night cometh when no Man &c.* latter end^t. I know I cannot do these things in a Hurry, and if they are not done before I dye I am undone, undone for ever.

Math. xxii. *And He stood speechless:* surpris'd by death before ye work of life be half done......

^{t} [i.e. Serm. xxix. on St. John ix. 4, near the conclusion, vol. ii. 324—327, in this ed.]

And w^n such a Person comes to dye, He lookes back with thankfulness upon ye Fav^r He has all His life rec^d fr. God— and with these thoughts He flings Himself into ye Armes of ye Divine Mercy and Goodness.

Supplement
No. XIV.

On ye other Hand, they who have done violence to their own lives by their intemperance, cannot but fear ye Punishm^t of those who have laid violent Hands upon y^{ms}.

Wicked Men. Tis true ye World will be no losers w^n such men go out of it.

Violent Death. More people dye violent deaths than we think—all y^t shorten their lives by Intemperance are properly enough *Felo de se.*

A time will come w^n all purposes to reform will be of no service to us, and who knowes but that time is just at Hand?

We have little Faith and Knowlege of w^t must come Hereafter if we can think of Death with^t concern.

We say every day one to another—"How suddenly this man dyed, How is this other taken off in ye midst of His sins. How young this other &c." But who takes warning? who says to Himself—"That wch is said of this man to-day may to-morrow be said of me?"

Death wch to good Men [is] the begining of their [joy] is to ye wicked the Begining of their Misery.

Need any man who knows Himself to be under the sentence of Death, and [that he] has no right of living one day longer, be advised to prepare for Death, yet this is ye case of every man living.

Luk. xxi. 23. Q. [Quesnel.]

It is not now the question as it was among Heathens, what will become of men w^n they dye—Our Lord X^t has told us, and we must believe Him, for He came fr. God—*They y^t have done good &c.*

1 Thess. i. 2. THE DAY OF Y^E LORD COMETH AS A THIEF IN Y^E NIGHT.

Thy Love w^d not have us surprised, therefore we are so often admonished &c. Let us never delude our S. [? souls.] Let us never delude our Selves wth imagining Hopes of a long life and with warning sufficient to prevent a surprise.

N.B. See Bp. Taylor's Life of Xt. p. 406, § 21, 22. *Dutys*

Supplement No. XV. *of a Sick and Dying person [on Restitution, and holy purposes.]*

Blessed is He y^t hath lived well and ended Happily.

XV.

[*Fragments from a MS. Book, marked* 10, *apparently by Dr. Wilson.*]

Of Prayer.

Pray^r is the desire of an Heart w^h ye H. Sp^t has made sensible of its Poverty, misery, and inability to help its self, beging of God to make Her w^t she ought to be.

May I always present myself before God with a firm Faith in His Mercy and Promises; with great *Reverence* to His infinite Majesty;—with the Humility of an Offender and a Beggar,—And with a Full purpose of obeying His commands.

May the Thoughts of *Death* and *Eternity* quicken my Devotions; my *Wants* make me earnest;—my Backslidings make me persevere; and may I wait wth patience, and leave it to God *How* and *Wⁿ* He will grant what I Pray for.

By Pray^r we own y^t we depend on God; and that we ought to be thankful for w^t we receive.

This will naturally lead us to *Love God,* and to *Fear* to displease Him;—For wch Reason He expects we sh^d Pray for every thing we want.

Pray with^t ceasing. Have God much in y^r Thoughts. He y^t w^d be *serious* in His Prayers must be *serious* at other times.

Pray^r puts us in mind of our wants, our misery and our danger—of the Power, Wisdom, Goodness and Promises of God.

God will not regard the Pray^{rs} of those who have no regard for His Commands.

Never undertake any thing y^t you are ashamed to Pray for, or to beg of God to Prosper.

All Power to do good is from God.

Qualifications. To be truly sensible of our Wants—To ask with the Humility of one who submits to His Father's Will. Never to Pray for any thing that it is unworthy of God to give or prosper—To attend to w^t we Pray for—To be assur'd y^t God will give us what is best for us.

Promises. *Call upon Me in the day of trouble, and I will deliver thee, and thou shalt glorify Me.* Ps. l. [15.]

Verily I say unto you, w^{t}soever ye shall ask ye Fath^r in My Name, He will give it you. Jo. xvi. 23.

Scripture Prayers—*Humble, Earnest, Plain*—Short and Full of Assurance—Such as follow.—*Lord if Thou wilt Thou canst make me clean:*—*Lord, help me:*—*Have mercy on me, Thou Son of David.*—*Have mercy upon my son, for he is a Lunatic.*—*Jesus master have mercy on us:*—*Say the word, and my servant shall be whole: &c.......*

Prayer. Is ye desire of a Soul, sensible of its own wants, misery and danger, and Beging of God to pity and Help it—He alone can do it.

Prayer. The condition wch God requires of us w^n we ask any fav^r is, y^t we earnestly desire it.

A Short Paraphrase on the Lord's Prayer.

Our Father which art in Heaven. In whom we live, and move, and have our being.

As a Father pityeth His own Children, so the Lord Pityeth y^m y^t Fear Him.

We are thine by Adoption, O let us be Thine by the choice of our own will, and ye Holiness of our Lives.

Eph. v. 1. *Be ye followers of God as dear Children.*

I will arise and go unto my Fath^r and say unto Him, Father I have sinned ag^{nst} Heav^n and before Thee, and am not worthy to be called thy Son.

Our Father, w^n therefore He denyes w^t we Pray for, we may be sure it w^d not be for our good.

Let Thy Spt. witness to our Sp^t y^t we are Thy Child^n. Enable us to crye *Abba Fath^r*.

What manner of Love is this that we sh^d be called the Sons of God? (1 Jo. 3, 1.)—*O that we may not sin, knowing that we are accounted Thine.* (Ecclus. v.) [Wisd. xv. 2.] That all X^{ns} may live worthy of this glorious Relation.—That we may Love, Fear, and Obey Thee, not as slaves but as Children.—That we may depend upon Thy Fatherly *Good-*

SUPPLEMENT No. XV.

ness to do what is best for us,—Thy *Wisdom* to choose for us,—Thy *Power* to help and defend us.

Hallowed be Thy Name. Thou art worthy to receive Hon^r and Glory and Power; For Thou hast created all things, and it is by Thy will that they all subsist. Rev. iv. 11.

Blessed be the Lord for all His mercys bestowed upon us.

Let y^r Light so shine before men y^t they may see y^r good works, and glorifye y^r Father which is in Heaven.

Whether ye eat or drink, or whatever ye do, do all to the Praise and Glory of God.

In this is my Fath^r glorifyed, y^t ye bring forth much fruit. Jo. xv. 8.

This is the Name of our God and Fath^r. "The Lord, ye Lord God, merciful and gracious, Long suffering, and abundant in goodness and Truth,—Keeping mercy for thousands, forgiving iniquity and transgression and sin, and y^t will by no meanes clear the guilty."

All that know Thy Name will put their trust in Thee.

They y^t Love Thy Name shall be Joyful in Thee.

May Thy Glory, O Heavenly Father, be the end of all our Actions.—May we never dishon^r Thee by Word or Deed.—May we all glorify Thee in a faithful discharge of the Dutys of our Calling.—That others, seeing our good works, may glorify our Father which is in Heav^n.—Fill all our Hearts with a zeal for Thy glory, *and for every thing y^t belongs to Thee. Let every thing y^t hath breath Praise ye Lord.*

Thy Kingdom come. May the Kingdomes of the world become the Kingdomes of the Lord, and of His Christ, that He may reign for ever and ever.

Do Thou, O King of Saints, reign in all our Hearts by the Spirit of Grace, and by the Pow^r of Thy Grace subdue whatev^r is amiss in us.

May Thy Kingdom of Grace here fit us for Thy Kingdom of Glory hereafter.

Bless the pious Endeav^{rs} of all that strive to propagate the Interests of Thy Kingdom;—And, by Thy grace, prepare the Hearts of Men to submit to it. May all y^t own Thee for their King, become Thy Faithful Subjects.—Deliver the world in Thy good time, From the Tyrany and Power of evil spirits; That all Nations may worship Thee and glorify Thy

Name. O subdue that wickedness wch hinders the coming of Thy Kingdom.

Thy Will be done in Earth as it is in Heav^n.

O that we may all be *fill'd with ye knowledge of Thy Will, in all Wisdom and Spiritual Understanding;—That we may walk worthy of the Lord, unto all pleasing.* Col. i. 9.

Blessed be Thou, O Heavenly Fath^r, for making Thy will known to us, in Thy Holy Word.—O give us *Light* to see, and Hearts to close with, and a *Power* to do Thy Will.—May we ever resign our Wills, and our Desires, to Thine, and the Orders of Thy Providence, as the very best y^t can be done for us, and for the world.—Subdue in us, whatever is contrary to Thy will;—and bring our wills into an entire subject^n to Thine; and to all the Orders of Thy Providence.

1 Thess. iv. 3. *This is the Will of God, even y^r Sanctific^n.*

Rev. xv. 3. *Just and True are Thy Ways, O King of Saints.*

1 Pet. iv. 19. *Let y^m y^t suffer according to ye will of God commit the Keeping of their Soules unto Him, as unto a faithful Creator.*

Let Thy will be the measure of all our desires. Let us never dispute Thy wisdom or Thy goodness.

Give me grace, O God, to Resign my will to Thine, to be directed and govern'd and disposed of both in body [and soul] by Thine Infinite Wisdom, Power and Love.

Give us this day our daily Bread.

Give us, O Heavenly Father, the necessarys and comforts of this Life, wth Thy Blessing. But above all things, give us the *Bread* y^t came down from Heav^n—The *Bread* that giveth Life unto the World.—The *Bread* that nourisheth to Eternal Life.—May we never forget that we depend upon Thee, for Life, and Breath, and all things.

We cast all our care upon Thee, knowing that Thou, being our Father, carest for us.

Give us grace to impart to such as are in want of what Thou hast given us more than our daily Bread: And withall give us contented mindes.

We offer, gracious Father, This Pray^r for all Thy children, as well as for ourselves.

Having Food and Raiment let us be therewith content.

Give us neither Poverty nor Riches, but feed us with food convenient for us.

Take from us all distrust, all fear and too much Thoughtfulness for the time to come—never distrusting Thy care.

Let us live as strangers and Pilgrims on Earth, content with Necessarys, and thankful for w^t Thou givest us.

Forgive us our Trespasses, as we Forgive them that trespass against us.

Thou, O Father, art good, and ready to forgive;—Thou art all mercy to us, O make us all so to one another. And that we may *Forgive,* and *Give,* and *Love,* as becomes the Disciples of Jesus Xt.

Make us ever sensible of our own Infirmitys, y^t we may treat others with Compassion.

We beseech Thee for all y^t are our Enemyes, not for vengeance, but for mercy, for their Repentance and Pardon, and for their Etern. Happiness.

May our Enemies ever have a place in our Prayers, and in Thy Mercy.

Even the Power to perform this merciful condition of Pardon, must be from Thy Grace, O Heavenly Fath^r.

O Lord forgive us, or w^t good will our Life do us? Give us the great gift of Charity, lest our Pray^r be turned into Sin.

Forgive us our Trespasses, wch are many and great, and render us unworthy of the least of Thy mercys.

With what measure ye mete, it shall be measured to you again.

Matth. xviii. 35. *So likewise shall my Heavenly Fath^r do unto you, if ye from y^r Hearts Forgive not every one his Broth^r their Trespasses.*

If thine enemy Hung^r Feed Him &c. Let us not discover that we have enemies any other way than by doing them more good than to others.

And lead us not into Temptation.

Leave us not, O Heavenly Fath^r, to ourselves, or to our own choices, lest we run into Tempt^n.

Support us in all our Saving Tryals, and grant that they may yield the peaceable Fruits of Righteousness.

Let not any confidence in ourselves provoke Thee, O God, to leave us to ourselves.

Thou, O Heavenly Father, knowest our Infirmitys, and the Power of our Enemys, be not, we Pray Thee, wanting to us in the Hour of Temptat^n.

In all Temptations succour us, that no Sin may ever get Dominion over us.

Fortify our souls, O most Powerful God, against all the Tempt. of the world, the Flesh and the Devil, for Xt's sake.

Jam. i. 12. *Count it all Joy when ye fall into divers Temptations, or Tryals.*

2 Pet. ii. 9. *The Lord knoweth how to deliver the godly out of Temptation.*

Matth. xxvi. 41. *Watch and Pray y^t ye enter not into Temptat^n.*

1 Cor. x. 13. *Let Him y^t thinketh y^t he stands, take heed lest he falles.*

[Heb. xii. 7.] *If ye endure Chastening, God dealeth wth you as with sons. For w^t son is he w^m ye Fath^r &c.*

Jam. i.12. *Blessed is ye man y^t endureth Tempt^n, for w^n He is try'd he shall receive a Crown of Life, wch the Lord hath promised to y^m y^t Love Him.*

Give us grace to avoid and Flee from all occasions of sin.

But deliver us from evil.

Grant, O Heavenly Fath^r That the great Adversary of our Soules may never find us off our guard, or from under Thy Protection.

Deliver us fr. the Evil of Sin, and fr. the Evil of Punishm. —From y^e *Guilt*, and fr. y^e *Power*, of Sin.

Grant y^t we may never fall into ye Sins we have Repented of.

Enable us to escape the Corrupt^n y^t is in the world thro' Lust, y^t we may be partakers of ye Divine Nature.

In all our saving Tryals give us grace to persevere, and overcome, to Thy Glory.

1 Pet. v. 8. *Be sober, be vigilant, bec. y^r Adversary the Devil as a roaring Lyon walketh ab^t seeking w^m He may devour.*

SUPPLE-
MENT
No. XV.

2 Cor. xii. 9. *My grace is sufficient for Thee, for my strength is made perfect in weakness.*

Phil. iv. 13. *I can do all things thro' Xt. y^t strengthens me.*

Deliver us from Sin and Wickedness, from our Ghostly Enemy, and from everlasting death.

For Thine is the Kingdom, and the Power, and the Glory, for ever and ever. Amen.

So we Thy Servants shall adore and advance the greatness of Thy Kingdome,—The Power of Thy Divine Majesty,—The Glory of Thy Mercy,—From Generation to Generation.—For Ever. Amen.

Thine is ye Kingdom, The whole Creation is Thine, and under Thy Governm^t.—Thine is the Power; Thou canst do whatever we Pray for, or stand in need of.—Thou canst cause Thy name to be sanctify'd in all the earth; and set up Thy Kingdom in all the world, and in all our Hearts.—Thou canst cause Thy Will to be done in Earth, as it is done in Heav^n, and incline all to submit to it.—Thou canst give us all things necessary for our souls and bodies.—Thou, and Thou alone, canst forgive us our sins; and dispose us to forgive one another.—Thou canst save us in the Day of Tempt^n and Deliver us from the Powers of Darkness, from ye Corrupt^n of our own Hearts, From an Evil World, and from Eternal Death.—To *Thee*, therefore, and to Thy *Blessed Son* and Holy Spirit, be Glory, Praise, and Thanksgiving for ever and ever. Amen. So be it.

St. Joh. xvi. 23. *Verily I say unto you, Whatsoever ye shall ask ye Fath^r in my name He will give it you.*

In full assurance of this, I most humbly Beseech Thee, O Heavenly Fath^r, to give me—The Spirit of Supplication and Prayer—The Graces of a True Repentance, of a Sincere Conversion;—of a saving Faith, of a teachable Temper, and an Obedient Will;—Of Humility and Self-Resignation; of Mortification and Self-Denyal.

Grant, O God and Father, according to Thy Son's Promise,—That I may be delivered from all Blindness and Hardness of Heart;—That I may feel the diseases y^t I lab^r under, and the woundes that sin hath made in my soul; and thankfully embrace the meanes wch Thy mercy hath provided for my recovery.

Grant, I humbly beseech Thee, that I may never *grieve* Thy *H. Spirit* by wch I have been sanctify'd;—That, thro' His Assistance, I may resist all the sinful Appetites of my corrupt Nature;—And y^t I may escape ye Corrupt^n y^t is in ye world thro' Lust—*The Lust of ye Flesh, ye Lust of ye Eye, and Pride of Life.*

Grant, that I may hunger and thirst after Righteousness;—That Christ may dwell in my heart by Faith;—That I may be rooted and grounded in Love:—And finally; That I may be restored to Thy image;—That the image of Satan may be destroyed in me;—That the end of all my actions may be Thy glory;—That my Heart may be entirely Thine, and that I may continue Thine for ever.—All wch I beg for J. Xt. his sake, the Son of Thy Love. Amen.

O that it may appear by my life y^t *Christ is Form'd in me,* as it appears by the Branch of the Vine, that it has its life and nourishment from ye tree in wch it is grafted.

[u] 1 Tim. ii. 1. *I exhort.... That Supplications, Prayers, Intercessions, and giving of Thanks be made for all men &c.*

O God, ye Creator and Redeem^r of all men, have mercy upon all whom Thou hast made and redeemed.

Ejaculations.

Let the Blood of J. Xt. O God, move Thee to have mercy upon a miserable Sinner.

Christian Perfection. May Thy Almighty and Powerful Grace make me as Perfect as Thou hast commanded me to be.

[u] [This and the following entries occur at wide intervals in MS. No. 10; the rest is a blank. A few entries have been omitted in the other MSS., as more convenient for insertion in the Memoir of the Bishop's Life.]

END OF "SACRA PRIVATA."

MAXIMS OF PIETY AND MORALITY.

[From MS. 5. p. 1*.]

1. *In Deo Quies.*
2. *Nervi et Artus sapientiæ, non temere credere*[a].
3. All is equal to a Soul truly resigned.
4. Serious Piety ye best security agst wicked error.
5. He y^t has a good Conscience has most skill in true Divinity.
6. The only way to peace is to give ye Heart entirely to God.
7. Common Practice ye worst Rule in Religion.
8. He has ye best Testimony of His sincerity who shews his Faith by its fruits.
9. It is not great, but useful Knowledg, y^t makes a Wise Man.
10. Perfect Resignation ye surest way to Heaven.
11. We receive Grace in ye same Degree we desire it[b].
12. Good purposes cost nothing and are worth nothing, wthout they are put in execution.
13. We can always do what is proper to our condition, and that is w^t is most pleasing to God.
14. The only way to perfection, is, to Live in ye Presence of God.
15. He y^t recounts his own good works, does but reckon up ye Gifts of God.
16. Have no other View but to please God.
17. Receive every thing y^t happens as God's appointment.
18. Those y^t commend our Faults, design to make a jest of us.

[p. 2*.]

19. All knowledge is vain y^t tends not to ye Practice of some duty.

---

[a] [Epicharmus, ap. Cic. ad Att. i. 19. Νᾶφε καὶ μέμνασ' ἀπιστεῖν· ἄρθρα ταῦτα τῶν φρενῶν. Bp. Wilson took it from the tract called "Q. Cic. de Petitione Consulatus," § 10.]

[b] [This recurs in the same MS., p. 2.]

20. He yt fancys he is perfect, may lose yt by Pride wch he attained by grace.

21. Nothing that pleases or displeases God is to be accounted little.

22. He lives to no purposes, who glorifyes not God.

23. Our greatest Hopes sh{d} lie beyond ye Grave.

24. No Man must go to Heav{n} who has not sent his heart thither before.

25. Be not ashamd of being a X{n}.

26. St. Aug. had ye sense of ye following verses writ in His Dining Room:—

"The Man in Railing bold, in Censure Free,
  Shall never be a welcom guest to me[c]."

27. The Change of a Sinner's Heart is as great a Miracle as any J. X{t} wrought on earth.

28. He yt is His own Pupil has a Fool for His Tutor.

29. A Man sacrifices to His own Net[d] w{n} He has taken nothing but dirt and Filth.

30. [e] *Concerning Maxims,* such as sh{d} not only be Believed but ever present upon ye mind:—

That Sin is the greatest evil.

That no pleasure sh{d} tempt one to commit ye least Sin.

That there will be a Future Judgm{t}, as sure, &c.

That a good Conscience is an inestimable Treasure.

31. [f] *Virtus est Vitium fugere.*

32. [g] *Christian Constancy.*

For having learn'd their [his] due Contempt to throw
  Upon those Interests and Baits which make
The Biass'd Hearts of men unmanly grow,
  And Cowardly Sin's Sneaking By Paths take,
In spite of all ye world wch dares say No,
He in the King of Heav'n's High way will go[h].

---

[c] [Possidius, Vita Aug. c. 22. "Contra pestilentiam humanæ consuetudinis in mensa scriptum ita habebat:—
Quisquis amat dictis absentum rodere vitam,
Hanc mensam indignam noverit esse sibi."]

[d] [See Habak. i. 16.]

[e] [MS. 5, p. 3*. otherwise blank, as is the whole of p. 4*.]

[f] In MS. 5*, a page otherwise blank, as is the whole of p. 6*.]

[g] [Ibid., p. 7*. This and p. 8* have apparently been inserted from another MS., or another portion of this MS.]

[h] [Beaumont's Psyche, canto xxiii. stanza 26.]

33. The King's Throne establish'd in Righteousness.
   Since to thine own Commands just duty Thou
     Expectest from thy Subjects; let thy Neck
   Not scorn to thine own Maker's Yoke to Bow;
     The precedent may dangerous prove, and wrack
   Thy Throne and Kingdom, If Thy People Read
   Highest Rebellion's lesson in their Head [i].

34. *Wicked Thanks.*
   Thrusting loud Thanks on God, as if their bold
   Sedition had been Patronized by Him.

35. *Anarchy.*
                        What Commonwealth
   Can Justify its name, where Subjects may
   Command, and Princes dare not but obey [k]?

36. *The Shepherds visiting X^t. &c.*
   Heaven sent us hither, and we need not fear
   But Heaven is able to supply our care [l].

[MS. 5. p. 8*.]

37. *Fleres, si scires unum tua tempora mensem,*
    Rides, cum non sit forsitan una Dies.

38. *Quicquid agunt alii sis memor Ipse Tui.*

39. *Cum duplicantur Lateres tunc venit Moses* [m].

40. *Seven Precepts of ye Sons of Noah:—*
    1. To Renounce Idols and Idolatrous Worship.
    2. To Worship ye True God.—The Sabbath.
    3. Not to commit Murther.
    4. Not to commit Fornication [or] Uncleaness.
    5. Not to Steal.
    6. To administer Justice, and Punish Malefact^{rs}.
    7. Not to eat Flesh with ye blood, or a member taken fr. a Beast alive.

41. *Fear of Man.* He that complains of ye Secular Power, is Ignorant of the Power of God.

42. In Time of Persecution for Righteousnes's sake, i.e. For doing one's duty. 2 Chron. xvi. 9, "The eyes of the Lord run to and fro thro' ye whole earth, to shew Himself strong in behalf of them whose [heart is perfect towards Him."]

---

[i] [Beaumont's Psyche, canto iii. stanza 157.]
[k] [Ibid., canto v. stanza 188.]
[l] [Ibid., canto vii. stanza 206.]
[m] [A Jewish proverb, answering to the English, "Man's necessity, God's opportunity." See Trench on Proverbs, p. 42. Cf. Exod. v. 9—19.]

43. [n]*Natural Religion, Moral Philosophy, Reason without Grace.* The vanity of all these will appear when men come to make use of them.

To a man, for instance, in affliction, in disgrace, &c., say all the fine things that Marcus Antoninus, Seneca, &c., ever said, and see if his mind will rest satisfied with them.

It is the grace of God w[h] makes the difference betwixt the Scriptures and the sayings of philosophers; the one is a two-edged sword; the other, wanting the Spirit, is a dead letter.

Hear the fair confession of one who was accounted a master of reason, &c.

D[r]. Radcliffe, in a letter to the Earl of Denbigh, Oct. 15, 1714, has these words: "Your Lordship is too well acquainted with my temper, to imagine that I could bear the reproaches of my friends, and the threats of my enemies, without laying them deeply to heart, especially when there are no grounds for the one, nor foundation for the other. [o] Give me credit w[n] I say, these considerations alone have shortened my days. . . The menacing letter inclosed will shew you fr. w[t] quart[r] my Death comes. . . I find these insupportable. And have experienced that tho' there [are] Repellent Medicines for diseases of y[e] Body, those of the Mind are too strong and impetuous for the feeble Resistance of the most powerful Artist," &c. A very fair Confession, one w[d]. think, fr. one who found y[e] truth of this, by experience, —for He dyed immediately [p].

---

[n] [Some portion of this, being lost in the MS., is supplied from the 4to. Ed., Works, ii. 354.]

[o] [MS. 5. p. 7. The pages numbered by Dr. Wilson are apparently torn out until we come to this, which is itself a little mutilated. It may seem that the pages now marked with * were considered by him as fly leaves, and passed over.]

[p] [See "Dr. Radcliffe's Life and Letters," 4th Ed. Lond. 1736. "Basil Fielding, 4th Earl of Denbigh, died March 18, 17$\frac{14}{15}$, having been Master of the Horse to Prince George of Denmark, and Teller of the Exchequer under George I."—Jacob's Peerage, ii. 511.

The letter, here reprinted at length, tells its own sad story better than it could be told any other way:—

"*Cashalton, Oct.* 15, 1714.
"My very good Lord,
"This being the last time that, in all probability, I shall ever put pen to paper, I thought it my duty to employ it in writing to you, since I am now going to a place from whence I can administer no advice to you, and whither you, and all the rest who survive me, are obliged to come sooner or later.

"Your Lordship is too well acquainted with my temper to imagine, that I could bear the reproaches of my friends and threats of my enemies without laying them deeply at heart; especially since there are no grounds for the one, nor foundation for the other; and you will give me credit when I say these considerations alone have shortened my days.

44. *Christian Virtue. Consists in order,* viz., in letting every Duty have its proper place and concern. The first Duty, for Instance, of a Clergy-man, is to take care of His Flock; of a Magistrate, to discharge His office; of a Parent, to take care of His children; of a Master, His Family; of a Servant, to do His Master's business faithfully. To engage in oth^r business before they acquit y^{ms} of these, is to go agst order, and all their virtues are useless.

45. *Whatever ye w^d y^t men sh^d do, &c.* To make this Rule of use, we sh^d suffer our Passions (*wouldings*) to plead freely on both sides, (as Councellors, not as Judges); see w^t can be said on one side as well as 'tother. This w^d calm our

"I dare persuade myself that the reports which have been raised of me, relating to my non-attendance on the Queen [Anne] in her last moments, are received by you, as by others of my constant and assured friends, with an air of contempt and disbelief, and could wish they made as little impression on me. But I find them to be insupportable, and have experienced, that though there are repellent medicines for diseases of the body, those of the mind are too strong and impetuous for the feeble resistance of the most powerful artist.

"In a word, the decays of nature tell me that I cannot live fourteen days; and the menacing letter inclosed will tell you from what quarter my death comes. Give me leave, therefore, to be in earnest, once for all, with my very good lord, and to use my endeavours to prolong your life, that cannot add a span's length to my own. Your Lordship knows how far an air of jollity has obtained amongst you and your acquaintance, and how many of them in a few years have dy'd martyrs to excess; let me conjure you therefore, for the good of your own soul, and the preservation of your health, and the benefit of the publick, to deny yourself the destructive liberties you have hitherto taken, and which, I must confess, with a heart full of sorrow, I have been too great a partaker of in your company. You are to consider (O that I had done so!) that men, especially of your exalted rank, are born to nobler exercises than those of eating and drinking; and that by how much the more eminent your station is, by so much the more accountable will you be for the discharge of it. Nor will your duty to God, your country, or yourself permit you to anger the first, in robbing the second of a patriot and defender, by not taking a due care of the third; which will be accounted downright murder in the eyes of that incensed Deity, that will most assuredly avenge it.

"The pain that afflicts my nerves, interrupts me from making any other request to you, than that your Lordship would give credit to the words of a dying man, who is fearful that he has been in a great measure an abetter and encourager of your intemperance, and would therefore, in these his last moments, when he is most to be credited, dehort you from the pursuit of it; and that, *in these days of your youth,* (for you have many years yet to live if you do not hasten your own death,) you would give ear to the voice of the preacher, whom you and I, with the rest of our company, have, in the midst of our riotous debauches, made light of for saying, '*Rejoice, O young man, in thy youth, and let thy heart cheer thee in the days of thy youth, and walk in the ways of thy heart, and in the sight of thine eyes: but know thou, that for all these things God will bring thee to judgment.*' On which day, when the hearts of all men shall be laid open, may you and I, and all that sincerely repent of acting contrary to the revealed will in this life, reap the fruits of our sorrows for our misdeeds in a blessed resurrection, which is the hearty prayer of,

"*My very good Lord,*

"*Your Lordship's most obedient and most obliged Servant,*

"JOHN RADCLIFFE."

He died Nov. 1.—Biogr. Brit.]

Resentments, make us *good-natured*, then Reason will be able to, qualify'd to, Judge what in such or such a case w^d be equally good and best for all Mankind, for Buyers and Sellers, for Masters and Servants, for Poor and Rich, &c. [MS. 5. p. 8.]

46. *Eternity.* Duration without beginning and without end. [om. in 4to.]

47. *Eternity.* Consider things as they have Regard to Eternity.

48. *World.* It may be used, but not enjoy'd.

49. *Riches.* He y^t considers an Estate as a Trust only, will often think of ye Acc^t He is to give.

50. *End of the World.* Now ye scenes change so fast, and all in such an hurry, 'tis most likely y^t ye opera is near an end. [om. in 4to.]

51. *Difficultys of X^{ty}.* If Grace will make everything easy, and if Grace may be had for asking, a Xⁿ has no reason to say y^t any thing y^t is commanded Him is hard.

52. *Take up the Cross.* This is design'd as a Peculiar Fav^r to X^{ns}. All men since the Fall are subject to unavoidable miseries, all ye difference is, X^{ns} suffer in obedience to ye will of God, wch makes y^m easy, while unbelievers suffer ye same things with an uneasy will and mind.

53. *Riches.* If X^{ty} forbids the *Love of Riches*, it is because ye Author of it knew that they are ye Root of all evil. [p. 9.]

54. *Charity.* A sincere and universal charity the most certain Rule never to be wanting in w^t we owe to others.

55. *Civility.* There is a civility y^t proceeds fr. vanity, there is also a civility y^t is [the] effect of Humility, Charity, and Zeal.

56. *Obedience.* The Dignity of the Master we serve ought to make our obedience most free and cheerful.

57. *Xⁿ Religⁿ.* To follow our own will, our Passions and our senses, is that w^d make us miserable in this world; 'Tis for this Reason, and that we may have a remedy for all our troubles, y^t X^{ty} obliges us to submit our will, our Passions and our Desires to ye will and Law of God.

58. *Libertin.* Why are too many pleased to Hear Religⁿ ridiculed, is it bec. 'tis ridiculous? No, but 'tis bec. men's lives are corrupt and they wish secretly y^t there were no truth in R.

59. *Xⁿ Religⁿ.* One of ye greatest proofes of Religⁿ is

this, y^t no man ever found a perfect certainty on ye side of Irreligion.

[p. 10.] 60. *Religion.* If a man has no Religion 'tis bec. He will have none. He loves Darkness better than Light, and He will not ask ye Gr. of God to assist and enlighten Him.

61. *Creed.* 'Tis not ye Evidence of its Articles I sh^d require, but Their Truth, i.e. whether I have undeniable Reasons that God has revealed y^m.

62. *Libertines.* The way to stop their mouths is to oblige y^m to lay down Principles and to prove y^m.

63. *Faith.* 'Tis Faith I want, saith a Libertine. But then he should know, that 'tis ye Gift of God. That it must be ask'd, and y^t a man must put Himself into a way to obtain it.

64. *Prayer.* A sinner y^t prays for any oth^r mercys, but ye Grace of Repentance and Conversion, must not expect to be heard.

65. *Virtues.* Account nothing a virtue but w^t God requires of you, wth respect to your station.

66. *X^n Duties.* Take care to practise ye Dutys of yor Station and Condition: Patience in Adversity—Content in Poverty—Humility in Prosperity—a Forgiving temper w^n at variance—Watchfulness in ye midst of Temptations—To [p. 11.] avoid vexation in going to Law.

67. *A desire to please G^d*—Is y^t in which X^n virtue consists; do this and mind not what the world Judges of you.

68. *Knowledge.* God is ye Auth^r of Light, to seek to be convinc'd of ye Truthes of Relig^n with^t asking God's Grace, shews y^t a man dos not know ye very first Principles of Relig^n.

69. *Truth.* Be not afraid of seeing the Truth, if you are God will not shew it.

70. *H. Scriptures.* He y^t Reads y^m with a purpose to profit by y^m, will find y^m clear, and his duty determind.

71. *Corrupt Heart.* The good X^n is not one who has no Inclination to vice, (for we have all of us ye seed of every vice in our Heart,) but who being sensible of such Inclinations, does not allow y^m to spring up and grow into ill actions.

72. *Pleasures, Amusemen^{ts}*. No pleasure is innocent wch hinders us from minding our salvatn.

73. *Shame.* Be not asham'd of being a X^n.

74. *Calamities, publick.* W^n we pray for ye removal of [p. 12.] them, we sh^d first lay aside ye sins y^t are ye cause of them.

75. *Apparel.* Religion only recommends modesty, and condemns singularity.

76. *Apparel.* All such dresses are forbidden wch incite irregular desires.

77. *Tests of Relig^n.* Such only may be depended on, as render a X^n more Holy and virtuous.

78. *Holiness.* Whatever is contrary to Holiness is forbidden to all X^{ns}, Laymen as well as Clergy.

79. *Religious.* One may be Religious in any Condition of Life, with^t fear of being laughd at, provided we own y^t we fear God, and our Life be all of a piece.

80. *World and Relig^n.* The Love of ye World and Relig^n are incompatible, and destroy one another.

81. *Business, Employment.* People generally lay ye fault wrong: there is no employm^t y^t obliges a man to sin. [om. in 4to.]

82. *Obedience.* God requires obedience to His Laws, only that we may not be miserable.

83. *World.* Love not the world, is a precept on wch depends our eternal weal or wo.

84. *Priests, X^n.*
Compounded all of sweetness is their might,
As being sent to Treat, and not to Fight.—*Psyche*^{s}.

85. *X^{ns}.* Few People consider y^t they are X^{ns}.

86. *Edification.* You say you were much edified by such a discourse, yet you continue still the same: you deceive yo^{r}self, you were not edified.

87. *Grace.* God gives Grace, but He gives it only to those y^t Labour and Pray for it.

88. *Covetousness.* They who toyl y^t their Heires may be lazy, and they who deny y^{ms} y^t their children may Live in Luxury, are condemn'd by Reason and Relig^n as Instances of Madness and Infidelity.

89. *Scruples.* Insincerity is the cause of more Scruples [p. 14.] than ignorance.

90. *Repentance.* There is no Repentance where there is not a change of Heart.

^{s} [om. in 4to. Beaumont's Psyche, canto xvi. stanza 93.]

91. *Disputes.* [Indifferent Things.] Strive not ab^t little things, lest you lose ye sight of ye mark of yor high calling^t.

92. [*Mark of*] *Sincerity.* He that shews the Power of [his] Relig^n by its Fruits, has the best Testimony of His sincerity.

93. *Custome.* Common Practice, y^e [very] worst Rule in Relig^n.

94. *Zeal.* People in affliction are apt to form great designes. This is wrong — A Convert by affliction sh^d only think of mastering his corruptions; all ye rest is vanity.

95. *Grace.* God has promised His Grace and Sp^t to those y^t ask, He has not done so in respect to any temporal good things.

96. *Despair.* Consider w^t God can do, and you'll never despair of success.

[p. 15.] 97. *Devout.* To be devout is most earnestly to desire to be sav'd, and to neglect nothing in order to that end; and [in] other concernes, is calld Application of ye Mind to the business you have undertaken.

98. *World.* 'Tis much easier to retire fr. ye world, than to live in it as one sh^d do.

99. *Religion.* W^n 'tis made a Science^u there is nothing more intricate, w^n 'tis made a Duty nothing more easy.

100. *Riches.* The best Estate or Inheritance has this condition annexed to it—*whatever is superfluous belongs to ye Poor.*

101. *Anger.* He that says y^t He designed no offence, and that He desires to be at Peace, if He says True, sh^d take immediate care to repair ye offence, wch He has given tho' unadvisedly.

102. *Enemys.* When we think of doing kindnesses, our Enemys ought to have the First place in our thoughts, for then we act as becomes X^{ns}.

[om. in 4to.] 103. *Reconciliations* made upon any other acc^t y^n that 'tis the Command of God y^t we sh^d forgive one another, are not X^{ns}, nor acceptable [to] God. Men are satisfy'd wth an outside Reconc., God requires ye Heart.

[om. 4to.] [p. 16.] 104. *Fundamental Truthes.* All Truthes are to be Believed, w^h we are convinced are Revealed in S.S.—But some are

^{t} [This and the two next entries occur also in MS. 5. p. 48.]
^{u} ["Speculation" written above in pencil by Bp. W.]

of more and some less necessity to salv., and consequently some are more and some less Fundamental.

105. *Religion.* One of the great ends of R. is to keep men in a constant Dependance upon God.

106. *Happiness.* The only solid Foundation of our Hap^{ss} is the distinct knowledge of ye moral attributes of God. He is *merciful*, He will therefore pardon sinners, on favourable conditions; He is true, therefore we depend on His Promises, Fear, &c.

107. *God's will be done.* He only knows w^t is best for us, so y^t w^t God gives me not, to be sure is not fit for me.

108. *Judgment.* Never judge by yor senses w^t is fit to be done, but first consider wheth^r 'tis not sinful, then wheth^r 'tis not agst Reason.

109. *X^n Charity.* Dos instruct us to *Love*, and as far as may be to Benefit all mankind.

110. *Resignation*—To ye will of God, is no less a Privilege [p. 17.] than a Duty.

111. *Peace.* The only sure way to Peace, is to give one's self entirely up to God.

112. *Temptation.* Wo to him y^t is alone. 'Tis a Duty [om. 4to.] and 'tis a Remedy to consult a Pious, able Friend, in these cases.

113. *Good Name.* He that loseth His good name, loseth the power of doing good.

114. *Feares.* He y^t attempts to get rid of His feares by runing from God, will infallibly encrease them.

115. *Faith. Never doubt or desert a certain Truth for an* [om. 4to.] *uncertain suggestion.* This is ye way of all Heretick. Tho' ye S.S. speak of Eternal Punishments, yet ye Socinians suggest that there is no proportion between temporal guilt and etern. punishm^t, therefore ye soul may be annihilated, but not, &c.

116. *Paternal Authority.* God may be a slow, but He will be a sure avenger of such as despise it. [om. 4to. [p. 18.]

117. *Simplicity.* 'Tis much better to be accounted, or to *be*, a weak man, than a wicked man.

118. *Difficultys.* A man may have Truth on His side, and yet be put to a stand by a subtil adversary.

119. *Morality* makes not a X^n, tho' no man can be a X^n with^t it. Faith must change mor. virt. into X^n Graces.

120. *Sacred Trinity.* Ardent Prayers joyn'd to serious reading, and especially ye S.S., will reveal X^t in us, and then we shall have another-gates feeling of this Truth than we had before.

121. *Holy Life.* The fruit of Righteousness is Peace.

122. *Spiritual Comforts* are great Blessings; but unless attended with Obedience, Self-denial, Humility, and other works of Faith and Lab^{rs} of Love, may be Delusions of Satan, or Effects of Temper.

[p. 19.] 123. *Cross.* He who had all things in His Power made choice of the Cross.

124. *Self-Denyal.* The very foundation of Spiritual comfort.

125. *Practical Truthes.* While these are *plain*, we have no need to cõplain of want of Light.

126. *Mercy of God.* 'Tis plain from w^t He has done for us, that He is more desirous to save us than we are to be saved.

127. *Meanes of Grace.* God evermore accompanys the ministrations of ye Preist, if there be no impediment on the part of the people.

128. *Preisthood.* Those only who can exclude fr. ye Sacram^{ts} can administer them.

[om. 4to.]
[p. 20.] 129. *Awakening Questions.* Have you ever seriously askd y^{r}self—what shall I do to be saved?

130. *Romances, Play, Opera, &c.* — are contrivances to corrupt the Heart, in wch the Devil and Man have shewd their utmost skill.

131. *Opinions, Prejudice.* There are some opinions fatal, as it were, to some men, 'tis therefore uncharitable to fall out, or to contend too eagerly ab^t y^m, unless they very nearly concern their Salvat.

132. *Sincerity.* The conduct of our Lives, the only proof of the Sincerity of our Hearts.

133. *Appetite.* We need but tast a Pleasure a very little while, to become a Slave to it.

[om. 4to.] 134. *Corrupt Affections.* The only way to overcome them is absolutely to deny their cravings.

135. *Prayer.* God knows our wants, but He commands [p. 21.] us to pray often, y^t we may often think of Him, wch we cannot do with^t actually Believing, Hoping in, and Loving Him as the only being able to satisfye our desires: now these acts beget Habits of *Faith, Hope,* and *Love;* and 'tis for this Reason y^t we are commanded to pray, that we may get these Habits.

136. *Zeal.* No further commendable than as 'tis attended wth knowledge.

137. *Eloquence.* That is to be avoided wch w^d raise the Passions, w^thout curing the Errors of the Understanding.

138. *Rules of Nāāl Rhetorick.* 1. *Never be Positive.* That upbraids the Ignorance of y^m we speak to; rather let y^m believe they know and do as you w^d have y^m, and they'll come up at last to w^t you suppose they are [p. 22.] already.

2. *Never tryumph.* Many w^d yeild but for ye shame of being overcome.

3. Let such propositions as are not attended with the clearest evidence be deliverd by way of enquiry.

4. A modesty in delivering our sentiments leaves us a Liberty of changing them without Blushing, w^n we find it reasonable so to do.

5. He y^t understands His subject well, and is heartily Affected with it, will not want ways of expressing Himself agreably.

6. To have our great end, viz. the Glory of God, in our thoughts and desires, is the best way of attaing knowlege and piety.

7. There are way[s] of Recommending Relig^n where it w^d be unseasonable to speak of them directly.

8. By running from one Argument to another you shew [p. 23.] a secret distrust of ye goodness of the First; and yor adversary lays hold of the weakest.

139. *True Wisdome* consists in knowing one's Duty exactly.

True Eloquence in speaking of it clearly.

True Piety in acting w^t one knows. To aim at more than this [is] to run into endless mistakes.

140. *Perswasion—Edification.* It is not he y^t teacheth

y^t convinceth. But we convince ourselves, w^n by God's grace we attend to w^t we Hear, and dwell upon it.

141. *Perswade.* There is a danger in being perswaded before one understands.

[p. 24.] 142. *Mirth.* ^{x} We think to laugh innocently, and we seldome ever laugh with^t crime.

143. *X^n Perfection* consists not in having no Failings, but in Resisting y^m always, and Victory in not consenting to them.

Neither dos it consist in doing extraordinary things, but in doing common things after a X^n manner.

God commands unlimited Holiness (Thou shalt Love wth all thy, &c.), that He may proportion His rewards to ye greatness of our endeav^{rs}.

The meanest of God's servants will be Happy, but some will be more Happy.

All y^t we can do (morally considering our Weakness, Temptations, &c.) is the Measure of our Duty.

144. *Devotion.* To desire to serve God in [that] State of
[p. 25.] Life His Providence has placed one in, endeavoring every day to serve Him in that State more perfectly, this is true Devotion, true Zeal, all besides is Vanity or Presumption.

145. *Self-Denyal.* We have reason to suspect every doctrin, wch w^d teach us to avoid sin with^t offering violence to nature, since ye S.S. every where speak of the *difficulty* of working out our salvation and being innocent.

146. *True Religion* cannot consist in any thing wch a wicked man can perform as well as a good man. So y^t external Forms, however necessary, are not of ye Essence of Relig^n.

147. *Self-Denyal* absolutly necessary to fit one to receive the gr. of God. It was for this reason y^t John the Bapt. was sent before X^t to prepare the way.

[p. 26.] 148. *Know your self.* Exterior order requireth a man to keep y^t Rank y^t belongs to His place.

My natural state obliges me to acknowlege my self perfectly equal with the rest of mankind, and consequently to be gentle, and sensible of the miserys of others.

---

^{x} [The 4to. reads, "When we think to laugh innocently, we should take care our mirth be not criminal."]

But w[n] I retire inward and consider the dutys of my calling, y[e] acc[t] I am to give, the temptations I have to struggle with, &c., I find cause to acc[t] myself amongst y[e] last of mankind.

149. *Deists* guilty of a double error. They suppose that [om. 4to.] men are governed by Reason, whereas they are generally governed by Passion.

2[dy]. They suppose y[t] y[e] Soul is capable of a constant attention, which it is not, and then passion will govern, as found [p. 27.] by woful experience; and y[t] 'tis easier to know w[t] is good than to follow it.

150. *Diversions.* Men of Business, men of Pleasures, and too often men of Learning, are all mov'd by y[e] same secret spring, viz., a satisfaction they find in Forgetting y[ms], and diverting the thoughts of dying.

151. *Riches, Prosperity.* To believe y[t] God gives for a Reward of virtue such things as raise in us the Love of the world, and all the vices y[t] flow from it, there cannot be a greater mistake in Relig[n]. The portion of y[e] Elect cannot be both Riches and Persecution.

152. *World.* It is not always necessary to oppose y[e] [om. 4to.] world, (J. X[t] Livd in y[e] world, and comply'd with its Laws and customes,) unless where we cannot otherwise oppose the [p. 28.] Love of the world.

153. *Damnation.* Men need not be at pains to go to Hell, they'll go there of course, if they make no resistance, but leave y[m]selves at Liberty.

154. *Truth.* Once Receivd upon satisfactory grounds, y[t] [om. 4to.] w[ch] is contrary to it will never take place.

155. *Talk.* Be sparing of yo[r] words, and never talk in passion.

156. *Injuries.* Be not offended at y[m], nor complain of men y[t] cause y[m]. But look unto Jesus, and w[t] and how He bore y[m].

157. *Humility.* Think meanly of yourself; and Remember y[t] all y[ts] good is Gods.

158. *Contentm[t].* Be content wth a little. J. X[t] was so, tho' all nature was at His command.

159. *Afflictions.* God will never forsake His Servants, [p. 29.] tho' He suffer y[m] to be afflicted for a season.

160. *Charity.* Love and Pray for all, especially yor enemies.

161. *God.* W^tever relates not to G. is not worth y^r care.

[om. 4to.] 162. *Contempt.* Affect contempt rather than applause.

163. *Injurys.* To say y^t an Injury is too great to be forgiven, is to forget both ye Authority and the Promises of God, as well as the greatness of our own offences.

The greater ye injury ye Great^r your obedience to G^d, if for His sake you forgive it.

He y^t says he never will Forgive, says in effect, y^t he will never go to Heaven.

[p. 30.] 164. *Enmitys.* A man y^t is at variance and refuses to be Reconciled has but one prayer to make, viz. y^t God w^d change his Heart.

165. *Enmitys.* You say you cannot see ye man y^t has injur'd you, and yet you must see him and forgive him too before you dye.

166. *Enmitys.* I forgive, but I'll have nothing to say to him. 'tis plain you do not forgive him.

[om. 4to.] 167. *Prayer.* If you desire to be heard, let yor enemies have ye first place in yor thoughts and prayers.

168. *Enemy.* To forgive him before He is sensible of his Fault, is to encourage him in his Sin: But not to forgive him, is to sin ourself—wch will you choose?

169. *Devotion* is a constant application to the Duties of one's station.

[p. 31.] 170. *Maxims of X^{ty}.* Become as little children.
    Love not the world.
    Watch and Pray continually.
    Take up y^r Cross, and bear it daily.
    Deny yo^rself.
    Love yor enemies.
    Be Poor in Sp^t—i.e. be disingag'd fr. ye things of ye world, and set not y^r affections on y^m.

[p. 32.] 171. *Religion.* He y^t is perswaded y^t true religion consists in the regulation of ye Heart, will not fear the Judgment of men, or be much concern'd at it.

172. *Patience.* The practice hereof consisteth—

1. In a Firm Belief y^t nothing [can] come by Fate or chance. Job v. 6; Lam. iii. 38; 2 Sam. xvi. 10; Job i. 21.

2. That all occurrences are consistent with ye Wisdom, Justice and Goodness of God. Ps. cxix. 75.

3. That ye most bitter things do, in God's intent, aim at our good. Job v. 17; Jam. i. 12; Prov. iii. 12; Heb. xii. 5; Rev. iii. 19.

4. Our duty therfore is—

To submit to God's will. Luk. xxii. 42; Heb. x. 34 [? 36]; Jam. i. 2.

To trust in God for ye removal of our afflictions, or for strength to bear y^m patiently. Lam. iii. 26; Ps. xxxvii. 7; Ps. xlii. 4 [5 ?]; 2 Cor. iv. 8.

To wait God's time and leasure. Heb. xii. 3.

To humble ourselves under ye Hand of God. 1 Pet. v. 6. i. e. by considering our Unworthiness, Weakness, Sinfulness, &c., and God's Holiness, Justice, &c.

To suppress all complaints. Neither to charge God foolishly, [p. 33.] Job i. 22; Ps. xxxix. 9. Nor to express any wrath or Revenge against the Instruments He employs, this being, thro' their sides, to wound His Providence. Matt. v. 44; Luke vi. 27; Rom. xii. 14; 1 Thess. v. 15; 1 Pet. iii. 9; Prov. xxv. 21; Rom. xii. 20.

To Bless God, and to own His Justice, His Goodness, in afflicting us for our Benefit. Job i. 21.

To be careful to avoid all sinful ways of redressing ourselves. 1 Pet. iv. 19.

§. To induce us to ye Practice of these duties, let us consider—

That it is the Right of God to assigne Our Station in ye world.

That He having promised to support, and to reward us, 'tis a great sin to distrust His word.

We being His servants He only has a right to dispose of us.

That being grievous sinners, we sh^d be content wth any thing less than Damnation.

That while we have our Reason, a good Conscience, assurance of God's Love, a sure title to Happiness, our condition [p. 34.] is not without comfort.

That afflictions bring us the nearest way to God.

§. But above all things let us look unto Jesus, w^t and How He sufferd; y^t we may know how to deport ourselves.

His whole Life was one continued exercise of Patience.
Is not this ye Carpenter's Son?
The Foxes have holes, &c. Matt. viii. 20.
The world hated Him. Jo. xv. 18.
They took up stones to stone Him.
They calld Him an Impostor, Matt. xxvii. [63], a Blasphemer, a Dealer with ye Devil. All this He received wthout any passion or disturbance, any Reflection, any Revenge.

To Judas—Friend, wherefore art Thou—

To one y^t smote Him—If I have spoken evil—

To those y^t spit on Him, scourgd Him, mocked Him, &c., not one angry word.

To the grossest slanders, not one dissatisfactory return.

To those y^t crucify'd Him—Father, forgive y^m, for, &c.

And now, shall we repine, w^n God made this ye portion of His dear Son?

[p. 35.] In this school He learnt obedience by the things He suffer'd, Heb. v. 8. And shall we, &c.

Was He silent w^n He was aspersed, Patient w^n He was Belied — entirely resigned w^n He was injured, condemnd, crucify'd—And shall we, who have ye same Joy set before us, not endure ye little injuries wch we meet wth with^t resentment?

O Lord Jesus, give us better mindes.

173. *Religion.* A man may have ye Form of Godliness with^t ye power, but He cannot have ye Power while He despises ye Form, i.e. ye outward practice.

174. *Humility.* He y^t is truly Humble, never thinks himself wrong'd.

175. *Love of God.* A sure Test y^t you Love God is this—y^t you receive Afflictions willingly;—bec. they are not desireable in y^{m}s. but only as they come from God.

176. *Reason and Faith.* Whatever is ye object of pure Faith cannot be the Object of Reason. Wthout ye knowledge [p. 36.] of Original Sin we are utter Strangers to ourselves, and yet nothing is more shocking to Reason than y^t ye transgression of Adam sh^d affect His whole posterity.

177. *Riches.* Tho not evil in themselves, yet one of the greatest snares; and almost inevitably lead to pride, &c. 1 Cor. i. 26. *Not many noble, not many mighty are called, &c.*

This will make a thoughtful X^n afraid, lest God gives Him Riches and Honours in His Anger and as a Judgm^t.

Pride, Ease, Hardheartedness, and Pleasure, ye too nāal consequence of Riches.

The Rich and Great have most need of being told the Truth, and yet they seldomest hear it.

178. *Greatness.* A gr^t Man is made so for others (not for himself)—To Relieve ye Poor—Comfort ye Afflicted—Protect—Correct—Deliver—the Oppressed, ye Vicious, &c.

179. *Worldly Wisdom.* He y^t Governes by the Rules of the Gospel, is surer of Success than if he observ'd ye best [p. 37.] Maximes of Worldly Policy. But then he is to know y^t ye Gosp^l enjoynes Discretion as well as zeal.

180. *Learning.* He y^t dos not prefer the knowlege of w^t belongs to the dutys of his calling to all other things, will not be able to give an acc^t of his time.

181. *Temperance.* The bounds w^h separate w^t is allowed and Forbidden, being almost imperceptible, it will always be dangerous to go to ye utmost bounds of w^t is allow'd.

182. *Labour.* In ye Sweat of Thy Face, &c. Lab^r therfore is a Duty fr. wch no man living is exempt, with^t forfeiting His Right to His Dayly Bread.

We are oblig'd to it as we are *Men,* by this Sentence; as we are X^{ns}, in conformity to X^t, whose Life was all Lab^r and [p. 38.] Sufferings; and as a *Sinner,* who cannot be reconcil'd to God but by Lab^r and Paines.

183. *Plays, &c.* [*Fear* (in pencil.)] He y^t is not satisfy'd they are unlawful Diversions, Let him, if he dares, Pray to God to Bless him in the way he is going; and to keep him from ye Danger, &c. 'Tis presumpt^n to depend on one's own str. with^t Grace, and 'tis impudence to ask it, w^n one is going wrong.

184. *Principijs Obsta.* One dos not begin to Fall, w^n the Fall becomes sensible.

185. *Diversions* are apt to make us lose the remembrance of ye dangers y^t encompass us, w^h is ye ready way to ruin. Fear being as necessary, &c.

186. *Heresies, Schisms,* Always break forth upon the prospect of worldly advantages.

187. *Ministry.* The Gospel Ministry is founded upon [p. 39.]

a Succession from ye Apostles; where that is wanting, there are no valid ministrations^y.

[om. 4to.] 188. *Deists* are forc'd to acknowledge y^t Reason alone is not sufficient for this world, and therfore confess the necessity of magistrates and a superior Authority to govern Men, who all have reason—They'll not see ye necessity with relatⁿ to anoth^r world. How absurd is this!

189. *Doubts of Conscience.* Never disobey ye plain Commands of God, and wⁿ there is nothing but probability of Sinning in obeying the Commands of yor Govern^{rs}, do not set opinion before Judgm^t. Obey Authority, if it is not very plain you shall sin agst God.

One may sometimes obey a sinful comand with^t sining. Thus Joab obey'd David in numbering ye People.

[p. 40.] 190. *Temptations.* Fearful X^{ns} may learn fr. ye Example
[om. 4to.] of X^t not to be frighted at the very worst of Temptat^{ns}. He was tempted to Self-Murder, to worship ye Devil, &c. This was consistent with Infinit Sanctity.

Temptations not only unavoidable but necessary in a X^s Life.

191. *Reason and Free Will.* Tryals have been made by Man, how far these will secure Him; In a State of Perfection—In the state of Nature after the Fall—And in the time of the Law—wth all outward Helps and Advantages, And [the] Conclusion has always been—Blindness, Wickedness, and gross error; and yet there are Men who call these sufficient, and w^d fain bring us back again to these, &c., even while we are under ye dispensation of an effectual Grace.

192. *Wilful Ignorance.* He y^t knows he's in the wrong ought not [to] be argued wth.—St. Luk. xx. 8, "Neither tell I you by w^t authority, &c."

[p. 41.] 193. *Election.* Our security is not to be derived from signes—but fr. *Duty*, wch is the best sign, and God's Mercy the best ground of Confidence.

194. *Grace.* Whatever fav^{rs} are showd to Men who either have no Right to y^m, or have forfeited their Right, must be said to be of Grace.

195. *Truth.* A sanctifyd Mind will see ye Tr. wⁿ an unpurifyd soul, wth much more Learning, cannot perceive it.

---

^y [The last clause blotted over in ink, apparently by Dr. Wilson.]

196. *Charity to ye Poor.* He y^t makes his own Imaginary wants a Reason for not giving to ye Poor, will never want pretences for his covetousness.

197. *Error.* Serious Piety is the best defence agst Wicked Doctrines.

198. *Sin.* Where there is a real abhorrence of Evil, there will be a proportionable care to avoid it. Abhor y^t wch is evil. Rom. xii. 9.

199. *Restoration to ye Image of God.* The most effectual [p. 42.] meanes of our Recovery to w^t we are faln from—Consists, First, in a firm Belief of the Rem. of Sins thro' J. X^t. who dyed for us, to *assure us* of the Sincere Love of God for his poor Creatures, and y^t He is fully Reconciled to y^m, If they will be Reconcild to ye Meanes He has proposed in the Gosp^l.

(2) *Secondly. A Firm Faith in the Power of God* for recovering the Image of God in us, consisting in Righteousness and true Holyness. Call'd therefore The Righteousness of Faith; bec. produced by a Firm Faith in ye power of God.

(3) *Thirdly.* In earnest Prayer to God for *Light* to discover w^t is evil in us, and for strength to overcome and Root it out.

(4) *Lastly.* In a wary and watchful walking in all external Right^{ss} such as is in our own power to perform. By wch we may be assured y^t our prayers are sincere; wⁿ we do w^t we can, and Pray for what we cannot do without the [p. 43.] especial Gr. of God.

200. *Test of being true X^{ns}.* They y^t are X^{ts} have crucify'd ye Fl. with ye Affections and Lusts.

201. *Charity.* 2 Thess. i. 3. Where Love abounds Faith increaseth. A *Test.*

202. *Obedience.* 2 Thess. i. 8. They y^t do not obey God, do not know God.

203. *A True Faith.* It is not a light matter w^t we believe, concerning God y^e *Father,* y^e *Son,* and *Sp^t.* Our salvatⁿ depends on it, y^t we believe as ye Saints of Old believ'd (Jude 3), not as we have a mind to believe and understand ye S.S. If ye believe not y^t I *am He,* ye shall dye in yor sins. Jo. viii. 24. He y^t speaketh agst ye H. Ghost shall never

be forgiven, &c. These are words w^h sh^d make us very fearful e'ther of dissembling or mistaking ye Truth. T. S. M.

204. *Mystery.* It is not possible y^t a Mystery be explain'd. If the Truth of it be prov'd that is sufficient.

[p. 44.] 205. *Happiness Eternal.* There may be degrees of Glory but not of Happ^{ss}. Vessels of different capacitys may all be equally fill'd. One Starr may differ fr. another in glory, but both are Stars and both bright according to their bulk.

206. *Afflictions.* Increase of Labors will be attended with an Increase of Rewards.

God will bring His faithful Servants ye easiest way (for He takes no delight in our afflictions) to Happ^{ss}. Therefore afflictions, and such a measure, are absolutely necessary.

All things work together, &c. ^{z}

207. *Religion* makes God one's Friend.

208. *Soul.* Remember y^t you are something more than body.

[p. 45.] 209. *Reproof, Convince.* To Reprove wth success, allow yor Adversary to be in the Right as far as he really is so, viz. as he takes the thing (for the Understanding as well as the Senses is not mistaken where it has a Right view of the Object). Then shew him y^t side of ye Object wch he did not take notice of, and he will hear with more patience. For to be *confuted* is but to be *better inform'd*, and if we do it with this caution, y^t we make not Pride and self Love our enemies, a man will hear us with the same attention and good will, as a Travailer w^d do w^n you tell him he is out of his way, and set him right.

210. *Grace.* The Gr. of God, amongst other ways, works upon us,—By setting certain thoughts strongly before us and by keeping off others, By diverting us out of ye way of [p. 46.] Temptation, and w^n we meet wth such, by suggesting such Reasons as are most proper to convince us, and by making us attend to y^m, &c.

211. *Christianity, or The Sum of ye Gospel.* J. X^t came into ye world to form unto himself a People y^t sh^d wholly depend upon God, and placing no confidence in any earthly support and comfort, sh^d be after another manner *Rich*, after anoth^r manner *Wise*, after anoth^r manner *Noble*, after anoth^r

^{z} [This last clause om. 4to]

manner *Potent*, in one word, after anoth{super}r{/super} manner *Happy*: designing to attain felicity by the contempt of those things y{super}t{/super} are generally admired.

A people y{super}t{/super} sh{super}d{/super} be strangers to Filthy Lusts by studing [? studying] in this Flesh y{super}e{/super} Life of Angels—That sh{super}d{/super} have no need of Divorce, as being able to mend or to bear all manner of evils.—That sh{super}d{/super} be wholly ignorant of Oaths, as those who will neith{super}r{/super} distrust nor deceive any body. That make not y{super}e{/super} getting of money their busines, as having laid up their treasure in Heaven—That sh{super}d{/super} not be transported w{super}th{/super} *vain Glory*, bec. they refer all to y{super}e{/super} Glory of X{super}t{/super} alone.—Void of *Ambition*, as disposed, y{super}e{/super} greater they are, so much y{super}e{/super} more to submit y{super}m{/super}s unto all men, for X{super}ts{/super} sake.— Sh{super}d{/super} avoid *wrath*, much more *Revenge*, as studying to deserve well of those y{super}t{/super} deserve ill of y{super}m{/super}.—That sh{super}d{/super} be so *blameless* as [p. 47.] to force Infidels to speak well of y{super}m{/super}.—That sh{super}d{/super} be Born again to y{super}e{/super} Purity and Simplicity of Infants.—That sh{super}d{/super} live like y{super}e{/super} Birds of y{super}e{/super} Air, w{super}th{/super}out solicitude—Among w{super}m{/super} sh{super}d{/super} be y{super}e{/super} same Concord as amongst y{super}e{/super} Members of y{super}e{/super} same Body—Where y{super}e{/super} Abundance of One sh{super}d{/super} supply y{super}e{/super} wants of Anoth{super}r{/super}, and evils of some be mitigated by y{super}e{/super} good offices of others. Who sh{super}d{/super} be y{super}e{/super} Salt of y{super}e{/super} Earth—As a City on an Hill, conspicuous to all y{super}t{/super} are ab{super}t{/super} y{super}m{/super}. Whose Abilitys sh{super}d{/super} make y{super}m{/super} forward to help others—To w{super}m{/super} this Life sh{super}d{/super} seem Vile—Death desirable—Fearing neith{super}r{/super} Death, Tyranny, nor y{super}e{/super} Devil, relying upon y{super}e{/super} Invincible Power of X{super}t{/super} alone. Who sh{super}d{/super} live as if every day were their last, and [as if they?] wisht for that day w{super}n{/super} they shall enter upon the possession of a true and lasting Happ{super}ss{/super}. [a]

---

[a] Erasmus, [Ratio veræ Theologiæ, Opp., t. v. p. 84, fol. Lugd. Bat. 1704. "Christum, cœlestem doctorem, novum quemdam populum in terris instituisse, qui totus e cœlo penderet, et omnibus hujus mundi præsidiis diffisus, alio quodam modo dives esset, alio sapiens, alio nobilis, alio potens, alio felix: quique contemtu rerum omnium quas vulgus admiratur felicitatem consequeretur: qui nesciret livorem aut invidentiam, nimirum oculo simplici: qui nesciret spurcam libidinem, utpote sua sponte castratus, Angelorum vitam in carne meditans: qui nesciret divortium, quippe nihil non malorum vel ferens vel emendans: qui nesciret jusjurandum, ut qui nec diffideret cuiquam nec falleret quemquam: nesciret pecuniæ studium, ut cujus thesaurus in cœlis esset repositus; non titillaretur inani gloria, ut qui ad unius Christi gloriam referret omnia: nesciret ambitionem, utpote qui, quo major esset, hoc magis sese propter Christum submitteret omnibus: qui nesciret, ne lacessitus quidem, vel irasci, vel maledicere, nedum ulcisci, quippe qui et de male merentibus bene mereri studeret: qui ea morum esset innocentia, ut vel ab Ethnicis comprobarentur: qui ad infantulorum probitatem ac simpli-

212. *Church.* Ch. on Earth ye only way to that in Heaven.

[om. 4to.] 213. *Holy Scripture.* The design of ye S.S. is to manifest to us ye Attributes of God—His Alm. Power in the creation—&c. His Provid., His Wisdom &c. This is Life Eternal, to know Thee ye only true God, &c. This is ye gr^t use of ye H. Sc.

[p. 48.] 214. *Infidelity.* There wd be no Infidels if X^{ns} w^d live as X^{ns} sh^d do.

215. *Sin.* No sooner comitted, but ye judgm^t is passed. No sooner did Ahab go to take possession—but ye Prophet is sent wth a Message. X^{ns} do not consider this.

216. *Bookes* have their Fate from the capacitys of y^r Readers, or rath^r from their Principles.

[p. 49.] 217. *Grace of God.* Not an infused Habit or Quality—but such circumstances, ordered by God, as incline a man to consider and attend to the things w^h concern his Salvation—Ex. Gr. A fit of Sickness, or some calamitous accident—This awakens the Soul, makes it hearken to Reason—These Reasons are eith^r suggested by ye Sp^t or by His Providence offerd, by a Booke, Sermon, or good freind—Temptations to ye contrary kept off, &c. All w^h produce an effect w^h if God had not so orderd everything all the Reason in ye world could not have wrought ye Man's convers^n.

[cm. 4to.] 218. *Reason and Nature.* Too weak to convert Men, If X^t had not taught and shewd us ye way—and assisted us in it.

[om. 4to.] Who w^d have given credit to ye Joyes prepar'd for Good Men, if He who is God had not made y^m known. Who w^d have believd y^t self-denyal is necessary to Happ^{ss}, if He who

[p. 50.] had all things in His power, had not shewd us y^t such a course is best, by denying Himself ye good things of this

citatem veluti renatus esset : qui volucrum ac liliorum ritu in diem viveret: apud quem summa esset concordia, nec alia prorsus quam membrorum corporis inter ipsa: in quo mutua caritas omnia faceret communia, ut sive quid esset boni, succurreretur cui deesset ; sive mali quippiam, aut tolleretur, aut certe leniretur officio: qui doctore Spiritu cœlesti sic saperet, qui ad exemplum Christi sic viveret, ut sal, ut lux esset orbis, ut civitas esset in edito sita, omnibusque undique conspicua: qui quicquid posset, id omnibus juvandis posset : cui vita hæc vilis esset, mors optanda immortalitatis desiderio: qui nec tyrannidem timeret nec mortem, nec ipsum denique Satanam, unius Christi præsidio fretus : qui modis omnibus sic ageret, ut ad extremum illum diem semper esset velut accinctus ac paratus."]

world? How few are capable of seeing the reason of this. And then by His Death, He has assur'd us, y^t the surest way of going to Happ^{ss} is to be crucify'd to all the Pleasures, delights, &c., of this world.

219. *Rule of Relig^n.* Where the S.S. are silent, the Ch. is my Text, where the S.S. speakes, the Ch. is my Comment; where both are silent, I follow Reason.—*Relig. Medici*, [§ 5. "In brief, where the Scripture is silent, the Church is my text; where that speaks, 'tis but my comment: where there is a joint silence of both, I borrow not the rules of my religion from Rome or Geneva, but the dictates of my own reason."]

220. *Hereticks.* Those y^t cannot be content to be the Authors or Espousers of Novelties, with^t desiring to [be] propagating y^m—Follow ye Example of Sathan, who w^d not fall without as many associates as He could. [Ibid. § 7. "Those have not only depraved understandings, but diseased affections, wch cannot enjoy a singularity without an heresy, or be the author of an opinion without they be of a sect also; this was the villany of the first schism of Lucifer, who was not content to err alone, but drew into his faction many legions of spirits."]

221. *Faith, Reason, Passion.* If Reason opposes Faith, Passion opposes the Dictates of Reason—must Reason be despised therfore? No. Why then must Faith be set aside [p. 51.] bec. w^t she directs seems absurd to Reason? [cf. *Rel. Med.* § 19. "As Reason is a rebel unto Faith, so Passion unto Reason; yet a moderate and peaceable discretion may so state and order the matter, that they may be all Kings, and yet make but one monarchy, every one exercising his sovereignty and prerogative in a due time and place."]

222. *Physician.* "I cannot go to cure the Body of my [om. 4to.] Patient, but I forget my Profession, and call unto God for His Soul." *Rel. Medici,* [pt. ii. § 6,] p. 146.

223. *Sleep.* "So like death, y^t I dare not trust it with^t" saying "my Prayers." *Rel. Med.* [pt. ii. § 12.]

224. *Prosperity.* A state full of danger. Both the Wise and Pious have been ensnar'd by it.

225. *Bp. Barrow's Epitaph.* "Exuviæ Is. Episcopi Asaph- [om. 4to.]

ensis in manum Domini depositæ, in spem lætæ Resurrectionis per sola Christi merita.

"O vos transeuntes in Domum Domini, Domum Orationis, orate pro conservo vestro, ut inveniat requiem in die Domini."

Mr. Thorndike's Epit. "Tu, Lector, Requiem ei et beatam in Xto. Resurrectionem precare."

[p. 52.] 226. *Grace before Meat.* "Every creature of God is good if it be sanctify'd wth ye Word of God and with Prayer."

227. *Merits.* He y^t reckons up His own good works, dos but recount the Gifts of God.

228. *Mediator.* Christ ye only M. of Redemption, all X^{ns} (even the Saints departed) may be M. of Intercession one for another.

229. *Law and Prophets.* The latter, Commentators on the former; to explain its true Spiritual meaning and to enforce it.

230. *By their Fruits, &c., &c.* Do Arianism, Deism, Socinianism tend to make men better than ye Orth. Doctrine? Do not they rather deprive us of many Helps, motives, and meanes of becoming better? therefore, &c.

231. *Mysteries.* We are in a state of Tryal, 'tis necessary y^t our Faith, as well as our Obedience, sh^d be tryed—To [p. 53.] humble that Pride, wch w^d have us Believe nothing but our Reason can comprehend,—but God will have us believe Him upon the sole authority of His word.

Besides, God designing y^t His servants sh^d worship His Son, it was necessary y^t we sh^d know y^t He was very God, otherwise we sh^d have been requir'd to be Idolaters.

232. *Whatever ye w^d y^t Men, &c.* That wch is equally best for all—Buyers and Sellers—Lenders and Borrowers, &c., is the Measure of our duty.

233. *Lord's Supper.* The Elements indeed are cheap and common, but ye Blessings annexed to y^m by ye H. G. are great and invaluable.

234. *Fav^r of God.* Jer. xxxi. 3. ["I have loved thee with an everlasting love."] Better than Life^c; For it lasts to Eternity.

^c [Ps. lxiii. 3.]

235. *Angels.* The Poorest has them for His guards, and consequently [is] greater y^n an Eastern Monarch.

236. *Commun. of Saints.* A X^n is mystically united to all ye worthys on earth and in Paradice: has an Interest in their Prayers, and in all ye Blessing asked and granted y^m.

237. *Afflictions* may make men esteem us less, but God loves us more, if we bear, &c.

238. *Grace before Meat. Man shall not live by bread alone,* [p. 54.] i. e. His meat w^d not keep Him alive, *but by ye Word of God,* spoken to Adam and to Noah—Every moving thing shall be for meat to you. By this general Blessing Heathens are nourished, but not being sanctifyed by Prayer, i. e. by ye Prayer (or Grace) of every particular person on every Meal, it preserves their Lives to no other purpose than y^t of ye Beasts, wheras ye Meals of X^{ns} are sanctify'd by Prayer, as well as by God's Genl Blessing.

239. *Riches.* They y^t flatter y^{ms} y^t their desires after R. [om. 4to] are only y^t they may be able with more wealth to do more good, do often Live to see themselves confuted,—and w^n Riches come do want Hearts to, &c. God's choices are therfore always best—He gives us not w^t we wish for bec. He answers y^t Pray^r—"*Lead us not into Temptation.*"

240. *Afflictions.* If God gives Fortitude and Patience in Affl., 'tis a certain Mark of His care and love.

241. *Wandering in Prayer.* The best way to remedy this, is, not to let ye mind wander too much at other times, but to have God always before you, in ye whole course of yor Life.—Be not overmuch disquieted tho' yor mind sh^d wander; Trouble and disquiet distract ye mind ye more; but rather endeav^r to possess yor soul in Patience, and God will pity [p. 55.] and help you.

242. *X^n Perfection.* One does not become Holy all at once;—do not run before Grace.—He y^t dos not advance, certainly goes backwards.

243. *Test of true Piety.* Where yor Treasure is, there will yor heart be. He y^t does not every now and then think of God, God is not His Treasure.

244. *Sickness, Afflictions, Pain.* If you consider sickness as a Pain to nature and not as a Fav^r fr. G—It will be a

Greif and Torment to you. To make it a Comfort, Believe y^t it is Orderd by God, a Loving Fath^r, a wise Physician. Tis ye effect of His mercy for yor Salvation. You become dearer to Him by being like to His Son. *Fastend to ye Cross*—He will loose you w^n tis best for you—we often hinder our Recovery, Health, Ease, &c., by trusting to Physick, worldly meanes, more than to God. Meanes succeed just as far as God pleases. God sends paines of ye Body to cure those of ye Soul. If He sends y^m, He only can cure y^m. Be not impatient to be at Ease. While you are chastend, you are sure God loves you, you are not sure of y^t w^n you are with^t chastisement.

245. *Despair.* God never leaves us till we forsake Him. We do this or are in danger of doing so, w^n we forget very often to think of Him, and *to Live as in His presence.*

246. *Devotion.* You desire to know How most assuredly to please God? Make your Soul a Temple, and serve Him there continually. Watch over yor self, y^t you neither Think, nor Speak, nor do any thing to displease Him. W^n you have done so, immediately ask Pardon, He's always in His Temple. [p. 56.]

247. *Afflictions* never intolerable but w^n we see y^m in a wrong Light, as ye effect of others' Malice—of our own folly—of chance—of Destiny, &c. But look up^n y^m as fr. God, a Fath^r, &c.—and all will be easy.

248. *Afflictions—Uniform Obedience.* All is equal to a soul truly Resign'd. [om. 4to.]

249. *Wickedness.* God can remedy w^n He pleases. W^t a X^n has to do is to pray for this—neith^r to wonder at it— nor be dejected.

250. *Dejected Sp^t.* You must not always expect sunshine, but to have your Turn of Darkness, &c. Let not this make you uneasy—you can do nothing of y^rself. He y^t gives you Joy, can and will give you strength to bear Sorrow.

251. *Ignorance.* Generally speaking, men have more need of a Confessor than of a Director. [om. 4to.]

252. *Dejected Sp^t.* Do every thing wth a desire to please God, let w^t will come of it; then you are safe: all will be well at last.

God has very often granted ye greatest Favours to ye greatest Sinners—as instances of His mercy and goodness, &c., y^t none might despair, who seek Him in sincerity.

253. *Resignation.* Perfect R. ye surest way to Heav^n.

254. *Take no thought for to-morrow.* Live without antici- [p. 57.] pating care. Look up to God at all times, and He will, as in a Glass, discover w^t is fit to be done.

255. *Religion* changes nothing in ye order of Providence; it leaves ye great in their Station—only makes y^m carefull not to abuse ye Favours of God—mak^g ye poor content, &c.

256. *Cross.* All we aim at is to be easy; The Gospel saith, *Blessed are they y^t mourn.* Strive to enter ye strait gate. Wo to y^t man who meets wth no troubles.

257. *Devotion* has its name fr. Devoting ourselves entirely to God—Universal Obedience to His Will—To His Commands, and to all ye appointm^ts of His Providence, in all circumstances of Life—To part with all for His sake—To obey Him without Reserve.

258. *Imperfect Conversions*—such as forsaking great sins, observing ordinances, &c., often more hazardous than Profligate Lives. These may startle—those keep ye mind at ease. The Gosp. ye only rule to Judg by—Bring forth fruits, &c.

259. *Faith.* What Fruits of Faith have we to shew? Do we live by F.? Do ye Promises and Threats of ye Gosp. affect us as if present? Do we regulat our Judgments, our choices, &c., by F.?

260. *Resignation.* Happ^ss consists not in being exempt [p. 58.] fr. sufferings, but in a voluntary acceptance of y^m as ye will of God.

261. *Resignation.* To repine at Sufferings is to charge God wth doing us Injustice. 'Tis to say we are innocent and have not deserved y^m. Alas! if it were left to ourselves to execute Justice for ye offences we have committed, we sh^d be too partial, or too cowardly to do it. 'Tis God only can do it, and we are angry.

262. *Prayer.* The Lukewarmness of our Pr. is the source of Infidelity. If Riches were to be had for asking, How earnest, constant sh^d we be at our Prayers.

263. *False Hopes.* We see plainly y^t we are not w^t we [om. 4to.]

sh^d be; we wish we were better—and sit still, and think there is something in ye very wish.

264. *Afflictions.* We ought to Judge of ye greatness [and] danger of our disorder, by the violence of the medicin wch our unerring Physician is forc'd to make use of. Let us beware lest endeavouring to leave ye Cross, we forsake Him who was for our sake fasten'd to it.

265. *Humility.* A sinner y^t deserves Damnat^n will not sure stomach it, to be commanded to be H. Learn of Me, saith X^t, for I am Lowly of Heart. The difficulty of this Grace appears in this—that ye Son of G^d was forc'd to take our nature to shame us out of Pride. He abaseth Himself, and we w^d exalt ourselves, and be esteem'd w^t we are not.—W^t Diabol. Pride is this?

[p. 59.]

To despair bec. we are poor and wretched is not Humility, but abominable Pride, we are not willing to owe our cure to God alone.

266. *Charity beareth long, &c.* True X^n Charity sees things in ye same Light y^t God dos. He can, and perhaps will, make a change for the better ye next moment. Grace dos not hinder us fr. seeing faults—but it teacheth us to bear wth y^m in submission to ye designes of Provid.—not to be surprised at ye corruption of ye world—To see ye Good as well as ye Bad—To consider our own faults—To think w^t trouble or offence we have given others—To consider the obligations we have to God—W^t hast thou y^t thou [hast not received?]

267. *Business.* We have but one great Business—That wch God has assigned us to do, all others are included in y^t. Let us be Faithful in our proper business, and Resigned as to ye success; to be anxious for *That*, is ye effect of Self-Love, Self-Will, and Pride.

268. *Death* inevitable, by our own confession, and yet we will not think of it. *Life* miserable, (we own it,) and yet afraid of that w^{ch}, if we please, will put an end to our troubles. W^t deplorable Blindness is this!

269. *Heaven.* There is no proportion betw. w^t we see, enjoy or wish for on earth, and what we hope for in H. The carnal man w^d reap with^t sowing—This is preposterous. To Hope much and do little is w^t Self-Love aims at, and yet

[p. 60.]

none but ye violent take ye K. of H. by Force, and wo to y^m who have their consolation in this world.

270. *Daily Bread.* That Br. wch nourisheth to Eternal Life. He who has lost his appetite is certainly sick; so is y^t soul y^t desireth not y^t Food wch cometh from God. We Receive Grace in ye same degree as we desire it.

271. *Inward Peace.* Jo. xiv. 27. Not to be found in the world, but in G. only. Neith^r Poverty, Crosses, [nor] Distress, can disturb yor P. All these are Fav^rs in ye Hands of God.

272. *The Beatitudes.* What new kind of Relig^n is this? [om. 4to.] will not most X^ns say—w^t strange Doctrine is this? Acts xvii. 19, 20.—Why verily if ye Son of G. had not reveald it, &c.—a thousand objections w^d have been made.

273. *Blessed [are they] y^t mourn.* For ye dangers y^t surround us—For ye contempt of God w^m we Love—For ye many sad occasions of sorrow.

274. *Worldly Wisdom.* Jam. iii. 15. *Earthly*—bec. its aims are no higher. *Sensual,* bec. it aims at gratifying ye passions. *Devilish,* bec. it imposes first on others, at last [p. 61.] upon those y^t practise and depend on it.

Blind are they who will be wise with^t grace—who can foresee all events, but those of ye greatest concern to y^ms: viz., Death and Eternity; and ye vanity of every thing they dote on.

275. *Losses.* God will take nothing from us, but w^t He knows w^d make us unhappy.

276. *The Fath^r of mercies, and God of Consolations.* 2 Cor. [om. 4to.] i. 3. God sometimes separates these two; He takes away ye comfort, but His mercies never fail His servants.

277. *Christ's Yoke.* Let not ye name affright us—Tis a Y. but easier and safer than full Liberty—Tis a Y. y^t makes the Practice of virtue pleasant—That secures us fr. ye violence of our corrupt nature—Fr. being ruind by false pleasures—That will make those Crosses y^t are unavoidable to be borne wth pleasure—That gives us a Liberty wch ye world knows nothing of, and a Reward unspeakable—That sweeten our Cross, recompense our Losses—make Death, to others frightfull, to X^ns a Blessing—A yoke to hinder us fr. ruining our selves.

278. *False Liberty.* A Liberty to ruin our selves—A

402   MAXIMS OF PIETY AND MORALITY.

Liberty to bring ourselves into Bondage [d]—They do not do w^t Pleases themselves.—They meet wth a thousand disappointments, mortifications, vexations. . . . . He y^t will not

[p. 62.] obey ye Laws of X^t must obey his own Passions, wch are the worst Tyrants—He must obey ye world and ye Humours of others—He must depend upon its fancys, customs, &c. In short—To serve God is perfect freedome—all els is mere slavery, let ye world call it w^t they please.

[om. 4to.] 279. *St. Paul's Conversion.* T.S.M. We have in this acc^t a model of God's dealing wth Sinners. We persecute X^t by our Infidelity, our crimes, &c. He strikes us to ye ground by Sickness, Afflictions, &c. He confounds our Pride, False Zeal, &c., by mortifying occurrences. He puts us into a consternation by ye sight of Death, Judgm^t, &c. He convinces us y^t it is hard to kick, &c.; i. e. to strive [with?] our Maker—what is all this for? but to make us crye wth St. P., *Lord, what wilt Thou have me to do?* i. e. To Devote our selves entirely to God.—To Resolve y^t nothing shall be too dear to be parted wth in obedience to Him—No Habit, no Friendship, no Sin, &c.

280. *The Religion of ye World.* Matt. vi. 24; 1 Kings xviii. 21. Setting aside Infidels—The rest of ye world believe y^t *some Religion is necessary.* The consequence is—They take w^t they like, not w^t X^t has prescribed. They^{ll} give God words and ceremonys;—They^{ll} serve Him, but ye world too—They^{ll} do *some* of ye things He has cōmanded, and some too y^t He has forbidden.—They flee to Him in distress, but t'is w^n every thing els forsakes y^m.—As far as ye custome of ye world allows they^{ll} serve Him.—But is this w^t we vowed w^n we were made X^{ns}? Is this to Love ye L^d with *all* ye Heart and Mind, &c. To Renounce every thing y^t He Hates?

281. *The night cometh w^n, &c. Time.* We seldom consider this till 'tis too late. Time is often a Burthen—And yet Eternity depends on it. We cannot always do w^t we

[p. 63.] wish to do, but we can always do w^t is proper to our condition, and y^t is w^t is best pleasing to God.—Vain amusements, Useless correspondencies — Unprofitable conversations,—all this is Time lost, &c.

[d] [Three lines are blotted here by Dr. Wilson, and the last could not be traced through his ink.]

282. *God's Presence.* Gen. xvii. 1. *Walk before Me, and be Perfect.* To live as in God's Presence, ye only way to perfection. W^n we lose ye sight of Him, we forget our dependance—We walk as in ye dark—We choose shadows for substances—We fall into snares, and errors—We are exposed to our Enemies— Our infirmities, &c. *I will lift mine eyes unto ye Hills, fr. whence cometh my Help.* Ps. cxxi. 1. Looking to our Feet, Human prudence, will not be sufficient to secure us. Look upwards. N. B. This last a Text.

283. *To Love God*—is to have no other will but His.— [om. 4to.] To Love w^t X^t (w^m He sent to teach us) Loved—Poverty, Humility, Sufferings.—To Hate w^t He forbid us to Love,— The world, and its vanities. Tis to desire to converse with Him, To know His will—To walk as in His sight, &c. All ye rest is mere Form of Words, learnt w^n we were young— and said wth out thinking w^t it meanes, w^t it requires—Men Love ye world, and every thing ye world dotes on,—Money, Estates, Titles, Power, Reputation, Figure—and yet they say they Love God.

284. *To know God.* T. S. M. No man can know God but he must love Him; Tis to know y^t He is ye Fountain of all Good—That He Loves me better than I do myself—That He pitys my sad condition—That He is ready to Help me— To Direct and assist me; That He is a Father to me, Forbids me nothing but w^t will really hurt me—will give me every thing y^t is good for me, and at last Eternal Life, if I continue to Love unto death. This is Eternal Life to know Thee and Jesus X^t.

285. *Take up the Cross.* Can God, who Loves us, take [p. 64.] pleasure in our sufferings? Could not He shew us a way to be good wthout afflicting us? We are to Judge of w^t is best, and w^t is necessary by w^t He dos, and w^t He requires. We are in a faln condition, and in order to be restored, we must of necessity be Humble, Depend on God entirely—Deny our own will, wch leads us fr. God—Believe Him—Put our whole Trust in Him—wean our Hearts from ye world, &c. All wch God dos, By Disappointing us very often.—By suffering men to injure us—By letting us Relaps into Sin, to convince [us] of our own weakness. Self Love wishes to be made Perfect

at once, but Self Love is w^t God will destroy, by a course of irksome Tryals. Our Disease is—an excessive Love of our selves, and of ye world; God orders or permits a Train of Events to cure us of This Love.—The cure is painful; but tis necessary. We suffer not fr. His cruelty, but fr. His Love and care. He is a Father, and cannot take pleasure in our misery.—He deprives us of what we love inordinatly, y^t we may Love Him—By correcting He amends us—We w^d do our selves Hurt, and He hinders us—We lament ye loss of a Freind, i. e. we are sorry y^t he has escaped a great deal of Sin, vanity, &c.—We are purifyed by afflictions, and made fit for Heaven—God forces us fr. a vain deceitful world, and we are in Distress for this—X^t was made a man of sorrows to teach us how useful sorrows are.

286. *Holy Scriptures.* Read y^m wth Humility, not to appear more knowing, but to edify.

287. *Troubled Mind.* Inward Tryals are as necessary as ye outw^d. Both come fr. G., on purpose to exercise us; and as [y^e] Outw^d shew us ye malignity of ye world, ye Inw^d shew us our own weakness, and to w^t dangers we are exposed, if God did not support us every moment. Our duty is—To keep our will submissive to God's Designe, Faithfully to depend on Him, to deal wth us as He pleases: For these Inward struggles are not in our own Pow^r no more than outward afflictions.

288. *God dwelleth in you.* Eph. iii. 7; 2 Cor. vi. 16; Jo. xiv. 23. We must therfore make our Addresses to Him as dwelling in us, making His abode in us—In *Us,* as in His *Temple.*—We must make our Address to Him—

As our *Master* and *Teacher*—and as Scholars beg of Him to shew ye way you sh^d walk in.

As a *King,* offer Him your Heart, y^t He may reign there, be ever ready to Receive His commands, &c.

As a *Father,* Reverence and Love Him above all things—and endeav^r to please Him—Go to Him wth Confidence and Freedom—He will excuse yor weakness, and pardon yor Failings—Crye Abba Father.

As a Physician, beg Him to look upon ye disorders of yor soul—If Thou wilt, Thou can[st make] me whole—Speak ye word and Thy Servant, &c.

As a *Shepherd*, Ask Him Food for yor soul. Keep close to Him, and never stray from Him.

As your *Redeemer*—Beg of Him to Deliver you fr. your captivity—" Lord I am oppressed, undertake for me."

289. *Walk before Me, &c.* Whatever happens to us (Sin [p. 66.] excepted) is the Will of God—Tis our Duty to accept it wth thankfulness—Sweet or bitter—wheth{r} fr. ye Hand of God, fr. ye malice of men—or fr. our own Imprudence.

Every day offer yor self to God, yt He may do in you, and with you as He pleases.

Read ye S.S., you'll find there fr. X{t} Himself wt you must do to please Him; but read to edifye, not to be more knowing.

Suppress all vain and useless thoughts, and live as in God's Presence, and ye Peace of God wch passeth all, &c.

290. *Mortification.* Every day deny yor self some satisfact{n}. Deny ye *Eyes* all objects of mere curiosity—The *Tongue*, every thing yt may feed vanity or vent enmity. The *Palat*—wt it most delights in, (but this not to be seen by others.) The *Earss*, by rejecting all Flattery—all Conversation yt may corrupt ye Heart. The *Body* all Delicatness, Ease and Luxury; by bearing all Inconveniences of Life for ye Love of God,—Cold, Hunger, Restless nights, ill Health, the negligence of Servants and Freinds, Contempt, Calumnies, our own failings, melancholy, and the pain we feel in overcoming the Corruptions of Nature.

Mortification and Prayer must ever go together, or prayer [p. 67.] will degenerat into Formality, dryness, &c. Do all this with ye greatest Privacy, as in ye sight of God, as having no other view but to please Him.

Don't make your self uneasy at ye Temptat{ns} to wch H. nature is subject, or disturb yor self with thoughts you cannot Help.

Be not over fond of talking ab{t} Relig{n}. Rather let the Inward opperations of ye Sp{t} appear in a Meek, Humble, Resigned and Chearful Behaviour.

Desire nothing with Passion and Eagerness. This is not of God, He dwelleth in Peace.

291. *Conversation* sh{d} be mild, well bred, without debate, without obstinacy; Bearing with others' Faults—With{t}

Reflecting on ye Absent—Backward to Believe Evil Reports—Speaking the Truth Simply—Not Judging others—Avoyding Flatterers and Flattery.

Choose for your Friends persons of Sense and Piety—But never such as take Freedoms—Don't be in pain to hear of yor Faults.—Suffer no body to take Freedoms with you; or to say any thing wch you ought not to Hear. Afflict no body—But Comfort ye Afflicted—Have no odd Humours. Never blame with^t Reason, and then you'll be always minded—Never Reprove with Passion—Make not yo^rself Familiar with y^r Servants—But Remember y^t they have a Title to yor Charity, weth^r Sick or Ignorant—Hurt no body—Be ready to pardon Injurys. Never make a jest of any body. Every moment implore ye Assistance of God, &c.

292. *The Design of X^{ty}* is to restore us to ye Fav^r of God by restoring us to His Image, in wch we were created, but [p. 68.] are since faln.—In order to this it proposes to [us] the Remission of our Sins—The aides of ye H. Gh. and eternal Happ^{ss} after death.

293. *Faith.* You say you believe the Gospel; you live as if you were sure not one word of it is true—This is madness not to be expressed.

[om. 4to.] 294. *Sinners.* Tis often said in excuse for an evil Life, *That we are all Sinners.* Tis not so often considerd, y^t some Sinners will be Saved, and some will be Damned. That makes a sad difference.

[om. 4to.] 295. *Custome.* Tis ye Custome of ye world to take ye Broad way to Hell.—Will you follow C . . . ?

[om. 4to.] 296. *Fundamental Truths.* Whatever is necessary must be easy to be understood.

297. *Grace.* To say we have not power to do w^t God requires of us, is Blasphemy.

[om. 4to.] 298. *Xⁿ Religion.* The great Mystery of X^{ty} consists in Restoring us to ye Image of God, fr. whence we—

[om. 4to.] 299. *Knowledge of God* is imparted according to ye proportion of Purity y^t is in us.

300. *Cross.* The most Consumat Wisdome made choice of ye Cross, of Poverty and Meaness.

301. *Consideration* is half Conversion.—We say we love our selves and yet don't care to converse wth our selves—

This is absurd — Tis for want of thinking, that we are undone.

302. *Death.* A timely preparation for D. frees us fr. ye Fear of D.—and fr. all other Feares.

303. *Injurys.* It costs more to Revenge than to bear them.

304. *False Hopes.* Miserable is ye case of those who have [p. 69.] no hopes but [that] ye God and Word of Truth will prove false.

305. *Life.* A true X^n is neith^r fond of Life nor weary of it.

306. *The end of Man.* We Reproach our Maker w^n we Act as if we were made only for little ends.

307. *Sensuality.* That you may [have] yor Portion wth Beasts in this world, you are content to have y^r Portion wth Devils in ye next.

308. *Love of God.* We cannot be happy wth one we do [om. 4to.] not Love—not wth God if we do not Love Him.

309. *Evil Speaking.* There is no man but knows more Evil of Himself y^n He dos of His neighbour.

310. *World.* He y^t has set his heart upon ye world is not in a capacity of understanding ye Gospel.

311. *Saving Knowledge.* Obedience to ye will of God entitles us to a peculiar promise of God's Assistance to guide us, &c.

312. *Children.* No inheritance can supply ye want of vertuous education.

313. *Debauchery* is only an Art ag^st Thinking. [om. 4to.]

314. *Prosperity.* If God denys prosp. to good men it is in order to something better.

315. *Charmes* are a kind of Magick wch ye D. gives Life [om. 4to.] to, tho' not visibly present, and produces some effects, w^ch [p. 70.] shall gain credit to y^m, and delude men into a fondness for y^m.

316. *Watch.* He y^t keeps a strict w. over ye first motions in ye mind, will avoid not only Wilfull Sin, but all vain, Idle, &c., wch God sees, and yet we sh^d be ashamed to speak y^m to men.

317. *Conscience.* W^n C. forsaks a man, ye Sp^t of God dos so too.

318. *Prayer.* We must never pray for such things (Riches, Hon^r, Prosperity), as it is not fit for J. X^t to intercede with God for. We may beg God's grace to despise such things.

[om. 4to.] 319. *Plays* destroy nãal modesty, wch is ye guard of Innocence—Creat boldness, assurance. Players—their very trade and livlyhood is to damn Soules.

320. *Sensuality.* Whoredom and wine (Hos. iv. 11) take away ye Heart, i. e. his right Judgment, Tast and perception of things.

321. *Covetousness* has such a Blinding Power y^t all the Argum. in ye world will not convince a man y^t he is Covetous.

322. *Catholick Truthes.* Tis a great Delusion to Receive
[p. 71.] ye Dictates of a Party, or the Opinions of Privat Men, for Cath. Truthes, w^thout Examination.

[om. 4to.] 323. *Plays.* Cato is always instanced as one of those Plays wch may be Read, or Seen by a vertuous person w^thout any danger.—A young Gent. (Admir^l Graydon's son) being in Love with a young Lady above his fortune, upon seeing y^t Play, came Home, and in a fit of Gallantry Kill'd Himself. Sist^r Patten, whose Relative He was, gave me this Acc^t.

324. *Original Corrupt^n.* Nature is certainly weak and Cor^t, but 'tis an error to ascribe all ye evils w^h proceed fr. Base Principles, Evil Customes, Education, Love of ye world, &c. To ye Cor. of N.

[om. 4to.] 325. *Unprofitable Servt.* A state of Idle living is a state of Damnable Sin. It makes no provision for Eternity. A man may be constantly employd in business; free fr. Scandalous Faults, &c., and yet not be in ye way of Life.—That Relig^n is of no value wch does not set men free from ye Love of ye World, ye Bondage of Sin—makes y^m not careful to maintain good works wch God has ordaind, y^t we sh^d walk in y^m.—They are a Sacrifice wth wch God is pleased—A Test of ye Love of God dwelling in us.

[p. 72.] 326. *Heaven and Hell.* That the Knowlege of Things so Amazing and Dreadful sh^d have so little effect upon our passions, and that things so desireable sh^d be despised, must be for want of Faith, consideration, and a due attention.

327. *The condition of a Sinner.* To be—Perpetually vexed at his own folly and weakness.—To do such things as he

inwardly condemns.—To be afraid of ye Light wch w^d discover him to himself and others.—To be afraid of w^t may come hereafter, &c.

328. *Marks of a worldly Sp^t.* A Concern for Pomp and Shew of Life—Gr^t exactness in ye modes and customes—A quick sense of Hon^r and Reputation and praise—Study of Ease and Pleasure—A desire to grow Rich, &c.

329. *Faith.* Where there is a True F. it works Miracles every day.—It casts out Devils—Spirits of Malice, Pride, Lust, Covetousness, Revenge, &c.

330. *Faith.* We are as much obliged to Believe God with Reluctance to our Understanding, as to obey Him wth Reluct. to our Will.

331. *Known Sin.* Every man who lives in known sin, is [p. 73.] advancing towards Atheism, i. e. To a State wch obliges him first to wish, and then to say—*There is no God.*

332. *Afflictions.* Preventive of Sin—Correct ye Corrupt^n of Nature—An exercise of Gr.—A conformity to X^t—A mark of Adoption to a sincere X^n. An Assurance of God's Love,—and a Preparative for Heaven.

333. *Baptism.* The H. Sp^t at B. takes possession of us, and keeps Possession, till men greive Him, y^n He forsakes us, and an Evil Sp^t succedes.

334. *Pale of ye Church.* The mercy of God, where there is Faith, sincerity and good works, can make good all canonical defects, but this sh^d not encourage men to despise ye Fav^r of being in a sound p^t of ye C. Ch. wch only has a right to ye Promises and ye Covenant, wch are inestimable.

335. *Love of God.* As He is our Lawgiver, is the keeping [om. 4to.] His Commandm^ts. As He is Omnipotent, is, &c.

336. *Happ^ss of Man* cannot consist in any thing wch will not last as long as He is like to last.

337. *Governm^t. of ye Heart.* There is no Gov. ye Outward Man, with^t first Gov. ye Inward.—W^n ye Heart is under no Restraint, we ourselves do not know whither it will carry us.

338. *Law, Gospel, Reason, Nāal Relig^n.* The Advantage [p. 74.] of ye Law above ye Gentiles—gave ye Jewes true and worthy notions of God, and prescribed y^m a certain way of worshiping acceptably. The Gentile world was destitute of these. Whenever the Jewes had offended, ye Law provided

y^m an Atonement, shewing to w^m and after w^t manner they were to apply for Pardon; In this ye Gent. were utterly at a loss.

The Advantages wch ye Gospel has added to ye Law are:— It has eased us of ye Burdensom ceremonies of ye Law—It gives us ye Assistance of ye H. S., and accepts of a sincere instead of an unsinning obedience.

Gives us better assurances of Life and Happiness after death, and full Instructions how to attain it.

N. B. No Atonement in ye Law for gr^t and wilful sins, under ye Gosp. no sin unexpiable^e.

339. *Afflictions, Patience.* Why sh^d a Living Man complain of ye Punishm^t of his Sins? All Sin *must* be punished, Here or Hereafter. *Justice* requires it, as well as ye nature of our condition; For Health and Prosperity is most likely to corrupt us; The Cross only can bring us back to God. We judge of our merit by ye worldly advantages we enjoy.— God is forc'd to shew us our mistake, and our dependance upon Him, by afflictions, &c. He y^t is uneasy under the Cross, w^d serve God wth y^t wch costs Him nothing.—Let us consider ye Issues of Prosp. and Adversity, and then we shall easily perceive by wch we have been most gainers.

[p. 75.] 340. *Dejection.* Be satisfyd y^t He who is Tempted, and sorry for it, is in a much safer condition than he y^t meets wth no uneasiness, disturbance in his sins.

341. *Discipline.* We have reason to bless God for those Sins wch awaken us, lead us to Repentance, make us to Love much, bec. much has been Forgiven.

342. *Error.* An error in Faith will almost necessarily be followd by an er. in Practice.

343. *Understanding.* Tis certain fr. H. S. y^t we are to be Judgd for the fault of our Understandings as for any other crimes.—If men *Hate knowledge—If they despise Wisdome and Instruction*, If they take no heed of ye light y^t is in them, but let it turn into Darkness, &c., they will certainly be punished for their Ignorance.

[om. 4to.] 344. *Indian Catechism*^f. The X^n Faith teaches us 2 Things—The corruption of nature, and our Redemption by

---

^e [This clause in the MS. has a pen drawn through it.]

^f [Dialogue ii. vol. iv. p. 155 of this ed.]

J. X^t.—These are Foundation Principles—No oth^r Relig^n dos or ever did teach y^m. *Pascal* ^{g}.

345. *Melancholy.* Be afraid to offend God—but be not [p. 76.] afraid of His anger, while you *fear* Him, for you are in y^t very state to w^h He has promised Pardon and Happ^{ss} if you persevere—And you w^d offend God, if you distrust His Promise, or His goodness wch has wrought that Fear in you.

346. *A Regenerate Person cannot Sin.* 1 Jo. iii. 9. i. e. He has by Faith and the Gr. of God got such an Habit of Holiness, such an inclination to vertue, y^t He cannot upon any Temptation knowingly consent to transgress the Laws of God. Having *overcome ye world* (5 ch. v. 4), i. e. all those Temptations, by wch men are led to commit Sin, *He is dead to Sin* (Rom. vi. 2), i. e. He can no more sin deliberately, than a dead man can breath.

347. *Sin.* All Sin includes in it *Atheism, Rebellion, and Idolatry.* This sh^d be well consider'd.

348. *Rash Judgment.* Remember—That [he] who takes upon him to Judge oth^{rs}, Usurpes the Right wch God has reserved to Himself.

349. *Worldly Advantages.* God could very easily give worldly affluence, but He kindly denys, Restraines, or de- [p. 77.] prives us of them, lest we sh^d set our H. upon them; and y^t we might Love Him above [all].

350. *Afflictions.* The Divine goodness has appointed these to be [the] portion of His own children, to make y^m fond of the Love of God, who will make y^m more than amends for all ye miserys they can suffer here.

351. *Greatness.* None so great as to be above giving an Acc^t to God of all his actions.

352. *Study.* Not to be more knowing, but to be more Holy, and to make others so.

353. *Poverty.* So far fr. being an Unhappyness, y^t it is a Security against Tempt. to gr^t Sins to wch the Rich are exposed.

354. *Death.* If you hope to dye well, take care to live well. In order to this—

1. Renounce the Love of the world, for *This* and the Love of God are inconsistent.

^{g} [Pensées, 2 par^{te}, art. iv. § iv., x.]

2. If you think this a difficult work, Rememb^r that the world is to be condemnd to Etern. misery, i. e. All that Love ye W. better than G.

3. The moment we dye our Fate is determind for ever and ever.

[p. 78.] 4. This consideration and a Fear for ourselves sh^d ever be present with us—Lest the Health we enjoy, and the seeming distance of Eternity, sh^d make us careless.

5. If we deny ourselves the pleasures of this Life, we shall enjoy Pleasures y^t shall last for ever.

6. Consider that there can be no Solid Satisfaction in this Life till we are got above the Fear of Death, and of w^t may follow, a miserable Eternity.

7. The Sting of Death is Sin—An Holy Life therfore is the only Cure for ye Fear of Death.

8. Let us therfore Devote our selves wholly to God, make [Him] the Object of our Love and Desires, and Resolve that nothing in this world, be it of never so great moment, shall prevail with us to do what we believe will displease Him.

9. Make the Word of God the Rule of y^r Actions, and pray for His Grace y^t you be able to observe it.

10. Keep a strict Watch over all yor Senses, lest Intemperance get the Mastery of you; and your outward senses be instruments of polluting the Soul.

11. Give Almes of your Goods, and so you will gather yor self a good Reward in the day of necessity. *I was an hungered, and ye gave, &c.*

12. Do not dare to sleep till you have made yor Peace with God, by confessing yor Sin, and by making Resolutions of amendment where you have done amiss.

[p. 79.] 13. Of all things beware of Lukewarmness and an Indifference for Eternity. To prevent this—

14. Let the awakening consideration of a Future Judgment be ever present wth y., and the consequences of y^t dreadful day to the Ungodly.

15. The Lord's Supper being a Sovereign Medicin for all the Diseases of the Soul, and especially agst y^t Universal Disease—*The Fear of Death*—it sh^d never be neglected.

16. In short, live as becomes a X^n, and then you may say wth ye Apostle, *To me to dye is gain.* Amen.

355. *Peace of Conscience.* Never to be obtained but by rooting out of Sin.

356. *Infidelity.* An obstinate Resolution of Believing only what pleaseth us, cannot alter the Truthes of X^{ty}, The Resurrection of the Body, and the Life Everlasting. [p. 80.]

357. *Charity to ye Poor.* If for want of This I shall be Shut out of Heaven, I need no other Argum^t to perswade me to give Almes.—*I was an hungerd.* [om. 4to.]

358. *Prayer.* Every Man y^t Prays ownes himself a Beggar, wch will make him Humble.

359. *Riches.* May not I do w^t I will wth my own? No, unless you w^d go to Hell wth [him] y^t Fared Sumptuously and let ye Poor Starve at his Gate.—Never were words more abused—Your own? Who made you a Proprietor?—Give an Acc^t of yor Stewardship—Talents, &c.—*Of Thy own do we give Thee.*

360. *Devil.* All the Power he has over us, is that of Temptation. Force us he cannot.

361. *Riches.* We are not forbid a moderate care—To acquire, To improve, To secure R.—Industry is a Duty.

To villifye y^m is a Fault—Honestly gotten may serve to good ends—That they are not our Treasure, y^t they are Uncertaine—That they are Temptations.—All this true, but y^t they are Useless, &c., is not true.

Tis certain no man ever found true Happ^{ss} in R. X^{ns} therefore are to be warn'd agst setting their Hearts upon them, Trusting in y^m, &c.—*All this will I give Thee.*—This *All* is nothing but vexation of Sp^t. X^{ns} sh^d be convinced—That to desire y^m wth eagerness—Is to desire to be furth^r fr. Salvation—To be in a condition—wch will make us unwilling to Hear the Truth—wch will lead us fr. God, and make us Love every thing better than God—wch furnishes men wth what will please the Senses, stifle Reason and Conscience—A condition directly opposit to Humility and a Teachable Temper—Few dare be sincere wth those y^t are above y^m—The Rich have all the Infirmities of other People, and have less time and fewer meanes of being cured. [p. 81.]

In short, R. oppose X^{ty} in all its parts.—This bids us set our affect^{ns} on Things above.—R. set before us whatever may allure our minds, and make us Love ye World—We sh^d Hope and put our Trust in God.—Riches Tempt us strongly to confide in y^m.—They lead to Covetousness, which is opposit to Charity, &c. The Rich young man is a sad Instance how hard it is to part wth y^m even for X^{ts} sake, and where He commands us.—Who can be Humble w^n every thing tēpts Him to Pride?

Well, then, must they be flung away? No—But They y^t Have y^m as they Hope for Salv. must be *Poor* in *Sp^t* —*Humble*, tho' tempted strongly to be otherwise—*Temperate*, tho' they have it in their power to make Provision for ye Flesh to fulfil ye Lusts therof—*Charitable*, tho' &c. *Watchful*; Have a mean opinion of y^{m}s, when every body ab^t y^m is admiring their good Fortune, and Happy Condition. *Teachable, Fearful, Devout*—as standing in need of more Grace, &c.

[p. 82.]

1 Tim. vi. 9. They y^t w^d be Rich, βουλόμενοι πλουτεῖν, ... compared wth v. 17 of y^t ch.

R.—apt to make men Lovers of Pleasures more than Lovers of God.—Vid. Sins of Uncleaness, 112^h.

That J. X^t might dispose us for Heaven, He first brings down the Price of all earthly Idols—He chuses a Life of Poverty—(See Prejudices agst, 143, 144^h). Blessed are ye Poor—Take no Thought what ye shall Eat, &c. How hardly shall they y^t have R. God hath made our Lives short, y^t we may have no pretence to set our Hearts on this world. *The Things y^t are seen are Temporal.* Don't let a X^n say—I must do this or I shall be undon for ever—My *all* lay at stake, &c. This is not true. Nothing lay at stake, but a short Transitory Life, &c.—Perishing Treasures, &c.

Take Heed and beware of Covet.—Our L^d w^d not have said this but there is Reason for it—Experience shews it, and w^n we come to dye we shall confess ye Vanity of R. (See Introduct^n to a Devout Life, 279.)

W^n R. increase, set not y^r Heart upon y^m, Ps. lxii. [10.] That's the Time of Danger—Those y^t are most able are very often the least inclind to do good wth y^m.

The Dutys of the Rich encrease as do their Riches. What will all the advantages they afford us, be to us, if it sh^d end in everlasting death?—That we may so pass thro' things Temporal, y^t we finally lose not the Things y^t are Eternal.

[p. 83.]

How hardly, &c. For such men think y^{m}s above *Censure*,

^{h} [These may be references to a Common-Place Book.]

Reproof—(Ecclus. xi. 24 [i]). *Fear of God or man,* above Advice.—Tis Hard to have y^m and not to Trust in y^m—Hard to submit to changes—Hard to believe ye next world better than this.

Who then can be saved? Why verily nothing but y^t Sp^t and Power of God can secure a man beset wth the Tempt. y^t R. bring fr. being overcome by y^m.

J. X^t declined R. He did it to teach us not to be fond of such things as lead to Ease and Idleness.—(See Chillingworth, 398 [j].) Those y^t make the best use of R. run Hazzards of being Ruin'd.

After all, Rich Men are not to be Ungrateful to God.—R. are His Gift.—The Apostle tells us w^t use we are to make of y^m, so dos our Lord,—" Make to yor selves Friends"—" Lay up y^r Treasure in Heaven"—" *Poor in Spirit*"—Having no Consolation in the Enjoym^t of Wealth and Hon^r.

A Soft and Sinful Life, too generally ye Effect of R. " Thou Fool—This night."

We are but Stewards—Not Proprietors. The not considering this makes us eager in Contending [for] our Rights—Fall out for Trifles—That we are Account^{ble} [k] only for so much as we can keep wth Peace and Charity—That God can supply all ye rest.—Let us Lay up for our Children a Tr. in Heaven, where the Unthrifty cannot squander it—Administrators cannot diminish it, &c.

Gen. xxxii. 10. " With my Staff I passed this Jordan"—Here Prosperity is ascribed to God alone—And so may ye Greatest part of men acknowledge.—R. got by Deceit make [p. 84.] a man no more Rich than a Dropsy makes him fatt. Ecclus. xxxvii. 3. [?]

The True character of a Gentleman.—One who has a good estate and authority, &c., and makes use of these to promote ye Glory of God, the Good of his Country, and to Help those y^t are in need.

The False Notion w^{ch} *people have.* — He is one who lives at Ease—with^t Lab^r and care—with^t Fear of Want—accountable to no body — Have whatever his Soul de-

---

[i] [" Say not, 'I have enough, and possess many things,' and what evil can come to me hereafter?"]

[j] [Sermon on St. Luke xvi. 9, § 19, subjoined to " Religion of Protestants," &c. 4th edition, 1674.]

[k] [That is, to those who come after us.]

sires—Fears no Changes—Respected weth^r he deserves or not, &c. This makes all desire Riches so impatiently.

362. *Way to Heaven.* All ways are indifferent to one who has Heaven in his eye; As a Travailer dos not chuse that Road wch is most Pleasant, but y^t wch is most safe, and wch will bring him soonest to his Journey's End. So Prosperity or Adversity, Poverty or Riches, if God so orders y^m, are equal to a X^n. But if he is to choose, The way of ye Cross is certainly the Safest; J. X^t made choice of *That.*

363. *Christianity.* The End of X^{ty} is to Perfect the Human Nature by participation of the divine.

364. *Evil.* Disobedience to God's Will ye Occasion of all Evil and Misery.

[p. 85.] 365. *Truth.* Τὸ ἀληθινὲς [qù. ἀληθινὸν] ἐν βραχεῖ κεῖσθαι. Truth lies in a little compass.

366. *The K. of God* is within you, i.e. The Power of X^t subduing all the Irregularities of the soul, and keeping the Passions in order.

367. *Sincerity.* The conduct of our Lives the only proof of the sinc. of our Hearts.

368. *Riches.* Tis seldom considered How difficult a thing it is to Answer all the Dutys wch such a Condition Requires of us.

369. *Humility.* An entire Submission to the Will of G. in all things; Receiving with Reverence whatever His Providence shall appoint for himself or others, looking upon it as the Gift of God to ye World in order to some greater good, tho' at present it seem grievous.—Dead to all Preeminency before others—not fond of Singularity, Praise or Glory, in the World.

370. *Looking unto Jesus.* Practical—What did I? What w^d He have done in these circumstances?

[p. 86.] 371. *Brazen Serpent.* Design'd not only to take away ye Pain but the very Poyson y^t caused it. So the Cross of X^t is not only intended to Ease ye Conscience for past guilt, but to root all Sin out of ye Soul—To crucify Sin wth ye Affections and Lusts.

372. *Lord's Supper.* The best Preparation a Serious Meditation of ye Passion of X^t. Therin to be Remember'd—To see Him sold for Money—Covetousness, &c.[1]

---

[1] [om. 4to. The pen drawn through it in the MS.]

373. *X^n Mysterys.* In great Mercy Reveald for our Use, not for our Curiosity—X^{ts} Divinity—That we might worship Him with^t fear of Idolatry, &c.

374. *Designe of X^{ty}.* To root out Sin, and to destroy y^e [om. 4to.] K. of the Devil.

375. *Ordinances.* Tho' God has not tied Himself to these, yet He has tied us to ye use of them.

376. *Oracle of Reason.* Tho' the Unhappy Auth^r of y^t Wicked Book^m boasted of his Performance, he did not con- [p. 87.] sider y^t The Oracle of God is not to be met wth but in the Temple of God, in an undefil'd Body, and in a purify'd Soul.

377. *Image of God.* This is an uncontested Truth—
That God loves His own Image and Likeness :—
That He is well pleased that this Image should be restored in men :—
That He will effectually Assist all such as sincerely desire His Help to perfect His Im. in y^m :—
That to endeavour this is ye True way of glorifying God.

378. *Study.* I am taught by experience y^t ye finding of divine Truthes, as well as the Receiving w^n found out by others, is the special gift of God, vouchsafed to Soules fit by Holiness to Receive such impressions. *Dr. Hen. More.*

379. *Things valuable. Bp. Hall*^{n}. A young Saint, An old Martyr, A Religious Soldier, A Conscientious Statesman, A [p. 88.] Great man courteous, A Learned man Humble, A woman loving Silence, A Friend not chang'd with Prosperity, A sick man Cheerful, A Soul departing wth Comfort.

380. *Disappointments.* Let yor Expectation be moderate, and yor disappointment will not be grievous.—Events fear'd, often prove best, and where we have expected Satisfaction, we often meet wth Crosses.—These are God's ways.

381. *Truth.* One may do mischief by following Truth uncharitably.

---

^{m} [Charles Blount; he committed suicide in the year 1693. "The Oracles of Reason" was published in that year.]

^{n} [Holy Observations, No. 5. Works, 1620, p. 125. "These things be comely and pleasant to see, and worthy of honour from the Beholder: a young Saint, an old Martyr, a religious Soldier, a conscionable Statesman, a great man courteous, a learned man humble, a silent woman, a child understanding the eye of his parent, a merry companion without vanity, a friend not changed with honour, a sick man cheerful, a soul departing with comfort and assurance."]

382. *Joy and Pleasure.* If you can be good with Pleasure, God dos not envy you yor Joy—but such is our corruption y^t every man cannot be so.

383. *Self Denyal.* He y^t takes all ye Liberty he may will certainly Repent of it. In all earthly Pleasures be satisfy'd wth a little, and you'll never Repent of doing so.

[om. 4to.] 384. *Tythes.* He who gives all sh^d have ye choice. The choice of our Age, Time, &c.

[p. 89.] 385. *Wickedness.* Whenever you are contriving or doing any evil thing, consider who it is y^t sets you at work—That the Devils drive you, y^t sh^d terrifye you indeed.

386. *Charity.* Nothing must hinder our loving our neighbour—many things may justly hinder familiarity with him.

387. *Peace of Mind.* Nothing but Innocency and Knowledge can make the Mind truly easy.

388. *Controversys.* In most Contr. there is some Truth on both sides; prejudice will not let us see, much less acknowledge it.

389. *Superfluities.* To desire Superf. is a signe of Weakness: to know what is enough, and to desire no more, is ye great Wisdome.

390. *Religion.* Those are not the greatest Enemies to Relig^n y^t are most Irreligious.—A formal X^n dos more Hurt sometimes than an Atheist.

391. *Backsliding.* He y^t intermits Dutys, will either lose ye Faculty of doing y^m, or will have ye Pain of recovering it.

[p. 90.] 392. *Resolution.* He can never be good y^t is not obstinate, i. e. In doing what he knows he ought to do.

393. *Learning and Grace.* Tell me not w^t Learning a man has, but what Grace. Honest Ignorance better y^n profane Kn.

394. *Atheists.* No surer proof y^t ye majority are Atheists w^n Sins agst men are punished wth severity, and those agst God scarce taken notice of.

395. *Magistrate, Justice.* While Justice on publick offenders is duly executed, publick calamities will not be sent.

396. *Sins of Impurity.* Twas these Sins wch brought destruction, an entire destr. upon ye Canaanites. People do not consider this.

397. *Divine Nature.* Communicated to us—By *sincerity*,

i. e. by doing what is in our power to please God, and by avoiding w^t will displease Him—By *Self-denyal*, by Denying the Animal Life even in things indifferent if they endanger captivating us—By *Earnest Prayer* to God for ye assistance of His Sp^t to enable us to know and do our Duty.—Thro' the Powerful Mediation of J. X^t whose mediation aims at this first of all, to obtain effectual Help for all y^t ask it, to subdue all sin, and to "purify unto Himself," &c. °

398. *Peace of Mind* preserved best—By doing our duty, [p. 91.] and expecting our Reward fr. G^d only, not fr. man, and then, tho' we sh^d be ill-treated, we shall not be disappointed, nor our minds disturbed.

399. *Knowledge.* Affect it not any farther than it is serviceable to virtue and an Holy Life. There is an Intemperance in seeking after High things, as much as High feeding.

400. *Reason—Grace.* Human Reason, tho' never so highly improv'd, will fall short of a true Knowledge and Insight into Spiritual matters if not assisted by Grace.

401. *X^n Knowledge. H. Script.* How by Repentance and [om. 4to.] Faith we may Recover God's fav^r Here, and be Happy for ever.

402. *Tests of a State of Grace.* Jo. x. 27. My Sheep hear My voice. This a distinguishing mark of X^{ts} Sheep.

Rom. viii. 13. If ye by ye Sp^t do mortify ye deeds of the Flesh, ye shall Live, i. e. eternally—

(1.) *He that is born of God doth not commit Sin.* 1 Jo. iii. 9, i. e. All Wilful Sin inconsistent with a Regenerate State.

(2.) Hereby we know y^t we are in Him—bec. we keep His Comm.—Especially such as are called Relative Dutys—As also such as no law nor censure of man can Reach; that is a sign y^t we have regard unto God indeed ^{p}. Evil thoughts, [p. 92.] Designes, Malice, Rejoicing in Iniquity, being all as offensive to God, as murd^r [and] Adultery are to good men.

(3.) *He that doth Truth cometh to ye Light.* W^n a man is willing to examine Himself and ye Stat of His Soul—Tis a good Signe.

(4.) *Blessed are they y^t mourn.*—If I find y^t God's Sp^t has so convinced me of ye Evil of Sin both in myself and others

° [The last sentence has a pen drawn through it.]

^{p} [From hence to the words "way of Salvation," p. 94, om. in 4to.]

—That I hate it,—Am Sorry that ever I was under the Dominion of it—I pray and strive agst all the Remaines of it—wch are a Burden and a grief to me—This must be fr. ye Sp^t of God—(for of my Self I am nothing) y^t has made me see my danger—Leave my Sins—and Lead a new life.

(5.) Hebrews xii. 6. *Whom ye Lord Loveth He chasteneth.* This another Test, especially if Afflictions are Rec^d with Resignation to ye Wisdom, Love, and Will of God.

(6.) *We Love God, bec. He first loved us.* My desire to Love God must arise from Hence, y^t He Loves me and caused me to Love Him, and y^t I Love Him I am sure bec. I desire to keep His commandm^{ts}.

[p. 93.] (7.) 1 John iii. 14. *We have passed fr. Death unto Life, bec. we Love ye Brethren;* i. e. all good X^{ns}—He y^t is born of ye Flesh will very naturally Hate him y^t is born of ye Sp^t—He that Loveth Him that begetteth, viz. God—will Love all y^m y^t are begotten of God's Sp^t, all X^{ns}.

(8.) *If ye forgive men their Trespasses, &c.* Nothing but ye Sp^t of God can bring our Hearts to this—To Forgive y^m y^t have injur'd me—To pray for them—To wish their Happ^{ss}, and y^t I may meet y^m in Paradise, &c.

(9.) *Believe in the Ld J. X^t—and Thou shalt be saved.* I earnestly desire to Receive Him in all His offices—Of King—To Receive His Laws—Of Preist—as He is our Advocate and Propitiation.—Of Prophet—declaring ye Will of God, &c.

(10.) *Be ye Perfect, as yor Heavenly Fath^r.* Matth. v. 48; i. e. Be as Perf. as you can—Grow in Grace—be always endeavouring to be more perfect—A man is not destitute of Gr. bec. he is not altogeth^r Perf.—But God requires Unlimited Holiness—y^t He may reward men according to their endeavours to be Perf. as He is P.

(11.) A man may be confident He has ye Sp^t of God and is under His conduct, if He dos sincerely ask it of God—*If ye being evil—How much more will yor Heavenly* [Father] *Give His H. Sp^t to y^m y^t ask Him.* I having Pleaded this Promise of ye Son of God—I have Pleaded ye Relation of a Fath^r and His miserable child. I have Pleaded my own [p. 94.] wants, &c. He cannot deny these motives—He has therefore given me His Sp^t—now *they y^t have ye Sp^t of God, they are ye Sons of God—and if Sons, then Heires.*

Fr. all wch one may conclude y^t he is under ye Conduct of ye Sp^t of God, and in ye way of Salvation.

403. *Take Counsel of God;* i. e. Ask His leave and approbat^n before you act—This will both shew us w^t is fit to be done, and Restrain us fr. doing w^t is not fit.

404. *Character of a X^n.* He endeavours after Holyness—Lives not in the Practice of any known Sin—Gives the whole Praise of this to God, and to J. X^t who obtaines this Grace for him and for all X^ns—Lives as in God's Presence—Conversation unblameable—makes ye H. S., and particularly ye Example of X^t, ye Rule of his Faith and Manners.

405. *Despair.* No man is faln beyond ye Power of God to Raise him—He y^t can raise ye Dead.

406. *Morality.* God is to be obeyd in every thing He commands.—This is most certainly the great Principle of [p. 95.] Morality—He y^t will not obey the *Positive* Laws of God, cannot be said to be a *Moral man*, w^n once those Laws are made known to him.

407. *Necessity of Faith.*—He y^t Feeles w^t a sad condition he is in, will see the necessity of a Faith wch will Remove Mountains: such a Confidence in ye Power, Goodness, Promises of God, as may make him such as God has commanded us to be—wch must be wrought by y^t Sp^t wch raised up X^t fr. ye Dead—to w^m nothing is impossible.

408. *Resurrect^n of X^t.* God signify'd to all ye world by *That*, y^t ye Debt was discharg'd, for wch He was made a Prisoner by Death.

409. *Detraction.* I will hear you speak evil of others, provided you will own y^t you deserve to be evil spoken of yor self.

410. *Self Denyal.* He y^t dos not practise This Duty dos not put himself into ye way of Receiving the Gr. of God.

411. *Knowledge.* There is [such?] Light arising fr. a sincere good Life, as dispells all Darkness.

412. *Vanity—all is V.* We run fr. one unsatisfying Ob- [p. 96.] ject to another.

413. *Divine Grace* repairs all the mischeif wch Sin has made in our Nature—Rescues us fr. ye Slavery of our Lusts —Dispels ye Darkn. of our Understanding—Heales the infirmity of our Will—Cures us of Self-Love—Carrys us fr. y^e

Creature to ye Creator—And fr. being an Enemy makes him a child of God.

414. *Lord's Supper.* Jesus X^t offer'd His body a Sacrifice to God—To satisfy His Justice—To return Him Thanks for His mercys vouchsafed to Men, and to pay in their Name all y^t Debt a Creature ows to his Creator—The Preist who commemorates ye same sacrifice ought to have ye same Intentions.

415. *Holy Scriptures.* They y^t Preach the Gospel so as to accommodate it to the maximes of the World, The Interests of This Life—and to the Inclinations of Nature, has forget [have forgotten?] y^t X^ts K. is not of this world, nor design'd to promote its Grandure.

[p. 97.] 416. *World.* He who sees nothing in the W. wch he Hopes for, or Desires — Feares not its Threats — Is not Tempted by its Promises and Baits of Profits, Hon^rs, or any of its Idols—is not driven to Shifts—Seeks no Freinds, no Composition wth it—Is free fr. Avarice, Envy, Hatred, Strife, &c. This is y^t noble Freedom wch the Son gives His Servants.

417. *Duty.* Tis dangerous to seek for expedients w^n we sh^d do our Duty—This Pilate scourged J. X^t in hopes y^t it w^d pacify ye Jews, and that he might not be oblig'd to Act ag^st his Conscience in condemning Him—wch yet he did.

418. *Disputes* are certainly necessary, where Fundamental truths are attacked and to be defended—or w^n very dangerous errors are broached.

419. *Preists.* The Master will not be—is not—Honoured, where His servants are slighted.

[om. 4to.] 420. *Necessary Truthes* are always clear and easy to be understood.

421. *Riches* are Blessings just as Poverty or Afflict^ns are, viz. w^n men comply wth God's ends in sending the one or ye other.

[p. 98.] 422. *The Devout* see things in a True Light — They enter ye Ch. with veneration, knowing it to be ye House of God—They consider ye Preacher as God's messenger—His Sermon as God's Word—The congregation as God's children—The Sacraments as effectual meanes of Gr. and as inestimable blessings.

423. *Religion* dos not depend on our opinion—Its principles are as sure and lasting as God Himself.

424. *Great and Small Sins.* There is not a more dangerous illusion than y^t of making a distinction twixt gr^t and small Sins, whereas there is no such dist. to be found in ye whole N. T.—As if God could not be offended, or a Soul ruind, but by the greatest Impietys.

425. *Comfort and Feares.* Relig^n brings the greatest Comforts along wth it, but then it sh^d ever be Remembered, That such comforts belong to true X^{ns} only; we sh^d be very careful not to administer y^m to such as have no right to y^m— They y^t want to be awakend are by far more than they y^t want comfort. To teach People to make the best Use of their Afflictions—To teach People how to dye well—To exhort Sinners to a sincere Repent.—To let men know [p. 99.] plainly w^n they are and w^n they are not in a State of S[alvation].—This is ye true and only safe way of administring comfort.

On ye other Hand, X^{ns} are not to be terrified wthout reason.

426. *X^n Perfection.* Attain'd as all other Perfection by Degrees—So y^t a X^n is not to be disheartend by his Imperfections; God suits His Graces to our present condition, and accepts of our Endeav^{rs} after Holiness, tho' often interrupted —provided they be sincere.

427. *Learning.* The end of L. ought to be Holiness of Life.

428. *Riches.* They have this Advantage—They put it into ye Power of those y^t have y^m to supply all their own real wants, and to help others; viz. To provide for both worlds, this and the next.

429. *Knowledge.* An eager desire of Knowledge ought to be Governd and restraind (being as Dangerous and Sinful) as any oth^r inordinate appetite, even as those y^t are confessedly Sensual. Happ^{ss} is promised—not to the Learned, but to ye Good. The very Sin of Adam consisted in a Desire of Knowledge, not necessary Knowledge, for that he was Master of already, but in a sinful Curiosity and Desire to know more than his present State required, wch is only such Knowledge as is necessary for the Advancem^t of Piety and a [p. 100.] good Life. All oth^r K. is sinful.

430. *Grace of God.* By this, if we w^d speak to be Understood, we must mean A Sanctifying Principle wch joines itself to, and cooperates w^th, Ordinary means of Providence: Not a Power y^t shall force men to be Good in Spite of their Resolution to be otherwise.

[om. 4to.] 431. *Socinian, Arian.* Guilty of a Double Blasphemy—First in Asserting y^t X^t is not God, [Though He thought it not Robbery to be equal wth God,] and *Secondly*—In Implying that tho' He was not God, yet y^t He had an Ambition to be Thought to be so. Tho' He was ye Humblest of men.

432. *Common Prayers.* In these we Joyn and Pray, not as Private men asking Blessings for y^ms, but as a Religious Society exercising that Charity wch is the peculiar Badge of the X^n Relig^n.

433. *Religion.* They that Live with^t Relig^n will dye w^th-out any Hopes of Happiness.

[p. 101.]
[om. 4to.] 434. *Deceitfulness of Sin—Temptation.* That a man be not led by it, Tis necessary y^t a man have a Presence of Mind—A lively Sense of his Duty—A clear Conviction of w^t is fit to be done—A watchful Eye over himself—Has [have] great things in his Mind—Can see before him—and distinguish between time and Eternity—Or els he will be apt to follow w^t Passion and not w^t Reason and Relig^n suggest.

435. *Meanes of Salvation.* Tis God who alone knows our nature, and what is necessary to make us Happy. He cannot err in ye choice of these meanes, His Goodness will not suffer Him to lead us wrong—And therfore with^t enquiring into ye Intrinsic nature of these meanes we may depend most securely upon y^m as the very best way to Happ^ss, viz. The meanes wch God has prescribed, not those of our own chusing.

And these are His Commandments. Matt. xix. 17. And if men will be wiser than God—consult their own Ease,—Employ their Reason and their wit—Dispute every thing He has prescribed, they will certainly come short of that Happ^ss they Hope for.

436. *Law and Gospel.* Both require the same obedience wth this difference—That ye Gospel allows place for Repentance, and pardon upon y^t condition. The Gospel, as a *Rule*, abates nothing of ye Rigour of ye Law—As a *Covenant* it admits of Repentance—What was Duty and Sin under the Law, is so

under the Gospel—Good works are still required, still neces- [p. 102.]
sary. With this Abatement, that instead of a perfect obedience, ye Gosp. accepts of Repentance and Sincerity—and
'tis this makes it indeed a Covenant of Grace. But then we
must Remember—That this being an Indispensable condition
—There is no Hopes for mercy, If we do not sincerely
endeavour to keep the commandments, and if we do not sincerely Repent us of all our Sins—so as to forsake y^m and
bring forth Fruits, &c.

437. *Temperance* has Respect to ye Good Estate of ye Soul,
as well as ye Body—Tis not enough y^t I injure not my
Health by Eating, Drinking, &c., but 'tis necessary y^t y^e
mind be not carried away to the lower pleasures of Sense
so as not to relish those Heavenly Pleasures wch we all Hope
to enjoy hereafter.

This shewes why Mortification and Self-Denyal are so
much insisted upon in ye Gospel—They are necessary to
take off our Minds fr. the Pleasures of this Life in order to
fit us for those of ye next.

438. *The Order to be observ'd in keeping God's Comm.*
Moral Dutys, where both cannot, must be observ'd before
positive injunctions; Matt. ix. 13. I will have mercy, &c.
Works of Charity before Works of Piety.

Religion of the End, viz. Those Acts of Religion, those
vertues wch have an Intrinsic goodness in y^m—Before y^t *Religion of ye Meanes*; i. e. Those Instrumental Dutys wch are
only meanes of attaining ye other.

For Instance—Prayer is a Direct Act of Relig^n expressing
Humility, Dependance on God—Gratitude, Love, Confession [p. 103.]
of His Power, His Truth or Faithfulness, Wisdome, Goodness, &c.: before Preaching, wch is only a meanes of Incul-
cating These.

439. *Degrees of Glory.* The Nature of Things prove this
—For Holiness being a Qualification for Happ^{ss}—The best
man must be the Happiest, and he y^t dos not desire to be as
Happy as he possibly can be, is in a fair way of not being
Happy at all.

For this reason a X^n sh^d begin betimes, y^t he may have a
greater Stock of Vertues to depend on—At least to lose no
Time w^n once he is Convinced of this Truth.

440. *True Religion Consists* in a prevailing Love of God, and in an Effectual Resolution of Obeying Him in all Instances.

441. *Repentance is*—The gr^t privilege of ye Gosp. obtain by ye satisfaction made by ye Son of God, y^t we may be pardon'd on our Rep., wch we never could have hoped for wthout that Satisfaction.

442. *The Love of God* will make our Duty easy and delightsome, and setting us above ye world, will secure us fr. falling.

443. *Purity of Heart* consists in such a Governm^t of ye Affections as not only to forbear outward Acts of, but even all consenting to, Sin, or Suffering it [—] any kind [of] entertainm^t in his Heart. This is a sure sign y^t a man acts upon a Principle of Conscience, y^t he is a Sincere X^n—Bec. he pays a Reverence to ye Laws of God in y^t part where no worldly consideration can reach—Neith^r Fear, Shame, Interest, Decency, &c. And 'tis a vertue most acceptable to God, being an Acknowledgm^t of all His glorious Perfections after ye best manner—His Wisdome, &c.

[p. 104.]

Tis this that Influences the whole Life. Matt. xxiii. 26. Cleanse first ye Inside of ye Platter, &c.

444. *Holy Scriptures.* A man y^t Reads ye S.S. as he dos other Books, for Diversion, for Improvm^t in Knowledge, &c. only, and not with a Design to order his Life according to the Rules, Examples of Piety, &c., he finds there, will never by all his Reading, become wise unto Salvation.

445. *The Word Preached*, tho' by a Weak Instrum^t (wch God generally dos gr^t Things by) is likelyest to do Good, w^n men wait for Edification in God's own way, and according to His own Appointment. 1 Thess. v. 12; Heb. xiii. 17. And as for personal Faults—a good X^n will make a distinction betwixt the *Treasure*—and the *Earthen Vessel*=2 Cor. iv. 7; Matth. xxiii. 2. And tho' he be our Inferior (wch yet Humility sh^d not suffer us to think) yet a X^n will consider y^t J. X^t Himself did accept of y^e Ministry of Angels, both for y^e Comfort of His Body and Soul.—Besides, The Weakest man may put y^e Greatest in mind of his Duty, wch is one great end of Sermons—2 Pet. i. 12. Thus David was brought to a Sense of his Sin by Nathan.

446. *Lord's Supper.* Not to be looked upon as a mere [p. 105.] Ceremony, but as an Act of Religious worship, Ordaind by X^t Himself—As a Sensible Representation of His Death, and of our Spiritual Communion with Him and wth His whole Family—A means of keeping up the Remembrance of the Passion, and of applying His merits, and of obtaining God's Graces and Fav^{rs}, particularly the Pardon of our Sins, to every one of His members—And as a Pledge to Assure us of all this—And therfore not to be neglected by any X^n or Rec^d wth negligence.

447. *Church Communion.* Being appointed by God under ye Law, and by X^t under ye Gosp. as a meanes to promote ye Glory of God—To preserve the Faith entire—A X^n will not look upon hims. as in a Private capacity, but as one United to X^t and His Church—Praying to, praising God, &c. for every Fav^r He vouchsafes to any Member, &c.

448. *Governm^t of ye Senses.* It being much more easy to prevent than to mortifye a Lust, A Prudent X^n will set a guard upon his senses, wch otherways w^d expose him to continual dangers—One unguarded look betrayed David—Job made a Covenant with his eyes—Evil Communications corrupt good manners.

The more we abstain fr. sensible pleasures, the easier we can be without y^m—And ye more we indulge y^m ye more desirous we are to gratifye y^m. Besides, if we consider how [p. 106.] much they unfit us for ye Joys of Heaven, we shall think ourselves obliged to forbear—To deny ourselves, by wch meanes a less degree of Grace will secure our Innocence, If ye Concupiscence, wch opposes it, be diminished.

449. *Governm^t of ye Understanding.* Understanding a Talent, and an acc^t will be required of the Improvm^t and Use we have made of it. Universal Knowledge being Impossible—Little Things below our consideration—Things of gr^t difficulty to be learn'd, unless of Equal Importance, Things of no use to our gr^t End, wch is Eternal Happ^{ss}. A X^n considering this will be content to be ignorant of many things wch others admire—And will only strive to be master of such Truthes as are of use to conduct him to his gr^t End. —Such are a Stock of Sound Principles, wch may defend him agst Error and Direct him in the way he sh^d go.—Con-

cerning Maximes tending to ye practice of a good Life,—Doctrines according to Godliness; 1 Tim. vi. 3, &c.—And he desires more Light for no End but that he may better see and not miss his way—Avoiding 2 Rocks—*Curiosity* and Vain Glory—Either to amuse himself or to be admired by others, The Fault of too many men; and indeed ye little use that many learned men make of their knowledge is ye true Reason y^t Human learning is so much despised—After all, the better a man knows the grounds of his duty, the better he is prepared to practise it.

N. B. 'Tis not the Habitual knowledge of Truthes of Importance—but the Actual Sense of y^m upon wch a good Life depends.

[p. 107.] 450. *Governm^t of ye Affections.* Our Affections being strongly inclined to sensible good, for the sake of which we are often tempted to Evil, and fall into great disorders—To prevent wch a Prudent X^n will resolve at all times to sacrifice his Inclinations to Reason, and his Reason to the Will and Word of God, if Reason clouded or Bribed by a present Temptation w^d lead him to do any thing contrary to *That* Word.

A good X^n also submits his will to ye Providence of God wch orders all things for the best, how much so ever it goes ag^st the grain and his own inclinations—For God Loves us, and will ever chuse better for us than we can do for ourselves.

And bec. our Passions, unless kept under a strict guard, w^d lead us to infinit evils, especially that great evil, The disturbing our Reason, and making us unfit to Act wth Prudence, a X^n will do all he can to keep y^m within bounds.

451. *Governm^t of The Tongue.* Many being the evils of Tongue: a X^n who knows that by his words he shall be Justify'd or Condemn'd, (Matth. xii. 37)—will pray God and endeavour to set a watch over his mouth and keep the door of his Lips. By avoiding—

1. *All Profane discourse*, all Oathes, or making light Appeales to God—Or making Free wth His Word, or any thing y^t belongs to Him, wch are ye more provoking, as having less Tempt^n.

[p. 108.] 2. *All Detraction, All censuring of others*, whether true or falsly—For who made Me Better than They? All making

Free wth other people's Reputation, considering ye almost Impossibility of making Reparation for such Injurys—All Flattery, making those Proud, incorrigible, &c. w^m we pretend to Love.

Propagating of Lying storys; as having this great guilt—That no man knows what additions may be made by others to y^m To the Prejudice, Trouble, Ruin of our Neighb^r.

3. All *Boasting*, wch is ye Offspring of Pride, making a man a Prey to Flatterers, &c.

4. All *Complaining* and Murmuring, as if there were no over-ruling Providence, or y^t God did not do well in permitting things to fall out as they do—wch is a degree of Blasphemy.

5. *Positiveness*, or being Wise in our own Eyes. Is. v. 21. As if we were not subject to Error.

6. *All speaking evil of Dignitys*, i. e. of God in His Representitives—All Filthy Talking and Jesting—wch sh^d not come out of That mouth wch must eith^r Glorify God in Heaven, or will Blaspheme Him in Hell.

To prevent these Faults, a Xⁿ will consider y^t the end of Speech is to Glorify God and Benefit our Neighb^r, And will Trye all his words by this Test; And by useing his tongue to These ends, he will avoid infinit troubles Here, and much [p. 109.] greater Hereafter.

452. *Governm^t of Conscience*. Conscience is y^t inward eye (Math. vi. 22,) by wch a man judges of the Lawfulness of his Actions wⁿ compar'd wth ye Law of God, wch being the Rule of Duty (and not our false persuasions), A Xⁿ will endeav^r first to know what is the will of God, w^t God w^d have him do (that he may neith^r Act agst His Rule, nor be answerable for not knowing it). And take care to act accordingly.

In order to this, a Xⁿ will do nothing hastily, but take Heed to his ways; And he will often call himself to an Acc^t, and Judge himself y^t he may not be Judged of God. By this meanes he will preserve his Conscience always Tender, i. e. very sensible of any thing y^t may hurt it, and secure y^t Peace of mind on wch all the comfort of Life depends.

Two things a Xⁿ will do—Never go agst ye best Light he has, This will prove his sincerity—And 2, To take care y^t his Light be not darkness, i. e. that he mistake not his Rule by wch he ought to go.

[om. 4to.] 453. *Religion.* How a man may be safe in his choice. Having first beg'd God's assistance, who having designed us for Happ^{ss}, will not deny to direct us in the way that leades to it.

Therfore seriously Resolving to find out the Truth and to stick to it wⁿ found—He first considers the gr^t Design of Religⁿ, wch is—To manifest The Goodness, The Wisdome,
[p. 110.] The Power, The Justice and other Perfections of God, And by the Knowledg and Belief of These, To make men Holy y^t They may be Happy.

These Perfections of God being best set forth in His Word, he resolves not to chuse y^t Church wch denyes him That assistance.

But [that] he may not be greatly mistaken in the true sense of Script.—he informes himself How the First X^{ns} understood it.

He then embraces all those Truthes wch he finds in the Scripture, but some being more, some less necessary to Salvation, his zeal for y^m is accordingly; Rejecting such things as he finds no grounds for in the Word of God.

As to Discipline and Worship, he compares the Script. and the Purest Ages, and concludes, that if he can be of a Church wch holds Communion wth ye first Followers of X^t who laid down their Lives for ye Truth; wch Rejects all Novelties, Singularitys, Doctrines, Ways of Worship, wch those first X^{ns} knew nothing of, wch Teaches the Word and Administers ye Sacraments and oth^r meanes of Gr. &c. And lastly, if he finds that continuing in the Practice of this Religⁿ, it makes him Serious, Holy, Temperate, Just and Charitable, &c., he concludes with Assurance, That he's in the way to Happ^{ss}, and obstinatly persists in it.

454. *The World.* A Xⁿ considers it as a Place of Ban-
[p. 111.] ishm^t where he's like to meet wth Difficultys and Dangers— Enough to make him despair, were he not secure of an Almighty Protection, and a Prospect of an Inestimable Reward, if He continue firm to his God.—He therfore will be very careful not to contract a fondness for a Place where he is not like to continue long; and where he is sure to

meet with no true satisfaction.—He sees his own danger from w^t he observes in oth^{rs}—who are every day led by ill examples, corrupt customs, wicked Principles, &c. As also by the Pleasures, Hon^{rs}, and Profits of the world.

He sees dangers in every state of Life, In Poverty, in Riches, &c., he therfore acts and Lives as one who sees his Dang^r and the advantage of guarding agst it.

In the first place he considers—That his Lab^r, whether it be to *know* or to *do* his duty, will not be in vain.—Happ^{ss} and the way to it are within his power—Nothing els is, all els is vanity.—There is one only thing that, w^n we come to Dye, we shall Repent of, viz. That we have not thought of our Latter end betimes—We shall not be sorry that we have not had Riches, Learning, Hon^{rs}, &c. But that we have not made the care of our Souls the gr^t concern of our Lives— Tis too often that men think not of this till very late—And then begin to study How to Live w^n they are going to dye.

A X^n that is wise for himself, will Consider w^t the Sp^t of God saith—*They that seek Me early shall find Me.* Prov. viii. 17.—i. e. They shall find that Wisdom and Grace, wch is necessary to secure y^m fr. ye Dangers they are liable to, thro' the whole course of their Lives — fr. y^{m}s, fr. ye World, or the Devil, who suites his temptations to all States and Conditions of Life—A X^n therefore will walk circumspectly, as one who Knows w^t he is to lose if he dos not,—he will walk by Faith, not by Sight—i. e. he will not be Governd by his Senses, but by his Reason, and by his [p. 112.] Faith, making this the measure of Truth — viz. w^t God has made known to us concerning another Life; wch a wise X^n will always have his eye upon, That he may attain Eternal Life, and that he may escape Eternal Death; w^{ch}, if considerd and Believ'd, will quench all ye Fiery Darts of ye Wicked one.

To be for ever miserable—To be for ever Happy—Let us dwell upon these—Let us consider what sort of Life we lead —where it will end. Tis for want of this y^t X^{ns} miscarry.

455. *Principiis Obsta.*—If we w^d put a Stop to the Beginning of Sin, we must begin there where Sin begins—viz. in the Heart and Thoughts, wch the Gospel has subjected to ye Law of God, as well as the Outward Actions, wch was y^e

Error of the Pharisees, who took care of yᵉ outward man only—This will make our Duty easy.

456. *The evil of Sin* may be known fr. the Atonemᵗ yᵗ was necessary to make Satisfaction to the Divine Justice, and fr. the Punishment wᶜʰ it will be attended wᵗʰ—everlasting Misery; wᶜʰ even Infinit Goodness has Assignd, &c.

457. *Solitude.* The School of Wisdom, 'tis there she teaches us Secrets wᶜʰ the World are utter Strangers to. Hos. ii. 14. I will bring her into yᵉ Wilderness, &c. We know the World by Conversing wᵗʰ others, but our selves by conversing wᵗʰ God and our selves.

[p. 113.]
[om. 4to.] 458. *Repentance.*—Not to be consider'd as a Reserve after an ill spent Life, but as a Remedy for past Sins.

[om. 4to.] 459. *Meanes necessary for saving the Soul.* That a man know the Truthes and Dutys of Xᵗʸ, and that he lives accordingly. This he cannot do wᵗʰout—Thoughtfulness—Prayer and Circumspection; Resisting Temptations, avoiding the occasions of yᵐ—A man who will neither eat, drink, nor take care of himself, will soon dye, 'tis yᵉ same wᵗʰ yᵉ Soul.

460. *Tests of True Religⁿ.* If men wᵈ consider how far they are influenced in their Religⁿ by Shame, by Law, by Custome, By Example, By worldly Considerations, &c., They wᵈ then see How much true Religⁿ they have.

461. *A man wᵗʰout Xᵗʸ* cannot but be—In a State of Doubt, Confusion, Fear, Distrust, &c.

462. *Happy Life.* Lay nothing much to Heart—Desire nothing too Eagerly—Rejoyce not excessively—nor grieve too much for disasters—And be not bent violently on any designe. And above all, let no worldly Cares make you Forget the concernes of yoʳ Soul.

463. *Indian Catechism* ᵍ. All men are Sinners—They know it yᵐˢ.—God has made known—That He will call all men to an acctᵗ—That J. Xᵗ is to be yᵉ Judg of Quick and Dead—That He will Judge yᵐ according to their Works—That their Works will be Judg'd Good or Bad as they agree wᵗʰ or are contrary to His Gospel—That it concernes every body to know wᵗ That Gospel Commands or Forbids, that whoever Receives and Believes in Him shall have Remission

[p. 114.]

ᵍ [Perhaps the first sketch or germ of that work as it occurred to the author's mind.]

of Sins—That that Gosp. was established by Miracles, and therefore no questⁿ to be made of it, for God Rais'd Him from the dead on purpose to convince all men that His Gospel, His Miracles, His Declaring y^t He was sent fr. God, &c., was true, and at our peril to be believed. Repentance and Remission of Sins was to be preached to all Nations—Luk. xxiv. 44.

464. *Faith and Practice.* If it were as Easy to persuade men to do w^t they know they ought to do, as 'tis to convince y^m that such things are fit and necessary, and commanded, we sh^d soon see a Reformation y^t sh^d surprize us.

465. *Old Testament and New.* The Patriarchs knew as well as we, y^t Faith and Repentance was the only way to please God—They had Faith in the Promise of the Messiah—They confessed their Sins, &c. See Ps. li.—And in their Prayers there was nothing concealed but ye name of *Christ*, wch they expressed by *The Tender Mercys, The Loving Kindness of the Lord, &c.* In short, both Churches had ye same Mediator, The same Sp^t as well as ye same God—and for this Reason we use ye same Psalms, ye same Pray^{rs} as they did, bec. dictated by ye same Sp^t. As far as they embraced the gr^t Promise, so far they embraced X^t.—Thus Moses esteem'd ye Reproach of X^t, &c. This is of gr^t moment to be understood, in order to understand the Bible,—and we only add the Gloria Patri, &c., To the Psalms of David to make them Xⁿ Hymns.

466. *Morality.* The true notion thereof—it consists in [p. 115.] ye Practice of Xⁿ Virtue, proceeding fr. Xⁿ Principles and Motives.

467. *Faith.* An inward disposition as necessary as External evidence. Pride, Wicked^{ss}, Hate y^t Light wch w^d force him to forsake his Sins—He may be careless of his Soul—Abuse ye Light God has given him, and he may neglect to Pray for y^t Grace wch is the gift of God, and wch alone can discover the Truth to him.

468. *The case of Faln Man.* Not as y^t of a Creditor and Debtor (Socinus^r), but as y^t of a Rebel and a Gracious Prince — The one offering a Pardon, ye other despising it, &c.

^r [Socinus de Jesu Christo Servatore, Pars iii. cap. i. Opp. tom. ii. 186.]

469. *Death.* It concernes us more than our Life is worth to know w^t will become of us w^n we dye.

470. *God's Will be done.* So we Pray, but then when God manifests His will by events y^t do not please us, we repine, and in effect Pray y^t His Will may not be done, but ours—A greater Sin y^n is thought.

471. *The L^d rebuke Thee* [S. Jude 9]—*Higher Powers.* [p. 116.] Since the Angels y^ms do not revile such as [are] exalted in Dignity and Authority, but referr y^m to ye Judgm^t of G., we ought never to Speak evil of Higher Powers, but mention y^m wth Respect, tho' they sh^d not be w^t they ought to be.

472. *Injury.* Much better to suffer an Injury than to commit one.

473. *Judgments of G.* W^n once ye most Scandalous Sins become generally matter of Mirth rath^r than of Sorrow and Shame, we have reason to Believe y^t ye Judgm^ts of God are not far off.

474. *Failings of Good Men.* God permits these, that men may see plainly that there is no person in w^m Nature is not corrupted.

475. *Contentedness.* Necessarys are seldom wanted—Tis sensuality wch is never satisfy'd.

476. *Knowledge.* That K. of wch we make no use will only serve to condemn us. Such Kn. is to be dreaded.

477. *Faith.* People who will not believe the Gosp. want Faith more than Proofes.

[p. 117.] 478. *New Testament.* Behold a greater than Solomon is here.

479. *Holy Ghost.* A Sinner has no Remedy to Reclaim him who Rejects the H. S., who alone gives Grace, Repentance, &c. Where the Root of Faith is pluck'd up, all principle of a Spiritual Life is extinguish'd.

480. *Riches.* Thou Fool, this night, &c. N.B. Thus God calls those whom ye world admires for having Gotten great estates for their children and in a short time.

481. *Charity to ye Poor.* The Poor work miracles every day—We give y^m—and they give us a treasure in heaven.

482. *Infidelity.* Is either pretended or Judicial—Eith^r they Reject the Light, or are given up to their own Darkness.

[om. 4to.] 483. *Punishm^t of Sin.* Proceeds fr. God's Mercy, who w^d have us saved, or fr. His Holyness to make us like Himself, or by His Providence to let us know y^t He is Just, or by meanes of Fear to put a stop to sin.

484. *Kingdoms of X^t and of Satan.* Whoever dos not belong to ye one must of necessity be a Subject of ye other.

485. *Instruction—true method.* To Instruct with^t Insulting—To see Faults with^t exposing y^m—To Silence men without triumphing over y^m. [p. 118.]

486. *World.* We never know how much we love ye world till we find pain and difficulty in parting wth its good things.

487. *Death and Judgm^t.* Who will pretend to say y^t he is not in a very few days to Dye and to appear, &c.

488. *Religion.* Wicked men, not being able to excuse their principles or their Lives, Endeav^r to ruin the Authority of That word and those Pastors wch Reprove y^m.

489. *Loyalty.* It is a very material part of Relig^n to Hon^r God in the most lively Image of His greatness and Power.

490. *Humility in Pastor.* The marks of Grandeur are a Burthen to an Holy Bishop—He beares y^m before men, but thro' Humility laments them before God.

491. *Sin will find out ye Sinner.* Siñers often find y^{ms} forced to see their Sin and their danger, w^n they endeav^r to shun ye sight of y^{ms} wth ye greatest care. [p. 119.]

492. *Afflict^n and Joy togeth^r.* 1 Thess. i. 6. This is a Secret and Priviledge peculiar to Faith and the Gospel.

493. *Fill up ye measure of, &c.* W^n a man is not only content to neglect his own salv^n, but is Industrious to ruin oth^{rs}—he then is filling up ye measure of his Sins.

494. *Pastor.* His final state and sentence will depend very much upon his Faithful discharge of his Duty. 1 Thess. ii. 19.—" For what is our Hope, &c., are not ye, our Flock?" i. e. All ye Hope we have is—That we have taken care of you.

495. *Consolation to Sinn^{rs}.* Tho' ye Sin be to us Inveterate and Incurable, yet it is not so to an Alwise, Almighty Physician.

496. *Afflictions* sh^d oblige us to think of ye Justice of God, whose Goodness will not suffer Him to afflict any but such as He finds Sinners—We need not fear applying this consideration to ourselves, but it may be Rashness in doing it [to] oth^{rs}.

497. *Infidelity.* Too many are pleased wth objections agst the truth of ye Gospel, for this very reason, that they may not be oblig'd to live according to its Lawes.

[p. 120.] 498. *Miracles.* There are Miracles of Grace as well as outward miracles—The former are wrought every day in the conversion of sinners, and are not minded, altho' the conversion of a Sinner is as g^t a Miracle as any X^t or His Apostles wrought on earth.

499 *Ordinances.* God can dispense wth y^m and save a soul with^t y^m, but He will not save those that despise y^m.

500. *Human Reasons.* Our Lord never gives human consolations. Jo. xiv. 1. Ye believe in God, &c. Nor Arguments fr. Worldly considerations—" Fear Him^s," &c.

501. *Afflictions.* Both the Righteous and ye Wicked suffer—The one is better for y^m, ye oth^r worse.

502. *J. X^t The Way—Deists.* To know God wthout J. X^t is to know God without knowing ye way to appease, to please or to enjoy Him—This ye knowledge of Deists—If any such y^t are not Atheists.

503. *Faith.* The excellency thereof, wch makes us know
[p. 121.] things wch we cannot comprehend—makes us possess y^t wch yet is not, and makes us find satisfaction in the greatest temporal evils.

504. *Test.* The Persecution of Pastors discovers the true Sheep. 2 Tim. i. 15.

505. *Instruction.* It is lost Labour to endeav^r to Instruct those who are neith^r desirous, nor are willing to know the Truth.

506. *Judge.* A good Judge sh^d never boast of his Power, bec. he can do nothing but w^t he can do Justly: he is not the Master but ye Minister of the Law. Authority wthout Virtue is a very dangerous state.

[om. 4to.] 507. *Authority.* Jo. xix. 11. In w^t hands soever lawful Authority is lodg'd, we ought to look upon it as our Sav^r did, as coming fr. above.

508. *Judge.* A Judge, if he w^d not abuse his Authority, must be free fr. a designe of making his Fortune by his
[p. 122.] place; if he is not, he will never do his duty; he is no longer Master of his Conscience.

* [St. Luke xii. 5.]

509. *Temp. and Spirit. Power.* The more X^t reignes in our Hearts, the greater is our Loyalty and Obedience to Temporal Sovereignes.

510. *Courtier.* The Fear of displeasing his Prince, and losing his place, is what chiefly prevailes wth such a Person, if he has not Fear of God, he will sacrifice conscience &c. to y^t desire, &c.

511. *Troubled Mind.* Grief and Fear are a very plain proof of our Love for y^t wch we fear we want.

512. *The H. Ghost.* A new Principle of a new Life.

513. *Cross.* God dos not require it of us, that we sh^d not feel any uneasiness under the afflictions of this Life, but y^t we sh^d strive to overcome it by His Grace.

514. *Truthes* wch can never be too often preached—The [p. 123.] Bondage of Man by Sin—The necessity of a Redeemer—His Incarnation and His Sacrifice—The great designe of the Gospel,—The Judgm^t of ye great day—The Power of His Grace to Restore us to God's Fav^r, &c.

515. *Servants.* One cannot be secure of ye Fidelity (Honesty) of a Serv. who is not faithful to his God: But one who feares God,—one may depend on him.

516. *Sin.* God often permits Sin, even in the Elect, that He may make their fall instrumental to their Conversion and Salvation.

517. *Deism.* Whoever rejects the Mediator, declares war agst God.

518. *Learning.* Human learning may be of gr^t use to explain the Faith, but it must not pretend to regulate it anew.

519. *Despair.* All people ought to be brought to despair of Salvation wthout Holyness of Life.

520. *Afflictions.* If God permits any evil to happen to [p. 124.] us, it is bec. that very evil is our good.

521. *Conversion.* Acts xiii. 7^t. Natural prudence may contribute towards the conversion of a man, but nothing y^t is natural can effect it.

522. *Melancholy.* W^n I advise you to search yor ways, I must also caution you, not to do it wth a mind full of Terror, for by that you'll only fill yor Soul wth dread and confusion, so y^t you'll not see yor way: Tis one of those arts

---

t [Sergius Paulus, *a prudent man.*]

wch ye Devil uses, to hinder well-disposed People fr. bringing forth fruits meet for Repentance.

523. *False Teachers.* God permits these sometimes, to confound the Negligence, Idleness or Unfaithfulness of those who by their Profession stand oblig'd to defend and propagate the Truth.

[p. 125.] 524. *Rash Judgment.* Men of corrupt Hearts and ill Lives, are willing to have all men as bad as themselves, and so very easily believe, that there is no more Virtue, Piety, or Sincerity in others than they know to be in y^ms.—This gives them a False Peace, &c.

525. *Original Sin.* Every man is sensible of an opposition wch the Law of ye Body maintains ag^st the Law of the Mind.

526. *Fasting.*—From pleasant meates, rather than fr. all, as it w^d answer ye Ends of Mortification, in not gratifying ye Palat, nor ministring to Luxury, so it w^d agree wth every constitution, and answer ye obj. That my Health will not suffer me to Fast.

527. *Self Denyal.* Not to lay ourselves under any unalterable obligations—Tis often a great snare.—Besides, when one has it in his Power to enjoy ye world, Tis then a great virtue, eith^r to Deny ones self at such and such times, or to use it as becomes a X^n.

If a man w^d seriously apply himself to mastering the Infirmities of his Nature, and the Inconveniences he is sure to meet w^th, he would have sufficient to exercise this virtue [p. 126.] —To learn to bear the Pride of one—the Stupidity of anoth^r —The Rudeness, The Neglect of a Third, with calmness— To submit to Hurry of business w^n Duty requires it—To Noise, disorder, negligence of Servants; Disappointments, Loss of Goods, of Friends—To bear wth the Humours, The Follys, The Tricks, The Indecencies of those wth w^m we have to do—These are Instances of gr^t self-denial, if they are done in a Sp^t of Piety, wth sweetness becoming a X^n.

528. *The Devil.* No good X^n ought to be afraid of him, or of his Instruments, bec. he is a Slave of Christ's and can do nothing w^thout His leave—But a Sinner ought to Fear him, bec. he is the Minister of God's Justice and vengeance. —Wherever X^t dos not reign ye Devil dos.

529. *Perswade.* Those must be taken by their senses, over w^m Reason has no Influence.

530. *Sin.* God sees in S. the good wch He designes to bring out of it, otherways He w^d never permit it.

531. *Knowledge of God.* There is a great Deal of Difference betwixt knowing God as a Philosoper, and as a X^n.— [p. 127.] The first has little or no effect upon ye Heart—ye Latter fills ye Heart wth Love, and causes us to Love and to embrace His Law.

532. *Almes.* He who makes use of the Beggar's Hand to ask our charity, is the very same from w^m we ask *our daily Bread;* and dare we Refuse Him w^n we have to give?

533. *Love of Enemies* consists in desiring their welfare, Praying for y^m, Speaking well of y^m, And assisting y^m as their occasions require—No Lawgiver but God who sees ye Heart could give such a Law, so contrary to sense wth hope of having it obey'd,—but God, who sees it necessary to fit us for Heaven—If God had not Lov'd us while we were His Enemies, we never, &c.

534. *Proof of Original Sin.* God can punish none but Sinners—Death is ye Punishm^t of Sin—God declares it—Those dye who never were capable of committing any Sin by their own will—Infants, &c.

535. *J. X^t on ye Cross.* All men were wth Him on ye Cross, bec. He there supply'd their place, as their victim.

536. *Two Kingdoms.* If we w^d know whose Subjects we are, let us examin what Love, what Habits reign in us. [p. 128.] [om. 4to.]

537. *The Law.* The designe of the Law was to discover Sin (Rom. vii. 7), eith^r by Informing ye Understanding or by awakening ye Conscience.

538. *Self Denyal.* A X^n who dos not find himself under a continual necessity of contradicting, Denying hims., has Reason to fear ye Safety of his Condition; he's very blind, or Harden'd. [om. 4to.]

539. *Prayer.* The Eloquence of Pray^r consists in our proposing our wants to God in a plain manner—Lord, if Thou wilt, Thou canst make me clean—Lord Help me—L^d increase our Faith—My Servant is sick, &c.—Lord save us, we perish.

540. *Pray^{rs}.* Wo to y^m whose Pray^r God Heares, as

He did the Pr. of ye Gergesenes, w^n they pray'd J. X^t to "depart out of...."

541. *Thoughts.* Math. ix. 4. How many pass in our soules, unfit, very unfit for God to behold.

[p. 129.] 542. *Human Motives.* Math. xiv. 5. W^n a man resists sin on human motives only, He will soon be overcome ⁿ.

543. *They y^t be whole, &c.* Math. xv. 34.ˣ. It is God's way to make us very sensible of our wants, and ye necessity of Extraordinary Help, before He thinks fit to afford it.

544. *Rich.* A Rich Good man is more afraid of not finding worthy persons to give to, than a poor man is of not finding one to give.

545. *X^t Crucify'd.* We ought to Humble ourselves for being so miserable y^t nothing but ye Death of ye Son of God could save us.

546. *Riches.* Great Riches are too often gr^t Obstacles to Salvation.

547. *Knowledge.* W^n one considers how very, very often ye Jewes perverted, mistook ye words of X^t, one cannot but set down this for a certain truth—That none but Good, sincere men are capable of Understanding ye Gospel.

[p. 130.] 548. *Afflictions.* We know not w^t we lose w^n we pray to be deliverd out of afflictions, bec. God always increases His Consolation and Gr. as afflictions abound. 2 Cor. i. 5.

549. *Persecution.* Mark vi. 11.ʸ. J. X^t permits not His Apost. to avenge y^ms by their Apost. power, or even to desire y^t He sh^d do it.—'Tis their part to Lab^r with^t ceasing, To suffer w^thout Resentm^t, and to leave their cause to God with a full Trust in Him.

550. *Sin.* Mark vi. 27. Tis extreme dangerous to take even one Step in the ways of Sin—since 'tis so difficult to retreat—and since it almost necessarily leades to anoth^r.

551. *Hereticks, Infidels.* By obliging y^m to explain their opinions, the surest way to put y^m to a shameful silence.

[p. 131.] 552. *Love thy neighb^r as thyself;* i. e. desire y^t he may be free fr. ye same evils, that he may enjoy ye same good things; especially y^t he may be Happy for ever.

553. *Poor.* It is great comfort to ye Poor y^t they can give

---

ⁿ [Que-nel, in loc.]   ˣ [33 ? Quesnel.]   ʸ [Quesnel.]

even more than the rich (Mark xii. 43[z]), and to surpass y^m in Liberality.

554. *Christian.* Tis an invaluable Blessing for a man to be within ye Pale of ye Ch.—a X^n.—But then the crimes he commits in that State are great^r, and more is expected fr. him.

555. *Take My yoak upon you.* The generality of ye World glory in nothing more than throwing off ye Yoak of X^t—of Relig^n—of X^ts Ministers. Do they get ease by this? Is this ye way to be Happy eith^r Here or Hereafter?

556. *Heretick—Libertin.* An hidden Heretick more mischievous than an open Libertin.

557. *Almes.* The Dutys of Charity are Acts of Justice, since God requires y^m, and bec. we are members of the same [p. 132.] Body, and beholding to one another.

558. *State of Tryal.* Man is in a State of Tryal—This Tryal is for Eternal Happ^ss or Misery.

559. *Art of Instructing.* There being a secret Pride in man, w^n ever we w^d Instruct to purpose, we must do it by such a method as may make y^m fancy y^t they are already knowing and able to Instruct us.—We must ask y^m Questions as if we wanted their Light.—This will oblige y^m to retire Inward, and consult their Reason, and w^n they have given us the answers wch Inward Truth dictates to y^m, we must lay y^m before y^m every moment, or els they'll depart fr. y^m, and forget y^t ever they allowd y^m. But w^n you put y^m in mind y^t they are their own, self-love will make y^m allow and think of y^m.

560. *Plays, Operas, &c.* The great Designe of those y^t [om. 4to.] compose y^m is to raise the Passions to as High a pitch as possible, and to bewitch ye mind—So y^t it must be unfit for serious thought—and subject those y^t frequent y^m to every Temptation y^t shall assault y^m. God is not there—He will not Hear those y^t sh^d call on Him there for Grace.

561. *Children, Parents, Riches.* You Love yor children, [p. 133.] therefore you w^d leave y^m Rich, i. e. you w^d leave y^m in a state of Life y^t shall be a Temptation and a Snare to y^m, and fill their minds wth Hurtful Lusts. Our Sav^r Lov'd ye young Rich man, and for y^t Reason He bid him Sell all y^t he had

[z] [Quesnel.]

and give to yᵉ Poor—Have you yᵉ same Love for yʳ children wᶜʰ Xᵗ had for this man? No, sure.

Put you on yᵉ same just thoughts of yᵉ world wᶜʰ J. Xᵗ had, and wᶜʰ you will have wⁿ you come to dye, and you will tell yᵐ—That Riches are a Snare, that they Hinder us fr. Loving God and our neighbʳ. That they are hastening to a State in wᶜʰ yᵉ world will signify nothing to yᵐ—That all yᵗ Indifference for God and Holyness is owing to yᵉ wrong opinion wᶜʰ men have of yᵉ world—and to their valuing it too much.—That it corrupts yᵉ Heart, blinds the Understanding, and leads to ruin—That no man can see his true Interest or follow it but he yᵗ is dead to yᵉ World.

[om. 4to.] 562. *Maximes of the World.*   *Xⁿ Maximes.*

Maximes of the World	Xⁿ Maximes
Live up to yoʳ Estate.	Sell all yᵗ you have.
Vindicate yoʳ Honʳ.	He yᵗ smiteth thee on one cheek.
Let us eat and drink, for tomorrow we dye.	Watch and Pray, yᵗ ye enter not into Temptation.
Every man has his Fault.	Be ye perfect as yoʳ Heavenly, &c.

After all, God will not Judge men according to Human Rules, and the Maximes of yᵉ world.

[p. 134.] [om. 4to.] 563. *Riches.* There is nothing but care and vexation in yᵐ, tho' never so justly gotten. Luk. xii. 17.

[om. 4to.] 564. *Inconsideration.* We are astonished to Hear a man deny the Truthes of yᵉ Gospel—Now 'tis in effect yᵉ same thing whether a man dos not believe yᵐ or dos not lay yᵐ to Heart.

565. *Prejudice.* Both wicked and good men see with their eyes—But if a man has yᵉ Jaundice he dos not see as others do—The mind may be disordered as well as the eyes.

566. *Walking warily.* One may easily foresee the success of yᵉ day, by our beginning it seriously wᵗʰ God or yᵉ world.

567. *Sensuality.* Religⁿ requires a greatʳ mortification of yᵉ pleasures of yᵉ Palat than is generally thought of. Sensual a man may be without Intemperance—Sensual, not having yᵉ Spᵗ, saith St. Jude—Earthly, Sensual, Devilish. Jam. iii. 15.

568. *Governm^t. Rulers.* The Sins of ye Rulers are fore- [p. 135.] runners of divine vengeance. Zeph. iii. 3, 4.

569. *Riches, Pride,* do very naally beget a contempt of ye Law of God.

570. *Church.* The Gospel represents the Church as a People who sh^d take up the Cross, Renounce the W. and all worldly maximes and Policys, and even themselves. Who sh^d despise the Pomp, the Wealth, and Pleasures of ye W., and only glory in their Sufferings, their Poverty and Mortifications, and in their good works;—who sh^d bring Unbelievers to X^{ts} Yoak by Mildness, by Humility, and the exercise of a sincere Charity.

571. *Spare Time.* A man has no time for wch he is not accountable to God. If his very Diversions are not governd by Reason and Relig^n, he will one Day suffer for ye Time he has spent in y^m.

572. *Faith in God.* Before ye Cock crow thou shalt deny [p. 136.] Me—This shewes us y^t God knows our Hearts better than we our selves do, and therefore we ought to believe w^t God has revealed and declared, tho' it be never so Contrary to our Imagination.

573. *Death, Funeral.* W^n we attend a Funeral, we are apt to comfort our selves wth ye Happy difference there is betwixt us and our Dead Freind—Let us at ye same time remember, That every wicked man is dead while he lives—Dead to all ye true ends of Life.—Let ye Dead bury their Dead. Math. viii. 22.

574. *Petty Governm^{ts}.* These are too often Govern'd wth more Fierceness, Authority, &c. than real empires.

575. *Love of Neighb^{rs}.* How can ye members of ye same body Deceive, Hate and Envy one another? 1 Pet. ii. 1. "Laying aside all Malice and Guile."

576. *The Serious Temper truly X^n.* W^n a X^n considers [p. 137.] the almost universal corruption of the Believing world—He cannot sure but be very serious—And therefore all ye Mirth and Jollity—and Foolish Entertainm^{nts} which are propagated wth so much eagerness—are really as unbecoming X^{ns} as it w^d be for a Wife or a Child to rejoice at ye Death of the Husband or Fath^r.

577. *Resignation.* W^n God deprives us of anything y^t is

most dear to us—Health, Ease, Convenience, Friends, Wife, Children, Estate, &c., we sh^d immediately say, This is God's Will—I am by Him commanded to part wth so much, for His sake—let me not therefore murmur, or be dejected, for y^t w^d shew plainly y^t I did Love y^t thing more than the will of God.

578. *God Almighty.* It will be a dreadful thing to be convinced of the Power of God, by the Terrors of His Justice rather than by the Greatness of His mercy to Sinners, and such as Trust in Him.

[p. 138.]
[om. 4to.]
579. *Design of X^t and X^y.* To free us fr. ye Power and Tyranny of Sin, the Devil, and our Corruptions.

580. *They y^t be whole, &c.* Nothing but the Sense of a present Unhapp^{ss} or a prospect of imminent danger, will put us upon seeking, looking out for relief.

While they y^t are in Love with their Maladies, and think y^{m}s. safe in ye midst of Enemies, and well under the most mortal diseases, &c.

581. *Poor.* Do not be dejected—You are Happyer by far than you imagine—1000 times Happyer than they who enjoy Riches, Pride, Luxury and all ye delights y^t Riches afford.

582. *Separation, Schism.* It will be found at last, y^t Unity and the Peace of the Church will conduce more to the saving of Souls, than the most specious Sects varnished with the most Pious Specious pretences.

[p. 139.]
583. *Sufferings.* He that resolves to do his duty, and is true to that Resolution, will infallibly meet wth variety of Sufferings: both from within and with^t.

The nāal unwillingness men have to suffer puts y^m too often upon unjustifiable meanes of avoiding such inconveniences.

This is not to follow ye example of X^t. *He* voluntarily chose to suffer, *We* studiously seek to avoid it; and every thing that is capable and designed to mortify our Corruptions.

And if Reigning wth X^t be ye consequence of suffering wth Him—How few, &c.

584. *Ridicule.* Nothing is more certain from Reason and Experience, than y^t wherever the Sp^t of Ridicule prevailes,

they y^t labour under it are incompetent Judges of w^t is serious and sacred. Bp. of S^t. David's Serm. of Reform.ᵃ

585. *Tythes.* Nehemiah x. 39. *And we will not forsake ye House of our God.* So y^t to withhold ye Tythes is to forsake ye House of God, in ye Judgm^t of ye People of God. See ye Place.

586. *Reformation of Manners.* The restraint wch Con- [p. 140.] science lays men under, is so much greater than the Restraint wch Temporal Lawes and Punishments can lay men under—That if ever a Reformat^n of manners be effectually brought ab^t, it must begin at Conscience.

587. *Prosperity—Charmes.* It is too sure a sign y^t God is angry wth those w^m He suffers to prosper by meanes wch He Himself has cursed.

588. *Dutys of Station.* W^n I see a poor man taking care of his children, teaching y^m their Duty, or bringing y^m to be taught—I conclude this man—

589. *Riches.—Their danger.* Vid. 1 Kings x. Unjustly [om. 4to.] got. Job xxvii. 8.

590. *Evil Conversation.* If you see any man industrious to propagate Impiety, Infidelity, a disregard to God's Lawes and Discipline, be assured of it, that man is an Agent of [p. 141.] Satan.

591. *Covetousnes—Riches.* Vid. Hab. ii. 9. [om. 4to.]

592. *Lord's Supper.* W^n duly rec^d a meanes of obtaining the blessings represented by it—i. e. a meanes of obtaining all ye benefits of X^ts death.

593. *Prayer.* By this there is a Correspondence and good Understanding kept up betwixt Heav^n and Earth.ᵇ

594. *Honesty and Diligence* Seldome go unrewarded long.

595. *Lord's Supper.* Called Communion—bec. every man brought something out of his store to communicate unto ye necessitys of ye Saints.

596. *Offertory.* It was one Punishm^t in ye Primitive Ch. not to admit certain sinners to ye Offertory, who yet might joyn in other partes of ye Service.—The Ch., saith St. Chry- [p. 142.]

ᵃ [Sermon preached to the Societies for the Reformation of Manners, Jan. 10. 1727, by Richard Smalbroke, Bp. of St. David's, (p. 14. London, 1728.) The concluding words of the original are "of all that is serious as well as sacred."]

ᵇ [In the 4to. this is blended with one which follows in MS., p. 194.]

sostom, receives not offerings from the injurious[c].—This went in those days for a very great punishm^t.

597. *Conscience.* God only needs to deliver a Sinner to his own Conscience to be avenged of His Sin.

[om. 4to.] 598. *Plays, Balles, Assemblys.* How is it possible for a X^n to be Innocent in an assembly where the Angels of God cannot be supposed to be present, nor where one cannot ask the Blessing of God—Where the Senses are filled wth Worldly, Sensual Pleasures, and the mind amused with Vanitys of all Sorts—Modesty laid aside, &c., no restraint, &c.,—Reason confounded—by giving the Devil an opportunity of tempting them.

[p. 143.] 599. *Sins particularly forbidden in the Gospel :—*

Unreasonable Cares and Feares—A Love for Worldly things—Sensual Lusts—Ungovernable Passions;—Anger, Malice, Envy, Hatred, &c.—Pride and vanity—Falshood, Hypocrisy, Murmuring, Discontent.

[p. 144.] 600. *Peculiar Blessings of the Gospel :—*
[om. 4to.] God has given us His Son to Redeem us—His H. Sp^t to change our Hearts and to assist us in our Duty—The Gospel to be our Rule—His Life our Pattern—His Ministers to be our Remembrancers, and Watchmen over us—His Sacraments, as Seales of those Bless.—The Blessings of Et. Life to encourage us—The most Fearful punishm^{ts} after death to, &c.

[d] 601. *Maximes or Rules of ye W.—*

All this will I give Thee.
Let us Eat and Drink.

Vindicate yo^{r}self.
A Servile temper—this
A Cowardly temper.
A Servile fawning.
An Unreasonable patience.
Charity begins at Home.

Maximes or Rules of the Gospel.

Sell all y^t thou hast, &c.
Hunger and Thirst after Right.

He y^t Smiteth thee, &c.
Blessed are ye Meek.
Forgive yor Enemies.
Love yor Enemies.
Bless y^m y^t curse.
Freely ye have Received—freely G.

---

[c] [Hom. 85 on S. Matth., ed. Field, t. ii. 500; 73, on S. John, ii. 861, ed. Savile.]

[d] [This occurs on a fly-leaf at the end of MS. 5.]

[e]602. *Controversies.* "Ex illorum lectione surgam nescio quo modo frigidius affectus erga veram virtutem, sed irritatior ad contentionem." Erasm.

[f] 603. "Difficillimum est simul et multa et opportune dicere."

604. "A man's errors cannot recommend him to God, but his behaviour under y[m] may be acceptable to Him." Dr. Conant [f].

605. Political Squabbles, w[ch] have too often their Rise fr. Covetousness, Pride or Ambition, ought not to be meddled with by Divines; they have something els to do, and are set apart for better purposes. They have neither precept nor example fr. S.S.

606. "Tanto melius nebulam vidit [? videt] qui extra nebulam est."

607. "They more exactly strive to know the List
    Of Cæsar's Acts, than w[t] was done by Christ [g]."

608. "Small is the Blind Man's Grief, to theirs who see
    Nothing at all but their own misery [h]."

609. "Profess not the knowledge wch thou hast not." Ecclus. iii. [25.]

610. Hearts are divided, bec. Interests are different.

610*. No Devotion, no Service acceptable to God, with[t] a precedent Resolution of Amendm[t] in the Offender.

611. *Atheist.* Every man that dos not believe that he ought to obey God is an Atheist, let him call himself w[t] he will.

612. A Contempt of God and of Relig[n] do necessarily undermine the Peace of every nation—and hasten its Destruction.

613. *Sin.* One sin very naåtly draws on anoth[r].

614. . . . . "Ubi non est *Pudor*
    Nec *cura Juris, Sanctitas, Pietas Fides,*
    Instabile Regnum est."—Seneca in Thyeste, [215.]

---

[e] [Here begins MS. 6. The paging (in Dr. Wilson's hand) continued at 615. The intervening sentences on a fly-leaf at the beginning, headed by the two mottoes:—
    Medijs immotus in Undis.
    Tuta et Parvula laudo.
From 602 to 614, omitted in 4to.]

[f] ["Though no man's error commends him unto God, yet his carriage under an error may." Sermons by John Conant, D.D. London, 1693. Serm. iii. p. 96.]

[g] [Psyche, canto xxi. stanza 105. The Poem has "But more," &c.]

[h] [Ibid., canto xxiii. stanza 74.]

[p. 145.]   [1] 615. *Peace of Mind.* The only way to Peace is to give the heart entirely to God.

616. *Corrupt Heart.* Will corrupt the Understanding and Judgment.

617. *Providence of God*—Is the Comfort of the Righteous—His wisdome cannot be surprised, His Power baffled, or His Love Shortend—W^n men forget this—Feares, Disquietudes, &c.

618. *Eternity—Death.* The only Happyness of this Life is to be secure of a Blessed Eternity.

619. *Repentance.* There is no other choice but Rep. or Damnat^n.

[om. 4to.]   620. *Life* is given us for no other end but to work out our own salvation.

[p. 146.]   621. *X^n Motives.* It is necessary to act upon X^n Motives in ye most common Actions of civil Life.

622. *Pride.* Think not too much of the Good you have done, lest you come to imagin y^t God is in yor Debt—And begin to Repine that you have not a Reward Here.

623. *Wisdome.* True W. consists in knowing how to make every thing instrumental to our Salvat^n.

[om. 4to.]   624. *Love of our Neighb^r.* We never despise others but w^n we do not reflect upon our selves.

625. *Humility.* A fault wch Humbles a man, is of more Use to him than a good Action wch puffes him up wth Pride.

626. *Pride.* The Devil never tempts us wth more success than w^n he tempts us wth a sight of our own good Actions.

[om. 4to.]   627. *God's Grace—Knowledge.* There is not a greater mistake, than for a man to think that he wants nothing but to know what He ought to do.

[p. 147.] [om. 4to.]   628. *Love of God—Morality.* A man never keeps the Law of God, but w^n he keeps it upon a Principle of Love to God.

629. *Crosses.* It is a most dreadful Judgm^t w^n God pmits a Sinner to meet wth no Obstacles in accomplishing His designes.

---

[1] [Here Dr. Wilson's paging recommences, being headed in Bp. Wilson's hand, "Maximes of Pietie, and of X^{ty}."]

630. *A minister of God* is not to Receive to himself the Homage Due to God—but to take care y^t it be p^d to Him.

631. *Pastors.* The Remissness of Pastors too often ye cause of the Faults and Miscarriage of ye Flock.

632. *Faith.* We often know the will of G. wthout knowing the Reasons therof. And even then to submit wth cheerfulness is the true Obedience of Faith.

633. *Submission to God's will.* The Servant is not greater than his Lord. Think often of this, and you'll never complain of ill usage, of Afflictions, or Humiliations.

634. *Knowledge* without Practice will only serve to increase our condemnation. Jo. xiii. 17.

635. *Prayer.* The way to be always Heard, is to ask [p. 148.] nothing of God but y^t His will may be done. To chuse y^t for us wch He Judges to be most conducive to His Glory, wch will ever be best for us.

636. *Consolation.* We have God for our Father, J. X^t for our Mediator, ye H. G. for our Comforter,—will not Faith in these assuage all our Sorrows?

637. *Security.* There is nothing more Dangerous than [om. 4to.] to think ourselves Holy enough—and to fancy y^t our work is done.

638. *Prayer.* The Word of God is to be the Rule of our Desires.

639. *A Test of X^y.* To be a Disciple of X^t and to be lovd [om. 4to.] by the World is impossible—Jo. xiv. [xv.?] 19.

640. *Preacher—The World.* To pretend to Preach ye Truth with^t offending carnal men, is to pretend to be able [p. 149.] to do w^t J. X^t could not do.

641. *Affliction—Prosperity.* Happy is that condition wch forces us to put our whole Trust in God.

642. *Suffering.* To suffer for Righteousness, as an evil doer, is the greatest Humiliat^n—But then it makes a X^n more conformable to X^t.

643. *Enemies.* We have more reason to Love than to Hate y^m, If we look upon y^m as Instruments of our Sanctification, as they really are w^n they give us occasion of exercising our virtue.

644. *God and the World.* Sad is ye Condition, and vain the Endeav^r of those that w^d please both these.

G g

645. *Concupiscence* consists in the Love of present pleasure.

646. *Authority.* Tis necessary that one sh^d sometimes forget y^t he is a Superior, and to remember y^t he is a Brother.

[p. 150.] 647. *Pastor.* The double duty of a Pastor is—To Instruct by the Word, and to Pray for Grace y^t it may become effectual to y^m that hear it.

648. *God's Ministers Protected.* Rev. iii. 10. God takes particular care of His Ministers, w^n they are truly careful to promote His Glory, &c.

649. *Human Misery.* Men feel by experience y^t they want that in y^{m}s wch is necessary to make them happy—They seek it in the creatures, and are disappointed.—If they w^d seek it in God, they w^d be sure to find it.

650. *World—Afflictions.* Those w^m God Loves, He weanes fr. ye Pleasures of this World. By Afflictions, &c.

651. *H. Scripture.* The reading of S. (w^n serious) is ever attended wth a Blessing—Acts viii. 28; for instance—The Ethiopian Eunuch.

[om. 4to.] 652. *Contempt* and evil treatment, is less to be Feard in a minister of ye Gospel, than Praise and kind Usage.

[p. 151.]
[om. 4to.] 653. *Sin—Temptation.* Whoever stops not at the first Temptation to, and degree of Sin, runs the Hazzard of arriving at the last and greatest.

654. *Calumny.* A X^n runs greater Hazzards from Commendation, than from an unjust Calumny.

655. *Christian.* To be a X^n is to follow the Rules and Precepts delivered by X^t.—To Love w^t He Lov'd and to despise w^t He despised, &c.

656. *Covetousness.* The fewer desires the more Peace.

657. *Happyness.* God will not suffer any soul to be Happy, wch seeks its Happyness in any oth^r but Himself. Hence disappointm^{ts}, &c.

658. *Progress of Sin.* W^n a man is once out of the way of God, he easily falls from one sin to another.

659. *Imperfections, Failings.* Let us not afflict our selves wth these. Our Perfection consists in opposing y^m.

[p. 152.] 660. *Misbelief.* Men very easily persuade y^{m}s that what is contrary to their Inclinations, is contrary to Reason and Religion.

661. *Good Works—Obedience.* Our Life is the only proof of our Faith.

662. *Perseverance—Confirmation.* The World, the Flesh, and the Devil are not so easily Vanquished as Renounced.

663. *Self-Denyal.* If God suffers us to follow our nāal Inclinations, we are sure to be for ever undone. We are therefore to Pray to Him to give us the Grace of Self-Denyal.

664. *Peace of Mind.* The sure way to attain it, is to be content to suffer one's self to be Govern'd and guided by ye Word of God, or a Prudent Pastor—who has ye care of our Souls.

665. *Rash Judgm^t.* The way to prevent it in our selves is to consider our own faults before we censure the conduct [p. 153.] of others.

666. *Poverty.* A man is not forsaken of God bec. he is in want. The very Disciples were forc'd to pluck the eares of Corn w^n J. X^t was wth y^m, w^n He c^d have supplied y^m wth one word.

667. *Humility—Pastor.* Far be fr. us the Pride of those [om. 4to.] who will not Impute the Faults and Unfruitfulness of their Ministry to y^{m}s, but to their Flock.

668. *Blindness* in Spiritual things is ye just and nāal Punishm^t of a Carnal Life.

669. *Ambition.* To be solicitous to better the condition of so very short a Life (unless oblig'd to it by the plain appointment of God) savours very little of a true X^n Faith.

670. *World.* Have no more commerce wth ye W. than is absolutely necessary. And if you w^d have it to Reverence [p. 154.] you, treat it always wth an Holy Severity.

671. *Poor in Spirit.* Mark vi. 8, 9, &c. A minister of ye Gosp. is not bound to part wth all, or to serve ye Ch. by depriving himself of all things—But whoever is not ready to be depriv'd of all, rath^r than be wanting to his duty, is not worthy of ye name of an Apostle of J. X^t.

672. *Eternity—Time.* Now is the time in wch we must chuse what and where we will be to all eternity; there is no time to be lost, to make our choice in.

673. *Prayer.* If we have not what we pray for, let us believe either that we have not asked as we ought to have

done, or that it is good for us that we sh^d not have ye thing we prayd for.

674. *Understanding.* The corruption of ye Heart is ye cause of the corruption of ye Understanding and Judgm^t.

[p. 155.] 675. *Afflictions.* Whatever befalls us, by meanes of the creatures, wheth^r we suffer by ye injustice of men, or fr. any unforeseen Accident, it still proceeds fr. God, either to restrain us by Fear, or to draw us fr. sin out of mercy : or to Punish us in this world, y^t He may not be oblig'd in Justice to do it in ye next. W^n we turn a deaf ear to these, 'tis God w^m we refuse to Hear.

676. *Life* is given and continued for no other end but to glorify God, and to save our souls. This is not often enough thought of.

677. *Salvation—Delusion.* Men flatter y^{ms} y^t their salvation is always in their own Hands, y^t they can set ab^t it, and secure it w^n they please. A very great Delusion. St. Luke xiii. 24.

678. *The Threats of Men* are nothing, so long as God permits y^m to do nothing.

[om. 4to.] 679. *Xty.* It is necessary to be X^{ns} (i. e. to Govern ourselves by motives of X$^{t.y}$) in the most common Actions of our Life.

[p. 156.] 680. *Business.* None is innocent w^n it hinders us fr. minding our salvation, and making y^t y^e gr^t business of Life.

[cf. 622.] 681. *Pride.* Tis a very dangerous thing to think too much of the good we have done, lest we sh^d imagin that God is in our Debt, and to expect our Reward here, and lest God sh^d give us our desires.

682. *Mercy of God.* Tis a False notion of God's mercy, viz. that it has no bounds or Rules, wch is the Ruin of many. Our L^d tells us (Luk. xvii. 30) y^t it shall be with Sinners, as it was wth Sodom ; let us judge by that of God's mercy and Justice.

683. *Sin and Wickedness.* The more we see in others, the more ought we to fear for our selves.

684. *Rash Judgm^t.* In order to Judge well of others 'tis necessary to know the Heart.

685. *Opportunity lost.* Zachæus, Luke xix. Men have

been lost for neglecting to take some certain steps, upon wch God has made their Salvat^n to depend.

686. *Conversion.* No true C. w^thout a Change of Life.

687. *Almes.* Let y^m be in some measure proportion'd to [p. 157.] our Substance and to our Sins.

688. *Sinners.* To punish Sinners, God need only abandon them to their own Passions; they'll soon be miserable.

689. *Inconsideration.* We are afraid of representing things of the greatest concern to us, to our minds by frequent meditation, lest it sh^d make us uneasy. And our misfortune is, we are not uneasy enough; but can this unthoughtfulness hinder what God has declar'd shall follow?

690. *Deism—Atheism.* He y^t acknowledges a God, w^thout knowing his own misery, is no more than a Deist; as he is an Atheist who sees his own misery w^thout know[ing] and confessing a God who is able and willing to Help him.

691. *Elect and Reprobate.* God's Mercy and Goodness towards ye former is more amazing than His Severity toward ye latter.

692. *Scruples.* There are very many cases where we must submit to the Judgm^t of others, or els we could not be said to Judge Reasonably.

693. *Afflictions* are always useful, especially w^n they oblige [p. 158.] us to have recourse to God.

694. *Miracles.* Men are generally fond of Hearing, and ready enough to Believe Strange things, unless w^n God is the Author of y^m.—'Tis then they begin to doubt of y^m.

695. *Miracles.* God works more invisible miracles than visible—The last were designed to strengthen ye Beliefe of the former—Tis a security y^t God will do ye former w^n there is occasion.

696. *Fear of Man, &c.* To neglect our Duty for fear of man or any Temporal evils, is to forget ye Ang^r of God.

697. *Knowledge.* Lu. vii. 31 (?). Humility opens ye Heart to Divine Truth, while Pride shuts it ag^st the Plainest Proofs.

698. *Knowledge—Faith.* Without the gift of Faith men [om. 4to.] see nothing but Absurdities in the mysteries of Relig^n.

699. *Knowledge.* To be distinguished by great Talents and excellencys will fill the mind wth Pride, will keep out of ye Heart and Understanding all saving Truth. [p. 159.]

700. *God and the World.* Wⁿever we take ye Part of Truth, if we w^d not be deceiv'd, let us not expect a good Reception fr. the World.

701. *Infidelity.* 1 Tim. iv. 1. Too often a just punishment of that curiosity wch leads men to lend an ear to the wicked Reasonings of Libertines. These are ye Seducing Spirits, &c.

702. *Penitent.* A penitent Sinner is no longer a Sinner in the sight of God.

[om. 4to.] 703. *Knowledge.* How knowing soever a man may be, whether in S.S. or Divinity, there is a way of knowing wch depends upon God alone, with^t wch their knowledge is of no use to y^m. By Humility and Prayer this is to be attained. While men fancy they have knowledge enough, they use not these meanes, and so continue ignorant, tho' their attainments otherways may be very great.

704. *Custome.* Disorders are not less criminal for being common, nor will they be less punished on this acc^t.

705. *Cause of infidelity.* Men pretend They want proofes wⁿ 'tis only that they may not obey the Truth if they sh^d see it made out.—Others say ye S.S. are obscure, that [they]

[p. 160.] may have a pretence not to study y^m—nor to follow their Directions.

706. *Weaknesses of Nature.* God will judge us not for the Affections of Human Nature, but for the Choices of our Will—J. X^t Himself was tempted, Fear'd Death, &c.

707. *Temporal Good things.* The more plentifully God bestowes y^m The more jealous we sh^d be of our selves—and the more earnest to beg of Him ye Gr. to make a good use of y^m, or els they are a snare, &c.

708. *God's Foreknowledge* imposeth no necessity upon ye Will—The Corruption of the Will is ye sole cause of Sin, God has no part in causing y^t Corruption: and if He foretells things, 'tis only bec. He foresees y^t they will certainly come to pass.

[om. 4to.] 709. *Miracles.* We wish for miracles—Why, 'tis a miracle y^t a Xⁿ avoides any wickedness, or chuses any Action y^t is good, Considering y^t he has within himself the Seedes of every Sin w^tever—and y^t ye Devil, if not restrained, w^d make them grow up. Tis by a Supernatural Power He is restrained.

710. *J. X^t Crucified.* A Sacrifice on wch depended the Salvation of the whole World.

711. *Almès* are due in Justice (wthhold not good, &c., [p. 161.] [Prov. iii. 27]), but we are at ye same time ye greatest gainers.

712. *God's own Time.* He has His own proper times and seasons, and He enables us by His Gr. to do that at one time wch we could not do at another.

713. *Knowledge.* Jo. xiv. 5. There are a great many [om. 4to.] Truths, wch become plain as occasion requires, and in proportion as we apply our minds to y^m, and as God opens our Understandings.

714. *Nature Corrupt.* It appears in nothing more than this—To see man forsaking his true good, and pursuing vanity wth all his might.

715. *X^t and ye World.* Jo. xv. 19. To be a X^n and to be lov'd by ye world, is a Paradox wch the Gospel does not allow of.

716. *Proof of Xty.* An Invincible proof of ye Truth of ye X^n Relig^n, y^t J^s X^t foretold exactly whatever sh^d happen both to Himself and ye Ch., and y^t His Doctrine sh^d prevail over the powers of ye World, and agst ye very Corruptions and Inclinations thereof: not by force, but by suffering, and by the Word and Sp^t of God alone.

717. *The Sins of others.* Shew us w^t we ourselves sh^d be [p. 162.] wthout ye Grace of X^t.

718. *H. S. obscure.* That we may apply ourselves to study y^m, and y^t we may have recourse to ye H. Sp^t by wch they were written for the Understanding of y^m.

719. *Members of one Body.* It is the settled order of Providence y^t men sh^d depend one upon anoth. For Instruction, for bread,—For Protection, for Advice, for Justice, For Prayer (viz. ye Poor for ye Rich), for Peace, &c.

720. *Truth.* Men are often more afraid to know it, than to be ignorant of it.

721. *Prayer* being the desire of the Heart, it follows, That he who leades an evil Life, is continually offering a wicked Prayer to God.

722. *Holy Scriptures.* He that is of a Teachable Temper, will submit to the Rules of ye Gospel in their plain and

obvious sense; and he y^t will not do so, will run into endless errors, even as much as if ye Gospel had never been preach'd.

[p. 163.] 723. *Virtue.* Every virtue consists in Denying some corrupt inclination of our depraved nature.

724. *Faith, obstacles.* Wherever there is an Inclination to Dispute the Faith, there can be no Disposition to Believe and embrace.

725. *Scepticks* determine peremptorily concerning those very things, wch they propose as Doubts.

726. *Error.* There is a Contagion of Minds as well as of Bodys, wch communicates its self by ye ways and manners of those wth w^m we converse. And this too often happens, w^n men instead of consulting inward Truth, they attend to ye sentiment of others, who have already corrupted y^ms, and by an Imposing air endeav^r to corrupt all ab^t y^m.

727. *Vanity.* The Remembrance of our own Infirmities and Miserys an excellent Antidote against ye Poison of Vanity.

728. *Cross.* Acts xiv. 22. Since the Fall there is no Salvat^n to be hoped for but by the Cross. In ye Sweat of &c.—We must thro' much tribulation, &c.—This is a Fundamental Truth. The good Lord engrave it upon my Heart.

729. *Glory belongs to God.* For 'tis He y^t gives Success to the Lab^rs of His Ministers—Let us beware of taking it to ourselves.

[p. 164.] 730. *Food—Intemperance.* Without the Grace of God, that wch is intended and necessary for ye Life of ye Body, becomes the Death of the Soul.

731. *Pleasures.* W^never we find y^t we use Pleasures w^thout Fear, we ought forthwith to forsake y^m.

732. *A X^n* ought to be such in the whole conduct of his Life, as well as in Acts of Religion.

733. *Difficultys.* W^n a man considers y^t God is as Powerfull ag^st all men as ag^st one single Person, A good X^n will not be cast down tho' the whole World strive to oppress him.

[om. 4to.] 734. *Authority.* All authority comes fr. God originally, and therefore do's never lose its Rights in those w^m He hath clothed wth it.

735. *Human Meanes.* The Designes of God are generally to be accomplish'd by Human Meanes—God assures

S^t. Paul, Acts xxiii. 11, that He w^d protect him fr. his enemies, and yet S^t. Paul, v. 17, applies to ye chief Captn for his security.

736. *Darkness.* This Life is truly calld so, bec. it hides [p. 165.] fr. us things of ye greatest concern to us—wch we mind not, understand not, while we are busy'd wth ye World.

737. *Wheth^r we eat or drink;* i. e. make all the Actions of [om. 4to.] yor Life an Holy Sacrifice to God.

738. *Watch and Pray.* He who thinks he can be a good X^n and secure his Innocence wthout doing so, must fancy y^t our Lord did not know w^t was in man w^n He made these ye standing meanes of securing X^{ns} fr. falling into Temptation.

739. *Holy Scriptures.* If we w^d not fall into endless Errors and Mistakes touching the Designes and Will of God, we must receive the Gospel in ye plainness and simplicity thereof, with^t wire-drawing it, to bring it to our own sentiments and desires.

740. *Strait Gate.* This is ye only passage to Heaven, for all X^{ns}, Rich and Poor, Great and Mean.

741. *Virtue* consists in a continual struggle and guarding [om. 4to.] agst contrary Vices.

742. *Prayer.* There cannot be a better way of Judging [p. 166.] of w^t Spirit we are of, as [? than] the trying to recommend our Actions to God in our Prayers. If we dare not recomend y^m to God—we may be sure they are evil. This is not to be understood of Trifles, but of things of Concern.

743. *Conversation.* The manner of our ordinary Conversation is that wch either Hardens People in Sin, or awakens y^m to a sense of Piety.

744. *Conversation.* We always do good or Harm to others by the manner of our Conversation.

745. *Learning.* All is impertinent and sinfull, that dos not make a man more sensible of his Duty, Fill ye Mind wth true and solid Light, Help to Reform the Heart, and the Manners, inspire us wth Temperance, Humility, Devotion, and Contempt of ye World, Give us right Notions of God and of our selves, of our Misery and Corruption, and how to cure y^m.—Whatever Learning dos not do this, is useless and [p. 167.] sinfull. He takes pains in y^t wch will do him no more good than the Miser's baggs w^n he is dead. His mind is taken

up wth false satisfactions wch separate him fr. God and Goodness.

746. *Troubles.* The difficulties we complain of are laid in our way, that we may make y^m so many steps to Perfection and Happ^ss.

747. *Spirit of ye World* is the Love of sensual Pleasures; wch fixes the Heart to this World, so y^t it cannot raise its self to God. God will have the Heart entire; w^n 'tis filled wth the World, there is no place for Him.

Relig^n accounts most of those Pleasures Criminal, and as leading to the greatest Sins, wch ye World calls Innocent; If we are to be govern'd by voices, Relig^n will lose ye cause.

748. *X^ts Yoak.* They that w^d make X^ts yoak easy by dispensing wth the Love of God, and permitting Men to Love ye World, are bad Directors.

749. *Sensible Pleasures.* Let y^m be what they will, wheth^r those of Youth or of Old Age, of the Rich or of ye Poor, of Learning or Ignorance, w^t ye world calls Innocent or Criminal, yet they separat us from God, and as such [are] to be avoided as we hope for Heaven.

[p. 168.] 750. *Scepticism.* Men that accustome y^ms in Human Sciences (in wch they find little or nothing certain) to Judge according to the Light of Reason, condemning every thing that dos not agree therto, are often rash enough to carry y^t Principle into ye concerns of Relig^n, and to Doubt of things Revealed, w^thout Remorse.

[om. 4to.] 751. *Learning.* Wretched is the man y^t knows every thing but God.

[om. 4to.] 752. *Love of God* will always be according to our Knowledge of Him, and His Perfections.

[om. 4to.] 753. *H. Scriptures.* Tho' we acknowledge ye H. S. to contain all things necessary to Salv., yet we deny the consequence that therfore nothing els is necessary.—For a man w^d very much mistake their meaning, who did not understand ye language in wch they were written—the Customes and Controversies of the Times,—and who did not read y^m wth an unprejudiced mind. For if people will read ye S.S. wth a desire to find, not ye Will of God, but their own Fancys, &c.

[p. 169.] 754. *Afflictions.* If Good men will scramble wth ye Wicked for that wch is properly their Portion and Happ^ss, 'tis no wonder that they come by ye worst, for "this is their Hour, and the Power of Darkness."

755. *Persecutions, Reformation.* When mild meanes will [om. 4to.] not do to Reform the Church (viz. by meanes of Lawful Magistrates), then God dos it generally by ye Meanes of Persecution.

756. *Knowledge of God.* In order to know God, y^t is, to have an Experimental K. of Him, we are required to meditate upon His Excelencys, Praise Him, Pray to Him, &c. That by such Exercises as These we may gain a settled Esteem for and Love of Him.

757. *Calamitys, Afflictions.* And many and many a Soul has dated its Salvation from some such happy calamity.

758. *Virtue.* Every — consists in opposing and resisting all Temptations to ye Contrary vice—Charity, in opposing continually Self-Love and Envy—Humility, all Tempt. to Pride.

759. *World.* There is no condition of Life (Poverty, [p. 170.] Riches, &c.) in wch a X^n is not oblig'd to Renounce ye World, as he hopes for Heaven. No man can Love God with all his Soul, who has not renounc'd ye Love of the World.

760. *Love of ye World.* We are equally oblig'd to Renounce the *World*, y^e *Flesh*, and y^e *Devil*—We see plainly the Sin of following the 2 last—We overlook this great Truth—That 'tis the Love of ye World wch gives the other all their Power over us—and ministers Occasions of such sins as we abhorr ye Thought of, till we are ruin'd by y^m.

761. *Who then can be sav'd?* Men are apt to say this— And at ye same time to Live as if it were the easyest thing in the World.

762. *Learn of Me, saith X^t.* So y^t we must endeav^r to possess our Souls with ye same Sp^t wch was in X^t w^n He was upon earth.

763. *Eternal Salvation.* This changes the nature of all Human things, wch are so far good or evil, as they thwart or [p. 171.] promote this one end of Life.

764. *All X^n Duties founded on Religion.* Not on the Sovereign authority of God, commanding w^t He pleases —Suffering becomes Sinners, therfore we are commāded

Self-Denyal—To be Thankful for Favours, &c.—To Fear w^t is truly Dreadful—To Rejoice for something wch we have Reason to be glad at—God cannot command us w^t is not fit to be believ'd or done, wth respect to ye condition He has plac'd us in; all His commands being founded in the necessities of our Nature; and to make us more Happy than we could possibly be with^t y^m.

765. *Self-Denyal.* A Life of Idleness, Indulgence, and Self-Love, is a Resignation of our selves to every vice, except such as cannot be committed with^t Trouble; and gives men entirely up to ye Power of the Devil.

766. *Faith.* I see the Heavens open'd, and ye Son of Man standing, &c. Faith discovers this to every X^n, but then it must be an Actual, present Faith—a Faith y^t is next to vision.

767. *Mercy and Charity.* Mercy is not to be purchased, but at the price of Mercy. Blessed are ye Merciful.

[p. 172.] 768. *Patience.* He that suffers Injurys wth an eye to the Justice of God, will bear y^m wth Resignation and wthout repining.

769. *Poverty.* None are poor but those y^t want Faith in God's Providence.

[om. 4to.] 770. *Temptation.* The advantage of Temptation is—To make us know our own Weakness, and to oblige us to go to God for Help.

771. *Self Confidence.* Tis the greatest of all maladies, to think ourselves whole—They y^t be whole, &c.

[om. 4to.] 772. *God's Protection.* God protects those whose mindes are taken up wth discharging their Duty wthout perplexing y^{m}s wth consequences.

[om. 4to.] 773. *Humility.* The great designe of ye X^n Relig^n is to make us Humble.

[p. 173.] 774. *Cases of Conscience.* Men too often consult Casuists
[om. 4to.] only to Justifye, if possible, their own corrupt Inclinations.

775. *State of Life.* If thou wilt enter into Life, Keep the Comm., so y^t to choose, or to continue in any Place or Condition, or State of Life, in wch we cannot keep God's Comm., is to choose not to be saved.

776. *Riches.* To be rich is a great Misfortune; X^t Himself affirmes it wth an Oath (Matt. xix. 23). And y^t such a

one cannot be sav'd wth an ordinary Grace (v. 24). The only way is to use y[m] not as a Proprietor, but as a Steward, and then a man may be said to be Poor in the midst of Riches. But this must be y[e] Work of God, who alone can root out y[e] Love of Riches from y[e] Heart (v. 26).

777. *Church* is called a Vineyard, bec. tis a Place of Labour, in w[ch] no man ought to be Idle.

778. *Heaven and Happ[ss]*. We have no Title to Heaven [om. 4to.] but by God's Promise, for all our Good Works are His Gift —And both the Gift and the Promise of Reward are from the Good Will of God in J. X[t].

779. *Persecution*. It must not be expected y[t] the Devil [p. 174.] will let those rest who are labouring to destroy his K.

780. *Truthes of y[e] Gospel*. Few People deny y[m], most live as if they were not true.

781. *The Creatures*. We sh[d] never look upon y[e] Cre. w[th]out considering their Relation to the Creator. How much of His Perfections He has communicated to y[m]— How He is present in y[m]—the use He w[d] have us make of y[m]—&c.

782. *Holiness*. It is y[e] greatest Blindness to pretend to Hope for Eternal Happ[ss] w[th]out preparing for it in the whole course of our Lives by Holy Living.

783. *Cares, Riches*. Tis not always great and crying sins y[t] creat a Forgetfulness of God, and a contempt of His Laws; very often y[e] cares of y[e] world extinguished [? extinguish] our Faith, &c.

784. *Faith in y[e] Power of God*. He that Believes in God [p. 175.] the Fath[r] Almighty, and is rooted in this Faith, will enjoy Peace in the midst of the most powerful Enemies. His Infinit Wisdom sees our Wants, His Infinit Goodness will incline Him to Help us, and His Infinit Power can do w[t] He pleases.

785. *Impurity*. An Habit of Impurity extinguisheth all the Principles of a X[n] Life.

786. *Afflictions*. What a mercy is it to be forc'd to turn to God by Afflictions, Diseases, or the Ill Usage of Men!

787. *Conversion*. It is as great a miracle to raise a Soul [om. 4to.] from the Death of Sin unto the Life of Righteousness as to raise a Person from Death to Life.

788. *Outward Performances* are more apt to puff up than to Sanctify w^n not animated by the Sp^t of God.

[om. 4to.]
[p. 176.]
789. *Unwashen Hands.* Let us take care to clean our Hearts from forgetting Him y^t Feeds us—Fr. Thoughts of Sensuality—and fr. [not?] sanctifying our Meales to ye Glory of God.

790. *Riches.* Mark x. 24. Whoever find in y^m his Rest, his Dependance, his Satisfaction, his Joy, his Safty, will never Heartily apply to God for these; Here lies ye danger of R.

791. *Ambition.* By such, every thing is accounted Just that is advantageous.

792. *Prayer.* A true X^n Pray^r is always heard, bec. such a one asks nothing more than that God's will may be done.

[om. 4to.]
793. *Forgive.* He y^t goes to his Pray^{rs} wthout a Forgiving temper obtains nothing but his own Condemnation.

794. *Reprobate.* It is one of the greatest Judgments in the World to be left to ourselves, and to be permitted to act as we please.

[p. 177.]
795. *Conviction.* To close wth the Truth w^n 'tis proposed, is oftentimes the necessary step to Conversion.

796. *World.* Mark xiii. 7. W^n a man throughly knowes this World, w^t its Spirit is, and w^t its end must be, he is prepar'd for all events, and is troubled at nothing; looking upon himself as a citizen of anoth. W.

[om. 4to.]
797. *Public Calamities, Afflictions.* Tis too often that people consider the calamities themselves rath^r than the Sins y^t have drawn y^m down.

798. *History.* To profit by reading of History, one must consider it as an Acc^t and Picture of the Instability, The Vanity of ye World, y^t every thing is nothing, and y^t God alone is all in all.

[mostly om. in 4to.]
799. *Calamities* are always Good—Both in their Original (wch is from God) and in their End—Either to Exercise the Good—To Chastise Offenders—or to punish the Wicked.

1. They exercise ye Good—In trying y^m—In strengthening y^m and making y^m exemplary.

[p. 178.]
2. They chastise Offenders—And are eith^r a Scourge to Punish Sins, or to prevent y^m.

We complain of Oppression, of our Lawes being trampled

on—Of Arbitrary Governm^t—Are we Wiser than our Physician?

3. Calamities are Punishments—Even as such these are good—Justice requires that Sin be punished—The Good of Society requires that offenders be stopp'd in their career of Mischief, and lastly, 'tis for the Good of the Sinner himself, if he be hindered from more Wickedness and a greater Damnation.

If therefore I am Good—I may conclude these calamities are to exercise me; If an Offender—To correct and recover me,—If Wicked—to punish me.

Our uncorrected manners require a lasting Scourge. We are Impatient:—Are we or our Maker to have our Wills done?

800. *Judgments of God* are hidden, but never unjust.

801. *Sin.* There is no Sin wch a man ought not to Fear and to think himself capable of, since we have in our Corrupt Will ye Seed of every Sin.

802. *Difficulties.* It is prudence to consider and foresee Difficulties, but then 'tis X^n Prudence, w^n God calls us to any Work, to obey God, and to depend upon Him for meanes of overcoming these Difficulties, wch we ourselves are destitute of. For God generally removes all those Obstacles, w^n a man undertakes any thing for His sake alone, wth Faith and Courage. [p. 179.]

803. *Hon^{rs}, Riches, &c.* The Love of Earthly things is always accompanied wth an Indifference towards Heavenly.

804. *Conscience.* W^n men have once suffer'd their Consciences to be govern'd by their Passions—The vilest Wickedness will be called a Zeal for God—Rebellion will be call'd a Concern for Law, &c., and the greatest vileness, Heroick Actions.

805. *Inheritance in Heaven, Charity.* He y^t expects an Inheritance in Heaven, will more easily part wth his Earthly Inheritance, wheth^r by Charity to ye Poor—or thro' Patience to those who wrong him of it.

806. *Do to oth^s as ye w^d.* That very Self Love wch blindes us wth respect to our Neighbour's Good and Rights, is made by X^t a meanes of Convincing and Informing us w^t we ought to do—by obliging us to change Persons, &c., wch will shew us our Injustice and our Duty.

807. *Do not y*^{e} *Publicans y*^{e} *same?* A man who findes nothing in his Life but w^t may be found in a Turk or an Heathen, will find at last y^t his X^n Name will be of little use, unless to condemn him.

[p. 180.] 808. *Love of Neighbour.* We love our Neighbor as X^{ns} w^n we Love him for God's sake—i. e. when we have an eye to God, and seek nothing but Him in doing our Neighb^r good.

809. *Good Works.* A Deficiency in these, is a certain Proof of a Defect in that Love wch we owe to God for the Pardon of our Sins, and for ye Graces He has given us.

810. *Love of God.* Luke vii. 47. He who fancy's y^t less Love is due fr. him to God bec. he has less Sins to be forgiven, dos not Understand w^t Sin is—what sad Fate he escapes who is pardon'd—What great mercy is necessary to preserve us fr. ye least Sin—what Sins, wthout the Grace of God, we are all subject to.

811. *H. Scriptures* are an Adorable mixture of Clearness and Obscurity, wch Enlightens and Humbles the Children of God, and Blinds and Hardens those of this World—The Light proceeds fr. God, and Blindness fr. ye Creature.

812. *Love of God.* There are 1000 things wch we love more than God wthout being sensible of it.

[p. 181.] 813. *Mark of Salvat*^{n}. Nothing can give us a greater assurance of our being in the way of Salv. than to see our selves rejected of and despised by those who will not think of another Life.

814. *Enemies.* Remember that you are the Disciple of Him who dyed for His enemies.

[om. 4to.] 815. *Take no Thought, &c.* He will always find sufficient who seeks no more than the necessaries of Life, 'tis only Sensuality y^t is never Satisfy'd.

816. *X*^{t} *the Only Physician.* Neith^r the Philosophers among ye Gentiles, nor Moses among ye Jewes, could find out a Remedy for Sin, they Saw and Felt ye Wounds of Sin, but could not Heal y^m. None but X^t can Relieve us.

817. *Grace Abused.* Graces and Blessings abused Harden the Heart.

818. *Knowledge.* Luke xii. 47, "That Servant wch knew his Lord's Will," &c. How much is Knowledge to be dreaded w. [when] our Works are not Answerable?

819. *To him y*^{t} *hath, &c.* Luke xii. 48. The more Graces [p. 182.] a man has Rec^d the more Reason he has to Fear, and ye Great^r Obligat^n to Lab^r for God.

820. *Repentance or Damnation.* Luk. xiii. 5. Except ye [om. 4to.] Rep. ye shall all likewise Perish, so y^t there is no Medium.

821. *Wisdom.* True Wisdome consists in knowing how to make everything instrumental to our Salvation.

822. *Wilful Sins.* Tis dangerous to commit the least wilful Fault, bec. it may have ye greatest evil consequence.

823. *Riches* are almost always abused wthout a very Extraordinary Grace; They Arm Injustice—They Support Pride; They encourage an Independancy; They are the Object of the most Violent Passions, and the Occasion of all oth^r Evils.

824. *Faith.* If Faith is not every day secur'd and in- [p. 183.] creased by Prayer, it will soon decay. [om. 4to.]

825. *Charity.* We never despise others, but w^n we do not know and think of our selves.

826. *Truth.* We too often judge of Things, not according to Truth, but according to our Inclinations.

827. *Principijs Obsta.* W^d men consider y^t there may be some things and circumstances, seemingly inconsiderable, on wch God has made their Salvation, perhaps, depend—They w^d never omit any opportunity of Good—nor admit the least Temptation to any evil whatever. For one evil is but the step to anoth^r, and the least degree of Grace rejected may be ye occasion of ye denyal of a greater.

828. *Sinner.* The greatest misfortune dos not consist in a man's being a sinner, but in his not knowing the Danger and the Remedy of Sin—And in Rejecting the Saving Hand of his Physician, who w^d Heal him, and the Meanes He proposes for his Recovery.

829. *Publick Pray*^{r}. Prayer is good in all places, but there is a particular Blessing attends it, w^n offered in the House of Prayer—The House of God Himself.

830. *Loyalty.* It is no small Part of Relig^n to serve God [p. 184.] in so lively an Image of His greatness and Power, as is y^t of Princes.

831. *Persecution.* It is Just and Reasonable y^t ye Mem- [om. 4to.] bers sh^d share in ye Different conditions of the Head.

832. *Relig*^{n} *not defended by Force.* Luke xxii. 49. "Lord,

shall we smite wth ye Sword?" They know X^t but Little who suppose y^t he is to be defended by Armes.

833. *Minister of X^t.* His Salvation dos in some measure depend upon that of others.

834. *Frugality.* We ought to manage our Temporal Riches to the best Advantage, not out of Covetousness, but bec. they are the Gift of God.

835. *Afflictions.* Afflictions, Temptations, Dangers, &c. are necessary to Awaken in us y^t Faith w^h is too apt to fall asleep in ye midst of an Undisturbed Prosperity—Tis then we are most sensible how much we stand in need of God; When [p. 185.] He withdraws His Fav^rs and the Light of His countenance, and w^n we are under the Apprehension of Evils, or Feel y^m.

836. *Disconsolate.* W^n Feares oppress a X^n he sh^d call to mind ye words of J. X^t to His Disciples (Jo. vi. 20), *It is I, be not afraid.* This will comfort us under all troubles, to believe y^t it is X^t who speakes to us.

837. *Reproches.* We are then Good X^ns w^n we are pleased to be treated as J. X^t was. Jo. vii. 12. Some said He was a good man—others said, Nay, but He deceiveth the people.

838. *Liberty.* We contend for Liberty, and 'tis too often seen, ye use we make of it, is to speak evil of J. X^t—of His Relig^n and His ministers, w^thout Fear, and wth Impunity— At ye same time y^t the least offences ag^st those y^t are but His Rep^esentativ's are punished w^h severity.

839. *Sermons* sh^d be Instructions, and not Declamations.

840. *Rash Judgment.* Tis too often we pass Judgments [p. 186.] upon men's actions, according to the Love or Hatred we have for the Persons, who have done it.

841. *Poverty—Riches.* James ii. 5. God hath chosen the Poor of this World, to make y^m Rich in Faith, and Heires of ye Kingdom, rath^r than the Great and the Learned—Twas such as they who first Rec^d His Word, &c., and yet this is the condition we flee from, wch we abhorr, and are afraid of more than death.

842. *If any man Thirst, &c.* Jo. vii. 37. In vain do we seek to quench and satisfye our Thirst and our desires amongst ye creatures, fr. Learning, Riches, Hon^rs, Pleasures, &c. Our drought will but increase till we seek J. X^t. —His Grace alone can Satisfye.

843. *Retirement.* We are apt to condemn those y^t are continually in the throng of business, &c. But if our Study and Retirement produces no solid good, 'tis e'en as good to be engag'd in Company and wth Business as to be alone.

844. *Vain purposes.* Men delude and please y^{ms} wth the [om. 4to.] Thoughts of Virtues w^h they will never put in Practice.

845. *Reason Insufficient.* The Heathen Philosophers thought it enough to lay good Reasons before men in order [p. 187.] to persuade y^m. They knew nothing of the necessity of Divine Gr., and therefore they are often forc'd to complain of the Insufficiency of Reason.

846. *Duty.* The Slothful and the Diligent are upon a level, if neith^r of y^m knows what to do, or dos it not.

847. *Happyness.* Most men, even the Philosophers, placed their Happ^{ss} in an agitation of ye mind, wch diverted y^m fr. thinking too much of thems. and their own miserable state—W^d to God most X^{ns} did not follow y^m in this.

848. *Despair.* We never seek X^t too late, or to no purpose, w^n we seek Him wth Sincerity, Humility, and a Penitent Heart.

849. *Dreadful Truthes* are not to be forborn, for fear of casting men into Despair. They are rath^r to be often Inculcated, to force Sinners by the sight of their Danger to throw thems. into His Armes who is the only Refuge of Sinners.

850. *God's Ministers.* W^d men really love God, they will [p. 188.] Hon^r Him in His Ministers—They that do not do so, do not consider that prejudices do easily pass from the Persons to the Truthes they preach, and to Ordinances they administer —Who dos not see ye fatal consequence?

851. *Judgments, Rash.* Jo. ix. 16. Envy Judges of the Works by the Person who dos y^m—Equity Judges of Persons by their Works.

852. *Truth.* Men often reject the Truth, tho' in itself evident enough, bec. the sight of it displease^h y^m—wch God punishes, very often, wth a Judicial Blindness; so y^t they canvass it so long till they lose the sight of that, wch to an Honest Lover of Truth is most evident.

853. *Knowlege,* when not accompanyed wth Humility, serves generally to no other end but to increase our Sins.

854. *Grace, Light, &c. Security.* Jo. xii. 35. If [we] w^d

preserve the present Light, let us dread the losing it—If we do not so, and make [no?] use of it, God will withdraw it. The more God bestows His gifts, ye more we sh^d pray for Grace not to abuse y^m.

855. *Justice and Mercy of God.* The Justice of God leaves those in Darkness, w^m His mercy dos not enlighten and draw out.

[p. 189.] 856. *Learning.* It is a worthless peice of learning to know every[thing] except the Love of God, and How to save our own Soul.

857. *Sins of others* shew us what we ourselves sh^d be w^thout ye Grace of X^t.

858. *Judges* ought to take care to examin every thing, but especially their own Hearts, lest Passion and prejudice sh^d pervert Justice.

859. *H. Scriptures.* A X^n Life is the great key of ye Gospel.

860. *The Life of Faith*—consists in a just knowledge and esteem of the X^n Relig^n—A Love for the Church in wch it is Taught and Practiced—A zeal for the Truth—A great Contempt for earthly things—A true affection for those that are Heavenly—A great value for X^t crucified—A desire to be united to Him—An Hatred for Sin—And Love of vertue—

[p. 190.] Joyfully closing wth ye means of Grace, The Sa[craments] and other Ordinances of God.—And Thankful for them—An entire confidence in the Grace of God—And as great a Diffidence in ourselves, and in our own works—A real Love and value for the Word of God—And in one word, a just esteem for every thing that has relation to ye world to come.

861. *Excommunication.* A man is cut off fr. ye Body of X^t as well by not living according to ye Gospel, as by not Believing ye Gosp^l.

862. *Resignation.* We ought to acquiesce in every dispensation of Providence, bec. God finds His Glory therin.

863. *Enemy.* A man who considers y^t perhaps his own Salvat^n depends upon ye Salv. of His Enemy, will not fail to pray for him, and Endeav^r his Conversion.

864. *Disappintm^nts.* It is happy for us, sometimes, to meet wth y^m, that we may be forc'd to adhere more closely to God, and to seek for consolation in Him alone.

865. *Happyness.* We plainly perceive y^t we have it not in [p. 191.] ourselves to make us Happy—If we seek for Happ^ss any where but in God—we are sure to be disappointed, and 'tis God who disappoints us, y^t at last we may go to Him.

866. *State of Tryal.* We continue here on earth only to be purify'd and to be rendred worthy of y^t Happ^ss for wch God has designed us.

867. *Charity.* Whoever showes mercy to men, will certainly find the same from God.

868. *Charity.* The gift of Charity is fr. G. A Gift more Precious than all ye World, bec. it prepares us for the reception of all oth^r Blessings.

869. *Flattery, Vanity.* The Remembrance of our In- [om. 4to.] firmitys and Misery the best Antidote ag^st the Poison of Flattery.

870. *Wickedness.* W^n it gets Head, one cannot attack it without suffering for it.

871. *Prejudice.* We easily perswade our selves that w^t [p. 192.] is contrary to our inclination, is contrary to Reason, Relig^n, &c.

872. *Grace before Meat, &c.* What a scandalous thing it is to take our food with^t being mindful and thankful to Him who bestowes it on us. St. Paul gave Thanks in the presence of ye Heathens (Acts xxvii. 35), and X^ns are ashamed to do it before X^ns.

873. *Faith ye Origin of w^t is Praiseworthy.* With^t Faith [om. 4to.] there is little Hon^r, Justice, Truth, Gratitude or Humanity.

874. *Providence of God.* God very often conceales His Alm. Power and Care over His creatures under meanes y^t seeme altogether natural and Human.

875. *Knowledge,* with^t Grace, produces nothing but Pride, Vanity, Presumption, &c.

876. *Corruption of our Nature.* This is ye First Principle of Piety and Relig^n.

877. *X^ns Indeed.* In vain do we bear the name of Be- [p. 193.] liev^s if we do not live like Believers.

878. *X^n Faith* makes Future good things present, eases temporal evils, Gives us a contempt for the pleasures of this World, and gives us a foretast of the Joys of Eternity.

879. *Prayer.* Is the groning of an heart sensible of its

own misery, poverty and inability, beging of God ye Gr. to know and to be able to ask w^t it wants.

880. *Martyrdom.* The World w^d use us just as it did the Martyrs, if we Lov'd God as they did.

881. *Election.* We cannot possibly perish if we adhere to J. X^t by a lively Faith in the power of His Grace, By a perfect Resignation to His Guidance and Direction,—And by a well grounded Confidence in His Goodness.

[p. 194.]

882. *False Shame.* Whoever is ashamd of his Master is not worthy to serve Him, much less to Reign wth Him.

883. *Prayer* shews the dependance Man has upon God, and by wch the correspondence betwixt Heaven and Earth is kept up.

884. *Faith.* Our Life must answer for our Faith.

885. *Unity, Charity.* We all belong to ye same Lord, United in ye same Hope—calld and assisted by ye same Grace, sanctify'd by ye same Sp^t—And shall we not have ye same mind, &c.

886. *Thro' J. X^t.* There is no Grace to be had but thro' J. X^t, no person being sav'd but in Him alone.

887. *Teachers.* Let us not attribute That to y^m wch belongs to X^t alone. He died for us, and 'tis He alone who by His Ministers do's all for us. We ought not therfore to minister occasions to the Fond Affections and Inclinations of men—Lest they sh^d be led to adhere to the Minister of the Truth rath^r than to ye Truth its self.

[p. 195.]

888. *H. Scriptures.* To despise the Simplicity of ye Word, and the Humility of ye Doctrine of ye Gospel, is too sure a Sign of Reprobation—on ye contrary, to esteem, &c.

[om. 4to.]

889. *Not many wise, not many, &c.* 1 Cor. i. 26. The Advantages of Learning, Birth and Authority, too often Hindrances to Salvatⁿ—greater and more certain than men will be persuaded to Believe.

890. *Humility.* The great design of God in relation to ye Childⁿ of Adam is to Humble y^m that no Flesh sh^d glory in His Presence. 1 Cor. i. 29.—He Humbles ye Learned, by the Foolishness of Preaching, wch they are confounded to see attended wth such success—He humbles the Preacher Himself, and those who are converted by his sermons, by convincing y^m of ye Folly of ascribing any thing to y^ms.—

He humbles the Great by requiring y^m to conform y^{m}s to J. X^t made of no reputation, and to Trust in Him alone.— He requires us all, as we hope for salvat^n, not to seek for it in ourselves (wch pride w^d suggest), but in J. X^t alone; who is to be our Wisdome by ye Light of His Word—Our Righteousness by the merits of His Sacrifice—Our Sancti- [p. 196.] fication and Redemption, by His Spirit and Grace. So y^t we owe all we have or Hope for to Him alone^m.

891. *Preacher.* No man can Speak of, or understand, ye things of God, as He ought, but He y^t is fill'd with the Sp^t of God. This Sp^t is given X^{ns} at Baptism—but they too often deprive y^{m}s of it, by a Carnal Life; and by adhering to their own Wisdom.

892. *Knowledge, Spiritual.* A man ought to be much disengaged from the things of ye Earth to be able to know the Mysterys of Heaven.

893. *Faith.* All X^{ns} Believe the Truthes and Mysteries of the Gospel—Only they y^t are Spiritual Understand y^m.—A man may please himself wth ye empty sound of words, and neglect or be very Ignorant of their Importance, and of ye Truths contain'd in y^m.

894. *Faith* in J. X^t as ye Mediator betwixt God and man is the Foundation of ye X^n Relig^n—as we Hope for Success in any thing we do, we must unite ourselves to Him, and [as?] Interceding wth us to God for success in that Act^n.

895. *Atheism—Judgments of God.* Josephus speaking of [p. 197.] the Jewish nation before its destruction (lib. v. ch. 16), saith there never was a more Atheistical Generation, γενεὰ ἀθεωτέρα.—They despised the Laws of men, and made a mock of the Lawes of God, and those that publish'd them— made no difference betwixt Good and Evil—A sure presage of a near desolation.

896. *Charity.* That person who is not concern'd y^t his Broth^r sh^d not Perish, is in great danger of Perishing himself.

897. *Indifferent Things.* A man who has the Interests of God and of his Neighb^r at Heart, will not too stifly insist upon Ind. Things.

898. *Idolatry.* There are few who have not their Idols,

---

^{m} [Cf. Quesnel, 1 Cor. i. 30.]

wch their Hearts adore, in wch they put their Trust, and place their Happ^{ss}; The worst of all is our selves.

[p. 198.] 899. *Charity.* 1 Cor. xiii. Suffereth Long. Beares the Imperfections of others, with^t vexation—waits for their amendm^t wthout Impatience—And begs it of God with^t being weary.

900. *Charity is kind,*—Good natur'd, far from creating needless trouble to any one.

901. *Charity envyeth not.* Rejoicing in the Happ^{ss} of others—and contented that others be preferr'd before her.

902. *Charity is not Rash*—dos nothing wthout consideration and order.

903. *Charity is not Puffed up.* Labours to forget herself, is little in her own eyes, and can easily bear a Superior.

904. *Doth not behave Herself Unseemly.* Never looks on others wth scorn, but always finds out something in others, for wch she may value y^m.

905. *Seeketh not her own.* Maketh her neighbour's Interests her own — and is ready to sacrifice her own to his.

[p. 199.] 906. *Char. is not easily provoked.* Never loses her tenderness for her neighb^r, however much she Hates the Sin, and therfore does not easily take Fire.

907. *Thinketh no evil.* Entertaines not groundless suspicions—but readily perceives w^t is good in others.

908. *Rejoiceth not in iniquity.* Whatever advantages she may reap fr. it, being always most concernd for the Hon^r of God, W^m all Iniquity dishonoureth.

909. *Rejoyceth in the Truth.* In ye knowledge of the Truth, however difficult to be Practised—Loves Goodness in every Body, and is pleas'd w^n it is embrac'd.

910. *Beareth all things*—With all wth w^m she converseth; never calling for, or accusing the Divine vengeance of being too slow.

911. *Believeth all things.* Knowing y^t the authority of
[p. 200.] God is equal in all things, even in the most difficult dutys of Loving our Enemies, w^m we are to Believe the best of.

912. *Hopeth all things*—both from the Power of God, and from ye Love she beares to others.

913. *Endureth all things,* rather than break the Unity of

the Church, or y^t her Neighb^r should be offended, and driven into Sin.

914. *Charity will never Fail.* Will never have an end, bec. it is that Bond w^h Unites us to God and to one anoth^r in Heaven.

915. *Sermons.* "Blessed are ye Poor, for yo^rs is ye K. of H.:" so y^t w^t is most proper and like to be of use to y^m is ye best way of Preaching. [om. 4to.]

916. *Scriptures.* A man may know all the Learned criticisms of the S.S. w^thout knowing ye Spirit, ye Piety, and the Mysterys therof.

917. *Humility.* The more God raises and exalts Good Men, the more they abase and Humble y^ms. They remember wth sorrow what they are of y^ms, and w^t they are capable of becoming. [p. 201.]

918. *Sufferings.* How useful are They—Since they do not only loosen our affect^ns fr. this world, but oblige us to Believe, to Hope for, and to expect a better. He cannot be miserable who has a Firm expect^n of Happ^ss Hereafter.

919. *Happ^ss Eternal.* The Measure of Love and Lab^r and Sufferings shall be the Measure of Glory.

920. *Mysterys, Faith.* The D—l ensnares us, by tempting us to Ask How such things *can be*, that he [may] make us disbelieve the things y^ms. Faith enjoyns us to rely upon God for the manner, [as well] as for ye Truth of the Revelat^n. [om. 4to.]

921. *The Cross, Afflict^n.* We know not w^t we lose w^n we pray to be deliver'd out of our Afflictions.

922. *The Cross.* The Dearer we are and the more devoted to God, the less ought we to expect to be spared. [om. 4to.] [p. 202.]

923. *Repentance—Despair.* The D—l aimes at 2 Things wth regard to Sinners, eith^r to hinder y^m fr. Repent^nce, or to make y^m Repent as Judas did.

924. *Gospel not Rec^d.* How sh^d they whose Hearts are set upon ye Riches, Pleasures, Hon^rs and all the Idols of this World, Love a Gospel wch condemns all these and recommends Mortificat^n, Self-Denyal, &c.

925. *Mediator.* It was necessary that our Mediator sh^d be both God and Man, y^t He might take care of the Interests both of the Creator and His creatures.

926. *Friendship* is to be purchased only by Friendship—A man may have Authority over others, but he can never have their Hearts, but by giving his own.

[p. 203.] 927. *Evil Conversat^n.* A man never converses with evil People (unless in order to convert y^m) who dos not leave y^m with his Heart infected — his mind obscurd—his senses tainted—his Faith weakened by their maximes—his Hope lessend, and all his Graces corrupted.

928. *Promises of God.* Let us often rep'sent unto ye eye of our Faith ye Greatness of God's promises, and His Faithfulness in performing y^m; nothing is more proper to animate us in ye way of virtue.

929. *False Charity.* To leave people in their Sins for Fear of awakening y^m and making y^m uneasy.

930. *Almes.* To give to Pious uses, is to put out our moneys to Interest upon the Security of God Himself.

931. *Purposes, Desires.* Let us not stop at Good purposes. They are the Gift of God—and not to improve y^m is to slight His Gift, and Graces, and to put our selves into ye number of Slothful servants and be liable to their sentence.

932. *Almes.* (Quesn. 2 Cor. viii. 13, &c.) God has not made all men equally Rich, that by His Grace in the Hearts [p. 204.] of men, He may provide for all, and that men may have opportunity of exercising their charity, and working out their own salvation by helping oth^{rs}. God has put the portion of ye Poor into the Hands of the Rich, to trye their Fidelity. And the Spiritual portion of ye Rich into the Hands of ye Poor, y^t members of ye same body may Love and depend one of another.

And He y^t wrongs ye poor wrongs himself most, by wthholding their portion or part.

A day will come w^n we shall be reduced to an equality.

933. *Faith and Obedience.* God has a Right to be Believ'd in y^t He has Rev.—as well as to [be] obey'd—in y^t He has commanded. The Authority is the same—And God expects submission in one as well as the oth^r instance.

934. *Love and Obedience.* Our Obedience will always be Answerable to our Love—This is the reason why God, to oblige us to obey Him, gave us in His Son the greatest reason to Love Him.

935. *Knowlege.* That wch Helps to Reform the Heart is of much more use to us than that wch only enlightens ye Understanding. [p. 205.]

936. *A messenger of Satan.* It is the Glory of X^{ts} Power —y^t He can make the greatest enemies of Mank. Instrumental to their Salvation.

937. *Temptations.* The most dangerous of all Tempt. is to believe that one can avoid or overcome y^m by our own strength and wthout asking the Help of God. [om. 4to.]

938. *Union.* X^{ns}, and especially the Clergy, will easily live in Peace one with an other, w^n they have most at Heart the Glory of God, and ye Interests of the K. of X^t. Hearts are divided bec. Interests are different.

939. *Evil Example.* Nothing is more contagious than evil example of persons in Authority—whether they be Lay or Clergymen.

940. *Morality.* The Moral Law leaves us under our own Inability and under Sin and the Curse, so y^t we may preach Morality long enough, as the Heathen Philosophers did, without any great effect, if we do not Preach J. X^t, who alone can give us Grace to fulfill the Law. [p. 206.]

With^t Faith in J. X^t we can do nothing profitable to Salvat^n. Faith being the Source of Prayer, Prayer of Grace, and Grace enables us to keep the Law. The voice of the Law is—*The man y^t doeth them shall live in them.* Gal. iii. 12. The knowledge of the Law can only make us sensible of our own Inabilitys—but cannot Help us—It is not only Remission of Sins that J. X^t has merited for us by His death, but Grace to do Good.

941. *Failings of others.* A Wise and Faithful Soul knows how to turn his own and the Sins of others to his own Spiritual advantage. [om. 4to.]

942. *Uncharitableness.* We are generally quick, Eager and Curious to know the Life of our Neighbour, but slow, backward and blind to observe, to condemn, and amend our own.

943. *Saints, X^{ns}.* X^{ns} cannot be too often put in mind y^t they that are Saints by Profession sh^d be so by their conversation. [p. 207.]

944. *Good Example.* There is no reproof more mild and

modest, no condemnation more effectual, no exhortation more effectual than a good Life.

945. *X^n Religion* consists in performing worthily the Duties we owe to God, our neighbour and our selves.

946. *Peace and Unity.* Phil. ii. 3, 4. The meanes of Preserving y^m. To be diffident of our own opinions—To despise worldly Hon^{rs}—To Love Subjection, and to sit loose from Earthly Things.

947. *Baptism.* We then contract and oblige ourselves to labour all our Life long to compleat and perfect ye Image of X^t in our selves.

948. *God's Faithfulness.* He never leaves those in error or under ruinous Temptations, who look to Him by Prayer, Study, and Endeav^{rs}.

949. *Thanksgiving.* He who forgets the Fav^{rs} he has Received deserves not to have new ones.

[p. 208.] 950. *Hæresies.* The subtilty of Human Reasoning has always been the Corruption of the Faith.

951. *Publick Judgments.* While the Church Gov^{rs} preserve the Purity of the Faith, the Order of Discipline, and Holiness of Manners, Conformable to ye Gospel, in ye Ch., and ye Civil Magistrate backs all these, by his Authority and his Power—There is no Fear of Pub. Judgm^{ts} in y^t nation—but w^n—&c.

952. *Human Learning.* The Church is not a School of Philosophy, where every one may utter the Imaginations of his own mind, &c. Vid. Col. ii. 8. Q. [i. e. Quesnel.]

953. *Baptism—its blessing and excellency.* Col. ii. 11. It separates us fr. Adam and engrafts us in X^t—It burys us wth X^t—Tis a Resurrect^n from Sin to Grace—It discharges us from the Debt owing to ye Justice of God by our Sins, now fully satisfy'd by Faith in ye Sufferings and Death of X^t—It cancels the Law of Death and Malediction wch was agst us.—In Bapt. our Sins did indeed dye and were buryed—but the [p. 209.] Seed and Root remain in us: these we are to mortifye all our life long [n].

954. *Covetousness.* Is call'd Idolatry, bec. it leades a man to do all that for money and Riches, wch he ought to do for the sake of God. [Quesnel.]

[n] [Cf. Quesnel, in loc.]

955. *Authority, Power, Greatness.* Nothing will distinguish a Great man from ye Poorest Slave, at the Tribunal of God, wth w^m there is no respect of Persons, so much as the severe Punishm^t the first will Receive for the Abuse of their Power, &c., and the Allowances the latter will have made y^m for the circumstances they lay under.

956. *Reprobate.* When, having laid aside the care of their own soules, men labour to corrupt and destroy others, tis then they are filling up the measure of their Sins apace.

957. *Revenge.* W^n God punishes it is to satisfy His own [om. 4to.] Justice, not to gratifye our Revenge—wch we sh^d avoid, as we w^d have God our Protector.

958. *Study.* It is one thing for a man to fill his Understanding and Memory with Truthes, and another to Nourish [p. 210.] his Heart wth y^m.

959. *Afflictions.* Happy is that Condition wch forces us to Trust only in God, and to be in the Hand of His Providence. Afflictions dispose us to Pray, and we are sure to want nothing if we find God in Pray^r.

960. *Worldly Pleasures.* They who give y^{m}s up to Pleasures, are making themselves chaines not easy to be broken.

961. *God's Assistance.* He y^t expects to do his duty as a X^n must have a Strength more than Human to go thro' wth it. He must have ye Pow^r of God wth him.

962. *Errors.* It is a dreadful but just Judgm^t y^t the mind sh^d fall into Error, w^n the Heart has resign'd itself to Sin.

963. *Persecution.* 2 Tim. iii. 13. He who wonders to see the wicked designes of evil men succeed dos not reflect upon [p. 211.] the conduct and designes of God concerning His Church.

We deceive ourselves with the Hopes of seeing an End of the Afflictions of the Ch. before the End of ye World.

The Grace wch supports us, and the Eternity we hope for, is the only Remedy and Comfort we ought to depend on ^{o}.

964. *Servants* ^{p}. One cannot be secure of the Fidelity of a servant who feares not God, but one may depend on one who lives by Faith.

965. *Form of Godliness.* Nothing is more provoking to

---

^{o} [Quesnel.] ^{p} [Cf. n°. 123.]

God than the use of Holy things without the Conversion of the heart.

966. *Art of Persuasion.* Heb. vi. 9. We shall hardly gain ye Mind and the Assent by perpetual Invectives—unless we raise their minds (at ye same time y^t we fill y^m with Fear) wth marks of our esteem and Hopes of better things [q].

[p. 212.]

967. *King's Courts.* The Providence of God teaches us in Moses that ye Court cannot with^t hazard be long the abode of true X^{ns} unless by the same Providence they lye under an obligat^n of being there [r].

968. *Not Fearing ye Wrath of ye King.* Heb. ii. 27. We have but little Faith w^n ye Fear of man hinders us fr. obeying God, who is omnipotent, and always ready to assist us.

969. *Singularity.* If a man is alone in doing his Duty he has the more reason to be thankful to God, and not to be asham'd of it before men.

970. *Holy Script.* Jam. i. 24. By these every man may see w^t he is—w^t he is not—and w^t he ought to be.—Let us therfore meditate upon y^m—Consult y^m as our Rule—and make y^m evermore our Pattern.

971. *The Tongue.* Intemperance in talk makes a dreadful havock in ye Heart.

[p. 213.]

972. *The Poor.* Having nothing upon earth to engage their affections too strongly, fix them more easily upon God [s].

973. *Riches and Power.* How great a Grace is necessary to keep a man from abusing them [t]!

[om. 4to.]

974. *Love of Neighb^r.* We Love our Neighb^r as our selves w^n we sincerely endeav^r y^t he may be sav'd.

975. *Test of Relig^n.* If nothing but ye outward profession of Relig^n distinguishes us fr. Infidels, we shall be X^{ns} only in order to a severer Condemnation [u].

976. *Libertines* fear nothing, ye Devils Fear and Tremble.

977. *Faith and Works.* Faith is the root of Works—A Root y^t produceth nothing, is dead.

978. *Call to ye Ministry.* A Lawful call gives a good ground to Hope for Mercy at ye great Day, and the Grace of God in the mean time.

[p. 214.]

979. *Tongue.* The disorders of ye Tongue are not to be

---

[q] [Quesnel.]   [r] [Quesnel on Heb. xi. 26.]
[s] [Quesnel on St. Jam. ii. 5.]   [t] [ib. 6, 7.]   [u] [ib. ii. 14.]

cured by Human Prudence—He alone can do it who has the Absolute Power over the Heart[x].

980. *Peace.* The Peace of Heav[n] is for none but those who Love it upon Earth[y].

981. *Content.* The Fewer desires, the more Peace[z]. [om. 4to.]

982. *Happ[ss] in God alone.* God suffers none to be Happy who seek their Happ[ss] out of Him.

983. *Knowlege.* That Person aggravates his Sin who boasts that he knows his Duty[a].

984. *Riches, their extreme danger.* See Jam. v. 1, &c. [om. 4to.]

985. *Magistrates.* In Magistrates we ought to have re- [om. 4to.] spect unto y[e] Authority of the Soverain, and in the Soverain [p. 215.] unto the Authority of God, who has appointed y[m]. They may abuse their Authority, but y[t] gives not subjects a . . . . . right to rebel[b].

986. *Example.* Good Example is a language and an Argument w[ch] every body understands[c].

987. *Publick Worship—The necessity of Joyning in it.* The Salvation purchased by X[t] is a *Common salvation,* (Jude 3,) of w[ch] we cannot Partake, but by Joyning with the Ch. or Body of men to w[ch] that Privilege was granted—We can receive no Influence fr. y[e] Head, except we are Members of y[e] Body, and joyn in those Outward Actions, the Sacr. [? Sacrifice and] Pray[s] by w[h] [we have] communion wth X[t]. We are all one Body, says y[e] Apostle, bec. we are all partakers of one Loaf or Bread. 1 Cor. x. 17.—Every branch of a Tree must be sapless and perish, if it has no communication wth y[e] Body of y[e] Tree.

988. *Error.* The mind is seldom corrupted before the Heart—God generally punishes the one by the other[d].

989. *Judgments delay'd* are generally most Terrible, w[n] [p. 216.] God suffers Sinners to fill up y[e] measure of their Sins.

990. *God's Hatred of Sin.* 2 Pet. ii. 4. How great must it be, w[n] He punished it so terribly in y[e] most noble of His creatures, y[e] very Angels[e].

991. *Number of Sinners* dos not hinder God from exer-

---

[x] [Quesnel on St. Jam. iii. 7, 8.]
[y] [ib. 18.]
[z] [ib. iv. 2.]
[a] [ib. 17.]
[b] [Quesnel on 1 St. Pet. ii. 14. This passage Dr. Wilson had blotted out with especial care.]
[c] [ib. 15.]
[d] [ib. on 2 St. Pet. ii. 2.]
[e] [Quesnel.]

cising His vengeance upon y^m, tho' it may sometimes prevent the punishments of men—He spar'd not the old world, &c. 2 Pet ii. 5 [f].

992. *Publick Worship.* Will a man say y^t he is of ye Household of God, who never eates the Bread of God in His House and wth His Family?

993. *Knowledge.* True Faith in J. X^t is an Universal Science, 1 Jo. ii. 20, and ye shortest way to knowlege [g].

[p. 217.] 994. *Love of X^t.* A man dreads ye coming of X^t just so far as he distrusts his own Love of X^t. [h]

995. *Afflictions.* How good is God in permitting y^m—Since 'tis only to force us to seek for Rest, and Ease, and Peace in Him for ever.

996. *Love of ye World.* Whoever Loves the World is more disposed than he imagines to Renounce God and His Relig^n.

997. *AntiX^t—Irrelig^n.* Let us adore God in these dispensations, waiting for the manifestation of the Good wch God will bring out of these great evils.

998. *Attributes of God.* The Angels Rejoyce in the Excellencys of God, the Inferior Creatures in His Goodness, Sinners only Rejoyce in His Mercy and Forgiveness.

999. *Come, let us Kill Him, and ye Inheritance, &c.* Mark xii. 7. This is still the language of wicked men—let us make His Ministers Contemptible—destroy their Order, &c., [p. 218.] and then they will no longer torment us.—We can then do w^t we please wth X^t, His Gosp. and X^ty, and live as we please.

1000. *Love of Controversys.* It is but a miserable Glory to be an Ingenious, a Learned disturber of the Peace of the Church or State [i].

1001. *Luxury.* They y^t make the Lab^r, the oppression of ye Poor, the support of their Extravagances—They y^t refuse to pay their just debts, bec. they cannot spare it fr. their vanity—They that waste their estates to please y^ms, &c. Will these call y^ms X^ns?—Will they expect to be Fav^rd by God?

1002. *Charity, Poor.* What a large stock w^d ye Poor have to the fore—If X^ns w^d but lay by for them all that they

---

[f] [Quesnel.]
[g] [ibid.]
[h] [ib. on 1 St. John iv. 17.]
[i] [" or State" om. 4to. ed.]

lay out in unnecessarys—Nay, if they were but to have all y^t X^ns lay out in Sin and Vanity—In Pride, intemperance, &c.? To comply wth evil customes, &c.—And in good truth I cannot see how any X^n can make amends, such as will be accepted of God, for all his idle expences, but by giving to ye Poor, in some way proportionable to the moneys he has misspent, and w^t he has by him.

1003. *Charity, or Love of our Neighb^r.* Tis not so much [p. 219.] our N. Interest as our own that we Love him—St. Jo. makes it the sure mark of a Spiritual Resurrection—"We know y^t we have passed fr. Death unto Life, bec. we Love the Brethren."

Signes of want of Charity—An Aversion to their company—Satisfaction in hearing y^m evil spoken of—A Joy in their misfortunes.

1004. *The same.* If you fancy that y^r Love of y^r Neighb^r is to go no further than desert, Consider w^t yor condition is like to be, if God shall so deal wth you, i. e. according to y^r desert.

1005. *Authority—Pastor.* Men generally look upon the Advantage, ye Pleasure, the Hon^r of Commanding, i. e. of having other People und^r their care. W^d they look upon it as a Charge, i. e. of having other Peoples faults to Answ^r for, as well as their own, tis probable they w^d not be so fond of Power, &c.

1006. *Love of X^t. Test.* He y^t Loves ye Lord J. X^t will [p. 220.] be affected with every thing wch relates to Him.—He will be glad w^n he sees Him Honourd in His Worship, His Ministers, &c. He will be concern'd w^n He is injur'd—He will strive to please Him, &c., and avoid every thing wch He has forbid: by this we frame the best Judgm^t of our Love of God.

1007. *Naūl Corruption. Mortification.* To root out this, must be the work of a X^ns whole Life—The task God has set us—For as Suckers, if not constantly rooted up, and taken away, do at last draw the sap to y^ms, and hinder the good fruit from thriving, so do growing Corruptions, if not narrowly *watched*, and w^n they appear, immediately plucked up.— This makes Mortification, Self-Denyal, Watching, so necessary X^n Duties, That by *Crucifying the Flesh*, we may in some measure conquer all its greater Corruptions at Last.—

The want of this care is the cause of so many Disorders amongst X^{ns}.

[p. 221.]

1008. *Religion.* "Non est res inventa, sed tradita."

Vinc. Lyrin.

1009. *High Places and Posts.* It is the most difficult thing for such as are in any Eminent Places to escape the Temptat^n of sacrificing Truth and Righteousness in some occasion or oth^r.

1010. *Test of our Condit^n.* Were we satisfyed of the safty of our Condit^n, we sh^d never seek out occasions of diverting our minds from thinking of our own Happ^{ss}; wch is y^t we sh^d Love above all temporal things.

1011. *Faith in ye Assistance of God's Sp^t.* Tis for want of this, y^t X^{ns} under ye Apprehensions of not being able to overcome all their Sins will set y^{m}s against none of y^m—Or will spare their darling sins, and avoid y^t Resignation, Self Denyal and Mortification wch are required of every true X^n.

Every X^n who believes the Gospel, may be assured y^t God, who calls us to Holiness, is both willing and able, if we are not wanting to our selves, to free us from all our corruptions, by the Assistance of His Sp^t.—And in truth this was the End of X^{ts} coming into ye World; And "Who gave Himself for us, y^t He might redeem us fr. all iniquity." Tit. ii. 13.

[p. 222.]

Whoever dos not faithfully Believe the Possibility of doing every thing thro' X^t who strengthens us, will neith^r Pray for such a Power, nor attempt to Act by it, nor trouble Himself ab^t it.

On the other Hand, w^n a X^n is fully perswaded y^t X^t by His Sp^t can and will assist us in overcoming the greatest corruptions y^t Human Nature is Subject to, why then we set ab^t it wth courage and confidence, and shall be changed fr. Glory to Glory, by ye Sp^t of ye L^d.—2 Cor. iii. 17.

1012. *Good purposes.* Tis not sufficient y^t our purposes be good, they must also be Regular.

1013. *Faith.* Faith is the measure of all other gifts of God—"according to y^r F. be it unto you."—Matt. ix. 29.

[om. 4to.]

1014. *Ignorant Pastor.* A great^r scourge to the Ch. than a vicious one, bec. he is more capable of destroying the Foundation, wch is Faith—and bringing in Superstition, Disorders and the very worst Abuses.

1015. *God sees all things.* This is ye comfort of Good [p. 223.] men, and a Plague to the wicked.

1016. *Loss of Goods, &c.* A man loses nothing w^n He only loses That wch must perish, wch he must leave at death.

1017. *Whosoever shall Confess, shall Deny Me, &c.* Math. [om. 4to.] x. We are willing to referr this to ye times of the Martyrs, only bec. we are unwilling to suffer.—We own X^t w^n we stand up for His Doctrin, own His Ministers, Support His worship, &c., and we deny Him, &c.

1018. *Love of God.* He w^m we Love most, is he w^m we are most concerned to Please, w^m we are afraid to offend. Let us trye our Love by this Rule.

1019. *Adam.* All right to Et. Happ^{ss} was lost in Adam. [om. 4to.]

1020. *Casuist.* Interest a Decisive Casuist — removes Scruples, easiest consulted, readily hearkend to.—After all, [p. 224.] tho' it may be consulted, it ought not to Govern or Determin by itself.

1021. *Test.* If we w^d really know our Heart, let us Impartially view our Actions.

1022. *To Him y^t hath shall be given.* The good use of [om. 4to.] one Grace prepares us for another.

1023. *Obstinacy.* Sad is ye condit^n of y^t sick person who is afraid of being cured—we do not consider, that this is the case of an infinit number of sick souls.

1024. *Affliction, Poverty, &c.* Do not make men wicked, but they discover—They shew w^t men are.

1025. *Temptations, Tryals*—God dos not usually permit [om. 4to.] His Servants to fall into Temp. and Tryals till they are able to undergo y^m.

1026. *Church Excom.* Tho' a man's being in the Ch. is [p. 225.] no certain mark of Salvat^n, yet his being out of it is too sure a proof y^t he is in the way of inevitable misery.

1027. *Worldly Motives.* W^n a man Resists, on human motives only—He will not hold out long.

1028. *Balles, Dancing, Plays, &c.* Whoever considers y^e [om. 4to.] case of John ye Baptist, cannot doubt but y^t these are great Snares, destructive of modesty and chastity—and a Pernicious contrivance of Satan to excite the Passions.

1029. *The Sp^t of Relig^n.* He y^t has not his eye upon this [om. 4to.] cheifly will be apt to call those Religious Actions wch are in y^{m}s indifferent—And will pass over wth indifference such as are really Sacred and Holy.

[p. 226.] 1030. *Riches, Prosperity.* When we take all the comforts they afford, they will make us forget ye necessity of passing thro' sufferings in our way to Heaven.

1031. *Sufferings.* To suffer is the lot of J. X^t and His ministers, and servants.

1032. *Comfort to Sinners.* Since nothing but ye death of X^t could save us, this shewes indeed the greatness of our misery, and ought to Humble us—But then how infinit is the Mercy of God to Sinners, since He w^d vouchsafe to give His only Son to dye for us—This ought to support us.

[om. 4to.] 1033. Math. xvii. 27. *Lest we sh^d offend y^m—cast an Hook, &c.* This condemns too gr^t an eagerness in us to defend our Temp. rights—But if we cannot recede from y^m wthout great prejudice to ourselves, and ye Ch. and Posterity......

[cf. 227.] 1034. *Men Pleasers.* Christ Himself abates nothing of the strictness of His Lawes for fear of giving people uneasyness and consequently His ministers ought not to Regard any thing wch the Corruption of Manners, or the Remissness of Discipline has introduced.

1035. *Resignation, Humility.* He y^t is truly humble, is always satisfy'd wth God's dispensation, bec. he knows y^t of himself he deserves nothing, and y^t his very virtues are the gift of God.

1036. *States of Life inconsistent wth Salvat^n:—*
1. The Idle voluptuous Life of men of Fortune.
2. The Busy Life, wch allows no time to consider.
3. The Professed Sinful Life.

1037. *Apparel, Fashions.* Singularity may be blamable, but Modesty in dress is not Singularity—Tho ye World be never so extravagant.

1038. *Greatness.* W^n a man looks upon Greatness as an Advantage, and values himself upon it, he acts like an Heathen. W^n he receives it wth Fear—and a Sense of his own [p. 228.] Unworthiness, and looks upon it as a Burden laid upon him for the Service of others, he then acts like a X^n.

1039. *Faith in God.* We believe a man like ourselves upon his bare word, and yet such is the Corruption of our Nature, y^t we make a difficulty of Believing ye Word and

Oath of God w^n it suits not wth our reason, or thwarts our passions.

1040. *The Goodness of God*—Who requires nothing of us, but w^t. is for our advantage—Who freely pardons our offences, and even rewards the good wch He Himself works in us.

1041. *J. X^t an example of, &c.* Math. xxvi. 57, &c. All the Malice of ye D—l and his Instrum^{nts} are made use of, all the Forms of Justice are violated, in order to oppress, calumniat and murd^r J. X^t.—And shall we complain of the Injustice of humane Judgm^{nts} as to our selves? Men think [p. 229.] they have a Right never to pardon a box on ye year—J. X^t takes one (v. 67) with a divine meekness.

That Diabolical method of revenging afronts by Hazzarding more lives y^n one.

1042. *Spirit of Law and Gospel.* W^n men have the knowledge of the Law, with^t the Sp^t of the Law, they are apt to oppose it, w^n they think they defend it.

Thus the Pharisees—condemn X^t for breaking ye Sabbath, &c. The Lawes of Relig^n are to be understood according to what they were designed for, viz. to promote the Glory of God and the good of men.

1043. *Sabbath.* God forbad Lab^r on the Sab. for Fear lest servants sh^d be oppressed by the Covetousness of their Masters, and that men might have sufficient time to mind their Salvat^n.

1044. *Lawes divine and human.* Let us always consider the Intent and designe of ye Legislator, this is the way to understand their true meaning, and to do nothing con- [p. 230.] trary to y^m.

1045. *Afflictions.* Mark v. 26. W^t a mercy is it to be forced to God by Misfortunes, Sickness, or the ill usage of men?

1046. *Meales* sh^d always put us in mind of God's benefits —who feeds us continually—This sh^d keep us fr. sitting down greedily to our meat; prevent Intemperance, and oblige us to offer this Action to God, and to beg that we may Receive His Gifts wth His Blessing.

1047. *Repentance.* Nothing is troublesome to us, so long as we are not obliged to change our Hearts.

1048. *Humility.* To Dispute wth Secular persons wch sh^d [om. 4to.] be ye greater, is very opposit to an Ecclesiastical Spirit.

[p. 231.]
[om. 4to.]

1049. *Riches.* Mark x. 17, 18, &c.

1050. *News papers.* If we w^d read these wth this view—That Wars and Commotions of Empires, Insurrections, persecutions, &c., are all the Judgments of God upon sinful men, that His Providence, and all His Glorious attributes are seen in y^m, &c., we sh^d especially read y^m to better purpose than to gratifye a curiosity, a Passion—or to pass away time, or to divert ye thought fr. other subjects.

1051. *Loss of Children.* God often takes y^m away lest they sh^d be Corrupted and Ruind eternally by the wickedness of ye World.—W^n we come into anoth^r world we shall see the Reason and the Mercy of those Providences, wch now we are apt to murmur at bec. we think y^m severe.

[p. 232.]

1052. *The World* Condemnes w^thout Mercy all those who eith^r Condemne, or will not follow its Max.

1053. *Human Frailty. Self Confidence.* Tis often that people want to be convinced that they are capable of Falling—And therfore tis necessary they sh^d fall w^n they least Fear it. St. Peter.

1054. *Truth.* W^n the speaking of Truth becomes a crime, then he who dares do it, must do it at ye peril of suffering.

[om. 4to.]

1055. *Fasting and Temperance* are absolutely necessary to secure a true Freedom of Mind and Thought—

This makes our morning thoughts more free, clear, and Reasonable, than after a *full meal*, wch in other words, is *Gluttony*, however harsh it may sound—If a man eates so much as unfits him for any duty of Pray^rs, or business, or

[p. 233.] Study—He eates too much, and eating too much is certainly *Gluttony*. A constant *full* Feeding is the very Death of the Soul—Destroyes ye very Spirit of Relig^n—as any oth^r notorious Sin.—Makes a man fit for nothing but dozing, Trifling, or Idleness.—Temperance, therefore, is an Universal Duty—A self denyal as absolutely necessary for a X^n who w^d get rid of ye Disorders of his Nature, as it is for a man in a Dropsy to abstain from Drink.—Tis the most general exercise of the X^n Life.—Its design being to destroy sensuality, Lessen the Corruption of our Nature, and enable us to enjoy Spiritual things.

The Duty here meant is not a Total Abstinence fr. all

Food for a certain time (all Constitutions not bearing this) but the Denying a man's self such dainties, or such a Quantity of Meat, as may indispose him for the Duties of his calling—Such a Self Denyal is a Duty, and a proper meanes of applying to God, in Hopes of being accepted.

In short—This duty makes our Repentance more affecting—calmes our Passions—Puts us in a Better state of Devotion—Disciplins the Body—Allays the Passions—Makes our Prayers more powerful with God for w^{t}ever we ask. (Math. xvii. 21.)

All this depends upon this Truth—That our Soules being United to a Body, y^t is more or less fit to Joyn in Acts of Relig^n according to ye state it is in. Now Temperance favours Piety—Luxury fav^{rs} Sinful Thoughts. The one gives [p. 234.] the Soul an Heavenly Tast, the other infects it wth dispositions, Earthly, Sensual, Devilish.

1056. *Of Judging by our Senses.* You see a poor man working hard for his daily bread, and but just able to get it.

You find yo^{r}self in easy circumstances, you want nothing, you Fear no want, you meet wth no trouble. You bless yor self and yor condition, and think yor self much happyer than ye poor man. You do not consider after all y^t this was in some measure ye case of Lazarus and ye Rich man—and y^t that poor man is in a surer way to Heaven than you are. This will make you thoughtful.

1057. *Repentance.* So long as there is no appearance of [om. 4to.] a new Life, of new manners, there is neith^r Rep. nor Conversion.

1058. *Eternity.* Where Et. lies at stake, he that loseth [p. 235.] one day, hazards all.

1059. *Hypocrisy.* X^{ns} do not take so much care to avoid the Sin, as w^t is scandalous in it. They bear Malice in their Hearts, and only take care to avoid to shew it in outward Acts.

1060. *Reproof of gr^t. mèn.* Jo. Bapt. Reprov'd Herod— [om. 4to.] bec. he neith^r Lovd the Good things, nor Feard the Evils wch he could give or Inflict on him.

1061. *Incarnation.* J. X^t according to ye will of God took upon Him our Nature, and the Sins of the World, in order to Undergo the penance and Punishm^t due to them, and to become a Sacrifice for y^m.

[om. 4to.] 1062. *Contracts wth ye Devil.* It is certain every X^n is incapable of making a Contract wth the Devil, i. e. He contracts for y^t wch is not his own; and wherof he has no Pow^r to dispose, J. X^t having purchased Him by His blood. But if X^{ns} [p. 236.] will renounce J. X^t—give y^{m}s up to the Devil—[those] who consent to Articles wth Him, God in Justice may give him power over y^m. Tho' with^t His permission the D—l himself is under an Interdict by the Authority of ye Supreme Justice.

[om. 4to.] 1063. *Advancem^t* wch comes not from God must needs be dangerous. How many are raised to High posts in the Ch. by ye Instigation of ye D—l, that their Fall may be more dismal.—If God raises a man, He is engaged by His goodness to support him—to prevent his fall, or to raise him ag^n.

1064. *Truth.* Provokes those w^m it dos not convert.

[om. 4to.] 1065. *Uncleanness—Sins of.* Our having so little abhorrence of such as to make a jest of y^m is too sure a sign y^t [we] app^{r}hend not the sad punishm^t due to such Sins.

1066. *Fear of Man—Pastor.* Those w^m Fear renders weak and cowardly in the exercise of ye ministry, forget that they exercise it in ye Name and Place of J. X^t to w^m they must acc^t.

[p. 237.] 1067. *Poverty —Power of Faith.* How glorious is it to God, to make Himself to be Beloved of those to w^m He denyes those things wch men most dote after! and purely for His own sake. This is a sure proof of ye X^n Relig^n and of the Power of Grace.

1068. *Charity to ye Poor.* Luk. vi. 34[k]. In cases of necessity all things ought to be as it were in common amongst those who possess X^t in common upon Earth, and who are to possess Him in Heav^n as their Joynt Inheritance.

1069. *Judge not, &c.* Luke vi. 37. How great is ye Goodness of God, in putting our Sentence as it were, into our own Hands, provided we do not usurp the Right wch belongs solely to Him, of Judging the Heart.

1070. *Condemn not, &c.* Luk. vi. 38. How desperatly mad and blind are we to expose ourselves to ye Severity of

---

[k] [35. This and the four following entries are taken from Quesnel on that chapter.]

God's Justice and Vengeance, by not shewing an Indulgence and Tenderness towards the Failings of our Broth^r!

1071. *World.* Whoever Loves ye World will never retain the Word of God in his heart.

1072. *God and ye World.* How oft do we see the Word [p. 238.] of God, Good desires, and even good Works, subsist for some time togeth^r with Vanity, Worldly Lusts, Ambition, Luxury, and even grow up togeth^r with y^m! Sooner or later the Thornes grow up and choke ye good seed if not rooted up in time.

1073. *Temptations* to a faithful X^n are only Tryals—To [om. 4to.] awaken our Faith—To make us more watchful in Prayer—And to make ye Power of God more manifest.

1074. *Faith—Good Works.* Our Lord praises it very [om. 4to.] often, not to oppose it to good Works, but to shew y^t it is ye Fountain of y^m.—And to take ye Jewes off fr. their confidence in the Works of the Law, wch they depended upon for their Justification, and in their own Righteousness.

1075. *Widowes Mite.* Every State of Life affordes us opportunities of doing Good, and wch God will reward, provided we take care to act up to ye opportunitys God gives us. This sh^d make us contented wth every Condition of Life.

1076. *Success.* We own this to be the Gift of God, and yet we value our selves, as if it was thro' our own power, [p. 239.] wisdome, &c. This is the sad effect of Self Love.

1077. *Learning, Knowlege.* How much is it to be dreaded, w^n the Love of God dos not accompany it, w^n this dos not make it useful, Edifying, Holy, Religious and mindful of our Salvat^n.

1078. *Neighbor,* Luk. x. 37. Is every one who stands in need of our Assistance, let him be what he will—The being Miserable gives any man a Right to our Mercy, wch is a *Debt,* not a *Fav^r* left to our discretion.

1079. *Covetousness.* A man Cov. not only in wronging others, but in holding his own wth too much concern and affection. Riches become not only the care, but the Torment of y^m y^t possess y^m, thro' fear of losing y^m.

1080. *Blessed—y^t mourn;* i. e. who are troubled at every thing y^t they believe displeaseth God.

1081. *Loss of Freinds, Goods, &c.* Afflictions have their

Use wⁿ they oblige us to consider that these are perishing things and y^t we must seek for Happ^{ss} in somthing wch cannot be taken away from us.

[p. 240.] 1082. *God's Ministers.* The sins committed agst these are not generally understood, they have a peculiar guilt in y^m—For they y^t despise y^m dishon^r Him y^t sends y^m, even J. X^t, and ye H. Gh.

1083. *Duty of Freindship.* It is a pernicious complaisance, to conceal from our Freinds Mortifying and Afflictive Truthes, wⁿ it is expedient they sh^d know y^m.

[om. 4to.] 1084. *The Life of Man* is to be valued only for its usefulness[1].

1085. *Regeneration.* The only certain Proof of R. is victory. He y^t is Born of God overcometh ye World, 1 Jo. v. Wⁿ we live by Faith—Wⁿ Faith has subdued ye Will—Hath wrought Repentance not to be repented of, 2 Cor. vii. 10—Hath Conquered our Corruptions—Then—To him y^t overcometh, &c.

1086. *Repentance.* By this we are to Understand a New Nature, a New Life. There is no difficulty in this.

[p. 241.] 1087. *Duty—Disconsolate.* Be more intent upon ye discharge of Duty, than upon the Fruit of it.

1088. *Xⁿ Perfection.* The way to advance in Xⁿ Perfection is to make Xⁿ Reflections upon every occurrence of Life, and to endeav^r to improve by them.

1089. *Meanes.* Acts ix. 25. To neglect meanes, to trust to an Unactive Confidence, is to Tempt God.

[om. 4to.] 1090. *Miracles—Libertine.* There must be somthing more than Miracles to convert a Libertin. Grace must make y^m effectual.

1091. *State and Grandeur.* It is the Love of State y^t makes it thought necessary to ye Episcopal dignity.

1092. *Time* is very precious wⁿ the Salvation of our Soules is concern'd.

[p. 242.] 1093. *Opposition* one meets wth in ye Way of Duty, a very necesary counterbalance to the Joy occasioned by any good works one has done, the poison of w^{ch}, and the commendatⁿ one may meet wth, is much more dangerous and

---

[1] [Mr. Stowell, Life of Wilson, p. 47, says, "This was one of his favourite Maxims." It is marked in the MS. with a ☞]

difficult to be overcome, than ye Contradiction one meets with.

1094. *Strange Relations.* To give credit to all strange acc^ts is lightness and Imprudence, to give credit to none is Ignorance and Rashness.

1095. *Reproof.* Any man who disturbes the false Peace of Sinners, must expect to be ill treated and reproched, and defam'd.

1096. *Magistrates,* unless they are upon their guard, will be made the Instruments of the designes of wicked men, or of their revenge.

1097. *Magistrates.* To Fear the displeasure of men and not to Fear doing injustice is an effect of Infidelity.

1098. *Riches.* X^ty dos not reject the Rich, but it inspires [p. 243.] them wth a contempt of Riches, and makes y^m as humble as if they were never so poor.

1099. *Providence.* That man is safe, who has Him on his side in whose Hands are ye Hearts of men, and all their power.

1100. *Prayer.* The condition wch God requires of us w^n we ask any Fav^r of Him is This, That we earnestly desire to obtain it. Men often ask y^t wch they are afraid sh^d be granted, the power of Leaving their evil ways.

1101. *Corruption of Nature.* He y^t will carefully look into His own Heart, will certainly Find eith^r all vices, or the seed of all vices, ready to grow up if not rooted out.

1102. *Unlearned.* Every body has understanding enough to be a X^n if he has but the will.

1103. *The Motions of Grace.* It is a sad misfortune to [p. 244.] strive to suppress the Motions of Grace, but a much worse to be successful in doing it.

1104. *Providence.* We see human events, but we see not [om. 4to.] the hand that directs y^m and makes y^m Answer His designes, concealed under ye designes of men.

1105. *Pomp, Pride, &c.* Act. xxv. 23. There is a great deal of difference betwixt the Distinction wch belongs to Dignity, and wch is not Condemned in the Gospel, and y^t Pomp and Magnificence w^h Pride Inspires, and w^h cannot but be displeasing to God.

1106. *Causes of Infidelity.* Men reflecting upon their own Actions, wth Fear of w^t may come hereafter, and being not willing to forsake their evil ways, or their false perswasions, despair of attaining ye Promises of ye Gospels and so turn Deists, y^t is, Infidels—first Hoping, and then affirming all Religⁿ to be false.

1107. *Duty.* Men are often set upon doing not w^t they ought, but w^t they desire.

[p. 245.] 1108. *Contempt of ye Clergy.* Exod. xvi. 7, 8. We may truly say w^t Moses did, "W^t are we? Yo^r murmurings are not agst us, but agst the Lord."

1109. *Riches,* unreasonably Heaped up and kept wthout Necessity, prove a Canker to ye owners, just as ye Manna did (Exod. xvi. 20), wch being kept contrary to God's Command, until ye next day, bred worms and stank, &c.

[om. 4to.] 1110. *Sabbath.* See Exod. xvi. 29. The Blessing of keeping it Holy.

1111. *Preisthood—Ministers.* A contempt of these dos most na^ally lead to ye Contempt of God, and of X^t—He y^t despiseth you, &c. We have X^{ts} own Word for it.

[om. 4to.] 1112. *Spirits.* The disbelief of Sp. is only to make way for ye denyal of a God, ye Fath^r of Sp^{ts}.

[om. 4to.] 1113. *Evil Habits.* If young people w^d but consider the Infinit trouble of breaking off evil Habits, of laying a Founda-
[p. 246.] tion for a bitter Repentance, or Damnation—They w^d, &c.

[om. 4to.] 1114. *Schism.* They y^t run away fr. their Father's House—the Ch. of God—don't consider y^t they run away fr. their Inheritance.

1115. *Authority.* He y^t is convinc'd by a lawful Authority, is convinc'd by Reason, for Reason bids us, in many cases, to submit to ye determination of Authority.—See "Reason and Authority Compar'd." Trapp's Sermons, vol. i., serm. 1.^m

1116. *Boldness of Wickedness.* We may expect in a short time to see all manner of Sins countenanced by the Magistrate, since men take the Liberty to avow their Sins with^t fear of punishm^t.

Other Ages practiced Wickedness, to our's is reserv'd the Impudence to Glory in them.

1117. *X^t our Pattern.* How unworthy an opinion w^d a

---

^m [See " A Preservative against Unsettled Notions and want of Principles in Religion, in several Discourses, &c., p. 10, by Joseph Trapp. Lond. 1715."]

Stranger have of X^t if he was to Judge w^t X^t was by the Lives of those who call y^{m}s His followers.

1118. *God's Omnipresence.* You will never be truly Happy untill you can say, I am glad that God sees all my Actions, [p. 247.] that He sees my Heart, and the very motives upon w^h I do every thing.

1119. *Daily Prayer—Family.* If we are once Convinc'd y^t nothing can prosper in our Hands—to wch God dos not vouchsafe to give His blessing, we can never think light [of], or omit this Duty.

1120. *Greatness, Honours, &c.* Those w^m God has abandon'd to ye Desire and enjoyment of Riches and Hon^{rs}, Deserve above all oth^{rs} our Prayers and our Compassion, As being in the most dangerous Circumstances of Life, wch renders y^m almost incapable of Grace and the Inspirations of Heaven. These are most miserable bec. they think y^{ms} Happy. A X^n is no otherwise Great in the eyes of God, than as he is Helpful to others—Feedes the Hungry, Protects ye weak,—Administers Justice Impartially, &c. Vid. Sp^t of Xt^y, pag. 52.^{n}

1121. *Atheism.* The true reason of the growth of Atheism is the Glaring Light of the Gospel, wch discovers plainly that there are Torments appointed for ye wicked. Wicked men, the more plain this is, the more Industrious they are to shut [their] eyes, to Hearken to any thing y^t may perswade y^m that this may not be—&c. till God gives y^m up to . . . .

1122. *Rich and Poor compar'd.* Blessed are the *Poor,* [p. 248.] They that *mourn,* they y^t are *persecuted,* &c., not one w^d in all ye S.S. like Blessed are the Rich, the Prosperous, the Great, and yet we all desire and strive after a Condition wch has no promise of a Blessing attending it.

1123. *The Gospel* affords us infallible Rules of Life, and provided we apply them Right, we cannot be wrong in our Judgm^t.

1124. *Mysterys and Maxims of X^t.* Men own the former bec. they do not make them Uneasy, but in their practice they deny the latter, bec. they condemn the Life they are resolved to lead. They will not Hear, nor see the Truth, y^t they may

---

^{n} [The substance of this passage is from "The Spirit of Christianity," (by Walter Kirkham Blount.) Lond. 1686.]

sin with^t Remorse.—They embrace errors with^t ever examining wheth^r they are such, bec. ye Truth w^d make y^m uneasy.

[p. 249.]   1125. *Schism.* W^n the mercys of God will not prevail wth X^{ns} to Unite, He often dos it by His Judgments.

1126. *Read ye Holy Scriptures.* Read ye S.S., but read wth attention—Read ye Parable of ye Prodigal—Read ye Parable of ye Rich man—Of him y^t built new barns, &c. Read these—and see if nothing in y^m belongs to you—Wheth^r you are not faring sumptuously every day, whiles others want Bread—wheth^r you are not laying out too much upon Fine Clothes, whiles oth^{rs} want clothes, to keep y^m warm, &c. &c. &c.

1127. *Death.* Our Happiness or Misery begins w^n we dye.

1128. *Hell.—I am tormented in these Flames.* Take notice y^t he who said this was a Jew, one who had Abraham to his Fath^r.—This sh^d make X^{ns} beware of depending upon a good Relig^n wthout leading of Lives answerable thereunto.

1129. *Fear.* Men are too apt to flatter y^{m}s y^t G. will not be so severe as He has threatend. This hardens men in Sin, and makes y^m boldly venture upon damnation—This is to represent God, as a God not terrible in Judgm^t.—Let a just
[p. 250.] Fear of God's vengeance have its proper effect, &c. The Sp^t of God makes use of Flames of Fire and Brimstone to awaken us, to represent to us.

You see therefore ye folly of those who say y^t there is one event to ye Righteous and to ye Wicked—Eccl. ix. 2. That it is in vain to serve God—Mal. iii. 14.

You hear on ye oth^r hand w^t ye Psalm. says, and wch is worth yor laying to Heart, y^t in keeping God's Com. there is great Reward—a Reward wch Eye hath not seen, &c.

1130. *Fear of God.* A man has no other Security of his virtue, but ye Fear of offending God.

1131. *Sin.* We have reason to bless G. y^t He has not taken us off by a sudden stroke of Death every time we have sin'd, as He did Ananias and Saph.

1132. *Original Sin.* Sad experience fr. our very Cradle shewes us how prone we are to Sin.

[p. 251.]   1133. *Consideration.* Repentance and Amendment ye naal consequence of consideration.

1134. *Things Sacred and Profane.* Mr. Mede (Book iv.

p. 1017 °,) is of opinion y^t the little regard of the distinction betwixt Things Sacred and Profane, is that wch will most surely bring down Judgments upon ye Protestant churches, wch are all more or less guilty of this *Sin, drawing down Judgm^ts*.

1135. *Riches.* Tis one of the most difficult things in Life, to know w^n one has enough of the World.

1136. *Hypocrite.* He that is angry at other men's faults, and is not angry at his own is an Hypocrite.

1137. *Learning.* It is not every body y^t can be scholars, but every body may be X^ns and even Saints [?] if it is not their own fault.

1138. *X^ns Privilege.* As you are a X^n you are the Pecu- [p. 252.] liar care of y^r Redeemer, and under the Guardianship of His good Angels.

1139. *Sin Punishable.* Few People are so blind, as to flatter themselves y^t God will permit their Sin to go unpunished—w^t then do they do to divert so uneasy a Thought —why they endeav^r to stifle, to Divert such Thoughts.

1140. *Visiting the Sick.* See Hosea, ch. vi. v. 1. margin. [om. 4to.] [The margin refers to Jer. xxx. 17.]

1141. *World.* Qu. [Quesnel?] May 4, 1731. A man will [om. 4to.] be sure to be well rec^d by the world, w^n he flatters it and complyes wth its ways, but if he opposes it, &c.

1142. *Conduct of ye Gr^t.* How careful sh^d they be to regulate it, w^n they see how ready the world is to follow their example.

1143. *Omniscience of God.* God sees every thing—This is matter of comfort to Good men and matter of Terror to ye wicked.

1144. *They that be whole.* The Sad Condition of those who are affraid of seeing their danger and of being cured is [p. 253.] more common than is imagined.

1145. *Why are ye S.S. somtimes dark?* Why to put us in mind that ye Knowledge of God and of the Mysterys of X^t are Fav^rs wch are to be asked of God, as ever we hope to understand.

° [p. 829, ed. 1672. "*Altius hoc animo meo insedit*, that the Reformed Churches, out of extream abomination of idolatry, have, according to the nature of men, incurred some guilt before God ἀμετρίᾳ τῆς ἀνθολκῆς, by taking away the distinction almost generally between things sacred and prophane, and that thay shall one day smart for it.... The present Judgments of God upon the Reformation do insinuate some such thing."]

1146. *Forgive Injurys, Love Enemys.* These must have no bounds in the Heart, tho' as to the outward behaviour, they may have some limitations.

1147. *Praise, Applause.* He who loves Praise loves Temptation.

1148. *Natural Religion.* There is Natural Reason—There are Natural Dutys—There are Lawes of Nature—But Natural Religion, there can be none—For ye Notion of Religion wch all people have, and wch the very Word imports, is a meanes of bring^{ing} men back to God, who have gone from Him—Now how can Nature, wch is corrupt and carrys us [p. 254.] from God, bring back to Him w^{thout} His Help[n]? . . . . We shall see an absolute necessity for a more commanding authority, and for more assistance than Nature can furnish us with.

[om. 4to.] 1149. *Plays.* 1 Cor. x. 7. Neither be ye Idolaters—The People sat down to eat (at the Sacrifices) &c.—Quesnel; See also v. 21.

1050. *Peace be unto this House;* i. e. All kind of *Happ^{ss}*—that yor Hearts can wish—Success in all Honest Undertakings—and Peace be unto you. Jo. xx. 21.

The World cannot give Peace—It may flatter us a while, but will deceive us at last.—Nay tho' one were sure of Prosperity all his days, wch no man on earth can be sure of.

1151. *Death.* It is only your Sins y^t can make you afraid of dying.

[p. 255.] 1052. *Afflictions* are designed by a gracious God, to do y^t for us, wch we are not able to do for our selves—They are a proof of our being within ye care of a Fath^r who cannot be pleased wth our ruin.

1153. *Study.* Be not solicitous to read any thing w^{ch} [has] no relation to virtue, Piety and being useful in y^r Generat^n.

1154. *Reason.* You will not be able by all ye Strength of Reason to subdue one lust, to support your minds under any great affliction, &c.

1155. *Peace of Conscience.* This will be sufficient to support you under all worldly afflictions—and enable you to go thro' every difficulty of Life—W^n you know y^t you are in ye way to Heaven, and endeavouring to please God.

---

[n] [Three lines in the MS. illegible through blotting.]

1156. *Condition of Life.* Every man's condition is ap- [p. 256.] pointed by the Wisdom of God, and no man ought to wish it otherwise than it [is], nor can do it wthout taxing God wth Injustice, &c.

1157. *Worldly Happ^{ss}.* See w^t it dos upon those y^t have their Hearts' desires—Their Faith is weak—They are less concerned for the Happ^{ss} of another Life—They desire to set up their rest here.

1158. *Goodness of Providence.* An Infidel is no reproch upon ye Goodness of Prov. He brings good out of evil—His Infinit Patience magnifys His Infinit mercy (if one may so speak).—He foresaw and foretold this by His Prophets and Apost., and especially by His Son, viz. Faith sh^d fail and Iniquity sh^d abound—That ye times of His Patience wth ye Gentile Church sh^d be fulfilld—That Iniquity sh^d abound, &c.—That ye ingrafted branches might be cut off.

1159. *Labour.* No man living is excused fr. L. of some [p. 257.] kind or other, eith^r of ye mind or body—Tho' his worldly circumstances be never so good—Innumerable are the evils occasioned for want of being convinced of this Truth—Plays, Assemblies, Clubs, Diversions of all kinds—Drunkenness, Tipling, &c.—All the Schools of Vice and Impiety—Gaming —The useless Lives of People of Estates—Useless to themselves and others—Idle visits—Impertinent Conversations —Debaucheries.

1160. *X^n Religion* is plain and Easy to be understood by [om. 4to.] all such as are desirous to understand it.

The most Unlearned can believe and embrace w^t God has made known to us, thro' the Gr. of God, and with^t this, the most learned know nothing to any good purpose, and are as far from ye K. of H. as ye most ignorant.

A X^n who leades a X^n Life knowes enough to carry him to Heaven and Happ^{ss}—And a good Scholar who leades a Useless or a Wicked life is in the very way to Hell.

The true Wisdom is to Know, to Fear, to Love and obey [p. 258.] God—This was the Wisdom of all such as are now in Paradise.—Study you to be saved—and w^n you dye, you will find y^t you were wiser than those y^t have Read and writ many bookes—and were not wise for y^{m}s. Envy not ye paines nor learning of these y^t are thus foolish.

1161. *Religion.* Nothing but R. can give us the Satisfaction and Peace we all so earnestly desire.

1162. *Vain Expences.* How odd w^d it look to hear one, upon giving moneys to a poor body, bid him go to ye Ale House and spend it—Go and venture at gaming—Go buy y^{r}self some foolish toy, &c.—Why do you y^t y^{r}self wch you own you sh^d be laught at to bid anoth^r do ?

[p. 259.] 1163. *Learning.* When it is made to serve Religion and Piety, 'tis truly commendable, but w^n it serves not to these purposes, 'tis the most impertinent employm^t and loss of time.

1164. *Quality and High Birth.* It was virtue wch first raised it above the Vulgar, and w^n that ceases in a Family, there is an end of ye real quality and 'tis a disgrace, &c. &c.

[om. 4to.] 1165. *Learning.* When 'tis serviceable to true Relig^n and virtue, 'tis a real ornament; when it ceases to be so, 'tis a Trifle.

1166. *Time.* Remember the advantages y^t may be made of it—Everlasting Happ^{ss}. Remember w^t you lose by losing it.

1167. *Clothes.* Decency and Cleanliness according to our Rank—All above y^t creates Contempt instead of Respect—They y^t are in King's Houses may without vanity wear soft raiment.

[p. 260.] 1168. *X^n Liberty.* Deprive not yo^{r}self of it—indulge not scruples—and dread Libertinism—some have run from one to ye other—Serve God and be cheerful °.

1169. *Death.* When it comes we shall either be Infinitly Happy or Infinitly Miserable : as sure as we now live, as sure as God is true,—so y^t there is no trifling in a matter of such concern.

1170. *Age of Infidelity.* Tis a sickly age of Infidelity— wch has not only depriv'd us of Relig^n but of Common Sense, even of ye Common Faculty of Thinking—A Foolish Generation—Tis a certain Signe of a sound and stedy Virtue and Judgm^t not to be carryed away wth ye current of Libertinism and Infidelity.—Let us make this wise choice, To be Happy [p. 261.] with the Few, rather than to go to Hell with ye Crowd.

1171. *Infidelity.* (T. S. M.) Is, no doubt of it, wonderfully and justly appointed, or at least permitted, as a Scourge to chastise those Formal Hypocrites, who profess the true Re-

° [Bishop Hacket's motto.]

lig^n. and yet in works deny it; and especially those whose duty it is to teach others by their examples, as well as doctrines, and [who] yet are so far from doing it, that they only harden ye Unbeliever and confirm him in his Infidelity. But God will be glorified in both.

1172. *Script. Reason.* " Divine Dialogues," 495. Let no [om. 4to.] X^n quit the Word of God (in his disputes wth Infidels) and fly to drye Reason with^t the assistance of ye H. Spirit, to maintain the Truthes of Relig^n.

We find by sad Experience w^t little good men have done by Subtiltys of Reason, and tedious deductions and sophistical Intricacies.—Infidels like these ways, bec. there is no end of y^m, and care not to be attacked by positive S.S.

1173. *To Serve God.* We then Serve or Glorify God, w^n we any ways acknowledge, and especially in a public [p. 262.] manner, The Wisd., Goodn., Power, Justice or Provid. of God.—And all this we do in our Publick Service.—We, by confessing our Sins, acknowledge His Justice; and by Praying to Him for w^t we want, His Provid., &c. &c. And so in every p^t of our Service.—See Rev. xiv. 7. " Fear God."

1174. *Infidelity.* How thankful sh^d every X^n be w^m God has preserv'd in this age of Infidelity, fr. falling from ye Faith, w^n we see so many, otherwise learned men, Infected wth this damnable vice to such a degree y^t they cannot see ye plainest truthes, bec. they are not disposed to receive y^m. And bec. they are possessed wth an evil Sp^t of Unbelief.

1175. *Wealth and Vanity.* The best Institutions have not been found proof agst wealth, and the consequence of Riches; i. e. Vanity and Pride.

1176. *States of Life inconsistent wth Salv.* St. Matt. xxii. 2. [om. 4to.] 1. A soft, easy, Idle, voluptuous Life—wherin a man only aimes at enjoying every thing y^t his Riches can furnish him [p. 263.] —Pleasures, Diversions, Feasting, &c.

2. A Life spent wholly in Heaping Wealth by all Ways, Employments, Trade, &c.

3. A Life profligatly Wicked, Sinners as it were by Profession, Enemies to Relig^n, God, and Goodness.

1177. *Jo.* xv. 7. " Ask what ye will and it shall be done [om. 4to.] unto you."

1178. *Prayer.* I ask nothing, O Jesus, but that my

Heart may be entirely Thine, that I may be restored to ye Image of God, and that I may continue Thine for ever.

That I may be fill'd wth ye fruits of the Spirit—Gal. iv. 22. Love, Joy, Peace, long Suffering, Gentleness, Goodness, Faith, Meekness, Temperance.

1179. *Faith.* Lord increase my Faith. Grant y^t it may purify my Heart—That it may work by Love—That I may Live by ye Faith in the Son of God—That at ye Day of Judgm^t it may be found to Praise and Hon^r and Glory.

[p. 264.]
[om. 4to.] 1180. *Ad Aulam.* 2 Chron. xv. 1, 2. "The Lord is with you, while ye be wth Him," &c. See also 2 Ch. xix. 2.

[om. 4to.] 1181. *Plays.* By wch the Soul and Affect^{ns} will be forceably Diverted and drawn fr. attending to and Loving those things wch are above: From these Entertainm^{ts}, the Primitive X^{ns} most religiously abstaind—As folly, Lewdness and Vanitys wch they had renounced at their Bapt.

[om. 4to.] 1182. *Reformation.* Let the Reform. be never so well founded, the Prov. of G. is not bound to secure it to those who take pleasure in unrighteousness. Dr. More [p].

[om. 4to.] 1183. *To ye Rich and Great.* To be miserable in the next World, after having our Hearts' desire in this, ought to awaken, to put men upon thinking.

1184. *External Worship.* We assemble together—To confess our Sin to God—To Pray for w^t we want—To give Thanks for His Fav^{rs}—To Hear His Will admonishing us to Repent and letting us know the consequence—To know the Mercy and Termes of our Redemption. To Receive and

[p. 265.] Commemorate the Pledges of God's Goodness and Mercy—By these Religious Acts, performed as they sh^d be, conscience is kept awake, and upon its guard—acquitting us w^n we do well—reproaching us w^n we do otherwise—These and many more are the Uses of outward and Publick Worship—wch w^n performed as it sh^d be, will be attended wth an especial Grace of God.

[p. 268.] 1185. *Death.* If we look upon Death only as a Punishm^t to which as Sinners we are justly condemnd, we could have little comfort in the thoughts of it.

---

[p] [Possibly this mention of Dr. More may have reference to his Exposition of the Epistle to the Church of Sardis, Rev. iii. 1—6, as prophetic of the dangers of Reformed Christendom. Theological Works, pp. 745, seqq., 762.]

But if we look upon it in anoth^r view, as a Sacrifice for Sin, wch God will mercifully accept of, in union wth the Death of His Son, for the Pardon of all our offences, provided we submit to it as due to our Sins, the Thoughts of Death will then be matter of real comfort to us.

Our only confidence is to be deriv'd from God's mercy in J. X^t, with full purposes of doing our Duty.

A good X^n will neither be fond of Life, nor weary of it.

The Sting of Death is Sin. Therfore a good Life is the [p. 269.] only Security ag^st the Fear of Death.

If God were pleas'd to kill us (said the Wife of Manoah to her Husband), He w^d not have receiv'd a burnt offering at our Hands, neither w^d He have shew'd us all these things.

Now this is the comfort of God's Servants—If God vouchsafes them time to consider their latter end—And grace to prepare for it—by Renewing their Vowes—By Receiving the Lord's Supper—By touching their Heart with the Dutys of Charity and Almes-deeds, &c. :—all these are proofes of God's tender regard for His poor Creatures, and groundes for a X^n to Hope y^t God will [perfect?] His Graces wth Pardon and Happyness.

Rom. v. 1. "Being Justify'd by Faith, we have Peace with [p. 270.] God thro' our Lord J. X^t." [These four texts

2 Tim. ix. 12. "I know w^m I have believed, and I am om. 4to.] perswaded that He is able to keep that wch I have committed unto Him against That day."

St. Jo. iii. 15. "He y^t Believeth in J. X^t shall not perish, but have Eternal Life."—Let it be, O Lord, unto Thy Servant, according to this Word.

2 Cor. v. 1. "For we know that if our Earthly House of this Tabernacle were dissolved, we have a Building of God, an House not made wth Hands, eternal in the Heavens."

"Whosoever shall call upon the Name of the L^d shall be saved—"

These, my Lord, are Thine own.

N.B. Much more of our Prosperity is owing to ye Pro- [p. 271.] vidence of God, than to our own contrivance or endeav^rs.

1186. *Proficiency.* By this we know that we are in the way of Heaven, as we know a tree is alive by its daily growth.

1187. *Moral virtue* consists in a Temper of Mind, and

Conformity of Manners, to Right Reason and the Commands of God.

1188. *Atheists.* All such as reject J. X^t are Atheists, according to St. P., Ephes. ii. 12, 'Αθεοὶ ἐν τῷ κοσμῷ.

1189. *Necessity of X^{ts} Death.* If nothing had been done to deterr us from Sin, both God and His Pardon w^d have been despised.

[p. 272.] 1190. *Conscience* is the present opinion a man has of his own Actions.

1191. *Atonement.* The offering such Conditions to ye Party offended, as He shall judge proper to accept for the offence committed, and sufficient satisfaction—Thus J. X^t offerd to God such satisfaction as He was pleased with, for the Sins of Mankind.

[om. 4to.] 1192. *Mediator.* A mediator must do three things—He must prevail with the person offended to accept of his mediation. 2. He must propose satisfaction for the offence, and see it made good if insisted on. 3. He must provide that the offender shall not offend in the like man^r ag^n.

1193. *God reconciled* to man w^n He forgives his offence.—Man reconciled to God, w^n he thankfully accepts of the pardon and endeav^{rs} to offend Him no more.

[p. 273.]
[om. 4to.] 1194. *Lord's Prayer.* Being in the Plural Number, seems design'd for a Society of X^{ns}—At least every X^n who uses it, sh^d consider himself as a Member of a Society, whose welfare he sh^d Pray for, as for himself.

1195. *Reason and Revelation.* It has been proved y^t Opium will kill a man—must we not believe this, but take any quantity at a venture, because our Reason cannot comprehend how it has this deadly effect?

The Mysterys of X^{ty} are above our Reason, but we believe y^m—bec. we have all ye Proofes necessary to convince any reasonable man, y^t God has reveald y^m as certain truthes.

1196. *Method of Reproving.* To do it with markes of Respect—with Mildness—To do it in so plain a manner as ye Person may be made ye Judge of the Reason, &c.

[p. 274.]
[om. 4to.] 1197. *The Sin, Crime of Satan*—was his not being content with the State of a creature (which depends entirely upon God). God therfore sustaind him no longer by His Grace, which was by him disownd.

The same befals men, who for want of Humility, do Arrogate (ascribe) to y^ms those things wch are God's; i. e. every thing that is good.

1198. *Ingratitude for Favours, &c.* This was Hezekia's crime for wch he sufferd. He forgat God, who had done wonders for him, and in ye Pride of his Heart, was lifted up, &c.

1199. *Rules and Maxims of the Gospel:—* [p. 287.]

Rash Judgm^t. Luk. vi. 41. He who well examines him- [om. 4to.] self, will not be ready to find fault wth others. Why beholdest Thou ye mote, &c.

We have then only a Right to Judge of ye Tree, wⁿ its Fruit appeares. v. 44.

Purity of Heart. (Blessed are ye Pure in Heart.) Is neces- [om. 4to.] sary to know God, and to distinguish that wch proceeds from God, from, &c.

Give me, O Lord, The true knowledg of the Spirit of [p. 291.] the Gospel. [om. 4to.]

Finish, O my God, the work of Thy mercy wch Thou hast begun in me.

Grant, O God, that I may employ and spend my Life for Thy sake.

1200. *Important Questions.* What assurance have I y^t [p. 295.] I am in a State of Grace and Salv. ? [om. 4to.]

1201. *Manks Proverbs :—* [p. 298.]

Hig shen dty hguale—"That will meet you;" i. e. Here- [om. 4to.] after: spoken of a Man's Good or Evil deeds.

Ta'n seihe cabbal corragh—"The World is a Tickle^q Horse^r."

---

^q [So Shakspeare, Measure for Measure, i. 3: "Thy head stands so *tickle* on thy shoulders, that a milkmaid, if she be in love, may sigh it off."— Henry VI., pt. ii., i. 1 :—
"The State of Normandy Stands on a *tickle* point."]

^r [Here end "Maxims of Piety and Morality," as contained in Bishop Wilson's MSS., numbered "Book V.," and "Book VI.," in the custody of Sion College.]

SUPPLEMENT

TO

MAXIMS OF PIETY AND MORALITY.

[THE following pages are printed from a MS. in the possession of Sion College; a thick volume, in 12mo., made up, *first*, of portions of a Common-place Book (pp. 1—111; then, by a mistake of the binder, 225—284, then 112—168, omitting 168—225); *secondly*, of a much smaller portion, unpaged, with the title "Collectanea;" *thirdly*, of the matter of two Sermons, or the greater part of them, nearly all in the Bishop's handwriting. On one of the fly-leaves at the beginning is an index to Texts of Scripture referred to in the Book; the heading in his own writing, the index itself in that of his friend and Vicar-general, Mr. Walker; and on the next leaf, in his own writing, "St. Luke xix. 14, 27, 'We will not have this Man to reign over us.' Deists, Infidels, all ungodly Christians, &c."]

1. *Apollonius Tyaneus* liv'd in the time of Domitian, and was accus'd for a Magician. Whoever pretends to magnifie [MS., p.1.] him must be one who has never read his Life, written by Philostratus; for that shewes him to have been an Impostor. His Miracles deserve not that Name, but are Impudent Forgeries, and even the Truth of these depends upon the Testimony of his Man Damis only, who tells us that he saw the chaines on Mount Caucasus with which Prometheus was bound, and many such like stories [a].

2. *Ad Clerum.* A sure Rule by which a Prince may know whether or no he has a faithful Servant; If he is more careful of his own affaires than of his Master's, and all his Actions and designes tend that way, that man will never be a good minister. Machiavel's Prince, ch. xxii. pag. 2.

[a] [This entry might be occasioned by some of the Deistical writers of that time, who, like the old heathens, would compare Apollonius with our Lord. e. g. Charles Blount, the Author of the "Oracles of Reason," published in 1680, a translation of two books of Philostratus' Life of Apollonius, with notes, of this character: see Leland, View of Deistical Writers, Letter IV., vol. ii. 67.]

SUPPLE-
MENT.
[p. 2.]

3. *Tithes.* An Acknowledgment that all we have is from God; and he loses the Advantage who pays not his Tithes with this thought.

4. *Ad Clerum.* God by the Prophet (Hoshea vi. 9) uses this terrible expression, "The Preists murder in the way by consent, for they commit enormities." Intimating that the ill examples of Preists are equal'd to ye greatest crimes of other men.—Pag. 10^b.

5. *Attributes of God—Goodness of God in the Works of Creation.* That Parents Love their Children and Children their Parents, is from an Instinct of Nature; it is from the same Instinct that Beasts Love their young ones, and these their Dams; Now God in Mercy to the Creature has so order'd this natural affection, that in Beasts it lasts but a very short while, otherwise it would be a Curse to them now they are under the Dominion of Man, who murders whole

[p. 3.]

sholes of them for his Profit, Pleasure or Humour. When any Superior Power doth so to men, 'tis look'd upon as a grievous calamity indeed, and it would be so to the Beasts, but that God in kindness has made affection short. They soon forget they have lost their Relations, and are at ease. 237.

6. *Atheism.* If the Belief of God were an Error, the mind would be extremly rejoyced at the casting off of such a Belief; but the contrary appears.

Those that make a Question whether these things are true, do yet act as if they were sure they are false. As if their doubting certainly made them so.

He that has no Religion has no Conscience; and therefore is not to be trusted, let his pretences be what they will.

7. *Modesty.* Of what great force and use this is, appears

[p. 4.]

from the Story of the Milesian Women (Plut., Of the Virtues of Women^c), who were cured of an uncommon melancholy, which made numbers of them to hang themselves, by a decree of the Senate ordaining that every woman who should afterwards lay violent hands upon herself, should be carryed naked through the Streets.

8. *Supper of the Lord.* There is a laudable Custome in the Greek Church, that such as Communicate, before they

---

^b [This and other like references indicate pages farther on in the MS.]

^c [Opp. ed. Reiske, vii. 22. Lips. 1777.]

approach the Lord's Table, they first go to the bottom of the Church, and in these words speak to the Congregation, συγχωρεῖτε ἀδελφοί· ἔργῳ καὶ λόγῳ ἡμάρτομεν. If no man finds himself injured or agriev'd, the People answer, Ὁ θεὸς συγχωρήσει ὑμῖν, ἀδελφοί.—Ricaut's State of the Greek Church, pag. 200.—Vid. pag. 19.

9. *Confession of Sins.* When the Penitent comes to Confession, the Priest saith to Him, Ὁρά· ἄγγελος Κυρίου παρίσταται λαβεῖν τὴν ὁμολογίαν σου ἐκ στόματος σου, καὶ βλέπε μὴ σιγῆς τι ἁμάρτημα αἰσχύνης ἕνεκα· ὅτι κἀγὼ ἄνθρωπος εἰμὶ ἁμαρτωλὸς ὡς καί σύ.—Ricaut, Of the Greek Church, p. 265.

10. Zech. viii. 16 :—*These are the things that ye shall do; Speak ye every man the truth to his neighbour; execute the judgment of truth and peace in your gates.* Here are many blessings Promised in this Chapter upon the Conditions here set down. We may guess at the reigning Sins of those [p. 5.] times, wch were Hypocrisie, Injustice, Malice, and Perjury.

It will be sufficient at one time to speak of the first of these. 1. What is the Duty here required of us? 2. What are the Acts? 3. What are ye Advantages? 1. [and 2. (?)] The Duty is such a Plain and Honest way of expressing our thoughts, as men may not be deceived by us, or more particularly, That neith^r by our Words or Actions we express more or less than what we really intend.

3. We shall never be believ'd if we do not do this, we shall be always apt to suspect others, and always be uneasie. We shall be forc'd to use unlawful asseverations to gain credit.

If you would be believ'd, Promise nothing but what is in your Power to perform, as well as in your Intention. Then keep your word though it be to your disadvantage.

Is it not a Reproch to us that a Sect of Men shall be sooner believ'd on their bare word, &c.

Ceremony and Complement nāally leads to Insincerity.

Test. If I can be content not to be believ'd.

If I am not over ready to use oaths to gain credit; for this is the Origin of vain Oathes.

11. *Origine of Unbelief.* Acts iv. 13, 14, &c. Hence it appears that it is not always for want of Reasons that men

do not Believe, but often from an Unwillingness to receive the Truth.

[SUPPLEMENT. p. 6.]

Therefore Jesus X^t is said to be a Stumbling Block, bec. Men of Wicked lives and Principles could not receive his Doctrine. Men cannot see because their deeds are evil. Or because they are under great Prejudices. Instance—A man of Pleasures cannot see the Pleasure nor the Advantage of Retirement, &c.

Take the Husbandman after he has long desir'd and Pray'd for Rain, and when God is pleased to send it, it will be very easy to convince that man of God's Goodness to men. He is pleased wth all you say, easily Understands you, and is from the Heart thankful for the Mercy. Now if at the same time you take a Citizen who is a Stranger to Husbandry, and use the very same Argum^{ts}, he shall Hear you without Concern, &c.

From this Instance you see how People come to differ, some believing and others slighting the very same Truths.

The reason of the Jewes' Infidelity. The Prophets plainly foretold the Messiah, they call Him a Prince, a Ruler, a King, &c. The Worldly minded Jewes, who thought of no greatness but such as was attended with Worldly Pomp, it was next to impossible they should receive J. X^t in His mean appearance, tho' had He not appear'd so, the greatest Part of men had wanted a Pattern, a Support, &c.

[p. 7.]

On the other side, they that were Meek and Sensible of their own Unworthiness, and Sins, were soon perswaded to receive one who promised them Pardon, &c., they easily saw the Prophecys accomplished in Him, and that He was indeed a Prince without a Retinue and Court, &c.

"Hearing ye shall Hear and not Understand," because of their Pride, Self-Conceit, Worldly-mindedness, &c. Now this was their Condemnation (Jo. iii. 19), which could not have been unless the Will of God had been plainly discovered by them.

The Natural man receives not the things of the Spirit, because they are spiritually discern'd. Nicodemus, though a Ruler, &c.

A Miracle do's not always affect the Understanding, but in most People startles [the mind] into a disposition of

[p. 8.]

Hearing and Receiving the Truth.—See "the Art of Knowing One's Self," ch. i. pt. 2.^d

The SS. tell us y^t if men have not their Senses exercised to distinguish betwixt Good and Evil, it is impossible for them to believe the Gospel.

Perverse Reasoning: see Math. xxi. 23, &c. Christ Heal'd Malchus at the very moment ye Jewes took Him.

I cannot indeed believe without Reason, but I may Shut my Eyes and not see the Reasons offer'd me, and I may Chuse whether I will Consider them or not.

If a skilful Artist makes a Curious Piece of Clock work, and yet for good reasons will not let us see the work within, must we denye him ye Hon^r of his work because we don't Understand every thing as well as he that made it? &c.

All men that are serious and do indeed desire to know the truth of these matters, First will be as fond of being instructed as any body will be to inform him [them].

He that wishes he could be satisfy'd will not set himself to oppose those that w^d Instruct him, will not laugh at and expose them purely on that Acc^t. [p. 9.]

If a Man is Sick, he Heares his Physitian with Patience, he is pleas'd with his Promises of Health, he follows his Advice.

12. *Call no man Rabbi, for one is y^r Master.* Matth. xxiii. 9. This Text abused by Quakers; in the true Sense they transgress this Command, for they pay as great and blind obedience to their teachers as the very Papists do to their Preists.

But yet these words have a very Instructive meaning; and for want of Observing this Rule Religion suffers very much.

People are apt to believe that those they esteem are always in the Right; they espouse their Principles in the Bulk, without examining which are sound, or which otherwise; they imitate their very Talk, Practices, &c.

---

^d ["Abbadie, James, a learned Protestant divine, was born at Nay, in Bearn, 1658; died 1727. Author of numerous theological works, which have been much admired, and several of them have passed through numerous editions, and translated,...as 'L'Art de se connôitre Soi-même: ou la Recherche des Sources de la Morale,' translated into English under the title of 'The Art of Knowing One's Self.' Oxf., 1698. 12mo." Watt, Bibl. Brit.]

SUPPLE-
MENT.

[p. 10.]

They do not so much Consider what the Gospel Saith as what their Teachers say.

This fills all their Thoughts, makes up their whole Conversation, exercises their Passions, their Desires, their Love, &c.

It is this makes Ordinary Conversation dangerous and sinful, Men are so Zealous for their Party that they forget the Words of X^t, &c.

This is a matter which should be mended, and the designe of this Discourse is to Contribute towards it.

The Concernes of a good Life are forgot.

13. *Ad Clerum.* I conferr'd not with Flesh and Blood. Vid. 19.

14. *In visiting the Sick.* Observe the method of the Liturgy, only take care to make that Service useful to the Sick Person: for Instance, In the Belief, Dost thou believe in God, i. e. Dost thou believe in Him, as that thou canst trust in His Power to do what He pleaseth; In His Goodness, that He will do what is best for thee, and all that trust in Him; In His Truth, that He will be faithful to His Promises, &c. ? And so of the whole Creed.

15. *Catechism.* Q. Who ordereth a good man's goings?

Q. To w^m must we look for a Blessing, &c. Except ye Lord, &c. ? pag. 11.

[p. 11.]

16. *History of the Bible.* By this way the Sp^t of [God] Instructed men most frequently, 1 Sam. xii. St. Stephen's Speech.

17. *Catechism.* Q. This is indeed a Happy Estate for those y^t are possessed of it, but I find in myself no inclinations. I am in this as I was in my Sickness; I envied those that Eat and Drank before me, but was not able to taste their Satisfaction.

A. But now you are return'd to yor Health you enjoy that Pleasure. And be you Assured that those who now take Pleasure in a Religious Life, were as great Strangers to it as you now are, &c.

18. *Quakers'* Light. *Snake* [e].

Q. Has every man this Light?

[e] [This is apparently suggested by Leslie's "Snake in the Grass," § 1. Works, fol., t. ii. p. 21. Lond. 1721. As it stands in Bp. Wilson's MS. there is plainly some mistake. Two or three slight emendations have been made, and are specified.]

Ans. Yes [f]. This is the Light wch lighteth *every man* that cometh into the World.

Q. Can a man do wrong that follows it?

Ans. Yes.

[Q.] Why then this Light is not Infallible.

[A.] No.

[Q.] Why then St. Paul did not do wrong when he Persecuted the X^ns, for he tells us (Acts xxvi. 9), I verily thought with myself that I ought to do this. Acts xxii. 34. So that a man may think he dos right and be mistaken.

[A.] He had the light but left it.

[Q.] But did he know when he left it?

[A.] Yes.

[A.] He did forsake it, but did not know it.

[Q.] Why then he dos not say the Truth, when he tells us that he was verily Perswaded that he ought to do, &c.

[Q.] Why then if a man may forsake the Light without knowing it, for ought you know you have forsook it. Vid. pag. 53.

19. *Club.* There are many plausible excuses made for this sort of Tippling:—To do business; and yet more business is hindered than forwarded by it.

It is not for the Drink, but for the Company. *A.* No man can always chuse his company, and he shall often meet with such as no serious X^n ought to converse with; besides, first people go for love of company, at last for love of drink.

It helps to pass away time. *A.* How is this consistent with Redeeming the time, &c.

After all, these are not the true Reasons, but the true reasons are—

1. Either a Man is uneasie with his Family.
2. Or with his Estate.
3. Or with himself, and goes into Company to divert himself and make his mind easie for ye Present.

1. But is not this that wch makes so many Families Uneasie.
2. Is it not an odd way of retreiving the Incumbrances of an Estate to do that which is ye Ruin of so many Estates?

---

[f] [The word "No" is omitted here, and [A.] and [Q.] are inserted in what remains of the Dialogue.]

512   MAXIMS OF PIETY AND MORALITY.

SUPPLE-
MENT.

3. But after all, that which generally leads men into this vice is an Uneasyness with themselves; all is not well within, and this for the present is a diversion.

Some men cannot rest till they are got to such a Pitch, or to such a time of night.

Evils of Tippling.

It Unfits men for the Service of God, and especially for that part of Worship wch every Xⁿ Family, &c.

It manifestly prejudices the Health. It often makes an ill Family, always an uneasie.

It is an Occasion of sad Reflections when one comes to dye.

Tis hard to determine who are Drunkards if these are not, for if none are so but those that tumble in the Streets, cannot speak Sense, &c., there are but few.

Why sure all that frequent the Ale House, spend much time there, Delight to be there, are Drunkards, &c.

[p. 14.]

20. *Spirits.* August 22, 1707. My Unkle [g] Legh, a Person of great Learning and Veracity, assured me, that about three Yeares after Mr. Bridges' Death (Rect. of Malpas), the same Mr. Bridges Passed by him as he was walking in day light; that the Spectre turnd and looked him full in the Face, and he being nothing afraid had time to consider the very garments he wore; that before he saw him he heard his gown rustle as he passed thro' some Burrs. Now this coming from a Person of his Integrity—a man not easily to be imposed on, &c.

21. *Marriage.* As you value your own Happiness, you will never Match with a Person of Unsound Principles, or of an Ill Life; for if you Love him as your self, as you'll be

---

[g] [i.e. his wife's mother's brother: for Mary Patten, the mother of Mrs. Wilson, was daughter of John Leigh, Esq., of Outrington, in Cheshire: of whose son John, the person here mentioned, Ormerod, Cheshire, i. 440, says, "John Leigh, of B.N.C., Oxford, afterwards of Edenhall in Cumberland, and of Ollerton in Cheshire, bapt. at Lymme March 27, 1645, married at Malpas, Aug. 31, 1685, Eliz., daughter of Randle Dod, of Edge, Esq."

"Tho. Bridge, M.A., was Rector of Malpas, the Higher Mediety, from 1624 to 1682, nearly 58 years. During the Rebellion he was ejected from his living, but in 1660 restored. He was also Vicar of St. John's Church, in Chester, where he rebuilt the parsonage, gave £50 towards erecting the Grammar-school, and £50 to the Poor. He died 1682, and was buried Oct. 7, aged 82:" so that it was in 1685 that Mr. Leigh saw what he related to the Bishop. See Ormerod, ii. 339, 40, who adds, "A fine portrait of Mr. Bridge is in possession of his descendant, the Rev. Ralph Bridge, who now (1816) fills, and has filled the office of curate to the same church for 40 years."]

apt to do, what a Torment will it be to you to fear continually, that he whom you love so dearly will probably be for ever miserable? Believe it for a certain truth, that to a thoughtful Person, the Loss of a Husband and a friend has nothing in it so afflicting as the fears we are under for their Eternal Welfare. T. W.

22. *Prophecy.* Echard, Eccl., Hist., p. 336, speaking of [p. 15.] Montanus, has these words: "Pride and Ambition first betray'd him, at which Breach Satan having entred, he was Acted by an evil Spirit, and was wont to fall into enthusiastick Fits and Ecstatic Raptures, which caused him in a frantic manner to pour out wild and unheard of things, and to Prophecy in a way and strain hitherto unknown to the Church;" reproaching the whole Christian Church for not acknowledging his Pseudo-Prophetick Spirit; he imparted his Demon to two Women, after he had corrupted them, by which they were immediately enabled to utter the most frantick, incoherent, extravagant Discourses. At the same time he own'd the Holy Scriptures, and the Principles of X^{ty}, but pretended greater Strictness, &c. Euseb. Epiph. &c.

23. *Dreames.* Joseph. Antiq. L. xvii. ch. 15. [c. xiii. § 4. t. i. 866.] gives an odd account of a Dream of Glaphyra of her first Husband, Alex., the son of K. Herod, who seem'd to chide her for forgetting the obligations of Love which were betwixt them formerly, and particularly for marrying his Brother. "However," saith he, "I will not forget our Antient Love, but will immediatly deliver you from this Reproche," and soon after she dyed.

24. *Types* are of Pure Institution, and Appointed by [p. 16.] God to be signes to represent the Favours He designes His Church in ages to come.

25. *Temple of Jerusalem in the days of Jesus Christ.* Its form. The outer Court, or that of the Nations, was a square enclosure, each side ab^t 500 Cubits. The Walls 15 foot thick, 36 f. high within, and without in many places 450 f., round which within was most magnificent Galleries. That on the South side being 105 feet broad, supported by 4 rows of Marble Corinthian Pillars, 6 feet Diameter,

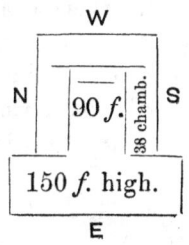

and 27 High. Out of this Court Christ drove the Buyers, &c. The whole Court was paved with Marble. A low wall (to which St. Paul alludes) parted this from the Holy Place, which was 10 feet above the level of the other, in the midst of which stood the Temple. On the Sides of the Holy Place magnifical Apartments. The Temple had its Porch 150 Broad, and High. The Body 90 f. broad and 150 f. high, with 38 chambers in 3 stories, the height of ye uppermost being 75 f., which encompassed the Body of the Temple. The Roof of which Chambers was encompassed with curious Ballisters, covered with Gold and making a Walk of 45 f. Broad. Mr. Jurieu [1].

26. *Death.* There are few of us but know more or less how very sensible is the affliction of Parting with our friends when Death takes them from us : scarce any misfortune so great. The only way of preventing the weight of this Calamity falling upon us seems to be this, First to take all possible care that those we love so dearly, our Wives, our Children, our Friends, be in the way of Life, and that our own Hearts be in Heaven; and then the Loss will more easily be born, when we can hope to see those whom we love so soon. But above all things, let us Love Him who Liveth for ever, who who is ever Present with us, who can comfort, help, defend us at all times, and then all other Losses, &c. Vol. I. pag. 42.

27. *Companion.* Ought to be chosen by reason, not for Humor and fancy. Such as are of a Worldly Spirit, an undisciplined Life, whose example may prejudice, whose Principles may corrupt, whose Discourse may infect, &c. As also such as are of weak judgments, who by their own conduct shew that they know not their true interest, for how can these advise you? Such as have not the command of their tongue, &c. But if you chuse such as are Virtuous and Wise, their example will edifye you, their wisdome will govern you, their conversation will be a credit to you. Besides it is against the express Rules of the Gospel, 1 Cor. v. 11, To be a Companion of loose and Idle People. *If any man, &c.* This is a most necessary Caution for young People,

---

[1] [Hist. Critique des Dogmes et des Cultes, depuis Adam jusqu'au J. C. Amstelod. 4to., 1704, pt. ii. c. 14; from which this is collected, not translated.]

who are most often ruind by an Unwise Choice of their Companions.

28. *Worldly Spirit*, as opposed to a true X^n Sp^t. 1 Jo. ii. 15. Such an one as finds no Pleasure but in the Vanities of the World. Eager after all sorts of Diversions, Gaming, Trifling Business, observing no Method of Living, Given to Apetite, to Ease and Luxury. Extreamly pleased with whatever Diverts the Mind from the Fears of what may come hereafter.

Now a man may be in this state, and yet not apprehensive of Danger, for being free from open Scandalous vices he may think himself (by comparison) better than those that are [not] so; and yet this is a sad condition to dye in, and consequently to Live in: for will a Person in this Temper pretend to Love [p. 18.] God with all his Soul? To desire to go to Heaven above all things? To Fear Him that can destroy both body and soul in Hell? Can such a Person be said to Live in a sense of an account which we must all give of our Time and of the opportunities we have of glorifying God, and doing good in our Generation? Can such Persons be said to Denye, to Mortifye, to Take up the Cross, &c. Or are not these any longer Christian duties?

29. *Fathers*, Antient. We must always make a distinction betwixt the Reasonings of the Fathers, and their Testimony; they often Reason as men, and as men may be mistaken, but when as Honest men they relate matter of Fact, done in their own, or their Cotemporaries Times, we must either Believe them, or els we must reject all Histories.—Dr. Potter, Church Government, pag. 173 [k].

30. *Penance.* You Sin without blushing, and yet are ashamed to do Penance; you do not scruple to offend God, but you think much to let ye World know y^t you are sorry for it.

31. *Image worship.* This Abuse was come to such a Height in the time of Michael, Emp. of Constantinople (812), that he was forc'd to publish an Edict to hinder Images of Saints fr. being accepted as Godfathers and Godmothers in Baptism, &c. See Du Pin, Ad An. 800 [l].

[k] [2nd ed., Lond. 1711.]
[l] [Transl. by Wotton, t. iii. p. 2, fol. Lond. 1695.]

SUPPLE-
MENT.
[p. 19.]

32. *Ad Clerum.* Those that make it their main business to gain the respect of such as are under their charge, and not to make Jesus X^t be Loved and Honoured by them, are Unworthy of the Sacred Ministry, bec. they designe to feed themselves, not their Flock. *Agobardus* [m]. Vid. Petri Damien [n]. Vid. pag. 19.

33. *Lord's Supper* [o]. Receive it as often as conveniently you can, y^t the Old Serpent seeing the Blood of the Lamb upon your Lips, may tremble to approach you. Pet. Damien, pag. 42.

34. *Dignity of Priesthood.* Whatever opinion other People have of us, we ought to give our selves a Just Esteem, as having the greatest Honour bestow'd upon us: when we consider for what we are to Answer. And indeed it is so with all sorts of Hon^{r}ble employment—A Govern^r, a Collonel, a Judge will none of them be High minded when they consider w^t acc^t they must give. And this will make People of Consideration a little more indifferent whether they obtain Posts of Hon^r and Profit, bec. the more they have to Answer for, the Greater the Authority, the Greater the Lab^r, the Greater the Acc^t.

35. *Ad Clerum.* Let us endeavour to bring People to a Carefulness of their Ways, a Tenderness of Conscience, an Inquisitiveness after their Duty, and of what may become of them, &c., by bringing them first to do such things as all People are agreed in are fit to be done.

§. Jer. xxiii. 22. If they had stood in My Councel, and had caused My People to Hear My Words, *then they sh^d have turn'd them from their evil ways,* &c. If then men have not been turn'd fr. their evil way, the Reason and the Fault is, they have not been made to Hear God's words; for where the People are instructed in the Right way, they shall be turned, &c.

[p. 20.]

---

[m] [Ep. ad Cler. et Monach. Lugdun. §§ 11, 12, 13, ap. Galland. Biblioth. Patr. xiii. 456.]

[n] [Perhaps in Opusc. xxii. *contra Clericos Aulicos:* in which it is proved that gaining preferment by adulation is a sort of simony. Opp., t. iii. 589.]

[o] [See Bp. Wilson's Parochialia, Works, 4to., i. 411. In Opusc. (Institutio Monialis), c. iii. Opp., t. iii. 336.

"Hujus corpus et sanguinem etiam ore carnis crebrius suscipe, ut hanc Ejus vocem merito possis audire: *Favus distillans labia tua, Sponsa; mel et lac sub lingua tua.* Terretur enim adversarius, cum Christiani labia Christi videt cruore rubentia." The treatise is addressed to "Blanche, who from a countess had become a nun."]

§. Zech. xi. 5. *Their own Shepherds pity them not.* A Clergyman stands charged with two things especially. The Honour of God, and the safety of such a Number of Soules. SUPPLEMENT.

§. It is their office to bless *in God's Name*, and to Pray for the People, and if it is not yor Fault, their Prayers will be Heard for you, whether they be good or otherways.

§. If you or I had the Management of an Estate of some thousands a year committed to us, we sh^d have a great Concern upon our Spirits, and think by what ways it was most to be improv'd: and are not, &c.

§. *Speak unto Aaron and His Sons that they Profane not My Holy Name, in those things wch they Hallow unto Me.*

§. *Shepherds.* And do's not a Shepherd, w^n any of his Flock are Lame, &c., not only apply Proper Remedies, but observe carefully what Effect his Paines have had, and whether other meanes sh^d not be used? and is not our Flock valuable?

§. 2 Cor. iv. 13. *Whilst we look at the things which are not seen, &c.*

This, we, of all men, sh^d bring our minds to, bec. we Profess our selves, and teach others, to Believe that Here we have no Abiding-Place, That Here we are strangers.

§. A Clergyman who sets X^t for his example will think no trouble too much, no office too mean, when he may do good, [p. 21.] and gain Soules. Exod. xix. 6; Levit. xxi. 4; St. Matth. xix. 24.

§. The ill consequences of speaking of the gr^t Truthes of Religion after an Unaffecting Way.

§. They that think our office and Business is easie, and that we have Tythes and Offerings for Nothing, will be convinc'd of their Mistake when they see us discharge the several duties of the Ministry faithfully: When they see us diligent in considering the wants of our Parishes, Visiting the Sick, Warning the Unruly, Instructing the Unlearned, Offending great men by X^n Reproofes, and Hazarding their displeasure; when they see the different sorts of people with whom we have to do, that some must be encouraged, others frightened, with the Judgments of God, some spoke to in Publick, others in Private. As these are thoughts which are enough to confound one who has this Burthen upon him, so they are considerations which will convince all thoughtful people y^t you well deserve w^t God has given you, while you do y^r duty.

A Clergyman that undertakes to teach others must understand himself what he ought to Speak; he must be good, that he may be able to Perswade; he must have Courage, that, &c.; Patience, that, &c.; Humble, &c.; Unblameable, that he may give none offence.

§. Unhappy is that Shepherd, and sad will be his Account, who receives the Fleece and Milk of the Flock, and yet suffers y^m to wander, or to be Infected, without putting to his Helping Hand, or Pitying their Ailm^{nts}.

[p. 22.] §. After all, if we find our People unmindful of their Duty, let us however mind our own, let us Pray for them, &c. And tho' we sh^d find some Refractory, we ought not to Repine, or despair and desist. Perhaps it is to exercise our virtues, that such an one is given to our Charge. Condescend to the Infirmities, Bear with the Impatience, Put up [with] his Injuries, do every thing to gain him, &c.

§. A man may, no doubt of it, perform all the outward obligations of his charge, and so the laws cannot Punish him for any Neglect, and yet be obnoxious to the Judgment and Severity of God's displeasure, &c.

§. *Why dost thou Preach My Laws, &c.*

§. Shall those that live by the Altar be Unconcerned, when the God of the Altar is despised? &c.

§. Those that are to Represent a Master who is Humble and Merciful, Just and Wise, should strive to have these qualities. Those who dispense the word and Sacraments sh^d discover that they have Purify'd thems. by that Word, and are Sanctify'd by those Sacred Mysteries. They that call themselves Messengers of the Gospel of Peace sh^d love y^t virtue and shew it, &c.

§. The Priest committing a Fault (Lev. iv. 3) was to attone for it by as great a Sacrifice as if the whole People had been guilty of that Sin. Intimating ye greivousness, &c. Vid. [Pol.] Syn. Critic. in Loc.; Math. ix. 36, 37, 38. The Mis-
[p. 23.] carriages of the Clergy are more Heinous, bec. they are supposed to know more of ye Powers of the World to come, to have thought more of Heaven, &c., than other men, and

for that Reason they may speak with more Authority, &c. Pag. 42.

36. *Debts.* Vid. St. Aug. de Civit. Dei, Lib. ii. ch. 18. The Commons, *Servili imperio,* were forc'd to Rebell, &c.

Men don't consider that all People deal with Bad Paymasters, upon the same Principle that Merchants Trade to ye E. Indies; they propose more than a double gain, if ever they have any Return, i. e. if ever you Pay them P. And they say in excuse for this, that they run as great Hazards of never being paid, as are the dangers of the Seas, Pirates, &c.

§. Hope deferr'd makes the Heart sick, (Prov. xiii. 12,) the Barbarity of those who make the Laborer to wait for his Hire, the Widowes Heart to fail, &c.

§. Justice and Peace have kissed each other; y^t is, one cannot be without the other. Ps. lxxxv. 11.

§. This affects both the Publick, and every man in particular who is concerned. It is very Naāl for men to make Repriseals wherever they can, and it is not a very Difficult matter for a Servant (and sometimes for oth^rs) to find an opportunity of paying themselves, at least in Part, very much to the master's disadvantage, and then the Mischeif is, the Debt is claimed, tho' really Paid.

§. When this Sin growes more Common, it will come to Sharp as Sharp can; w^t has been may be, &c.

§. Vid. Lock, Hum. Und. p. 195 : "Nor is there one of ten Thousand able to bear^q," &c.

§. Will it move Pity or Scorn more to see one who calls [p. 24.] himself a Gentleman, skulking out at a Back door to avoid his Creditors? To avoid the sight of a Petition, as of a Warrant, and to leave the Town, as People do in a Plague, shuning the sight of men for fear of Infection. To see an English man of Quality live at Home as in a Jail, and Abroad in perpetual Uneasiness, &c.

§. Makes all his Friends Uneasie to see nothing but Bills,

---

p ["I am ready to make it out, whenever your Lordship shall think it your interest to enquire into this matter, that you pay constantly one third more for what you want than does any other person." Bp. Wilson to Lord Derby, Cruttwell's Life, p. xiv.]

q [197. fol. 1700. B. ii. c. xxviii. § 12: "Nor is there one of ten thousand, who is stiff and insensible enough, to bear up under the constant dislike and condemnation of his own Club."]

SUPPLEMENT. Accounts, Petitions, &c., to Hear nothing but Complaints, or Curses, &c.

§. Psalm ix. 9, 10, 12, 18, 19, 20; Ps. x. 16, 19, 20; Luk. xviii. 7; Job vii. 2. *As an Hireling desires the Reward of his Lab^r.*

§. Prov. xxiii. 10, 11. *Enter not into Fields of the Fatherless, &c.* Jer. xxii. 13. Wo unto Him that buildeth his House, &c. Hab. ii. 9; Levit. xix. 13; Ecclus. x. 8. Bec. ["Because of unrighteous dealings, injuries, and riches got by deceit, the kingdom is transferred from one people to another."] And why not Estates and Honours, &c. Deut. xxiv. 14. Vide p. 55. v. 2.

37. *Disputes* in Religion. Tis more safe as well as Commendable to stick to an old Opinion, tho' one is not able to defend it against all opposition, than to Forsake it, without being able to give a Reason of our Change.

38. *Schisme.* The true notion of it, the same fr. the Beginning.

[p. 25.] Every true and Lawful Bishop is the Representative of Christ in his own Diocese. Whoever holds Communion with him, and with those ordain'd or appointed by him, Holds Communion with Christ. And whoever departs from his Communion, forsakes the Communion of Christ, opposeth that Authority which Christ has given His Bishop over him, and is guilty of Schisme.

This true Primitive notion of Schism destroys the Pretences of both Papists and Dissenters.—The first are for having all Bishops to derive their Power and Authority from the Pope, and not immediately from X^t. The Dissenters on the other Hand, &c. Now in these matters we are not to Govern our selves by the Judgments or Fancys of men, but by the Gospel of X^t, and the Judgment of the First Churches upon that Gospel.

If a man be inclin'd to Compassion, he will be apt to Hope and speak Favourably of such as are in Schisme, even of Jewes, Turks, &c. But then we must observe to such— That if God has given us Rules and Lawes (as we say He hath about Ch. Governm^t) to which *we* are bound, tho' God by them has not bound up Himself from having mercy on whom He will besides, we say that this is the Ordinary [way] of Salvation; and that such as are for trying experiments how far God will be merciful beyond the bounds He hath set us,—we say such People run a great Hassard; we do not Judge of their Final Condition, for X^t has forbidden us to do so.

The Promises of the Gospel are all made to us not as to men, but as to members of Christ's Body; he that Holds not Communion with him who represents Christ in the Church where He lives, is no member of Christ, &c. For he that is not a Member of the visible Church, cannot be a Member of the Invisible; he holds not the Communion of Saints, &c. [p. 26.]

39. *Scruples, Melancholy.* See pag. 343. To believe that our Sins are Pardon'd implyes two things. That *God* is faithful to His Promises, and that *we* have truly Repented. The first of these is necessary, but not the second; the Centurion had faith in Christ, tho' he believed himself Unworthy. Math. viii. 10. Kettlewell, X^n Believ^r, pag. 19, fol. [Works, Lond. 1719, t. i. p. 517, 18.]

§. "But I seek myself in all I do;" i. e. your own good: and doth not God do so too? You may propose to yo^{r}self the same end y^t he doth.

§. Let His Rod as well as His Staff comfort you. Nothing a Sin but what I consent to; i. e. am pleased wth, for if I am not Pleased (with Evil Thoughts), for Instance, I shall oppose them, and then I do what God would have me do; and God is so far from being Angry with me when He suffers the Devil thus to vex me, that He is Pleased to see me offended at any thing that I suspect is an offence to Him. And therefore I ought to rejoyce that I have an opportunity of shewing my Love to God.

§. Why should I expect to meet with no Disturbance? I have no Promise for such a Thing, but rather the contrary. Self Love indeed would have it so, but Self Love is what it is my Duty to oppose.

§. Afflictions are indeed sent as Punishments of Sin, but not always signes of God's Anger, they shewe indeed how hateful Sin is, since it requires such sharp usage. [p. 27.]

They serve to Convince us y^t we are Sinful Creatures. That we have no Power to Help ourselves. That we are

SUPPLE-
MENT.

under the continual Protection of God, or els the Devil w^d soon get the mastery of us.

We may from hence conclude what a dreadful thing it is to deserve the wrath of God, when even they that have forsaken their evil ways, do even yet feel such Instances of His displeasure.

We are hereby brought to Remember and Confess many sins which we had quite forgotten.

We are warned hereby to avoid falling into sin, since, &c.

§. Consider the Behaviour of J. X^t in the like case.—He was tempted to worship the Devil, was He the worse for being tempted to so vile a thing? &c. He was tempted to kill Himself,—*Cast Thyself down, &c.*

The greater your trouble is, the less danger there is of your yielding, &c.

"But if I am Belov'd of God, why do such things befall me?" Why, did not He suffer such things to Befall His Beloved Son? and many good men, &c.

Greater is He that is with you (so may every good X^n say), than he that is, &c.

§. "What then would you advise to be done?"

[p. 28.] 1. Solemnly Protest before God and His Holy Angels, that you disown every evil Thought, Word, or Designe, that shall enter into your heart, or come out of yor mouth during this disorder. 2. That you do not depend upon your own strength, but you will call upon Him, who, &c. Having done this, endeav^r to be content, casting your care upon Him who careth for you, and then none of yor disorders, or the consequences of them, will ever be laid to your charge.

§. Resist the Devil and he will flee from you, viz. take the sword of the Sp^t, the *Word of God* [give Instances of S.S. proper for the several circumstances], slight, despise, pass by, the things wch cannot Hurt you, &c. See v. 2, p. 107.

[p. 29.] 40. ^{r} *Confirmation.* To be children of God and Heires of Heaven, are very desirable things, but then we sh^d take this along with us, An Heir of the K. of H. must *deny himself,* a Child of God must *take up the Cross, &c.* Take up the

---

^{r} [Here is an entry, "*Natural Rhetorick. Rules,*" which has been given before, almost word for word, in the former "Maxims," No. 138.]

MAXIMS OF PIETY AND MORALITY.   523

Cross, i. e. &c. Deny yo^rself, i. e. you must be content if you are poor, and tho' an Opportunity of getting Riches unjustly comes in yor way, &c. Be not asham'd of X^t and His Gospel, &c.

§. This whole Congregation will be Witnesses against you, if you forget this Promise, and fall into Scandalous Sins.

§. The Heart is deceitful above all things, &c. An Instance, Jer. v. 6. [? xvii. 9.]

§. It concernes you to know it, and it is my duty to tell you, that it is much easier *now* to begin to Lead a Xⁿ Life, than it will be hereafter. Remember thy Creat^r, &c.

§. All People hope to go to Heaven, and there are few who don't purpose to fit themselves for it, and yet under these Hopes, many are undone by deferring their Reformation. Those that are wise will begin to do so, before evil Habits, evil Company, evil Manners, &c. [p. 30.]

§. By this Act of your own, you secure to yourself the Protection of God, under which you will be secure from fear of evil.

§. If Parents w^d but consider what a Comfort it will be (wⁿ they are ab^t to leave the world) to them to have seen their Children in the Way of Salvation, to have put them under the Government of God's H. Sp^t, who can *deliver*, Guide, and Support y^m better than, &c.

§. *By which you are sealed*—secured, made sure, confirm'd—for so is a deed by a Seal. You have an Impression as with a Seal, made upon your Soul, which will never be defaced unless you break it.

§. It is now your duty to take all opportunities of learning yor Duty, to come constantly to Church, to Pray constantly to God, &c. 195, 178, 188, 236.

41. *Discipline*, Church Discipline^s. The Laws of the Church, which are its Discipline, aim at the same things as the Lawes of the Land do, viz. To Punish evil doers, &c., that the Judgments of God may not overtake us for our Sins. In the first ages of Christianity, the Church had no power but to Admonish the Unruly, to keep Notorious Offenders from the Lord's Supper, and to turn such out of the Church as would not be Reformed by these Meanes; [p. 31.]

^s [Probably a sketch of a sermon for a Tynwald.]

and even these were Punishments which then they fear'd more than death; but when Kings and Princes became Christians, and knew that they were answerable to God for the Lives and Manners of their Subjects, they began to ease themselves of that Burthen by Putting it into the Hands of the Church to Punish offenders with Fines and Imprisonments, which has had this unhappy effect, that People are more afraid of Temporal Punishments than of excommunication, w^{ch}, to a Person who knows the meaning of it, is the most terrible Judgment that can befall any Christian Man.

Now while this Power, and these Lawes are exercised, *not* to satisfye any Private Spleen, nor to give People unnecessary Trouble, nor to put them to needless expence, but only in order to mend their manners, and to appease the Anger of God, why then I doubt not, but you'll think this Power a Real Blessing, and all Good, and all Wise Men will wish us to go on and Prosper. For this we may be well assured of,

[p. 32.] that where Church Discipline is conscientiously exercised according to God's Word and the Lawes of the Land, God will never be so far displeased with that Nation, as to Unchurch it. "Lest I come, and Remove thy Candlestick" (viz. the Light of the Gospel), was never threatened until the Discipline of the Church was slackened. *Rev.* ii. 5.

§. And that *you* may know the Power wch Christ hath given us for Edification, read *Math.* xviii. 17, which words, &c.

§. Instead of taking it ill that you are call'd to an Account for your offences, you ought to be glad, and very thankful, that the Church takes notice of you, and is concern'd for your Welfare. As a man who has a wound or an ulcer, is pleas'd to find People of Judgment ready and willing to Help and to Cure him.

§. "But People now-a-days will not esteem it a Punishment to be debarr'd from coming to the Ch. and Sacrament." How do you know that? He is the same God, Now as well as Heretofore, who made men feel, and fear and tremble under, the Censures of the Church. Let us do our Duty, and leave events to Him; and let us conclude, as we ought, that a Person who despiseth the wholesome orders of the Ch., is neither an Hon^r nor Blessing to any Ch. And what if He do's forsake us? &c. But after all, excommunication, &c., will not be so very easie to the minds of Careless People as may be imagined at first sight. Begging, appointed by Law as a Punishment for Theivery (in the Island of Ceylon), an Intolerable hardship.

In short, Grace we cannot give (that is the work of God's Spirit alone), God only expects from us that we do our duty, and that we do it without *Respect of Persons, without Preferring one before Anoth^r,* (vid. loc. [1 Tim. v. 21.]) without fearing the face of man. A wise and a Good man had rather have the ill will, if it must be so, of all the ill men in the world, than be rejected of God for not doing his Duty. *Blessed are ye when men shall say evil of you for My sake.*

§. "Other People don't do this." But are we to be judg'd by what other People do? they have not such opportunities.

§. I speak of these things at this Time, y^t all the good People of this Island may know whose Fault it is if in any Particular Parish offenders escape, &c.

§. Let us Remember the Character wch the Spirit of God gives of the Sons of Levi, who, when the Honour of God, and the welfare of the whole Congregation lay at Stake, it is said of y^m that they had neither Friend nor Brother, &c. [Ex. xxxii. 27—29.]

§. A Thoughtful man will be better satisfy'd with a congregation of six People, who communicate out of Conscience, &c., than with six hundred who only come out of Custome, and who, because they have no Root (as our Saviour speaks), no foundation of saving knowledge, when they are required to Live like X^{ns}, fall away.

§. Not only Adulterers, &c., are to be Presented, but litigious, Busy bodys, Tipplers, for these are Sins which will ruin men, if not, &c.

§. Great care is to be taken that when offenders have been brought to Publick Penance, that they either live orderly for the Future, or be excommunicated, &c. You'll easily see that if this is not done, our Church Discipline will be of little use, and will soon degenerate into a formal Custome, which People will submit to for Fear, but not for Conscience' sake.

But w^n People shall be made sensible that there is reall danger in being excom., That there is no Peace for them while they continue careless, That the faithful are warn'd to avoid y^m, That they will as sure be shut out of Heaven, as they are out of the Ch. on Earth, they'll then begin to look ab^t them.

§. If there shall appear any vexatious treating of Penitents, any Undue Severity when People have given true Signes of sorrow, any Notorious Remissness, any Undue Fees exacted, then let the Blame remain with us, and the Reproach of Betraying the Discipline of the Church.

§. That *Schoolmasters* be Instructed and enjoyned to teach the Children How to behave themselves at Church, —not to sit or lean, or lye along at Pray^{rs}, not to laugh, yawn, &c., but to Consider where they are, and w^t ab^t. Vid. pag. 48.

42. *Custome.* Enquiries ab^t it.

1. From what mistakes it drawes its force?

2. What considerations are of force to disarm it of its Power?

3. What way we may deliver our selves from its slavery?

Following of a multitude no excuse for Wickedn. No Comfort in being undone for Company.

Tis fit y^t we sh^d have so much Xⁿ Courage as to despise the good opinion of the world, if it will think fit to deny us it, for such things as really deserve it.

To suffer Reproach for well doing, this is, &c. Vid. pag. 62, 63.

43. *Errors.* To guard the Mind agst y^m.

1. Let the *will* fix the Understanding upon such objects as are fit to be consider'd.

2. Don't Judge of a Thing wch you don't apprehend.

3. Suspend your Assent till you see cause to give it.

4. Determine nothing till the clearness of the evidence oblige you to it.

5. Withdraw the mind from bodily things.

6. Engage not so far in any opinion as to make it necessary it sh^d be right to Preserve yor own Reputation.

7. To embrace the Truth, though oppos'd to our Humours, designes, or former sentiments.

8. Look up to God for illumination, *In His Light we shall see light.*

Truthes which have no Influence upon Practice, are of

very little use. They may serve to make us love our selves, but not God.

9. Resolve never to change your opinion wthout good Reasons for so doing.

An easie assent to things inevident, is the source of all that novelty which the world is full of.

§. Never be afraid to own your Ignorance, those to whom you own this know that they themselves are ignorant of many things.

§. The Reason of Peoples changing their opinions, is generally bec. they took y^m up without Reason, and this if not timely prevented will end in Scepticism.

44. *Uncontested Truthes.* That we sh^d endeav^r to be as Happy as we can be.

That we ought to spare no Paines to be so.

45. *Passions.* Government of them.

1. Never suffer your Inclinations to determine the *will*, till you have examin'd, according to your knowledge, the good and evil that is before you.

2. Keep the mind in a Temper betwixt mirth and melancholy, and you will be fitted to Receive all accidents that may befall you.

3. Fix not your Heart too much on the business or the Pleasures of this World, lest you be at last Tempted to believe *this* the best Place.

4. Make your Passions serviceable to Religion, and Occasions of true Piety. If you are afflicted by the world, turn y^t sorrow into a sorrow for yor Sins, &c.

5. Endeav^r to be satisfy'd in all God's choices. I must not pretend to have Hope in God, wⁿ I am concern'd for every event.

6. Never oppose Passion with Passion, Be prepar'd to meet discouragments, Don't too easily conclude that yor Arguments and Lab^r are lost.

46. *Jesus Christ*, His Life, Example, Doctrine. Wonderfully suited to the Condition and Necessities of Sinful men. *We are born to trouble;* He shew'd us how to bear afflictions so as to make *us* and *them* well Pleasing to God, to be gainers by them. Our whole Dependance is upon God. His whole life was such, having not a *Place where to lay*

SUPPLE-
MENT.

[p. 38.]

His Head, and yet He was the Beloved Son of God. The Poor therefore ought not to despair, &c. We have Enemies both Spiritual and Temporal; He taught us by His example how to overcome the one, and how to bear the Injuries of the other. He knew that the Condition of our Nature required that we sh^d converse with ye World; He taught us how to do so without being defiled with it. He did not Himself, nor hath He commanded us to run out of the World, to become a useless part of the Creation, but He set us an example of conversing with men for their good, of meeting and Resisting Temptations, of Glorifying God, whose Power is made manifest in delivering His Servants from the Power of the Devil, &c. He knew that mortification and self-denyal was necessary, but then He required only such as are consistent wth the rest of yor virtues, &c.

47. *Infirmity.* Sins of Infirmity.

No Sin of Infirmity, which one do's not Strive Against.

No Sin of Infirmity, which Proceeded from carelessness, or want of due Consideration.

No Sin of Infirmity, which a man commits often, having had experience of his weakness, and was not careful to avoid Temptation, or has neglected to Pray for Grace and Strength, &c. He that always Proposes in his Heart to do

[p. 39.] the Will of God as far as it shall at any time be made known to him, is willing to be inform'd both of his own weakness and duty, Prays Constantly to God, &c.—When he sins, his failing may be said to Proceed from Infirmity; it is what his Nature is Subject to, &c. Sins of Infirmity, such as one commits contrary to ye settled Purpose of his Heart, through surprise, violence, &c.

48. *Faith, with^t wch it is impossible to Please God.* Tis dangerous to be mistaken in a matter wch so much Concernes us; he that has *True Faith,* has a Principle of a New Life, and it will easily be seen, both by him that has it, and by others.

If I ask myself what sort of confidence I had in my Father when I was a child; that I never question'd his Love for me; that I loved him even when he corrected me; that I laid before him all my complaints, &c. ? I shall soon see whether I *so* behave my self towards God;

but if instead of doing this, I am apt to Question the Love of God, as often as He corrects me; if in Poverty I am ready to despaire, if I faint in the Day of Adversity as if I had no helper, if I forget who 'tis that took me from my mother's womb, &c., then is my Faith weak, and my Strength but small.

If a man of Credit, whose Breath is in his Nostrils, gives you his word, you are entirely satisfy'd, and yet God, who hath said, *I will never leave thee nor forsake thee*, His Truth [p. 40.] shall not entirely be rely'd upon; and is not this for want of Faith?

But how must we gain such a degree of Faith? Why, as we do all other Graces; by Praying to God, and by accustoming ourselves to go to Him upon all occasions, to Ask His Favours and w^t we want, to Thank Him for His Mercies; by Acknowledging at all times His Power, His Wisdome, and His Goodness, &c.

Tis natural for men to deceive themselves. A man that is in good circumstances, and finds himself chearful under the Blessings of God, and judges of his Faith at this Time, is apt to conclude that his Faith cannot be reproved. Such a man w^d do well to ask himself, "w^t sh^d I be, if I were stript of all these things, and exposed to a Wide and Unmerciful World?" The same Good God brings all this to pass, and often thus visits His best Servants, &c.

§. Do you Believe our Saviour's Sermon on the Mount? Why do you Believe that *they that Mourn are Blessed*, i. e. Happy? and so of the Rest. It is for want of true Faith if you do not, for, &c.

§. Impediments of Faith.

Why is not a man permitted to be judge in his own Cause? Bec. his own Interest and a love to himself will be apt to bias him. Tis this which hinders us Believing the Truth of the Gospel. I dearly love my own Ease, I see [p. 41.] they that Mourn, i. e. &c.,—are in Pain. I don't consider that a short affliction for God's sake will be rewarded, &c.

If a man Preaches up Liberality to a Mixed Congregation, they that are in want will more easily be convinced and believe you, than they that are Rich, because, &c.

We Believe the Historys of the Bible, we are fond of the

Promises therein contained, but because the Threats are uneasie to Flesh and Blood, we dare not think of them; we are apt to wish, if not to hope, they may not be true, &c.

Did Balaam believe in God when he said, "if Balak w^d give me his House full of, &c. ?" One w^d have thought that this was a pretty sure Testimony of his Faith, and yet the wages of Unrighteousness made him wish y^t God w^d go against His word.

§. Faith necessary before Knowledge. We Believe a man has skill before we think fit to trust his Judgment, or learn from Him. We honour our Parents, bec. we believe common Report that they are so, without wch belief we sh^d not Hon^r y^m, &c. Pag. 197.

[p. 42.] 49. *Death.* If the Bitterness of Death were past wⁿ men leave this world, it w^d not be of such Consequence w^t end men make, but wⁿ we are assur'd from &c. Pag. 51.

50. *Ad Clerum.* We cannot keep too strict a watch over our selves that we may be examples in so corrupt an age. Pag. 47.

51. *Lord's Supper.* As oft as the Childⁿ of Israel eat the Passover, their Faith in God was increased: (here explain the Passover :) for Remembring what He did for them when He deliver'd them out of Egypt, and that His Arm is not shorten'd, they had Reason to expect His Favour in all their distresses, if they did not forfeit it; so when we consider the great Love of our Saviour J. X^t thus dying for us, this raises our Spirits, and is as acceptable to us, as it w^d be to a criminal to speak to him of the mercifulness of the Judge before w^m he was to be tryed. So comfortable is the Lord's Supper to them that receive it worthily.

[p. 43.] "But some People who do their best do not meet with Joy and Comfort." Why, then, such People may be sure that Joy is not the best for them at Present.

If you had a Child who was apt to grow bold and careless the more kind you were to him, w^d not you think fit to withdraw yor Favours a little (though you lov'd him never so well), and not always to smile upon him? and shall not we allow God to know our temper and our failings as well as we know our Children, and how to treat y^m for their future good?

Compel, O Lord, all those to come to Thee whose Corrupt Hearts w^d excuse y^m from Thy service.

Abana and Pharpar in the eye of Reason were as like to cure a Leprosie as the waters of Jordan, but then the command of God makes a vast difference: so Bread and Wine. . . . .

This Holy Sacram^t very proper to preserve us from falling into a State of Security. We are obliged to examine our selves, viz. Whether our Righteousness be such as we may hope will be accepted of God. Whether I do the Duties [p. 44.] which God has commanded me? In a State of Grace or Damnation, &c.

It is not enough not to be scandalously Wicked, and yet too many depend upon this Preparation. It is not enough to do some things in Religion, &c.

§. Let me ever Remember Thy Love, and especially w^n I am under affliction of Mind, let me call to mind *this Pledge* of Thy Love to sinful men.

§. Let this H. Sacr. be to me Health and Salvation according to Thy Word.

§. *Judge your selves, Brethren.* I am a very grievous Sinner, O be merciful unto me in that day.

I am a Sinner, and Sinners can best understand and set forth Thy beloved Attributes of Mercy and Goodness.

Thou that art the Saviour of them that put their trust in Thee.

§. We Receive this Sacr. to Preserve the Unity of the Church, declaring our selves, though many, yet to be, as Partakers of one Bread, so of the one Body, w^h ye Bread Represents, viz. the Body of X^t. 1 Cor. x. 17.

Sacraments are not only meanes of Grace, but signes of [p. 45.] our Communion with God and with one another; by these we are all united in one Body, &c.

§. Let the Remembrance of Thy death, O Blessed Jesus, be ever Seasonably Present with me w^n Temptations assault me. Let Thy Good Sp^t preserve my Body evermore a fit Temple for the Lord God † to dwell in.

[The] Lord's Supper is an occasion of exercising all our X^n Graces. We Confess our Sins, we Pray for Grace, we Humble our selves before God, we exercise our Charity, &c.

† ["Holy Ghost" interlined here.]

§. Here the greatest Sinner may hope for Pardon, the weakest, Strength, and all Salvation, if they Receive with Devotion, and resolve to live, as becomes the Gospel of X^t, to the best of their Power.

You are admitted to the Table of the Lord in token of His being Friends with you.

§. Give me desires as great as my Necessities—That all who are Partakers of one Bread may all be United, and of one Heart and Soul, at Peace with God, and one with another.

And be in Charity with all men. If you wish no man any Hurt, Rejoyce not in their Misfortunes, are ready to do any Good w^h may reasonably be expected from you, you are then in Charity.

[p. 46.]

§. By the mighty Power of Thy Death, destroy in us whatever is contrary to Thy Divine Will. Vid. [Ostervald's] Cause of Corrupt., pag. 470, and Bp. Andr. Devot.

It is for X^{ts} sake that God will forgive us our Sins and Receive us into Favour; it is by His death He has obtained this Favour for us. We must therefore never forget His death, y^t remembering That at all times we may have [? it] to comfort us in our Afflictions.

As meat will not nourish us unless our bodys are prepared to receive it, so, &c., &c.

§. Grant that by the constant use of this Holy Sacrament, I may be enabled to run the Race that is set before me, looking unto Jesus, &c., and that I may continue Thy faithful servant unto my lives end.

Give all Thy Faithful Servants a share in these Mercies, &c.

[p. 47.]

O God, who hast given Thy Son to be unto us both a Sacrifice for Sin, and also an ensample of Godly Life, give us grace, &c.

Let me never forfeit these Blessings by any Wilfull Disobedience, &c. See p. 77.

52. *Ad Clerum.* Qualifications of a *Good Confessor.*—A Blameless Life. Of an Unviolable Secresy, a Sweet Behaviour to Allure and to comfort Sinners. Courage to Reprove, and Prudence to Apply fit Remedies to Troubled Consciences, and to let them know that God respects Sincerity of Heart above all things. Pag. 47.

53. *Ad Clerum.* J. X^t, after He was declared to be the Son of God, and ordain'd to the Ministry, *Hear yee Him,* Fasts 40 days and nights, to teach His Ministers how Necessary it is to starve the Animal Life, before they take upon them to be Instructors about *Divine Matters.* SUPPLEMENT.

§. We have now greater Reason than ever to be Zealous in turning men from darkness to light, and from the Power of Satan unto God, because the Prophecies concerning better Times seem to be near an accomplishment, and consequently (as it was in the Apostles' times) we may expect greater Assistances, if we are not negligent in carrying on the Work of Righteousness, &c. [p. 48.]

§. It lookes like an Hardship to Present a man for Fornic., Drunkeness, &c., who was never made truly sensible of the greatness of these sins, How to overcome Temptat., How to cure Himself, &c., by Plain Discourses suited to the Capacitys of the People.

§. It will be a Reproach upon us if a man is brought as a Criminal before a Temporal Judge, before ever he has been Reproved, Presented, or censured by us. *Nemo repente fit turpissimus.* Pag. 49.

54. *Discipline. Penance.* Let us consider w^t an injury it is to a notorious evil Liver to admit him to the Lord's Supper, with^t admonishing him, and without signes of repentance; it will make him secure and easie, though he Lives in such a course as will exclude him from the Communion of Saints and the Supper of the Lamb for ever.

§. The Church is sufficiently furnished wth meanes of Saving soules, tho' she never make use of the Temporal Sword. Pag. 85.

55. *Bishop.* Is a Pastor set over other Pastors, as appears from the following Script. They were to ordain Elders; they might Receive an Accusation against them; they were to charge them to preach such and such Doctrines, and no other; to stop the mouths of deceivers; to set in Order the things that were wanting. Tit. i. 5, 11; ii. 15; 1 Tim. iv. 12; v. 19, &c. This was the Form of Church Government in all Places and Ages of the Church, and to Reject this, goes far towards rejecting the ordinance of God. [p. 49.]

56. *Ad Clerum.* If you have Occasion to speak Com-

534   MAXIMS OF PIETY AND MORALITY.

SUPPLE-
MENT.

fortable Words to Persons in Affliction, at the Hour of Death, under great Calamities, let it be done so as y^t Standers-by may perceive y^t you do it upon Presumption that his Past Life has been Regular, not as if his Present Sorrow could obtain it of God, for y^t were to encourage others in Sin.

§. If Divine grace is Necessary for the Salvation of every Particular Xⁿ, much more is it necessary for those who are to take care of the Soules of others. Vid. Dodw., 1st Letter, &c. § 3.

[p. 50.]

In Visiting the Sick, and the Healthful also of his Parish, he fits himself better for all the other duties of his calling[u], ... than by any other Study. It Teaches him how to Live, how to Preach, how to Suffer with Patience, how to Dye, &c.; to be easie, charitable, &c. It makes him to be Beloved, to be sought unto, to be Believ'd.

The faithful discharge of this duty will bring to our minds the Words of our gr^t Master—He y^t will be gr^t among you, let him be Servant of all; for in very deed we must be so, &c.

One of your Flock is a Profane Person; perhaps ye Providence of God permits this, to see your love and concern to reduce him.

You must expect to meet with disrespect, even for your calling's sake; but then, this is not for yours, but y^r Master's sake, so y^t you have reason to Rejoyce, and be exceeding glad, &c. Vid. pag. 57.

57. *Charmes.* Deuteron. xviii. 10, 11, 12, 13, 14; Isaiah lix. 4, *They trust in vanity;* Psal. xxxi. 6, "I hate them that regard lying vanities, but Thy law do I love." Vid. pag. 58, pag. 122 ^v.

[p. 51.]

58. *Customes.* The Emperor is a gainer by Christianity, which obliges us not to defraud him of his Rights, or cheat his Exchequer[w].

59. *Death.* The thoughts of Death will teach us more than we think of. Not to be fond of the World, w^h we are soon to Leave; not to be Proud, since we shall all soon be equal'd in the dust; not, &c.

---

[u] [The MS. has one or two unintelligible words.]

[v] [This reference in Mr. Walker's hand.]

[w] [This refers, no doubt, to the contraband trade of the Isle of Man. Cf. Tertull. Apol. § 42: "Vectigalia gratias Christianis agent ex fide dependentibus debitum, qua alieno fraudando abstinemus."]

It puts an End to Sorrowes, Infirmities of old Age; it Relieves the oppressed, and such as had no Helper; it puts an end to our state of tryal, &c.; these things w^d be intollerable if they had no end. Only let us take care that we go not from a troublesome, but short Life, to an endless misery.

The Sting of Death is Sin, 'tis y^t makes it terrible indeed.

It is a Comfortable Truth, that our Lives are in God's Hands, death cannot take us without His leave.

Terrible, indeed, to such as are not at Peace with God. [p. 52.] Let us, however, not forbear to speak of Death, for come it will, whether we are prepared or not.

60. *Conscience* is that which in every man excuses or Accuses him for what he do's well or otherways. See pag. 49.

61. *Rebellion.* They who contend for Defensive arms against the Government w^n *they think* it becomes Unreasonable, have not well consider'd the corruption of Human Nature, wch seldom keeps within due bounds w^n Provoked and let loose, so ye Defensive Armes often turn to offensive &c.

St. Ambrose, in Oratione contra Auxentium, [§§ 2, 9, ed. Venet., t. iii. 915, 917] :—" Coactus repugnare non novi, sed Dolor, et Fletus, Orationes et Lachrymæ fuerunt mihi arma adversus milites; talia enim sunt munimenta sacerdotis, aliter nec debeo nec possum resistere; et relinquere Ecclesiam non soleo." . . . . " Servum Christi non custodia corporalis, sed domini Providentia, sepire consuevit."

62. *Quakers* slighting the Laudable Institution of X^t and [p. 53.] His Church, a certain sign of their Pride, when X^t Himself, to teach us Humility, submitted to be Baptized, &c., though He had no Sin to be cleansed of.

63. *Controversies* engage our own and our Peoples minds and affections in things that are often unprofitable, at least for them to know, in the mean time neglecting, or not minding with concern, the great busness of our Soules.

64. *Christianity.* Nothing so desirable, or so fit to be proposed to Men, as the X^n Faith in the Simplicity thereof.

Our eternal Welfare depends upon the knowledge of X^t bec. He is the only Sacrifice for Sin, and because we can be accepted of God by Faith in Him.

SUPPLE-
MENT.

[p. 54.]

65. *Scripture. Inspired Writings.* The Prophecies of things to come—the Nature of the Subject seems to require, that not only the sense, but the very words must be inspired; the writer was to write thus and no otherways.

2. The Gospel and Acts are an Historical Account of what our Blessed Saviour Did and Suffer'd for us; here the Holy Ghost presided over the Evangelists, and directed them to such and [such] Parcels of History as sh^d be most proper to establish the Truth of the X^n Religion, and kept them strictly to the Truth of Historians, while the Style and Expression and Method might be left to them.

[p. 55.]

3. St. Paul useth such Expressions in his Epistles (and so the other Apostles in theirs) and Arguments, as his great wisdom and experience might suggest, and if the Holy Ghost inspired him and the others with an extraordinary share of Wisdom, watched over them lest they sh^d utter any thing but Sound Doctrine, directing them in all doubtful and difficult cases, one cannot see what other Degree of *Inspiration* could be necessary to establish the authority of what they said, tho' the Words and Manner of Arguing were left to them. Pag. 83.

66. *Debts.* Not paying of Debts where a man can do it has more of Evil and Injustice in it, than at first sight is apprehended; for to Put off this duty bec. it is not so Convenient for me now as it may be hereafter, is to act as if all the world were made for me. I may very likely disappoint and afflict a man who is in the same Circumstances, and in Debt; this Person by my Injustice is forced to put off and disappoint another, he a third, and so on, to God knows how many; and all these really suffer bec. of me: and as I am the Cause of their troubles, so I shall too likely be the Subject of their curses.

[p. 56.]

Italian Prov., "He y^t has p^d his Debts has got an Estate." Charity is called in Script. a Debt, what Name then shall we give [to] that Injustice wch withholds from Poor People y^t for w^h they have Labour'd, that w^h is their own, if they could get it? Those who make their Creditors wait till even the Debt will not Pay for the Attendance, who makes [make] the Needy eyes wait, and forces [force] from distress'd

Creditors a mixture of Teares, and Pray^{rs}, and Curses, &c., wch are all reserv'd to the day of Judgment.

Supplement.

And by the way, this sort of Dealing supposes that there will be a Day of Judgment, which hard-hearted men are loathe to believe or hear of. For if there is a Just God, He will some time or other do those Poor People Right and Justice, which Here they could not obtain; and call gr^t Oppressors to an Acc^t before a Judge more Powerful than themselves.

Let us Hear the Words of Job, he was a greater man than any of the East, and yet he, &c. Job. xxxi. 13, 14, 15, 16. [p. 57.]

Entail'd Estates no security agst God's Justice, for He can cut off the entail by the destruction of the whole Family, the most effectual way of doing it.

1 Thes. iv. 6. *That no man go beyond or defraud his Brother in any matter, for God is the Avenger of all such.*

67. *Ad Clerum.* The best Argument to Persuade a man to the Practice of any duty is to let him see by my Actions that I am convinc'd my self of, and think my self happy in doing w^t I w^d recommend to him, i. e. I must let him see the fruits of Temperance in my self, if it secures the Health of my Body, and the Quiet of my mind, my Charity, my Estate, my Gratitude, my Friends, and my Chastity, my Reputation, &c. p. 68. [p. 58.]

68. *Grace* of God, i. e. A Sanctifying Principle which joynes its self to, and cooperates with, ordinary Meanes; it dos not force men to be good in spite of their Resolutions to be evil, nor doth God deny this grace to such as earnestly desire it, &c.

69. *Charmes.* One need not scruple to affirm that those evil Spirits (which make a Jest of the destruction of men)— that they gain a Power, tho' limited, over the Bodies or goods of those who are so ignorant or so wicked as to have to do with their Instruments, viz. Charmers, Witches, Fortune-tellers, &c. No man who calls himself a X^n ought to have to do less or more with such People and Practices, lest he becomes [become] a Subject of Sathan and his kingdom, while he thinks the least of being so. Vid. p. 122^x. [p. 59.]

70. *Conscience.* When a man acts against his Conscience,

---

^{x} [In Mr. Walker's hand.]

SUPPLE-
MENT.

tho' the thing he dos be lawful, yet he do's evil, bec. there is a Readiness in that man to what is evil, if either Fear or Intrest, or any great Temptation comes in His way.

71. The character of a People designed for destruct^n, see St. Aug. de Civit. Dei, lib. ii. cap. 20, 21.

72. *Repentance.* That we have Time to Repent, that we have grace to do so, and that we have the Comfort of Living to bring forth fruits meet for Repentance, are great Favours, mighty Blessings; but still 'tis to be consider'd that it had been better not to have willfully done that wch will stand in

[p. 60.] need of these Helps and Fav^{rs}. For 'tis certain 'tis better not to Sin, than to Sin and after to Repent; by the last I may escape damnation, but by the first I may hope for greater degress of Happ^{ss}.

I have ever been with Thee, and never disobey'd at any time Thy com̃ands. To him the answer is—*Son, all that I have is thine.*

A proper Consideration to keep men from making experiments, how gracious God may be to them upon their Repentance; Abstain from the Sin, and be sure God will be gracious to you, and treat you better than after y^r Repentance.

73. *Repentance.* One great hindrance to Religion is this, That its duties are Recommended, Pressed upon us, and looked upon as Burthens, &c. For Instance, Rep. is said to

[p. 61.] be a Precept of the Gospell, &c., when in truth it ought to be esteem'd a *Priviledge*, the greatest y^t ever was offer'd Mankind; 'tis plain the Jewes thought so, (Acts [xi. 18.]) *Then hath God to the Gentiles granted Repentance unto Life.* A Favour the Jewes thought God w^d never have vouchsaf'd y^m. Page 65.

74. *Spirits.* What I shall say upon this subject is not designed to gratify your Curiosity, but to shew you how Watchful we ought to be, how constantly evil Spirits are employed to ruin us, if we suffer them to get the Dominion over us; and w^t Power they have to ruin, if God did not continually interpose, &c.

On the one hand, we sh^d not stint, nor slight their Power, lest by despising w^t they can do to us, we fall into a sinful carelessness; on the other hand, we ought not to equal y^m

with God, and the Powers of His Holy Spirit, lest we fall into despair, &c.

75. *Custom.* "This is My Beloved Son, *Hear Him*"—He y^t heareth not *Me* is not of God. How do we Believe this Truth, (tho' from the mouth of God Himself and His Son,) when we do not consider what God has taught us, but w^t lesson, w^t example the World has sett us? [p. 62.]

The World saith, 'tis Honble, 'tis Praiseworthy to be able to do good (i. e. to be Rich and Great), tho' you sh^d not have the will. But the Blessed J., by His example, set us another Pattern. He has made it Honble to be Poor, if in y^t Condition we do all the Good we can, &c.

We see then y^t if we w^d make a true judgment of w^t is good, what is to be despised, what ought to be feared, what we ought to set our Hearts upon, what we may Depend upon, what will and what will not Deceive and Disappoint us, we must be taught of God, or we shall most certainly be misinformed; for *Custome,* indeed, will pretend to teach us these things, and the world will count us very singular, if we will not follow its ways; but they are the Ways of Deceit, and Sin and Death. See p. 78. [p. 63.]

76. *Custome.* Vid. McKenz.'s Essay of Reason, p. 121.

"Be not conform'd unto this present evil World," "Love not ye World, &c." These things we profess to Believe to be the will and comand of God, and y^t our Salvation depends upon Acting suitable to this Belief; at the same time, the World has got such an hanck upon us, y^t we follow its ways contrary even to our most serious and well-grounded profession. Pag. 78.

77. *Repentance.* It is readily own'd by all X^{ns}, that unless we Repent we shall Perish everlastingly. How then do People make their minds easie who are not in a State of Repentance? Why one of these ways—either they call that R. wch is no such thing, as confessing their Sins, leaving off some one or more ill Habits, &c.; or, 2^{ly}, they purpose to Repent hereafter, &c., hoping that God is to be found when *they* please, tho' He has expressly declar'd the contrary; Prov. i. And in the mean time they go on to provoke God by a wicked life, to deny them His Grace, without wch no man can Repent. [p. 64.]

SUPPLE-
MENT.

He y^t Lives without Repentance, or puts it off till his Death, must expect to Despair w^n he w^d have the greatest comfort—Sorrow and Despair are his due, 'tis folly to think it sh^d be otherways; and if a man expresses any hopes of mercy (who has liv'd a vicious life, and has not Repented and brought forth fruits meet for Repentance), his hopes are vain, or else he is deluded by ye comfortable words of Ignorant People who know not the terms of Salvation.

When we preach up the Necessity of Repentance, People are apt to conclude this is spoken of scandalous Sinners only, such as Adulterers, &c. But let us not deceive our selves—Such a Repentance as will be accepted of God consists in an hearty sorrow for all our sins, those y^t are not of y^t black dye; a Resolution of Keeping all God's Commandments; asking pardon continually where we have failed, mending *still* where

[p. 65.]

we have done amiss, in short, leaving nothing to be done w^n we come to dye, but calling ourselves to an acc^t for this one thing—Whether our Life has indeed been a state of true R., i. e. whether R. has been the Duty of our Lives, at least so long as to bring forth worthy Fruits. Pag. 60—224, 158.

78. *Absolution. Death-Bed Repentance* (187), *Auricular Confession.* Tis certainly true, *none can forgive Sins but God only.* Mark ii. 7. And yet those are not vain words—Whose sins ye Remit they are Remitted. Jo. xx. 23.

These Script. are easily Reconcil'd by this other Instance out of these Holy Records—The Leper, under the Law (Lev. xiii. 6), was Healed by God only, the Preist alone could pronounce him clean, he had certain Rules given him by wch he was to goe; if he neglected these, he acted Presumptuously —If he followed them, he had Authority to pronounce him

[p. 66.]

clean, and as such he was received into the congregation, a Type of Heaven. Apply this to the *Ministry of Absolution*. We are to enquire diligently into the Motives, Steps, Signes, Fruits of Repent. If we find them to be such as the Gospel Requires, we declare them Pardon'd. If not, we pronounce y^m unclean, and not fit for the Kingdome of Heaven.—To His People *being Penitent*, of which the Preist is appointed the Judge—by *Gospel Rules*, and he w^d mightily abuse his Power, if he sh^d Pronounce one Penitent, who has been persuaded to tell his Faults, without considering seriously how to leave y^m, and purposing sincerely to do so. And certainly the best way to satisfye one's conscience whether we are truly penitent, is for a while to try whether we keep up sincerely to our Resolutions of Forsaking every sin. 94, 187, 224. See page 69.

SUPPLE-MENT.

79. *Sensible Pleasures. Riches, Self-Denyal.* Gen. xiii. 10, 11. "And Lot lifted up his eyes and beheld all the Plain of Jordan, &c., and he chose." Here is the exact description of a Person making choice of *Good* by his sense *only*. A [p. 67.] Rich Country, to be amongst People that abound with all the conveniences of this Life, is most desireable to Flesh and blood, and w^t we are most ready to choose, without considering the consequences. But this Good Man in time felt the error of Choosing ag^st the Rules of Reason and Experience, and found that it had been better for him to have chosen the Poorest Part of the Land of Canaan; for besides the Temptations and Vexations he every day met with, because of their abounding in every thing, and especially in wickedness,—besides this, they were nearer that signal destruction which soon after they met with, in which he also had been overwhelmed but that the Mercy of God deliver'd him by a Miracle.

He had nothing but Reason and Prudence to guide him, but we have a surer word of Prophecy, by wch we sh^d Govern our selves, and by wch we are told how hard it is for them y^t Trust in Riches, &c., That look for Happ^ss from the good [p. 68.] things of this World.—On the other [hand], this Word of God assures us, y^t we must deny ourselves such things as please us—And y^t we cannot relish the Good Things of the oth^r life, nor Receive them, nor understand them, while we are overfond of, and full of the Delights of this, &c.

80. *Ad Clerum.* See the 3rd ch. of the 1 Ep. Cor., which in the main treats of Teachers, and their Labours, and the Reward the faithful Labourer may Hope for, and the careless loseth. See ye Oxford Annotat. on that ch. Pag. 68.

81. *Ad Clerum.*

"He who dares nothing but his Maker Fear,
Against all Monsters may proclaim a War [y]."

82. *Conscience.* Our Church is very sollicitous that all her

[y] [Beaumont's Psyche; Canto iii. § 154.]

[Supplement.]

[p. 69.]

children sh^d come to ye Sacrament wth *a quiet Conscience,* and w^d have them take some Paines herein, &c. Let us consider what is meant by a *Quiet Conscience.* Tis a Full assurance or Perswasion that God is at Peace with me, or that I have made my Peace with God, who for the sake of His Blessed Son (His Precious Blood), upon my Repentance and Faith, has forgiven me all my sins; that I am now Really a child of God, and an Heir of Heaven, &c. Let us see how far we can with truth say we believe this—for just so far we have Peace of Conscience, and no further. *Vid. Placette of Conscience,* pag. 404. 79.

83. *Counsels and Precepts.* In ye Oxford Annotations on St. Paules Epist. tis often said, particularly on 2 Cor. viii. 8, that there are higher degrees of Charity and other X^n virtues,

[p. 70.]

y^t are not *in Precepto,* and may be omitted without sinning, yet are *in Consilio,* and the performance of them highly Acceptable to God.—Now, how a man can be said to Love God with all his heart, &c., and yet omit ye doing of what he believes is Highly acceptable to Him, is at present not accountable to me, especially when I find the Apostle in y^t very Place declaring that he dos not com̃and *the Thing,* but speaks it to trye the *Sincerity of their Love.*

84. *Confession of Sins.* Repentance. *He that Confesseth and Forsaketh his Sin shall have Mercy.* Prov. xxviii. This shewes the folly of those who depend upon bare Confession and Absolution, and quiet their Consciences wth y^t, without taking care to Forsake their Sins for ye Future. See p. 78, 225.

[p. 71.]

85. *Duels.* That which men call Honour is really no better than *Rank Pride,* so that if nothing els sh^d deter men from this Wickedness, *this* sh^d, that they are under the Dominion of a most foul Sin, when they hassard their Lives, in plain words, they *are in a State of Damnation at y^t very time.* I said *Pride,* and w^t is it els? How contrary to ye example of J. X^t.

86. *Astrology.* See the vanity of this Art sufficiently proved by Dr. More, *Myst. of Godliness,* ch. xv. B. vii.

87. *Light within.* What the true Light is, and what the Quakers' false Light, see Dr. More's *Myst. of Godl.,* pag. 408.

88. *Last Judgment. Day of Judgment.* The Burning of

[p. 72.]

Sodom and Gomorrah a lively Type of the Day of Judgment,

when the Wicked shall be overwhelmed with Fire and Brimstone, and the Righteous (as Lot was) shall by the Angels be snatch'd out of y^t Destruction, &c., and Rescued from the Power of Hell and Death, and out of the Hands of the Devil.

89. *Christian Religion. Best for all People, y^t it sh^d be obey'd, &c.* Tis agreed on all hands that it w^d be best for the world, and for every body in it, if all *People w^d do as they w^d be done to.* If our Children had no Examples,—Temptations to Debauchery, Swearing, &c.—If men were not swayed by Private Interest more than Public Good—If Envy, and Hatred, and Wrath, and Strife, and Sensual Lust, &c.—If every body might Peaceably enjoy what they or their Ancestours had justly gotten. If People w^d be *Temperate* in their way of Living, and *content* with w^t they can get honestly.—If we w^d be kind and obliging one towards another, and bear with such Infirmities as most People are subject to.—If all men w^d but Believe that Industry will be certainly Blessed from above, and y^t Idleness will cover a man with Rags—That if Malice and Envy were banished from amongst men, it w^d be happier for ye World; and y^t Covetousness and Ambition do a World of Mischief, even to those that are subject to these Vices, as well as to others,—&c. Every body is thus far agreed ab^t these things.—Now 'tis a most certain Truth—That the X^n Religion, w^d People but embrace it, w^d bring all this ab^t. Tis the most Proper, the most effectual, the only Thing y^t can do it, &c.— [p. 73.] For it gives us all the assurance possible, that there will be a Future Judgment, when every body's Thoughts and Actions will be laid open, and Rewarded or Punished, &c. In the mean time, the X^n R. assures us y^t God sees all we do, or Think, or speak—That He has given us Lawes, for the Observation or Breach of wch we are most certainly accountable —And that we may not be discourag'd, the same Religion shewes us that, if we are not wanting to ourselves, we shall be enabled not only to do w^t God requires of us, but to do it willingly and of choice. That we ought to do all these things with all our Hearts, because Heaven and Hell are not things to be despised or trifled with, &c. The X^n Religion obliges Magistrates to be just, diligent, faithful, &c. And

544   MAXIMS OF PIETY AND MORALITY.

SUPPLE-
MENT.

the People to be Obedient, Dutiful, &c. And all this for conscience' sake; for no other consideration can do this.

So that upon the whole it will appear that ye X^n Religion (even those that have no Religion being Judges) dos serve very evidently towards bettering the World, and making it a Happyer Place to live in, so long as God pleases to continue us in it.

People y^t look up to God on all occasions for Help will not Rebell, &c.

Magistrates who believe y^t Government is God's Creature, κτίσις, will Govern as in the Sight of God, and will have no reason to use Tricks, Unlawful Methods, &c., to secure their $Governm^{nt}$.

Nay, lastly, this will more terrifye foreign Enemies than is usually thought of.—Achior's Advice to Holofernes, Balaam's Advice to Balak, &c. 79, 238.

[p. 74.]

90. *Trinity.* See Dr. More, Myst. of Godl., B. 9. ch. 2.

91. *Covenant.* New Testament or $Coven^{nt}$. The X^n Religion is a $Coven^{nt}$ by which God has bound Himself to Man, and Man to God; the $Mediat^r$ of this Cov. is J. X^t, whose blood is the Blood of this Covenant ('for both among Jewes and Heathens covenants were made with sprinkling of blood, intimating a mutual imprecation of destruction to one another, if they dealt treacherously in the covenant so ratified), which being shed to procure peace betwixt God and Man, a Peace of the Highest Concern to Men, the Breach of this Covenant will be attended with the most fatal consequences. Heb. x. 26, &c.

Now we may be assured y^t we keep, and shall keep, this Cov. if we observe these Rules—

1. Never consent to known iniquity—Immediatly return to God and ask His Pardon w^n we are sensible we have done amiss. 1 Jo. 2. *That ye sin not—But if any man sin.*

2. That we always keep in our minds the Power of God's Sp^t to help us in all our straits—*According to thy Faith be it unto thee.* He y^t Believes 'tis in his Power to overcome Temptations, will, &c.

2 [3]. To love X^t and to keep His Comandments, for ye Love of X^t will constrain us, &c.[x]

[x] [More, Myst. of Godl., ix. 10.]

92. *Affections.* Corrupt Affections. The only way to Master is to deny them. Affect not applause, and *Pride* will hang down his head and dye. Give not vent to your *Anger*, and it will soon leave you. Answer not your *Lust*, and it will not Sollicit you. Dare to do good against the Inclinations of yor Heart, and *Hatred* will vanish; and *Covetousness* will not triumph, where you force yor self to good works. *Myst. of Godl.*, p. 486 [y].

Supplement. [p. 75.]

In short, ye outward Actions God has put in our power [z]; if we use them aright, His Grace will come in to our Help.

93. *Conversation.* If you would Converse with the World without Scandal to others, or injury to your self, observe 2 Rules—

1. Not to Judge of others by External Circumstances, in Diet, Clothes or Behaviour, but only for w^t is Christian or otherways.

2. Not to make others' Liberties a Measure for your self, but do w^t *you* are perswaded *you* ought to do [a]. 295.

94. *Religion.* So far true and indispensably necessary— 1st. As it sets forth the Wisdom, Goodness, and Love of God to Mankind. [p. 76.]

2nd. As it Magnifies the Person of our Sav^r, and warrants Divine Hon^r to be paid Him.

3rd. As it Advances the Divine Life in all his Members.

4th. As it therefore becomes Recommendable to those y^t are without. *Myst. of Godl.*, p. 497 [b]. (160.)

All the rest are (in Comparison of these) idle Curiosities [c].

95. *Sacrifices.* The Sacrifice of X^{ts} death was represented by the Sacr. under the Law, and so Represented as to give the *Sincere Observers* of the Law a Right to all the Benefits of that Death wch they Represented. [p. 77.]

96. *Lord's Supper.* "A Lively Faith," &c., may thus be explain'd: by an offer of great kindness from some great man. If I am assured by good tokens of His good will towards me, if I am assur'd that the Person He sends hath Authority from Him to confer the Favour upon me, &c., then I rest satisfied, &c. Without this I sh^d have reason to be in Doubt; any body might pretend to bring me a fair

[y] [340. Ed. 1708.]
[z] [Ibid.]
[a] [342, in substance.]
[b] [348-50, B. x. 3, 4.]

[c] [Five references to the *Mystery of Godliness*, and one to Inett's "English Church," are omitted here.]

SUPPLE-
MENT.

[p. 78.]

Promise; so I might be deceived, but if I am sure 'tis His Messenger, sent by Him, [&c.] For, in short, the Sacraments are only of any Benefit to us, as they are ordain'd of God, and Receiv'd by us with an eye of Faith to His Institution. And tho' a Person, not sent of God, sh^d never so devoutly beg God's Blessing to descend upon the Elements of Br. and W., and distribute, &c., this were no Sacram^t, no Pledge to assure us of God's Grace and Fav^r, &c. Vide p. 87 ^{d}.

97. *Predestination.* Certainty of Foreknowledge implies no more than certainly knowing before hand that Free Agents will choose and Act so and so, upon such and such Emergencies, Temptations, Assistances, &c.; this Foreknowledge in God, dos by no Meanes oppose ye Freedom of Will wch is in Man. Cannot Free Agents be Free, tho' God in His Infinit Wisdome and Knowledge knows how they will act long before?

98. *Confession and Absolution.* Pag. 187. See *Chillingworth's Sermons*, pag. 408 ^{e}.

99. *Custome.* See *Reflections on Men's Prejudices, &c.*, pag. 129, &c., pag. 147 ^{f}.

[p. 79.]

100. *Separation from ye Ch. of Rome.* Did the X^{ns} do well in separating from the Synagogue, which had Pronounc'd our Lord a Deceiver, and His Miracles false? And whether had not they a Right to examine this Judgment by the Rules of Scripture and Reason, altho' the Synagogue was in Possession of Authority, &c. Whatever the Ch. of R. alleges agst the Reform'd, to prove y^t we are not permitted to enquire and dispute, but to submit, all this the Synagogue might have insisted on, agst ye Primitive X^{ns}. *Placette, Conscience,* pag. 30. [in Kennett's transl., 8vo., 1705, p. 311.]

---

^{d} [The reference in Walker's hand.]

^{e} [and 409 : " In obedience to His gracious Will, and as I am warranted, and even enjoyned, by my holy mother the Church of England expressly, in the Book of Common Prayer, in the rubrick of Visiting the Sick . . . . I beseech you, that by your practise and use, you will not suffer that commission which Christ hath given to His ministers to be a vain form of words, without any sense under them; not to be an antiquated, expired Commission, of no use nor validity in these days: But whensoever you find yourselves charged and oppressed, especially with such crimes as . . lay waste . . the conscience, that you would have recourse to your Spiritual Physician, and freely disclose the nature and malignancy of your disease. . . . . and come not to him only with such a mind as you would go to a learned man experienced in the Scriptures, as one that can speak comfortable, quieting words to you, but as to one that hath authority delegated to him from God Himself to absolve and acquit you of your sins."]

^{f} [This reference, with those in Nos. 114, 119, 129, 132, 133, the Editor has not been able to verify.]

101. *Despair.* Vid. *Placette, &c.*, pag. 42. [Kennett's Supple-transl., p. 402.] It w^d be unjust to Judge hardly of those ment. who have no hopes of themselves thro' an Unreasonable Despair: for when once the Mind is so much alienated as to deprive a man of the free use of his Reason, wch may proceed from Melancholy, &c., his Actions are Involuntary, and in a Moral Acc^t are not Criminal.

102. *Lord's Supper.* 68. [*Placette on*] *Conscience.* [Kennett's translat., p. 423.] No man can communicate worthily who is not in a state of Grace. Tis for this Reason [p. 80.] we are commanded to examine our selves.

103. *Superstition.* Is such an apprehension of God [as] renders Him Grievous and Burdensome to the Thoughts, and so destroys all cheerful converse with Him; begetting instead thereof, a forc'd Devotion, void of Inward Life and Love. *Smith's Select Disc.* pag. 36^g.

104. *Soul. Its Immortality* needs not be Prov'd, bec. it is embrac'd by all sorts of People, and never question'd till after men have taken Paines to root ye Belief of it out of their minds.

Whatever checks and controules ye senses must be of an higher Nature than the Senses. No such Principle in Beasts. A Beast's senses (nor indeed a Man's) are not deceiv'd w^n the Moon appears to y^m no bigger than a Sive, Reason can only correct y^t Error.

A Good man sees ye Immortality of his own Soul in a better Light than that of Arguments drawn from Reason.

The Immortality of the Soul, *The Main Basis of all Religion.* The SS. do rather suppose than positively prove this Truth; they suppose an Antecedent knowledge, and only teach us how to behave ourselves so as y^t our Immortal Soules may not be miserable for ever.

105. *Glory of God.* The true way of Glorifying God, is [p. 81.] so to conform our selves to His Image, as y^t we may Convince our selves and others that we think nothing better than He is, and y^t we desire nothing more than to be like Him.

106. *Justice. Divine Justice.* It does not primarily intend Punishment, but takes it up as a mean to prevent wickedness, and to promote Goodness.

g [35, 4to. Lond. 1673.]

SUPPLE-
MENT.

God Himself is not without Law, nor, in a Sober Sense, above Law. His Love and Goodn. are the Foundation of all His Works and Commands; He did not, therefore, nor could He designe to make His creatures Miserable to Manifest His Justice; and if men are tortured in seeking *after good*, and often miserably disappointed, it is to make y^m renounce all earthly enjoyments, and to desire to return to the Author of their Being. And therefore they have such Principles as may serve to conduct y^m back to Him from whom they have stray'd; and they are then miserable when

[p. 82.]

they refuse to Act by such Principles. And those Laws wch we call Positive Laws of God, proceeding fr. ye Free Pleasure of God, these were added *bec. of Transgression*, (Gal. iii.) i. e. to secure the Eternal Law of Righteousness from Transgression; and therefore the Observance of these has been omitted wthout Sin, when they have stood in competition with any other Law of Moral Duty or Human Necessity.

Two sorts of People in fault; 1st, Those who think they are above ordinances, w^n indeed they have need of y^m as a Hedge to secure y^m from straying, and, 2ndly, Those who Place all Relig^n in these, w^h are only intended to Help us in our Pursuit of some *Higher Good*. This is y^t *Everlasting Righteousness*, spoken of Dan. ix., to be brought in by the Messiah, in opposition to *That Righteousness* mentioned Math. iii.[h]

107. *Sin—Evil.* The Body an occasion of Evil to the Soul two ways,—1. As it hinders its mental operations, presenting its Idols to it continually; 2ndly, As it craves its Passions to be gratified by a Sinful Inordinacy[i].

[p. 83.]

108. *Prophecie.* The way wherby Reveal'd Truth is Convey'd to us[k].

109. *Holy Scriptures.* The H. Penmen may be supposed not to speak by Inspiration in these following cases:—

1. Where they treat of the common occurrences of Life, wch have no Relation to Divine Truths: as Rom. xv. 24; 2 Cor. i. 16, &c.

2. When they speak of such things as are matter purely of Humane Prudence. 1 Cor. vii. 11; 2 Cor. xi. 17; 2 Cor. viii. 8, 10.

---

[h] [Abstracted from Smith, ubi supra, pp. 135—156.]

[i] [Ibid., p. 158, from Plotinus.]

[k] [Ibid., 162.]

3. When they discourse of such things as our Lord told y^m they must be content to be ignorant of, as of the Day of Judgment, &c., which God has not (as the Apostles themselves have recorded) imparted to any creature.

4. *In all other cases they writ and spake by the particular Direction and Assistance of the Sp^t,* being Appointed by God the Founders of the Universal Church; and therefore endued wth a Power of confirming their Doctr. by Miracles, ye Seal of God, wch justified their Commission. 2 Cor. xiii. 3. *We speak the things of God in the words wch the Holy Ghost teacheth.* 1 Cor. ii. 12, 13; 1 Cor. xiv. 37. And therefore w^n St. Paul was design'd for the Apostolate, he was not taught by the rest of the Apostles, who could have inform'd him of every thing wch Jesus did and Taught, Luke i., but *purely* by *Revelation,* Gal. i. 11. Comp. wth v. 12 and 1, 1 Cor. ii. 10. The Despising of y^m was the despising not men, but God. 1 Thess. iv. 8. Pag. 86. [p. 84.]

110. *King's Evil, cured by Touching, &c.*[1] See Bp. Bull's Thoughts of this, and why some are not cur'd, &c. Vol. 1st of his *Sermons,* pag. 217 [m].

111. *Infant Baptism.* Children are therefore Baptized, bec., if they Live, they will Sin, and tho' their sins are not Pardon'd before hand, yet in Baptism they are admitted to that State of Fav^r, that they are within the Covenant of Repentance and Pardon. Bp. Taylor, *Unum Necessar.,* Append., p. 38 [n].

112. *Sacrifices.* It was some comfort to a Sinner, that God w^d accept of the Life of a Beast instead of the offender's. But this was not the only Use of Sacr. They were chiefly intended to preserve the Knowledge and Remembrance of the Promised Seed, &c. And this custome being Universal, must have a Beginning as early as Mankind.

113. *Law of Nature* is y^t Power wch Teaches and enables men to put a Difference betwixt w^t is Good and Evil, Pure and Impure, Beauty and Deformity. This was the Law [p. 85.]

---

[1] [The Registry of Winwick, Jan. 3, 1684, contains "a Certificate signed by Doctor Sherlock, Rector of Winwick, and Churchwardens, for Henry the son of Ralph Bate, of Croft, who had the Evell, and was toucht by his Maiestie."]

[m] [Serm. v. p. 99, Oxford, 1840.]

[n] [*Deus Justificatus*, obj. 4, answer 6, Heber's Ed., t. ix. 347.]

SUPPLE-
MENT.

written in the Hearts of all men, wch made y^m liable to punishment.

114. *Tithes, Præscriptions, &c.* Vid. Long's Exercit. of Things given to Religious Uses, p. 96.

115. *Clothes, Pride, Modesty.* Vid. *Sins of Impurity*, pag. 116, 117. [Osterwald, De l'Impurité, § iii., c. iii., no. 5, Amsterd. 1707.]

116. *Confession; Private, Publick.* Vid. *Sins of Impurity*, 151—154, &c. [ibid. § v. c. ii.] p. 96.

117. *Penance, Publick.* *Sins of Impurity*, pag. 160, 161. [ibid. c. iii.] Pag. 97.

118. *Goodness. God's Goodness and Mercy. Lawes Good.* Those that depend upon God's Mercy without Reforming their Lives, have not consider'd that God dos not shut *this* man out of Heaven, and make *that* man eternally Happy,

[p. 86.] purely bec. it pleases Him so to do.—But bec. in His Infinit Wisdom He knew y^t men cannot possibly be Happy without observing such and such Rules—without abstaining from such and such vices, He has therefore forbidden the one and commanded the other.

So y^t the Lawes of God are like Land marks to sea-men; they direct us in our way to Heaven, and shew us where dangers lye, w^t will Hinder us from getting to Heaven.

119. *Romances, and the Virtues they Teach.* Vid. *Prejudices agst Relig^n*, p. 261, &c.

120. *Scriptures.* He that w^d profit by y^m must not trouble himself with the Hardest parts of SS., but wth such as are most edifying. Remembring that the design of J. X^t was not only to procure us the Pardon of our Sins, but to make

[p. 87.] us *like God;* in order to wch the Pardon of our Sins was indeed necessary; but ye gr^t design of X^{ty} is to raise us above this world and its vanities. p. 167.

121. *Calling.* He that dos not faithfully discharge the duties of his calling for ye good of men, cannot wth a good conscience Receive the Profits thereof.

122. *Pride.* Whenever you are Prais'd, even deservedly, offer the Praises to God, for to Him they are due; wch is a worthy Sacrifice, well-pleasing to G^d, and a cure of Pride.

123. *Youth. Nil dictu fœdum visuque hæc limina tangat,
   Intra quæ puer est.*

124. *Law and Gospel.* The first shewes us our Misery and danger, the Latter our *only Remedy.*

125. *Lord's Supper.* Little do People know w^t they do, w^n they turn their Backs upon this ordinance. For my own part, w^n I consider the many Staines and Pollutions of my Soul, and that all these, wch are not blotted out by the Blood [p. 88.] of the Lamb will most certainly Rise up in Judgm^{nt} agst me, I w^d not for the world despise such a Remedy. The Brazen Serpent, &c. 187.

126. *Self-Denyal. See Affections,* p. 75. A choice Receipt for those that will use it. *Dr. Hen. More.* See his *Ethicks,* lib. iii. ch. iv.

To Deny ones self in Things Indifferent (consistently wth Health, and a Civility of Behaviour to others,) he call'd a *Secret,* the greatest one Freind could communicate to another. You must please yo^{r}self in nothing. *Ibid.* There is no Pleasure comparable to the not being Captivated to any external thing w^{t}ever.

"He that knows not how to Resist the Present importunity of Pleasure or Pain, for the sake of w^t Reason" (Religion) "tells him is fit to be done, wants the True Principle of Virtue and Industry."—(Yes, and of Pietie too.) *Lock of Educat.,* sect. 45 º.

127. *Suspect yourself in whatever you have a strong in-* [p. 89.] *clination for. Ibid.* ᵖ He that cannot command his *Thoughts* will soon lose the command of his Outward Actions.

Rom. x. 3. *Even X^t pleased not Himself,* as appears in the Meanness of His Birth and Relations,—the Company (Sinners) He conversed with,—The Form of a Servant He took upon Him,—the Death He underwent.

Eccles. i. 8. *The eye is not satisfy'd wth seeing, nor the ear with hearing,* and so of all the senses and appetites.

Luke vi. 24, 25, &c. Wo unto you that are rich, for ye have Received yor Consolation—Wo unto you that are full—that laugh now.

It qualifies us for God's Favours, and Gracious Assistances. —*The Meek will He guide in Judgm^t,* and *"teach y^m His Ways."* Ps. xxv. 9.

º [An extract from the Life of Bonnel, p. 122, is here omitted, being given in *Sacra Privata.*]

ᵖ [[Life of Bonnell,] 126, 8vo., Lond. 1707, by Archd. Hamilton.]

SUPPLE-
MENT.
[p. 90.]

The Greater our Self-Denyal, the Firmer is our Faith, and more Acceptable to God.—Therefore the Sincere Devotion of the Rich; the Almes of the Poor; the Humility of the Great; the Faith of such whose condition is desperate (*leaning upon his bed-staff* q); to contemn the Good Things of the World when one can command y^m at Pleasure; to continue instant in Prayer tho' we find not that comfort we expected:—These are great Instances of self denyal, and such as God will Highly Reward.

They that imagine that *Self-Denyal* entrenches upon our Liberty, do not know, it seemes, that this only can make us Free indeed; that it gives us the Victory over our selves; Frees us from the Bondage of our own Corruptions; enables us to Bear Afflictions (wch will come one time or oth^r)—to foresee y^m without any Amazem^t.—That it enlightens the Mind, Sanctifies the Will, makes us slight those Baubles wch oth^rs so eagerly contend for, &c.

He that thinks it his duty to deny himself will not take it ill w^n oth^rs deny him w^t he expects, i. e. Crosses [cross] him, &c.

"Mortification consists in such a Sparing use of the Creatures, and in such a well Governed Abstemiousness, even fr. lawful Pleasures, as may deaden his Love for y^m, and make him more Indifferent in the enjoyment of y^m. . . . By doing this a X^n lessens the weight of Concupiscence wch carries us to evil, and Renders the Grace of God more effectual to turn the Ballance of the Will." Norris, *X^n Prudence*, pag. 300^r.

[p. 91.]

128. Tis a Part of Special Prudence, *Never to do any thing merely because any one has an Inclination to it;* but bec. eith^r 'tis my duty, tis Reasonable, &c. He y^t will follow his Inclination, *because he wills,* in one thing, will do it in anoth^r.

129. *Miracles.* God is a Sp^t, and if He w^d make Himself visible to us, it must be by the effects of His Power.

Tis true He can make Himself known by Inspiration; but then a Bare Inspiration can convince the mind of him only that is Inspir'd, and if he w^d convince anoth^r he must give him a convincing Proof of his being so Inspir'd; y^t is, of

---

q [Gen. xlvii. 31; Heb. xi. 21.]   r [Not word for word.]

God's Presence with him, and of the Authority he has to speak in His Name.

Miracles, therefore, are necessary to testifye the Mission of him by whom they are wrought.

For a *Miracle* is an Action that in its *self* or *circumstances* is a sign to us of the Presence or Operation of some Invisible or Supernatural Power, being done out of the way of Nature, or above its Power, in which there is an appeal made to the Senses and Reason of mankind.

Now the Devil having in all ages enabled his vassals to do Wonders, viz. Miracles, it was necessary that God (when He purposed to reveal Himself to, and Chuse a People out of, the Idolatrous World) sh^d make manifest a Superior Power, over all the Powers of Darkness, or Dæmons, wch ye World [p. 92.] worshipped as gods.

He therefore so ordered it, that there was a Contest in the Face of the World, betwixt the servants of these Dæmons and His Servant Moses, by whom He design'd to reveal Himself to the Israelites; Moses wrought 1, 2, 3, Miracles; the Magicians did the very same. But then God restrain'd and comptrowled them, they could go no further, but acknowledg'd that *the Finger of God*, a Greater Power than that wch assisted y^m, was present wth Moses—who still went on heaping Miracles upon Miracles, wthout Stop, or Limitation, by wch he convinc'd the Israelites, *That the Lord is God, and that there is none besides Him*, and wherin the gods of Egypt "acted Proudly," i. e. did all they could to keep their Vassals in their Power, *He was above* them.

The Israelites being thus prepared to Believe the Lord and His Servant Moses, God by Moses gave them the Law, &c., made known to them what w^d Please Him, what worship He expected from His Servants, what Blessings they might expect fr. Him if they strove to Please Him, and w^t w^d follow if they forgat Him.—And He forewarn'd them particularly (Deutr. xiii. 1), that if the Devil (as he w^d do) empower'd any of his Prophets to work wonders in order to draw them fr. the Service of God, to Worship False Gods, they sh^d not hearken to him, but Remember that God, whom they served, was superior to them all.

By this way both Jewes, and Gentiles afterwards, came to

SUPPLE-
MENT.
[p. 93.]

know the True God, and to Receive a Revelation fr. Him. For J. X^t, besides Infinit other Miracles, cast Devils out of those they had taken possession of, wch effectually prov'd His Superiority over them; so did His Apostles. And if the Jewes did not Believe, for all this, that He came fr. God, J. X^t has given the Reason, viz. *They hated the Light, bec. their Deeds were evil.*

And bec. the Devil will still use his utmost Power to seduce X^{ns} as well as Jewes, J. X^t has Forewarn'd us of False X^{ts}, &c., wch shall work Miracles [σημεία, the same word wch is used to express our Lord's works] to Deceive X^{ns}. Well then :—

What must a X^n do to distinguish Lying W[onders] from True Miracles? Why, he must "trye the Spirits, whether they be of God;" "Beware of False Prophets: ye shall know them by their Fruits." And, " if there come any, and bring not *This Doctrine,* Receive him not ;" viz. we must enquire into *the Power* by wch they perform them, and the *Evidences* of that Power.

Jesus X^t Himself Appealed to His workes. He appeal'd also to the Revelations wch went before of Him—To the Tendency of His Doctrine, and its agreeing with Former Revelations, wch the Jewes own'd to be of God; and lastly, to the Nature of His works—To destroy the K. of Darkness.

[p. 94.]

Nicodemus (St. Jo. iii. 2,) Judges of the Doctrine of X^t by His Miracles, not of His Miracles by His Doctrine. He had Reason, since J. X^t neith^r spoke against God, nor agst Moses. The only Rules wch the Jewes had to distinguish False Miracles fr. True.

Texts of Scripture, &c., relating to this Subject :—

Numb. x. 28—30=Gal. i. 8, 9. Miracles are as the *Seales,* Doctrines as the *Contents* of a Divine Commission; thus a Prince's Commission may be detected of Forgery—eith^r by the False Seal, or by some Absurdity in the Contents, or by both.

The Doctrines wch Receive their Authority fr. Miracles, are not the same wth those which are known antecedently to Miracles. J. X^t (Mark ii. 3) cured a man of the Palsie with a word—to give Evidence of *This Doctrine,* that He had Power to Forgive Sins.

See Dr. Jenkin's *Observations upon ye Life of Apollonius Tyanæus*.

130. *Excommunication, Discipline, Absolution.* Being cut off from the Church (Regularly and in the Fear of God), you are thereby cut off from all Right wch X^{ns} have to the Promises of God in the Gospel.

In the Primitive Church, not only Refractory Sinners were Excom̃., but even very Scandalous Offenders were not Admitted to Penance, till after some time at least, tho' they desired it. A Milder Censure not being thought sufficient to make ye Sinner sensible of his guilt and danger; or to secure the Ch. fr. the Scandal of giving Countenance to Sin, by admitting the most profligate to Peace upon the same Termes, &c. Some, therefore, were left to God's Judgm^{ts}, and not admitted to Penance. "There is a Sin unto Death, I do not say," i. e. I do not command you, [p. 95.] to admit such to Publick Penance, or to intercede with God, by Pray^{rs} for such in the way or course of their Censures; bec. Profligate Sinners were not presently to have this Comfort; and some, as Apostates, never, but to be left to God's uncovenanted Mercy.

Imposition of Hands was not, in the Primitive Church, the Absolution of Penitents, but the way to it; by Imposition of Hands, Sinners were first Admitted to Penance.— Then, in the course of their Penance, dismiss'd wth ye Pray^{rs} of ye Faithful, &c.

Such in the Primitive Church as dyed in a State of Penance, and did not live to bring forth Fruits meet for Repentance, or to perform what was appointed by the Church,—their Salvation was questioned.

131. *Tythes.* Matth. Paris tells us, ad Ann. 1075, that [p. 96.] Pope Gregory VII., having Publish'd a Decree y^t the Laity sh^d not own those Clergy that were married, and refused to put away their wives, the Layity not daring to pay them their Tythes, nor to make use of [them] themselves, were forc'd to burn them rather than be guilty of so great a crime as to touch the goods of the Church, or mix y^m with their own. See Prideaux, pag. 287 [s]. See p. 103.

132. *Obedience to Higher Powers.* "The Powers *that be,*

---

[s] [*Original and Right of Tithes*, 8vo. Lond. 1710.]

are of God." This is the fixed and standing Rule for Private Conscience; not such intricate Points of Right and Title, of wch the Generality of Mankind are no Judges. Bp. of Cork [Peter Browne], *Of Drinking Healths,* pag. 99. [Lond. 1715.]

133. *Confession, Absolution, &c.* Those Priests who give hasty Absolutions exceed their own Power, and sadly abuse it to their own and others' destruction. None can be Absolved who is not truly Penitent—Such as bring forth no Fruits of Penitence, are not Absolv'd, but deluded with a shew of Absolution. Jo. Episcopus Casteriensis, *de Recto usu Clavium,* lib. ii.: see 97, 98, and back, 65, 94.

134. *Absolution.* Those who make a Mock of Absolution as it is pronounced in our Daily Service, &c., have not well considered y^t ye very same Person Baptiseth for ye Remission of Sins, and Administers ye Lord's Supper as a Seal of the Forgiveness of the Sins of all Worthy Communicants. It is neith^r water y^t will wash away Sins, nor Bread and Wine; but these duly administer'd, by one rightly ordain'd, to Persons duly qualified by Faith and Repentance; then ye Sacraments avail for ye Forgiveness of Sins; and ye Daily Absolution is of the very same value, and preacheth for the correction of Sinners, where 'tis administer'd and Receiv'd as it sh^d be. For our L^d has given His Vicegerents this Power. Jo. xx. 23.

135. *Church Censures.* There is no Forgiveness of Sins out of the Communion of the Church. Pag. 166.

The Graces of the Gospel, the Promises of God, ye Forgiveness of Sins are all made over to X^{ns} by ye Ministry of ye Sacraments. If these are justly deny'd, Grace, Forgiveness, Promises, &c., are all Deny'd. Whoever, therefore, is Separated from X^{ts} Body, wch is ye Church, is separated from X^t ye Head. 166.

136. *Absolution.* In the Daily Service—only Declarative. Dr. Hammond, *View of ye New Directory,* 147, 148 ^t. And

---

^t [§ 30. Works, fol. Lond, 1674. t. i. What Hammond says is, that even Knox approved our Absolution, regarding it as declarative. He calls it himself "This exercise of the keys of the Kingdom of Heaven, this pronouncing God's Pardon, and actually giving the Pardon and Peace of the Church to all her penitent children;" calls the omission of it "a barbarous inhumanity," and "a rare example of despight to Christ's command:" and says, "There is more reason to wish for more of this nature, than that what we have already were omitted."]

yet he adds y*t* in our Liturgy, it is not only y*e* Pronouncing, but actually giving the Pardon and Peace of the Church to all her Penitent children.

*The Power of Remitting Sins, only y*e* Power of Preaching y*e* Gospel.*—This is one of y*e* Socinian positions, &c. Dr. Ham., *Power of y*e* Keys*, pag. 226 [u].

Absolution, absolutely necessary only to those who have been bound by Excommun. All other Absolution with*t* this precedent Binding Censure, being (tho' it may be allowed very useful and profitable for y*e* comfort and satisfaction of y*e* Penitent) neither Commanded or prescribed y*e* Preist to give, or y*e* penitent to Receive, by these S.S., "W*t* soever [ye] shall bind," &c. *Ibid.* p. 254 [x].

Binding and Loosing belong peculiarly to y*e* censures of y*e* Ch. In this case the Ministers of X*t* Act *Authoritatively* (by commission from X*t*) when*r* they excom. or absolve offenders. *Ibid.* 258 [y].

It was on this acc*t* that Novatus was censured, (*Conc. Nicen. Can.* 8,) viz. bec. he deny'd Absolution to y*e* *Lapsi* *Ibid.* 263 [z].

Excommunication is a super-addition to y*e* Band in Heaven, by w*ch* y*e* Sin is made Indissoluble before God, till it be Absolv'd on Earth, or [Absolution] duly sought for from the Church. Nay, in y*e* case of a sincere Repentance (if y*e* Sin was open and Scandalous) the Sinner is bound before God, until by submitting to Penance he obtain Absolution fr. the Church. *Ibid.* 265 [a].

This kind of binding and loosing, a Judicative Power, p. 200. *Ibid.* [b]

"Whosesoever Sins ye Remit," &c. In Ordaining of Presbyters, thus much is by these words conferr'd,—

1. The Declaring of Absolution in y*e* Church after Confession of Sins.

2. Absolving y*e* Penitent by way of Pray*r* before y*e* Sacram*t*.

3. On Special Confession on the Sick bed; and these not only by way of Pronouncing and declaring, but (as a Minis-

---

[u] [c. iv. § 25, from Volkelius.] [x] [Substance of c. iv. § 93—101.]
[y] [Ibid. § 105.] [z] [c. v. § 19.]
[a] [c. vi. § 1, 4.] [b] [c. i. § 2.]

SUPPLE-
MENT.

terial Act) Actually absolving him. *Ibid.,* pag. 217. But all this do's not amount to ye Power of Excommunication, wch is reserved to ye Bp. *Ibid.* [c]

In all ye Formes used in the Romish Ch. the Preist pronounces ye Absolution *Judicially and Authoritatively*, wch our Church has changed into, *He pardoneth, &c. Nicholls on ye Com. Prayer,* verb. *Absolution.*

Our Church do's not look upon Absolution to be Absolutely necessary for ye Forgiveness of Sins, as ye Ch. of Rome dos;

Neither do her Preists act *Judicially* and Authoritatively, for wch we are curs'd by ye Ch. of Rome. *Concil. Trident., Sess.* 14, *Can.* 9 : " If any one shall say y^t ye Absolution of ye Preist is not Judiciall, but only Ministerial—Let him be accursed," &c. Ours is only a Ministerial Act, &c. *Nicholls on ye Absolution in Office for Visit. ye Sick.*

[p. 100.]

"From all this it is apparent—That this Absolution is more than *Declarative*, it is *Effective and Judicial,* Insuring and conveying to the proper Subjects thereof, the very Absolution or Remission its self. It is as much ye bringing God's Pardon to ye Penitent, as an authoriz'd Messenger bring^g a Pardon from his Sovereign to a condemn'd Criminal is effectual to his Present pardon." *Wheatly on ye Absol. at Morning Pray^r,* pag. 93, 94.

See also his observations on ye Visitⁿ of ye Sick, pag. 252. [in substance.] If ye Penitent be duly prepar'd (wch the Preist ought to see to), he will as well convey as declare a Pardon to ye Sick person.

The first *Absolution* in ye Daily Service is *declaratory;* ye 2nd in ye Communion Service, *Precatory;* the 3rd in Visit. of ye Sick, *Judiciary* ; what we blame ye Ch. of Rome for, is y^t she uses this *last* Form to every confession, she sells Pardons, and places her Preists in God's Throne. " Sacerdos est Judex condemnare vel salvare." *Bellarmine* [d], [*ap.*] *D^r. Comber* [e].

Abp. Usher. " Whether the Ministers of the Gospel may be accounted Judges in some sort we will not contend. For, saith S. Jerome, ' Having ye Keys of ye K. of Heaven, they

---

[c] [c. iii. § 14, 15.]   [d] [De Pœn., l. iii. c. 2, Ap.]
[e] [Pt. i. sect. iv. § 1.]

Judge after a sort, before ye day of Judgm^t,' i. e. They Forgive or Retain Sins, while they Judge and declare, that they are forgiven by God, or Retain'd." *Answer to Challenge,* pag. 146, 162.

☞ " Behold I *certifye* thee y^t thy Sins are forgiven thee, I *Pronounce* unto thee, that thou hast God favourable unto thee. W^tever X^t in Baptism and in His Gospel hath promised unto us, He doth now declare and Promise unto thee by me; of this thou shalt have me a witness, go in Peace," &c. *Ibid.,* pag. 163.

A.Bp. Cranmer. See ye Preface to *Divine Right of Episcopacy* ^f.

^g " Ye shall Reverence God's Ministers, and w^tsoever they do to you, as wⁿ they baptize you, when they give you *Absolution,* &c., these you shall so esteem as if X^t Himself, in His own person, did minister unto you: He, tho' not seen, is present with His ministers, and worketh by ye H. Ghost in ye Administration of His Sacraments. And yet His ministers may not do w^tsoever they please; our Lord has given them plain Instructions w^t they are to teach and do:—They are to declare unto us the Forgiveness of our Sins, wⁿ we truly Repent and Believe in X^t; and wⁿ they do so, whose soever sins they forgive on earth, their sins be forgiven in heaven. But if he sh^d give Absolution to Unrepentant Sinners, they w^d but deceive, &c. We ought not to despise this great Authority wch God has given unto men, but thankfully to use it. This is matter of great comfort to an afflicted Conscience, wⁿ we Receive *Absolution* of y^m to w^m X^t hath promised—' whose sins ye shall forgive, &c.'

"When I have sinned, I ought to go to the minister of God and confess my sin, and pray him according to God's Commandm^t to give me Absolution, and then I ought stedfastly to believe y^t my Sins are forgiven me in heaven, and this faith will stand agst all assaults of ye enemy, being built upon God's Word and Work. For he knoweth y^t ye minister hath forgiven him, and he knoweth y^t ye minister hath Authority from God so to do. And whosoever do's despise

[p. 101.]

^f [Edited by Hickes, 8vo. Lond. 1708, p. xxv., &c.

^g [These passages are a kind of abstract from "*Cranmer's Catechism,*" which was really the work of Justus Jonas, but was edited by Cranmer in 1548. See the Oxford edition, 1829, pp. 196—204.]

560   MAXIMS OF PIETY AND MORALITY.

SUPPLE- this Order, he shall not find ye forgiveness of Sins, neither
MENT. in his own good works, &c., to wch God has not promised forgiveness of Sins. Wherefore despise not Absolution, for it is the Com̃and and Ordinance of God.

[p. 102.] "For wheth^r God's ministers do Excommunicate open offenders, or do give Absolution to those wch be truly Repentant, these Acts of the ministry have as great Power and Authority as tho' our Ld J. X^t Himself had done ye same. These things our Sav^r did appoint, y^t our Consciences might be comforted, and assured of ye forgiveness of our Sins."

Dr. Barrow, *Exposition on ye Creed*, pag. 600 [h].

Altho' forgiveness is proposed to all y^t Repent and Believe, yet He requires (and 'tis our Duty to Comply with it) that this Repentance be approved and declared by ye Church, and Confirmed by Baptism, Absolution, &c.

The Ministers of ye Gospel may be said to Remit Sins—

1. *Dispositivé*, by working fit Dispositions.
2. *Declarativé*, by publishing ye Conditions.
3. *Imputativé*, by praying for.
4. *Dispensativé*, by ye Sacraments, Absolution, &c. Wherby Grace is exhibited and Ratify'd by Imposition of Hands. *Homilys*, pag. 213. [*of Com. Prayer and Sacraments.*]

"For altho' Absolution hath the Promise of Forgiveness of Sins, yet it hath not this Promise annexed to ye outward sign, ye Imposition of Hands, and, consequently, no Sacrament."

Dr. Potter, *Of Ch. Governm^t*, pag. 364 [i], calls ye Power of Remitting and Retaining sins a *Judicial Power*, and Answers Objections.

[p. 103.] 137. *Tythes.* The first and chief end of Tythes is *this, they are a Worship and Tribute due to God*, and an Acknowledgm^t y^t we owe all to Him. The second is, that since God Himself dos not need y^m, they are to maintain His ministers.

The Canonists (to please ye Pope, who had appropriated most of ye Tythes to his Creatures ye Monks) found out a new Distinction, viz. that ye Clergy had only a Right to a decent Competency. As for a *Tenth*, y^t was only of Eccle-

[h] [Works, t. ii. pp. 514, 518, 519, fol. Lond. 1686.]   [i] [342—354, 2nd. ed. 8vo. Lond. 1721.]

siastical Institution, so y^t modified Stipends, &c., are of Popish Original. *Lesly*, pag. 128 [j].

After this the Begging Fryars, in opposition to ye secular Clergy, asserted y^t Tythes were only Almes, y^t might be given or withheld at pleasure. This, too, is Popery. At last ye Pope sold y^m all (y^t were not appropriated to Monasterys) in Italy to Lay Gentlemen, and made y^m part of their Estates. *Ibid.* pag. 130.

138. *Blood, Eating of.* Forbid before ye Law, by the Law, and after the Law. See this set in a just Light. *Fidde's [Body of Divinity]*, vol. ii. 171 [k].

139. *Juries of Enquiry* [l]. A defence therof where ye Life [p. 103.] of ye offender is not in Hazard.

In the Chancery of England, if a Bill of Complaint be put up agst a person for Misdemean^{rs} in prosecuting his suit, he's oblig'd to answer upon oath, tho' it be to his shame.

The same Court compels men to answer to Interrogatories wch very often hurt both their cause and Reputation. [p. 104.]

Men are every day required to give in their Acc^{ts} upon Oath, wherein if they have dealt fraudulently, they are exposed both to shame and punishm^t.

If it be alledg'd by the plaintiff y^t a Jury, after they were together, receiv'd a Letter from ye Defendant, they shall be sworn upon it.

Executors and Administ^{rs} are upon Oath to give Inventories; is there not danger of Perjury? Must the Oath be therefore laid aside?

Proofs from SS. 1 Kings viii. 31, 32. "When a man shall, &c." ["trespass against his neighbour, and an oath be laid upon him to come to swear, and the oath come before Thine altar in this house: then hear Thou in heaven, &c." Cf. Lev. v. 1; 2 Chr. vi. 22, 23.]

Prov. xxix. 24. "He that is Partner wth a Thief hateth his own Soul: he heareth Cursing," (i. e. an Oath with a Curse laid upon him by the Magistrate if he speak not the truth,) "and bewrayeth it not," &c.

Judges xvii. 1—3. "About wch thou Cursedst," that is in

---

[j] [Essay concerning the Divine Right of Tithes, § 10. Works, fol. Lond. 1721, t. ii. pp. 846, 847. (in substance.)]

[k] [fol. Lond. 1720.]

[l] [This entry is in Mr. Walker's handwriting, all but the heading.]

our Language, "[didst] put out a Jury of Enquiry, laying a curse upon all to discover what they know of the matter."

Deut. xxi. 1—5, &c. "And they shall Swear, 'Our hands have not shed this blood; neither our Eyes have seen him who shed it.'"

Exod. xxii. 7, 8, and ver. 10, 11. In both these cases a man's reputation lies at stake, besides the Restitution if he has done amiss, and yet an Oath is given. He must either discover his own wickedness, or be sinfully forsworn.

Lev. vi. 2—5. A Sacrifice appointed for one that had stolen, and forsworn himself upon Inquest made.

Numb. v. ver. 14. The Bitter Waters. This is a Capital Crime; and don't our Laws, pursuant to this, oblige People suspected to clear themselves, or do Penance?

Objections Answered. "Nemo tenetur seipsum accusare vel prodere, sive propriam turpitudinem revelare."

This is only meant of Crimes altogether secret; but wⁿ once the Crime is publick, then follows the other part of the rule: "Proditus tenetur seipsum ostendere, et suam innocentiam purgare." It was so in the case of murder, as above.

The best method for restoring Juryes of Enquiry would be, to receive the Jewish Law, That ye guilty person should (upon his confession, or refusal to swear) be obliged to pay a certain sum more than the thing, and all charges.

140. *Troubled Mind.* See ye Epistle for the 3rd Sunday in Advent. Gauther. [inter Rodolph. Gualtheri, Homill. in Epistolas, Tigur., 1588, f. 48, b.]

141. *Intercession.* Tho' God can give His blessing without the intercession of His Servants, yet 'tis plain He has otherways order'd it. See Gen. xx. 7; 1 Sam. i. 17; ii. 20.

142. *Indian Catechism.* See More's Works (new Edition, [1708,] *Mystery of Godliness*), pag. 322 ^m.

143. *Justice*; viz. Righteousness (one of ye Beatitudes) ought to be set above all by Regards; that nothing be done by Partiality. Act as in ye sight of God, and in Fear of His Justice; for infinite are ye cases wch a man may be unjust in if he only Feares man. Avoid Covetousness and

---

^m [b. ix. c. iii., containing hints on the best way of imparting Christianity to simple persons.]

Ambition, ye great Temptations to Injustice. Study Industry and Frugality. [SUPPLEMENT.]

144. *Melancholy Scruples. Parochialia.* Amongst ye many [p. 107.] objects of compassion wch a Clergy man will meet with in the way of his duty to exercise his Charity and Patience, the Dejected, &c., will Require Assistance to secure y^m from ye malice of ye D—l, and the sad effects of such Disorder.

They'll complain—That they have been gr^t Sinners, &c.; they are subject to gr^t Infirmities; they want Faith; they question the Love of God bec. He hides His Face fr. y^m; and they despair of ever getting ye Mastery of their corruptions, &c.

This is the Coven^t of God,—"Their sins and their Iniquitys I will Remember no more."

Tis want of Humility y^t makes us Impatient. Humility makes us content wth ye measure of Grace and Perfection wch God vouchsafes, while we strive to do our part.

This Dispensation very proper (and to be sure ye most proper in yor case) to wean us fr. ye world, &c.

Doubts and Feares afford this Test and Comfort, y^t we Fear God—else why are we concerned y^t we offend, &c.

In ye Darkest moments God is Present to Deliver us.

Epr.[n] Unprofitable Feares, perplexing Thoughts, Fretfulness, Despondency, Apt to think Endeav^rs fruitless, Oppression of mind—Often ye effect of Pride, Impatience, and Self Love.

This a Life of Tryal and Sorrow. God permits us to struggle wth our Infirmitys, y^t we may be sensible of our Weakness and Dependency, be Humble. "Behold we count [p. 108.] y^m Happy y^t Endure." Jam. v. 2.

Sin ag^st ye Holy Gh. always accompanyed wth hardness of Heart, Resisting ye H. G., Hating Duty.

"He y^t Cometh unto Me," (i. e. who desires it,) "I will in no case cast out." No man y^t desires this can be abandoned of God, or have sinn'd ag^st ye H. G.

If a man hopes to get rid of his Feares by running fr. God, he'll find his mistake to his sorrow:—"Come unto Me all y^t," &c. Rest is only to be found this way. Vid. *Remarkable Passages,* pag. 122, &c.

[n] [Query the meaning of this abbreviation.]

SUPPLE-
MENT.

Text. Rom. xvi. 20. *And ye God of Peace shall bruise Satan under y^r Feet.*

If God will accept of this Temporal Affliction instead of an Etern., wch y^r sins may have deserved—If He sh^d be extreme—you'll have no reason in the end to Complain.

If you were giving yor Child a Medicine, and he sh^d be very Untowardly and Fret, and be peevish, and crye, "You designe to poyson me," w^d not you tell him, 'tis bec. you loved him you did this; that if you had a mind to have destroyed him, you w^d not have taken so much care of him?

God loves you better than you do yor children, and knows better w^t is good for you.

He will have us to Glorify Him by Methods of His own choosing, not of ours. Do yor duty as well as you can. Do not require satisfaction in doing it, till God sees fit—Pride.

[p. 109.] Nothing uneasy to a mind truly Religious. He whose Heart goes along wth his Lips in this Petition, "Thy Will be done—"

They y^t have no Feares, but pass their days wthout Concern,—They are ye people in danger.

But they y^t see their own Corruptions—who strive agst y^m—have no Conceit of themselves—God resisteth ye Proud.

If you recover ye Tranquillity of mind, wch you so Impatiently wish for—you'll have more reason to watch and Pray then, even than now—You'll have more need of Advice.

Formality and Negligence are too often ye Effects of those Comforts we pray for.

Don't omit any known duty—such as ye L^{ds} Supper, &c. tho' you go wth all yor Feares, Scruples, &c.

W^n God removes this Cloud, then Consider ye dangers of a Prosperous Condition.

If I sh^d tell you y^t all this proceeds fr. a Rebellion of yor Will, wch is not pleased wth w^t God wills—If you recover y^r Peace with^t submitting to His will—Remember it is not ye Peace of God.

There is something in yor Case wch God sees w^d be a Hinderance to yor Happ^{ss} wthout this Thorn, this Messeng^r of Satan to Buffet you.

One moment of ye Happ^{ss} of ye next world will recompence you. You beg of God to shew you, Why He suffers, &c. Must God give His creatures an Acc^t of His ways?

W^n your mind is more Composed, tis then and not before that I w^d have you call yo^{r}self to an Acc^t. Till then you must follow ye Advice of y^r Director.

Satan cannot go beyond his commission to touch one Hair of yor Head. [p. 110.]

W^n you Charge yo^{r}self wth faults, be sure they be those of yor proper calling. They are easily seen; 'tis not so in oth^r matters.

The same everlasting Arm is still able to support you wch has hitherto done it.

You will not say y^t you are so perfect y^t God cannot purify you in ye Furnace of Affliction; He dos so by His dearest Children.

Resolve to be w^t He thinks fit you sh^d be. Fling yo^{r}self humbly at His Feet; Own y^t you have no Power in yo^{r}self; Neith^r Light nor power; y^t you expect both fr. His Goodness. Trye to exercise this one Virtue, and be not sollicitous ab^t any thing els.

Let this suffice—That you do not live in any known sin; that you will leave any such w^n you know it.

Be not sollicitous to be assured of ye Pardon of yor sins; leave y^t to God, and mind you yor duty.

This is one way God orders to shew us to our Selves.

St. Paul had his Buffettings; are you better than he?

You Forbeare going to ye Sacram^t; why y^{ts} w^t ye Devil w^d bring you to! Go in Obedience to X^{ts} Command, then you are safe, wth all yor Feares.

You say yor case is Singular; alas, you do not know w^t passes in ye Hearts of oth^{rs}.

I could tell you of one who suffered a great deal more, &c., who yet at last blessed God for it, and declared very solemnly y^t He w^d not for ye whole world not have gone thro y^t Furn. of Affliction. [p. 111.]

Temptations have their mighty use—Keep us humble, Keep us close to God, Run to Him for Help, Depend upon Him, make us concerned for our Salvation.

Complain not much to others—y^t argues Impatience. p.155.

145. *Tythes* are for the maint. of *God's Word*, as well

SUPPLE-
MENT.

as of His *Ministers*. 'Twould soon be forgot, as it has been wherever His ministers have been despised.—Nehem. x. 32 [? 37, 38]; Prov. iii. 9, 10; xx. 25; xxiii. 10; Mal. iii. 8—10; Luk. x. 7; 1 Cor. ix. 4—6, &c.; Gal. vi. 6; Phil. iv. 17; 1 Tim. v. 17, 18.

The most proper maintainance—for by this meanes the Preist and People mourn together, and rejoyce also together, weth^r in Plenty or Famin.

Stipends—Uncertain. In dear yeares ye Clergy would want, &c.

Patron. So called from defending ye Parsons' Rights.

Preist. Let "ye Preist, ye Minister of ye Lord, say,"—'tis not enough y^t I say,—"Lord have mercy on me." Jam. v. 14. "Let him call for ye Elders," &c. This ye only publick Acknowledgm^t you make to God Alm.

[p. 112.] 146. *Itching ears.* 'Tis our Lord y^t has said—y^t ye seed wch is the Word of God, if it fall into good ground, will take root. Take you care—That ye seed be sown by one sent by X^t, and y^t ye ground be good.

147. *There is a Way, &c.* [Prov. xiv. 12.] (228.) That we are liable to error, needs not to be prov'd; the Reasons plain.—That we (knowing this) may be oblig'd to depend on God; that we may be careful not to offend Him fr. w^m we Look for Light and power; that we may not Consult wth Flesh and Blood,—wth corrupt reason, but ask counsel of God.

148. *Preists of God.* Exod. xvi. 8, 9. "Your murmurings are not agst us, but agst ye Lord."

149. *Text, Sanctification.* (See p. 124.) 1 Thess iv. 3. "This is ye will of God, even yor Sanctification."

There cannot be a more Comfortable revelation. God wills—He desires—our Sanctification, bec. He knows y^t wthout this we cannot be Happy; He therefore sent His Son to assure us of this—That our Sins sh^d not make us despair of His Fav^r—But y^t we sh^d close wth so much Goodness of God, wch nāally leades us to Repentance.

He w^d have ye whole creation Happy as soon as 'tis capable of H. God is as it were Gratify'd by our being w^t He w^d have us be—Good. God extends His Love to all y^t make not y^{ms} Uncapable of it.

150. *Tythes.* See Lev. xxiv. 4, 6. The shew-bread a continual Testimony of ye Peoples' dependence on God for Life, &c.

SUPPLEMENT.
[p. 113.]

151. *Preist.* See Numb. vi. 24. The Solemn Blessing wch ye Preists were directed to make use of—to the end y^t God might bless ye People.

152. *Prayer.* If God sh^d grant our Desires for Temporal things, there could not be a greater Plague to us. See Numb. xi. 33.

153. *Regeneration.* That wch it concerns us to know is— our lost Estate by Nature, and our Recovery by Grace.

Whatever we see amiss eith^r in ourselves or others (we see how perverse oth^rs are w^n they injure us, &c.), all this was quite otherways in ye State of Innocence, there was nothing blameable.

Regen. is the work of ye Sp^t of God—"Except ye be born of ye Sp^t, &c."

They y^t think Reason and Free Will Sufficient to Regen. suppose this Absurdity, That a man may make himself Holy by a Will y^t is corrupt. That wch is born of ye Flesh, is Flesh. Jo. i. 13; iii. 6.

God's Grace and Man's Free Will are very consistent; for if God by His Sp^t makes me see my own bad Estate by Nature, and the infinite advantage wch will be to me to close wth ye offers of Mercy, then my will freely chooses y^t wch I see to be best for me.

[p. 114.]

By Regeneration we are made partakers of a Divine Nature. This we are to have in our eye evermore as the *mark* we aim at. The whole Dutys of X^ty aim at this as *meanes* of attaining it.

1. We are *baptized.* That being brought w^thin the covenant of Gr. we may have the Assistance of God's Sp^t (we are thereby put into a capacity of Salvation), to enable us to become *New Creatures.*

2. *Prayers* are necessary, bec. by y^m we obtain of God a sense of our evil condition by Nature, and strength to overcome his [our?] Corrupt Affections, y^t he [we?] may be restored to ye Image of God.

3. By hearing Sermons, we learn ye manner of our Redemption, the Enemys we have to deal with, ye way of over-

SUPPLE-MENT. coming y^m, the Dutys required of us, &c., that we at last become perfect, as—

4. If we give *Almes* on any oth^r Acc^t y^n in obedience to God's will, in gratitude to Him for being so good to us, and in Compassion to our fellow members, we are wrong.

5. The Lord's Supper is a solemn acknowledgm^t of our being in Communion wth X^t and His Ch.; but what a X^n [p. 115.] is to aim at is—To be made like unto X^t in [all] things, y^t as He died, &c.

These are all necessary meanes of Restoring us to ye Image of God—as such only to be valued.

Things necessary to Regeneration—That we be dedicated to God in Baptism, "Except ye be born of Water;" That we receive His Word as our Law, "Except ye be born of the Sp^t;" That we receive it into an Honest and True Heart, y^t it bring forth ye Fruits of Obedience, "Every one y^t doth Righteousness is Born of God."

By Baptism we become Related to God. We are His children; we can go to Him as a Child to His Fath^r; we are of His House and Family; we come to ye Knowledge of X^t—of all Knowledge the most necessary.

Born of ye Sp^t; i. e. we have Anoth^r Sens of things wch we had not before. We Love God; we hate Sin; we Love Holiness.

All Wilfull Sin Inconsistent wth a Regenerate State. Such are Regenerate as are under such a Lively Sense of their Duty, as y^t they cannot Knowingly Sin.

He y^t Sincerely Loves God, Feares His anger, Hopes for ye greatest Good from [Him], Believes His Commands to be Holy, Just, and Good,—To such a one ye Comands of God cannot be grievous.

It is much to be feared y^t ye Generality of X^ns do not know, at least they don't consider, w^t is required of y^m in [p. 116.] order to their Salvation, viz. an Inward change of Heart, as well as an Outward Profession of ye Gospel, "Except a man be born, &c."

If we could effect this, this w^d be striking at the root of Sin, and all our after work w^d become easy.

How this change is to be wrought is well worth your hearing with ye utmost attention.

How we may recover y[e] Image of God, His Fav[r] here, and Eternal Happ[ss] hereafter. SUPPLEMENT.

First, Every man in w[m] this change is not already made, ought to Consider y[e] danger of Dying Unconverted; he ought to Reflect upon his former evil or careless Life. This of course will lead him to wish he had lived better, and by degrees to abhorr himself for all his evil actions and omissions, and to beg of God to have Compassion upon him, and to help him to amend what is amiss in him.

W[n] a man becomes sensible of his own bad condition, and in all Humility flies to God for mercy, he is then qualified for God's especial Grace to perfect what is begun in him; i. e. God will stir up the seeds of Grace w[ch] were given in Baptism, but w[ch] have been since quench'd and smother'd (as it were) by evil habits.

And if a man finds himself inclin'd to condemn his past Life—afraid of offending God, willing to hearken to what his conscience tells him he ought to do or avoid; if he finds himself restrained fr. Sins w[ch] before he was fond of, he may depend upon it, 'tis y[e] work of God, y[t] God has a merciful designe to make him Holy, y[t] he may be qualify'd to be made Happy.

But let him have a care of neglecting these attempts of y[e] Holy Sp[t] of God to convert him.

God is indeed merciful, long-suffering, abundant in goodness, forgiving Iniquity, has no Pleasure in y[e] Death of a [p. 117.] Sinner. But then Sinners must take care not to Resist His gracious designes for their good.

A man may know y[t] he is in a State of Salvation—that his heart is changed for y[e] better,—by y[e] Fruits of that Good Sp[t] w[ch] wrought that change in him,—Love, Joy, Patience, Faith, Temperance, Obedience to God's Laws, and mortifying all y[e] Works of y[e] Flesh, w[ch] are manifest.

If God afflicts us wth Calamitys, Sickness, Disappointments, &c., we sh[d] look upon these as the most merciful Instances of His Fatherly Kindness, to make us Hate y[e] Sin w[ch] He hates for our sake, and to wean us fr. y[e] Pleasures of Sense, and to bring us to love God, and whatever He loves.

Use—In way of Examination. Let every X[n] consider

SUPPLE-MENT.

w^t Sp^t it is y^t leads him (for led every man is, eith^r . . . .).

— If I pray to God out of a Sense of my wants, &c., but if I only go to church out of custom, &c. If I abstain fr. Sin only for fear of Reproach or Punishm^t, and not out of Love to God. . . . .

Our Corrupt Nature leads us fr. God, and if we are not brought back by ye Grace of God, we shall live and dye wth Affections close to ye World.

Unless a man be truly Converted, i. e. translated fr. a State of Corrupt Nature to a State of Grace, whereby a man becomes restored to ye Image of God in wch he was at first created.

New Man. This shewes y^t we must be wholly chang'd. Our soules were made holy and righteous; as such we were like God. God made us after His own Image. Able to obey any Law wch God sh^d think fit to give him, God gave our first Parent a Law for ye Tryal of his obedience, wch Law

[p. 118.] he broke, and his and our Nature became therby Corrupt and prone to evil Continually.

For ye Sp^t of God forsook him, and instead of having a Race of children Holy and Righteous, his children became deprav'd as he was now become. This we cannot but be sensible of, viz. Our Understandings are blinded, our will perverse, our affections disorderly and rebellious, not only agst our Reason, but agst our God.

Now this disorder must be mended before ever we can be Happy, before God can take any pleasure in us. And this is to be done only by embracing and obeying ye Gospel of X^t.

For by *that* our Understandings are enlighten'd; we know w^t God expects fr. us; our wills are brought to Submit to God's Will, and our affections are drawn off fr. ye World and placed upon God.

All this is brought ab^t by ye Power of God's Sp^t; and therfore our Lord says—That "except a man be born," i. e. made a new man by ye Sp^t, "he cannot enter into ye K. of Heaven."

Regeneration.—The work of God's Sp^t given to every X^n in Baptism; and if every X^n is not Regenerate, it is not bec. God wills not his Conversion.—Some resist ye Sp^t of God, some grieve Him, &c.

The Cause of Regeneration.—The Word of God. Jam. i. 18. "He begat us by ye Word of Truth."—You see w^t a dangerous thing to despise God's Word.

Necessity of Regeneration. Consider w^t it is that makes Heaven a Blessed Place.

It is bec. there we shall have Reason to Love God with all our Soules—Love w^t He Loves, Obey His Will, &c. Will any expect to go to Heaven, &c., You must Love all y^t God Loves—perhaps y^t very man w^m you hate here. [p. 119.]

You take no Pleasure here in admiring ye Goodness of God, and yet y^t must be y^r Happ^ss in Heaven.

Will y^t mouth wch is filled wth oathes and curses here, be fit to Praise God.

You'll there see none but Pure and Holy Soules, ye very sight of w^m offended you here.

See God. To see God is to see Him as He is—in all His Attributes. To see an Infinit Just God—How will a Sinner endure this Sight. To see an Infinit Good—How will one who has all along abused y^t Goodness, &c.

X^ns, tis to be feared, have a confused notion of Heav^n.—Tis a place of Happiness, y^t all agree in, but w^t sort of Happ^ss?

All Spiritual Duties must needs be burdensome to a Carnal mind, but let ye Heart be Spiritual, all will be easy and pleasant.

If a man parts wth his Sins, as a man in a Storm flings out his goods, wch w^d otherwise sink ye vessel, 'tis plain he w^d not part wth y^m if [he] could help it.

Proofs of being in a Regenerate State. Rom. viii. 16. "The Sp^t itself beareth Witness with our Sp^t y^t we are ye children of God."—This Witness is Infallible.

"Give diligence to make yor calling Sure." [p. 120.]

How may I be assured y^t I Love G^d? Why, by keeping His commandments. How may I be assured y^t my Obedience is Sincere? by taking care to do w^t is in my own Power by ye Gr. of God.

"Behold all things are become new"—A new Heaven, new affections, new Life.

If Death comes before Grace has wrought a change in yor Inward as well as outward man, you are for ever Undone.

Now is ye Day of Salvation. Let no man deceive you

SUPPLE-
MENT.
(saith St. Paul, Eph. iv. 6,) "wth vain words ;" as if the Sins he had been mentioning were Consistent wth ye Hope of Salvation.

. . . . But be assured of this—That a Worldly, Carnal man is no more capable of being Happy in Heaven, than a sick man is capable of taking delight in a Fine Feast.

Rom. [Gal.] vi. 15. In ye X^n Relig^n, "neith^r Circumcision nor Uncirc. availeth any thing," i. e. is of any effect or Use, "but a New Creature."

Rom. vi. 16; 1 Cor. vii. 19; 2 Pet. i. 4. "Wherby we might be Partakers of the Divine Nature."

[p. 122—121 is blank.]
154. *Divinity. Method of Studying it.* See Du Pin, Eccl. Hist., Cent. 16, ed. Wotton, 1710, pag. 313.

155. *Sorcery, Witchcraft, Charmes.* Corn. Agrippa, his opinion of. Ibid. p. 403.

156. *Lord's Day.* A Set of useful Conclusions on this Subject by the Faculty of Paris. Du Pin, ed. Wotton, vol. xi. pt. iii. p. 130.

157. *State of man before the Fall.* [Abstracted from Bp. Bull.] Created in ye Image of God, Gen. i. 26, wch consisted in an Understanding Soul and a Free Will—These are part of his Nature, and still remain.

He was conditionally Immortal—For he might Eat of ye Tree of Life, Gen. ii. 16, and he was forbid to eat ye Forbidden Fruit on pain of becoming Mortal, Gen. ii. 17.

He had also Supernat. Powers, by wch he knew and Lov'd God—Righteousness and True Holyness; i. e. he was able to act conformable to any Law G^d sh^d give him.

God made a covenant of Life wth him, Gen. ii. 16. This was a very gr^t Tryal of his obedience, laying a vast restraint both upon his Rational and animal Appetite.

His Duty had been to have perfected ye Divine Life, so y^t he might have been fit for, and translated to Heaven;

[p. 123.]
but having a Free Will, he gave way to his appetites, and breaking ye Covent, he and his posterity became subject to Death; for ye Divine Sp^t forsook him, and instead of propagating an Immortal Race, he (Gen. v. 3) begat a Son after his own Image, y^t is, with such a Corrupt nature as his own was now become.

God foresaw all this, and the disorders y^t w^d follow, wch yet He permitted, that by a Redeemer He might discover

His own most Glorious Attributes, His Goodness, His Patience, His Tender Compassion, His Justice to Obstinat Sinners, &c. Pag. 225.

158. *Justification* is that Act of God by wch we are Adjudg'd Righteous before Him, and as such Accepted to ye Reward of Et. Life.

None Justify'd but such as have fulfill'd ye Law by wch they are Judged. God must Judge according to Truth, Rom. ii. 13. By ye Law of Works, therefore, wch we have not fulfilled, we cannot be Justify'd.

We are therfore Justify'd by Faith, i. e. such a F. as engages us to Good Works. This is *the Law* of ye Gospel. But forasmuch as this Law admits of Repentance, we fulfill the Law, not only w^n we observe it punctually (wch we cannot do), but also w^n we truly Repent, w^n we shall be so Unhappy as to have broken it.

And w^n we are said to be Justify'd by *Faith,* ye meaning [p. 124.] must be—That it is Faith wch sets before us Etern. Life and Etern. Misery, wch whosoever Believes to be ye Portion of all men, eith^r as they keep God's Laws or break y^m, will set himself to such good Works as will please God.

And notwithstanding this, our Justification is of mere *Grace*, and not of *Debt*; for it is God's mere Fav^r thro' J. X^t y^t He will accept of our Repentance, and has made this the Law by wch we shall be judged. In short, we are all Sinners, and cannot be justify'd without God's Pardon for X^t's sake; but then this Pardon will be granted to none but such as obey ye Gospel, and in that sense we may be said to be Justify'd by Works. And thus were all the Patriarchs Justify'd, viz. by Faith and obedience. See pag. 127.

159. *Sanctification.* All X^ns are Sanctify'd, or Holy, as they are dedicated to God in Baptism.

But the Sanctification here spoken of consists in leading a life agreeable to ye Gospel of X^t. This and this only can give us any comfortable Hopes of being Happy w^n we dye. This Holiness we attain (not by infused Habits, but) by the assistance of the H. Sp^t upon our closing with ye meanes of Grace. And therefore we are commanded to be *Holy,* i. e. to use ye meanes of becoming such sincerely, and we shall be so.

SUPPLE-
MENT.

[p. 125.]

160. *I find then a Law, y^t w^n, &c.* The gr^t Enmity betwixt ye Flesh and the Sp^t—This every X^n experiences, until eith^r ye Sp^t or ye Flesh has got ye Mastery. Tis a Condition Miserable enough, and therfore to be Remedied as soon as may be, and by no Meanes to be made a Reason why we sh^d continue in it, bec. of ye Opposition we feel in ourselves, as some perverse people do, who eith^r complain agst God for suffering us to be thus made wth Appetites, and Reason checking y^m; or as an Excuse for Sin, for who can help it, say they, Have not I a Law wthin me, &c.

Maxims. Whatever God has commanded must be Just and Good, and Worthy of Him, and will be for our Advantage if we obey Him.

The Law complained of is no Law to X^{ns}, bec. X^{ty} forbids us to submit to it, enables us to get ye Mastery, Rewards us if we do so, Threatens us if we do not. In short, we are in a state of Tryal, by wch God w^d manifest His Glory, His Power in enabling weak Creatures to overcome gr^t Difficultys, His Patience, His Goodness, &c., His Justice, &c.

He has given us ye Knowledge of our Duty, Assistance to perform it, will accept of our Repen^{ce} w^n we have done amiss, will Reward, &c. Men endure very great Hardships in ye Ways of Vice, Feares of w^t may come Hereafter, &c.

[p. 126.]

The Law complained of; is a Law of our own Making. God gives us His Sp^t—we grieve Him, we get ill Habits, we run into Temptations, and then we complain; we run into ill comp., we are advised agst it; Habits become strong; God in His Word forewarnes, Threatens, &c.; we mind it not, we profess His name, and say, Who can Help it? We Drink, Whore, &c., Steal, &c., and say, I was born to it, &c.

Is. iii. 10, 11. "Say ye to ye Righteous, it shall be well wth him," &c. This is ye Law we are under.

If men encourage y^{ms} in Sin, Contrive to keep up their Lusts and Passions in Rebellion agst God's Laws, Refuse to Hearken, or to be Reformed by Sickness, Visitations, &c.

Men must not plead and call Wilful Sins Sins of Infirmity, and so hope they'll be pardoned. *Sins of Infirmity*, w^n we strive and Pray agst y^m.

Men are angry wth God—not so much for giving y^m Laws to check their Appetites, as for this, That He has not given them leave to sin wthout Comptrowl, and wthout Fear of a Future Acc^t.

He y^t w^d make his Life easy, and have an Happy Death, must first of all Resolve upon this work, To get ye Mastery of his corrupt Affections.

Difficulties. God has so ordered it, we must meet with [them.] We shall find a struggle in following ye Laws of God. To make us amends, we have a Promise, &c., and to deterr us, &c. He who offers ye Reward has a Right of naming ye Conditions.

We are Subject to diseases; we may Complain of being so, but yet we don't sit still, but look out for Help. Let us have ye same concern for our Soules. [p. 127.]

Let us endeav^r to be under no Law but one, that of J. X^t, wch will fit us for Heaven.

161. *Justification.* Justify'd, i. e. Accepted of God thro' J. X^t. ☞ To meet wth these expressions—I hope God will be merciful for X^{t'}s sake to me, tho', &c.

Tho' a man is accepted of God, yet his Faith must work by Love; i. e. he must still go on in works becoming ye Fav^{rs} he is called to. Heb. x. 38. "If any man draw back"— Tho' upon our Receiving J. X^t our Sins are forgiven, yet our Pardon shall be cancelled if we neglect Acts worthy of our Faith. Col. i. 22, 23.

Attributes of God manifested in our Justification.

His *Goodness*, in not requiring sinless Obedience, because He knows our frailty.

His *Wisdom*, in requiring the Heart to be reformed, and not to rest in outward Performances.

His *Holiness*, in requiring all to be Holy, &c.

The Faith y^t Justify'd Abraham. He Acted as one who believed w^t God had promised could and w^d be made good— that God had Power to do it, &c.

☞ God's Gracious Designe is to set forth His own Glory by Restoring us to a Condition of being made happy; and this must be by bringing into ye Soul those Holy Qualitys, wch we have lost, and ye loss of wch makes us miserable. [p. 128.]

Those qualitys are—The Believing God to be w^t He really is, *Infinitely Good, Powerful, Just, Faithfull, Holy,* and then to Act accordingly.—That we Love His Goodness, Imitate

His Holiness, Obey His Commands, Fear His Power, &c.; and all this to the best of ye power He affords us.

This *Faith* (ye Principle of our Justification) is to be wrought in us, by considering ye Gospel. There we have X^{ts} Miracles to establish the Truth of His Doctrines, His Doctrines to direct us, His example to encourage us, God's Goodness to accept our sincere endeav^{rs}, His Justice to make us Fear His Ang^r, and His Promises to incite us. If we give Attention to these things, ye Sp^t of God will work in us—A Fear for our selves—A desire to please God—We shall be sorry we have offended Him—Resolve to do so no more. In short, he will become a new man, and his Faith will be accepted, and so will his person—He being now become such as God, who knows his weakness, will accept of.

The Termes insisted on to Adam were perfect Obedience; The Termes of ye Gospel are Faith and Sincerity. And This will be Imputed (made to pass) for Righteousness, thro' Faith in X^t, for oth^{r}wise it could not have Justify'd us.

[p. 128*.]

He (i. e. J. X^t) is our Righteousness; i. e. He has obtain'd these Conditions for us—These Termes of Reconciliation—We shall therfore have reason to Love ye Ld J. X^t, and to shew our Love by keeping His Commands. Jo. xiv. 15; and especially ye new one—*That we Love one anoth^r, as He hath Loved us*—y^t is, That we bear one anoth^{rs} burthens—Not let our Love center in our selves—That we use our Riches, Wisdom, Power, &c., to make others Happy as well as our selves.

N.B. Whether I shall be Justify'd, acquitted, or Condemn'd, when I shall appear before God's Judgm^t Seat, is a matter of no small Concern.

Man is faln fr. Happ^{ss} by Sin—Tis by Holyness he must be restor'd—Faith must bring this ab^t—A Faith in God's Mercy thro' X^t. W^n this Faith has made a real change in ye Heart, Resolutions, &c., then a man is Justify'd, i. e. put into a Way of Salvation, and if we walk worthy of this Faith, we are sure to be saved.

Gal. ii. 20. "And y^e Life y^t I now live, I live by y^e Faith."

A Faith y^t has power to change y^e Heart and Life, i. e. to restore us to y^e likeness of God.

162. *Righteousness*—A conformity to a Law.

R. of Faith—*Evangelical R.*, A X$^{n's}$ Conf. to y^e Gosp., which is His Law—Repenting for Defects, and trusting in God for pardon thro' X^t, being Fav^{rs} obtained by our Law giver. [p. 129.]

Christ's R. His Conformity to y^e Law of Mediation.

Legal R. A Conformity to y^e Law of Moses by wch y^e Jews hoped to be Justify'd.

God's R. God's way of accounting men Righteous; by ye Termes of ye Gospel with^t ye Law.

163. *Providence.* Luk. xxii. 35. *"W^n I sent you wthout Purse, &c., Lacked ye any thing?"* Whatever God orders, He will take care of ye consequence. See Exod. xvi. 29. See Eph. v. 6. Oxf. Annotat.

Carest thou not y^t we perish? If God is our Fath^r, He will take care of us—if we strive to please Him.

Prov. xviii. 10. *The Name of ye Lord is a Strong Tower—ye righteous flee into it and are safe.*

164. *Text.* Jo. xvii. 3. *This is Life Et., to know Thee ye only true God, and J. X^t.*

Pascal's Thoughts. [p. i. Art. 15. n. 2, ed. Lond. 1704.] 168.

To desire to know more than God has reveal'd is folly.

To know God as Reveal'd to us in ye O. T., and J. X^t in ye New.

H. Script. call'd God's Testimonys—bec. they bear Witness of His Attributes. Ps. cxix. 14. Almighty by ye Creation—All-Wise by His Providence—Terrible in Judgment —Merciful—Faithful to His Promises, &c.

He y^t knows God to be Almighty, will Fear Him, &c. [p. 129*.]
He y^t knows y^t this is God's word, will attend to it.

No necessity of proving y^t there is a God. Ps. ix. 16. This Lord is known by ye Judgments He executes. Ps. lviii. 11. *So y^t a man shall say, Verily there, &c.* Phil. iii. 8. *I count all things but loss, for ye excellency of ye Knowledge of X^t J. my Lord.*

165. 1 *Jo.* iii. 9, 10. *Whosoever is born of God doth not commit sin. In this ye Children of God are manifest, &c.*

Whosoever Receives ye Word of God (by wch we are born ag^n, Jam. i. 8,) dos not Commit Sin—doth not Live in any known Sin. But if he falls into any, he forthwith Repents—for lead a Sinful Life he cannot—i. e. while ye Sp^t of God abides with him and Governes him.

And in this ye Children of God, &c. By this any man [may know] whether he is a Child of God, and in ye way of Happ^s, or a child of ye Devil, and in ye way of Perdition.

The knowledge of this of great use—Men hope to go to Heaven at ye same time y^t they [are] governed by ye Devil. We see ye Reason why all ye Arguments in ye world will not prevail wth some people. We wonder at it, but ye reason is plain—they are of their Fath^r ye D—l, and his works they will, and must do.

All we have y^t is Good is fr. God—Absurd to be proud—I could no more make my self a Child of God, than a Child of Nature.

[p. 130.] The children of God are not distinguished fr. [others] by any External Works, wch an Hypocrite may do as well as a ch. of God—but by an Holy Life, Humility, Justice and Purity, Faith. X^{ns} have an Immortal seed in their Hearts—A man may suffer his crop to be spoil'd.

166. *2nd Series. Sins of Impurity.* To such as have had ye misfortune to fall into S. of Im.

They are first to be made sensible of their danger—That they [have] lost ye Fav^r of God—Hopes of Heavⁿ—Are under ye Gov. of ye Devil.

This concernes not only publick offenders, but all y^t know y^ms faulty in this way.

Consider w^t is required to a True Repentance.

The error of ye Ch. of Rome, wch we have laid aside, concerning Confession and Absolution, and w^t we retain—Mistakes people run into—I have left off ye Vice—I have done Penance—I will marry her w^m I have debauched.

You hope God will touch yor Heart—You do not consider y^t Sins of Impurity Blind ye Understanding, Stifle Conscience, Blot out all Good purposes, Grieve His Sp^t, Drive Him fr. Men, Leave you under the Governm^t of Satan—and yet you'll Hope y^t, &c.

Avoid Temptations—Tis a Sp^t y^t will return wth 7 oth^r Sp^{ts}. Upon a Tempt. flee immediately to God for Help—"O God, Arise, Help me and deliver me."

People think it very easy to break off Habits of this Vice —they'll be sadly mistaken.

The paines people take to hide these Vices, shews how shameful they are.

Such as w^d avoid falling into these Sins, must keep a strict watch over y^{m}s—Observe a very strict sobriety—Avoid Idleness—Pray Constantly. Filthy Talk—

W^d you know wheth^r yor sins of this kind are forgiven— Set before you ye Parable, "A certain Creditor," &c. If yor Sorrow make you Love God more, &c.

God will not so easily pardon these Sins [this sin], bec. of the Honest Remedy He has provided agst falling in it, and to prevent it.

How can a man make Reparation to a woman he has abused?

If young people will suffer y^{m}s to hear filthy words, they'll soon lose their modesty.

He y^t will not give Glory to God in openly acknowledging his Faults, will have no reason to Hope for pardon.

W^n you Come to dye, Then yor Conscience will set these things before you—You have been a Fornic., an Adult.—You have been ye Cause, it may be, of anoth^r body's Damnation. —You have by yor Example made other people think lightly of these Vices.—Gracious God, in w^t a Condition must that Soul be? You live in this sad state, tho' you do not see it till—

The Commonness of this Sin sh^d not make us slight it—it sh^d rath^r make us afraid, since corrupt nature is so apt to fall into it. It sh^d make us conclude, y^t all y^t do so are in ye Broad way.

Are you Angry y^t we preach agst Sins wch provoked God to punish y^m wth Fire and Brimstone—such Sins as will certainly, if not some way restrained, bring down Judgm.? W^d you have people treated as Worthy to Continue Members of X^{ts} Ch. who are manifestly ye Child^n of ye Devil? W^d you have us, by treating y^m wth fav^r, lead y^m into a Belief, that the Sin is small, their Repentance, the Way to Pardon, easy?

I do now testifye agst all such as have Sin'd and have not Repented—That their Repentance will not be accepted of

SUPPLE-
MENT. God, unless it bring forth fruits. Remember I tell you y^t Repentance and Conversion upon a Deathbed, &c.

All people live in y^t Sin wch they have not Repented of—tho' they are not actually guilty as formerly.

You do y^t very thing wch you dare not so much as think of, wch you dare not utter wth yor lips.

[p. 133.] You dare not (for Instance) say, "I will not believe one word of y^t worm y^t dyeth not and ye Fire y^t is never to be quenched, I will not Believe these things, tho' X^t has declared y^m to be so. I will go on, let w^t will follow. I'll go on, tho' Fire and Brimstone sh^d be my Portion—W^t signifys Eternity?" You dare not speak, but you'll Act, at this mad rate.

After all, you'll get nothing by braving it out in this World—By making yo^{r}self easy bec. you can hide it fr. men. A time is coming w^n God will bring to Light ye Hidden things of Darkness, w^n ye Stoutest, Stubbornest, Hardest Heart shall be made to tremble.

Prov. xxii. 14. "He y^t is abhorred of God, shall fall into these sins."—You were abhorr'd of God for yor oth^r Sins, before God gave you up to Uncleanness.

167. 1 *Cor.* xii. 25, &c. *If one Member suffer, &c.*

In ye Civil Governm^t, Inferior and Superior as Necessary as Head and Members in a Human Body—Tis our Interest as well as our Duty to endeav^r ye welfare of ye Society, and y^t every one sh^d be as happy as we wish to be.

That all men sh^d be good X^{ns}, good Neighbours.—That we sh^d be really affected wth ye Sins of oth^{rs}—We are all one Body—And if one Member Suffer—

"Every man for himself" is a wicked principle—utterly inconsistent wth the Sp^t of X^{nty}.

[p. 134.] The Happ^{ss} of any Society consists in this—That the Generality of its people are Wise and Good men, as ye Health of ye Body Naāl, &c.

Sin is of a Contagious Nature, it will not only increase by our Example, but by our Silence.

The more Sin increases, the nearer Destruction.

Evil Examples may corrupt yor child, yor servants, yor self, &c.

The designe of X^{ty} is to make us one Family, y^t we may

Love one anoth^r. How? "Thou shalt in any case reprove thy Broth^r."

Our own Happ^ss is bound up in the Welfare of ye Church.

A Seasonable Severity is very often Necessary to put a stop to growing vices, evil examples, &c.

Private people say tis not their business to reform ye World, and yet they will censure, oppose, and weaken ye Hands of those whose business it really is, and who must answer to God and to Society, if they do not.

We are Commanded—To "Exhort and Convince gainsayers"—To "warn y^m that [are] unruly," &c. Shall we obey God, or Fear man?

They y^t w^d Hinder ye Correcting of Vice, are no Friends to God or their Country.

168. Text, Prov. xiii. 12. "*There is a way y^t,*" &c. "*It is not in man that walketh to direct his steps.*"

Dr. Y., [Edw. Young?] *Wisdome of Believing*, and answer [p. 135.] to remarks on it.

Ps. lxxi. 12. "*So I gave y^m up to walk in the way of their—*"

Necessity of Revelation to free us fr. ye Mistakes of Naāl Relig^n.

"*I thank thee, O Father,*" [&c.]

Erasmus—*de Milite X^no.* [cap. iii. ?]

Prov. xxviii. 26. [*He that*] *Trusteth in his own heart is a Fool.* Dr. Barrow, vol. ix. 45, 6.

The designe of ye Sp^t of G^d in this S.S. To teach us y^t we are not able to chuse w^t is best for ourselves—y^t we may not with too much Confid. rely upon our own wisdom, but consult God's Word, and depend upon y^t, when our Reason, Passion, or Interest w^d perswade us to ye Contrary— For this is the meaning—There are ways of Reasoning, and of Living wch seem right, and men are satisfy'd wth y^m, and yet they are such as lead to destruction; i. e. Men are apt to be, and often are, deceived, w^n they least think so,—Ease, Humour, Pleasure, Interest, all combine to make y^m judge amiss. And sad and constant experience convinces us y^t men are often ruin'd, even where they have been most confident of their own Wisdome and Safety. And 'tis Happy for us that we know this, and very Happy if we mind it. [p. 136.]

W^n I know y^t I am apt to be mistaken—y^t my Reason is

SUPPLE-
MENT.
short—That my prejudices are many and great—My Temptations Strong—this will make me to close wth God's Word,
wch alone may be depended on, for a Rule to walk by, &c.

The way here meant is ye way of Worldly Wisdom, in
opposition to y^t of Faith.

See [*Bp. Gastrell's Christian Institutes,* or] *Sincere Word
of God,* p. 3; *Jurieu's* [?] *Devotions,* p. 22.

Whenever men choose to Govern y^ms, they are by ye Just
Judgm^t of God left to y^ms, and then they never fail to choose
w^t will hurt y^ms.

Men reason falsly w^n they Follow ye example of oth^rs as
blind as y^ms.

W^n they place Relig^n in things y^t do not make men
better, &c.

But why is he to be punished if he dos y^t wch he believes
to be right? Bec. he dos not follow his Reason, but his
Passions—Bec. God has given him anoth^r Rule wch he neglects—Bec. he neglects to ask for Gr. w^n he may [have?]
it for Asking, and wch w^d—

If Reason were Sufficient, why are Laws made to Restrain?
W^t one man thinks Reasonable, anoth^r thinks hard and unjust—The Commandment of God is exceeding broad; i. e.
it reaches to all.

[p. 137.] *Inference*—That you are liable to be deceived, will be no
excuse for Wickedness. The same Light wch discovers to
us our Condition shews us a Remedy.

Pride and Ambition, and Carnal knowledge, and Flattery
are grateful to Flesh and Blood—None of these will stand
a man in stead in ye day of Adversity.

The Lips of a Strange Woman drop as an Honey-comb—
but her end is bitter as Wormwood.

This is ye end of following Sense—w^thout Grace. Wisd.
ch. i. [16.] *" While they think to have a friend, &c."*

All ye world have had a Rule to walk by—The Gentiles
had Reason and Conscience—They w^d not mind this—Their
minds became dark—their lives polluted wth all manner of
Wickedness. Rom. i. The Jewes had a Law, this they perverted. X^ns have the Gospel, and they'll be Wiser than
God, they'll only have Reason to go by—

" W^n there was no K. in Israel."

Eccles. xi. 9. "*Walk in y*^{e} *Ways of thine Heart, &c.*" SUPPLEMENT. God's Word, not our wishes, ye Standard of Duty; otherwise, Right and Wrong w^d be just as People sh^d fancy, or find their Interest—"*Whatsoever ye w*^{d} *y*^{t} *men, &c.*"

"Tis only ye Vulgar y^t follow their Senses"—Pray don't ye men of Education do so too?—don't they follow evil [p. 138.] Customes, Passions, Prejudice, &c.? "I must have satisfaction for such an affront."

The Rules of ye Gospel will shew us w^t is already in us— That we have reason—but y^t we have corrupted it. The Gospel requires nothing but w^t is agreable to Reason freed from Error.

God punishes those wth a Judicial Darkness who will not make use of ye Light God affords y^m—Thus He dealt wth ye Jewes, &c.

God did not designe y^t men sh^d governe y^{m}s by their own Reason only—He therefore gave man a Law fr. ye first.

The Corruption of Hum. Nature—Degeneracy of ye world —Many Truthes lost once well known.

Uncertainty of Hum. Reasoning—Imperfect knowledge.

The H. Scr. gives us, not only Rules, but Examples, ye conduct of Providences, &c.

Inferences. No Reasoning—not an angel fr. Heaven to be followed contrary to Revelation.

"*How can ye, being evil, think y*^{t} *w*^{ch} *is good?*"—Corrupt ss. lives will ever be ye occasion of corrupt Reasoning.

"*Until I went unto the Sanctuary of God.*"—There he ss. found a Cure for his doubts, wch all his Reason could not resolve before.

Pool, Synops. in Loc., for a 3rd Conclusion °.

Custom—Prevails agst Reason in Infinit Instances.

Temporal Interest—Will make y^t seem reasonable to one [p. 139.] wch anoth^r abominates.

Pleasure, will blind ye Understanding.

A Profane Habit. Tis not Naāl to man to blaspheme ye God y^t made him.—How many do so.

Many call evil good, and good evil. Is. v. 20.

"I have sin'd, and w^t harm hath happened." Ecclus. v. 4.

° [Perhaps the great danger of God's leaving us to ourselves: for Pool's notes refer mostly to the *irony* of the text in Ecclesiastes.]

SUPPLE- The H. S. are given to supply ye defects of Reason, and to
MENT. secure us ag^st ye Corruption of Nature.

"*All ye ways of a man are right in his own eyes.*"

We look upon Riches, as able to make us Happy—The S.S. say they cannot—Experience finds this true—Men in Health value many things, wch Death shewes y^m to be vanity and vexation of Sp^t.

The S. tells them so before, but they'll not believe.

This shewes us y^t ye SS. are fr. God, who only Knows w^t is in man.

Why sh^d Riches got by Vanity be diminished? Why a man in possession of a Great Estate got by Injustice sh^d not leave it to late posterity,—Reason will not be able to answer such Questions as these.

Circumstances often make people judge differently; w^n a man y^t is Injured has justice done him, he sees very easily ye Advantage of Governm^t, and confesses it. At another time—

[p. 140.] How readily was a Levelling Principle embraced by ye lesser People, who thought they had as good a Title to ye good things of ye world, &c.

Inference.—No man sh^d go into ye world w^thout praying for God's direction.

The folly and the Danger of Questioning any thing wch God has revealed.

If He has threatend Sinners, y^t will come to pass.

How dangerous to make Experiments ag^st SS.

{ The Provision God has made for our Security—The H. Scr.—*A Light unto our Feet*—His H. Sp^t—*This is ye way, walk ye in it.*—Governm^t to restrain men fr. their ruin.

If once we are convinced, That we are liable to be deceived; That we often are so; That we love to deceive our selves; We sh^d then be prepard to Hear w^t God in His H. Word has [said].

"*He gave y^m up to a Repr. Mind.*" Rom. i. 28. They w^d not be Governd by Reason—God "*gave y^m therefore up to follow their own Hearts' Lusts*," the greatest Judgm^t y^t could befall y^m.

We must not blame God w^n we fall into error. He has

given us a Rule—we neglect it, are made miserable by doing so, and complain.

Tis agreed y^t an Universal Liberty for every man to do w^t is right in his own eyes, w^d ruin us all—Who must give y^m Laws? Must every man be a Law to himself? and a Judge for himself and oth^{rs}? Must ye Voice of Nature determine? W^n shall we all agree w^t that is? In short, w^n all Expedients have been tryed (as all have been), we shall find —That God only can set bounds and Lawes, &c., for He only knows our Nature, and w^t will hurt us. [p. 141.]

The Ch. of Laodicea received a severe check—She s^d she was rich, &c. Is not this ye case of an Infinit number of X^{ns}, who see not their wants, &c.? If men were left entirely to y^{m}s, they w^d naally aim at Power, Riches, &c.; these w^d as naaly make y^m Proud, Insolent, Hated, &c.

There are People y^t will be Rich at any rate, be Unjust, Oppress their Neighbours, Take all Advantage. This seemes Right to y^m—They dont believe w^t God saith on this Head.

If a man is very Rich, he'll be apt to be very easy, very secure, Fear nothing, &c.—"*Thou Fool, this night*"—"*Riches profit not in ye day of wrath.*"

"*Are not Abana and Pharpar,*" &c. So it appeared to him. Prov. xxiii. 4. "*Cease fr. thy own wisdome.*" ss. ss., ss.

"*Slothfulness casteth into a deep sleep*"—And yet men think they have a Right to indulge y^{m}s, if they need not Lab^r. ss.

Twas thus Saul Reasoned, and he thought it was right, w^n he disobey'd God, and lost his Crown.

Is Reason then of no use? Yes, sure—It bids us depend on God. [p. 142.]

The designe of this disc. is to shew ye Dang^r of Governing our Faith or Manners by Mistaken Rules and Maximes—Evil Customes, Examples of Great Men—Inclination of Corrupt Nature.

That people may abuse ye Light of Reason and Nature, St. Paul assures us, and gives sad Instances of it—"*God shall send y^m strong Delusion y^t they shall believe a lye.*" 2 Thess. ii. 11.

Conclusion. You will perceive w^t I have been aiming at— To convince you and myself—That "*it is not in man y^t walketh, &c. [to direct his steps]*"—That we may, as poor bewilder'd people sh^d do, Seek to God for Light—be thankful

SUPPLE-MENT.

for it—not to be wise above what is written—to depend entirely on God for Light and power.

A Formal Religⁿ seemes Right,—Here men set up their Rest, Fear no Evil, and [are] yet in ye way [to Evil].

Placette, 248, 249.

Luk. xi. 34. My Bible, [with MSS. notes by Bp. Wilson; now in the Bodl. Lib.]

See Educat. of a Prince, [by Ramsay?] 117. That whole discourse.

[p. 143.] 169. Tinwald^p. *"Ye shall not Fear ye Face of man. For, &c. [the Judgment is God's."* Deut. i. 17.]

Amos v. 10.	Ps. lxxxii. 1. *"God standeth in the Congregation of ye Mighty. He is a Judge among ye Gods;"* i. e. Over those y^t are His Representatives upon Earth.
Is. xxix. 21.	
	Jam. iv. 12. *"There is one Lawgiver, who is able—"*
Sons of God.	Jam. iii. 6. *Where Envying and Strife is—There is confusion and every evil work.*
Of Magistrate.	The Great Sanhedrim (ye great Court of ye Jewes) sat in ye room Gazith, looking towards ye Holy of Holys, where was ye Presence of God^q. This was no doubt the reason why your Pious Ancestors Contrived to have yor Tinwald and a House of God so near one anoth^r.

Educat. of a Prince. 140.

They y^t put ye Laws in Execution sh^d be exceeding Careful to Administer Justice wthout partiality.

If ye Judgm^t is God's, we must be obedient, not only for Wrath, but Conscience' sake; i. e. Magistrates w^d not dare to oppress, tho' they have it in their Power—And ye Subject w^d not dare to rebell, were they sure to get ye better.

It is not our business, properly speaking, to deal in Civil matters, unless as Subjects ye Laws have devolved it upon us. But this is our charge, and we have ye same Authority as Princes and Govern^{rs} have in the way of their duties :

[p. 144.] To put you always in mind—That you are Account^{ble} to God.

That in all you do you ought to have regard to His Laws in the first place.

^p [1704, 1709, 1712. He preached in 1725 on the same text, but not quite the same Sermon. See Serm. lii., vol. iii. p. 1, above.]

^q [Lewis, Origines Hebrææ, b. i. ch. vi.]

That where He has left you to Reason, you ought to be very careful not to pervert Justice—*For ye Judg^{nt},* [&c.]

That that is Justice, which God Himself w^d declare, were He on ye Bench.

There is no power but of God. Rom. xiii. 1. To Him all oth^r Powers are Accountable.

For ye Good of Mankind He has given some, Power over ye Bodys, Goods, Estates, Lives of oth^{rs}—wch God, ye Auth^r of Life and Death, has given y^m.

But then, lest any man finding himself vested wth so much Power, sh^d be tempted to Abuse it, all nations (almost) have agreed to have Laws to restrain and to direct y^m—If they judge according to those Laws, that is God's Judgm^t.

Both ye Magistrate and People answerable to God—The one, if he makes not ye Law his Rule, and ye oth^r, if he Lives not in all dutiful Obedience.

2 Chron. xix. 6. *"Take Heed w^t ye do—For ye Judge not for man, but for ye Lord,"* &c. i. e. Let ye Judgment you give be worthy of God—let not ye Smiles nor the Frownes, the Hopes nor the Feares of any worldly Good or Evil prevail to Biass you—only Fear Him who is able to save and to destroy. Make no man's will yor Law—he's but a M.—*ye Judgm^t is God's*—He cannot deliver you in ye day of wrath.

Whenever [men] forget this—That ye Judgm^t is God's, and y^t to Him they are accountable,—

Interest will prevail wth y^m,—Friendship will gain upon y^m, —Passion will hurry y^m into Error,—Bribes will blind their eyes,—W^t ye world will say will influence y^m.

But if a man Considers himself as in ye Place of God— Answerable to Him for any wrong he does—

I set God always before me—That he might do nothing unworthy of God.

The great end of Civil Gov^{nt} is to secure ye Hon^r of God, by being a Terror to evil doers, and an Encouragm^t to those y^t do well.

Every Magistrate (wheth^r Eccl. or Civil) stands Charg'd wth this—To Promote, to Consult, to Countenance, &c., ye Hon^r of God, and the Cause of Religion—Bec. they claim Obedience, not by any right of their own, but as they Judge for God.

SUPPLE-
MENT.

There is neith^r Wisdome, nor Understanding, nor Counsel agst ye Lord.—God will soon shew y^m their Mistakes, who think to Rule wthout Him.

Laws always do, or sh^d speak ye same Thing, to ye Poor and Rich—To Friends and Enemys. It was for this reason y^t ye wise Heathens pictured *Justice* with a vail over her Face—That she might not consider ye person, but ye Cause of, &c.

Laws made, That Judges, as well as People, might have a Rule to go by; and y^t Obedience may be more cheerful, w^n they y^t give ye Law shew y^t they are y^{m}s Governd by Laws.

General Rules for ye Direct^n of Magistrates where ye Law is silent.

That all men are equally men, and have a right to be treated as men, with Justice and Charity.

That no man ought to be Judge in his own Cause—bec. all men are subj. to error and prejudice.

That we are all Members of one Body, in [?] Society— and if one, &c. [1Cor. xii. 26.] *Whatever ye w^d y^t men, &c.*

That no man be Condemned Unheard.

That no Advantage be taken of men's Weakness, Inadvertency, Poverty, or want of Help.

[p. 146.] *Rules of Charity.* That we sh^d always believe ye best where ye Contrary is not Manifest.

We sh^d punish wth Compassion, w^n we are forced to—

Magistrates sh^d consider, That they are in ye Place of a Judge, Who is Infinitly *Just, Holy,* and *Good*—They sh^d endeav^r to be so, or they Dishon^r Him for w^m they Act. And for ye encouragem^t of Faithful Judges, &c., He can sufficiently Reward His Faithful ministers, He can Protect y^m agst, &c.

He can also punish those y^t betray—So y^t neith^r ye Hopes or Feares of those above y^m, nor ye unjust clamors of those belowe y^m, may be able to shake y^m, &c.

Fear not ye Face of man, for, &c. Shall ye Feet say to ye Head? [*&c.*] *He y^t resisteth, Resisteth not man, but God.*

Concl. And may there ever be found in this place a set of Magistrates, Civil and Eccl., who shall concur in such things as shall promote the Hon^r of God, and the Good of this Place.

170. 1704. *Except ye Lord build ye House.* The very Heathens made this Observation, *Dei ope et auxilio multo magis Remp. Romanam quam Ratione Hominum et consilio Gubernari* ^r.

Tis 150 years ago since Mr. Camden ^s said of the People of this Isle, y^t they Hated thieving and Lying—is it so now? where is it found? Will a magistrate say—That ye Judgm^t is God's, w^n he countenances Sins, Injustice, Fraud, Litigiousness, Robbing God of His Tythes, Countenancing a Rich or a Poor man in his Cause,—both wch are equally forbidden,—w^n those y^t w^d punish vice meet wth discouragem^t?

He must be a Son of Belial y^t can be pleased wth the misfortunes of oth^rs—But to spare Vice out of pity, &c. These are "ye tender mercys of wicked men," and are " cruel ^t." Tis to desire y^t our Friends may be easy here, tho' they sh^d be Damned hereafter.

The Judgm^t of God is—That wickedness be punished, that Sin be made Uneasy to men, that they sh^d be made to take shame to y^ms who fear'd not to sin ag^st God.

Thou y^t Judgest anoth^r and dost ye same thing.

" Thou y^t sh^dst punish a man for," &c.

To keep ye wicked fr. doing mischief to ye Society—Josh. xxii. 20. *Did not Achan commit a Trespass, and wrath fell on ye whole Congregation?* Sins of Privat men, not punished, bring down Judgments upon ye whole nation.

To be remiss in punishing offenders—It is ye Interest of all, to Discountenance and Punish Vice.

By this ye Judgm. of God may be turned away—This ye best for offenders y^ms.

We wish y^t our children may not have evil Ex.

Tis for want of Piety, Courage, and Honesty y^t Vice is so triumphant—This Drunkard may debauch my Son or my

---

^r [The Editor has not succeeded in verifying this passage. There is a well-known one to the same effect in Cic. *De Harusp. Respons.*, § 9.

^s [Rather Bishop Merrick, in a letter to Camden. *Britannia*, ed. Gibson, col. 1052. "Stealing, and begging from door to door, is universally detested." Merrick was Bishop from 1576 to 1599. Camden's work came out first in 1586.]

^t [Prov. xii. 10.]

SUPPLE-
MENT.
Friend—This Fornicator may, &c.—This Unjust man, this Knave, w^m I now fav^r or countenance, connive at his villany, may hereafter cheat my Heir. Some are wicked for want of consideration, some bec. of multitude of evil examples; many take evil ways bec. of Countenance of great men, or negligence of Magistrates, and some in Hopes of baffling Authority.

[p. 149.] A Magistrate who Feares God, will accept no man's person, Court no man's Fav^r, Fear no man's Face.

To see a Magistrate profane, who is to punish others for being so—To see a man make light of an Oath, who expects y^t such as come before him for Justice sh^d stand in Fear of Him by w^m they swear [&c.]

To take care of growing Vices,—To root y^m out betimes, lest they become too many to be cured by ye Eccl. or Civil Magistrate, or any Power but y^t of God's Judgm^{nts}, wch certainly will come, w^n eithe^r ye magistrate cannot, or will not do his duty, [&c.]

That we all who have a share in the Governm^t of this Church and State, may truly and Indifferently minister Justice to ye Punishment of Wickedness and Vice and to ye maintenance of true Relig^n and Virtue [&c.] Amos v. 10, Is. xxix. 24.

171. *Restitution.* I have purposely avoided such cases as are commonly put, ab^t Restitution, bec. I w^d encourage all people y^t have Scruples of Conscience on y^t Acc^t to go to their Pastors, who can best advise y^m, Direct, and Comfort y^m.

If a man dos all he can towards undoing his sin—

The Heart, from whence ye Sin proceeded, must first be cured of its corruption, be made sensible of ye guilt, &c.

What a man is bound in Conscience to do, not w^t ye law will oblige him to do.

Rest. a Condition of our Pardon fr. God.

What hinders the Practice of this Duty?—A False Shame—A covetous Temper—A False Hope y^t it is not necessary.

[p. 150.] Method of making R. Proportionable to ye Damage—This will oblige me to prefer a Poor man's less debt to a greater of a Rich man, bec. ye Poor man's little loss may affect him more. Let the Necessity of Restit. be ever present wth us all, to hinder us fr. doing, fr. speaking, wrong.

Zech. v. 4. *The curse shall enter into ye House of ye Thief, and it shall consume it, wth ye Timber and ye Stones.* Ezek. xxxiii. 15. *If ye wicked give ag^n y^t wch he hath robbed, he shall live, &c.* Lev. vi. 1, 2, 3, 4, 5. The Laws of wrong and Restitution—Twill not be sufficient to say, "Let those look to it, who did ye wrong"—But he must look to it who is a gainer by ye Injustice.

Tis Astonishing to see people easy under ye Guilt of this sin—as if 'twere nothing.

It must be known to be a Sin, by every body, because every body calls for Satisfaction w^n injured.

They y^t think y^t Repent. consists only in asking God's Pardon, don't consider.

Let not ye Good Patriarch's [u] Advice be slighted, he knew his Interest as well as any of us.

God dos not require Impossibilities. [He does require] a desire to do every man Justice—Doing w^t is in our Power.

☞ Heads—
1. What Restitution is.
2. That tis necessary to Salvation, not to be dispensed wth.
3. In w^t cases to be made.

How little of X^{ty} have they who must be compelled to do Right to their Neighb^r? X^{ty} obliges us, even where my Neighb. knows not y^t I have wronged him. [p. 151.]

W^t ye Law w^d oblige me to, y^t Conscience will, &c.

Remedy agst Injustice—Pray God to bless ye work you—

Let every man free his Conscience fr. a Burthen, &c. Restit. and Asking Forg. proofs of a sincere Repent. A cursed Proverb—Happy is ye child, &c.

What shall it profit a man, &c. People are too apt to make nothing of words, and a man may be injured in his good Name, more than in his Goods, and Rest. must be made. Better children sh^d be left to starve, than to be left wth goods wch will corrupt their very morals. Trust y^r childr. wth God.

Hindrances. A false opinion y^t we want more than indeed we do—A too great fondness for our childr.—An Unjust

---
[u] [Perhaps Jacob. See Gen. xliii. 12.]

SUPPLE-
MENT.

Compliance wth ye vanity of ye world wch makes more necessary than really is so.

He y^t has made Restitution to ye best of his power may enjoy w^t he has left wth Peace—Eat his bread with cheerfulness—and leave w^t he has wth God's blessing to his children.

[p. 152.]   *Debts.* A man who sincerely desires to pay his just debts, will deny himself some conveniences of Life, rath^r than oth^r people sh^d want w^t is their own.

If Theeves are of ye number of those who must not enter, we sh^d beware of such Sins as come any way near that vice.

The same justice wch obliges me to restore w^t I have borrow'd, will oblige me to make Rest. of y^t wch is anoth^r man's.

Heires and Executors will be more unwilling to make Restitution, tho' never so earnestly desired—therefore ye best way [is] to do it one's self. Tis better to go to Heaven wth a little, wth one eye, one hand, &c., than go to Hell with Covetousness—in *Complaint of a Sinner.* See pag. 155.

176. *Prayers. Remove this Cup—Not My Will, but Thine be done*—This our Pattern. Lay yor desires before ye Th. of Gr.—such Pet. as are lawful:—Then submit y^m to God's Will.

177. *Lord's Supper.* Br. and Wine Commem. Sacrifice of X^ts Death past, as ye Paschal L. was of His Death to come.   187.

178. *Account of X^ty.* It dos most effectually promote virtue and restrain vice.

It lays restraints upon ye very Thoughts, fr. wch all vice proceedes—It secures the Peace of Familys and Kingdoms—It commands w^t is good, and gives Assistance—H. Sp^t:—It provides a Remedy for Miscarriages—Repentance:—It has proper Hopes and Feares, to hinder Negligence and Back[sliding]. It brings us ye Readiest way to ye Knowledge of Truth. *He y^t will do His will, &c.*

179. *Two Covenants.* Man created after ye Image of God, was to Govern Himself by the Law of Nature—He Fell, and was not able to Observe y^t Law.—That Law could not possibly be changed—viz. Piety towards God, Justice towards men, &c., must always be Dutys, they cannot but be so.

God in mercy therefore granted a New Law, TheCovent SUPPLE-
of Grace—By wch He accepts of Repentance, &c. MENT.

God's Designe in this New Cov^ent is to bring man back to ye Image wch he has Lost—That he may be qualify'd for Happ^ss, wch he cannot possibly be w^thout being Regenerated.

To bring this ab^t—He sent His Son into ye world to declare His Readiness to Forgive men upon their Repent- [p. 154.] ance and Returning to their Duty.

To shew y^m that it is possible by the Divine Gr. to do w^t God expects—He did this in our Nature.

He died for us, and procured our Pardon and ye H. Gh. He gave us a Rule, ye Gospel, containing God's Displeasure ag^st Sin, His Grace, and our Duty.

They y^t will not Receive this shall be Damned. Mar. xvi. 16. And even they that Hold ye Truth in Unrighteousness.

But if we Believe ye Gospel and Live accordingly, we shall be made Etern. Happy.

The Decalogue is a Copy of ye Law of Nature, Com[mand-ing] w^t is in its own Nature Good, and Forbid[ding] Evil.

So y^t ye Designe of the Gospel is to Recover man to a State of Perfection, by Outward Meanes and Inward Aides—By rooting out original Sin. And so much is every man Restored to God's Image, as he gets ye mastery of his corruptions.

180. *Fear.* Job xxxi. 23. *Destruction from God was a Terror*—Tho' I could get over all other considerations, I could not think of God's Anger and be easy.

Worldly Restraints of very little force to keep men from Wick^ss—But ye Dread of Him who can destroy, ye weight of His Arm, &c.

And indeed ye Corruption of our Hearts is such y^t nothing but this Fear can conquer it.

This Fear, however, very consistent wth Peace of Conscience. [p. 155.]

181. *Religious Melancholy*, (pp. 26, 107). If you did not Love and Fear God, you w^d not be Uneasy y^t you have offended Him. And if God had not Loved you, you could not Love Him. (Pag. 228.)

182. *Restitution, Confession.* Ps. xxxvii. 21. *The Wicked borroweth.* W^n we come to perform either of these Dutys, we shall then see how shameful Sin is. W^d it not be better to think of this before we commit y^m? (P. 169.)

594   MAXIMS OF PIETY AND MORALITY.

SUPPLE-   183. *I Thank Thee, O Fath^r. The Gr^t Oracle*, 672. The
MENT.   Wisdom of ye World is so far fr. teaching us our duty, y^t it
is y^t wch still renders y^e × of Ch^t of none effect.

184. *Custome.* W^t is it but C. and ill example y^t makes
Modest Women imitate ye Habits y^t were Invented by y^e
Unchaste in order to beguile ye simple. *Educat. of a
Prince*, 174, &c.

185. *Visiting ye Sick.* If a man going to give an Acc^t to
[p. 156.] his Judge sh^d give this Answer—" I did not know that this
was my Condition—That I was to answer for these things—
I w^d have made all ye Satisfact^n and Restit. in my power, if
I had known it so necessary a Duty—I w^d have made my
Peace and dyed in Charity wth [&c.]—I w^d have bewayled
my careless mispent Life, and warned oth^{rs} fr. following my
example—I w^d have done some good wth the Unrighteous
Mammon I have left—My Past^r did not deal truly wth me;
he only Pray'd for me, and bid me Hope in God's Mercy,
but never search'd into ye disorders of my Soul." [*Scupoli's*]
Spirit. Combat. 164; *Ench. Precum.* [8vo. Lond. 1707,] 290;
Spirit. Academ. [*Rous's Heavenly Academie*,] 628, 629.

186. *Ministry.* 2 Cor. iv. 7. *We have this Treasure in
Earthen Vessels, that y^e, &c.*; i.e. God magnifyes His Power
and Glory in making use of weak men and weak instruments, to destroy so powerful an Adversary as ye Devil; and
to pull down a kingd. supported by Men and Devils. 159.

187. *Thou shalt Love thy Neighbour, &c.* (*Indian Catechism*, [*Dial.* 16]). He that w^d take ye most effectual way
[p. 157.] to Teach the Dutys of X^{ty} must follow X^{ts} method. He must
endeav^r to possess men's Hearts wth a Principle wch will lead
y^m to all dutys. *Rouse*, [*Heavenly Academie*, B. v.] 630.

188. *True way of Preaching to Purpose.* (*Indian Catechism.*)
To shew men their Corruption, their Weakness, and their
Danger—That they may lay hold of ye Grace offer'd y^m.

Thus ye Apostles First Convinced their Hearers—That
neither ye Law of Nature, nor ye L. of Mos., nor even a
state of Innocence, was secure wthout ye Grace of God.
The Jewes had an Holy Law, and yet they were become a wicked People. The Gentiles, notwithstanding all
the Improvements of Reason they boasted of, were fallen
into ye most monstrous sins. J. X^t came into ye world then,

w^n all might have been convinced y^t the Condition of man stood in need of some furth^r Help, besides Free-will, Reason, Philosophy, &c.

189. *Law.* All Mankind are under one of these three Laws:—

1. The Law of Sin; all y^t commit being slaves to it.
2. The Law of y^e Letter—who abstain fr. Sin for fear of Punishm^t.
3. The L. of y^e Sp^t, under wch there is perfect Liberty. *Cudworth, L$^{d's}$ Supper,* 177 ^{x}.

190. *My K. not of this world.* See *Men's Prejudices,* 143, 144.

191. *My Peace I give—not, &c.* *Ditton on y^e Resurr.*, [p. 158.] p. 15 ^{y}.

192. *And his Heart fretteth.* *Young's Serm.*, vol. i. 364, 365.

193. *Spendthrift.* You greatly mistake if you think y^t you may do what you will wth yor own. If it was left you, it was left you in trust, and wth an intent y^t you sh^d leave it posterity, unless by some stroke of Providence, wthout yor fault, you are forc'd to part wth it, or any part of it. You are bound in conscience, and you are answerable to God if you do not, to leave it to posterity, as much as to restore a Sum of money, given you to keep for anoth^r.

194. *Repentance not to be rep. of.* When a Man remembers his sin wth detestation, &c.

195. *Repentance.* He y^t rep. of any sin, must rep. of all y^t attend it. Of Adult., for instance, he must rep. of Uncleanness, Wrong to his Neighb^r, Breach of his own Vowes, tempting anoth^r to Sin, it may be to Damn. (181.)

196. *Sins Unpardonable.* When ye Fath^{rs} speak of such, they only meant that ye Ch. did not grant y^m Absolution, not y^t God w^d not pardon y^m. Therfore they always exhorted even such to rep. *Unum Necessar.*, 486 ^{z}. [p. 159.]

197. *Composing differences.* (*Pastoralia.*) He y^t considers his own offences agst his neighbour, wch yet he hopes

---

^{x} [Rather Serm. ii. subjoined to that discourse, and to *Intellectual System,* &c., iv. 384. London, 1820.]

^{y} [In which he shews that "the peace of wise men" can only be had by faith in the Resurrection, and contrasts it with the "mechanical tranquillity" of the world. Lond. 8vo., 1712.

^{z} [By Bp. Taylor, c. ix. § iii. n. 2°, 23.]

God will forgive him, will be prevailed on to hearken to reason, &c.

198. *The Head cannot say to ye Feet, &c.* Charity. A love for God and man being so necessary to Salv., God has so ordered it, y^t as we all depend on Him, and so ought to love Him, so we shall all depend one on anoth^r. The Clergy depend on the Layty for their subsistence—the Layty on y^m for their Pray^rs and Blessing—the poor depend on ye Rich for a share of their plenty, and the Rich on y^m for their Lab^r. Gosp., 8th Sund. after Trin.[a]

199. *Preists, Ambassadors.* Not to be despised bec. they don't appear in grandeur. J. X^t did not do so. He y^t despises a Clergyman for being poor, w^d have done ye same to X^t. If they are Rich, then they say they are proud—if Poor, they are to be despised.

200. *A short Acc^t of ye X^n Religion.* (See back, 75.) Epiphany. Jo. xiv. 22; 2 Cor. v.

Man was made perfect, and God required of him Perf. Obedience.

Upon his transgression, the Law of Perf. Obed. remained in force; and the Dutys of N͞aal Relig^n Unalterable—viz. it must ever be a Duty to Hon^r God, and Love our Neighbour, &c.

Now Man's Powers being lessened and his Duty still the same, he must needs be in Bondage;—to know and allow w^t is good, and not to be able to do it, and to fear the consequence.

He saw y^t he could not be justify'd by Unsinning Obedience—and the Laws whether of Nature or of Moses had no Reservations for Pardon upon Repentance.

This made men Fearful, Humble, Afflicted, Weary and Heavy laden—and this disposed all y^t were so, for Receiving the Gospel w^h gladness w^n it was first published.

The meaning of ye word *Gospel* is, *Good Newes*—or *Glad Tidings;*—you see it must be so to all thoughtful People—its design being to free us fr. those Feares wch we must labour under till we know for certain how God will deal with us, as we are sinners.

---

[a] [? some mistake in this reference.]

Now the Great Blessing of the Gospel appeares in *this*, that it instructs us how, at ye Day of Judgment, we may escape the Punishment due to our sins—and how we may be found in God's Fav^r, and Receive that Blessing wch His Son shall then pronounce—*Come*, &c.

[Supplement. [p. 161.]]

The G., I say, puts us in a way of being secure of this Blessing.

First; by making known to us, y^t God, for His Son's sake, has enter'd into a *New Covenant* wth man. By wch Cov^t He has promised to accept of our Repent.—to Receive us into Fav^r—to assist us wth Helps sufficient to do our Duty.—And wch is an astonishing Fav^r, He will make us Eternally Happy w^n we dye—Provided we suffer ourselves to be Governed by His H. Sp. while we Live.

Secondly. The Gosp. puts us in a way of Happ^ss. By giving us Rules, and directing us to such meanes, as are necessary and sufficient to carry us thro' all difficultys wch we can possibly meet wth in our way to Heaven. But that we may be more sensible of ye Blessing of X^ty, let us take a view of our Condition by Nature, and w^t it w^d end in.

We are born of sinful Parents—we have been in Rebellion ag^st God ever since we could break His Laws—His Laws have been grievous to us—we have taken a Pleasure in doing ye very thing He has forbidden us. In short—our own Cons. bear witness ag^st us, y^t we have not done what we know we ought to have done. [p. 162.]

We must not believe that it was always thus wth man. And we see for certain, y^t he w^d be a much better creature, if he could command his appetites—if he could wth pleasure obey his Maker—if he could always see w^t was best for him, and follow y^t wch he approves to be best. Why, just so it was wth our First Parents before the Fall. For he and everything els was created in ye very best manner. Every thing was *very good*—as good as it could be in its kind. And particularly man was created *in Righteouss^ss and True Holyness*—Able to obey any Law wch God, for his tryal, sh^d give him.

It is not so with us now—we see and we feel it otherwise—we cannot but confess y^t we are in a State of Rebellion ag^st God—ag^st an Holy, Just, and Powerful God—who therefore must be highly displeased to see His Laws broken

SUPPLE-
MENT.

[p. 163.]

by His creatures, that know His Will, and His Power, and yet go on to offend Him.

This is the condition we are in by nature, from wch it plainly appears, y^t no man Living can be Justify'd before God, If God in mercy had not found a way to restore us to His Fav^r—By accepting our Repentance, and giving us greater assistance and Power than we have by Nature.

This is the Designe of ye Gosp., to make known to us God's will and purpose, and Gracious Intention to Receive us into Fav^r—Upon condition y^t we thankfully embrace this offer—Forsake every evil way, and strive to please Him, as far as we are able by the assistance He shall give us.

So y^t there is a New Covenant, a *Coven^t of Gr.*, suited to ye Frailty of our condition.

But how shall we be assur'd y^t God will accept of our Repentance—Receive us into Fav^r—and assist us powerfully to do His Will?

Why to give us ye Utmost Assurance of this, His Bl. Son came down fr. H.—Took our Nature upon Him—made known to us w^t w^d please G.—w^t is necessary to fit us for Heav^n and Happ^{ss}—and w^h Things they are wch will shut us out of Heaven.

[p. 164.]

Particularly He assur'd us—That it is no great Matter what our Lot is in this world, provided we can secure God's Fav^r—For y^t this is a very short Life, and only a Passage to a Life y^t is to last for ever.

To convince us more effectually of this—He made choice of a very poor Life Himself—was very easy and content wth any thing y^t ye Prov. of God afforded Him.

That men may not think it indifferent whether they close wth this New Coven^t or not—He has made known to y^m this Important Truth, wch before they knew little of—That after this Life is ended, we shall all be adjudged to an everlasting Life of Happ^{ss} or Mis.—According as we have kept or broken this New Cov^t.

And most effectually to convince us of ye Truth and Importance of these things—After He had wrought infinit Miracles for Confirmation of this Truth—That He came fr. God—He laid down His Life and seal'd this Covenant wth His own Blood. And God to assure us y^t w^t He had said was true, and that w^t He had done was accepted by Him—God therefore Rais'd Him fr. ye Dead—Rec^d Him up into Heaven—And sent down ye H. G. to be wth His faithful servants unto ye end of ye world—To assist our weakness—To Renue our Nature, and by *that* to fit us for Heav^n.

Thus you see how matters stand wth us—Man was created Holy—while he continued so, God was well pleased with him—After he fell, and became unfit for Heaven, God had however compassion on him—Entered into a New Covent^t wth him. The Designe of this New Cov. is to restore man to that Holy Temper, y^t he may be fit and capable of y^t Happ^{ss} in Heaven for wch he was first created. [p. 165.]

In this Cov^{nt} God has had a merciful Regard to all our weaknesses. The most Ignorant may know w^t God expects fr. them—The greatest Sinner may be sure of Pardon if he truly Repents—The weakest X^n may depend upon all needful assistance—The meanest servant of X^t is certain not to be overlook'd. Lastly, every X^n may be assur'd y^t his Lab^r will not be in vain; That he will be for ever happy, if it is not his own fault altogether.

And now, X^{ns}, you see why ye Gospel is called a *Covenant of Grace;* It is of God's mere goodness y^t He will accept of our Repentance—That He sent His Son to teach us our Duty, and to Lay down His Life for us—That He sends His Holy Sp^t to assist, and even to strive wth us, to make us Holy, y^t we may be Happy—and that after all He will make us poor creatures, Dust and Ashes, equall to, and Happy as, the Angels in Heaven.

You see the Reason why J. X^t has commanded us to deny our selves—Not to do many things wch we are fond of—To take up ye Cross, &c.—Tis to wean us fr. this world, and make us set our hearts upon the next. In short, These things are commanded us for our good—and to secure us in ye way to, and fit us for, Heaven. [p. 166.]

In one word, nothing but ye Gospel—embracing and following the Rules of the Gosp., can give mankind any real satisfaction, any real comfort.

Life and Death is set before us. We may put ye thoughts of y^m from us—But whether we mind y^m or not—one or ye oth^r must be our portion.

SUPPLE-
MENT.

201. *Discipline.* Gal. vi. 1. *If a man be overtaken, &c.*

202. *Lent.* Ps. cxxvi. *They y^t sow in Tears*—To press a serious Temper.

203. *Charity Sermon.* 2 Cor. viii. 8, 24. *Shew y^e to y^m and before ye churches, the Proof of yor Love.* 2 Cor. ix. 13; Phil. iv. 17; Deut. xv. 11. *Osterwald* on 2 Cor. viii.

204. *Lord's Supper. Labour not for ye Bread y^t perisheth, but for y^t bread wch endureth for ever.*

[p. 167.] 205. *Swear Falsly.* Paral. Text, Lev. xix. 12.

206. *Easter.* "*This day shalt thou be wth Me in P.*" Misery and Happ^{ss} not so far off as people are apt to imagin and perswade y^{m}s.

207. *Disputes.* "*This is ye will of God, y^t wth well doing ye may put to silence ye ignorance of Foolish men* ^{c}."

208. *Propagat^n of Gosp. abroad.* Amos vi. 1. "*Wo to y^m y^t are at ease in Zion.*" Blair, [*Sermons,* 8vo. Lond. 1722,] vol. ii. p. 47.

209. *Two Kingdomes of X^t and Satan.* 2 Cor. xi. [? iv.] 3, 4. *In w^m the God of this world, the Prince of the Power of ye Air, y^t now Ruleth, &c.*

210. *Holy Scriptures.* (Dr. Nich. [W. Nichols] on xix. Ps.) Jo. viii. 47, *He y^t is of God Heareth God's Word, &c., therfore*—All y^t Love God will be glad to know what will please G^d. *What shall I do y^t I may inherit Et. Life?*

The answer is plain—*How readest Thou?*

Whoever will do His will. Jo. vii. 17; 2 Cor. iv. 3, 4. *If our Gospel be hid,* be not understood, &c.

Rom. vi. 7. *The Form of sound words.*

These are ye words of J. X^t ye Son of God—Pray consider their meaning, and How much they concern us.

"He y^t is of God" (belongeth to God)—"Heareth," i. e. Takes delight in Hearing, "God's Word" and will—and he

[p. 168.] y^t dos not do so dos not belong to God.

"To the Law and to ye Proph" ["testimony"]. You see it is not as we imagine, or conclude, or Hope for, or Fancy —But God's Word,—wch is ye Standard of Duty.

Right and Wrong is to be Judg'd of by ye Word—W^n

---

^{b} [This and the nine following entries have ("Txt") prefixed to them in the MS., being plainly memoranda for sermons.] ^{c} [1 St. Pet. ii. 15.]

People forget y^t they have a Rule to walk by, it is then they run into endless errors.

We were never designed by God to Govern our selves. Experience shews y^t we are not able.—We sh^d not know half ye Things y^t concern us, if G. had not Revealed y^m to us.

"Riches got by Vanity^d," &c. A Person in Possession of a gr^t Est. got by Injustice, &c. That ye 3^d and 4th Gener. may feel ye effects of my sin—That Sin will find us out, tho' never so secretly committed—" Cast thy bread upon ye waters," &c. Eccl. xi. 1. Who could say these things, but He who brings y^m to pass?

Human Reason and Policy w^d teach us anoth^r way of increasing our Riches.

God only knows w^t is safe and good for us—w^t will Hurt and Ruin us.

With^t God's word we know not our own ailments—our own Weaknesses, nor our Dang^{rs}—nor our Enemies—nor w^t will become of us w^n we dye.

Advantages we have by God's Word—a Light unto our Feet—We shall not depend on our own Judgm^t where God's Word says, &c. We shall not so much as wish y^t things were otherways y^n He has declared.

[From p. 168 to p. 225 is wanting in the MS.]

211. [*Existence of the Devil.*] . . their Master's work, who is [p. 225.] the Devil. And therfore that evil Sp^t (lest that thought sh^d startle men) has put it into the Hearts and Mouths of as many of his servants as he can seduce so far, to deny that there is any such a being as the Devil.

But then all such must deny the H. Scr. and do despite to ye Sp^t of God; are abandoned of God and left to y^{ms}, and to their own Master.—To prevent as much as may be people fr. falling into this dreadful error and condition— It will be necessary to set the Truth in as clear a Light as one can. (Pag. 230.)

212. *State of man before ye Fall. Bp. Bull.* (See back, 122.)

A Covenant of Eternal Life made wth Adam, for him and his Posterity—This Covenant by his Transgression made void for himself and them.

---

^{d} [Prov. xiii. 11.]

SUPPLE-
MENT.

[p. 226.]

They then became subject to the Law of Nature and Reason—This Law has not ye Promise of Etern. Life annex'd to it.

The words of ye Coven^t are, *In ye day Thou Eatest Thou shalt surely Dye.* It followes then y^t if he had not eaten, he sh^d surely have lived, and not been subject to mortality.

This was a Coven. of Grace, or Fav^r. For Adam had no Right but by ye Fav^r of God—having no Title by Nature to Immortality—And this Covenant depended upon a condition to be performed by Adam.

Paradise was to Adam a Type of Heaven; Here he was to undergo a certain Tryal of his Obedience, and then by virtue of ye Covenant, he was to be translated to Heaven, after he had been fitted for y^t blessed place, by Acts of Obedience, Devotion, &c.—i. e. w^n he sh^d have given such a Proof of his Virtue and Obedience as God sh^d have approv'd of.

It was Impossible y^t nāal powers sh^d enable a man even in the state of innocency to attain a Supernatural end, and therfore God added a Supernatural power, even His H. Sp^t —wch H. Sp^t J. X^t has obtained for every Faithful Believer (it having been lost to all men by ye Fall of Adam), and it is given in Baptism. And as this was the Principle of the Divine Life for wch Adam was designed, so is it ye Principle of Divine Life in every X^n—And may be lost (as it was by Adam) if it is not preserved by Prayer, Obedience and Charity —and avoiding every thing y^t may grieve it.

In short, man not being able by the condition of his nature to subsist for ever, God gave him His Sp^t that he might be able to persevere in Blessedness. And considering that the will of man was flexible to good or evil—God, to secure the grace He had given him, gave him a Law, y^t having a due regard to y^t he might at last be perfect, and fit for Heaven—And it is this Spirit wch restores all X^ns who obey it to ye Image of God.

From all y^t has been said it followes,—That there is an Absolute Necessity of Divine Grace in faln man to Restore him to ye Image of God—viz. ye Holyness wch is necessary to fit him for Heaven.

If the Nature of man stood in need of ye Grace of God to

continue in that Innocence in wch he was created, how can Supplement.
it possibly w^thout the Grace of God recover that Innocency
wch it hath lost? [p. 227.]

213. *Propag^n of ye Gospel*^e. Rom. iii. 29; Rom. v. 21. Unconverted Gentiles. Acts xi. 29. [Quesnel.] Math. viii. 11. Acts xiii. 46, 47; Rom. iii. 21. Q. [i. e. Quesnel in loc.] True X^ns think y^ms oblig'd (bound) to help those who are utterly unknown to y^m. This is peculiar to X^ns.—To know y^t any of our fellow-creatures are in Darkness and under ye Power of ye Devil is motive sufficient.

214. *Resurrection.* Acts xiii. 30. But God rais'd Him from the Dead. See Quesnel, [*in loc.*]
"The Resur. of X^ts Human Nature an Indubitable proof of His Divine—Of ye Truth of His Relig^n—Of His Gospel, and of every thing He taught on Earth—It was the Seal of all ye Truths He deliver'd."

215. *God's Providence.* Txt. Esther vi. 1. "*In y^t night ye K. could not sleep, &c.*" From the surprising occurrences (to be first set forth) of this mystery, proceed to shew y^t every thing y^t befalls us is by God's Ordering or Permission. —"A Sparrow falls not, &c." Math. x. 30; Lu. xii. 6, 7. See Acts xxv. 12; xxvii. 44. Quesnel. Wicked men generally execute upon y^ms ye sentence of Divine Justice—Lame, Blind, Idiots—not so by chance—Let those y^t are free fr. these Infirmitys Praise God, Acknowledge His mercy to y^m, &c. (224.)

216. *Christmas Day.* "*To this end was I born, y^t I might bear witness to the Truth,*" i. e. that I might lead [p. 228.] men to ye True Good—To their true Happiness—To know God, &c. And this by setting up His Kingdom amongst men—The World is a Lye, it leads men into Error and Death. Acts xiv. 15. "*We preach unto you y^t ye sh^d turn fr. these vanitys unto ye Living God.*"

217. "*There is a Way w^ch.*" "Who in times past suffered all nations to walk in their own ways." Acts xiv. 16. And if God sh^d suffer us to do so now, we sh^d fall into as great Follys, as ever the Heathen did. The Light of ye Gospel wch we have had might make us a little more refin'd in our

---

^e [These four entries are headed with ("Txt.")]

Folly, but we sh^d be as much estrang'd from God, and ye way to Heaven and Happ^{ss}, as they were—It is ye Sp^t of God can only keep us in ye right way. [Back, 112—135, or 263.]

218. *Religious Melancholy. Cast all yor care upon Him; for He careth for you.*

A full Trust in God ye only Comfort of dejected soules— "The very Haires of yor Head are all numbered."

N.B. The disorders of ye soul, as well as those of ye Body, are both fr. God.—Both Signes of His Love and care of us. —We cannot see the Reason of Things, but God can.

"Trust in the Lord and be doing good"—i. e. Go on in ye way of yor Duty, and leave yor self in God's Hands, for 'tis the work of God^f.

God afflicts the Soul as well as the Body, y^t we may learn to look up to Him—wean our affections fr. ye world, and see ye vanity of every thing besides.

God will eith^r Remove ye Sorrow or give Gr. to bear it.

Wicked or Careless, Thoughtless people—Tis fit, and a Blessing, wⁿ they fall into trouble of mind.

Good people have no reason to suspect y^t they are forsaken bec. &c.

God's Love is ye same wⁿ He hides His Face, as wⁿ He Smiles—and both sh^d have this effect, to make us keep close to Him—Joy is not always proper—God only knows it—He sees y^t Pride, Negligence or Self-Sufficiency w^d be ye effect.

A man is certainly more acceptable to G. who pursues and perseveres in his duty under disconsolatⁿ, than he, &c.

"My soul is sorrowful even unto Death"—It was then "He was heard in y^t He feared."

Blasphemous Thoughts, no sins if we reject y^m, no sign of God's displeasure; no more our Fault than wⁿ we are dirty'd in going [along] ye streets.—They are such afflictions as sickness, Loss of Goods, &c.

Employ yor Thoughts upon good Subjects—Converse wth yor Friends—Be ever employ'd—Despise y^m—Strive not wth y^m—Beg of God to deliver you fr. evil, and leave it to Him to chuse how long this affliction shall [last,] as you w^d if you pray'd to be deliver'd fr. pain of Body.

---

^f Is. xxxii. 17: ["The work of Righteousness shall be peace,"] &c.

Now you see how much you want God's Help, how little any body els can help you—these are real Blessings got by this dispensation, as irksome as it is.

"Is any afflicted? let him pray." Be sure forbear not y^t duty—Yo^r perseverance in duty is most acceptable, bec. you have no sensible pleasure in doing it.—But let yor Prayers be short.

219. *Two Kingdomes of God and Sat^n.* (Ecclus. xxxix. 28.) The Devils are a body Politick, or Kingdom—To deny this, or their Power, Malice, Being, &c., is in effect to deny the X^n Relig^n—wch enables us to overcome y^m [g], Promises Help, Rewards, Punishm^{ts}, as we oppose, or are led by y^m. (Backward, 225 and 233.)

As ye power of ye Devil was every where lessen'd, as ye K. of X^t prevail'd; so now X^{ty} begins to decline, and as that [p. 231.] day approaches when ye Son of God shall come and scarce find Faith, Satan begins to enlarge His power and His K. ag^n.

Saducism—Deism—Atheism.

Greater is He y^t is wth us, &c.

He y^t Soweth Tares is ye Devil.

Why is this permitted? To exercise our virtues; as ye Canaanites were left—'Twill redound to y^r benefit in the end.

As ye Holy G. makes ye Soules of Good men His Temple, so dos ye Devil those of Bad.

Satan entered into Judas; see Math. viii. 16. Q[uesnel.] The Discipline of ye Primitive Ch. aim'd at this, to keep up the knowledge of these 2 Kingd. in ye minds of X^{ns}.

220. *Justification.* No man can be Justify'd, y^t is, Counted Righteous by God, till he is really Righteous; now no man is really so, till he is Sanctify'd, in Body, Soul and Sp^t.

221. *Publick Justice.* W^n men have no mind to see the Truth, and who is in the right, they Industriously avoid the Settled Courts of Judicature, wch is ye way to discover w^t ought to be done, and proceed by violence to oppress those, w^m by common course of Justice they cannot condemn.

222. *Apparel.* See Quesnel, Acts xxv. 23. (Pag. 232.)

---

[g] 1 St. John iv. 10 [? 4]; Matt. xii. 28—30; xiii. 38.

SUPPLE-
MENT.

[p. 232.]

223. *Propagation of Gosp.* Math. v. 14. "Ye are ye Light of ye World," &c. If an Infidel, instead of seeing ye effects of an Holy Faith shine in X^{ns}, sees nothing but Covetousness, Corruption of Manners, Insincerity, &c., he is confirmed in his Infidelity, instead of being brought out of Darkness to Light, and fr. y^e Power of Satan unto God. See Math. viii. 11, 12, Quesnelle; Math. ix. 37, and x. 6—8; Rom. x. 19; Luk. xiii. 29; Jo. xii. 46.

224. *And they laughed Him to scorn.* Math. ix. 24.

Thus do Infidels—speak to y^m of y^e Great Mysteries of X^{ty}, and they laugh us to scorn. Here is Consolation for X$^{t's}$ Ministers—y^t He Himself was laughed at.

225. *Luxury in Apparel.* Math. xi. 8. *Behold they that wear soft clothing are in King's Houses.* See Quesnelle. (P. 231.)

226. *Excommunication.* Tho' one's being in the Ch. dos not infallibly secure his Salvat^n, yet w^n a Person is justly turned out of ye Ch. and obstinately continues so, he is in ye sure way of Perdit^n.

[p. 233.]

227. *Two Kingdoms of X^t and Sat.* (230, back.) It is sure of ye greatest moment to know wheth^r we belong to X^t or to Satan. Jo. xiv. 30. The Devil,—the Minister of God's Justice—Wherever God dos not reign, there dos ye D—l.

The D. supports his Empire by engaging men to follow their Passions and their worldly Interests.—J. X^t supports His by destroying these Passions, and by obliging men to Renounce ye world. [See K. of X^t, pag. 240].

228. *Death Bed Repent^{ce}.* Tis then a man w^d give all ye world for salvation. While he has it in his Power, he will not think of it; w^n tis (in a manner) out of his Power, then he is for doing everything. W^n there is no more time, there is no more Hope for Eternity.

229. *Lord's Supper. Do this in remembrance of Me.* How is y^t to be done? Suppose yo^{r}self at ye Foot of ye Cross—J. X^t speaking to you after this manner—"I suffer all these Torments for yor sake—To Reconcile you to God—To make atonem^t for yor sins—To deliver you fr. Death and Hell, &c."—w^t w^d yor thoughts be? "I abhorr ye sin for wch you are forc'd to bleed and dye—I will never willingly commit it ag^n—I am astonish'd at yor Love for so contempt-

ible, so miserable a Creature—I Thank you wth all my soul—I will depend upon ye Satisfaction, &c." See 1 Cor. xi. 23—28.

230. *Providence.* This to carnal eyes may seem to be the effect of meer chance, yet we see tis the Decree of a steddy Providence; and Regulated by the Hand of God. [p. 234.]

231. *Masquerades and Plays.* See Mark vi. 22, 23. Quesnel.

232. *Calamities, Publick.* Mark xiii. 14. Tis then [&c.] The Generality of people seek how to save their Goods and their Lives more than their soules—and tis bec. men Reflect more upon ye Calamities y^ms, than upon ye sins y^t draw y^m down.

233. *Repentance, Death Bed.* What affliction can be equal to y^t man's, who upon his Death bed can find nothing in His whole Life but w^t must render him unworthy of mercy?

234. *Charity Sermon.* Your Almes will oblige those w^m you Relieve to Pray for their Benefactors, and those Pray^rs will obtain fr. God greater degrees of Grace, &c. 2 Cor. ix. [14.] [p. 235.]

235. *Faith.* Tis a great mistake and delusion to think y^t Miracles are sufficient to oblige men to believe, and to cure Infidelity. Faith is ye gift of God, to those only who Pray for it, and are Disposed to Receive it—To Desire to see Miracles, is no good Disposition.

236. *Supper, Lord's.* The song of Simeon a pattern of Thanksgiving after ye communion—Lord, now lettest Thou, &c. Quesnel.

237. *Repentance.* (Luke iii. 3, 4, 5. Quesnel, that whole chapt^r.) We ought to preach Repentance more than any oth. thing, it being ye foundation of X^n Piety. The world dos not love it, bec. they do not love to see their ailments.

238. *Angels.* See Quesnelle, St. Luke iv. 10, 11, &c.

239. *Anti X^t.* The absolute necessity of Believing ye Incarnation.

240. *Incarnation.* W^t Corruption, w^t Blindness are we subject to, since y^t God was oblig'd to take upon Him our Flesh to convince us y^t He ought to be fear'd above all things—for J. X^t gave up His Life to convince us of this [h]. [p. 236.]

241. *Confirmation.* They run ye hazard of making atheists,

[h] [Three entries, mere references to Scripture, omitted.]

who bring persons to be confirm'd before they have instructed y^m in the Principles of X^ty and y^r Duties. Luk. xiv. 28.

242. *Almes.* (Luk. xvi. 5, 6, 9.) Are not only profitable to us, as they engage the Poor to pray for us, but as they help the poor to Praise God for His Goodness, and prevent them from sinning by taking away all occasion of their Repining at ye sadness of their Condition, in Comparison of y^t of those who enjoy all y^t their Hearts desire.

243. *Riches.* Luk. xvi. 19. For a man to have gr^t Riches, and to take no care of the Poor, will be ye cause of his Damnation.

May God open ye eyes of the Rich, y^t they may see their Danger, and prevent it, by giving to y^m to w^m tis due (as Superfluities are to ye Poor)—Ps. xli. 1.

A man who leaves his Heir an Ill example, and Riches to enable him to gratifye his own Passions, leaves him ye meanes of damning himself; this is not thought of as it sh^d be. See 2 Tim. iii. 2.

244. *Penance, Publick.* A man y^t is unwilling to bear ye shame and the confusion of Penance, is no true Penitent.

245. *Thanksgiving.* The designe of God in conferring blessings upon us is to be glorify'd for y^m.

246. *Attributes of God.* Luke xix. 23. It is of the utmost importance to know God well.

247. *Govern^ts.* The more zealous they are to cause their subjects to Fear and Hon^r God, the more faithful will God make their subjects to them, both in their Obedience, and paying them their dues, and w^t of right belongs to them.

248. *Warr.* Luk. xxi. 9, 20, &c.

249. *Marks of ye True Relig^n. Paschal*[1]. A Religion wch teaches us to Love our Creator, and to avoid displeasing Him.

W^ch discovers to us the Corruption of our Nature, y^t there is somthing in us wch ought to be Hated, such as Pride, Ambition, Envy, Covetousness, &c.

W^ch affords us effectual meanes of curing this disorder, and of restoring us to a better condition.

---

[1] [Pensées, p. 2, art. 4—9.]

W^ch sets before us the Difficulties we are to struggle w^th, and how to overcome and avoid y^m.

W^ch is fitted for all capacitys—Poor, Rich, Learned, &c.

A Relig^n wch subsists by y^e pure power of God, for as much as it is not only continually opposed by y^e world, but by every man who embraces it, for we are n$\bar{\text{a}}$ally averse to its precepts, and are dotingly fond of w^t it forbids.

It commands us to love God above all things, and tis so we love our selves. [p. 239.]

Tis y^e X^n Relig^n y^t discovers to us y^e Remedy of all our evils, we see plainly that this Remedy is not in our selves.

It prevents our *Pride*, by assuring us of ye Corruption, Sin, and Death to wch we are all subject. And it prevents *Despair*, by assuring us of ye Divine Grace, Fav^r, and Pardon.

The mystery of ye Incarnation shewes us ye greatness of our danger.

W^n we read ye Law and the Prophets, let us always have our eye upon y^m as they are explained by X^t and His Apostles. Then we shall see plainly that our Enemies are our own carnal affections, our Redeemer a Spiritual Conqueror — That He is to come first in Humility to abase ye Proud, and secondly, in Glory to exalt ye Humble—That He is to be God as well as man. Christ has told us w^t is meant by a True Israelite; to be truly Free; w^t is meant by Circumcision, viz. y^t of ye Heart; the true Bread of Life. The Land of Canaan is Heaven. Moses and David meant ye same thing w^n they speak of enemies; viz. our Sins.

250. *The H. Scriptures.* St. Jo. xii. 34. Quesnel. (Back, 167.)

251. *Riches.* (Back, 237.) How angry are we at Those y^t Steal, and wth w^t severity do we punish y^m!

We do not consider y^t it is as great a Sin for those y^t have Riches to spend y^m Idly, as it is for a Poor man to Steal, and y^t ye one will as certainly go to Hell as ye oth^r.

Riches. You say you love yor child, and w^d therfore leave him a Competent Estate. Our Ld Loved ye Rich young man as well as you do yor child; and He advised him to sell his Estate, that he might be sure of a Treasure in Heaven. [p. 240.]

252. *This Life a State of Tryal.* 2 Cor. v. 9. Let us but look upon this Life as *a State of Tryal—a State of Re-*

pentance, and we shall see w^t a change it will make in our selves, and all y^t confess this. It will oblige us to Renounce ye world, and all its vanitys—To deny our selves—To mortifye all our evil and corrupt affections—not to set up our Rest Here. We shall then see the reason of all ye Truthes of ye Gospel, wch at present seem strange to us.—*Blessed are they y^t Mourn.* For sure it becometh sinners to do so all their Life long. *Take up ye Cross.* For J. X^t w^d not have suffered such things for sin, if *Sufferings* were not necessary for Sinners, &c., 2 Cor. v. 10. A Future Judgm^t shewes y^t this Life is a State of Tryal.

253. *Kingdom of X^t*, not of this world. Jo. xviii. 36. Consisteth in a Spiritual Influence upon ye soules of men, producing in y^m Virtue, Joy, and Peace. Rom. xiv. 17.

Not to be carried on by worldly meanes, or supported by wealth and Pomp, force or violence. 2 Cor. x. 4; 1 Cor. i. 27.

Imposeth no Lawes but such as are necessary for Edification and Order. Math. xv. 9; Col. ii. 20, 21; Gal. iv. 10.

Purely spiritual—Administered by meek Perswasion. 2 Cor. i. 24; 2 Cor. iv. 5. Without domineering. 1 Pet. v. 3. The Ministers of this King are to be Patient—Gentle, &c. 2 Cor. vi. 4; 1 Tim. iii. 3; Tit. ii. 2. To Rebuke in Meekness. 2 Tim. ii. 24, 25.

[p. 241.]

In short, it is not to be upheld by ye same Arts, Forces, Policys, whereby secular Governm^{ts} are maintained, for then it w^d be of this world.

Tis true, an Ecclesiastical Society may be invested wth oth^r Powers than those now mentioned, for the Order, Peace and Good of ye Commonwealth; but then this is not to be call'd, so far as it uses these things, the K. of X^t. but an Human institution.

J. X^t has granted to His Church certain Powers and Rights—viz. The Power of ye Keyes—To enact Lawes for Order and Decency,—to Receive in and Shut out Offenders—To Ordain Pastors, &c. Every Ch. consists of Bps., Priests, and People, observing ye Institutions of X^t, and y^t sort of Governm^t wch ye Apostles did ordain.

Rebellion or Schism in this Kingdom of X^t consisteth in Disturbing ye Order and Peace of any single Church, In withdrawing fr. its obedience—In Obstructing Good Correspondence and Peace betwixt oth^r Churches—In Condemning oth^r Churches without just cause, and in Refusing to maintain Communion wth y^m without manifest Reasons.

The true way in this Kingdom of X^t of Reconciling dissentions among X^{ns} is—for each Church to let others alone in ye Enjoym^t of their freedom in Ecclesiastical Administrations—Declaring agst apparently hurtful errors, &c.

In ye mean time tis hence plain y^t all who withdraw y^{m}s fr. ye Com^n of Particular Churches once established, and holding the Faith entire—are Schismaticks, &c.

254. *Idolatry.* Every man has his Idols and does not see it, some ye works of his Hands, others of their Brain, some Gain, others Glory, &c. [p. 242.]

255. *Perfection, X^n.* (*Mr. Law's.*) Is what every soul, wch hopes for salvation, must aspire after. It consists in the Right performance of ye Duties of our Calling—Proceeding fr. such an Holy Disposition as ye Gospel requires, viz. fr. a Love of God, and of our Neighb^r. For it is the Habit of Mind fr. wch all our Actions are, in ye Sight of God, *Good* or *Bad*. So y^t all X^{ns} who Pray and Labour after such a Habit, may be equally *Perfect;* A Poor Widow may be as charitable as ye Richest—and a man y^t cannot pay his Debts, as Honest and Just—and one y^t is Faithful in a few things, as acceptable to God as he y^t is so in many—and he y^t lives up to that measure of Light, tho' less, wch God has given, is as accepted and as *perfect*, as he y^t lives up to a greater. In short, there is one only Rule of X^n Perfection for all men, *To love God, and to keep His Commandments.* To this all men are call'd, and men will be rewarded or punished, as they fail or come nearer to this Rule^k. [p. 1—9 ^{l}].

X^{ns} are in the Flesh like other men; but then they are also Members of that Society wch has the Son of God for its Head and Govr. [p. 14.]

The way we come to be Members of that Society is by Baptism, by wch we are devoted to God, and engage ourselves to Live as becomes Members of so Holy a Society:—

---

^{k} X^n Perfection is a daily advance towards ye Holyness wch we shall attain to in Heaven.—St. Aug^t.

^{l} [These references are made to Law's Christian Perfection, 8th Ed. London, 1807.]

SUPPLE-
MENT.

To follow that wch is *Good*, and to avoid every thing that is *Evil*. [p. 26.]

[p. 243.]

But then we are not to Judge of *Good* and *Evil* by our senses, but by our *Faith*, and by the *Gospel*, wch makes known to us things of the greatest concern to us, and wch by Nature we were utterly ignorant of.

Such as these—That we are a Race of Fallen Spirits, sent into this world as a Place of Tryal, and that as we behave our selves *Well* or *Ill* here, we shall be happy or miserable for ever. [p. 19.]

That therefore we ought to have nothing so much at Heart, as how we may mend our nature, be deliver'd from the Power of our Sinful Passions, be Restor'd to a New Nature, and to ye Fav^r of God, y^t w^n we dye we may be Happy. [p. 28.]

That we are in great danger of being Diverted from this work by the cares, the pleasures, and the amusements of the world; and y^t nothing but X^ty can secure us from Ruin.

The end of X^ty being—To gather out of ye Faln Race of men all such as are willing to become the Subjects of X^t, and who will oblige themselves to follow His Commands and Example in order to be Eternally Happy.

Now the first thing He requires of y^m is—That wth ye Simplicity of Children (Luke xviii. 16) they suffer y^ms to be Taught by Him what they are to Believe, w^t they are to Fear, w^t to Hope for, what to Do, and what to avoid; never opposing their own reason or Wisdome to ye Wisdome of God. [p. 34.]

For instance, they must believe—That the World is nothing but Vanity, that Riches are a Snare, that Prosperity is Dangerous, Pleasures most Mischievous, Afflictions Favours. And that Mortification and Self-denial, however uneasy to Flesh and Blood, are absolutely necessary to fit us for Heav^n and Happ^ss.

[p. 244.]

Now we cannot possibly receive these Truths, until God gives us a new Heart, by giving us another Spirit very different from that wch we are born w^th.

Which Spirit will be a Principle of a New Life, y^t is, it will give us new Thoughts, new Judgments, new Desires, and will enable us to see and to do those things wch we have naturally neith^r Inclination nor Power to do.

A man y^t has this Spirit *cannot commit Sin*, (and there- fore will always be in God's Fav^r,) i. e. he will not, he cannot make Sin his Choice, (no more than a man who is govern'd by a spirit of Covetousness will be extravagant,) tis contrary to the main bent of his soul, tis pain to him. [p. 30.] SUPPLEMENT.

The Holy Spirit being so necessary to our Salvation, our Lord has assur'd us that we may obtain it, *God will give His H. Spirit to them that ask Him,* and make y^ms worthy of so Holy a Guide.

The way to do this is—*To Renounce the World, the Flesh, and the Devil;* wch are all equal Enemies to that State of Holyness to wch we are call'd. This we did at our Baptism, but we must do it every day of our Lives.

And that we may not Deceive ourselves in a matter of so gr^t Moment, we are assur'd—That it is not only the vices and vanitys of ye world y^t we are to Renounce, but that the very Cares and Business of the World, if they possess ye Heart, and hinder us from making ye care of our Soules our chief concern, are equally sinful. [p. 44.] [p. 245.]

So y^t he who forgets God in the most lawful business of Life, will come short of Heaven as sure as ye greatest Sinner, and consequently every state of Life wch is not devoted to God is sinful.

Tis for this Reason y^t J. X^t Denounces a wo against all that are Rich, not that have got Riches unjustly, but who live in the Enjoym^t and Pleasures wch Riches afford—" Thou hast received thy good things," is the only Reason given why ye Rich man in the Gospel was sent into Hell. [p. 62.]

This is the Reason y^t our Lord made this a standing Rule for His Followers, *He that forsaketh not all that he hath cannot be My Disciple.* [p. 55.]

Accordingly it was His express command to ye Rich young man—*Sell all that thou hast and give to the Poor, and thou shalt have Treasure in Heaven.*

That is—Resolve, as you hope for Heavⁿ, to have as little regard for yor Estate as if you had sold it, and cheerfully part wth w^t is more than necessary for yo^rself and family to those y^t are in want.

And this is what all Rich men are oblig'd to do—To Renounce, to be dead to, to be crucified to ye world :—*the* meaning of selling all y^t they have, wch is the only way to gain such affections as are necessary to fit us for Heaven.

Because all Enjoyments and ways of Living wch make us to Love the world and forget that God is our only Good, are to be parted wth at the Hazard of our Soules.

Tis true the Distinctions of Civil Life are necessary, but a Rich man is as much oblig'd to Renounce ye world, to avoid Pleasures, Vanity, Excess, and Indulgence, and to Love God *with all his heart*, as ye Poorest man alive.

These are Gospel Rules for *all;* and our Salvation depends upon observing y^m. *Take no thought for to-morrow.—Labour not for ye meat y^t perisheth.—Lay not up for yo^{r}selves Treasures upon Earth.—Ye cannot serve God and Mammon. —Having food and Raim^t, be therwith Content.* [p. 79.]

Our Lord Confined the Rich man to one only way of Employing his incomes—*Give to the Poor.* Had there been a better, He w^d certainly have told him. [p. 84.]

If we are to Love God with all our Heart and Soul and Mind, as we are requir'd to do, we must first be persuaded y^t He is our only Happ^{ss}; we must renounce all other, and suffer y^m not to take possession of our Hearts. [p. 86.]

And if we w^d Love our Neighb^r as our selves, wch is ye next gr^t Duty of ye Gospel, we must beware of placing our Happ^{ss} in worldly Interests and Enjoyments—for if we do this, we shall Love and hate, Envy, and be Unjust, Speak Evil of, and be Unkind to others, in proportion to the Love we have for the world, as they Fav^r or oppose our worldly Views and Happ^{ss}. [p. 94.]

There is indeed a Sober and a Reasonable Use of the world, w^n we keep with^n the bounds of Necessity and Decency, and Suffer it not to take possession of our Hearts. [p. 98.]

This makes *Self-denyal* an Indispensable Duty; every one y^t will be X^{vs} Disciple, *must Deny Himself, and take up his Cross daily.* [p. 107.]

Self-denyal and Suffering being a Debt due for Sin, J. X^t suffered for the Sins of ye whole world, not to Free His followers fr. Sufferings, but to make their Sufferings accepted of God. [p. 103.]

He therefore pronounces y^m *Blessed that Mourn,* who not

only by y^s shew their Indignation agst that Sin wch cost Him His Life, but [try?] also to pay some part of the Debt y^t is due for Sin.

This mourning must arise from a true sense of our Condition, as we are faln spirits, separated fr. God by Sin and Vanity, and is to be express'd by abstaining from Pleasures, wch blind ye mind, corrupt the Heart, and Remove us still furth^r fr. God. [p. 248.]

For ye same Reason He pronounces *those Blessed who are Poor in Sp^t,* whose minds are exercised ab^t their Spiritual wants, and who cease to Live the Life of the World. [p. 119.]

Not to Resist Evil is another Command of X^t and another Instance of Self-denyal; i. e. To Suffer wth patience even such ill usage as we might prevent by resistance, or remedy by going to Law; wch our Lord forbids expressly, bec. y^t w^d Raise the Passions, Embitter the Mind, and Destroy X^n Charity. [p. 120.]

Human Lawes, therfore, are not to be a X$^{n's}$ Rule, in cases where the commands of X^t have set us the Termes of our Salvation, wch is the Doctrine of the Cross; He Himself being made perfect thro' Sufferings; wch are real Fav^{rs} in the Hands of God; serve to Mortifye our Flesh, purify our Soules, and are the Safest way to Glory. Heb. ii. 10.

And therefore w^n our Lord pronounces those *Blessed who are Revil'd and Persecuted for Righteousness sake*, He dos not speak of y^m as Hardships, but as matters of Rejoycing, to suffer any thing rather than depart fr. our Duty. [p. 128.]

Now Self-denyal is a Duty, not bec. God requires it, but bec. tis both Reasonable and Necessary, as all oth^r X^n Dutys are, to our Happ^{ss}; They are necessary to change our Nature, to restore us to ye Image of God, and make us such as God can take pleasure in. [p. 130.] [p. 249.]

Fasting and Abstinence, for example, are necessary to lessen the power of Bodily Passions, and Free the Soul from their Dominion, which w^d otherways hinder us fr. seeing ye Truth, and fr. following w^t we are convinc'd is good. [p. 139.]

For nothing destroyes ye Spirit of Piety more than Indulgence of ye Body; Fasting, therefore, is by our Lord joyned wth Pray^r as the most effectual way of applying to God. [p. 151.]

And tho' every one cannot abstain altogether from food, yet every one can, and is indispensably bound, to abstain fr. such food, such degrees of Eating, and such Pleasures as are necessary to destroy sensuality, and make us fit for spiritual exercises and enjoym^{ts}. [p. 146.]

St. Paul knew how much the state of ye Soul and its health depended upon the body, and our manner of living. He therefore Judg'd it necessary to exercise this virtue in order to secure his own Salvat^n. And every X^n who desires to overcome the World, ye Flesh and ye D—l, must do so too. [p. 155.]

After all, Temperance in Meat and Drink is but a small part of Self-denial, there are other things w^{ch}, if indulged, will as certainly ruin us. [p. 163, 176.]

Such are Blindness in the Understanding, Perverseness and Vanity in the Will—Self-Love, Anger, Pride, Revenge in the Passions; Falsness, Hypocrisy, Hatred and Malice in the Heart;—these are all to be opposed, being as odious to God and as ruinous as Intemperance and Lust. [p. 158.]

[p. 250.]

So far therefore as we see the corruption of Nature, whether in our selves or others, so far we see the necessity of an *Universal Self-Denyal,* y^t we may heartily close with all the Dutys of Relig^n, wch are necessary to recover us to a state of Holyness. Wthout a sense of this, the Dutys of Relig^n have no meaning. [p. 164.]

But there is still another, and a more important reason for *Self-Denyal,* and y^t is—To prepare our selves for the Grace of God, with^t wch we can do nothing y^t is good; *none being the Children of God, but they that are led by the Sp^t of God.* [p. 178, 180.]

Now indulgence dos not only nourish corruption, wch increases or abates as we give way to or deny our appetites, but it provokes God to leave us to ourselves, to withhold His grace or hinder us from improving under it, and to suffer us to sink under our own corruption.

X^{ns} sh^d consider themselves not only as men, acted by Reason, but as men endued wth the Sp^t of God, wch is the Principle of our new life, so y^t whatever it be that grieves and drives away this Spirit, whether it be an Idle or a Busy Life, whether it be vain amusements, useless Learning, or

[p. 251.]

what are called innocent pleasures, it ruins us as effectually as the most profligate Life. [p. 182.]

X^{ns} are often amazed w^n they come to dye, and wonder y^t they were all their lives long so blind as not to see the Importance of an Holy Life, the Vanity of the world, and the evil of Sin. They w^d have seen all these very plainly had they not griev'd that Spirit wch was given y^m at Baptism and at Confirm^n, and forc'd Him to forsake them. [p. 188.]

If we w^d avoid this Judgm^t, we must remove all hindrances of Divine Grace, all vain and foolish, Idle and Unprofitable Conversation, all business, cares, Pleasures, Studies and Diversions, wch make us unfit for the serious thoughts of Eternity, and for the fellowship of the Divine Sp^t. [To p. 200.]

The more serious we are, ye more sensible shall we be of our own misery, and more devoutly apply to God for Help. [p. 265.]

We cannot be Devout w^n we please, we must alter our Life before we can alter our Heart. He y^t is Humble, has Renounced the World, and has mortify'd his corrupt affections, will be Devout of Course; while he y^t has not done so, will go to Church, and say his Prayers, and confess his Sins, and ask for Grace, wthout Devotion, and without any benefit. [p. 252.] [p. 267, 275.]

True Devotion Consists in a Constant serious temper of mind, always adoring God, and aspiring after ye Happ^{ss} of the other world. [p. 270.]

Prayer is but one way of Expressing our Devotion, but it is a very necessary one, especially if we consider it not only as it is an Address to God, but as it is an exercise of Holy Thoughts and Desires concerning things of the Highest moment. And that it is not to inform God of our wants, but to fill our hearts wth Devout affections, such as may render God propitious to us. [p. 277.]

Now concerning Pray^r we ought to make this a Law to ourselves. To meditate before we Pray what we are ab^t, what we Pray for, and to W^m. To make a Pause, and to ask our selves wheth^r our Hearts go along wth our Lips; wch will be means to make us truly devout. [p. 284.]

Let us not think it Sufficient to confess y^t we are miserable Sinners, for y^t is only Confessing y^t we are men; but

SUPPLE-
MENT.
we are to Confess our particular failings, and ask for ye particular Grace our case requires. [p. 288.]

He y^t has learned to Pray as he ought, has got the Secret of an Holy Life. [p. 290.]

[p. 253.] J. X^t is the Way, the Truth, and the Life. No man cometh unto God but by Him. He is the Way, by His Example wch all X^{ns} are bound to Imitate. The Truth, by His Word, wch we are bound to Receive; and the Life, by His Grace, wch we are oblig'd to Pray for. Out of this Way there is nothing but Wandering, without this Truth nothing but Error, and wthout this Life there is nothing but Death. [p. 292.]

Can any one tell why we sh^d be fonder of the World than He was? Are we less in Danger of being Corrupted by Prosperity than He was? Can we finish ye work we have to do wth more ease and less distraction? Is less Mortification, Self-denyal, Watching and Prayer necessary for us than for Him? [p. 306.]

Was He more meek and lowly than we need to be? Did He avoid Hon^{rs}, Riches, and Shewes of Life, Pleasures and Indulgence, and can we say we follow His Example? [p. 309.]

If we continually read His Life in the Gospel, not so much to know His Actions, as to Attain His Spirit, we shall see how far we come short of our Pattern, and we shall follow it more perfectly. [p. 314.]

In short—Xⁿ Perfection, wch we are to aspire after as we Hope for Heaven, consists in Devoting our selves wholly to
[p. 254.] God; in a constant universal Self-Denial, in opposing and Renouncing all such things as gratify our corrupt nature, and in striving to mend its disorders. [p. 315.]

In fitting ourselves by pureness of Living, for the fellowship of the H. G., avoiding every thing y^t may grieve Him.

In continuing Constant in Prayer, and other Acts of Devotion, and in Imitating the H. Jesus.

He that strives after this Perfection will be Happy now and to all Eternity. [p. 316.]

And let a man be doing w^t els he will, he is losing his time and his Lab^{rs}, and wch is worse than all, his soul. [p. 323.]

Let him be never so studious, never so learned, never so Rich, never so Powerful, never so admired, never so Happy in his circumstances, never so famous in his Generation;— Supplement. all will be lost wth him at Death, and himself too, if he has not minded *this one thing needful,* the being Perfect as our Heavenly Fath^r is Perfect. [To p. 326.]

God only knows what allowances He will make for any man's coming short of every Degree of Holyness wch he is capable of, so that we can have no security of our Salvation, but by doing our very best, this being the only Test of our Sincerity. [p. 326.]

Our very best will be imperfect, and will be accepted only [p. 255.] bec. it is our best. *Thou shalt Love the Lord thy God wth all thy Strength;*—this is our Rule.

Our Encouragem^t is—That ye more Perfect we are, the more happy we shall be; every Prayer, every Almes, every Self-Denyal, every good work will be remember'd to our everlasting Comfort. [p. 332.]

If these things do not affect us now very sensibly, it is bec. our minds are filled wth other thoughts and amusements.

But let us spare one minute to Think y^t the Hour is at Hand w^n we are to be what we must be to all Eternity.

What our thoughts will then be if we are not prepar'd for such a change, no mortal can describe.

256. *Devotion* is only known in its effects—An earnest desire of conversing wth God—Of hearing his Word, and laying our Wants before Him—Of Devoting ourselves wholly to God—for thence it has its name. We all own y^t w^thout a Devout Disposit^n all our Pray^rs are not only in vain, but [p. 256.] sinful.—And yet we pray w^thout this Disposition. And where the Heart has no part in our Pray^rs—this is a Terrible Disorder, and ought to Humble and Force us to go to God for Help. In business of Importance, wch concerns our Body, or ye World, we find no such distractions—we can attend whole Houres upon Things that Delight us. Tis bec. we have got an Habit of Wandering and Indevotion, y^t we go on to Approach Him with^t Fear and without Concern. We do not enough consider the Sin of Indevotion, or we sh^d strive most Heartily to amend. Tis too sure a sign we do not Love God. Tis a Crime wch deprives us of God's Blessing and Favours—He will not be found but of them that seek Him. We think Indevotion a small Fault,

SUPPLE-
MENT.

but will God, are we sure, think y^m [it] so? If it offends God it can be no small fault.

That we may mend so great a Fault, let us consider fr. whence it Proceedes? *Now nothing disorders the Heart but an Habit of Sin.* God will have no regard to their Pray^{rs} who have none to His Commands—Nor will He accept of an Heart divided betwixt Himself and the World, and Worldly Pleasures. Men may cheat even themselves, and think to make amends wth a Day's Fasting, or an Almes, for ye Debaucherys of a Month, but God is not to be cheated. Innocency of Life is necessary therefore to true Devotion—Sin renders us utterly uncapable of it.

The next Source of Indevotion is the Love of ye World. Tis this distracts our Hearts; we cannot serve God and Mammon. We cannot tast the Pleasures of Devotion while ye World is our Delight. Dangers and Feares, and Hopes and Despair, Pleasures, and wor^d [worldly?] Things come across the mind wⁿ it sh^d be employ'd ab^t the Greatness, the Majesty, the Goodness and Love of God; wⁿ Faith, and Hope,

[p. 257.] and Charity, and Thankfulness sh^d possess our Hearts, and make y^m Devout. If we w^d be Devout, we must first possess our Hearts wth a deep Sense of the Vanity of ye World; it will not then return so very often into our minds. But this must be the work of Grace, and this the Fruit of Prayer.

The Cares of ye World are anoth^r Source of Indevotion.—The Dread of Poverty, of Loss, of Disgrace, of Disappointments, &c., come cross ye mind wⁿ it sh^d be intent on God. If we w^d consider y^t our Feares change nothing in ye state of our affaires, but only break our Rest and Disturb our Devotions, we sh^d make our Saviour's Command a Law to our selves.—Take no thought for to-morrow.

Multiplicity of business anoth^r Source of Indevotion. And yet this is thought the most Innocent way of spending ye Time wch is given us in wch to secure Eternity. Tis true we must serve the Necessities of Nature—And man is born to Lab^r—But God has reserved at least one day in Seven, one Hour in Seven, not so much for Himself, as for us; if those were shut out whose time was spent in so necessary affaires as buying of Land, Proving of Oxen, bec. it took up all their

Thoughts, w^t will become of ye bulk of mankind? Neith^r the goodness nor the Innocency of the Employm^t will be taken for an Excuse if it keeps fr. God.

Letting the Mind Rove, anoth^r Source of Indevotion. A Soul acustom'd to Wander, cannot fix w^n it w^d or sh^d. We must resolve to set bounds to our roving thoughts, use our selves to think of Few and Good Subjects. A great compass of Learning (wch too many Covet) is a greater hinderance of Devotion than is thought of. How can ye Soul think upon God and His Attributes, wch is filled wth Sciences, Sublime Speculations, Experiments, Discoverys, Projects, &c. ? Wretched is the man who knows every thing but God. If we w^d be devout we must do violence to our minds, and keep y^m fixed on God. Help me, O God, in this attempt, and I shall despise all oth^r Sciences wch the world boasts of.

Long Interruption of Holy Exercises ye last Source of Indevotion. Let us often renew our Intercourse wth God, and we shall at length be delighted wth it. The exercise of Piety becomes a Lab^r bec. we are not used to y^m. Let us bring our Soules by Violence to God.

But above all Enemies to Devotion, *the Spirit of the World,* i. e. the Love of Sensual Pleasures, is the greatest. The closer Union we have with sensible things, the more our Union with God is lessened. Every Age of Life has its peculiar pleasures, but all in general are Enemies to Devot^n. Tis true y^t God originally design'd, that men, fr. the things He made, sh^d see and adore His Wisdom, Power, and Goodness, &c. But now, by reason of our Corruption, they are all become snares, and we abuse these favours to our destruction. If Grace dos not prevent us, i. e., we suffer y^m to possess our Hearts wholly, so that no place is left for God.

As matters therfore now stand wth us, *sensible pleasures, whether in their use or abuse, are Enemies to Devotion.* Nothing but a Devout Disposition fits a man for Death. But then, How bitter, O death, is the Remembrance of thee to him that Lives in peace, with all his good things ab^t him. He lives in Feares, he dyes with Reluctancy, while they y^t have Renounced Pleasures, find less difficulty in leaving the World, since they have already renounced all y^t was charming in it.

[p. 258.]

SUPPLE-
MENT.
[p. 259.]

Let us consid^r J. X^t, who, tho' Lord of ye Universe, yet chose not to have an House where to lay His Head!—To have no meanes of Furnishing Himself with sensible Pleasures—Going on foot from place to place. Let us look unto Jesus, the Auth^r and Finisher of our Faith, &c.

After all, Relig^n dos not say y^t all Pleasures are Criminal. There are pleasures wch necessarily follow most of ye Actions wch are designed to preserve Life and Health; these, w^n kept within bounds, cannot be Criminal. Tis impossible, for instance, not to be pleased with drink w^n one is athirst. The great Concern of a X^n sh^d be, To make Necessity, not Pleasure, his Rule. The bounds wch separate Good from Evil, are not to be perceived but by gr^t care; God w^d have us pass thro' this world wth some difficulty, and thro' Dangers, y^t we might always depend upon God, and look up to Him for Help, who alone is able to conduct us thro' so difficult a way.

The more the Soul is used to be mov'd by Bodily Pleasures, the less capable it is of Tasting Spiritual Joyes. He y^t w^d be Devout, therfore, must resolve to Tast sensual pleasures very moderatly. When men consult their Hearts, their Senses, and their Passions, they forget their Reason, their Duty, and their God. Hence all evil comes. Out of ye Heart proceed Evil Thoughts, &c., and to walk in the ways of one's Heart, &c., is in Solomon's words to lead a Wicked Life. Tis Devotion alone that leads to True Pleasures; we shall always find it so, after we have been a thousand times deluded and disappointed by every thing els.

[p. 260.]

We very ill understand our Intrest w^n we imagine y^t we lose y^t time wch we give to God and to Devotion.

Helps y^t lead to Devotion. The first, earnestly to desire it; he y^t seeks after God, is not far off finding Him. He y^t Hungers after Right^{ss} will certainly be fill'd. Such desires are the effects of Grace, and Grace dos nothing in vain, Provided we call upon God for Help to second y^m.

The Second Help to D.—is to lead a virtuous Life. God is light, and cannot unite wth Darkness. Tis not the magnificence, but the cleaness of the Place y^t makes it a Temple for ye H. G. To do Good to one's neigh^r, to ye Miserable and Needy, &c., Disposes the Soul to Devotion. This makes yᵉ Active Life so much preferable to yᵉ contemplative. The *Active* is yᵉ very School of Virtue and Piety, and is so far fr. distracting Devout Soules, that it is the shortest way to Devotion. The World is made for the Exercise of all Xⁿ Virtues; the Heavens afford matter for our *Wonder*—The Lightning fills us wᵗʰ Fear—The *Wisdom* of God is seen by every one yᵗ has eyes; the Poor and Miserable are made to be objects of our Pity and Liberality—The Sick of our Assistance, the Ignorant of our Instruction—Those yᵗ Fall, yᵗ we may lend yᵐ an helping Hand, and to be a warning to our selves—Some are vain yᵗ we may see and Despise yᵉ Vanity of yᵉ World—others fall yᵗ we may Fear and look to our own steps. Good men are Rewarded, yᵗ we may *Hope*—so yᵗ we are surrounded wᵗʰ motives to Virtue and Piety, if we will but mind them—And let us always remember that virtue consists not in doing no ill, but in doing Good. The Unfruitful Tree and yᵉ Unprofitable Servant are both Instances of this Truth.

The Third Help to D.—*To guard the Senses;* by wᶜʰ Temptations seize upon the Soul, and by meanes of a Corrupt Heart, yᵉ things wᶜʰ in yᵐs are good become Snares. Let, therfore, the Devout Soul be as Reserv'd as is consistent wᵗʰ Prudence and Good manners.

In seeking out Innocent Diversions we often meet with Criminal. Never be curious to know all that passes, 'twill distract the Mind, wⁿ it wᵈ be intent upon better things, and Fill the Thoughts, and take room wᶜʰ God shᵈ possess entirely.

The Fourth Help to D.—*is to persevere in Holy Exercises.* As the D—l never leaves off to tempt us, so must we never leave off to resist him. Relax not your daily Devotions on frivolous pretences; wⁿ you think to return to yᵐ with vigour, you'll find yoʳself like Samson, wⁿ his Hair was cut like other men, very cool and indifferent. Nor let the World be a pretence to run from yʳ Devotions.

The next Help to D.—*To have God always before our eyes.*

Other particular Helps—*To have Set Regular Hours of Prayer.* The Primitive Hours were, 6, 9, 12, 3, 6, 9.—A strict observance of these for some time wᵈ make the Returnes of Duty easy.

SUPPLE-
MENT.

[p. 262.]

Solitude, another Help. W^n thou Prayest, enter into thy closet.

Prayer, attentive, persevering, and ardent, anoth^r Help.

Fasting and Mortification—The flesh never thrives but to ye Cost of the Soul—A great Meal is but an ill preparation for Devotion—The less the Soul is united to ye Body by sensual Pleasures, and full feeding, the easier it raises its self to God. But then let us always remember that Mortification is to go further than the Body; Self-Love, Pride, Envy, Jealousy, Hatred, Malice, Avarice, Ambition, must all be mortify'd, by ceasing fr. ye occasions of y^m. Wo to y^m y^t are drunk, but not wth Wine—A person may be besotted wth Vanity, wth Pride,—The true Sobriety of ye Soul consists in Humility, and in being Content wth Necessarys.

257. *Mysteries. Trinity, &c.* God can make known to us things wch we cannot Comprehend—We our selves can do so—We can make known to a man y^t is born Blind, That we can see things at a million of miles distant fr. us, the Sun, for Instance, as soon as those that are wthin 20 yards of us. Tis Impossible for him to Comp'hend this—and yet he will believe it upon a Sober man's assuring him it is so upon his own knowledge.

So y^t the Truth of a Thing may be made known to us, tho' the manner how it is, or can be, may be a mystery y^t we cannot Comp^{e}hend.

Hence it followes—That a Doctrin may be true, tho' 'tis mysterious. There may be an order of beings wch may comp^{e}hend w^t we cannot—as one man can comp^{e}hend such things as another can have no notion of.

So likewise we have evidence Sufficient, y^t a Thing is true, wthout having distinct conceptions of ye manner or the Reasons of it.

[p. 263.]

We may be assured y^t J. X^t is ye Son of God, and this Perswasion may make us very grateful for the Fav^r of His taking our Nature upon Him, &c., and this without being able to understand the manner of ye Union of ye Divine and Human Nature. Nay, we may reap the benefit of this perswasion wthout being able to answer all the Questions y^t may be asked concerning it.

It will be acknowledg'd—That God can, if He pleases,

make known to us certain Mysteries, wch we, in this state, cannot comprehend—These we receive purely bec. God has made y^m known to us; to endeav^r to explain y^m is impertinent, bec. impossible; and dangerous, bec. of ye Disputes they may raise, and the Errors they may occasion.

SUPPLEMENT.

We do not deny our Reason wⁿ we Believe Mysterys, it being the highest Reason to Believe w^t God has Reveal'd; at the same time, we are assured y^t God cannot require of us to believe any thing y^t carryes in it a plain Contradiction.

258. *There is a Way y^t, &c.* See Jo. ix. 16, in my Bible. See back, 228.

259. *Lord's Supper.* Ends therof—1st. The Remembrance of His Death: specify'd by Himself—2dly. To Testify our Union wth X^t, and communion with one anoth^r: mentioned by St. Paul. These ye only ends mentioned in S.S.

260. *Magistrate.* There is this difference betwixt the punishm^t inflicted by a Just Magistrate, a Fath^r, or Master, and a Revengeful man; ye one punishes out of Love, and a design of amending ye Fault; ye oth^r out of Malice, and to gratify a Revengeful Sp^t. [p. 264.]

261. *Of Prayer.* (Back, 76.) Wⁿ men pray for Temporal things, it sh^d always be wth submission to God's Will— "While ye meat was yet in their mouths, ye wrath of God came upon y^m," &c. See Numbers xi. 33.

262. *The Lord's Prayer.—Our Father wch art in Heaven.* [p. 265.] Thou art my Father, I will leave it to Thee to give me w^t is best.

Thou art our Fath^r, and we all are Brethren. I pray not for myself only, but for all my Brethren. I am a very Child, Weak and Ignorant, be Thou a Fath^r and a Guide and Help to me.

Thou art our Fath^r. I will not Fear to go to my Fath^r, He will not cast me off.

God is my Fath^r, He has a right to correct me, and I will bear it patiently, bec. I know tis for my Good.

God is my Fath^r. I will therefore behave myself like the son of such a Fath^r.

I have done amiss, but I will go to my Fath^r, and will say unto Him, &c.

SUPPLE-
MENT.

He is "in Heaven," and sees all things—I will therefore live as under His all-seeing Eye.

He is "in Heaven," and to be Feared as well as Pray'd to—"Fath^r:" I will therefore Love as a Child, not Fear Him as a Slave.

My Fath^r is in Heaven—This Earth therefore is not ye Inheritance of those whose Father is in Heaven^m.

[p. 267.] *Hallowed be Thy Name.* "How excellent is Thy Name in all ye World, Thou y^t hast set Thy Glory above ye Heavens."

"As for me, I will be talking of Thy Worship, Thy Glory, Thy Praise and Wonderous works: I will also tell of Thy Greatness, so y^t men shall speak of ye Might of Thy marvellous works."

"All Thy works praise Thee, O Lord, and Thy Saints give thanks unto Thee." Ps. cxlv.

"My mouth shall speak the Praise of the Lord, and let all Flesh give thanks unto His H. Name for ever and ever."

"Let all ye Earth Fear ye Lord. Stand in awe of Him all ye that dwell in the world."

"The Fool hath said in his Heart, There is no God."

"He y^t Confesseth Me before men, him shall, &c."

"That God in all things may be glorify'd." May I, Great God, ever Glorify Thy Name, by promoting the Knowledge of Thy Glorious Perfections and Excellences—By shewing respect to every thing y^t has ye Name of God call'd upon it—wheth^r it be Thy Name, Thy Day, Thy House, Thy Word, Thy Ordinances, Thy Ministers, wch Thou hast appointed to set forth Thy Glory.

"That ye Name of God be not blasphem'd through you."

Grant y^t this may never Happen thro' any neglect or fault of mine. Rom. ii. 24.

May I not only Pray for it, but Hallow Thy Name in My Dayly Conversation.

Math. v. 6. "That men seeing y^r good works, may Glorify yor Fath^r wch is in Heaven."

Jo. xv. 8. "In This is My Fath^r Glorify'd, y^t ye bring forth much Fruit."

^m [p. 266 is blank in the MS.]

Rev. iv. 11. "Thou art worthy, O Lord, to Receive Glory, and Hon^r, and Pow^r, for Thou hast created all things, and for Thy Pleasure they are and were created."

SUPPLE-
MENT.
[p. 268.]

May all our Actions tend to Thy Hon^r—y^t we may speak and Live worthy of y^t relation we bear to God.

That all men may come to ye knowledge of Thee and of J. X^t.

May I never Blaspheme Thy Holy Name—never take it in vain—never speak lightly of any thing y^t has Thy Name call'd upon it.

Let us never speak of God but with reverence—nor Hear others speak lightly of Him but wth Abhorrence.

To think of God always wth Devotion and Reverence, is ye true, sure way to be transformed into His image and likeness. Ps. cxlv. "All Thy works praise Thee, O God." May they Help us, teach us to Glorifye Thee.

"Let every thing y^t hath Breath praise ye Lord."

May we always use Holy Things after an Holy Manner.

1 Cor. x. 31. "Wheth^r ye eat, drink, or whatsoever ye do, do all to ye Glory of God."

Math. v. 16. "Let yor Light so shine before men, y^t they may see yor good works, and Glorify yor Fath^r wch is in Heaven."

1 Sam. ii. 30. "Him y^t Honoureth Me, I will Hon^r."

2 Thess. i. 12. "That ye Name of our Lord J. X^t may be Glorify'd in you and ye in Him."

"Hallowed be Thy Name." Fath^r, Son, and Holy Ghost to be worshiped and Glorifyed. Nicene Creed.

Upon any gr^t Deliverance or Mercy rec^d—"Hallowed, &c. Not unto us, O L^d, but unto Thy Name be the Glory."

"*Thy kingdom come.*" Luk. xvii. "The K. of G. is within" (among) "you"—A Power subjecting the wills of men to the Law of God—Tis ye Rule of ye Sp^t of God in ye Soul.

[p. 269.]

O take possession of this Thy K. in Me, and rule Here as thou dost in H. Destroy all ye Powers of Darkness within me.

May the Gospel be Rec^d and have its saving effects in all ye w.—That we may become one Flock under one Shepherd —ye K., ye Lord Jesus.

May we not only pray for this blessing, but strive to advance it. May all Thy Subjects, O K. of H., shew to w^m they belong by their works.

Bring in everlasting Right^{ss}, O God, and remove ye wickedness w^h hinders ye increase of Thy K.

"We will not have God to rule over us." This is in effect w^t all [the] wicked say. Every Xⁿ is bound to establish ye K. of G. by opposing ye Corruptⁿ of ye w.

I own Thee for my K., do Thou make me Thy faithful Subject.

Wherever the Gospel is Rec^d and Obey'd, there X^t Reignes.

May the Unbelieving Nations be Converted.

Protect Thy Subjects from the Malice of Men, and Powers of Darkness.

Protect Thy Ministers—Bless Thine Ordinances.

"Thy K. come," to destroy all those Heresies and Schismes wch distract Thy Church, and that "Holyness wthout wch no man, &c."

Since the Hearts and Soules of men are ye Subjects of Thy Govern^t, let us acknowledge Thee, O Fath^r, and Thee O J. X^t, and Thee O H. Ghost, to be ye only Lord God and K. of all ye Earth.

"That Thy Ways may be known upon Earth, Thy saving health among all nations." Ps. lxvii. 2.

That our Lord's K. may attain those blessed ends for wch it was designed and set up.

Whoever Prays for this is bound to promote—engages himself—

That Thy Name may be great (adored) among ye Heathⁿ.

Ps. lxxxvi. 9. "All nations w^m Thou hast made shall come and worship Thee, O Lord, and shall Glorify Thy Name."

Is. lx. 2. "I will give Thee for a Light to ye Gentiles, and y^t Thou mayst be for Salvation to ye ends of ye Earth."

Let Truth and Righteousness be established in this place.

Convert or Confound all the Adversaries of Thy K.

May Satan never set up his K. here.

Make me Thy Subj. out of Love: and [to] yield Thee a willing ob.

L^d, do Thou ever dwell and Govern in my Heart.

Make me Instrumental in promoting ye Interests of Thy Kingd.

Thy will be done in Earth as it is in Heaven. That men may imitate ye Angels in obeying ye will of God with readiness and pleasure.

That we may obey w^t He Commands, and submit to all the dispensations of His Providence.

God having made known His will in the H. S., our duty is to endeav^r to know it. He has also given us this Rule to understand it, Jo. vii. 17, "If any man will do"—i. e. desire to do—"ye will of God," &c.

May all X^{ns} do Thy will, and walk worthy of their Xⁿ Name. In this Pet. we acknowledge ye wisdom of God,—that He knows w^t is best; His Justice,—y^t He will Command w^t is best; His Goodness, &c., in all dispens. of Prov. At ye same time we disclaim our own Wisdom, Desires, [&c.]

That we may know wheth^r we are brought under ye Pow^{rs} of X^{ts} Kingdome, This will be a Test—Can we deny our own will and submit to God's?

Knowing Myself to be a Sinner and worthy of Punishm^t, I cannot but own ye Justice of God in treating me as I deserve, nor can I wonder at any Misfortunes, Troubles, Afflictions, distresses, y^t befall me.

Give us this day our daily Bread. Bread, i.e. The Necessarys of this Life—All things needful both for our Soules and Bodys.

Give us—i. e. Give a Blessing to our Honest Lab^{rs}—For Lab^r is a Duty fr. wch no man is exempt, with^t Forfeiting his Right to his daily Bread.

Bread—not Superfluitys—not goods for many years.

Bread—But w^t if God gives us more—We are then to consider w^t He probably intends by it. Is it not to try me—Is it not y^t He may Give it thro' my Hands to those y^t want, y^t there may be an Equality—Is it not to trye my Resignation, wⁿ He takes it away?

That we be neither puffed up wth Pride, nor cast down wth Fear.

Give us—For all y^t we enjoy is Thy Gift—our Wisdome, our Lab^r—our Friends—our Estates, &c., all in vain wthout God's Blessing.

Give us—for Thou alone knowest w^t is fittest for us—w^t a measure of necessarys, [&c.]

Give us—and give us Grace to be Content wth w^t Thou givest us—not to envy oth^{rs} or endeav^r to get by unjust meanes.

The Gift being every day fr. God, must every day be askt fr. G.

Give us, &c. That we may be enabled to serve Thee during our banishm^t.

Our daily Bread—This puts us upon the necessity of Praying every day of our Lives.

Labour and Care necessary as well as Pray^r—*In the sweat of thy brow.*

Our daily Bread—such a Measure of Necessarys as to Thee seems meet.

To be Content and Thankful for our present portion.

The Bread of Idleness—of deceit—of dishonesty.

Bread—Give us Bread—and give us Thy Blessing wth it.

Give me—for I acknowledge Thee to be giver of all good gifts.

Ours—by honest Industry—By Thy Gift—By Imparting what is not necessary to those y^t want, y^t there may be an Equality.

Give us—If it is Thy Gift, a Blessing comes along wth it.

Give us—And let us never Sacrifice to our own nets: or ascribe ye success to ourselves.

Give *us*—not only to me, but to all y^t want, ye necessarys, the conveniences of Life.

See Levit. xxiv. 5. Shew-Bread.

And forgive us our Debts (trespasses), as we, &c. May I cheerfully close with the conditions of Pardon wch J. X^t. has ordained.

Blessed be God y^t we have, every day we live, a Remedy for the sins we every day commit[n].

Since so much depends upon our Forgiving oth^{rs}, we sh^d pray daily for a Forgiving Temper—That God w^d inspire us wth this Grace.

Our own Pardon depends upon our Forgiving oth^{rs}—we are not to expect forgiveness any furth^r than we forgive oth^{rs}.

---

[n] [See S. Aug. Serm. xviii. 5, "quotidianam medicinam, ut dicamus, *Dimitte,* &c.; ut his verbis lota facie ad altare accedamus,...et corpore Christi et sanguine communicemus:" cf. clxxxi. 8; ccxiii. 8, &c. &c.]

Give me this sure Mark of my love to Thee and my Neighbour—To Thee in complying wth this most difficult comm^d.

Take fr. Me ye Sp^t of Pride, y^t I may not think myself too good to receive an Injury—tho' I am apt to injure oth^rs.

Give me a meek and quiet sp^t, y^t remembering my own Infirmities I may bear wth those of oth^rs.

Let me not so far despise Thy Gospel as to act ag^st one of its most important precepts.

Preserve me fr. a sin wch will shut me out of Heav^n. Forgiveness belongs to those only who forgive.

Ps. ciii. 1, 2. "Praise ye L^d, O my Soul, and forget not all His benefits—Who forgiveth all Thy sins."

N.B. We are to go to our Pray^rs as well as to ye H. Sacr. wth charity in our Hearts, Charity to all ye world. "To Lift up Holy Hands, with^t wrath or dissention." 1 Tim. ii. 4. I own this condition to be Just, and I expect God's pardon no other wise than as I do forgive oth^rs—We are [p. 276.] neith^r qualify'd for Pardon nor can Hope for it, on any other terms.

Forgive us every day, for we need forgiveness every day of our Lives.

"If we confess our sins God is Faithful and Just, &c." 1 Jo. i. 8; Is. lix. 1. "Our Iniquitys have separated betwixt us and our God." Jer. v. 25. "Our Iniquitys have withholden good things fr. us."

Forgive both ye Sin and ye Punishm^t.

Lay aside Thy Just displeasure, and receive us into Fav^r.

Not only my offences, but the sins of all my Brethren.

Forgive us, especially all those who have faln into sin by my Fault, by my Example, &c.

Forgive us, my enemies especially—Forgive and it shall be Forgiven—Blessed be God for so reasonable a Condition.

We use it as an Argum^t wth God to forgive us, "Forgive us our sins, for we forgive every one y^t has offended us." Luk. xi. 4.

Forgive—wth all our Hearts,—for so we desire God to forgive us. To do y^m good.

The repeating these words ought to Humble us, since there is occasion as often as we Pray to ask forgiveness.

<small>SUPPLE-MENT.</small> Forgive —Keep Thy servant from presumptuous sins—Forgive my Secret Sins—Keep me fr. Backsliding.

As we forgive—Not aggravating ye faults of others—Bearing with their failings.

"Be not overcome of evil, but overcome evil wth Good."

I will forgive my Enemy—For he is an Instrument in Thy Hand eith^r to punish, or to prevent my Ruin.

[p. 277.] *And lead us not into Temptation.* We pray God y^t we may never provoke Him to leave us to ourselves—for then—

Forgive w^t is past, and suffer me not to backslide for ye time to come.

And since ye Devil cannot Tempt me wthout Thy leave and permission—restrain his Power—Interpose Thy Alm. aid—Suffer me not blindly or wilfully to follow my own mind, evil customes, Infectious Examples — Flatterys of ye world—Fear of man.

Let us ever hearken unto Thy voice, lest Thou deal with us as Thou didst wth Thy own People, Ps. lxxxi. 11, 12—"give us up to our own hearts' lusts, and let us follow our own counsels."

Jer. x. 23. "It is not in man y^t walketh to direct his steps."

Do Thou restrain my Appetites, wⁿ sensible objects press on.

[p. 278.]
[p. 279.] *But deliver us from Evil.* From ye evil One.

From Sin, the root of all oth^r evils—whether Penal or Afflictive — Diseases — Disappointments — Ill Success—Disgrace, Reproach—Dangers—Difficultyes—Distress, troubles of Mind—Being deprived of God's Grace—of His assistance—of ye Comforts of His Holy Sp^t—Hardness of Heart—Blindness in ye Understanding—Want of Love to God.

[p. 280.]
[p. 281.] *For Thine is the Kingdom, ye Power, &c.*
[p. 282.] 263. *Sin agst the Holy Ghost.* Math. xiii. 32. The Mercys of God, and the Merits of J. X^t being Infinit, no Sin can be Unpardonable, but w^t is Incurable. No Sin can be Uncurable to Faith,—All things being possible to Him that Believeth. The Sin therefore of ye H. G. must be That wch obstructs all meanes of Conviction, and Cure of Infidelity. Now the Miracles of J. X^t being, as it were, the Seal and Markes of

the Undoubted Hand of God, w^n these were despised, and attributed to the Power of ye Devil—tho' He who wrought y^m endeavour'd by His Doctrine to oppose y^t Power—there could be no other meanes of Conviction, and consequently the Person was faln into a Sin wch was Incurable, and therefore Unpardonable—i. e. The Sin agst ye H. G.

264. *Charity Schools.* Mark ix. 41. For "Whosoever shall give you a Cup of"—i. e. Whoever dos any thing towards promoting the Truth and Hon^r and K. of God—shall have a suitable Reward.

265. *Propag^n of Gospel.* "God who hath given His Son ye Heathen for His Inheritance, and ye Uttermost part of ye Earth," &c. It becomes all X^{ts} subjects and servants, and especially His peculiar Ministers, to endeav^r to get Him into the possession of all parts of His Rights and Kingdom.

266. *Irreligion.* The Jewes never suffer'd Strangers w^{ch} [p. 283.] dwelt among y^m to Live with^t Lawes; They oblig'd y^m to observe ye Sabbath, and at least ye Precepts of the Sons of Noah—w^t a shame is this to X^n Princes and Magistrates, who suffer even X^{ns} to Live wthout any sign of Relig^n or Law?

267. *Confirmation.* Let such as have been (or are to be) confirmed, be asked concerning the *motives* to take upon y^m the X^n profession.

Don't you see y^t all serious X^{ns} are likelier to be despised than respected for their profession.

If you resolve to Live as ye Generality of ye world dos, you had better not to be Confirm'd—you will deserve to be Excomm. And tho' for want of Discipline you sh^d not be excom. while you live—yet you'll be shut out of Heaven w^n you dye.

On ye oth^r Hand, if you resolve and continue to Live like a X^n, you will certainly be Eternally Happy w^n you dye.

If you are unhappy in this world, this is a sure sign y^t God will make you amends in ye next, if you strive to please Him. The Happyness of this Life is not necessary to ye next. Prosperity leades men too often to Pride and forgetfulness of [p. 284.] God — so y^t men lose ye reward of ye world to come by striving to have their Portion here—God dos not afflict X^{ns} wth a purpose to Hurt y^m but to preserve y^m.

SUPPLE-
MENT.

268. *Confirmation.* Every thing y^t must have an end is of little consequence to perswade. Eternal Happ^{ss}, wch Vice and Corruption of Manners will certainly exclude us from, —this ought to be cheifly insisted [upon] and Thought of.

269. *Self-Denyal.* If a Physician prescribes Self-Denyal to His sick Patients, ye Fear of Death prevailes wth y^m to follow his directions—Jesus X^t, who knows w^t will hurt us, Ruin us Eternally, prescribes ye same, and we regard Him not—He forbids us ye immoderate use of Riches, of Joy, of Pleasures, and prescribes Temperance, Fasting, Teares, &c., and He practised Himself w^t He taught His followers. And this is w^t we must do if we will attain Eternal Life.

INDEX TO MAXIMS OF PIETY AND MORALITY.

(The letter S. means Supplement.)

ABSOLUTION, S., 78, 134, 136.
Adam, 1019.
Ad Aulam, 1180.
Ad Clerum, S., 2, 4, 32, 35, 50, 52, 53, 56, 67, 80, 81.
Advancement, 1063.
Affections, S., 92.
Affliction—Poverty, 1024.
——— Prosperity, 641.
Afflictions, 159, 206, 237, 240, 244, 247, 248, 264, 332, 350, 496, 501, 520, 548, 675, 693, 754, 786, 835, 959, 995, 1045, 1152.
——— Patience, 339.
——— and Joy together, 492.
Age of Infidelity, 1170.
All is equal, &c., 3.
All Knowledge is Vain y^t tends not, &c., 19.
Almes, 532, 557, 687, 711, 930, 932; S., 241.
Ambition, 669, 791.
Anarchy, 35.
Angels, 235; S. 237.
Anger, 101.
Antichrist, Irreligion, 997; S., 238.
Apparel, 75, 76; S. 221.
——— Fashions, 1037.
Arian, 431.
Art of Instructing, 559.
——— Persuasion, 966.
Ask what ye will, &c., 1177.
Astrology, S., 86.
Atheism, 1121; S., 6.
——— Judgments of God, 895.
Atheist, 611.
Atheists, 394, 1188.
Atonement, 1191.
Attributes of God, 998; S., 5, 245.
Augustine, St., 26; S., 71.
Authority, 507, 646, 734, 1115.
——— Pastor, 1005.
——— Power, Greatness, 955.
Awakening Questions, 129.

Backsliding, 391.
Balles, 598.
Balles, Dancing, Plays, &c., 1028.

Baptism, 333, 947, 953.
Beatitudes, The, 272.
Be not ashamed, &c., 25.
Bishop, S., 55.
Bp. Barrow's Epitaph, 225.
Blessed are they y^t Mourn, 273, 1080.
Blindness in Spiritual Things, 668.
Blood, Eating of, S., 138.
Boldness of Wickedness, 1116.
Bookes, 216.
Brazen Serpent, 371.
Business, 267, 680.
——— Employment, 81.
By their Fruits, &c., 230.

Calamitys—Afflictions, 757.
Calamities always Good, 799.
——— publick, 74; S., 231.
Calling, S., 121.
Call no man Rabbi, S., 12.
——— to ye Ministry, 978.
Calumny, 654.
Cares—Riches, 783.
Cases of Conscience, 774.
Casuist, 1020.
Catechism, S., 15, 17.
——— Indian, 344, 463; S., 142.
Catholick Truthes, 322.
Censures, Church, S., 135.
Change of a Sinner's Heart, 27.
Character of a Christian, 404.
——— of a People, S., 71.
Charity, 54, 160, 201, 386, 825, 867, 868, 896, 899—914.
——— *beareth long*, 266.
——— Love of our Neighbour, 1003, 1004.
——— Poor, 1002.
——— to ye Poor, 196, 357, 481, 1068.
——— Schools, S., 264.
——— Sermon, S., 203, 233.
Charmes, 315, 587; S., 57, 69.
Children—Parents—Riches, 312, 561.
Christ Crucify'd, 545.
——— and the World, 715.
——— the Only Physician, 816.
——— our Pattern, 1117.

Christian, 554, 655, 732.
——— Constancy, 32.
——— Charity, 109.
——— Duties, 66.
——— Faith, 878.
——— Knowledge, 401.
——— Liberty, 1168.
——— Maximes, 562.
——— Motives, 621.
——— Mysteries, 373.
——— Perfection, 143, 242, 426, 1088; S., 255.
——— Privileges, 1138.
——— Religion, 57, 59, 298, 945, 1160; S., 89.
——— Virtue, 44.
Christianity, 363, 679; S., 64.
——— Account of, S., 178, 200.
——— A Man without, 461.
——— Designe of, 292, 374.
——— or the Sum of the Gospel, 211.
——— Proof of, 716.
——— Test of, 639.
Christians, 85.
——— Indeed, 877.
Christmas Day, S., 215.
Church, 212, 570, 777.
Civility, 55.
Clothes, 1167.
——— Pride—Modesty, S., 115.
Club, S., 19.
Come, let us kill Him, &c., 999.
Comfort and Feares, 425.
——— to Sinners, 1032.
Commandments—Order to be observed, 438.
Common Practice, the Worst Rule, 7.
——— Prayers, 432.
Communion, Church, 447.
——— of Saints, 236.
Companion, S., 27.
Concerning Maxims, 30.
Concupiscence, 645.
Condemn not, &c., 1070.
Condition of a Sinner, 327.
——— of Life, 1156.
Conduct of ye Great, 1142.
Confession and Absolution, S., 98, 133.
——— of Sins, S., 9, 84.
——— Private—Publick, S., 116.
Confirmation, S., 40. 240, 267, 268.
Conscience, 317, 597, 804, 1190; S., 60, 70, 82.
——— He y^t has a good, &c., 5.
Consideration, 301, 1133.
Consolation, 636.
——— to Sinners, 495.
Contempt, 161, 652.
——— of God, 612.
——— of ye Clergy, 1108.
Content, 981.
Contentedness, 475.

Contentment, 158.
Contracts with ye Devil, 1062.
Controversys, 388, 602; S., 63.
Conversation, 291, 743, 744; S., 93.
Conversion, 521, 686, 787.
——— St. Paul's, 279.
Conversions, Imperfect, 258.
Conviction, 795.
Corrupt Affections, 134.
——— Heart, 70, 616.
Corruption of our Nature, 876, 1101.
Counsels and Precepts, S., 83.
Courtier, 510.
Covenant, S., 91.
Covetousness, 88, 321, 591, 656, 954, 1079.
Creatures, The, 781.
Creed, 61.
Cross, 123, 256, 300, 513, 728, 922.
Crosses, 629.
Cum duplicantur, 39.
Custome, 93, 295, 704; S., 42, 75, 76, 99, 184.
Customes, S., 58.

Daily Bread, 270.
——— Prayer—Family, 1119.
Damnation, 153.
Darkness, 736.
Death, 268, 302, 354, 469, 573, 1127, 1151, 1169, 1185; S., 26, 49, 59.
Death-Bed Repentance, S., 227, 232.
——— Funeral, 573.
——— and Judgment, 487.
Debauchery, 313.
Debts, S., 36, 66.
Deceitfulness of Sin, 434.
Degrees of Glory, 439.
Deism, 517.
——— Atheism, 690.
Deists, 149, 188.
Dejected Spirit, 250, 252.
Dejection, 340.
Designe of X^t and X^{ty}, 579.
Desire to please God, 67.
Despair, 96, 245, 405, 519, 848; S., 101.
Detraction, 409.
Devil, The, 360, 528.
Devotion, 144, 169, 246, 257; S., 256.
Devout, 97.
——— The, 422.
Differences, Composing, S., 197.
"Difficillimum est simul," &c., 603.
Difficultys, 118, 733, 802.
——— of Christianity, 51.
Dignity of Priesthood, S., 34.
Disappointments, 380, 864.
Discipline, 341; S., 41, 201.
——— Penance, S., 54.
Disconsolate, 836.
Disputes, 91, 418; S., 207.
——— in Religion, S., 37.

MAXIMS OF PIETY AND MORALITY. 637

Diversions, 150, 185.
Divine Grace, 413.
——— Nature, 397.
Divinity, Mode of Studying, S., 154.
Do not ye Publicans ye same ? 807.
Do to others as ye w^d, &c., 806.
Doubts of Conscience, 189.
Dreadful Truthes, 849.
Dreames, S., 23.
Duels, S., 85.
Duty, 417, 846, 1107.
——— Disconsolate, 1187.
——— of Friendship, 1083.
Dutys, All Xⁿ, 764.
——— of Station, 588.

Easter, S., 206.
Edification, 86.
Elect and Reprobate, 691.
Election, 193, 881.
Eloquence, 137.
Employment, 81.
End of Man, 306.
Enemy, 168, 863.
Enemys, 102, 643, 814.
Enmitys, 164, 165, 166.
Error, 197, 342, 726, 988.
Errors, 962 ; S., 43.
——— A Man's, 604.
Eternal Salvation, 763.
Eternity, 46, 47, 1058.
——— Death, 618.
——— Time, 672.
Evil, 364.
——— Conversation, 590, 927.
——— Example, 939.
——— Habits, 1113.
——— Speaking, 309.
Example, 986.
Except the Lord build, &c., S., 170.
Excommunication, 861 ; S., 130, 225, 1026.
External Worship, 1184.

Failings of Good Men, 474.
——— of others, 941.
Faith, 63, 115, 259, 293, 329, 330, 467, 477, 503, 632, 766, 824, 884, 893, 1013, 1179 ; S., 48, 234.
——— Xⁿ, 878.
——— in ye Assistance of God's Sp^t, 1011.
——— in God, 572, 1039.
——— Good Works, 1074.
——— in J. X^t, 894.
——— and Obedience, 933.
——— Obstacles, 724.
——— the Origin, &c., 873.
——— in ye Power of God, 784.
——— and Practice, 464.
——— Reason, Passion, 221.
——— A True, 203.
——— and Works, 977.

Fallen Man. The Case of, 468.
False Charity, 929.
——— Hopes, 263, 304.
——— Liberty, 278.
——— Shame, 882.
——— Teachers, 523.
Fasting, 526.
——— and Temperance, 1055.
Fathers, Ancient, S., 29.
Father of Mercies, 276.
Favour of God, 234.
Fear, 1129 ; S., 180.
——— of God, 1130.
——— Man—Pastor, 41, 696, 1066.
Feares, 114.
Fill up the Measure of, &c., 493.
Flattery—Vanity, 869.
Fleres si scires, 37.
Food—Intemperance, 730.
Forgive, 793.
——— Injurys, 1146.
Form of Godliness, 965.
Friendship, 926.
Frugality, 834.
Fundamental Truthes, 104, 296.
Funeral, 573.

Glory belongs to God, 729.
——— of God, S., 105.
God, 161.
——— Almighty, 578.
——— dwelleth in you, 288.
——— and the World, 644, 700, 1072.
——— reconciled to Man, 1193.
——— sees all things, 1015.
God's Assistance, 961.
——— Faithfulness, 948.
——— Foreknowledge, 708.
——— Goodness and Mercy, 118.
——— Grace, 627.
——— Hatred of Sin, 990.
——— Ministers, 850, 1082.
——— Ministers Protected, 648.
——— Omnipresence, 1118.
——— Presence, 282.
——— Protection, 772.
——— own Time, 712.
——— Will be done, 107, 470.
Good Example, 944.
——— Name, 113.
——— Purposes, 1012.
——— Works—Obedience, 661, 809.
Goodness of God, 1040.
——— of Providence, 1158.
Gospel, 338, 1123.
——— not Received, 924.
Government of ye Affections, 450.
——————— of Conscience, 452.
——————— of ye Heart, 337.
——————— of Rulers, 568.
——————— of ye Senses, 448.
——————— of ye Tongue, 451.
——————— of ye Understanding, 449.

Governments, S., 246.
———— Petty, 574.
Grace, 11, 87, 95, 194, 210, 297, 393, 400, 430.
———— Abused, 8, 817.
———— before Meat, 226, 238, 872.
———— of God, 217, 430; S., 68.
———— Light, Security, 854.
Greatness, 178, 351, 1038.
———— Honour, &c., 1120.

Happiness, 106, 657, 837, 865.
———— Eternal, 205, 919.
———— in God alone, 982.
———— of Man, 336.
Happy Life, 462.
Have no other View, &c., 16.
"Heart fretteth," S., 192.
Hearts are divided, 610.
Heaven and Happiness, 778.
———— and Hell, 326.
"———— sent us hither," 36.
———— Way to, 362.
He lives to no purposes, &c., 22.
Hell, 1128.
Heresies, 186, 950.
Heretick—Libertin, 556.
Hereticks—Infidels, 220, 551.
He yt fancys he is perfect, &c., 20.
— yt is his own Pupil, &c., 28.
— yt recounts, &c., 15.
High Places and Posts, 1009.
History, 798.
———— of the Bible, S., 16.
Holiness, 78, 782.
Holy Ghost, 479, 512.
—— Life, 121.
—— Scripture Obscure, 718.
H. Scriptures, 70, 213, 286, 415, 444, 651, 722, 739, 753, 811, 859, 888, 970; S., 109, 210, 250.
Honesty and Diligence, 594.
Honours and Riches, 803.
Hopes, our greatest, 23.
Human Frailty, 1053.
———— Learning, 952.
———— Meanes, 735.
———— Misery, 649.
———— Motives, 542.
———— Reasons, 500.
Humility, 157, 174, 265, 369, 625, 773, 890, 917, 1048.
———— Pastor, 490, 667.
Hypocrisy, 1059.
Hypocrite, 1136.

Idolatry, 898; S., 254.
If any Man Thirst, &c., 842.
I find then a Law, &c., S., 160.
If one Member Suffer, &c., S., 167.
Ignorance, 251.
Ignorant Pastor, 1014.
Image of God, 377.

Image Worship, S., 31.
Imperfections—Failings, 659.
Important Questions, 1200.
Impurity, 785.
———— Sins of, 396; S., 166.
Incarnation, 1061; S., 239.
Inconsideration, 564, 689.
In Deo Quies, 1.
Indifferent Things, 897.
Infant Baptism, S., 111.
Infidelity, 214, 356, 482, 497, 701, 1171, 1174.
Infidelity, Cause of, 705, 1106.
Infidels, 551.
Infirmity, S., 47.
Ingratitude for Favours, 1198.
Inheritance in Heaven—Charity, 805.
Injuries, 156, 163, 303.
Injury, 472.
Instructing, Art of, 559.
Instruction, 485, 505.
Intercession, S., 141.
In Time of Persecution, 42.
Irreligion, S., 266.
Itching Ears, S., 146.
I Thank Thee, O Father, S., 183.

Jesus Christ, S., 46.
———— an example, &c., 1041.
———— Crucified, 710.
———— on the Cross, 535.
———— the Way—Deists, 502.
Joy and Pleasure, 382.
Judge, 506, 508.
———— not, &c., 1069.
Judges, 858.
Judging by our Senses, 1056.
Judgment, 108.
Judgments delay'd, 989.
———— of God, 473, 800.
Juries of Enquiry, S., 139.
Justice, 395; S., 143.
———— Divine, S., 106.
———— and Mercy of God, 855.
Justification, S., 158, 161, 219.

Kingdom of Xt, S., 253.
———— of God, 366; S., 190.
Kingdoms of Xt and of Satan, 484; S., 218, 226.
King's Courts, 967.
———— Evil, cur'd by Touching, S., 110.
———— Throne, establish'd, &c., 33.
Knowledge, 68, 399, 411, 429, 476, 547, 627, 697, 698, 699, 703, 713, 818, 853, 935, 983, 993.
———— Xn, H. Scripture, 401.
———— Faith, 698.
———— of God, 299, 531, 756.
———— without Grace, 875.
———— without Practice, 634.
———— Spiritual, 892.

MAXIMS OF PIETY AND MORALITY. 639

Known Sin, 331.
Know your self, 148.

Labour, 182, 1159.
Last Judgment, S., 88.
Law, S., 189.
—— The, 537.
—— and Gospel, 436, S., 124.
—— Gospel—Reason—Naāl Relig^n, 338.
—— of Nature, S., 113.
—— and Prophets, 229.
Lawes divine and human, 1044.
Learning. 180, 427, 518, 745, 751, 856, 1137, 1163, 1165.
—— and Grace, 393.
—— Knowledge, 1077.
Learn of Me, saith X^t, 762.
Lent, S., 202.
Lest we sh^d offend y^m, Matt. xvii. 27, 1033.
Libertin, 58, 556.
Libertines, 62, 976.
Liberty, 838.
Life, 305, 620, 676.
—— of Faith, 860.
—— of Man, 1084.
Light within, S., 87.
Looking unto Jesus, 370.
Lord's Day, S. 156.
—— Prayer, 1194, S., 262.
—— Supper, 233, 372, 414, 446, 592, 595; S., 33, 51, 96, 102, 125, 177, 204, 228, 229, 259.
Losses, 275.
Loss of Children, 1051.
—— of Goods, 1016.
—— of Friends, &c., 1081.
Love of Christ, 994, 1006.
—— of Controversys, 1000.
—— of Enemies, 533, 1146.
—— of God, 175, 308, 335, 442, 628, 752, 810, 812, 1018.
—— of Neighbours, 575, 624, 808, 974.
—— *thy Neighbour as thyself*, 552; S., 187.
—— and Obedience, 934.
—— of ye World, 760, 996.
Loyalty, 489, 830.
Luxury, 1001.
—— in Apparel, S., 224.

Magistrates, 985, 1096, 1097.
Man sacrifices to, 29.
Manks Proverbs, 1201.
Mark of Salvation, 813.
Marks of a worldly Spirit, 328.
Marriage, S., 21.
Martyrdom, 880.
Maximes of X^{ty}, 170, 562.
Maxims of the Gospel, 601.
——— or Rules of the World, 562, 601.

Meales sh^d always put us in mind, &c., 1046.
Meanes, 1089.
—— of Grace, 127.
—— necessary for Saving the Soul, 459.
—— of Salvation, 435.
Mediator, 228, 925, 1192.
Melancholy, 345, 522.
Members of One Body, 719.
Men pleasers, 1034.
Mercy and Charity, 767.
Mercy of God, 126, 682.
Merits, 227.
Messenger of Satan, 936.
Method of Reproving, 1196.
Minister of X^t, 833.
———— of God, 630.
Ministry, 187; S., 186.
Miracles, 498, 695, 709; S., 129.
—— Libertine, 1090.
Mirth, 142.
Misbelief, 660.
Modesty, S., 7.
Morality, 119, 406, 466, 628, 940.
Moral Philosophy, 43.
Moral Virtue, 1187.
Mortification, 290.
Motions of Grace, 1103.
Mysteries, 231.
———— Faith, 920.
———— and Maxims of X^t, 1124.
Mystery, 204.

Nature Corrupt, 714.
———— Religion, 43, 338, 1148.
———— Rhetorick, Rules of, 138.
Natural Corruption, 1007.
Necessary Truths, 420.
Necessity of X^{ts} Death, 1189.
———— Necessity of Faith, 407.
Nervi et Artus, 2.
Neighbor, 1078.
Newspapers, 1050.
New Testament, 478.
"No Devotion," &c., 610.
"No Man must go to Heaven," &c., 24.
Not fearing ye wrath of ye King, 968.
"Nothing that pleases," &c., 21.
Not many wise, &c., 889.
Number of Sinners, 991.

Obedience, 56, 82, 202.
———— to Higher Powers, S., 132.
———— Uniform, 248.
Obstinacy, 1023.
Offertory, 596.
Old Testament and New, 465.
Omniscience of God, 1143.
Opera, 130, 560.
Opinions, 131.

Opportunity lost, 685.
Opposition, 1093.
Oracle of Reason, 376.
Ordinances, 375, 499.
Original Corruption, 324.
—— Sin, 525, 1132.
—————— Proof of, 534.
Origin of Unbelief, S., 11.
Outward Peformances, 788.

Pale of ye Church, 334.
Parents, 861.
Passions, S., 45.
Pastor, 494, 647.
Pastors, 631.
Paternal Authority, 116.
Patience, 172, 339, 768.
Peace, 111, 980; S. 191.
—— be unto you, 1150.
—— of Conscience, 355, 1155.
—— Inward, 271.
—— of Mind, 387, 398, 615, 664.
—— The only way to, 6.
—— and Unity, 946.
Peculiar Blessings of the Gospel, 600.
Penance, S., 30.
———— Publick, S., 117, 243.
Penitent, 702.
Perfection, Xⁿ, 143, 242, 426, 1088.
————— Only Way to, 14.
Persecution, 549, 779, 831, 963.
Persecutions—Reformation, 755.
Perseverance—Confirmation, 662.
Perswade, 141, 529.
Perswasion—Edification, 140.
Physician, 222.
Piety, Serious, the best Security, 4.
Plays, Balles, Operas, &c., 183, 319, 323, 560, 598, 1149, 1181.
Pleasures—Amusements, 72, 731.
Political Squabbles, 605.
Pomp—Pride, &c., 1105.
Poor, 553, 581.
—— The, 972.
—— in Spirit, 671.
Poverty, 353, 666, 769.
———— Power of Faith, 1067.
———— Riches, 841.
Tower, Temp. and Spirit, 509.
Practical Truthes, 125.
Praise—Applause, 1147.
Prayer, 64, 135, 167, 262, 318, 358, 539, 593, 635, 638, 673, 721, 742, 792, 879, 883, 1100, 1178; S., 152, 261.
Prayers, 540; S., 176.
Preacher, 891.
———— The World, 640.
Preaching, True Way of, S., 188.
Precepts, Seven, of the Sons of Noah, 40.
Predestination, S., 97.

Prejudice, 131, 565, 871.
Pride, 569, 622, 626, 681; S., 122.
Priest, S. 151.
Priesthood, 128.
Priesthood—Ministers, 1111.
Priests—Ambassadors, S., 199.
—— Xⁿ, 84, 419.
—— of God, S., 148.
Principijs Obsta, 184, 455, 827.
" Profess not," &c., 609.
Proficiency, 1186.
Progress of Sin, 658.
Promises of God, 928.
Propagation of Gospel abroad, S., 208, 212, 222, 265.
Prophecy, S., 22, 108.
Prosperity, 151, 224, 314.
————— Charmes, 587.
Providence, 1099, 1104; S., 163, 229.
—————— of God, 617, 874 ; S., 214.
Publick Calamities—Afflictions, 797.
———— Judgments, 951.
———— Justice, S., 220.
———— Prayer, 839.
———— Worship, 987, 992.
" Pudor, tibi non est," &c., 614.
Punishment of Sin, 483.
Purity of Heart, 443.
Purposes—Desires, 931.
————— Good, 12.

Quality and High Birth, 1164.
Quakers, S., 62.
———— Light, S., 18.
Quicquid agunt, 38.

Rash Judgment, 348, 524, 665, 684, 840, 851.
" Read ye Holy Scriptures," 1126.
Reason, 338, 400, 1154.
—— and Faith, 176.
—— and Free Will, 191.
—— without Grace, 43.
Reasons, Human, 500.
Reason Insufficient, 845.
—— and Nature, 218.
—— and Revelation, 1195.
Rebellion, S., 61.
" Receive every thing," &c., 17.
Reconciliations, 103.
Reformation, 1182.
————— of Manners, 586.
Regenerate Person, 346.
Regeneration, 1085; S., 153.
Religion, 60, 80, 99, 105, 171, 173, 207, 255, 390, 423, 433, 453, 488, 1008, 1161; S. 94.
———— not defended by Force, 832.
———— of ye World, 280.
Religious, 79.

MAXIMS OF PIETY AND MORALITY. 641

Repentance, 90, 441, 458, 619, 1047, 1057, 1086; S., 72, 73, 77, 194, 195, 236.
—————— or Damnation, 810.
—————— Despair, 923.
Reprobate, 794, 956.
Reproches, 837.
Reproof, 1095.
—————— Convince, 209.
—————— of Great Men, 1060.
Resignation, 110, 253, 260, 261, 577, 862.
—————— Humility, 1035.
—————— Perfect, 10.
Resolution, 392.
Restitution, S., 171, 182.
Restoration to ye Image of God, 199.
Resurrection of X^t, 408; S., 213.
Retirement, 843.
Revenge, 957.
Rich, 544.
—— and Great, To the, 1183.
—— and Poor Compared, 1122.
Riches, 49, 53, 100, 177, 239, 359, 361, 368, 421, 428, 480, 546, 561, 563, 569, 589, 591, 776, 790, 823, 1049, 1098, 1135; S., 242, 251.
—————— and Power, 973.
—————— Prosperity, 151, 1020.
—————— their extreme Danger, 984.
—————— Unreasonably Heaped, 1109.
Ridicule, 584.
Righteousness, S., 162.
Romances, Plays, Operas, &c., 130; S., 119.
Rule of Religion, 219.
Rulers, 568.
Rules and Maximes of ye Gospel, 1199.
—— of Natural Rhetorick, 138.

Sabbath, 1043, 1110.
Sacrifices, S., 95, 112.
Saints—X^{ns}, 943.
Salvation—Delusion, 677.
—————— Mark of, 813.
Sanctification, S., 149, 159.
Satan, Messenger of, 936.
—— Crime of, 1197.
Saving Knowledge, 311.
Scepticism, 750.
Scepticks, 725.
Schism, 1114, 1125; S., 38.
Schisms, 186, 582.
Scripture—Inspired Writings, S., 65.
Scriptures, 916; S., 120.
—————— Reason, 1172.
Scruples, 89, 692.
—————— Melancholy, S., 39, 144.
Security, 637.
Self-Confidence, 771.

Self-Denyal, 124, 145, 147, 383, 410, 527, 538, 663, 765; S., 126, 269.
Sensible Pleasures, 749; S., 79.
Sensuality, 307, 320, 567.
Separation fr. ye Ch. of Rome, S., 100.
—————— Schism, 582.
Sermons, 839, 915.
Servants, 515, 964.
Serve God, To, 1173.
Shame, 73.
—————— False, 882.
Sickness, 244.
Simplicity, 117.
"Since to thine own Commands," 33.
Sincerity, 8, 132, 367.
—————— Mark of, 92.
Singularity, 969.
Sin, 198, 216, 347, 516, 530, 550, 613, 801, 1131.
— Evil, S., 107.
— Evil of, 456.
— Original, 1132.
— Progress of, 658.
— Punishable, 1139.
— Temptation, 653.
— and Wickedness, 683.
— will find out the Sinner, 491.
Sinner, 828.
—————— Condition of a, 327.
Sinners, 294, 688.
Sins Great and Small, 424.
—— of others, 717, 857.
—— particularly forbidden in the Gospel, 599.
—— Wilful, 822.
—— Unpardonable, S., 196.
Sleep, 223.
"Small is the Blind Man's Grief," &c. 608.
Socinian—Arian, 431.
Solitude, 457.
Sorcery—Witchcraft, S., 155.
Soul, 208; S., 104.
Spare Time, 571.
Special Prudence, S., 128.
Spendthrift, S., 193.
Spirit of Law and Gospel, 1042.
—— of Religion, 1029.
—— of the World, 747.
—— Worldly, S., 28.
Spirits, 1112; S., 20, 74.
Spiritual Comforts, 122.
State and Grandeur, 1091.
—— of Life, 775.
—— of Man before the Fall, S., 157, 211.
—— of Tryal, 558, 866.
States of Life inconsistent with Salvat^n, 1036, 1176.
Strait Gate, 740.

T t

Strange Relations, 1094.
Study, 352, 378, 958, 1153.
Submission to God's Will, 633.
Success, 1076.
Suffering, 642.
Sufferings, 583, 918, 1031.
Superfluities, 389.
Superstition, S., 103.
Supper of the Lord, S., 8.
"Suspect yourself," S., 127.
Swear Falsly, S., 205.

Take Counsel of God, 403.
Take My Yoak upon you, 555.
—— *no thought for to-morrow*, 254, 815.
—— up the Cross, 52, 285.
Talk, 155.
"Tanto melius nebulam," 605.
Teachers, 887.
Temperance, 181, 437.
Temple of Jerusalem, S., 25.
Temporal Good Things, 707.
Temptation, 112, 770.
—————— Tryal, 1025.
Temptations, 190, 434, 937, 1073.
Testament, Old and New, 165.
Test, 504, 1021.
—— of being true X^{ns}, 200.
—— of X^{ty}, 630.
—— of our Condition, 1010.
—— of true Piety, 243.
Tests of Religion, 77, 975.
—— of a State of Grace, 402.
—— of True Religion, 460.
Thanksgiving, 949; S., 244.
Thanks, Wicked, 34.
The Case of Vain Man, 468.
—— *Head cannot say to the Feet*, S., 198.
—— *Lord rebuke Thee*, 471.
—— *Night Cometh, &c.*, 281.
—— Serious Temper truly X^n, 576.
—— Tongue, 971, 979.
—— Threats of Men, 678.
—— Word preach'd, 445.
There is a Way, &c., S., 147, 168, 216, 258.
"They more exactly," &c., 606.
———— *that be whole, &c.*, 543, 580, 1144.
This is Life Eternal—Text, S., 164.
—— Life a State of Tryal, S., 252.
Things Sacred and Profane, 1134.
—— Valuable, 379.
"Those y^t commend our Faults," 18.
Thoughts, 541.
Thro' J. X^t, 886.
Time, 1092, 1166.
Tinwald, S., 169.
To him y^t hath, 819, 1022.

To know God, 284.
—— Love God, 283.
Trinity, S., 90.
———— Sacred, 120.
Troubled Mind, 287, 511; S., 140.
Troubles, 746.
Truth, 69, 154, 195, 365, 381, 720, 826, 852, 1054, 1064.
Truthes, 514.
———— of ye Gospel, 780.
True Wisdome, 139.
Two Covenants, S., 179.
—— Kingdoms, 536; S., 209.
Types, S., 24.
Tythes, 384, 585; S., 3, 114, 131, 137, 145, 150.

"Ubi non est Pudor," &c., 614.
Uncharitableness, 942.
Uncleanness, Sins of, 1065.
Uncontested Truthes, S., 44.
Understanding, 343, 674.
Union, 938.
Unity—Charity, 7.
Unlearned, 1102.
Unprofitable Servant, 325.
Unwashen Hands, 789.

Vain expenses, 1162.
—— purposes, 844.
Vanity, 412, 727.
Virtue, 723, 741, 758.
Virtues, 65.
Virtus est, 31.
Visiting the Sick, 1140; S., 14, 185.

Walk before Me, 289.
Walking warily, 566.
Wandering in Prayer, 241.
Warr, S., 247.
Watch, 316.
———— *and Pray*, 758.
Weaknesses of Nature, 706.
Wealth and Vanity, 1175.
"We can always do," 13.
"What Commonwealth," 35.
Whatsoever ye w^d y^t Men sh^d do, &c., 45, 232.
Whether ye eat or drink, 737.
Whosoever is born of God, S., 165.
———— *shall Confess me, &c.*, 1017.
Who then can be saved? 761.
Why are ye SS. sometimes obscure? 1145.
Wickedness, 249, 385, 870.
Widowe's Mite, 1075.
Wilful Ignorance, 192.
—— Sins, 822.
Wisdome, 623, 821.
Wise Men, 9.

World, The, 48, 83, 98, 152, 310, 416, 454, 486, 670, 759, 1071, 1141.
—— Afflictions, 650.
—— The, Condemnes, 1052.
—— End of, 50.
—— and Religion, 80.
Worldly Advantages, 349.
—— Happiness, 1157.
—— Motives, 1027.
—— Pleasures, 960.

Worldly Spirit, S., 28.
——————— Marks of, 328.
—— Wisdom, 179, 274.

Youth, S., 123.
Yoak, Christ's, 277, 748.

Zeal, 94, 136.
Zech. viii. 16, *These are the things*, S., 10.

www.ingramcontent.com/pod-product-compliance
Lightning Source LLC
Chambersburg PA
CBHW071215290426
44108CB00013B/1185